What Is the Argument?

What Is the Argument?

An Introduction to Philosophical Argument and Analysis

Maralee Harrell

The MIT Press
Cambridge, Massachusetts
London, England

This book was set in ITC Stone Serif & ITC Stone Sans by Jen Jackowitz. Printed and bound in the United States of America.

Library of Congress Cataloging-in-Publication Data is available.

ISBN: 978-0-262-52927-3

10 9 8 7 6 5 4 3 2 1

Contents

Preface ix

I Doing Philosophy 1

1 Introduction 3

1.1 What Is Philosophy? 3
1.2 How Do We Do Philosophy? 6
1.3 Purpose and Structure of This Book 11
1.4 In-Class Exercise 12
1.5 Reading Questions 13

2 Types of Arguments 15

2.1 Vocabulary 16
2.2 Necessary versus Sufficient Conditions 22
2.3 Deductive versus Nondeductive Arguments 24
2.4 Forms of Valid and Invalid Deductive Arguments 24
2.5 A Priori versus A Posteriori Deductive Arguments 27
2.6 Types of Nondeductive Arguments: Induction, Argument by Analogy, and Abduction 28
2.7 Answers to Self-Assessment Exercises 29
2.8 In-Class Exercises 30

3 Argument Analysis and Diagramming 33

3.1 Visual Representations of Reasoning 34
3.2 Understanding and Representing Argument Structure 39
3.3 Interpreting Arguments to Create Diagrams 51
3.4 Diagramming Objections and Replies 59
3.5 Summary 65
3.6 Answers to Self-Assessment Exercises 66
3.7 In-Class Exercises 72

II Philosophy of Religion 85

Introduction 87

4 Deductive Arguments for the Existence of God 93

4.1 St. Anselm, *Proslogion* 93
4.2 St. Thomas Aquinas, *Summa Theologica* 101
4.3 In-Class Exercises 113

5 Deductive Arguments against the Existence of God 119

5.1 Michael Martin, "Three Reasons for Nonbelief" 119
5.2 John Mackie, "Evil and Omnipotence" 126
5.3 In-Class Exercises 132
5.3 Reading Questions 136

6 Nondeductive Arguments for the Existence of God 137

6.1 David Hume, *Dialogues Concerning Natural Religion* 137
6.2 William Paley, *Natural Theology* 144
6.3 In-Class Exercises 156
6.4 Reading Questions 161

III Epistemology 163

Introduction 165

7 The Definition of Knowledge 171

7.1 Plato, *Theaetetus* 171
7.2 Edmund L. Gettier, "Is Justified True Belief Knowledge?" 175
7.3 In-Class Exercises 180
7.4 Reading Questions 184

8 Justification and Certainty 187

8.1 René Descartes, *Meditations on First Philosophy* 187
8.2 John Locke, *An Essay Concerning Human Understanding* 206
8.3 David Hume, *An Enquiry Concerning Human Understanding* 212
8.4 In-Class Exercises 221
8.5 Reading Questions 227

9 The Problem of Induction 229

9.1 Hans Reichenbach, *Experience and Prediction* 229
9.2 Karl Popper, "Science: Conjectures and Refutations" 234
9.3 Nelson Goodman, *Fact, Fiction, and Forecast* 241
9.4 In-Class Exercises 247
9.5 Reading Questions 252

IV Theory of Mind 253

Introduction 255

10 Dualism 259

10.1 René Descartes, *Meditations on First Philosophy* 259
10.2 Gilbert Ryle, "Descartes' Myth" 267
10.3 In-Class Exercises 273
10.4 Reading Questions 275

11 Materialism 277

11.1 J. J. C. Smart, "Sensations and Brain Processes" 277
11.2 Jerry Fodor, "The Mind–Body Problem" 281
11.3 In-Class Exercises 283
11.4 Reading Questions 288

12 Antimaterialism 289

12.1 Thomas Nagel, "What Is It Like to Be a Bat?" 289
12.2 Frank Jackson, "Epiphenomenal Qualia" 293
12.3 Paul Churchland, "Knowing Qualia: A Reply to Jackson" 296
12.4 In-Class Exercises 300
12.5 Reading Questions 305

13 Consciousness 307

13.1 John Searle, "Can Computers Think?" 307
13.2 Dan Dennett, "Consciousness Imagined" 311
13.3 In-Class Exercises 314
13.4 Reading Questions 316

V Free Will and Determinism 317

Introduction 319

14 Hard Determinism 323

14.1 Baron d'Holbach, "Of the System of Man's Free Agency" 323
14.2 Galen Strawson, "The Impossibility of Moral Responsibility" 328
14.3 In-Class Exercises 333
14.4 Reading Questions 336

15 Compatibilism 337

15.1 David Hume, "Of Liberty and Necessity" 337
15.2 W. T. Stace, "The Problem of Free Will" 341
15.3 In-Class Exercises 346
15.4 Reading Questions 348

16 Libertarianism 349

16.1 Roderick M. Chisholm, "Human Freedom and the Self" 349
16.2 Peter van Inwagen, "The Powers of Rational Beings: Freedom of the Will" 354
16.3 In-Class Exercises 360
16.4 Reading Questions 363

VI Ethics 365

Introduction 367

17 Meta-ethics: Divine Command Theory 373

17.1 Plato, *Euthyphro* 373
17.2 James Rachels, "Does Morality Depend on Religion?" 379
17.3 In-Class Exercises 385
17.4 Reading Questions 388

18 Meta-ethics: Relativism 389

18.1 Ruth Benedict, "Anthropology and the Abnormal" 389
18.2 James Rachels, "The Challenge of Cultural Relativism" 393
18.3 In-Class Exercises 397
18.4 Reading Questions 399

19 Normative Ethics: Virtue Ethics, Egoism, and Contractarianism 401

19.1 Aristotle, *Nicomachean Ethics* 401
19.2 James Rachels, "Egoism and Moral Skepticism" 405
19.3 Thomas Hobbes, *Leviathan* 412
19.4 In-Class Exercises 418
19.5 Reading Questions 428

20 Normative Ethics: Utilitarianism and Deontological Ethics 429

20.1 Jeremy Bentham, *An Introduction to the Principles of Morals and Legislation* 429
20.2 John Stuart Mill, *Utilitarianism* 435
20.3 Immanuel Kant, *Groundwork for the Metaphysics of Morals* 440
20.4 In-Class Exercises 445
20.5 Reading Questions 448

Notes 451
Index 457

Preface

I consider myself to be very fortunate to be a philosophy teacher—it is one of the few academic disciplines in which a student can, even on the first day of an introductory course, engage in *doing* the subject rather than merely *learning about* the subject. As an instructor, I strive to build on this advantage to engage my students in not only studying philosophers and their ideas, but actually participating in philosophical discourse. If we think of philosophy as a great, centuries-long conversation, then I want my students to enter into that conversation rather than just understanding what the conversation is about and what others have to say.

To enter into this conversation, students need to read and wrestle with original sources. We can gain great insight from those who have either started new conversations, or advanced old conversations in significant ways. Having introductory students enter into this conversation with some of the greatest minds in history is, of course, a rather lofty goal—one that would ideally be met by engaging in a wide variety of philosophical endeavors.

One subset of these endeavors concerns the way in which we read philosophy. There are many ways to do this; Jay Rosenberg, for example, has very usefully and succinctly laid out six different ways in his excellent book, *The Practice of Philosophy*:[1]

1. For conclusions: Reading for *what* the philosopher thinks.
2. For arguments: Reading for *why* the philosopher believes what he does.
3. In the dialectical setting: Reading for *how* the philosopher thinks—the dialectical setting, contribution.
4. Critically: Reading to determine whether the argument a philosopher gives is good.
5. Adjudicatively: Reading to determine which of two or more different philosophical positions is more reasonable.
6. Creatively: Reading to inform and enhance one's own thinking about a particular issue or problem.

What Is the Argument? is straightforwardly engaged in the most basic of the six ways, as is appropriate, I think, for beginning students: numbers 1, 2, and 4, above: What is the position, why is the position held, and are the reasons for holding it any good?

Reading for the dialectical setting and contribution, as well as reading adjudicatively or creatively, are certainly worthy ways to read, but they are not my aim here. For classes that aim for these goals, I think this book maybe usefully paired with extended classroom discussion of the historical, social, and philosophical situations of each author and/or a text that approaches philosophy from a historical perspective.

Critical Thinking

During the past decade, I have taught an introductory philosophy course nearly every semester. At Carnegie Mellon, this course fulfills a general education requirement in each of the colleges that make up the university. Thus, the students taking my class are quite diverse, both in their demographics and their intellectual interests. Carnegie Mellon's mission statement, like those of most colleges and universities around the country, includes a promise to develop the critical thinking skills of its students.

However, we have no general education requirement that specifically targets the development of these skills. Thus, I have always viewed my role in teaching this course as not just introducing students to great philosophical thinkers, ideas, and texts, but also as explicitly and deliberately improving my students' critical thinking skills.

Argument Diagramming

Most philosophers can agree that one aspect of critical thinking involves the ability to reconstruct, understand, and evaluate an argument—tasks we may call, for the sake of brevity, "argument analysis." And if we think of an argument the way that philosophers and logicians do—as a series of statements in which one is the conclusion, and the others are premises supporting this conclusion—then an argument diagram is a visual representation of these statements and the inferential connections between them.

For example, at the end of *Meno*,[2] Plato argues through the character of Socrates that virtue is a gift from the gods. While the English translations of Plato's works are among the more readable philosophical texts, it is still the case not only that the text contains many more sentences than just the propositions that are part of the argument, but also that, proceeding necessarily linearly, the prose obscures the inferential structure of the argument. Thus, anyone who wishes to understand and evaluate the argument may reasonably be confused. If, on the other hand, we are able to extract just the statements Plato uses to support his conclusion and visually represent the connections between these statements (as shown in figure 0.1), the structure of the argument is immediately clear, as are the places where we may critique or applaud it.

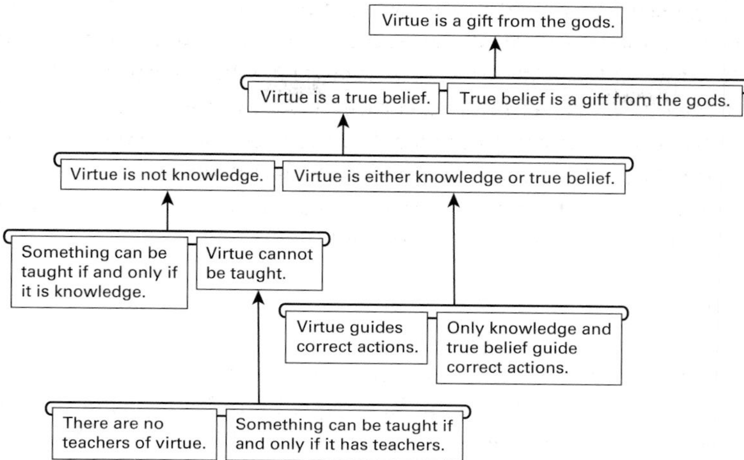

Figure 0.1
An argument diagram representing an argument in Plato's *Meno*.

As another example, in the *Third Meditation*, Descartes argues that the idea of God is innate.

It only remains to me to examine into the manner in which I have acquired this idea from God; for I have not received it through the senses, [since] it is never presented to me unexpectedly, as is usual with the ideas of sensible things when these things present themselves, or seem to present themselves, to the external organs of my senses; nor is it likewise a fiction of my mind, for it is not in my power to take from or add anything to it; and consequently the only alternative is that it is innate in me, just as the idea of myself is innate in me.[3]

The argument presented here can be diagrammed as shown in figure 0.2.

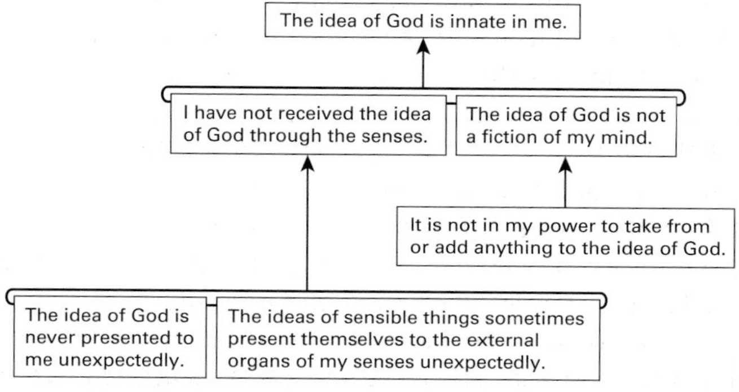

Figure 0.2
An argument diagram representing an argument in Descartes's *Third Meditation*.

Argument Diagramming Software

Recent research on argument visualization (particularly computer-supported argument visualization) has shown that the use of software programs specifically designed to help students construct argument diagrams can significantly improve students' critical thinking abilities over the course of a semester-long college-level critical thinking course.[4]

But, of course, one need not have computer software to construct an argument diagram; one needs only a pencil and paper. However, in my experience over the past several years, it is not only easier to construct a diagram using a software program, but using a program in class is superior to using either the chalkboard or static overhead slides.

The first time I diagrammed arguments in the classroom, I did not use any argument-diagramming software; in the first half of the semester I used the chalkboard, and, since this proved to be messy and time consuming, in the second half I presented fully formed diagrams on overhead slides. For their part, most of the students submitted diagrams drawn by hand, while some used the drawing tools in Word to produce their diagrams. Even this static presentation and the cumbersome drawing of the diagrams, though, helped the students tremendously. Nearly all of my students learned how to construct a diagram that accurately represents the argument given in a text, and as I said above, these students improved their critical thinking skills significantly more than the students who did not learn this skill, both in my section and in the other sections of the introductory course.[5]

Even with these great results, I still want the students to experience more tangibly the way that I construct diagrams: how I move boxes around, create and erase arrows, set aside smaller subarguments to be connected to the overall argument later. Until now I had done all this with pencil and paper, and showing the exact steps of *that* process to the students would, I believe, be at best unhelpful.

I originally created figures 0.1 and 0.2 in Microsoft Word, using the drawing tools. This is very cumbersome and time consuming, not to mention static. With this sort of tool, I must work out the argument diagram ahead of time, construct it in Word, and then present it to my students fully formed. The advantage of software systems is the potential to construct the diagram "on the fly" both for my own use and the students' use, and for presentation to the students. It is especially important to be able to present a diagram dynamically to my students so that they can see, as well as participate in, its construction. This kind of practice allows the students to construct argument diagrams themselves that represent both arguments in texts and their own arguments.

There are many sorts of argument diagramming software packages on the market; some of the more prominent are Araucaria,[6] Argutect,[7] Athena Standard,[8] Inspiration,[9] and Rationale.[10] Since I teach the use of argument diagrams in all of my classes for the purposes of both understanding and evaluating texts, and creating novel arguments, I reviewed the advantages and drawbacks of each of these packages from this perspective. Ultimately, I conclude that they are each too powerful in some aspects and too deficient in others to suit my purposes.[11]

Thus, I have collaborated with Matthew Easterday, formerly a PhD student at Carnegie Mellon's Human and Computer Interaction Institute, to design and build a program that I can use for classroom demonstrations and the students can use to practice constructing argument diagrams themselves. I have presented earlier versions of this software at both the 2005 and 2006 North American Computing and Philosophy Conferences.[12] The latest free version of this software (in Java or Air) can be found at http://www.phil.cmu.edu/projects/argument_mapping/.

In chapter 2, I cover some basics of deductive and nondeductive logic, while the basic technique of argument diagramming is the subject of chapter 3. All of the materials in these two chapters are covered in an online mini-course I have developed at Carnegie Mellon University, called Argument Diagramming. This course is free and open: https://oli.cmu.edu/teach-with-oli/review-our-free-open-courses/. I generally do not cover the material in chapters 2 and 3 in class, but have the students take the mini-course within the first week of the semester. This course teaches not only argument diagramming, but also how to use the iLogos argument-diagramming software mentioned above.

Teachers: Purpose and Structure of This Book

I have developed this book as part of my "flipped classroom" style of teaching, in which I ask my students to do a substantial amount of analytic work outside of class and engage in discussion and problem solving in class. So, in my introductory philosophy course, I use this book in conjunction with either a text anthology or course packet of primary sources. For example, in a typical class period, my students will have read the primary source text, plus my analysis and evaluation of part of the argument. In class, I give short lectures interspersed with discussions in which we will tackle, as a class, other parts of the argument. These are in the "In-Class Exercises" at the end of each chapter. Thus, this book is really meant to be a *companion* textbook to the primary source readings in an introductory philosophy course.

The design of this book as a companion textbook is also the reason I have included "Reading Questions" at the end of each chapter, along with the In-Class Exercises. The Reading Questions presuppose that the student has read a substantial portion of the text from which the argument I analyze came.

Part I of the book contains the first three chapters, and it is here that students are introduced to the study of philosophy in general (chapter 1), the basics of argumentation and logic (chapter 2), and argument diagramming (chapter 3). In chapter 4 I begin to do in-depth argument analysis on parts of primary source texts using argument diagrams. In these analyses, I use the following notation: the conclusion (if it is explicit) is in purple text. The red sentences and sentence fragments are the individual claims the author makes, while the green words are "indicator phrases," that is, phrases that indicate how the claims are supposed to fit together to support the conclusion. The blue sentences are illustrations of some of the author's specific claims, and despite being introduced by premise indicators, they do not seem to be meant as reasons to believe the claim as much as concrete examples of the claims given to aid understanding.

In Part II, after my presentation of how to analyze arguments, I consider in detail several objections to various arguments in philosophy of religion. This is to model some ways to criticize arguments, so that the students can start doing it on their own. Thus, my analyses of objections to the author's arguments taper off starting in Part III, on epistemology, because I start discussing objections to the arguments with the students in class.

In my own teaching, I also think it is important to emphasize that argument analysis involves an interpretation of the text. I generally share this disclaimer with my students: "Keep in mind that the following interpretation and analysis of the argument is *my* interpretation and analysis. I use the text to support my interpretation, but the way I have reconstructed the argument may not be the only reasonable way. Any interpretation, though, must be supported by the text, according to the principles of fairness and charity."

I Doing Philosophy

1 Introduction

1.1 What Is Philosophy?
1.2 How Do We Do Philosophy?
Philosophy in Ancient Greece
Western Philosophy since Ancient Greece
Thinking Philosophically
1.3 Purpose and Structure of This Book
1.4 In-Class Exercise
1.5 Reading Questions

Learning Objectives

At the end of this chapter you will be able to:

- Describe key philosophical questions, and to identify the methods and goals of philosophy
- Define the following terms:
  - Epistemology
  - Metaphysics
  - Value theory
  - Logic
  - Paradox

1.1 What Is Philosophy?

Many Introduction to Philosophy textbooks begin with an admonition that people generally don't understand what philosophy is. I don't find this to be the case, though. On the first day of class, I always ask my students to think of questions they think are particularly philosophical; and they always do a great job. They hit on all the major areas of philosophy, and ask the same questions that philosophers from Ancient Greece to contemporary times ask. Usually the list goes something like this:

Does God exist?
What is human nature?
What can we know?
Is science the best way or the only way to gain knowledge?
Why is there evil in the world?
What is real?
What is consciousness?
Is truth relative?
Is morality relative?
Is abortion permissible?
Do animals have rights?
Should we always make decisions based on what is best for everyone?
Do I have free will?
What is time?
Can computers be conscious?
Do we know that we are not living in a Matrix?
Is democracy the best political arrangement?
Is beauty really in the eye of the beholder?

And of course:

Which came first, the chicken or the egg?

As I said, these questions illustrate the four major areas of philosophy: epistemology, metaphysics, value theory, and logic. *Epistemology* is the study of knowledge, and generally concentrates on three major questions: (1) what is knowledge? (2) what can we know? and (3) how can we know it? Thus, these questions that students usually pose are all epistemological questions:

What can we know?
Is science the best way or the only way to gain knowledge?
Do we know that we are not living in a Matrix?
Is truth relative?

Metaphysics, for philosophers, is not usually adequately represented by the "metaphysics" section in most bookstores, where the books generally are about spirituality, the paranormal, and alternative healing methods. Instead, metaphysics spans all questions about what there is in the world. For example, these questions from the students are all metaphysical questions:

Does God exist?
What is human nature?
Why is there evil in the world?
What is real?
What is consciousness?
Do I have free will?
What is time?

Value theory, broadly construed, concerns questions about what we value and is divided into three subgroups: aesthetics, moral theory, and social and political theory. Aesthetics includes questions about beauty, for example; moral theory includes questions about the right way to behave; and social and political philosophy concerns the right way to organize groups, such as governments. Thus, these questions belong to value theory:

Is beauty really in the eye of the beholder?
Is morality relative?
Is abortion morally permissible?
Do animals have rights?
Should we always make decisions based on what is best for everyone?
Is democracy the best political arrangement?

Finally, *logic* is the study of reasoning, with an emphasis on how people ought to reason (not just how they do reason). Logic began with Aristotle, who identified different kinds of reasoning patterns and classified them as either good reasoning or bad reasoning. Logic was greatly extended at the end of the nineteenth century with the work of Gottlob Frege and Bertrand Russell, but it was still essentially about discerning the difference between good reasoning patterns and bad ones. And this is why, even though the student who asks the question is usually just trying to be funny, I classify questions like

Which came first, the chicken or the egg?

as genuine philosophical questions, falling under the heading of logic.

A great deal of the advancement of logic and mathematics, for example, has traditionally come from the study of paradoxes. A *paradox* is a set of two statements that we have good reasons to believe are true, but which contradict each other. Consider, for example, Zeno's paradox. Zeno of Elea (~490–~430 BC), as recounted by Aristotle, argued that one could never cross from one end of a room to another.

Example
"Zeno's arguments about motion, which cause so much disquietude to those who try to solve the problems that they present, are four in number. The first asserts the non-existence of motion on the ground that that which is in locomotion must arrive at the half-way stage before it arrives at the goal" (Aristotle, *Physics*, Book 6, chapter 9).

So, to reach the other side of the room, first you must go half the distance to the other side, which takes some amount of time. But, to get halfway across the room, you must first get a quarter of the way across the room, which also takes some amount of time, and so on. Since any distance can be cut in half infinitely many times, there are an infinite number of distances to cross, each of which takes a finite amount of time. Crossing an infinite number of distances would take an infinite amount of time, and could never be done. So, you can never get to the other side of the room. This is a paradox, of course, because you can demonstrate that you can get across the room; you just do it. So we have a puzzle—what is wrong with Zeno's reasoning? It wasn't until the eighteenth century when the theory of infinitesimals was developed with a theory of continuity that this question could be answered (can you figure it out?).

Definitions
Epistemology: the study of knowledge
Metaphysics: the study of what there is
Value Theory: the study of what we value
Logic: the study of how we ought to reason
Paradox: a set of two statements that we have good reasons to believe are true, but which contradict each other

1.2 How Do We Do Philosophy?

Now that we have identified some of the questions at the heart of philosophy, we turn to a discussion of how we go about trying to answer these questions. One misconception students have when they first come into my classroom is that philosophy never makes any progress. This makes a certain amount of sense, if we think that many of the philosophical problems we struggle with today are the same questions that the Ancient Greeks and philosophers of the past debated. This, however, is not entirely true; there are many philosophical questions that we have answered, or at least made a fair amount of progress on. Unfortunately for philosophers, each time this happens, the people working on that question carve themselves away from philosophy and create an entirely new discipline.

Consider, for example, the question: What is a proof? This is a question that consumed philosophers from Aristotle (384–322 BC) to Gottlob Frege (1848–1925). When we began to combine the insights from all the philosophers who have studied this question, we created modern computer science. Or consider the question: If a game of poker is interrupted, what is the fairest way to divide the money in the pot? Sure, you could just give everyone back the money that they put in during that hand, but philosophers like Blaise Pascal (1623–1662) and Gottfried Leibniz (1646–1716) were interested in determining how the money could be divided according to how the players would have likely fared if they had continued the hand. This led to the modern mathematical theory of probability.

Here's another question: What is a rational belief? This question drove Thomas Bayes (1701–1761) to develop Bayes' theorem, which gave rise to Bayesian statistics. This kind of question is related to the question of what is a rational decision. And philosophers' research here eventually gave rise to modern economics. Finally, the ancient question: What is the nature of the mind? Answers to this question combined with questions about proofs eventually became modern cognitive science.[1]

So, how do philosophers tackle these and other problems? We reason our way through them. Besides being a subdiscipline of philosophy, logic is also the main tool philosophers use to find answers. Thus, philosophers are primarily concerned with arguments. Good arguments are logical, that is, the premises are true and they support the conclusion. Philosophers' solutions are the conclusions of their arguments.

Ultimately, philosophers are interested in the truth. We are not interested in supporting particular preconceived ideas. We are interested in finding out what is actually the case. The oldest example of this sort of attitude that we have in print is a man named Socrates who lived in Athens, Greece, in the fifth century BC.

Philosophy in Ancient Greece

The earliest written works we have of philosophy in Ancient Greece are Plato's dialogues. (We know some of the earlier philosophers' works only because they were included in later philosophers' texts.) Plato lived from about 427 BC to 347 BC and lived primarily in Athens. Like many of the youth of Athens at the time, he considered himself a pupil of Socrates (469–399 BC). After Socrates' death, Plato traveled extensively around the region; and in 387 BC, he returned to Athens to found his own school. He named it the "Academy," after a sacred site that had olive trees dedicated to Athena (goddess of wisdom and courage), right outside of the walls of Athens, called "Akademia." The Academy had a continuous span of 900 years, until it was closed in 529 AD because it was perceived as a threat to Christianity.

Most of Plato's works take the form of dialogues between Socrates and other speakers, but contemporary scholars believe most of these conversations did not actually take place. It is not clear how much of the content in the dialogues belongs to Socrates and how much belongs to Plato; we get some clues by things Plato says in the dialogues—for example, taking care to mention when he was or was not present. Plato wrote these dialogues over a span of about fifty years. Contemporary scholars divide the dialogues into early middle and late periods, with the selection below, Plato's *Apology*, being one of the early dialogues.

As Socrates explains in *Apology*, his friend Chaerophon had visited the Oracle at Delphi. He asked the Oracle whether any man in Athens was wiser than Socrates. The Oracle's answer was that no one was wiser. The phrase "Know Thyself" was inscribed above the Oracle's temple, and was the "first commandment" of the god Apollo. As Socrates explains, he does not consider himself to be wise, so he commits his life to trying to understand the Oracle's pronouncement.

Plato's *Apology* may seem to be misnamed, for Socrates is anything but apologetic in this dialogue. The name actually comes from the Greek word *apologia*, meaning "defense." In Athens, all free men were allowed to vote, and it was a true democracy. The judicial system consisted of trial by a jury of 501; the plaintiff and defendant were each able to speak, and call witnesses, and the jury voted. In this dialogue, Plato tells us that he was present at the trial of Socrates, so contemporary scholars think it's probably an accurate portrayal.

Aristotle (384–322 BC) was born in Macedonia and came to Athens as a teenager. In Athens, he studied with Plato at his Academy for about twenty years. After Plato's death in 347, he traveled, collecting biological data, and eventually became the tutor of Alexander the Great. In 335, he returned to Athens and founded his own school, the Lyceum. This school had a very visible colonnaded walk (*peripatos*) that Aristotle and his followers used to roam while engaged in their discussions. As such, they were dubbed the Peripatetics. However, after Alexander's death in 323, there was a wave of anti-Macedonian sentiment and Aristotle was charged with impiety. Rather than suffer the fate of Socrates (who was ultimately sentenced to die by drinking poison), he fled Athens, and died shortly thereafter.

Most of Aristotle's works actually consist of lecture notes and accounts of lectures written by others. Scholars in the first century BC are credited with giving his work its present organization, and copies were transcribed over the centuries. In 1831, the Berlin Academy published the first critical edition of Aristotle's works, and these are what scholars still use today.

The first books of Aristotle's works are on logic, language, and scientific inquiry. In the *Prior Analytics*, Aristotle presents his invention: the logic of the categorical syllogism. Then, in the *Posterior Analytics*, he applies this logic to science. Next is the *Physics*, in which Aristotle presents his doctrine of four causes. We will encounter this doctrine first in Part II, when we consider teleological arguments for the existence of God, and second in Part VI, when we encounter Aristotle's ethical theory. The doctrine of the four causes is that the explanation of any thing is given by describing each of its four causes—the material cause (what it's made out of), the efficient cause (the maker), the formal cause (its form or essence), and the final cause (its purpose). After the *Physics* is the *Metaphysics* (which literally means: "what comes after the physics"), and last is Aristotle's practical philosophy—*Nicomachean Ethics* and *Politics*.

Thinking Philosophically

Philosophy, as a conversation about all of the issues we discussed above, has been going on for thousands of years. As Bertrand Russell suggests,[2] the value of philosophy is not so much in the resolution of problems, but in the investigation of the problems themselves. In order to join in the conversation, philosophers, broadly speaking, engage in (at least) three different kinds of activities:

1. Argument Analysis

We work to understand the arguments that others have made. For example, the only way to find a solution to Zeno's paradox is to understand clearly the argument Zeno made that led to the paradox in the first place. As we noted above, Aristotle relays this paradox as follows:[3]

> Zeno's arguments about motion, which cause so much disquietude to those who try to solve the problems that they present, are four in number. The first asserts the nonexistence of motion on the ground that that which is in locomotion must arrive at the half-way stage before it arrives at the goal. (Aristotle, *Physics*, Book 6, chapter 9)

As Aristotle gives the argument, it can be represented like this:

Premise:	If you cross the whole room, you must cross half the room.
Conclusion:	Motion is impossible.

But, of course, the argument is much more complicated than this. What we really want to understand is how Zeno thought the premise supports the conclusion. We can fill in Zeno's argument as follows:

Premise:	If you cross the whole room, you must cross half the room.
Premise:	If you cross half the room, you must cross a quarter of the room, and then an eighth, a sixteenth, and so on, ad infinitum.
Subconclusion:	If you cross the room, you must cross an infinite number of finite distances in a finite time.
Premise:	An infinite number of finite distances adds up to an infinite distance.
Subconclusion:	If you cross the room, you must cross an infinite distance in a finite time.
Premise:	It is impossible to cross an infinite distance in a finite time.
Subconclusion:	You can never cross the whole room.
Conclusion:	Motion is impossible.

2. Argument Evaluation

Once we adequately understand the arguments others have made, we can begin to reason our way through them to determine whether they are good arguments. With the invention of calculus, beginning with Isaac Newton and Gottfried Leibniz in the seventeenth and eighteenth centuries, mathematicians identified the problem with Zeno's argument—the third premise. The infinite number of finite distances can be represented as a series of reciprocal powers of 2:

$1 + \frac{1}{2} + \frac{1}{4} + \frac{1}{8} + \ldots \ldots$.

This series, however, is a convergent series, which means that the sum of this infinite series of numbers is actually a finite number. In this case the series converges to 2. Thus, while the first subconclusion is true, the third premise is not. Thus, the second subconclusion may or may not be true—the argument supporting the second subconclusion is bad. Thus, since the final conclusion depends on this subargument, the overall argument is bad.

3. Argument Creation

Finally, as philosophers, we are not merely interested in determining whether others' arguments are good or bad; we are also, and perhaps more importantly, interested in offering our own solutions to philosophical problems. But solutions are not enough; we also need to present good arguments for our solutions. After identifying the problem with Zeno's argument, we can present a new argument that demonstrates the dissolution of the paradox, and thus, the solution to the problem:

Premise:	If you cross the whole room, you must cross half the room.
Premise:	If you cross half the room, you must cross a quarter of the room, and then an eighth, a sixteenth, and so on, ad infinitum.
Subconclusion:	If you cross the room, you must cross an infinite number of finite distances in a finite time.
Premise:	An infinite number of reciprocal powers of 2 adds up to a finite number.
Subconclusion:	If you cross the room, you must cross a finite distance in a finite time.
Premise:	It is possible to cross a finite distance in a finite time.
Subconclusion:	You can cross the whole room.
Conclusion:	Motion is possible.

It is these activities of finding solutions that philosophers, like Socrates, believe will lead us to the truth. And, in fact, these activities are not the sole province of philosophy—scholars in a wide variety of disciplines analyze, evaluate, and construct arguments all the time. Consider the various sections of a research paper in psychology. The primary goals of the author are to present a hypothesis inspired by recent research, and to argue that the results of the studies support the hypothesis of the paper. In addition, in the discussion section, the author must evaluate her own argument to determine potential problems with the studies and future studies to perform.

Or consider a proposal by the engineers of a company that designs and builds nuclear power plants. These plants cost a lot of money, and so of course the purchaser wants to compare bids from several companies. Now, there is no one way to build a nuclear power plant—the best way to build one will depend on a variety of factors, and the purchaser probably has several criteria for judging which is the best proposal. So each company proposes a design for the plant and a price to build it. The proposal must present an argument to the purchasers that this company's design is the best according to their criteria. In addition, if proposals of other companies are known, the proposal must evaluate these other arguments and show theirs to be superior.

There is no doubt that philosophers engage in other activities, two of the most important being the generation of questions and possible answers. But the hallmark of the philosopher is that she does not stop with possible answers—rather, these are the just first steps. The crucial part is defending the answers with arguments.

1.3 Purpose and Structure of This Book

The purpose of this book is twofold. First, recall the questions from section 1.1. Throughout this book, you will read how various philosophers in the Western world have argued for particular answers to these questions. Philosophy was not always as specialized as it is today, and until quite recently, philosophy was not even different from science. Thus, many of the philosophers we will read wrote about, and have had an influence on, a wide variety of current views of philosophy, science, and religion.

In particular, we want to consider the following series of questions:

- Does God exist? Can we prove that God exists? Can we prove that God doesn't exist?
- What is knowledge? How do we get knowledge? Is science the best way to gain knowledge?
- What is the nature of the human mind?
- How can we have free will if our bodies are biological machines?
- Do we have the freedom to act on our moral beliefs?
- Why and how are we morally responsible?

Second, you will be introduced to particular tools for *doing philosophy*. Thinking philosophically requires the analysis and evaluation of arguments, so in the next two chapters you are going to learn:

- different types of arguments
- argument diagramming as a tool to analyze arguments
- logical principles such as validity and strength

You will see many of the different types of arguments in action in chapters 4, 5, and 6, as well as the use of argument diagramming in the analysis of arguments throughout the book. In the exercises at the end of each chapter, you will be asked to do your own analysis of arguments using the tools you learn in Part I. In the subsequent chapters in Parts II through VI, I use the following notation in my analysis: the conclusion (if it is explicit) is in purple text. The red sentences and sentence fragments are the individual claims the author makes, while the green words are "indicator phrases," that is, phrases that indicate how the claims are supposed to fit together to support the conclusion (see chapter 3). The blue sentences are illustrations of some of the author's specific claims, and despite being introduced by premise indicators, they do not seem to be meant as reasons to believe the claim as much as concrete examples of the claims given to aid understanding.

By the end of the book, or by the end of the course in which you are reading this book, you will gain some understanding of the history and methods of philosophy, but the real point is to get you asking important questions, reasoning clearly and capably, and sharpening your critical thinking skills—developing abilities, in other words, that will make a difference in your life long after specific content details have faded from memory. I want you to begin to understand philosophy as a process and as a tool for critical evaluation, and to develop confidence in your abilities as philosophers and as students.

1.4 In-Class Exercise

1. Consider Aristotle's reconstruction of another of Zeno's paradoxes:

> The second is the so-called "Achilles," and it amounts to this, that in a race the quickest runner can never overtake the slowest, since the pursuer must first reach the point whence the pursued started, so that the slower must always hold a lead. This argument is the same in principle as that which depends on bisection, though it differs from it in that the spaces with which we successively have to deal are not divided into halves. The result of the argument is that the slower is not overtaken: but it proceeds along the same lines as the bisection-argument (for in both a division of the space in a certain way leads to the result that the goal is not reached, though the "Achilles" goes further in that it affirms that even the quickest runner in legendary tradition must fail in his pursuit of the slowest), so that the solution must be the same. And the axiom that that which holds a lead is never overtaken is false: it is not overtaken, it is true, while it holds a lead: but it is overtaken nevertheless if it is granted that it traverses the finite distance prescribed. (Aristotle, *Physics*, Book 6, chapter 9)[4]

As we did in the section titled "Thinking Philosophically" above, (a) analyze and (b) evaluate Zeno's argument, and (c) construct an argument that comes to the opposite conclusion of Zeno's.

1.5 Reading Questions

Consider Plato's *Apology*.

1. What is the charge against Socrates? Can you imagine what might be similar charges that could be brought against a philosopher today?
2. At the beginning of his defense, Socrates denies the accusation that he is a teacher. Why does he say this? Do you think he is a teacher? If not, what do think it is that Socrates is doing? If yes, what is he teaching, and how is he teaching it?
3. Socrates says that the Oracle at Delphi proclaimed him to be the wisest man. What does Socrates think wisdom is? Does Socrates believe that he is the wisest man? If Socrates, as he claims, does not know what justice, knowledge, and so on are, how can he be the wisest man?
4. Why does Socrates believe that "no evil can happen to a good man"? Do agree? Why or why not?
5. Why does Socrates choose not to flee Athens? What would you do in similar circumstances?
6. What is your evaluation of Socrates' arguments? Which of his arguments are good? Which are bad? Why?
7. Is there anyone today whom you consider to be similar to Socrates? Why? If Socrates were alive today, who (or what kinds of people) do you think he would try to engage in the type of dialogue for which he was famous?

2 Types of Arguments

2.1 Vocabulary
2.2 Necessary versus Sufficient Conditions
2.3 Deductive versus Nondeductive Arguments
2.4 Forms of Valid and Invalid Deductive Arguments
2.5 A Priori versus A Posteriori Deductive Arguments
2.6 Types of Nondeductive Arguments: Induction, Argument by Analogy, and Abduction
2.7 Answers to Self-Assessment Exercises
2.8 In-Class Exercises

Learning Objectives

At the end of this chapter you will be able to:

- Identify several types of arguments commonly used in philosophical discourse
- Define the following terms:
  - Statement
  - Argument
  - Validity
  - Soundness
  - Cogency
  - Strength (of an argument)
  - Deductive argument
  - Non-deductive argument
  - A priori
  - A posteriori
  - Necessary and sufficient conditions

One of the essential components of doing philosophy is considering well-known views on the subject at hand. The first step in considering someone else's view consists in reconstructing his or her argument with fairness and charity. In this chapter we will first review some vocabulary before explaining various types of arguments.

2.1 Vocabulary

Before we can learn about different types of arguments, we need to become familiar with some important definitions.

Statement: A statement is a sentence that can either be true or false.

> *Example*
> "I earned an A on the final paper in my introductory philosophy course."

The above statement is either true or false depending on my actual grade on the paper. We say that this sentence has a *truth-value* (either true or false), and perhaps we can even know what the truth-value is. Not all sentences in English are statements—questions and commands, for example, are not statements. Some nonstatement sentences can, however, be transformed into statements with some rewording.

> *Example*
> "Go to class!"

The above command can be usefully transformed into the statement, "You should go to class," if the context permits.

Conditional statement: Conditional statements are special because they occur so often in arguments. A conditional statement has two parts: the antecedent and the consequent. A conditional statement generally has the form of an "if, then" statement, in which we have "If [the antecedent], then [the consequent]."

Consider the following:

> *Example*
> If you earn an A on the final paper, then you earn an A in the class.

The entire statement is the conditional, "you earn an A on the final paper" is the antecedent, and "you earn an A in the class" is the consequent. It is important to remember that a conditional statement, just like a regular statement, is a sentence with a truth-value. This conditional statement is either true or false depending on the instructor's policies in the course.

Self-Assessment

1. Rewrite the following conditional statements in standard "if …, then …" form:
   a. If you have a dog, you will have fur all over your clothes.
   b. You will never get an A if you keep falling asleep in class.
   c. If I knew you would be late, I would have brought a book.
2. Choose one. A statement is:
   a. a sentence
   b. a sentence that is true
   c. a sentence that can either be true or false
3. Choose one. An antecedent is:
   a. the part that comes after the "if" in a conditional statement
   b. the part that comes after the "then" in a conditional statement
   c. the part that comes before the "if" in a conditional statement
4. Which of the following sentences is a statement?
   a. "What time is it?"
   b. "I wish it were 8:00 already."
   c. "Come here at 8:00."
   d. "8:00, yeah!"

One thing to keep in mind about conditional statements is that they are not always presented in the "If *x*, then *y*" format. Often the "then" is omitted; sometimes it's presented in a "*y*, if *x*" format; and sometimes it's presented in a "*x*, only if *y*" format.

The rule of thumb is that the antecedent is always the part that immediately follows the "if," *unless* it immediately follows an "only if." The part that immediately follows "only if" is actually the consequent.

Self-Assessment

5. Rewrite the following conditional statement in standard form: "You get an A in this class only if you have perfect attendance."

Confusing? Let's look at what the sentence actually says. This is not a claim that if you have perfect attendance, then you will get an A; there may be several other things you have to do besides having perfect attendance. What it does say is that having perfect attendance is *necessary* for getting an A. Thus, if we know that you got an A, then we at least know that, regardless of your performance in other areas, you had perfect attendance. Thus, in standard form this statement would be rewritten as "If you get an A in the class, then you had perfect attendance."

Argument: For our purposes, an argument is a technical term that has a precise meaning: an argument is a set of statements, one of which is the conclusion, and the others are premises, which are supposed to provide support for the conclusion. In other words, the conclusion is asserted to be true on the basis of the premises.

> For example, you might make the following argument to your philosophy instructor: "It says in the syllabus that if a student receives an A on the final paper, then he or she will receive an A in the class. I did, in fact, receive an A on my final paper, so I should get an A in the class."

In this case, the premises are: (1) *It says in the syllabus that if a student receives an A on the final paper, then he or she will receive an A in the class*, and (2) *I did, in fact, receive an A on my final paper*. And the conclusion is: *I should get an A in the class*.

We often represent arguments like this:

Premises:	Premise 1.
	Premise 2.
Conclusion:	Conclusion.

In the next chapter we will learn about a different way of representing arguments that makes the relationship between the statements in argument much clearer. But for now, this representation will do.

> **Self-Assessment**
>
> 6. Identify the conclusion in the following argument:
> "According to the handbook, if a student cheats on an assignment, then that student should receive a failing grade. Sam did, in fact, cheat on the last homework assignment in Calculus, so Sam should get an F in the class."

> *Definitions*
> **Statement:** Declarative sentence; a sentence that could be true or false.
> **Conditional statement:** A statement that can be put into an "if ..., then ..." form.
> **Argument:** A set of statements in which one or more statements (the premises) are given as reasons to believe another statement (the conclusion).

Validity: A valid argument is one in which it is not possible for the conclusion to be false if the premises are true.

This is a very bold statement, not about what is actually the case, but about what could possibly be the case. Consider a course you may take in college; maybe it's Philosophy 101. And imagine that the instructor has written in the syllabus: "If you earned an A on the final exam, then you will receive an A in the class." Then consider the following argument:

Premises:	If you earned an A on the final paper, then you will receive an A in the class.
	You earned an A on the final paper.
Conclusion:	You will receive an A in the class.

The premises may not be true in your case, but *if* they are true, then the conclusion is guaranteed to be true. Or, to put it another way, it can't be the case that the premises are true at the same time that the conclusion is false. Thus, this is a *valid* argument.

Conversely, an invalid argument is one in which it is possible for the premises to be true and the conclusion false. Consider the following argument:

Premises:	If you earned an A on the final paper, then you will receive an A in the class.
	You will receive an A in the class.
Conclusion:	You earned an A on the final paper.

Here, it is possible for the premises to be true, but the conclusion false; there may be conditions other than earning an A on the final exam that would lead to an A in the class. You can imagine, for example that the syllabus said the following:

"There are two ways to guarantee yourself an A in this class. (1) If you earned an A on the final exam, then you will receive an A in the class. (2) If you earned an A on the final paper, then you will receive an A in the class."

In other words, even if it were the policy of the instructor that if you earned an A on the final exam, then you will receive an A in the class, just knowing that you will receive an A in the class doesn't tell us whether you earned an A on the final exam. Thus, for this argument, it is possible for the premises to be true and the conclusion to be false.

It is important to note that, given our definitions, a statement cannot be valid or invalid, and an argument cannot be true or false.

Soundness: A sound argument is a valid argument in which all the premises are actually true in our world.

This means that any argument that is either invalid, or valid with at least one false premise, is unsound. Consider the following example:

Premises:	If Barack Obama is the president, then Barack Obama lives in the White House.
	Barack Obama is the president.
Conclusion:	Barack Obama lives in the White House.

This is a sound argument at the time I'm writing this, but is probably valid but unsound at the time you are reading this because at least one of the premises will not actually be true.

Consider again the invalid argument from above:

Premises:	If you earned an A on the final paper, then you will receive an A in the class.
	You will receive an A in the class.
Conclusion:	You earned an A on the final paper.

This argument is unsound because it is invalid, regardless of whether the premises are actually true.

Self-Assessment

7. For each of the following arguments, determine whether it is valid or invalid.
   a. Either the Pirates won the game, or the Braves did. The Pirates didn't win, so the Braves did.
   b. If Holly was going to be late, she would have called. But she's not going to be late, so she won't call.
   c. I will either go to law school or move back in with my parents. I will not move in with my parents, so I'll go to law school.

Strength: Not all unsound arguments are bad; an invalid argument may be a good or strong argument.

Consider the following argument:

Premises:	Ninety percent of Americans are afraid of snakes.
	Jane is an American.
Conclusion:	Jane is afraid of snakes.

This argument is invalid because it is certainly possible that Jane is part of the 10 percent of Americans who are not afraid of snakes. Thus, it is possible for the premises to be true and the conclusion to be false. However, it is unlikely that Jane is a part of the 10 percent rather than the 90 percent, so it is unlikely that the conclusion would be false if the premises are true.

A *strong* argument, then, is an invalid argument in which it is likely that the conclusion is true, given that the premises are true. Unlike validity, strength can come in degrees. Consider a similar argument:

Premises:	Ninety-nine percent of Americans are afraid of snakes.
	Jane is an American.
Conclusion:	Jane is afraid of snakes.

Here, it is even more likely that the conclusion is true given that the premises are true. And since it is more likely, we say that this argument is stronger than the first, although they are both considered strong.

Conversely, a weak argument is an invalid argument in which it is not likely that the conclusion is true, given the truth of the premises.

Consider the following argument:

Premises:	Thirty percent of Americans speak French.
	Jane is an American.
Conclusion:	Jane speaks French.

While it is possible that Jane is part of the 30 percent of Americans who speak French, it is more likely that she is part of the 70 percent who do not. Thus, this is a weak argument.

Cogency: Just as we can evaluate valid arguments in terms of the actual truth or falsity of their premises, we can evaluate invalid arguments. A cogent argument is a strong argument in which all the premises are actually true in our world.

This means that any argument that is either weak, or strong with at least one false premise, is uncogent. Consider the following argument:

Premise:	All swans observed so far have been white.
Conclusion:	All swans are white.

This is quite a strong argument, but, unfortunately, black swans have now been observed in Australia. Thus the premise is false, and the argument is uncogent.

Self-Assessment

8. For each of the following arguments, determine whether it is strong or weak.
   a. Most Americans brush their teeth every day. Shauna is an American, so she probably brushes every day.
   b. Nearly two-thirds of college students have cheated on an assignment. Manny is a college student, so he has probably cheated on an assignment.
   c. Almost half of people over sixty-five have some sort of hearing loss. Clark is over sixty-five, so he likely has some hearing loss.

Definitions

Valid: In a valid argument, if all the premises are true, then the conclusion must be true.

Sound: A sound argument is valid and has all true premises.

Strong: In a strong argument, if the premises are all true, then the conclusion is likely to be true.

Cogent: A cogent argument is strong and has all true premises.

2.2 Necessary versus Sufficient Conditions

When we try to think of a definition of something, we may be tempted to list all the things that fall into that category. For example, when Socrates asks for a definition of "virtue," Meno gives him a list of virtues: piety, justice, charity, and so on.[1] But, as Socrates replies, a good definition does not list things that satisfy the definition; rather, a good definition provides *necessary and sufficient conditions*. So let's look at this idea of giving necessary and sufficient conditions.

Example

Let's say that in one of your courses, the syllabus says that earning As on all your assignments is a necessary and sufficient condition for getting an A in the class. What does this mean? Well, it certainly means that if you get As on all your assignments, then you get an A in the class. But this conditional explains only a *sufficient* condition—after all, if it only said "You get an A in the class if you earn As on all your assignments" (which is another way of expressing the same conditional) you may well think that there are other ways to get an A in the class (like acing the exam, washing your professor's car, etc.). If this were the case, then earning As on all of your assignments would be sufficient for getting an A in the class, but not *necessary*.

So what makes the condition necessary? Well, if earning As on all your assignments is necessary for getting an A in the class, then you can't get an A without doing that. Thus, we way express the necessity is by saying "You get an A in the class *only if* you earn As on all your assignments." This makes it clear that the very least you have to do is earn As on all your assignments to get an A in the class, although if this were the only statement in the syllabus, you may think that there are other things you need to do as well.

So, what we need for necessary and sufficient conditions is *both* of these conditional statements. We can express these two conditional statements as one by saying: "You get and A in the course *if and only if* you earn As on all your assignments."

Similarly, a definition of something should express the necessary and sufficient conditions for being that thing. Consider the definition of a bachelor: A bachelor is an unmarried adult male. That is, we can say: a person is a bachelor *if and only if* that person is: (a) unmarried, (b) an adult, and (c) a male. This states the *sufficient condition* that if someone has (a), (b), and (c), then that person is a bachelor, and the *necessary condition* that someone has (a), (b), and (c) only if that person is a bachelor (alternately, if someone is a bachelor, then that person has (a), (b), and (c)).

Definitions

x* is a necessary condition for *y: *y* only if *x* (alternately, if *y*, then *x*); *y* cannot occur without *x*.

z* is a sufficient condition for *y: if *z*, then *y*; *z* is enough for *y*, although *y* could obtain another way.

2.3 Deductive versus Nondeductive Arguments

Most of the arguments we will see in this book aspire to a very high standard in attempting to establish their conclusions. Philosophers usually want to claim that their conclusions come with a 100 percent guarantee of being true, provided that they show that their premises are also true. In other words, philosophers generally aim to give sound arguments.

Sometimes, however, arguments do not live up to this standard. Still, we would like to be able to classify arguments not just according to their actual logical form, but also according to what the author intended the logical form to be. The reason is that we do not want to criticize an argument for being invalid if the author didn't intend for it to be valid, but instead intended for the argument to be strong. Thus, we will make the distinction between *deductive* arguments and *nondeductive* arguments. A deductive argument is one that makes the claim that if the premises are true, then the conclusion is guaranteed to be true. A nondeductive argument is one that makes the claim that if the premises are true, then the conclusion is likely to be true. We call a "successful" deductive argument *valid*, and a "successful" nondeductive argument *strong*.

Definitions

Deductive argument: An argument that is intended to be valid.

Nondeductive argument: An argument that is intended to be strong.

2.4 Forms of Valid and Invalid Deductive Arguments

There are some valid and invalid argument forms that are so common that they have been given names.

Valid Argument Forms

The first example on page **19** has the form of *modus ponens*. In that example, A stands for "you earned an A on the final paper," and B stands for "you earn an A in the class."

Valid Argument Forms

Modus Ponens

Premises:	If A, then B.
	A.
Conclusion:	B.

Modus Tollens

Premises:	If A, then B.
	Not B.
Conclusion:	Not A.

Hypothetical Syllogism

Premises:	If A, then B.
	If B, then C.
Conclusion:	If A, then C.

Disjunctive Syllogism

Premises:	Either A or B.
	Not A.
Conclusion:	B.

Constructive Dilemma

Premises:	Either A or B.
	If A, then C.
	If B, then D.
Conclusion:	Either C or D.

Categorical Syllogism

Premises:	All As are Bs.
	C is an A.
Conclusion:	C is a B.

A similar argument is the following:

Premises:	If you earn an A on the final paper, then you earn an A in the class.
	You did not earn an A in the class.
Conclusion:	You did not earn an A on the final paper.

This argument has the form of *modus tollens*.

Four additional common valid argument forms are illustrated by the following arguments. The following has the form of *hypothetical syllogism*:

Premises:	If you earn an A on the final paper, then you earn an A in the class.
	If you earn an A in the class, then you graduate with honors.
Conclusion:	If you earn an A on the final paper, then you graduate with honors.

The following argument has the form of *disjunctive syllogism*:

Premises:	Either you earn an A on the final paper or you earn a B on the final paper.
	You did not earn a B on the final paper.
Conclusion:	You earn an A on the final paper.

The following argument has the form of *constructive dilemma*:

Premises:	Either you earn an A on the final paper or you earn a B on the final paper.
	If you earn an A on the final paper, then you graduate with high honors.
	If you earn a B on the final paper, then you graduate with regular honors.
Conclusion:	Either you graduate with high honors or you graduate with regular honors.

The following argument has the form of *categorical syllogism*:

Premises:	All grades are relative.
	This score is a grade.
Conclusion:	This score is relative.

There is one more deductive argument form we should consider before proceeding—*reductio ad absurdum*. In this sort of argument, we first assume that the negation of the conclusion is true. Then we use that assumption to draw a contradiction. Finally, since the assumption leads to a contradiction, we conclude that the negation of the assumption (in this case, the conclusion) is true.

This is basically the form of Zeno's argument from the previous chapter—he assumed that "An infinite number of finite distances add up to an infinite distance." Using this assumption, he was able to show that you can never cross the whole room. But of course he could demonstrate, by doing it, that you can cross the whole room—hence the paradox. Since we have a contradiction, then the assumption must be false. And we saw that if we use the premise "An infinite number of finite distances add up to a finite distance" instead, we do not reach a contradiction, and we can resolve the paradox.

As a simpler example, consider the following argument:

Premises:	All birds can fly.
	Penguins are birds.
Conclusion:	Penguins can fly.

This conclusion, of course, contradicts our experience that penguins, in fact, cannot fly. We can use this contradiction to show that the assumption "All birds can fly" is false (if, of course, the claim that penguins are birds is true):

Assumption:	All birds can fly.
Premise:	Penguins are birds.
Subconclusion:	Penguins can fly.
Statement of fact:	Penguins can't fly.
Subconclusion:	Penguins can fly and penguins can't fly.
Conclusion:	Not all birds can fly.

Invalid Argument Forms

An invalid argument may be a bad argument, but not because it is weak or uncogent; rather, it may be bad because the premises do not support the conclusion. A formal fallacy is an argument that has a similar form to one of the valid forms we have named, but is not valid.

One example we used above has the form of *affirming the consequent*:

Premises:	If you earned an A on the final paper, then you earn an A in the class.
	You earn an A in the class.
Conclusion:	You earned an A on the final paper.

Although this argument seems to resemble the form modus ponens, it is actually invalid. The rule (the first premise) doesn't say that earning an A on the final paper is the only way to get an A in the class; perhaps it is also the case that if you earn an A on the final exam, then you earn an A in the class. Thus, the truth of the premises does not guarantee the truth of the conclusion.

Another formal fallacy is *denying the antecedent*:

Premises:	If you earned an A on the final paper, then you earn an A in the class.
	You did not earn an A on the final paper.
Conclusion:	You did not earn an A in the class.

Again, although this argument resembles the form modus tollens, it is actually invalid because it is possible that the premises could be true while the conclusion false. Recall the example above: if you earn an A on the final exam, then you can earn an A in the class without earning an A on the final paper.

Self-Assessment

9. Determine the form of each of the following arguments.
   a. Either the Pirates won the game, or the Braves did. The Pirates didn't win, so the Braves did.
   b. If Holly was going to be late, she would have called. But she's not going to be late, so she won't call.
   c. According to the handbook, if a student cheats on an assignment, then that student should receive a failing grade. Sam did, in fact, cheat on the last homework assignment in Calculus, so Sam should get an F in the class.
   d. If the cat is sleeping, she snores. If the cat snores, I can't sleep. So if the cat is sleeping, I'm not.

2.5 A Priori versus A Posteriori Deductive Arguments

In a philosophical context, *a priori* means "prior to experience." An a priori proposition is one whose verification does not require experience; it is something that can be verified purely by reason. In particular, the assertion is that once you understand the concepts and definitions involved in the proposition, you don't need any particular experience on top of that understanding to know that the proposition is true. Rather, you can reason directly from the concepts and definitions to the truth of the proposition.

An example of an a priori proposition is: 2 + 3 = 5. Once you understand the concepts of addition and equality, and the definitions of 2, 3, and 5, you can understand through reason alone that this proposition is true. There's no experience that you need to have, no "checking with the real world" that you need to do to verify that it is true. A priori reasoning, or an a priori argument, then, is reasoning that uses a priori propositions as premises; that is, it is reasoning from concepts and definitions.

In contrast, *a posteriori* means "after experience." An a posteriori proposition is one whose verification does require experience; it is something that can be verified only by experience. In particular, the assertion is that even if you understand the concepts and definitions involved in the proposition, you still need to "check with the real world" to verify that it is true.

An example of an a posteriori proposition is: There are two cows in that field. Even after you understand the concepts of "cow," "field," and "being in a certain place," and the definition of "two," you would still have to verify, by some experiential means, whether the statement is actually true. A posteriori reasoning, or an a posteriori argument, then, is reasoning that uses a posteriori propositions as premises; that is, it is reasoning from facts about the world.

Definitions
A priori: Prior to experience; independent of any particular experience
A posteriori: After experience; dependent on particular experiences

2.6 Types of Nondeductive Arguments: Induction, Argument by Analogy, and Abduction

Strong arguments are not always those with premises that assert percentages. Many (if not all) scientific laws are actually the conclusions of strong arguments, the premises of which are assertions about what we have experienced so far, and the conclusions of which are assertions about what we will continue to experience in the future. These are often referred to as *arguments by induction*.

Example

Premise:	All of the massive objects observed so far fall to the ground at a rate of 9.8m/s2.
Conclusion:	All massive objects fall to the ground at a rate of 9.8m/s2.

In addition, many arguments by analogy are strong arguments. This type of argument is one we come across quite frequently in philosophy. The premises generally are (1) that two situations are analogous (or alike in some important respects), and (2) that certain things are true of one situation. The conclusion is then that those same things will be true of the second situation. The strength of arguments by analogy depends on how good the analogy is for the purposes of the argument.

Example

Premises:	My bowl fell off the counter and broke.
	Your bowl is very similar to my bowl.
Conclusion:	If your bowl falls off the counter, then it will break.

Finally, many *abductive arguments* are strong. An abductive argument is often called an *inference to the best explanation*, and it is structured as follows. Some fact about the world is presented as needing explanation. A claim is made about what the best explanation is for that fact, and then the inference is that this explanation must be true.

Example

Premises:	There is not enough visible matter in the universe to account for all of the gravitational effects we observe in space. The best explanation for the extra gravitational effects we observe is the presence of matter we cannot see (dark matter).
Conclusion:	The universe contains dark matter.

Self-Assessment

10. Determine the type of each of the following arguments.
    a. Erica will probably make the shot since her average is 0.75.
    b. Hannah smelled smoke and something sweet coming from the hood of her car, so there's probably a leak in the antifreeze reservoir.
    c. Ivan fixed Greg's computer, and I have the same computer, so Ivan can probably fix mine too.
    d. There is beauty all around, so there must be a spirit looking out for us.
    e. An atom is like a miniature solar system. The planets revolve around the sun, so the electrons must revolve around the nucleus.
    f. Most Labradors weigh over 75 pounds when they're full grown, so I'm sure my Lab will weigh over 75 pounds when he grows up.

2.7 Answers to Self-Assessment Exercises

1. Rewrite the following conditional statements in standard form:
   a. *If* you have a dog, *then* you will have fur all over your clothes.
   b. *If* you keep falling asleep in class, *then* you will never get an A.
   c. *If* I knew you would be late, *then* I would have brought a book.
2. c is correct.
3. a is correct.
4. b (although c could plausibly be interpreted as "You should come here at 8:00," which is a statement.)

5. *If* you get an A in this class, *then* you have perfect attendance.
6. Conclusion: "Sam should get an F in the class."
7. For each of the following arguments, determine whether it is valid or invalid.
   a. Valid.
   b. Invalid—fallacy of denying the antecedent.
   c. Valid.
8. For each of the following arguments, determine whether it is strong or weak.
   a. Strong.
   b. Strong.
   c. Weak.
9. Determine the form of each of the following arguments.
   a. Disjunctive syllogism.
   b. Fallacy of affirming the consequent.
   c. Modus ponens.
   d. Hypothetical syllogism.
10. Determine the type of each of the following arguments.
   a. Induction.
   b. Abduction.
   c. Argument by analogy.
   d. Abduction.
   e. Argument by analogy.
   f. Induction.

2.8 In-Class Exercises

1. Which of the following sentences is a conditional statement?
   a. "If you leave the door open, the dog will get out."
   b. "If you don't want the last donut, can I have it?"
   c. "The cat will come in if she hears the can opener."
   d. "The dog will come only if you call her name."
2. The following are conditional statements. Identify the antecedent and the consequent in each.
   a. "If we set our clocks back an hour, we will get an extra hour of sleep."
   b. "I am going to be really annoyed if she's late again."
   c. "You can get a driver's license only if you are at least sixteen."
   d. "If you try to pet the cat he will probably bite you."

3. Complete the following sentences in your own words.
   a. An argument is ____________________.
   b. The conclusion of an argument is ____________________.
   c. A premise of an argument is ____________________.
4. For each of the following arguments determine whether it is valid, invalid, strong, or weak.
   a. My dog will come only if I call her name. I did call her name, so she will come.
   b. Eric will probably make the shot since his average is 50 percent.
   c. Jana is a good lacrosse player. She scores a lot of goals and the other team always puts their best defender on her.
   d. Either I'm going to do it or you're going to do it, and I'm not going to, so you are.
   e. My friends all say I will like this restaurant, and they know me pretty well, so I will probably like it.
   f. If the cat is sleeping, she snores. If the cat snores, I can't sleep. So if the cat is sleeping, I'm not.
   g. If Rob gets gas first, then he'll be late. Rob wasn't late, so he didn't get gas first.
5. For each of the following arguments, determine the form or type.
   a. Jana is a good lacrosse player. She scores a lot of goals and the other team always puts their best defender on her.
   b. Kenny gets a Wi-Fi signal all the way over here, and you have the same phone, so you'll probably get a signal too.
   c. If I don't pass Calculus, then I will be put on academic probation, and if I get put on academic probation, then my parents won't let me keep the car. So if I don't pass Calculus, then I'll lose the car.
   d. Nearly two-thirds of college students have cheated on an assignment. Manny is a college student, so he has probably cheated on an assignment.
   e. You're either with us or you're against us. You're clearly not with us, so you're against us.
   f. Almost half of people over sixty-five have some sort of hearing loss. Clark is over sixty-five, so he likely has some hearing loss.
   g. If you can't swim, then you can't play water polo. But you can swim, so you can play.
6. For each kind of argument, construct an example of your own, and explain why you think it is that kind of argument.
   a. Valid
   b. Invalid
   c. Sound
   d. Unsound
   e. Strong

f. Weak
g. Cogent
h. Uncogent
i. Deductive
j. Inductive
k. Argument by analogy
l. Abductive
m. Modus ponens
n. Modus tollens
o. Hypothetical syllogism
p. Disjunctive syllogism
q. Constructive dilemma
r. Denying the antecedent
s. Affirming the consequent

3 Argument Analysis and Diagramming

3.1 Visual Representations of Reasoning
3.2 Understanding and Representing Argument Structure
 3.2.1 Structural Indicators: Premises and Conclusions
 3.2.2 Multiple Statements within Sentences
 3.2.3 Linked Arguments
 3.2.4 Convergent Arguments
 3.2.5 Chain Arguments
 3.2.6 Complex Arguments
3.3 Interpreting Arguments to Create Diagrams
 3.3.1 Fairness and Charity
 3.3.2 Implied Premises and Conclusions
 3.3.3 Implied Premises and Conclusions: A Complex Example
3.4 Diagramming Objections and Replies
3.5 Summary
3.6 Answers to Self-Assessment Exercises
3.7 In-Class Exercises

Learning Objectives

At the end of this chapter you will be able to:

- Analyze and diagram arguments
- Define the following terms:
  - Linked argument
  - Convergent argument
  - Chain argument
  - Complex argument
  - Subargument
  - Fairness
  - Charity

3.1 Visual Representations of Reasoning

Consider the following story:

"Ten o'clock? I'm not sure if I'll be able to make it. Let me call you back, okay?" Alexis closed her phone and turned to Brandy, "That was Char. She wants go out to see the Wanderers later. I really want to go …"

"Are you kidding? No, you shouldn't go! You know we're going to have a quiz in math tomorrow. You're not doing so great in the class, and you really should study. Look, I'll study with you, okay?"

Alexis sighed, "My mom said the same thing. Not about the studying; about the not going. She thinks I haven't been getting enough sleep lately. She wants me to go to bed early. And not just tonight—for the next few." She sighed again and sat down.

"Well, she has a point." Brandy sat down too, "Even if we weren't almost definitely going to have a quiz tomorrow, that's a good reason why you shouldn't go."

"Yeah, maybe," Alexis trailed off. She flopped back on the bed, "Ugh! You know my dad's in on it too."

"What do you mean?"

"He says I've been spending too much money. He says the tickets are too expensive. If I want to buy them," Alexis raised both her hands up to do air-quotes, "I'll have to 'crack open someone else's piggy-bank.' Ugh," Alexis sighed again, "But I really want to go!"

Brandy stood up again, and looked at Alexis. "So let me get this straight. You have three separate reasons, and good reasons at that, and you still don't believe it? That you shouldn't go out?" Brandy laughed and threw a pillow at her friend, "You're unbelievable!" She laughed again, as Alexis threw the pillow back.

"You're right, you're right. I'm convinced; I won't go," Alexis lowered her voice conspiratorially, "but please don't tell my parents that anything they said made a difference."

Brandy is certainly right about one thing; Alexis was presented with three different reasons for her to believe that she should not go to the concert. Or, to put in another way, Alexis was presented with three separate arguments that all had the same conclusion. Let's look at these arguments one at a time. We can write the first argument like this:

Alexis should not go to the concert because she should study for her math quiz.

We can break this argument up into two parts: (1) Brandy wants Alexis to believe that she should not go to the concert, so (2) Brandy gives Alexis a reason to believe it. Alternately, we can say that Brandy is telling Alexis that her belief that they are going to have a quiz the next day supports her belief that Alexis should stay home.

We can represent that way of looking at the conversation visually, with this diagram:

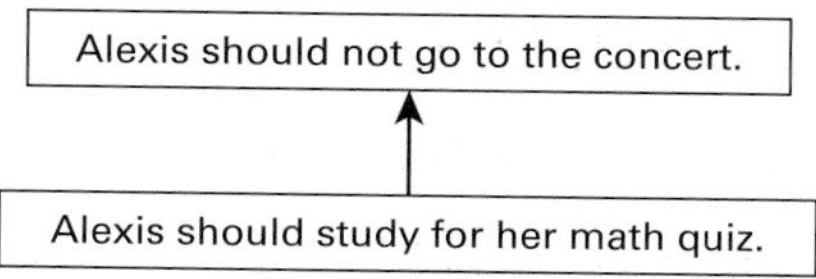

Here, the sentences in the boxes are each of Brandy's beliefs, and the arrow indicates that the bottom belief supports the top belief.

We can do the same thing with the arguments that each of Alexis's parents give. From what Alexis says, it seems that her mother believes that she's not getting enough sleep, and so she should go to bed early. Alexis's mother also thinks that this supports her belief that Alexis should not go to the concert. And again we can represent this with a diagram,

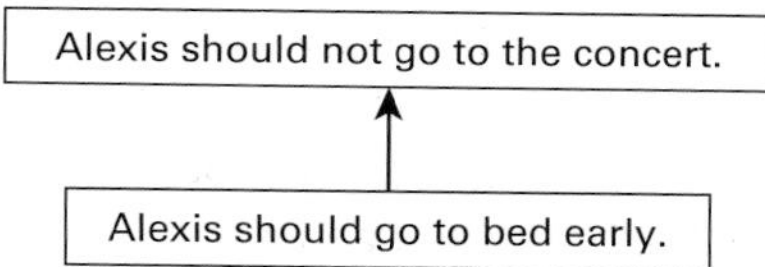

where again the sentences in the boxes are Alexis's mother's beliefs, and the arrow represents the fact that Alexis's mother thinks that the bottom belief provides support for the top belief.

Similarly, it seems that Alexis's father thinks she's spending too much money, and so should not spend money on a ticket to the concert. Alexis's father also thinks that this supports his belief that she should not go to the concert. This reading of Alexis's description can be represented with this diagram:

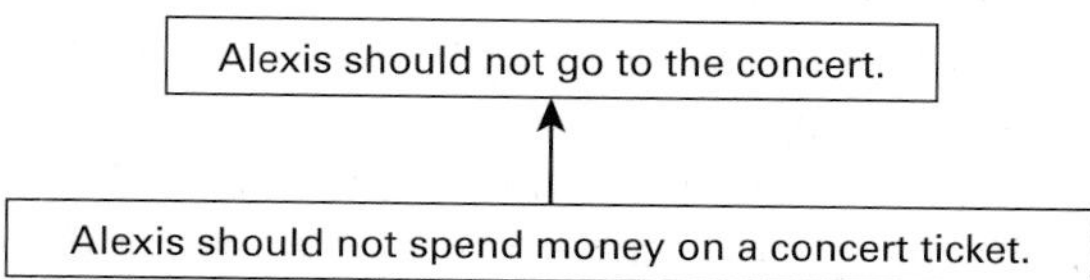

In fact, since all three arguments have the same conclusion, we can represent them in one single diagram:

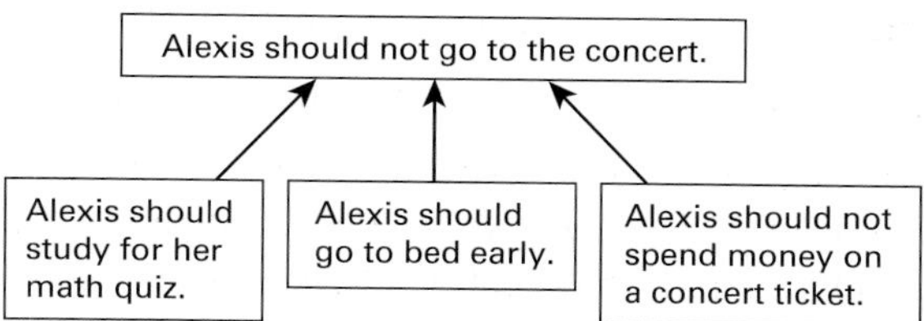

Let's consider another exchange:

Dr. Jordan reached her hand into the paper bag and pulled out a lemon. She placed it on the table, and looked out at the class. "Do lemons conduct electricity?" she asked, looking into her students' faces.

Jaime raised his hand, and Dr. Jordan nodded toward him. "I don't know—let's plug it in and find out," Jaime smiled.

"Yes, we could do that," Dr. Jordan smiled back, "and we will ... tomorrow. But right now, I want you to use what you know about chemistry to make a conjecture."

"Okay," Jaime said, "how do we start?"

"Well, what do you know about lemons?"

"They're sour," said Jaime, dryly.

"Yes! And why is that?" probed Dr. Jordan.

"Um ... citric acid?" Jaime asked.

"Right," said Dr. Jordan as she walked to the chalkboard. "So let's write this down. We know that lemons contain citric acid," she said, as she wrote this on the board. "What else?"

"Water and fructose."

"Good. So we have citric acid and water—we don't care about the fructose right now. What do we call a combination like that?" Dr. Jordan inquired.

"Electrolyte!"

"Yes, good. Lemons contain an electrolyte. OK, now for 'plugging it in.' We want to hook up an ammeter or some other device, like a lightbulb, to see if we can get a current. In order to do this, we would have to stick metal into the lemon in two places. So now," she asked as she turned back to the class, "what do we know about electrolytes and metal?"

"Let's see," began Jaime, "The electrolyte will oxidize certain metals, like zinc. So, if you stick something like a zinc-plated nail in the lemon, the Zn atoms will oxidize to Zn^{++} ions."

"OK, good," continued Dr. Jordan, "now what if we put in another piece of metal, like copper?"

"Well, copper won't oxidize; it's just a conductor."

"Right. What will happen, though, is that the Zn^{++} ions and the H^{+} ions will be attracted to the copper, and if we connect the piece of zinc to the piece of copper outside of the lemon, they will draw the free electrons from the zinc around the circuit to the copper."

"Oh, yeah! And then the H^{+} ions will reduce to hydrogen gas around the copper, right?" Jaime asked.

"Right. And the negatively charged citrate will be attracted to the zinc. So the electrons will 'flow' from the zinc to the copper outside the lemon, and positive charge will flow from the zinc to the copper inside the lemon. And this will continue as long as there is zinc left to oxidize. So electrolytes can conduct electricity."

"Cool," said Jaime, "a lemon could be a battery."

"Okay," replied Dr. Jordan, "so we seem to have what seem like good reasons to believe that lemons conduct electricity. How confident are you?"

"Pretty confident," replied Jaime, "I definitely believe it now."

"Good," Dr. Jordan smiled, "tomorrow we'll see how well we've argued."

Dr. Jordan has made a good point; after this exchange Jaime does have good reasons to believe that a lemon could conduct electricity. Let's look at these reasons. The first thing Dr. Jordan notes is that lemons contain citric acid and water. Jaime says that this combination is an electrolyte, and Dr. Jordan concludes that lemons contain an electrolyte. We can represent this reasoning like this:

Lemons contain a combination of citric acid and water.
All combinations of citric acid and water are electrolytes.
So, lemons contain an electrolyte.

The first two facts are given by Dr. Jordan as reasons to believe the third. And, as we did above, we can represent this reasoning visually, with a diagram:

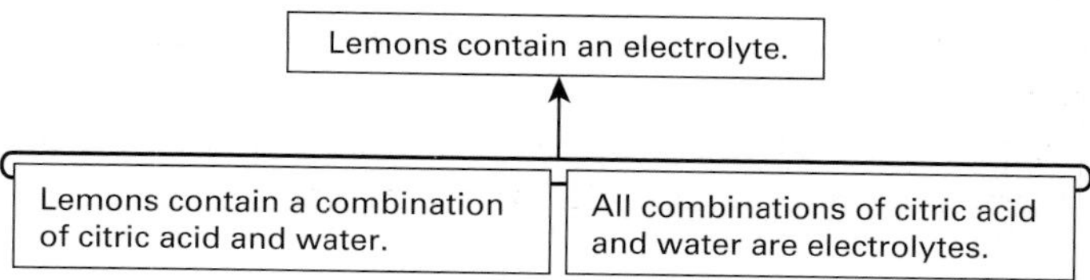

This diagram is noticeably different from the diagrams above. Why? Recall that we noted above that Alexis was given three different reasons to believe her conclusion. That is, if one of the reasons were taken away—if, for instance, Char had bought Alexis's ticket for her—she would still have had good reasons to believe that she shouldn't go out.

Here, however, the two reasons that Dr. Jordan gave for her conclusion must work together to support the conclusion. In other words, if we took away the fact that "All combinations of citric acid and water are electrolytes," then the fact that lemons contain this combination would not be a reason to believe that lemons contain electrolytes.

To create accurate argument diagrams we need to keep in mind that we write statements inside of boxes, and connect the boxes with arrows. More explicitly, the rules are:

1. Each box contains only one statement.
2. The arrows begin at one box, or one grouping of boxes, and end at one box.
3. The box at the end of the arrow is the conclusion of the argument.
4. The box(es) at the beginning of the arrow is (are) the premise(s).
5. The arrow is the inference from premise(s) to conclusion.
6. Separate arrows indicate separate lines of reasoning (the inferences).
7. Attached boxes indicate that these premises are supposed to work together to support the conclusion.

Self-Assessment

1. Consider the following argument diagram. Which part represents the conclusion of the argument? Which part represents the premise of the argument? Which part represents the inference in the argument?

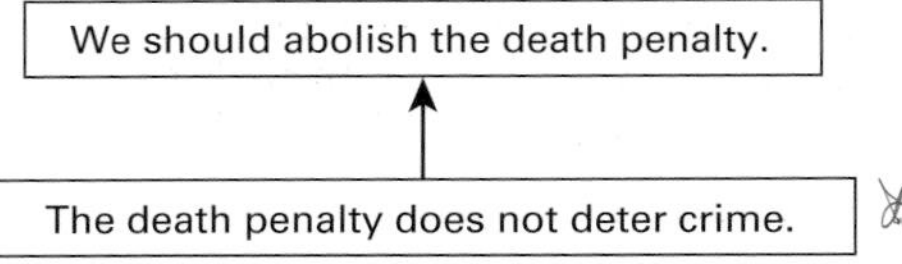

Recall the following example:

Example
"If a student receives an A on the final paper, then he or she will receive an A in the class. I did, in fact, receive an A on my final paper, so I should get an A in the class."

The statements of the above argument have been placed into boxes:

If a student receives an A on the final paper, then he or she will receive an A in the class.

I received an A on the final paper.

I should receive an A in the class.

Self-Assessment

2. The two diagrams below present two possibilities for representing the argument above. Determine which of the diagrams is correct and why it is correct. Choose one:

a. Diagram A is correct because the premises have separate lines of reasoning to support the conclusion.
b. Diagram A is correct because the premises work together to support the conclusion.
c. Diagram B is correct because the premises have separate lines of reasoning to support the conclusion.

continues

d. Diagram B is correct because the premises work together to support the conclusion.

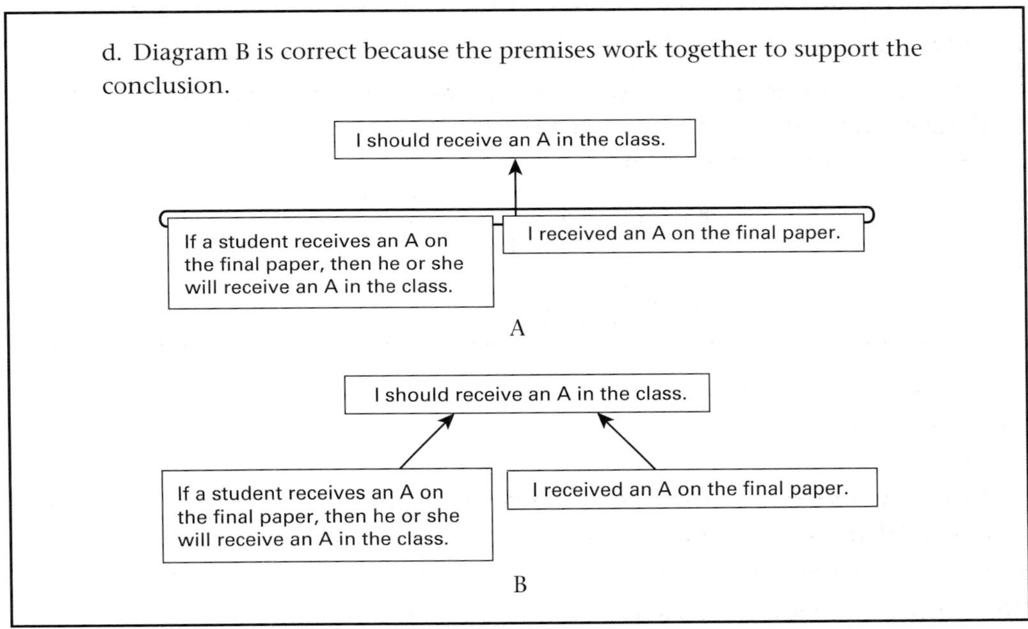

3.2 Understanding and Representing Argument Structure

It is important to remember that any representation of an argument is an *interpretation*, and any interpretation must be supported by the text. In long, complex texts, the task of interpretation is more difficult, and the same text may be subject to many different interpretations. What follows in this and subsequent sections are various methods we can use to probe the text in order to develop the best representation possible.

3.2.1 Structural Indicators: Premises and Conclusions

We can often identify the premises and conclusions of arguments by the signals the author uses.

Example: Consider the following argument.
"We should abolish the death penalty. This is because it does not deter crime."

Here, the author uses a common premise indicator: "because." This alerts us that what follows "because" is supposed to support (act as a premise for) some other statement.

This argument is diagrammed as:

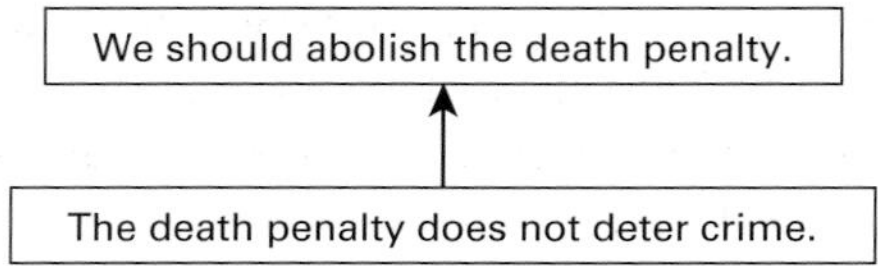

Common premise indicators include:

because	for	given that	the reason is that
since	as	recall that	assuming that
consider that	after all	it is evident that	based on the fact that

Self-Assessment

3. The following arguments contain one premise and one conclusion. Identify the premise indicator and the premise in each.
   a. "Consider that it's already 8:00. We are going to be late for the movie."
   b. "People should be allowed to own guns. The reason is that people have the right to protect themselves."

There are also words that signal a conclusion. Common conclusion indicators include:

so	therefore	we may infer that	wherefore
thus	accordingly	implies that	proves that
hence	consequently	shows that	it follows that

Self-Assessment

4. The following arguments contain one premise and one conclusion. Identify the conclusion indicator and the conclusion in each.
   a. "The death penalty does not deter crime. So we should abolish it."
   b. "Jack stopped to pet the dog. Hence, we will be late for his appointment."
5. Identify which of the following diagrams is the most appropriate representation of this argument: "I have the most experience. It follows that I should be in charge."

3.2.2 Multiple Statements within Sentences

Premises and conclusions are not always stated in complete, independent sentences. Previously we learned that premises and conclusions are statements, which are types of sentences. However, we also then saw that sometimes these statements are not actually given as complete, independent sentences in the text.

> *Example*
>
> Consider again the argument above: "We should abolish the death penalty. This is because it does not deter crime."
>
> The same argument could be contained within a single sentence: "We should abolish the death penalty, because it does not deter crime."

In both arguments, "because" serves as a premise indicator. This is an *argument* because the author is asserting the truth of one statement:

(the conclusion: We should abolish the death penalty

on the basis of another:

(the premise: The death penalty does not deter crime).

Each of these are *statements* because they are expressions of propositions that are either true or false (though we may not know their truth or falsity), even though they were both contained in the same sentence. And once we separate the premise from conclusion, we can diagram the argument:

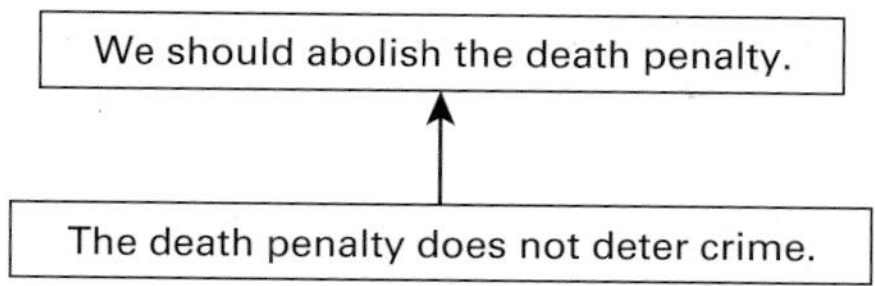

Notice that we put "The death penalty does not deter crime" in the premise box, even though the text says "it does not deter crime." The problem is that "it does not deter crime" is not an independent sentence—it cannot be understood unless we have the information about what "it" is. Thus, we rewrite the text as "The death penalty does not deter crime" so that this premise can be understood on its own.

This is a general rule about argument diagrams. Each sentence in a box should be a complete and independent statement that can be understood on its own.

We can similarly rewrite the arguments from the examples above.

Examples
"Consider that it's already 8:00. We are going to be late for the movie"

can be rewritten as

"Considering that it's already 8:00, we are going to be late for the movie."

"People should be allowed to own guns. The reason is that people have the right to protect themselves"

can be rewritten as:

"The reason that people should be allowed to own guns is that people have the right to protect themselves."

Self-Assessment

6. Identify the indicator in each of the following arguments, and say whether it is a premise indicator or a conclusion indicator.
   a. "Soda is bad for you because it rots your teeth."
   b. "We should start since she has given us the signal."
   c. "It's my car; hence, I should be the one to drive it."

It is also the case that parts of an argument can be contained in a single sentence, even if the entire argument is given in more than one sentence.

Example
"Brain states have only instrumental value; therefore they do not have intrinsic value. So, since states of consciousness have intrinsic value, brain states are not states of consciousness."

Here, the entire argument is given in two sentences, but two of the statements are contained in the first sentence, and two are contained in the second. Let's take them one at a time. Consider the first sentence:

"Brain states have only instrumental value; therefore they do not have intrinsic value."

"Therefore" indicates that the second part of the sentence is supported by the first part.

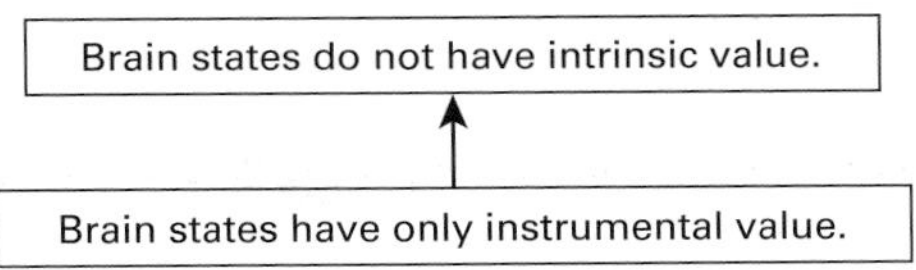

Then, consider the second sentence:

"So, since states of consciousness have intrinsic value, brain states are not states of consciousness."

"So" indicates that something in the second sentence follows from the conclusion in the first sentence. Having "so, since" indicates that before we find out what follows from the first sentence, we are going to get another statement that supports the same conclusion.

This means that both "Brain states do not have intrinsic value" and "States of consciousness have intrinsic value" support the claim "Brain states are not states of consciousness."

The entire argument can be diagrammed like this:

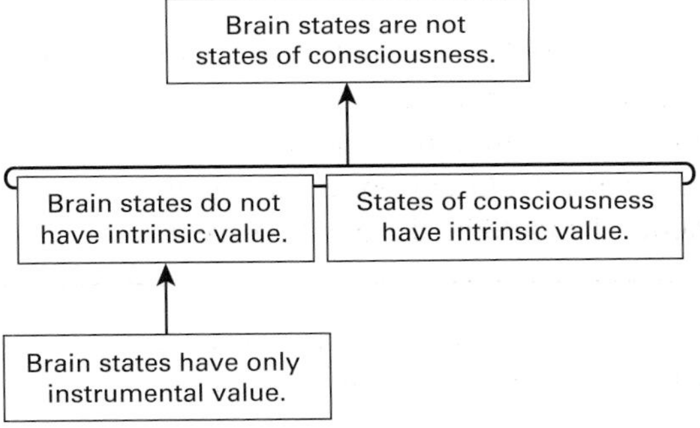

Self-Assessment

7. Identify all the indicators in the following argument, and say whether it is a premise indicator or a conclusion indicator. "The price of gas is rising at an astronomical rate. So, since we have a limited budget, we need to start driving less."

3.2.3 Linked Arguments

As we saw with the two conversations at the beginning of this chapter, arguments—even those we encounter in everyday life—have many kinds of structures. One of the great things about argument diagramming is that it forces us to understand the structure of the argument.

As in the conversation with Dr. Jordan and Jaime, as well as other arguments discussed above, some premises need to be combined in order to support a conclusion. You may have learned (in a logic class, for example) about certain argument forms, such as modus ponens. Consider the following argument:

> *Example*
> "In the syllabus it says that if I received an A on the final paper, then I will receive an A in the class. I received an A on the final paper. Therefore, I will receive an A in the class."

There are three statements in this argument: (1) If I received an A on the final paper, then I will receive an A in the class. (2) I received an A on the final paper. (3) I will receive an A in the class.

This particular argument exhibits the form of *modus ponens*:

Premises:	If A, then B.
	A.
Conclusion:	B.

In this case, neither premise alone could support the conclusion; rather, the premises act together to create a deductively valid argument. An argument in which two or more premises must be combined in order to support a conclusion is called a *linked argument*. This would be clearer if we had some sort of visual way of representing the argument. This is what argument diagramming does.

The above argument can be diagrammed as follows:

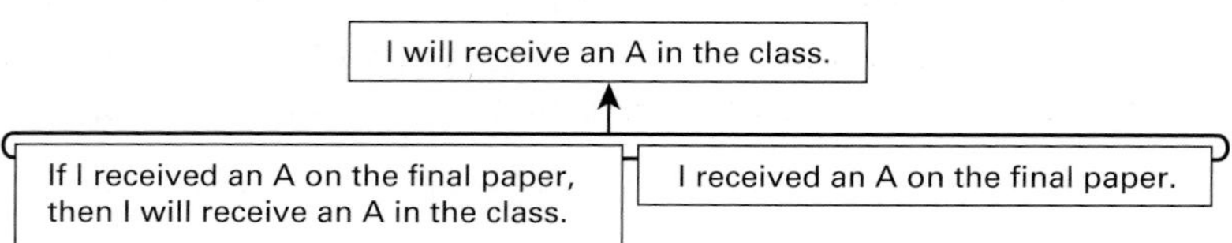

The oval around the top of the two premise boxes means that the premises are *linked*—that the intention of the author is that these premises work together—and the arrow means that they support the conclusion. It is most common to use this kind of representation when the author's argument is an example of a known valid argument form. Sometimes, though, premises are meant to be combined even if the argument does not exemplify one of these forms.

How do we know when the premises are supposed to be combined, and when they are supposed to be separate lines of reasoning? The answer is that we have a variety of words and phrases that indicate the difference. In this section, we will concentrate on premises that are supposed to be combined.

Definition
Linked argument: An argument in which two or more premises must be combined in order to support a conclusion.

Common combination indicators include:

and	thus, since	besides	in addition to the fact that
but	so, because	as well as	plus the fact that

Indicator phrases such as "thus, since" and "so, because" are special because they indicate both (1) statements that are to be combined and (2) the conclusion that those statements are supposed to support. Consider a different way of expressing the argument above.

Example
"In the syllabus it says that if I received an A on the final paper, then I will receive an A in the class. Thus, since I received an A on the final paper, I will receive an A in the class."

The word "thus" generally indicates a conclusion, so what follows "thus" is supposed to follow from what comes before it. In this case, this means that the first statement is a premise that supports either the second or third statement. The word "since" generally indicates a premise, so the second statement is also a premise. The combination "thus, since" then indicates that what comes before combines with what comes after to support the conclusion.

In other words, we could easily rewrite the second sentence above:

"*Thus, since* I received an A on the final paper, I will receive an A in the class"

like this:

"*This, combined with the fact that* I received an A on the final paper, *supports the claim that* I will receive an A in the course."

Self-Assessment

8. Diagram the following argument: "Medical researchers are constantly discovering new ways to treat and cure diseases, and the health of our citizens should be a top national priority. Thus, doctors should be eligible for government grants to support their work."

3.2.4 Convergent Arguments

Often the premises given by the author are not supposed to be combined, but rather are supposed to provide independent reasons for believing the conclusion; that is, each premise by itself would support the conclusion, and using all of them merely makes the conclusion more likely.

> *Definition*
> **Convergent argument**: An argument in which two or more premises are given, but each is a separate, independent reason supporting the conclusion.

How do we know when premises are involved in independent, separate lines of reasoning? The most common way that an author indicates that he or she is presenting different, independent lines of reasoning to support a conclusion is to list the reasons explicitly, using numbers (first, second, third, …), letters (a, b, c, …), or something similar.

> *Example*
> "Eating animals is wrong for a variety of reasons. First, many animals are sentient creatures that have thoughts and emotions. Second, we should not cause animals to suffer if we don't need to. Finally, raising animals for food uses resources, like grain, that could be used to feed hungry people around the world."

Here, the author gives a list of different reasons that support the conclusion. The implication of such a list is that each reason can stand on its own to support the conclusion, and each reason added just makes the argument stronger.

We can rewrite this argument as:

Premises	Many animals are sentient creatures that have thoughts and emotions. We should not cause animals to suffer if we don't need to. Raising animals for food uses resources, like grain, that could be used to feed hungry people around the world.
Conclusion	Eating animals is wrong.

In this case, however, the important structure is not well represented by this rewriting of the argument. In particular, it does not show us that each of these premises provides independent support for the conclusion. That is, each premise by itself can support the conclusion; none of the premises needs to work with any of the others to provide this support. We could, in other words, reasonably view the overall argument as a combination of the following arguments:

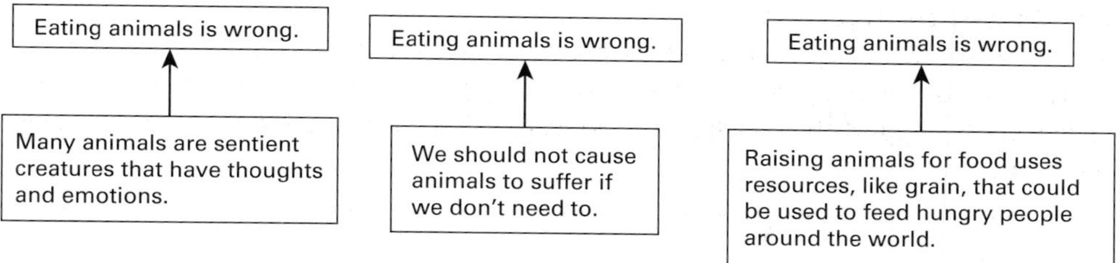

The idea is that if a premise can support a conclusion by itself, then we say that it is a separate line of reasoning.

If we diagram this argument, these details about its structure become apparent:

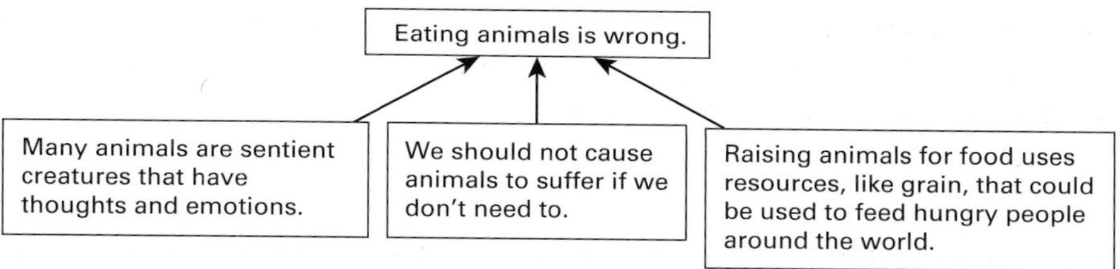

How do we know when the premises involved are independent, separate lines of reasoning? The idea is that if the premises are independent, they could each be taken alone to support the conclusion (though each of these arguments by themselves may be weaker than the argument taken as a whole).

Unfortunately, some of the same words, such as "and," that indicate convergent arguments are often used to indicate linked arguments. There are, however, words that are often used to indicate separate lines of reasoning in an argument:

besides	also	moreover
furthermore	another reason	furthermore

Self-Assessment

9. Diagram the following argument: "Dogs are good pets because they give unconditional love. Moreover, dogs can provide protection at home."

3.2.5 Chain Arguments

Finally, an author may be making a chain of inferences in the argument. A *chain argument* will always have at least one *subargument*, meaning that one statement will be both a premise and a conclusion within the argument.

Example
"Since cats like milk, they will try to tip over a glass of milk. So, you shouldn't leave yours on the table when cats are around."

How do we diagram this argument? We have two indicator words here, "since" and "so," but they don't occur together, so they are not indicating a linked argument. Let's take the sentences one at a time. The premise indicator occurs in the sentence "*Since* cats like milk, they will try to tip over a glass of milk." This tells us that "Cats like milk" is supposed to support "Cats will try to tip over a glass of milk."

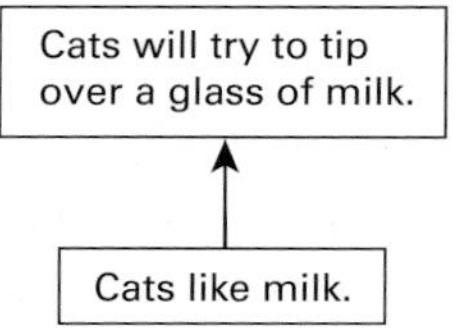

The conclusion indicator occurs in the sentence, "*So*, you shouldn't leave yours on the table." This tells us that "Cats will try to tip over a glass of milk" is supposed to support "You shouldn't leave your glass of milk on the table when cats are around."

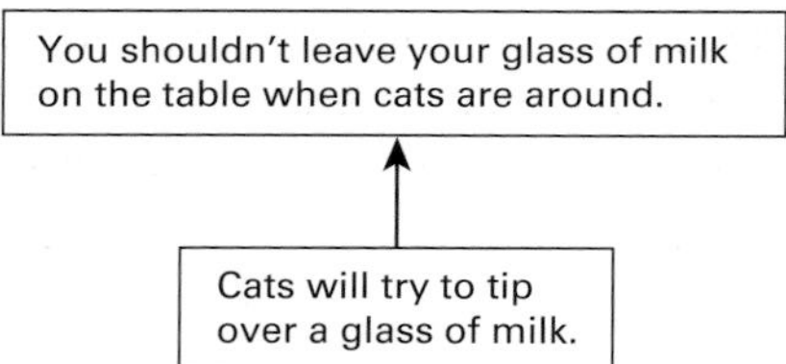

Notice that each part looks like an argument in its own right. When the conclusion of one argument is used as a premise in another argument, we call the first argument a *subargument*, and the conclusion of that argument a *subconclusion*.

Definition
Subargument: An argument in which the conclusion is used as a premise in another argument.
Chain argument: An argument that contains one or more subarguments.

Accordingly, the entire argument can be diagrammed as follows:

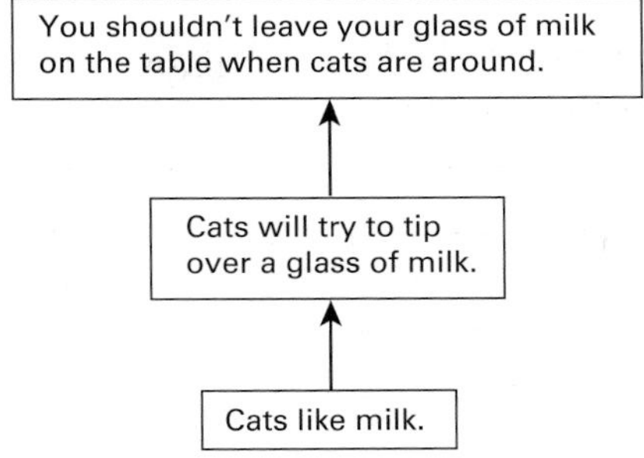

Self-Assessment

10. Diagram the following argument: "The semantic properties of mental states (i.e., what they are about) are not intrinsic, because they depend on facts about the individual's history and environment. Therefore, mental events do not cause other events by virtue of their semantic properties."

3.2.6 Complex Arguments

Most real arguments—those you would find in an article, an editorial, or a speech, for example—are more complicated than the ones we have studied so far. Real arguments usually have some combination of linked, convergent, and chained premises supporting either the main conclusion, the subconclusion, or both. We call this kind of argument *complex*.

Definition

Complex argument: An argument in which more than one of the above types of argument (linked, convergent, sub-, and chain) appear.

Example

"Four-wheel-drive cars cost more than two-wheel-drive cars, so we shouldn't buy a four-wheel-drive. Furthermore, we don't really need a four-wheel-drive, and we shouldn't buy things we don't need."

There are three indicator words in this argument: "so," "furthermore," and "and."

The first indicator word tells us that "We should not buy a four-wheel-drive car" is the conclusion supported by the claim "Four-wheel-drive cars cost more than two-wheel-drive cars." So, this first part of the argument has the following basic structure:

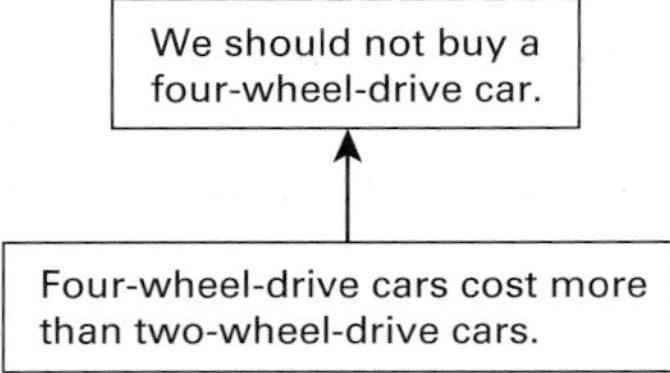

The second indicator word tells us that the author is giving us a separate line of reasoning to support the same conclusion. But, unlike the first line of reasoning, there are two statements here: "We do not need a four-wheel-drive car" and "We should not buy things we do not need." The third indicator tells us that these two claims are supposed to work together.

So, the second part of the argument has a linked structure:

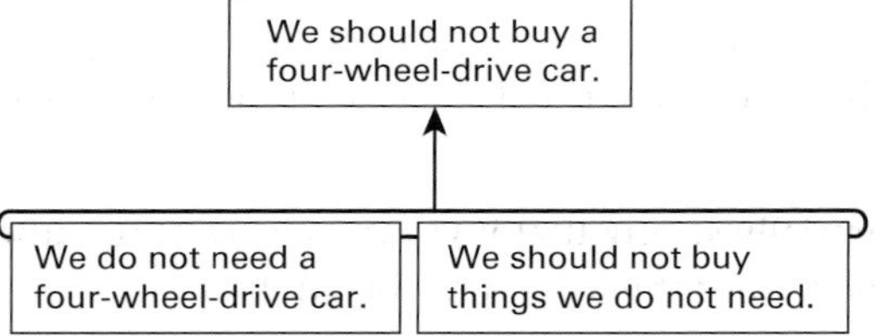

Overall, then, the argument has a convergent structure:

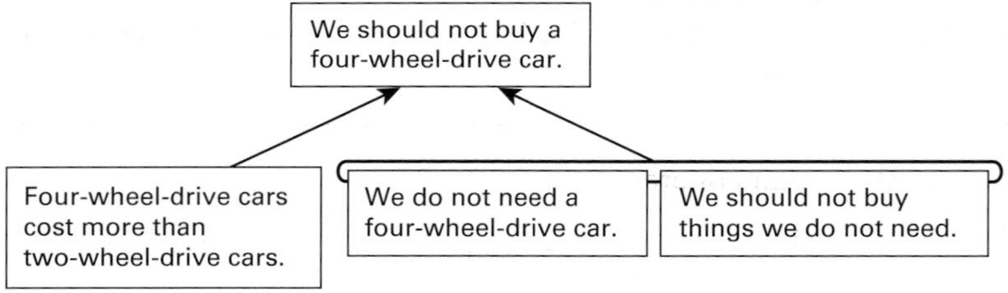

Self-Assessment

11. Diagram the following argument: "Pool maintenance can cost hundreds of dollars a year and we really don't have that kind of money. So, I don't think we should put a pool in this summer. Besides, pools pose a real drowning danger to small children."

3.3 Interpreting Arguments to Create Diagrams

3.3.1 Fairness and Charity

Diagramming arguments is a visual way of representing an argument. But representing an argument always involves *interpretation*. What we have been doing so far is learning ways to interpret arguments as accurately as possible. When we evaluate arguments, we don't want to misrepresent what the author of the argument is saying, for then our evaluation would be worthless.

The principles we have seen so far—for example, using premise and conclusion indicators and identifying the structure of the argument—offer relatively concrete steps to take when reconstructing an argument.

The principles of fairness and charity, however, are somewhat more abstract.

Fairness: We should always interpret the argument in a way that is consistent with the author's intentions. For example, we should always use language that is as close as possible to the language the author uses. We should not put words in the author's mouth, or take words out of the author's mouth.

Charity: If there is some uncertainty, we should always put the argument in the best possible light. If there is ambiguity, always choose the interpretation that makes the argument stronger rather than weaker.

These principles are essentially saying that if we are unsure of our understanding of an argument, we should give the author the benefit of the doubt.

> *Example*
> "Even though logging is a big industry that employs a ton of people, the government should ban it in national forests. Logging disturbs local ecosystems; and we can't survive without our ecosystems."

The premises of this argument are:

Premise 1	Logging disturbs local ecosystems.
Premise 2	We can't survive without our ecosystems.

But how should we rewrite the conclusion? Here are three options:

1. The government should ban logging.
2. The government should ban logging in national forests.
3. The government should ban all logging everywhere.

The first option is not the best interpretation. The author does not say that logging should be banned, period. The author says that logging should be banned *in national forests*. Similarly, the third option is not the best either, because the author does not say that logging should be banned everywhere. Again, the author says that logging should be banned *in national forests*.

> *Example*
> Consider a twist on the argument above: "Even though logging is a big industry that employs a ton of people, the government should ban logging in national forests. Logging disturbs local ecosystems; how are we going to survive without our ecosystems?"

The first sentence contains the conclusion: The government should ban logging in national forests. The second sentence contains the premises, the first of which is: Logging disturbs local ecosystems. But how should we rewrite the rhetorical question into a statement? Here are some options to consider:

1. We might not be able to survive without our ecosystems.
2. We could probably survive without our ecosystems.
3. We can't survive without our ecosystems.

The author seems to be saying something much stronger than the first option, so interpreting the rhetorical question this way makes the argument weaker than the author probably meant it. And the author doesn't seem to believe the second option. The author seems to be implying that we can't survive without our ecosystems, and interpreting the rhetorical question this way would make this premise not support the conclusion. The third option seems to be the most accurate, and makes the author's argument as strong as possible.

Fairness

When arguments are complex, many people tend to interpret them in a way that supports the positions they already hold. Often, people may reword important claims in a way that the author didn't intend, or restate them with emotionally loaded words. Also, people may omit important premises, or add premises not provided in the original. (There is indeed a legitimate place for adding implicit premises and conclusions. We'll get to this in the next section in the chapter.)

The principle of fairness says that we should not let our biases and/or preconceived ideas influence the reconstruction of an argument. For example, if an author presents a conclusion that is qualified in some way, we shouldn't represent the conclusion without the qualification.

> *Example*
> Consider an argument advocating the use of medical marijuana. It would not be accurate or fair to represent the author as being in favor of legalizing *all* drugs.

Charity

When authors use rhetorical questions, ambiguous language, or hedges in their arguments, it can be very difficult to interpret the argument fairly or accurately. We always rewrite rhetorical questions as statements if they seem to be intended as premises. But formulating a claim that masquerades as a rhetorical question can be tricky.

> *Example*
> "It should be illegal for Occupy Wall Street protesters to camp in parks. They make the parks dirty and it is unsafe for both the campers and the rest of the public. How important is freedom of expression, anyway?"

There are a few different ways to rewrite the rhetorical question at the end of this argument:

1. Freedom of expression is not important.
2. Freedom of expression is not the most important thing.
3. Freedom of expression is very low on the list of important things.

The most charitable interpretation here is probably (2). The author seems to be arguing that cleanliness and safety, for example, may be more important than the perceived need of the protesters to be able to sleep where they protest. It seems to be an uncharitable interpretation to say that they author thinks that freedom of expression is unimportant or of very little importance.

In the absence of other information in the text, then, the principle of charity says that when parts of the argument are ambiguous, we should interpret them in the best light possible. This means interpreting a claim in a way that makes it true, rather than false; or interpreting a claim in a way that makes the premises support the conclusion, rather than not supporting it.

Sometimes, though, the principles of fairness and charity conflict. This happens when, for example, we have the choice to rewrite a premise either (1) in a way that makes it true, but not support the conclusion, or (2) in a way that makes it false, but does support the conclusion.

> *Example*
> "All CMU sophomores are students, but aren't all Pitt sophomores, too? So, no Pitt sophomore is a CMU sophomore."

How would we rewrite the rhetorical question in this argument using the principle of fairness? Here are two options:

1. All Pitt sophomores are students.
2. No Pitt sophomores are students.

The two options would work in the argument like this:

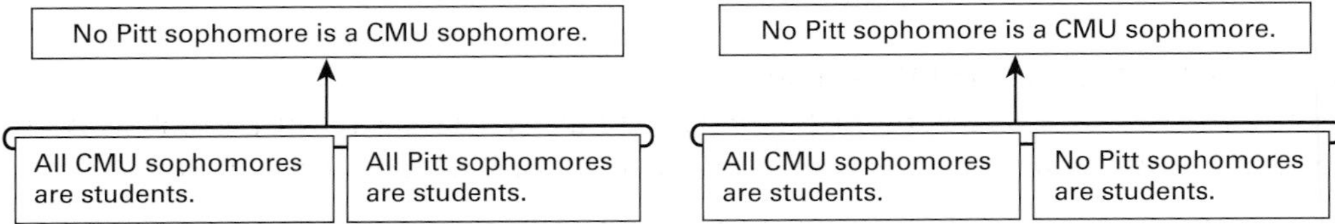

The principle of fairness dictates that we interpret the argument as closely to the original intent of the author. The second option violates the principle fairness because the way the question is phrased implies that the author thinks Pitt sophomores are also students. Thus, the first option is in accordance with the principle of fairness.

How would we rewrite this argument using the principle of charity? Consider the same two options. The principle of charity says that if you have the choice, you should interpret the argument in such a way that the premises do support the conclusion. The first option violates the principle of charity because, even though the premises and the conclusion are all true, the premises don't support the conclusion. Thus, the second option is in accordance with the principle of charity because, even though the second premise is false, these premises do logically lead to the conclusion.

The conflict here is that it seems that the rhetorical question should be rewritten as "All Pitt sophomores are students," because this seems to be what the author intended. However, if we rewrite the question this way, the premises do not support the conclusion—if it we substitute "college student" for "Pitt sophomore" for example, this argument would make no sense. On the other hand, the principle of charity requires that we rewrite the rhetorical question as "No Pitt sophomores are students," because that makes the conclusion follow directly from the premises. However, this way of rewriting the premise is clearly false and not what the author intended.

So what do we do? Well, it depends. The convention in logic is to represent the argument in such a way that the premises directly support the conclusion, and leave the question of whether the premises are true to the evaluation stage. In practice, though, it may not always be so clear-cut. The intuition here, for example, may be to do something different from the two options above: add an extra premise or two that allows the rewritten premise to be true *and* the premises to support the conclusion. For example:

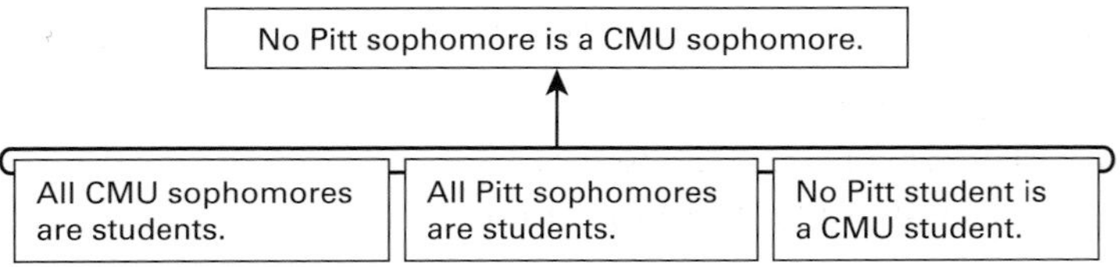

Adding premises (and/or conclusions!) that seem to be implied by the author is the subject of the next section.

3.3.2 Implied Premises and Conclusions

Recall from the previous section that authors don't always include all claims that are necessary for the argument they are making. Arguments of this sort are called *enthymemes*.

> *Definition*
> **Enthymeme**: An argument in which a premise and/or the conclusion is implied but not stated.

In particular, some authors seem to assume that the conclusions of their arguments are so obvious that the conclusions don't need to be stated explicitly. Just as when we are trying to restate something the author explicitly says, though, we should always apply the principles of fairness and charity when trying to formulate a claim that the author is using implicitly.

> *Example*
> "It seems obvious to me that people in the future will never develop time travel. Really, if they do, wouldn't we have heard from them by now?"

According to the principles of fairness and charity, what is the best way to rewrite the rhetorical question in this argument? Here are some options:

1. If people in the future develop time travel, then we may or may not have heard from them by now.
2. If people in the future develop time travel, then we would have heard from them by now.
3. If people in the future develop time travel, then we definitely would have heard from them by now.

Option (2) seems to accord best with the principles of fairness and charity. The way the question is phrased implies that the author is more confident than "may or may not," so (1) is out. In addition, we shouldn't put words into the author's mouth, and the author did not say "definitely," so (3) is out as well. Now we can ask a further question. What other premise does the author seem to believe but doesn't state? Here are some options:

1. People in the future develop time travel.
2. We have heard from people from the future.
3. We have not heard from people from the future.

Option (1) would make the argument circular (i.e., it assumes what it is trying to prove), so would not be charitable. And option (2) would definitely make the argument bad, and also does not seem to be what the author is implying.

We can diagram the original argument as follows:

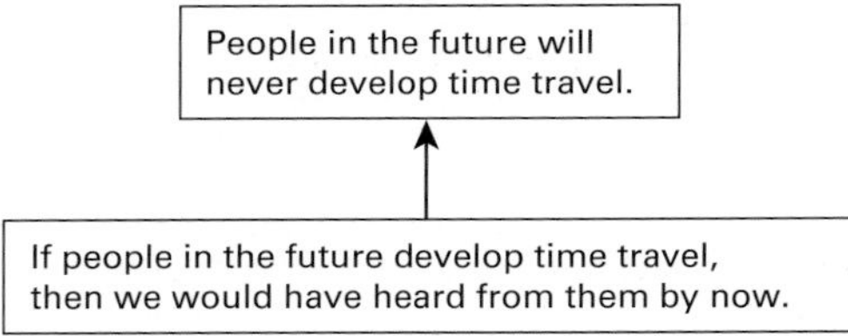

Here, the argument looks like part of a modus tollens argument. Recall that this valid argument form can be expressed as:

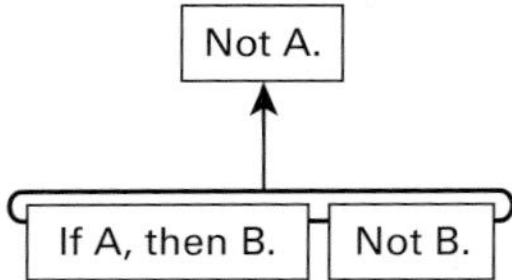

Let "People in the future develop time travel" be A, and "We would have heard from people in the future by now" be B. Then, what we have in this example is:

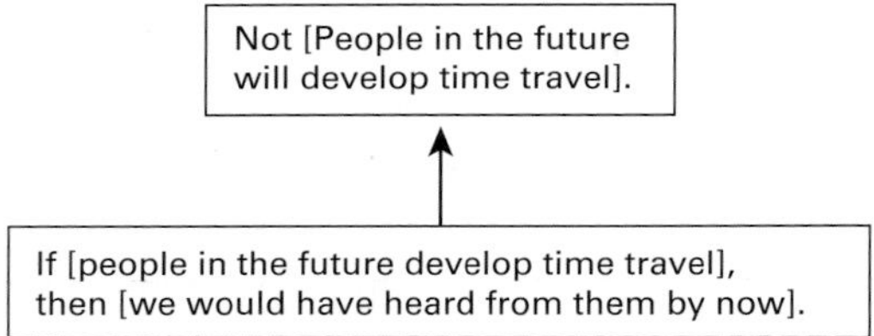

But, it seems clear, as we saw above, that in giving this argument, the author believes that we have not heard from scientists in the future. In fact, the conclusion doesn't really follow from the premise if we don't assume that this is true. This is equivalent to filling out the entire modus tollens argument.

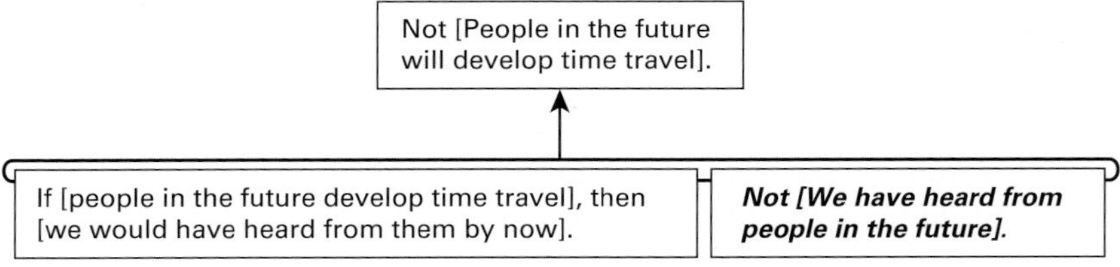

There are of course, better ways to represent this second premise and the conclusion: "We have not heard from people in the future" and "People in the future will never develop time travel," respectively.

So, the complete diagram would be:

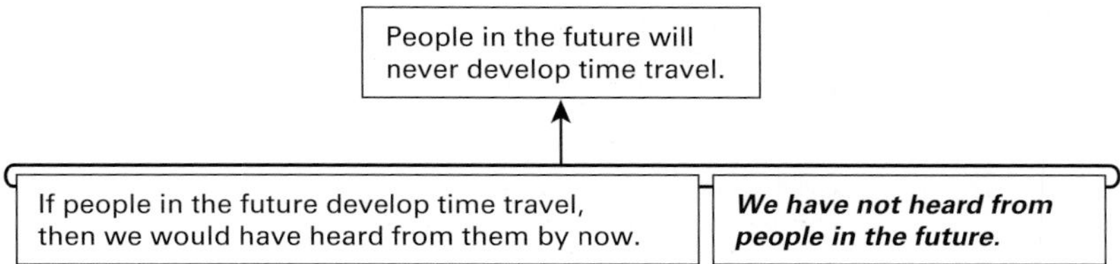

Here, by convention, we have italicized the implied premise to indicate that it is not something the author actually said, but rather something we believe the author implied.

Notice in this diagram that the implied premise is linked with the explicit premise to support the conclusion. This is a result of the way that we decided what is implied in the argument: we determined that the implied statement is a premise by figuring out what the explicit premise needed to help it support the conclusion. If the implied premise helps the explicit premise by connecting it to the conclusion, then it is a linked argument.

Sometimes, though, what is implied or missing is not a premise, but rather the conclusion. In this case we have to insert the implied conclusion when we reconstruct the argument, or it wouldn't be an argument at all.

> *Example*
> "If you want to do well on your test, then you should turn off all your electronic gadgets and study; and I know you want to do well on it."

The two statements here are:

Statement 1	If you want to do well on your test, then you should turn off all your electronic gadgets and study.
Statement 2	You want to do well on your test.

What is the conclusion of this argument? First, the "and" indicates that this is a linked argument. Second, this argument has the form:

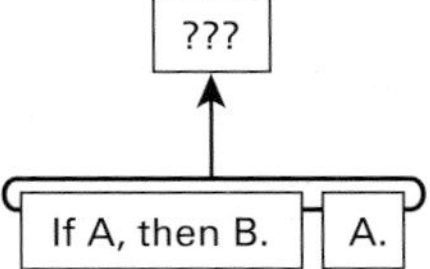

The conclusion that would make this a valid argument is: "You should turn off all your electronic gadgets and study."

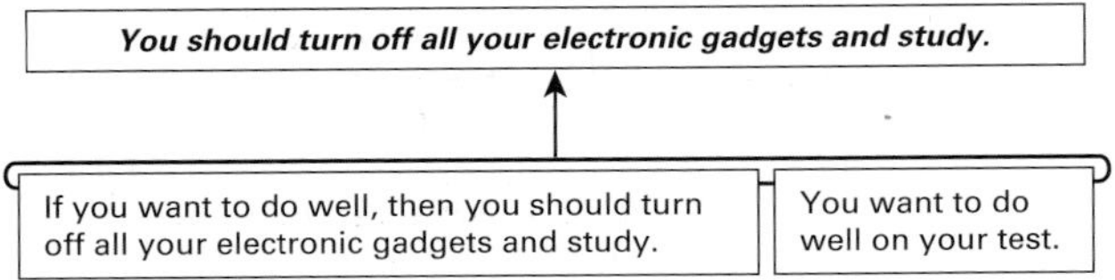

Now, let's look at an argument that has both a missing premise and a missing conclusion.

> *Example*
> "*Harry Potter* is just like *Star Wars*, which has remained immensely popular because it reiterates the classic tale of a good individual's triumph over evil."

The statements in this argument are:

Statement 1	*Harry Potter* is just like *Star Wars*.
Statement 2	*Star Wars* is immensely popular.
Statement 3	*Star Wars* reiterates the classic tale of a good individual's triumph over evil.

First, it seems as though the author is not just saying that *Harry Potter* is like *Star Wars*, but also that it is like *Star Wars* in a particular way—immensely popular—because it is like *Star Wars* in another way—reiterating this classic tale.

Thus, is seems plausible to assume that the conclusion of this argument is that *Harry Potter* will continue to be immensely popular.

If we include this implied conclusion, we can represent this argument as:

Premises	*Harry Potter* is just like *Star Wars*. *Star* Wars is immensely popular. Star *Wars* reiterates the classic tale of a good individual's triumph over evil.
Conclusion	*Harry Potter* will remain immensely popular.

And we can diagram this argument as:

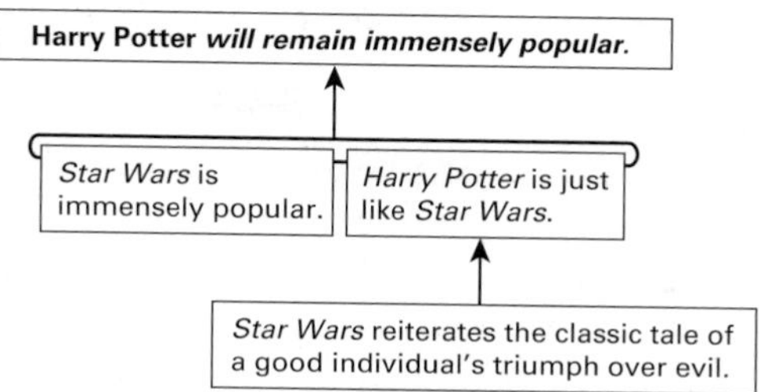

This is good, but there also seems to be a missing premise here—one that helps support the claim that *Harry Potter* is just like *Star Wars*. Such a statement is "*Harry Potter* reiterates the classic tale of a good individual's triumph over evil."

So we can change the representation to:

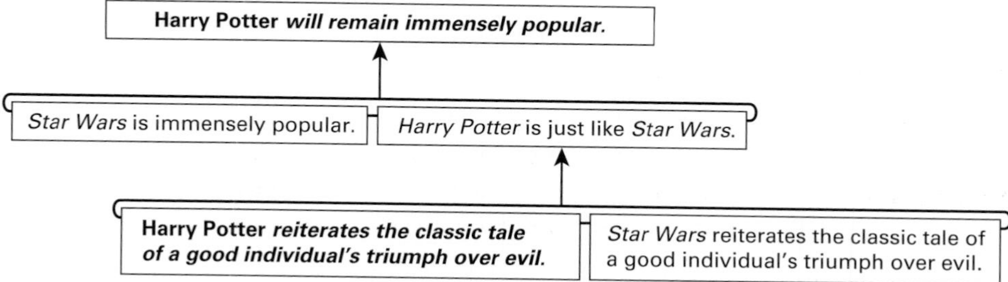

Self-Assessment

12. Here's a tough one! Diagram the following argument, made by Seth Waxman in *Dickerson v. United States*, including any implied premises and conclusion: "If the *Miranda* decision is reversed, police will no longer be compelled to give those warnings; and if they aren't compelled to give them, they won't give them. But because police interrogations take place out of public view, the integrity of such interrogations can be safeguarded only if those *Miranda* warnings are invariably given."

3.4 Diagramming Objections and Replies

Often, authors will include possible objections to their arguments, along with replies to those objections. Authors do this because it makes their arguments less susceptible to attacks, because the positions of opponents are considered and refuted beforehand.

Example

"We should all be vegetarians for several reasons. First, it is wrong to kill sentient animals unless it is in self-defense. Second, the grain that we use to feed the animals we eat could be used to alleviate hunger throughout the world, since the ratio of grain used to meat we get is 10 to 1. Finally, being a vegetarian is much more healthy than being a meat-eater.

Of course, some people would argue that we should eat the animals that we hunt, and that there are some animals that need to be hunted. After all, if it is immoral to kill animals for food, it is also immoral to allow animals to starve to death from overpopulation. My reply would be twofold. First, deer are overpopulated because we killed their predators, so that we could raise animals for food. Thus, deer don't need to be hunted in order to save them from starvation. We could curb overpopulation more humanely by instituting a sterilization program until predators are reintroduced and the population is under control. Second, hunting doesn't lead to less suffering. Bullets and arrows that end up wounding rather than killing deer lead to slow, painful deaths."

First, let's diagram the main argument that occurs in the first paragraph. The listing of reasons indicates that these premises converge to support the conclusion in the first sentence.

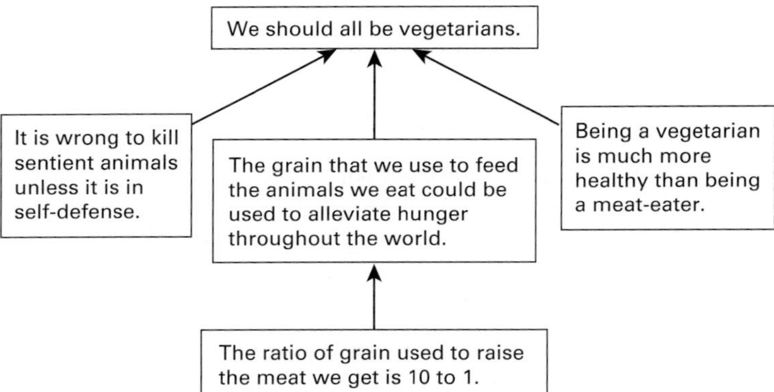

Then, what should we do about the second paragraph? How do we represent objections and replies to those objections? Just as we use black arrows to indicate that one statement supports the truth of another, we use red arrows to indicate that one statement contests the truth of another.

> *Definition*
> **Objection**: A statement that contests the truth of a statement, set of statements, or an inference in an argument. The objection may be included with the text of the argument, or may be introduced by another argument.
> **Reply**: A statement that answers an objection. The reply may be included in the text of the argument, or may be introduced by another argument.

In this section we will be concerned only with objections and replies that occur in the same text as the argument.

The author offers the statement "We should hunt animals like deer, to control overpopulation" as a possible objection to the conclusion in the previous paragraph. We can tell this is the author's intention by the author prefacing the objection with "Of course, some people would argue that …" This kind of phrase is an indicator that the author is laying out an objection.

The author is considering the objection that we need to hunt deer to control overpopulation. And the reason we need to do this is that if, as the author concedes, it's immoral to kill animals for food, then it's equally immoral to allow animals to die of starvation.

We can represent this objection with a *red* arrow:

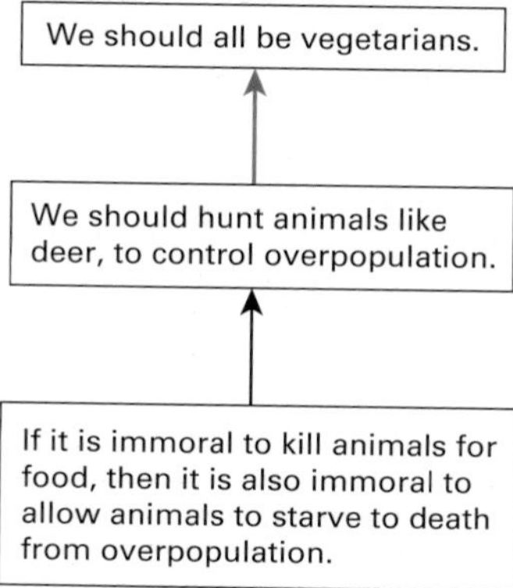

The list here indicates that the author is considering two replies to this objection. The first is that deer don't need to be hunted to control over population. And the reason for this is that we could sterilize deer to control the population instead:

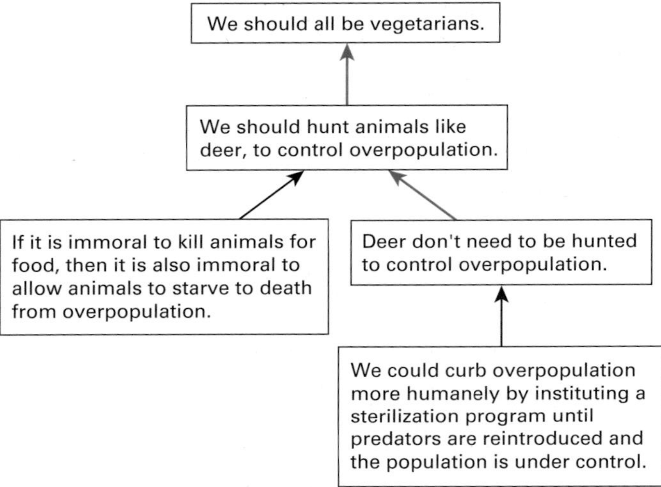

The second is that hunting deer can also lead to unnecessary suffering. And the reason given for this is that hunters who only wound the deer make them suffer agonizing deaths:

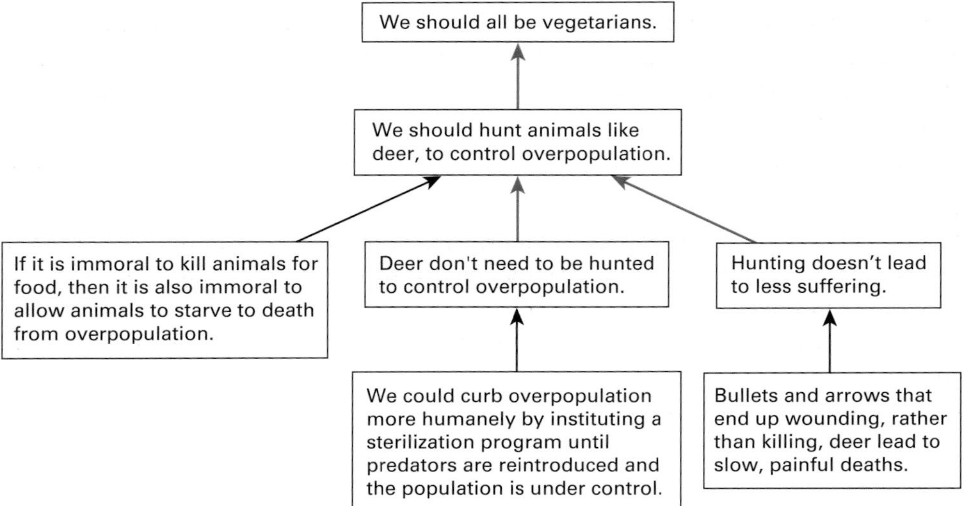

Then, if we combine the diagram of the original argument with the diagram of the objections and replies, we get this:

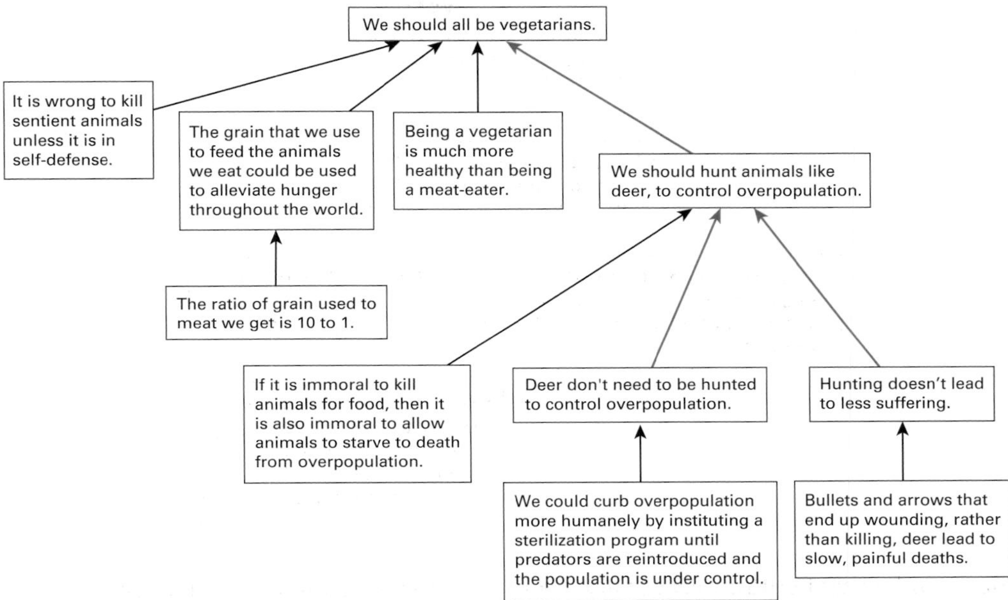

It is important to emphasize here that we are still only diagramming the argument that is actually presented in the text. That is, we are only diagramming the objections that the author presents; we are not diagramming our own objections to the argument. We will consider our own objections to arguments in the following chapters. But, now, let's look at another example.

Example

"I told you that you had to earn an A on the exam, or you would fail the class. But, you did not earn an A on the exam; therefore, you will fail the class. You claim that you shouldn't fail the class because you worked really hard all semester. My reply is that grades reflect performance, not effort, and you did not perform well enough to pass the class."

The word "therefore" indicates that "You will fail the class" is the conclusion of the argument, and the word "but" indicates that the two premises should be combined to support this conclusion. We can diagram this part like this:

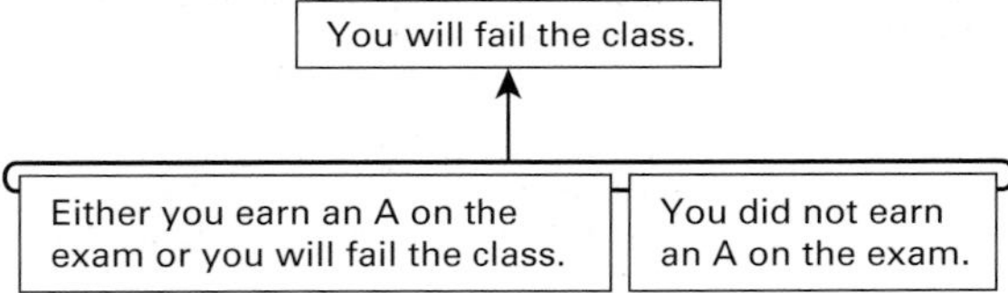

Then, the phrase "you claim that" indicates that the author is considering an objection: "You shouldn't fail the class because you worked really hard all semester." This is also a subargument, which we can represent like this:

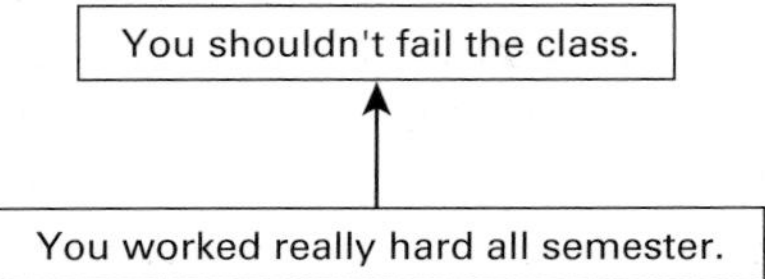

As this is an objection to the conclusion, we can diagram these two parts by having a red arrow (indicating objection) going from the subconclusion of the objection to the main conclusion of the argument.

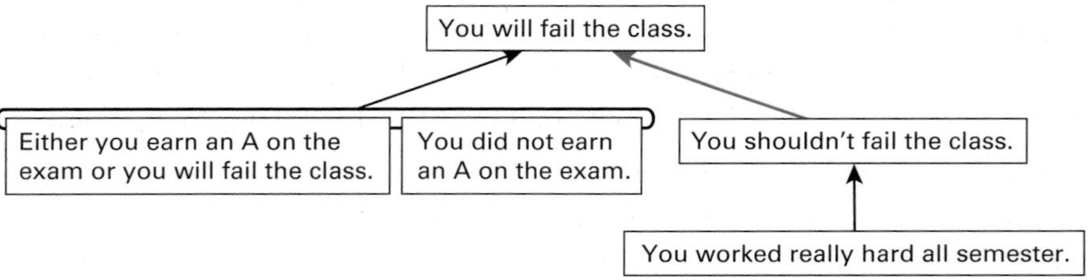

Finally, as indicated by "my reply is that," the author offers a reply to the objection. In essence, a reply is an objection to the objection, so we represent a reply with a red arrow as well.

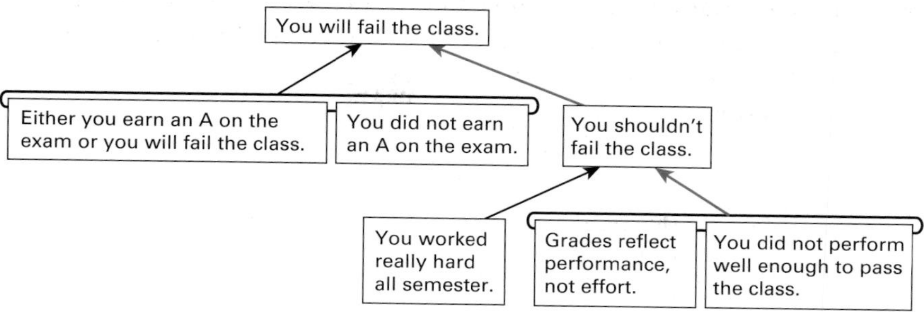

3.5 Summary

Thus far we have been practicing argument diagramming on short, relatively simple arguments. The arguments presented in following chapters are much longer and more complex. It is important to remember that any representation of an argument is an interpretation, and any interpretation must be supported by the text. In long, complex texts the task of interpretation is more difficult; the same text may be subject to many different interpretations.

Not all interpretations are equal, however. An interpretation can be better or worse depending on how much support the text offers for it. What we have seen in this chapter is a variety of methods for ensuring that we develop the best representation possible. Even so, different people using the same methods may still come to different conclusions about what the best representation is. In what follows, I will take you through my own reasoning in developing the representations I present. These are by no means the only reasonable representations possible. Alternatives may be equally well supported by the text. As you read through my explanations, I encourage you to develop alternatives of your own.

Before we move on, though, let's review the steps for constructing an argument diagram:

1. Identify all the claims being made by the author. Rewrite them as complete, independent sentences, according to the principles of fairness and charity.
2. Using structural indicators, identify which statements are premises, subconclusions, and the main conclusion.
3. Identify the main conclusion if it is implied.
4. If your objective permits, identify the implied premises as well.
5. Put the statements in boxes and use arrows to connect them, indicating support *from* premise(s) *to* (sub)conclusion with an arrow. Keep in mind:
   a. Multiple statements (or groups of statements) that each provide independent support for a (sub)conclusion should have their own arrows.
   b. Multiple statements that must be combined to support a (sub)conclusion should be linked and have only one arrow.

6. Identify any objections and replies to those objections, and rewrite them as complete, independent sentences.
7. Enclose the objections and replies in boxes. Draw red arrows from objections to the statements they contest and from the replies to the objections.

3.6 Answers to Self-Assessment Exercises

1. The top box represents the conclusion, the bottom box represents the premise, and the arrow represents the inference.
2. Diagram B is correct because the premises work together to support the conclusion.
3. a. Premise indicator: "Consider that." Premise: "It's already 8:00."
   b. Premise indicator: "The reason is that." Premise: "People have the right to protect themselves."
4. a. Conclusion indicator: "So." Conclusion: "We should abolish [the death penalty]."
   b. Conclusion indicator: "Hence." Conclusion: "We will be late for his appointment."
5. B.
6. a. "Because" is a premise indicator.
   b. "Since" is a premise indicator.
   c. "Hence" is a conclusion indicator.
7. "Since" is a premise indicator. "So" is a conclusion indicator.
8. There are two indicator words here. First, the word "thus" in the second sentence indicates that "Doctors should be eligible for government grants to support their work" is the conclusion of the argument. Second, the word "and" in the first sentence indicates that there are two premises here that need to be combined to support the conclusion, since neither claim can do the job by itself. We can represent the argument like this:

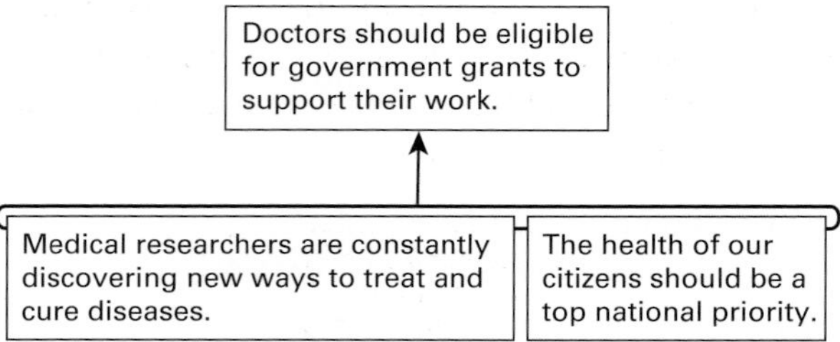

9. Here "because" indicates that "Dogs give unconditional love" is a premise that supports the claim that dogs make good pets. Additionally, the word "moreover" indicates that there is another, independent reason to believe that dogs make good pets.

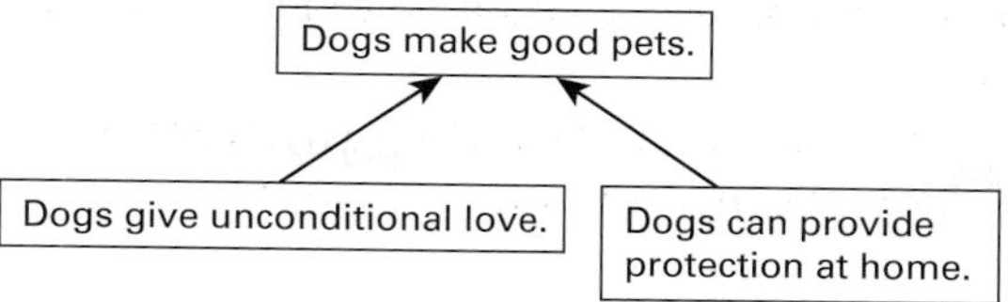

10. The indicator word "because" in the first sentence tells us that "The semantic properties of mental states are not intrinsic" is a subconclusion supported by the statement "[The semantic properties of mental states] depend on facts about the individual's history and environment." The indicator "therefore" in the second sentence tells us that the subargument in the first sentence supports the main conclusion, "Mental events do not cause other events by virtue of their semantic properties."

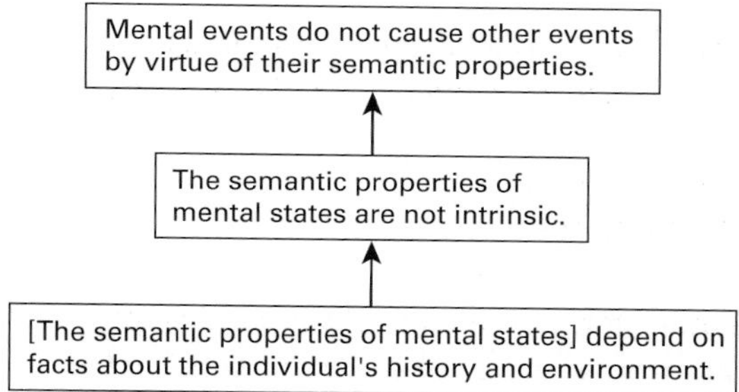

11. The indicator word "so" tells us that "We should not put in a pool this summer" is the conclusion supported by the two statements in the first sentence. It is clear that these two statements are not intended to be two separate reasons for the conclusion, but rather are supposed to work together. So, this first part of the argument has a linked structure. The final sentence gives us an additional reason to believe the conclusion, one that doesn't have anything to do with money. Thus, we add this to the map with its own arrow, indicating that, overall, the argument has a convergent structure.

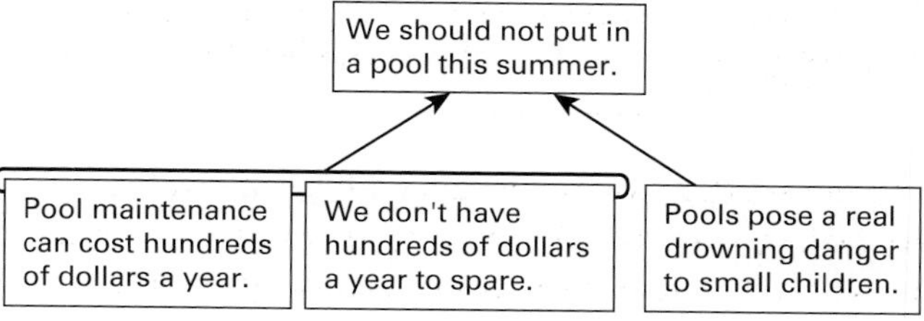

12. This argument is rewritten as:

Premises	(1) If the *Miranda* decision is reversed, police will no longer be compelled to give *Miranda* warnings.
	(2) If police aren't compelled to give *Miranda* warnings, then police won't give *Miranda* warnings.
	(3) Police interrogations take place out of public view.
Subconclusion	(4) The integrity of police interrogations can be safeguarded only if *Miranda* warnings are invariably given.
Main conclusion	*???*

It seems clear that the author is arguing against reversing the *Miranda* decision. So we can represent the conclusion as something like: "The *Miranda* decision should not be reversed."

Now, let's look at the implied premises. Of course, keep in mind that whether you provide the implied premises depends on what kind of reconstruction of the argument you are giving. If, for example, you are trying to represent just what the author actually says, then you should not add any extra premises; doing so would be "putting words into the author's mouth." If, on the other hand, you are trying to represent the most charitable interpretation of the author's words, then you may want to add any premises that seem to be either implied or assumed by the author.

To see how to add implied premises—if that is what we want to do—look again at the argument against reversing the *Miranda* decision. First, let's fill in the conclusion we think the author had in mind (for the rest of this example, the explicitly stated statements will be numbered, and the implied statements will be lettered):

Premises	(1) If the *Miranda* decision is reversed, police will no longer be compelled to give *Miranda* warnings.
	(2) If police aren't compelled to give *Miranda* warnings, then police won't give *Miranda* warnings.
	(3) Police interrogations take place out of public view.
Subconclusion	(4) The integrity of police interrogations can be safeguarded only if *Miranda* warnings are invariably given.
Main conclusion	(A) *The* Miranda *decision should not be reversed.*

Next, let's look at the inferences the author makes. The premise indicator "because" indicates that statement (3) is meant to support statement (4).

The missing premise here is that if (3) is true, then (4) is true, that is, "If police interrogations take place out of public view, then the integrity of such interrogations can be safeguarded only if *Miranda* warnings are invariably given by police."

Let's put this implied premise into this subargument:

Premise	(3) Police interrogations take place out of public view.
Implied premise	(B) If police interrogations take place out of public view, then the integrity of such interro*gations can be safeguarded only if* Miranda *warnings are invariably given by police.*
Subconclusion	(4) The integrity of police interrogations can be safeguarded only if *Miranda* warnings are invariably given.

And, we can diagram this subargument like this:

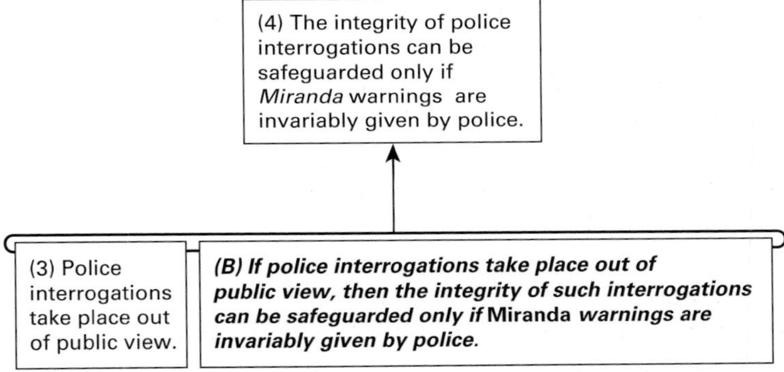

It also seems clear that the author wants to draw a conclusion from (1) and (2). The conditionals in these statements can be represented as: (1) If A happens, then B will happen, and (2) if B happens, then C will happen. The natural conclusion from this is: If A happens, then C will happen. So, we can write the implied subconclusion as: "If the *Miranda* decision is reversed, then police won't give *Miranda* warnings."

Let's put in this implied subconclusion:

Premise	(1) If the *Miranda* decision is reversed, police will no longer be compelled to give *Miranda* warnings.
Premise	(2) If police aren't compelled to give *Miranda* warnings, then police won't give *Miranda* warnings.
Implied subconclusion	*(C) If the* Miranda *decision is reversed, then police won't give* Miranda *warnings.*

And, we can diagram this sub-argument like this:

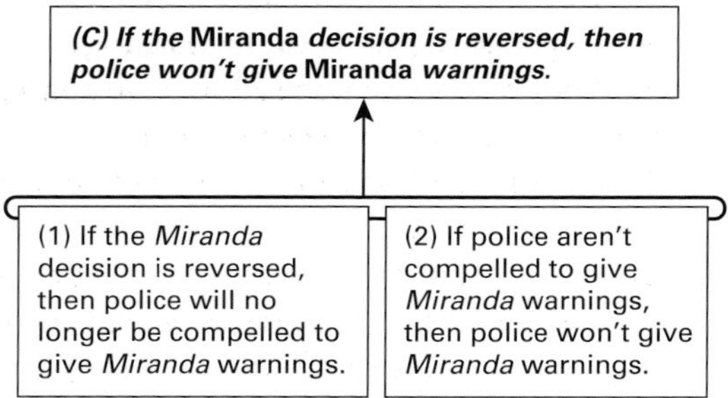

The author also seems to be assuming that safeguarding the integrity of police interrogations is something that should be done. If we add this to the argument as an implied premise, we can see that if we combine subconclusion (4) with this implied premise, another subconclusion (that we will supply, since it was missing) follows naturally:

Subconclusion	(4) The integrity of police interrogations can be safeguarded only if *Miranda* warnings are invariably given by police.
Implied premise	(D) *The integrity of police interrogations should be safeguarded.*
Implied subconclusion	(E) Miranda *warnings should invariably be given by police.*

Then, if we combine the two implied subconclusions (C) and (E), the main conclusion (A) follows:

Implied subconclusion	(C) *If the* Miranda *decision is reversed, then police won't give* Miranda *warnings.*
Implied subconclusion	(E) Miranda *warnings should invariably be given by police.*
Main conclusion	(A) *The* Miranda *decision should not be reversed.*

And we can diagram it like this:

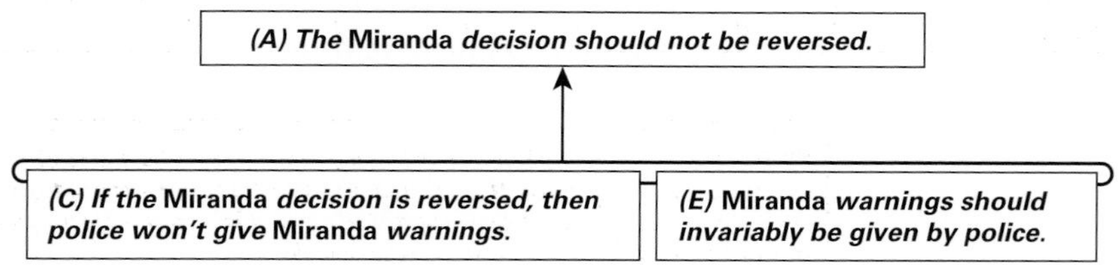

So, the whole thing looks like this:

Premise	(1) If the *Miranda* decision is reversed, police will no longer be compelled to give *Miranda* warnings.
Premise	(2) If police aren't compelled to give *Miranda* warnings, then police won't give *Miranda* warnings.
Implied subconclusion	(C) *If the* Miranda *decision is reversed, then police won't give* Miranda *warnings.*
Premise	(3) Police interrogations take place out of public view.
Implied premise	(B) *If police interrogations take place out of public view, then the integrity of such interrogations can be safeguarded only if* Miranda *warnings are invariably given by police.*
Subconclusion	(4) *The integrity of police interrogations can be safeguarded only if* Miranda *warnings are invariably given.*
Implied premise	(D) *The integrity of police interrogations should be safeguarded.*
Implied subconclusion	(E) Miranda *warnings should invariably be given by police.*
Main conclusion	(A) *The* Miranda *decision should not be reversed.*

And it can be diagrammed like this:

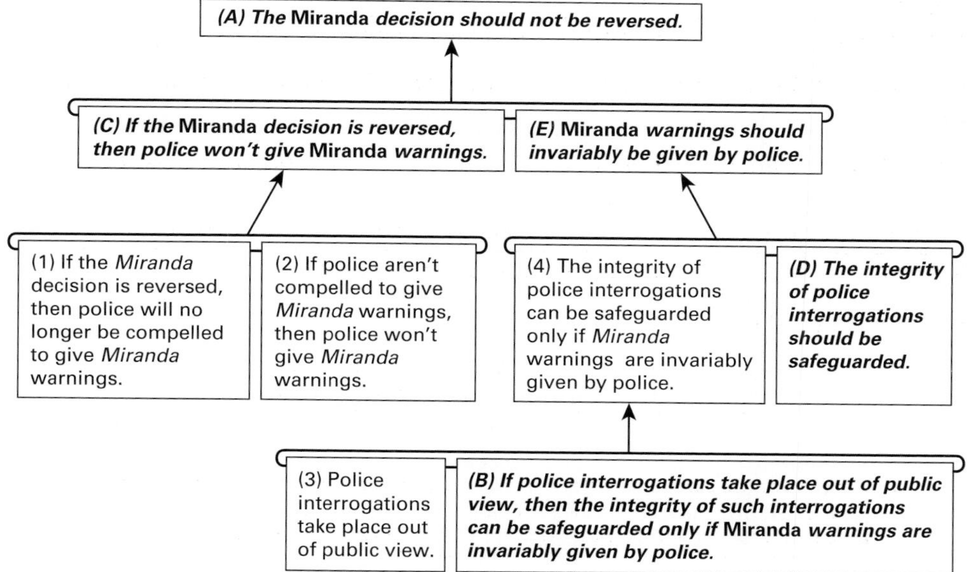

3.7 In-Class Exercises

An asterisk (*) indicates more challenging questions.

Section 3.2.1: Structural Indicators

1. Diagram the following argument:

Premise	Some brutally violent criminals should be put to death.
Conclusion	We should not abolish the death penalty.

2. Diagram the following argument:

Premise	Pizza is my favorite food.
Conclusion	We should order pizza tonight.

3. Identify all the premise or conclusion indicator(s) in each of the following arguments.
   a. "Soda is bad for you. This is because it rots your teeth."
   b. "We should start. For she has given us the signal."
   c. "The identity theory inappropriately requires that any creature with mental states must have a central nervous system like ours. Thus, the identity theory can't be right."
   d. "States of consciousness have intrinsic value. So, since brain states only have instrumental value, they do not have intrinsic value. Therefore, brain states are not states of consciousness."

4. Using premise and conclusion indicators, identify the diagram that best represents the following argument: "I earned an A on the final exam. So, I should get an A in the class."

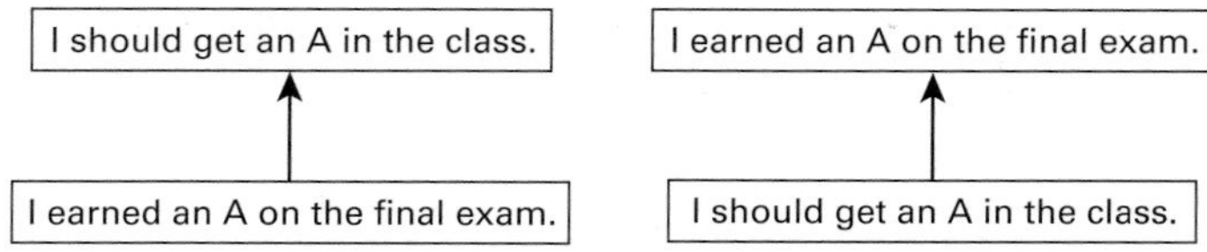

*5. Using premise and conclusion indicators, identify the diagram that best represents the following argument: "To every existing thing God wills some good. Hence, since to love any thing is nothing else than to will good to that thing, it is manifest that God loves everything that exists."—Thomas Aquinas, *Summa Theologica*

A.

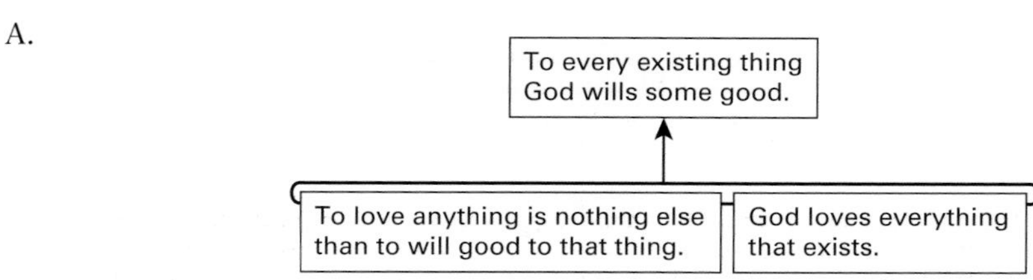

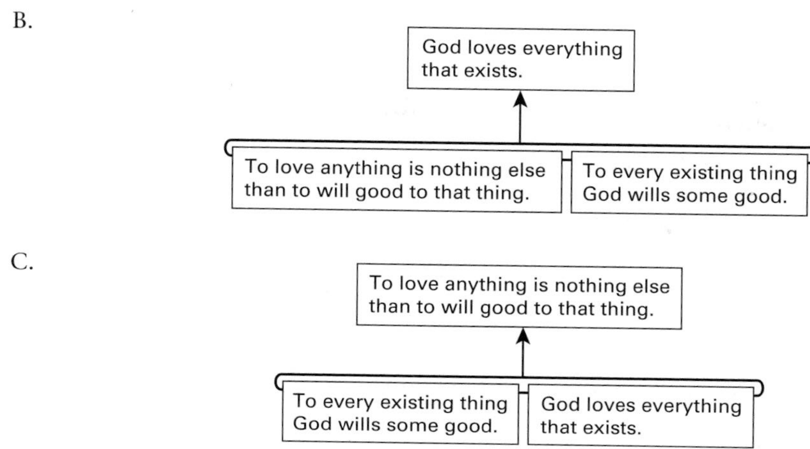

*6. Using premise and conclusion indicators, identify the diagram that best represents the following argument: "Taxation of earnings from labor is on a par with forced labor … it is like forcing the person to work *n* hours for another's purpose. Therefore, since it is wrong to force one person to work for another's purpose, it is wrong for the government to tax our earnings."—Robert Nozick, *Anarchy, State, and Utopia* (1974)

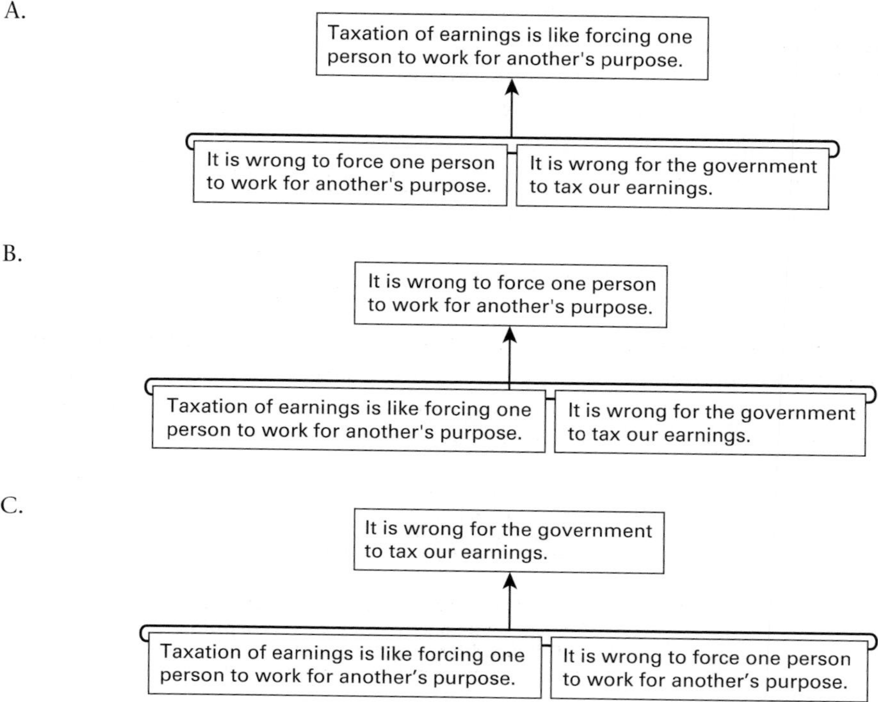

Section 3.2.2: Multiple Statements within Sentences

7. Identify the diagram that best represents the following argument: "Soda is bad for you, because it rots your teeth."

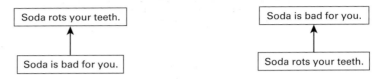

8. Identify the diagram that best represents the following argument: "We should start, for she has given us the signal."

9. Identify the diagram that best represents the following argument: "Farm-raised fish are bad for the environment, so you shouldn't eat them."

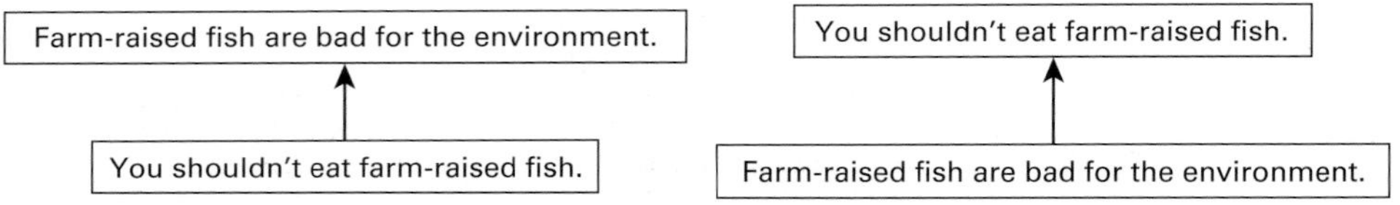

10. Diagram the following argument: "You shouldn't believe that Kiera was home studying, since I saw her at the movies."

11. Diagram the following argument: "I should be the one to drive the car; after all, it's mine."

12. Using premise and conclusion indicators, identify the diagram that best represents the following argument.

"All of your poetry is bad. So, since no one wants to sit through a reading of bad poetry, you should not be surprised that I am leaving."

A.

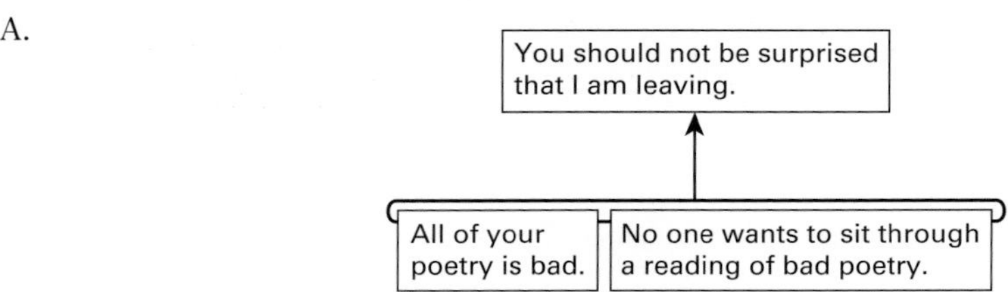

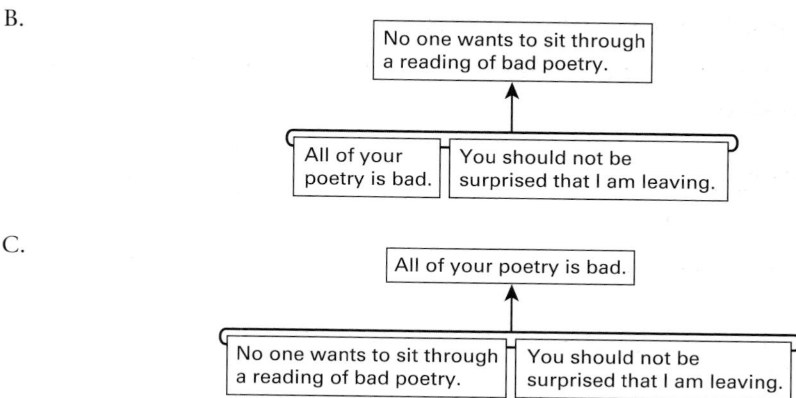

Sections 3.2.3–3.2.5: Linked Arguments, Convergent Arguments, Chain Arguments

13. Choose the diagram that best represents the following argument: "David is a good student. One, he studies hard; two, he always participates in class discussions; and also he comes in for help on all of his papers."

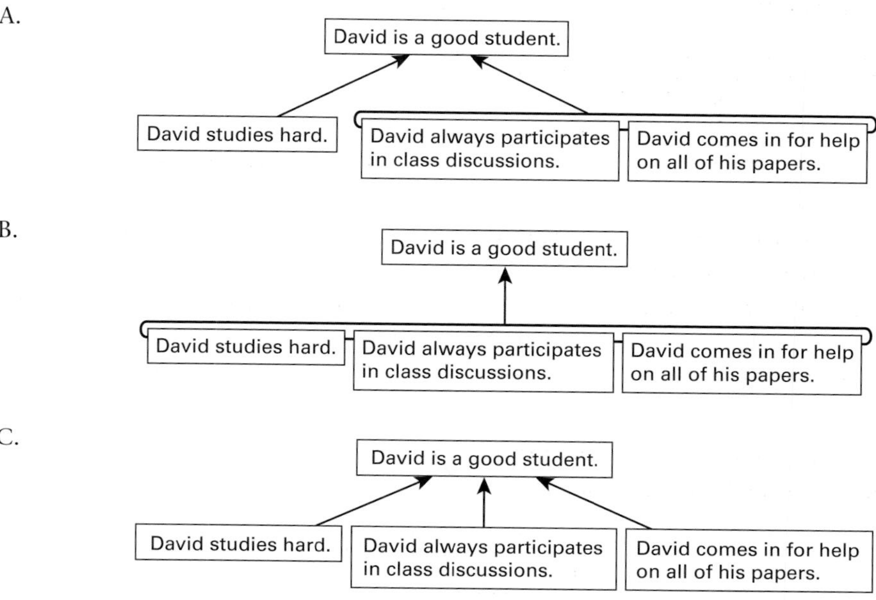

14. Choose the diagram that best represents the following argument: "Labrador retrievers make good pets because they are very friendly and also easy to train."

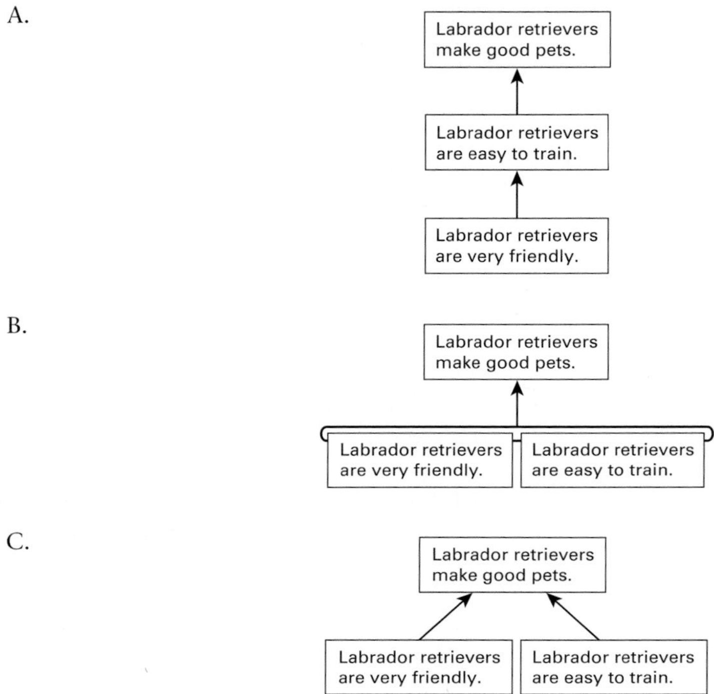

15. Choose the diagram that best represents the following argument: "Labrador retrievers make good pets, since they are very friendly. I know because every one I've ever met has wanted to lick my face and be petted."

A.

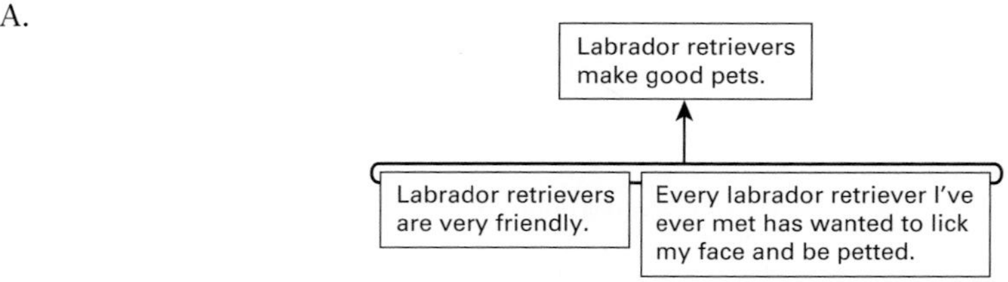

B.

C.

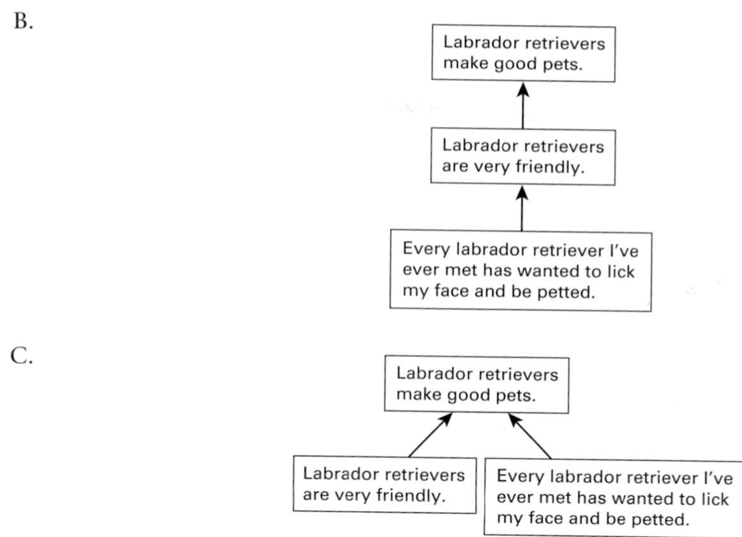

16. Choose the diagram that best represents the following argument: "Labrador retrievers are very easy to train. So, since easily trained dogs make the best pets, these dogs are great pets."

A.

B.

C.

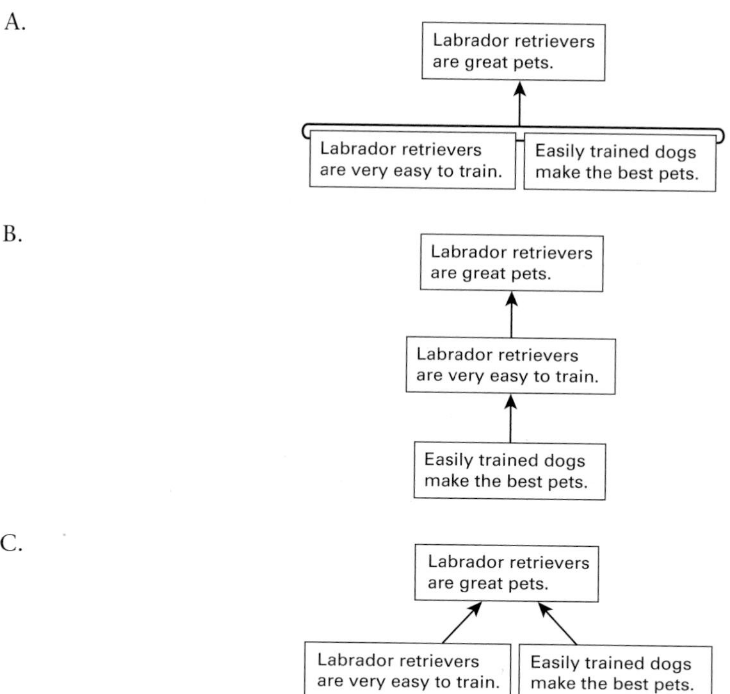

17. Choose the diagram that best represents the following argument: "Either Boris drowned in the lake or he drowned in the ocean. But Boris has saltwater in his lungs, and if he has saltwater in his lungs, then he did not drown in the lake. So, Boris did not drown in the lake, and thus he drowned in the ocean."

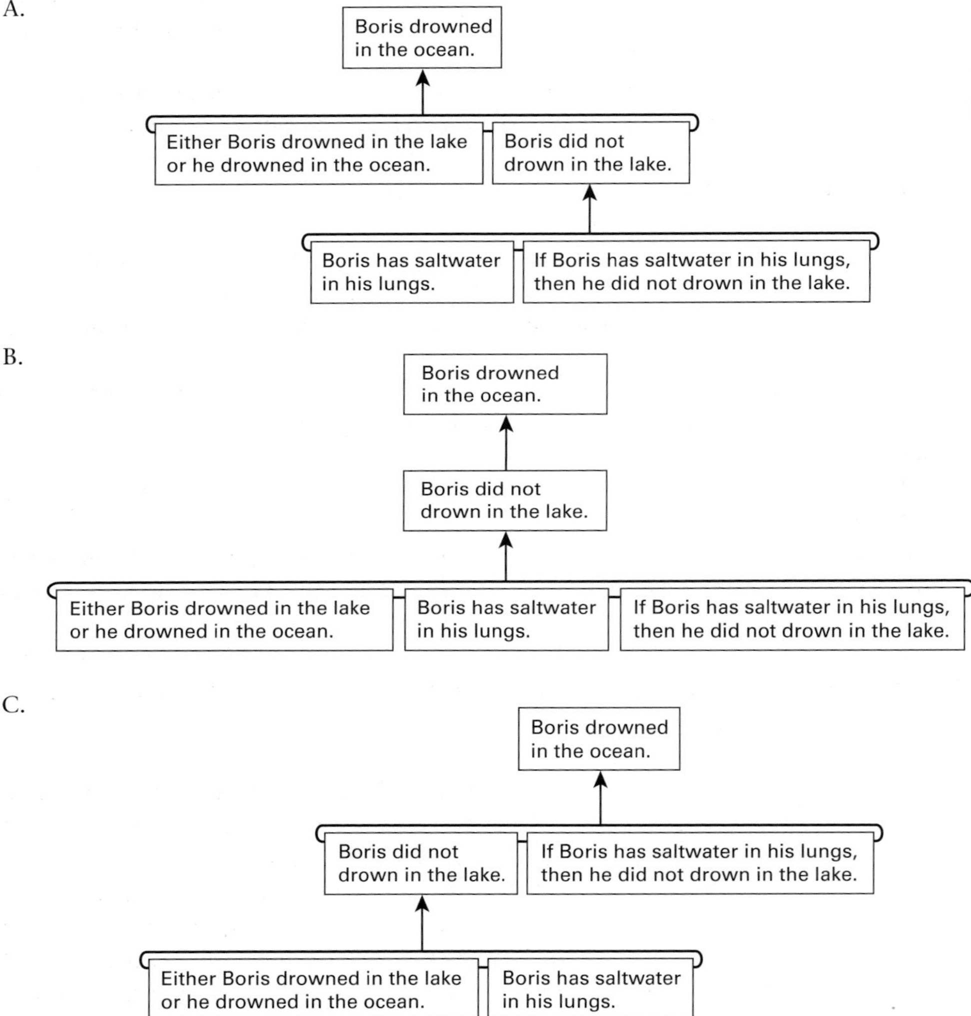

18. Diagram the following arguments:
    a. "Playing sports like soccer or basketball is fun. Playing sports also teaches children about discipline and teamwork. Thus, children should be encouraged to play sports."
    *b. "There should be a standard format for all university websites. A standard format would make it easier for students to navigate websites of schools to which they are interested in applying. Also, a standard format would make it easier for small schools to develop and maintain their own websites."
    *c. "High-tech corporations can't make their products in the United States for many reasons. For one thing, American schools aren't producing citizens with the skills that these companies need. Also, suppliers for their products won't relocate to the United States. Furthermore, American workers are just too expensive."
19. Diagram the following arguments:
    a. "Politicians should not be trusted, because they lie all the time. I know this because every time I see them on TV, they say something that just isn't true."
    b. "The defendant is guilty. After all, he was undoubtedly present at the scene of the crime since his fingerprints are on the safe."
    c. "If China attacks Taiwan, Taiwan will fight, for the Taiwanese are ready to defend themselves because their navy is well trained and well equipped."
20. Diagram the following arguments:
    a. "We need to take this animal somewhere to treat its injuries, but we can't take it home. So, I think we should take it to the vet."
    b. "Taxing our earnings is the same as the government forcing us to work without pay. Thus, since it is morally wrong to force someone to be a slave, taxing our earnings is wrong."
    c. "A government is responsible for the safety and security of its citizens. That, plus the fact that you can't protect anyone without any resources, supports the claim that the government is right to tax our earnings."
21. Diagram the following arguments:
    a. "The existence of an all-good, all-powerful, and all-knowing God, it is said, is logically inconsistent with the existence of evil in the world. Hence, since we cannot deny that there is such evil, we should conclude instead that God does not exist."
    b. "The defendant is guilty. After all, he confessed to stealing the jewels. In addition, he was undoubtedly present at the scene of the crime since his fingerprints are on the safe."
    *c. "Using contraceptives is immoral. For whatever is unnatural is immoral since God created and controls nature. And contraception is unnatural because it interferes with nature."

Section 3.3.1: Fairness and Charity

22. Choose the best representation, according to the principles of fairness and charity, of the following argument: "Cigarette smoking causes lung cancer. Therefore, if you continue to smoke, you are endangering your health."

A

Premise	Cigarette smoking guarantees that you will get lung cancer.
Conclusion	If you continue to smoke, you are endangering your health.

B

Premise	Cigarette smoking is a positive causal factor that increases the risk of lung cancer.
Conclusion:	If you continue to smoke, you are endangering your health.

23. Choose the best representation, according to the principles of fairness and charity, of the following argument: "Americans of this generation read less than those of the previous generation. Isn't the explanation obvious? We should get rid of all of our televisions."

A

Premises	Americans of this generation read less than those of the previous generation. Watching television causes kids to not want to read.
Conclusion	We should get rid of all of our televisions.

B

Premises	Americans of this generation read less than those of the previous generation. Watching television contributes to children reading less.
Conclusion	We should get rid of all of our televisions.

C

Premises	Americans of this generation read less than those of the previous generation. Watching television causes kids to hate reading.
Conclusion	We should get rid of all of our televisions.

24. Choose the best representation, according to the principles of fairness and charity, of the following argument: "Contrary to the opinions of some, welfare recipients do not like being on welfare. I mean, does anyone like being poor? Does anyone like being unemployed?"

A

Premises	Some people don't like being poor. Some people don't like being unemployed.
Conclusion	Welfare recipients do not like being on welfare.

B

Premises	Most people don't like being poor. Most people don't like being unemployed.
Conclusion	Welfare recipients do not like being on welfare.

C

Premises	No one likes being poor. No one likes being unemployed.
Conclusion	Welfare recipients do not like being on welfare.

25. Choose the best representation, according to the principles of fairness and charity, of the following argument: "We need to have the death penalty. You can't deny that people fear death more than they fear life in prison. So wouldn't the death penalty be a greater deterrent than life imprisonment?"

A

Premises	All people fear death more than they fear life in prison. The death penalty is just as much a deterrent than life imprisonment.
Conclusion	We need to have the death penalty.

B

Premises	Most people fear death more than they fear life in prison. The death penalty is just as much a deterrent than life imprisonment.
Conclusion	We need to have the death penalty.

C

Premises	All people fear death more than they fear life in prison. The death penalty is a greater deterrent than life imprisonment.
Conclusion	We need to have the death penalty.

Sections 3.3.3: Implied Premises and Conclusions

26. The following argument is an enthymeme. Choose the diagram that best represents it: "Farm-raised fish are bad for the environment, so you shouldn't buy them."

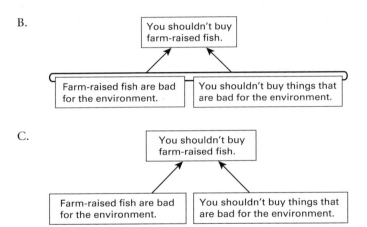

A.

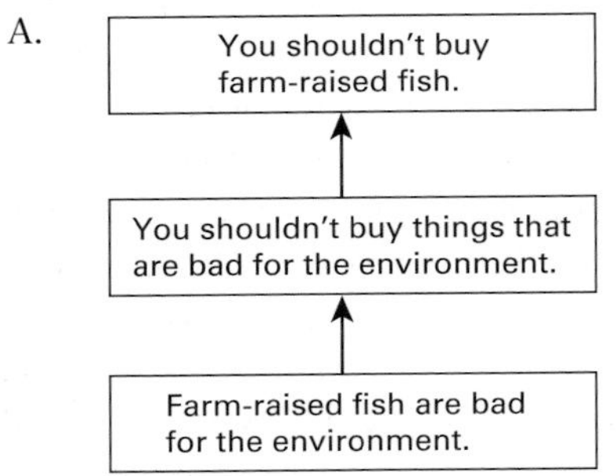

B.

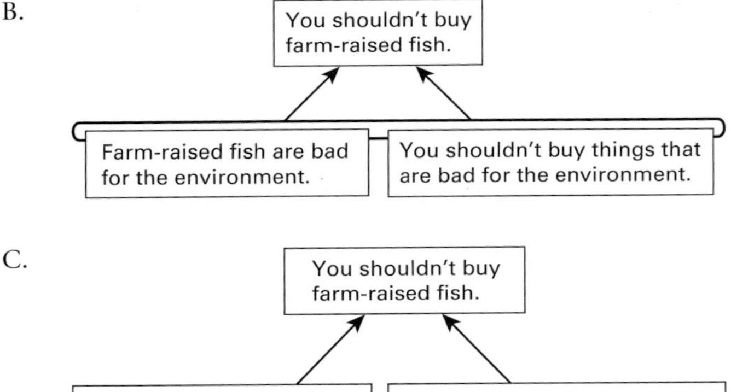

C.

You shouldn't buy farm-raised fish.

Farm-raised fish are bad for the environment.

You shouldn't buy things that are bad for the environment.

27. Diagram the following argument, adding in any missing premise or conclusion: "Everyone knows that people have the right to defend their property. So, the government shouldn't pass laws restricting how we treat trespassers."

28. Diagram the following argument, adding in any missing premises or conclusions: "I think you want to go to law school. If so, you should study hard for the LSAT."

29. Diagram the following argument, adding in any missing premises or conclusions: "Self-absorbed people don't help charities, and I know Clara is not self-absorbed. We should expect a check from her soon."

30. Diagram the following argument, adding in any missing premises or conclusions: "There is no law against composing music when one has no ideas whatsoever. The music of Wagner, therefore, is perfectly legal."—Mark Twain.

Section 3.4: Diagramming Objections and Replies

31. Diagram the following argument, including the objections and replies: "A government is responsible for the safety and security of its citizens. That, plus the fact that you can't protect anyone without any resources, supports the claim that the government is right to tax our earnings. Of course, some people would say that taxing our earnings is the same as the government forcing us to work without pay, and so taxing our earnings is wrong. But, that's wrong, because we are getting paid, and then using that money to buy protection."

32. Diagram the following argument, including the objections and replies: "I think all citizens should be allowed to vote, even if they can't read English. Someone who disagrees with me might argue that people who can't read English shouldn't be allowed to vote, because they can't be well informed about politics. And if you can't be well informed, then you shouldn't be allowed to make decisions about the community. So, people who can't read English shouldn't be allowed to make decisions about the community, and so they shouldn't be allowed to vote. But first, the right to vote doesn't depend at all on your ability to gather information, and second, people can get information from sources other than print media."

II Philosophy of Religion

Introduction

We begin with philosophy of religion, and in particular, arguments for the existence of God. Why begin here? The reasons are these: Many of the arguments offered as proofs for the existence of God are short and relatively easy to understand, and so they are a good place to begin our argument analysis and evaluation practice. In addition, these arguments are good examples of many of the types of arguments we discussed in Part I, so we can further our understanding of these types by seeing them instantiated in various ways. Finally, many of these arguments are variations on arguments you may have encountered before—like the design argument or the argument from evil. Thus, since you may be familiar with some of these, the arguments should be easier to evaluate once we understand their content and structure.

There are, of course, topics in philosophy of religion other than arguments for or against the existence of God. Here is a list of questions that also interest philosophers about religion:

- What is religion? Can we define it?
- If God exists, what is the nature of God?
- What is the significance of holy books?
- What is the role of faith? Is faith compatible with reason?
- What is the role and significance of religious experience?
- Does a person have an immortal soul?

Tackling all of these questions would require an entire book just on philosophy of religion, so we are going to confine ourselves with the question of whether we can show, via reasoned argument, that God either does or does not exist.

Learning Objectives for Part II

At the end of Part II, you will be able to:

- Describe four historically influential philosophical attempts to prove that God exists.
- Discuss the strengths and weaknesses of these four arguments.

- Describe the following kinds of arguments:
  - Ontological argument
  - Cosmological argument
  - Argument from incoherence
  - Argument from evil
  - Teleological argument
  - Design argument
- Define the following terms:
  - A priori deductive argument
  - A posteriori deductive argument
  - A posteriori nondeductive argument by analogy
  - A posteriori nondeductive abductive argument
  - Natural theology
  - Quantifier switch fallacy

Preliminary Questions for Part II

1. What is religion? What is its purpose in general? What are the purposes of religious rituals?
2. Do you think it's necessary to have rational reasons for belief in God for the belief to be justified or legitimate?
3. Is there a difference between believing in God and believing in the Greek gods, the Roman gods, or the "Flying Spaghetti Monster"?
4. What is your concept of God? Are you religious? Does your religion include a belief in God?
5. Where do your religious or nonreligious beliefs come from? Does it matter?
6. How does your religion view other religions?
7. Are we hardwired to believe in God? Does it matter?
8. What is the big bang theory? Does the big bang theory support the existence of God?
9. What is the anthropic principle? Does the anthropic principle support the existence of God?
10. How do you define evil? What kinds of things are evil?
11. How do you explain the existence of evil in the world? If you believe in God, how do you reconcile this with the existence of evil?
12. Do you believe that the world displays evidence of intelligent design? What is this evidence?

The Rise of Natural Philosophy

The Christian religion, which emerged in the first century AD, began to have serious problems in the second and third centuries, and these problems only grew worse in the following centuries. The first problem was the heresies—schisms within the faith that became increasingly became commonplace. For example, in the second century, a new prophet arose, Montanus, and a new heretical movement, Montanism, which became one of the principal targets of the new Catholic church. Other rifts included the Arian schism, the Nestorian schism, and the Miaphysite schism.

Also in the first few centuries, as the new scripture of Christianity was growing, those who could read began to recognize more and more conflicts between the Old Testament (the Hebrew Bible), and the new scripture. Usually, the solution was to take the New Testament (the developing scripture) as literally true, and the Old Testament, when there was conflict, as not literally true, but rather as containing metaphors and analogies. And finally, Jesus had not yet returned to establish the Kingdom of God, which had been expected during the lifetime of the apostles.

In the fourth and fifth centuries, the debate within Christianity turned mainly to the problem of evil. How, people asked, can there be so much evil in the world if God is both all-powerful and all-good? Evil seemed rampant at the time—Rome, the center of the Christian world, was sacked; innocent children (including children who had not yet been baptized) died regularly; and natural disasters causing much pain and suffering were common. Each of the splinter groups had their own answers, but many were not satisfactory at all.

Natural theology is the attempt to know God through reason and ordinary experience.

Philosophers began tackling these problems as early as the third century, with the work of Plotinus (204–270 AD). St. Augustine (354–430 AD) coined the expression *theologia naturalis* ("natural theology"). Natural theology is the attempt to know God through reason and ordinary experience, and is opposed to *revealed theology*, the theology of the Church, which is the attempt to know God through (only) scripture and religious experience.

Plotinus, who was born in Egypt and studied in Alexandria, fused philosophy and religion by combining Platonic principles with Christian teaching. He is generally considered the last of the ancient Greek philosophers, and his major work is *The Enneads*. In his works, *The Confessions* and *The City of God*, St. Augustine, who was born in Roman Africa (now Algeria), continued Plotinus' project of combining Platonism and Christianity,

Deductive and Nondeductive Arguments

Recall our discussions from chapter 2 of (a) deductive and nondeductive arguments and of (b) a priori and a posteriori arguments. Deductive arguments are those that are intended to be valid—intended to have premises that guarantee the truth of the conclusion. Nondeductive arguments, on the other hand, are intended to be strong; these are arguments that are technically invalid, but in which the truth of premises is supposed to make the conclusion likely to be true. We discussed in some depth three kinds of nondeductive arguments: induction, argument by analogy, and inference to the best explanation (abduction). An a priori argument is reasoning that uses propositions as premises whose verification do not require experience; that is, it is reasoning from concepts and definitions. And an a posteriori argument is reasoning that uses propositions as premises that do require experience for verification; that is, it is reasoning from facts about the world. In this section, we are going to consider four types of arguments for the existence of God:

a. a priori deductive argument
b. a posteriori deductive argument
c. a posteriori nondeductive argument by analogy
d. a posteriori nondeductive abductive argument

An a priori deductive argument is one that uses a priori propositions in a (intended-to-be) valid argument. The idea is that you can just use your reasoning abilities, and don't have to rely on any particular experience of the world, to determine whether the premises are true. Likewise, an a posteriori deductive argument is one that is intended to be valid, but uses a posteriori propositions, ones for which you have to have experience to know whether they are true, to support the argument's conclusion.

Nondeductive a posteriori arguments also use a posteriori propositions to support the conclusion. A posteriori arguments by analogy generally rely on experience in the world to determine whether two things are similar, or how similar they are. This type of argument, then, is judged by how good the analogy is, how relevant the similarities are for the purposes of supporting the conclusion. A posteriori abductive arguments depend on observations about the world that need explanation; they are judged by the number of alternative explanations considered and how well they actually do explain the observations.

Deductive Arguments

Ontological arguments show that God exists based on an analysis of the concept of God.

Born in Italy, St. Anselm (1033–1109) continued the work of Plotinus and Augustine before him, combining the philosophy of Plato with Christianity. He is famous for (among other things) one version of an a priori deductive argument for the existence of God—the *ontological argument*. In this argument, Anselm aims to show that if you truly understand the idea of God, then you will be forced to come to the conclusion that God exists. He does not depend on any particular experiences of or facts about the world—he depends just on your reasoning about concepts. We will consider this argument first in chapter 5, and then turn our attention to St. Thomas Aquinas (1225–1274).

Cosmological arguments show that God exists based on certain factual features about the universe.

Aquinas was also Italian, but combined the philosophy of Aristotle (instead of Plato) with Christianity. He is famous for a different kind of deductive argument—the *cosmological argument*. This is a class of a posteriori arguments that depend on particular observations about the world. These facts could have been otherwise (they aren't necessarily true), but they happen to be true in our world. In the second part of chapter 4, we will consider Aquinas's argument that depends on the fact that in our world there are things that are in motion. It didn't have to be the case that things are in motion—you might imagine a world in which there is no motion—but in our world it is the case, and we have to experience the world to know this.

Arguments from incoherence show that God does not exist based on an analysis of the concept of God.

In chapter 5, we will consider two contemporary arguments against the existence of God. First, we consider Michael Martin's "Three Arguments for Nonbelief." We will examine in detail his first argument, the *argument from incoherence*. This argument begins with a convergent nondeductive subargument that the many descriptions of God in the Bible are inconsistent with each other. This inconsistency is then used in a deductive argument that the concept of God is incoherent, and if we take the Bible seriously, then we have reason to believe that God does not exist.

Arguments from evil show that God does not exist based on the existence of unnecessary evil in the world being inconsistent with the existence of God.

In the second part of chapter 5, we consider John Mackie's *argument from evil*. This is a deductive argument against the existence of God, based on the fact that evil exists in the world. It is interesting not least because it is a contemporary a posteriori deductive argument, and a very good example of a reductio ad absurdum argument.

Arguments from religious experience show that God exists based on the religious experience of the arguer or some other person.

There are other kinds of arguments for the existence of God that we will not cover in this section, but which are important, nevertheless. One is the *argument from religious experience*. In this type of argument, the arguer claims that he or she has had an experience of God, and so God must exist. This is often a kind of abductive argument in that the arguer claims that the best explanation of the religious experience is that it was a genuine experience of God. Another is a *theodicy*. This type of argument is often given as a counter to the argument from evil. The arguer denies the existence of unnecessary evil, and so denies a basic premise of the argument from evil.

Theodicies are counterarguments to the argument from evil, based on denial of the existence of unnecessary evil in the world.

Nondeductive Arguments

In chapter 6, we will consider two kinds a posteriori nondeductive arguments that have an important commonality: they are both *teleological* arguments. To understand this, let's go back to Aristotle. In Aristotle's *Physics* he gives his account of the four causes of any thing. For example, consider a table.

- material cause: what it's made out of—wood
- efficient cause: what made it—a carpenter

- formal cause: what makes it what it is—flat surface
- final cause: what is its purpose—for putting things on

For Aristotle, everything has a purpose. The purpose is the thing for which it was designed and created. The table's purpose is to be something that we can put other things on, whether they are magazines, flowers, or plates. Aristotle also believes that each living thing has a purpose—the end for which it was designed and created, the thing that guides its behavior. Humans, for example, are designed and created to exercise their innate rationality. How does Aristotle know this? By investigating the world, we can determine what is unique about a particular object or organism, the thing that the organism does better than any other. According to Aristotle, the thing that separates humans from animals is our ability to reason.

Teleological arguments show that God exists based on features of the world that demonstrate purpose.

Generally, then, a teleological argument is one that relies on observations of design and purpose in the world. And usually a teleological argument for the existence of God depends on our experience of things that seem to have a design and a purpose, but were not created by human beings—if something has a design and purpose, and was not created by humans, then it must have been created by something else, which we call God.

David Hume (1711–1779) was a Scottish philosopher and historian, and in his *Dialogues Concerning Natural Religion*, he presents a clear and influential version of a teleological argument by analogy for the existence of God. Here, one of the characters in the dialogue presents an argument based on the similarity between a human-made machine and the universe. We will consider this argument in the first part of chapter 6.

Design arguments are teleological arguments that show that God exists based on features of the world that demonstrate intelligent design.

In the second part of chapter 6, we turn to William Paley's teleological argument, with his famous watch analogy. Paley (1743–1805) was an English philosopher who gave a slightly different argument for the existence of God that combines an argument by analogy and argument to the best explanation. Like Hume, his main premises are claims about the similarities between human-made machines, like a watch, and natural "machines," like the eye. Both Hume's argument and Paley's argument rely on observations that natural objects seem to have a purpose; for example, the eye has the purpose of allowing an organism to see. These natural objects are complex, with parts that need to be combined exactly as they are to function properly.

4 Deductive Arguments for the Existence of God

4.1 St. Anselm, *Proslogion*
4.2 St. Thomas Aquinas, *Summa Theologica*
4.3 In-Class Exercises

4.1 St. Anselm, *Proslogion*

St. Anselm (1033–1109) was an Italian philosopher and theologian who is credited with founding scholasticism, originally aimed at reconciling Christian theology with the philosophical writings of the ancient Greeks in an academic setting. As a young man, Anselm entered the Benedictine Abbey of Bec, where he spent the next thirty-three years. Then in 1093, he was made Archbishop of Canterbury in England. The king had thought Anselm would bow to his every wish, but Anselm was adamant in his opposition to the king's usurping of the pope's authority. Anselm became famous for being the archbishop who openly opposed the Crusades, and for originating the ontological argument for the existence of God.

In one of his two earliest philosophical works, *Proslogion* (the other being the *Monologion*), Anselm gives an argument that is supposed to prove not only that God exists, but that God exists *necessarily*. Thus, it is an a priori deductive proof. It is intended to be valid, which makes it deductive, and there is no particular observation about the world one has to make to know that the premises are true, which makes it a priori. Thus, Anselm's argument is a version of the ontological argument—an argument that intends to show that God exists based solely on an analysis of the concept of God.

Anselm states the basic argument in chapter 2 of the *Proslogion*, and makes additions in chapters 3 and 4. He purports to show that since God is by definition the greatest being, then he must exist, because existence is greater than nonexistence. Ultimately, then, this is a reductio ad absurdum argument. Anselm shows that denying God's existence leads us to deduce a contradiction—that God is both the greatest being and not the greatest being—which leads to the conclusion that the denial of God's existence must be false. The whole argument, though, is made from subarguments that are instantiations of the argument forms we saw in the previous section. Here we explore Anselm's argument from chapter 2 of the *Proslogion* in detail, leaving the analysis of chapters 3 and 4 as exercises.

Let's look at part of Anselm's text in more detail. Specifically, we will analyze and diagram the argument, and then discuss criticisms of it.

From *Proslogion*.[1]

Preface

AFTER I had published, at the solicitous entreaties of certain brethren, a brief work (the *Monologium*) as an example of meditation on the grounds ahead ahead of faith, But But in the person of one who investigates, in a course of silent existence existence reasoning with himself, matters of which he is ignorant; considering that this book was knit together by the linking of many arguments, I began to ask myself whether there might be found a single argument which would require no other for its proof than itself alone; and alone would suffice to demonstrate that God truly exists, and that there is a supreme good requiring nothing else, which all other things require for their existence and well-being; and whatever we believe regarding the divine Being.

...

Chapter 2: That God Really Exists

THEREFORE, Lord, you who give knowledge of the faith, give me as much knowledge as you know to be fitting for me, because you are as we believe and that which we believe. And indeed we believe you are something greater than which cannot be thought.[1] Or is there no such kind of thing, for "the fool said in his heart, 'there is no God'"? (Ps. 13:1, 52:1)? But certainly[A] that same fool, having heard what I just said, "something greater than which cannot be thought," understands what he heard,[2] and[B] what he understands is in his thought,[3] even if he does not think it exists. For it is one thing for something to exist in a person's thought and quite another for the person to think that thing exists. For when a painter thinks ahead to what he will paint, he has that picture in his thought, but he does not yet think it exists, because he has not done it yet. Once he has painted it he has it in his thought and thinks it exists because he has done it.[*] Thus[C] even the fool is compelled to grant that "something greater than which cannot be thought" exists in thought,[4] because[D] he understands what he hears,[5] and[E] whatever is understood exists in thought.[6]

And certainly[F] "that greater than which cannot be thought" cannot exist only in thought,[7] for[G] if it exists only in thought it could also be thought of as existing in reality as well,[8] which is greater.[9] If, therefore,[H] that than which greater cannot be thought exists in thought alone, then "that than which greater cannot be thought" turns out to be that than which something greater actually can be thought,[10] but[I] that is obviously impossible.[11] Therefore[J] something than which greater cannot be thought undoubtedly exists both in thought and in reality.[12]

In the preface, Anselm tells us that he wants to provide an argument for the existence of God. The particular kind of argument he wants is one "which would require no other for its proof than itself alone." Thus, Anselm wants a sound deductive argument, the conclusion of which is that God exists.

In chapter 2, Anselm's first claim is that God is something greater than which cannot be thought (1). This is a mouthful, so let us abbreviate this phrase with "Greatest Conceivable Being" (GCB). By "great" Anselm means "perfect," and the idea here is that one cannot even conceive of something more perfect than God—God is by definition the greatest being possible.

Anselm then proceeds to show us that since we can understand the concept of a greatest, or best, being, that being must exist. Let's see how this works.

The "But certainly" (A) indicates that what follows is an answer to the question posed immediately before: is there such a thing as a GCB? And the "and" (B) indicates that claims (2) and (3) are to be combined to answer the question—that is, to support the claim that a GCB exists at least in our minds (4), as indicated by the "Thus" (C) right before it. Before we get to this subconclusion, however, Anselm wants to make clear the distinction that he is drawing. There are two kinds of existence: one is existence in reality, and the other—the lesser one, as we see below—is existence in thought. To help his readers understand this distinction, he gives us the example of the painter (*). At one time the painting only exists in the painter's thoughts, and later the painting exists both in reality and in the painter's thoughts. After the example, Anselm restates his subargument from above; as indicated by the "because" (D) and the "and" (E), the fact that the fool understands what a GCB is (5)—which is a restatement of (2)—is to be combined with the fact that whatever is understood exists in thought (6)—which is a restatement of (3)—to support (4).

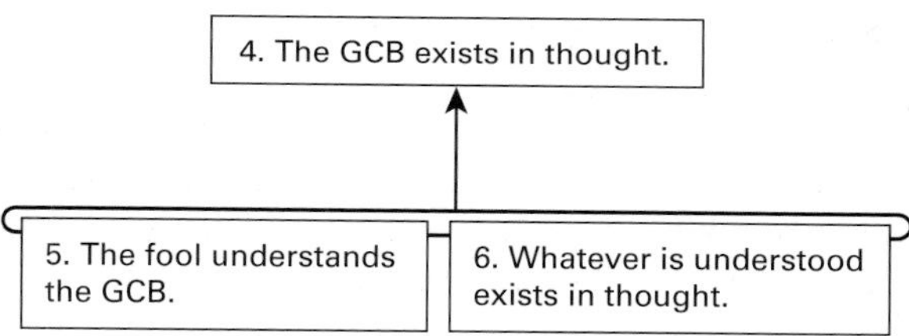

This is a variant of a modus ponens argument:

(5) The GCB is understood.
(6) If the GCB is understood, then it exists in thought.
So, (4) The GCB exists in thought.

But this is just one part of the overall argument. The rest is a subargument for the claim that the GCB cannot only exist in thought (7). As indicated by the "for" (G), the reason for (7) starts with the claim that if something exists in thought, like the painting, we can also think of it as existing in reality (8), and the claim that existing in reality is better than existing only in thought (9). These two claims combine, as indicated by the "therefore" (H), to support the claim that if anything, and so the GCB in particular, exists only in thought then we have a case in which something that is the best conceivable thing is at the same time not the best conceivable thing (10).

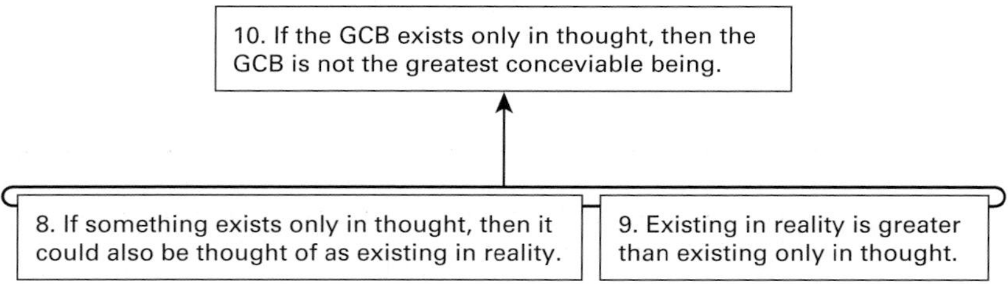

There's a lot packed into this subargument, so let's pick it apart. In (9), Anselm is referring to what is better or more perfect. For any thing, existing in reality is better than (or more perfect than) existing in thought only. So, as in his example, the actual painting is better than the thought of the painting. Proposition (8) is the claim that it is possible that anything we can conceive of could really exist, even if it doesn't happen to exist. So the painting may not happen to exist, but since we can conceive of it, it is at least possible that it could exist. If we instantiate the "something" in (8) with the GCB, then this is an example of a hypothetical syllogism:

(8) If the GCB exists only in thought, then the GCB can be thought of as existing in reality.
(9) If the GCB can be thought of as existing in reality, then the GCB that exists in reality is greater than the GCB that exists only in thought.
So, if the GCB exists only in thought, then the GCB that exists in reality is greater than the GCB that exists only in thought.

The second part of the consequent of this conditional says that something is greater than something that nothing can be greater than. And this is a contradiction. We can, thus, write this alternate version of the conclusion as:

So, (10) if the GCB exists only in thought, then the GCB is not-GCB.

As indicated by the "but" (I), this subconclusion is meant to be combined with the claim that this state of affairs—the contradiction—is impossible (11) to support the negation of the claim that the GCB can exist only in thought (7).

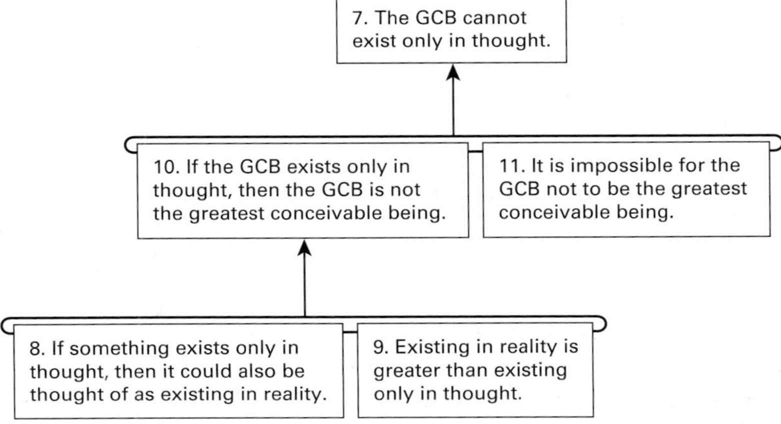

Then, as indicated by the "Therefore" (J), claim (7) combines with claim (4) to support the claim that the GCB exists in both thought and reality (12).

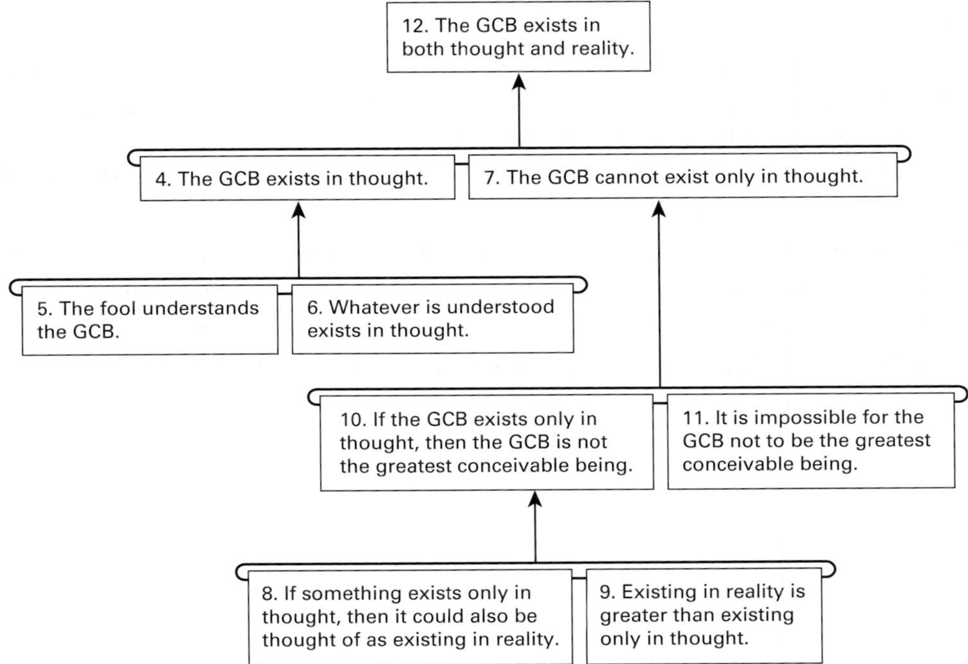

Ultimately, then, claim (12) can be combined with claim (1), to support Anselm's final conclusion that God exists.

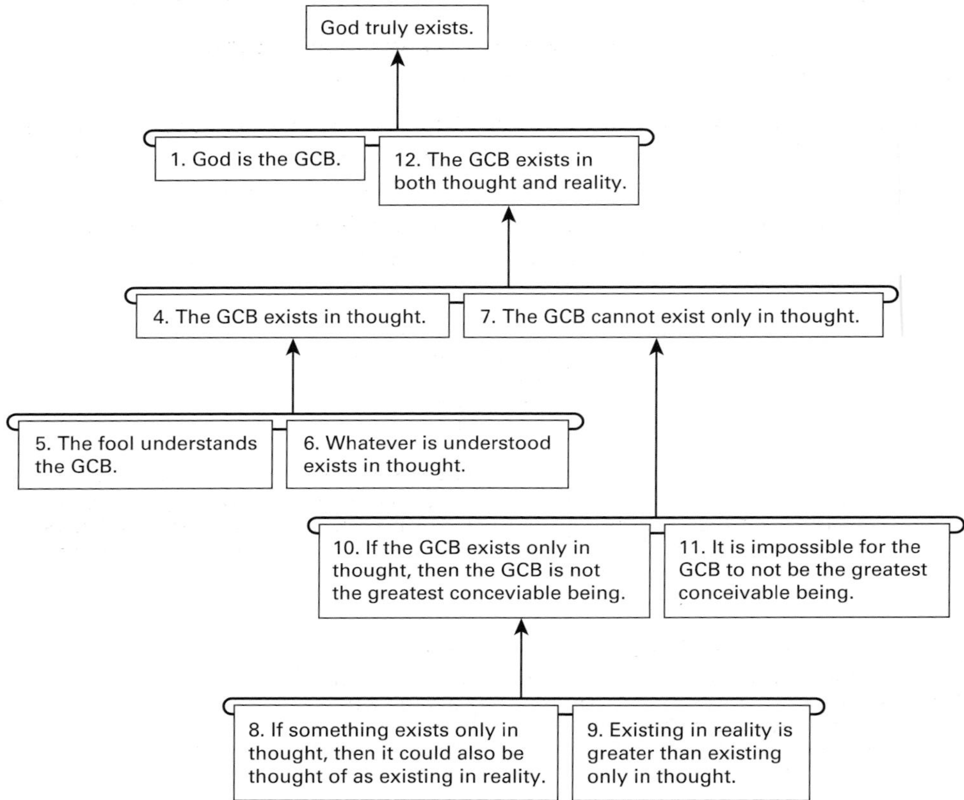

The upshot of Anselm's ontological argument is that merely understanding the idea of God, as you must if you are to deny the existence of God, proves God's actual existence, since to deny God's actual existence generates a contradiction. Thus, this argument is a priori, since one does not need to have any particular experience of the world to understand the contradiction.

Now that we're clear about what the premises of Anselm's argument are, and how the premises are supposed to work together to support the conclusion, we can begin to evaluate the argument. Remember that in evaluation we are interested in the soundness (or cogency) of the argument. This means we are interested in (a) whether the premises are true, and (b) whether the premises actually support the conclusion. In terms of the argument diagram, this means we are interested in the content of the boxes and the plausibility and strength of the arrows.

Against Anselm's argument for the existence of God, we can consider two major objections.

1. Existence in reality is not obviously better than existence in thought.
2. There is a difference between possibility and conceivability.

Let's take these objections in order, considering the objections from the point of view of the argument diagram. But first, let us consider the second part of Anselm's argument. While the subargument comprising claims (8), (9), (10), (11), and (7) looks like a deductively valid argument, it is not, as it stands. Anselm's argument can be made clearer if we rewrite the statements and add to the subargument the premises that seem to be missing.

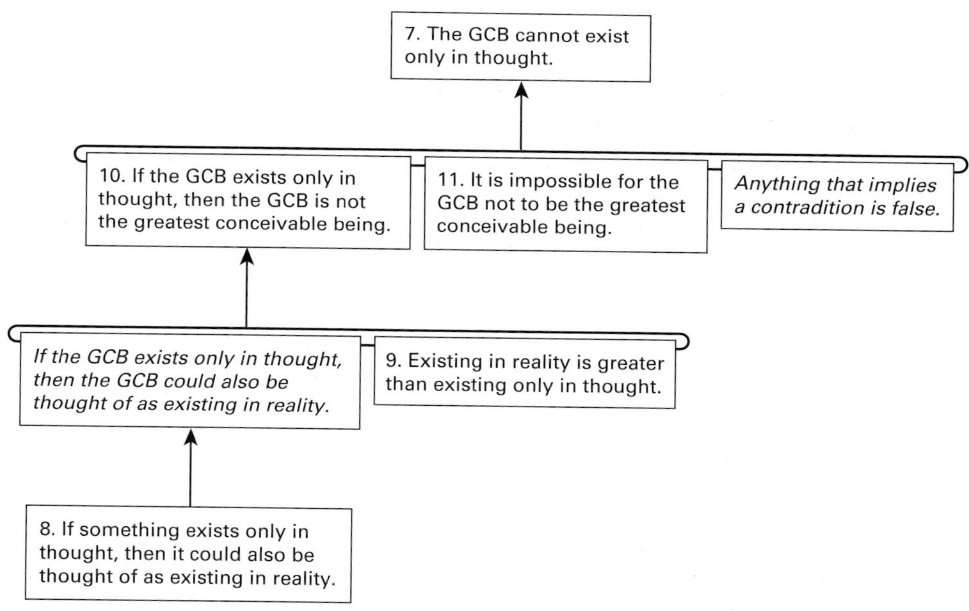

Now the logic looks airtight, right?

First Objection

Not so fast, says Gaunilo of Marmoutiers, a Benedictine monk who approved of most of the *Proslogion* but criticized Anselm's proof of the existence of God. Gaunilo published his criticism as "What Someone on Behalf of the Fool Replies to These Arguments." The first objection is essentially this: Take the argument above and substitute Greatest Conceivable Island (GCI) for GCB; then the same argument form proves that the GCI actually exists. Gaunilo gives this example not to prove that the best island does actually exist, but rather to show that there must be something wrong with the *form* of the argument, since it can be used to prove all manner of crazy claims.

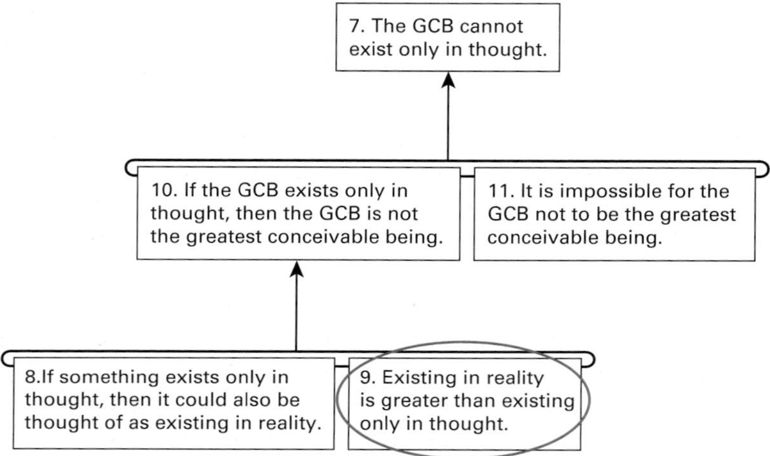

One way to interpret Gaunilo's criticism is to reject Anselm's claim (9)—that is, reject the claim that existing in reality is better than existing only in thought. After all, Anselm does not give any reasons for believing this claim, and it seems perfectly natural to wonder what these reasons could possibly be.

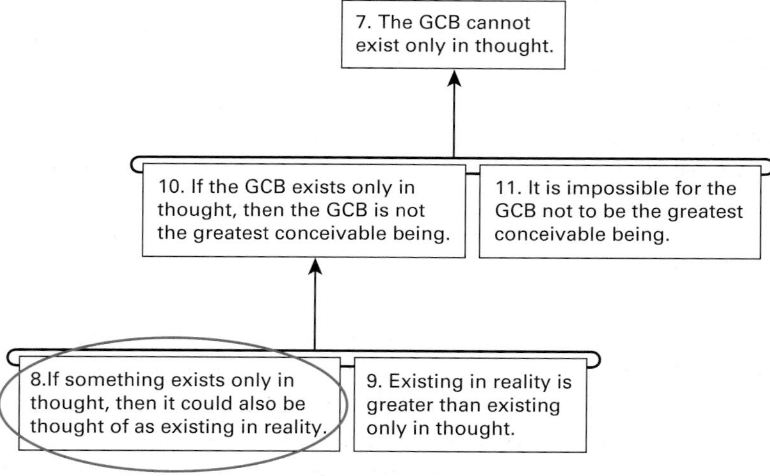

Second Objection

The second objection is to the claim that is paired with (9). As with (9), Anselm does not provide an argument for (8), the claim that anything that exists in thought can be thought of as existing in reality. In fact, there are good reasons to think that this is *not* true.

In making this claim, Anselm seems to be conflating two ideas: conceivability and possibility. In attempting to provide a proof of the existence of God, it would seem that Anselm has to assume that it is possible that God exists. What Anselm actually says, however, is that it is *conceivable* that God exists (this is what he attributes to the fool—that to deny God's existence, one must first be able to conceive of God).

The problem is that conceivability does not imply possibility. Let's look at an example. When Isaac Newton published his *Philosophiae Naturalis Principia Mathematica*, in which he laid the foundation of the branch of physics called mechanics, he held a certain view of the universe that served to support his theory. In particular, he thought that space was absolute and that light traveled at an infinite speed.

Albert Einstein decidedly removed this support with his introduction of the general theory of relativity. One important component of this new theory is that light travels at a finite speed, and that nothing can travel faster than light. If we accept this new view of the universe, then light traveling at an infinite speed, though conceivable to Newton, is nonetheless not possible.

So, one might argue that while Anselm and the fool may both be able to conceive of the existence of a God who is all good, all knowing and all powerful, the actual existence of such a God might nonetheless be impossible. We haven't shown, of course, that it *is* impossible; we've merely shown that conceivability does not imply possibility—which is to say that something existing in thought does not imply that it could actually exist, and that we reject claim (8).

So it seems that Anselm's proof has serious problems. But what does this mean? Have we shown that God does not exist? Far from it! All we've shown is that *this* argument does not give us adequate reasons to believe the conclusion; we have not shown that the conclusion is false. To show that the conclusion is false, we would have to provide good reasons for thinking that God does not exist, that is, an argument against God's existence. And this is just what we will see in the chapters to come. First, however, we will look at a few more kinds of argument *for* God's existence.

4.2 St. Thomas Aquinas, *Summa Theologica*

Born in Italy, St. Thomas Aquinas (1225–1274) was a (perhaps *the*) preeminent philosopher and theologian of the Middle Ages. In his early years, Aquinas studied both at the Benedictine Abbey of Monte Cassino and the University of Naples. He joined the Dominican order and left for France for further study. In Cologne he studied Aristotle's works, which had been recently reintroduced to the West. Aquinas adapted Aristotle's philosophy to provide a foundation for Christian thought and natural theology. Aquinas believed that the existence of God was not revealed knowledge, but rather was knowledge justified by argumentation, reasoning from naturally occurring phenomena.

In one of his greatest works, *Summa Theologica* (written around 1260), Aquinas provides five proofs of the existence of God. The fourth is a proof that concerns how properties come in degrees, and the fifth is a proof from intelligent design. The first three, however, are *cosmological* proofs, from the Greek *kosmos*, meaning "world" or "order." Recall that a cosmological argument is one that intends to show that God exists based on some contingently true feature of our world.

These proofs are a posteriori deductive proofs—they are intended to be valid arguments, while ultimately resting on a premise that is an observation about the natural world; Aquinas treats this observation as an effect that requires a causal explanation, and he ultimately traces the cause back to God. In the proofs, he combines this observation with some other premises about how the world works, to argue that God must exist. Here we explore Aquinas's first argument in detail, leaving the analysis of his other arguments as exercises.

This type of argument is called the *cosmological argument*, and is an example of an a posteriori deductive argument. Now, let's look at Aquinas's text in more detail. Specifically, we will analyze and diagram the argument, and then discuss criticisms of it.

From *Summa Theologica*.[2]

The existence of God can be proved in five ways. The first and more manifest way is the argument from motion. It is certain, and evident to our senses, that in the world some things are in motion.[1] Now[A] whatever is in motion is put in motion by another,[2] for[B] nothing can be in motion except it is in potentiality to that towards which it is in motion;[3] whereas a thing moves inasmuch as it is in actuality.[4] For[C] motion is nothing else than the reduction of something from potentiality to actuality.[5] But[D] nothing can be reduced from potentiality to actuality, except by something in a state of actuality.[6] Thus that which is actually hot, as fire, makes wood, which is potentially hot, to be actually hot, and thereby moves and changes it.[*] Now[E] it is not possible that the same thing should be at once in actuality and potentiality in the same respect, but only in different respects.[7] For what is actually hot cannot simultaneously be potentially hot; but it is simultaneously potentially cold.[#] It is therefore[F] impossible that in the same respect and in the same way a thing should be both mover and moved, i.e. that it should move itself.[8] Therefore,[G] whatever is in motion must be put in motion by another.[9] If that by which it is put in motion be itself put in motion, then this also must needs be put in motion by another, and that by another again.[10] But[H] this cannot go on to infinity,[11] because[I] then there would be no first mover,[12] and, consequently, no other mover;[13] seeing that subsequent movers move only inasmuch as they are put in motion by the first mover;[14] as the staff moves only because it is put in motion by the hand.[§] Therefore[J] it is necessary to arrive at a first mover, put in motion by no other;[15] and[K] this everyone understands to be God.[16]

Aquinas tells us up front what he is doing: providing a proof of the existence of God. By "proof" Aquinas means "a sound deductive argument," and so the conclusion of his argument is just what he wants to prove—that God exists.

As indicated by the final "therefore" (J), the short version of Aquinas's argument comes at the end of the paragraph. The claims that there must be a first mover (14) and that God is the first mover (15) work together, as indicated by the "and" (K) between them, to support the conclusion that God exists.

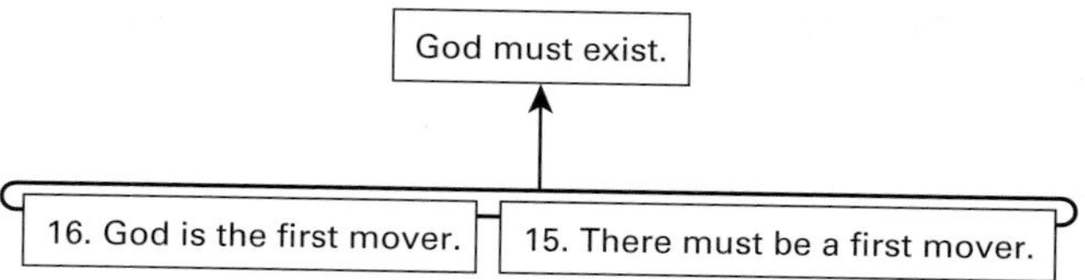

Aquinas seems to take (16) as obviously true, because he does not provide any argument for it. But he does think that (15) needs support, and this is what the rest of the paragraph does—provides an argument for the claim that there must necessarily be a "first mover." The basic idea of this argument is this:

Something can be in motion only if another thing put it in motion.
If we keep going back, finding the causes of motion, we must eventually get back to the being that put the first thing in motion.
That being is the "first mover," otherwise known as God.

Using this last part of the argument as our goal, let us go back to the beginning of the argument, then, to see how the argument gets there. The first claim Aquinas makes is (1): in the world there are some things that are in motion. This, he says, is obviously true and needs no argument, but let's set this to the side for the moment. His next statement, introduced by "now" (A), which indicates that it will be used with (1) somehow, is (2): whatever is in motion is put in motion by another. But notice that this is the same as statement (9). This indicates that everything that occurs between statements (2) and (9) is going to be a subargument with that as its conclusion. After claim (2), but still in the same sentence, Aquinas indicates by the word "for" (B) that the next two claims—something can be moved only if it has the potential to be moved (3) and a thing can move something else only if it has actual motion (4)—will be a reason to believe (2). What does this mean? In slightly different language, the claim is that something can be moved only if it has the potential to be moved. Aquinas takes (3) to be unproblematic, but he offers a further argument for (4) using the indicator word "for" (C) again, and using "but" (D) to indicate that the combination of the next two claims—causing movement is changing something from having the potential to be moved to having actual motion (5), and only something that has actual motion can change something from having the potential to be moved to having actual motion (6)—is a reason to believe (4).

He gives an example involving fire and wood (*) to explain these premises. So now we have a chain of reasoning: (5) and (6) support (4), and (3) and (4) support (2).

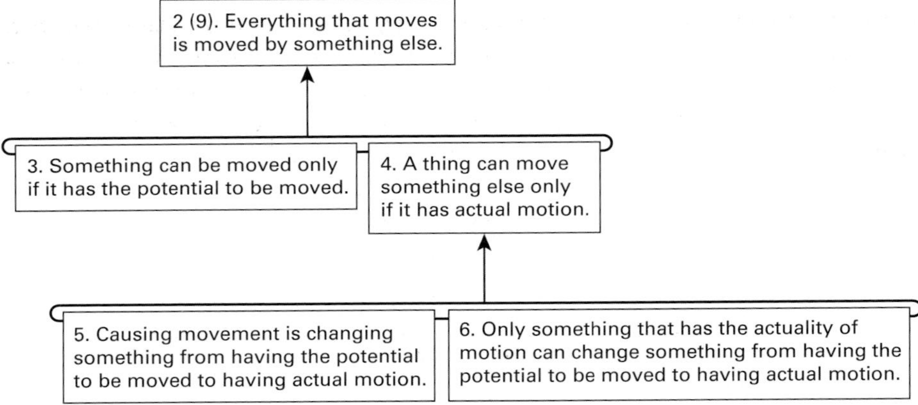

The chain isn't complete yet, however, because there is the possibility that something could have both the potential to be moved and actual motion, and so could cause itself to move. Aquinas thinks this is obviously false (7), and he gives an example to show why (#). By the words "therefore" (F) and "now" (E), he indicates that (7) will be combined with what came before, to support the claim that it is impossible for a thing to move itself (8). This, then, as indicated by the "therefore" (G), is the reason to believe (2), which is restated in (9). Aquinas says that this then leads to a chain of movers and those moved (10).

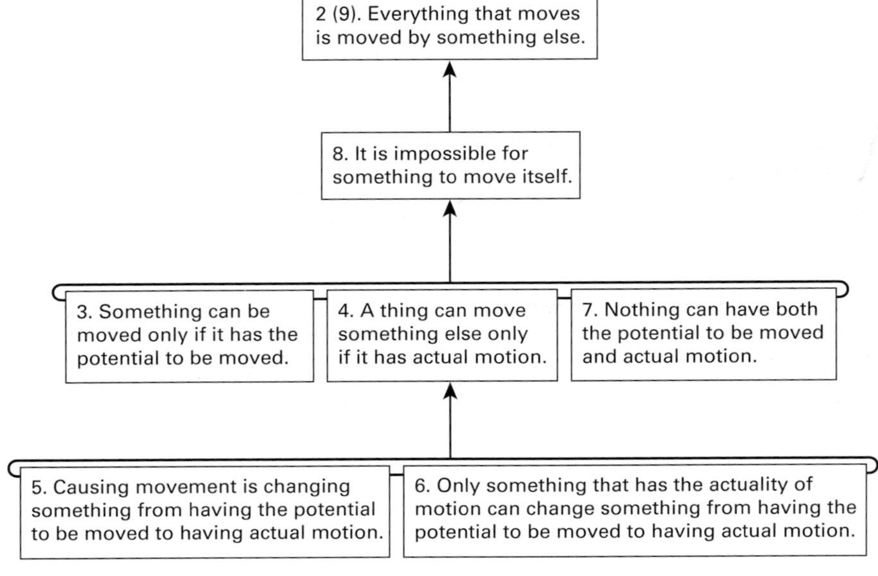

As a result of this subargument, we have two claims, (1) and (10), which are supposed to support claim (15) somehow. They cannot provide this support by themselves, however, because the first is a just a statement that some things move and the second is the subconclusion that anything that moves must have a mover, whereas (15) is a claim that there is a being who can move things, but who does not need anything else to move it—a first mover. Thus, we need some bridging claims to get from (1) and (10) to (15), and this is exactly what the claims following (10) do. By the indicator word "but" (H), we see that (10) is to be combined with the claim that there cannot be an infinite chain of movers (11).

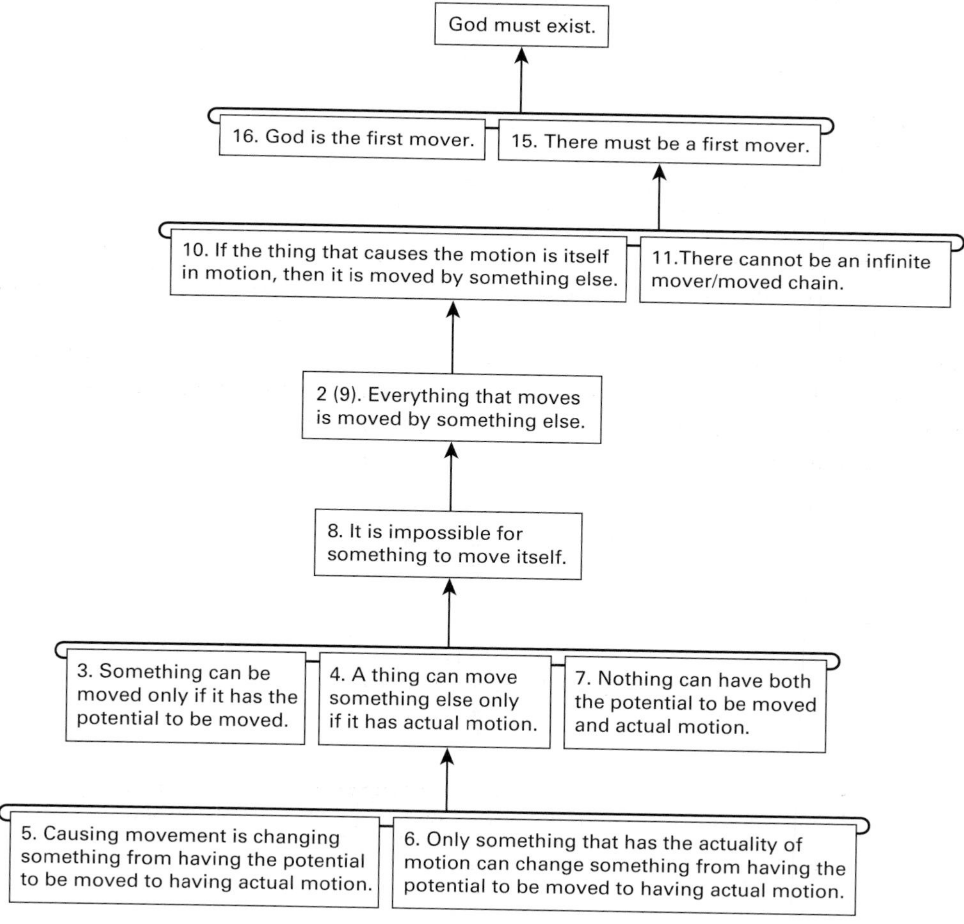

Claim (11), however, is not merely asserted; rather, it is the conclusion of another subargument, indicated by the word "because" (I). The reason given for believing that there cannot be an infinite chain is that if there were an infinite chain of movers, there would be no motion now (13). This claim is in turn supported by the claim that if there were an infinite chain of movers, there would be no first mover (12), combined with the claim that if there were no first mover, there would be no subsequent motion (14). The statement (§) is an example that illustrates this reasoning. If we combine (13) with the fact presented at the beginning—that some things are in motion (1)—the chain of reasoning leads to subconclusion (11), and we have come back to where we began.

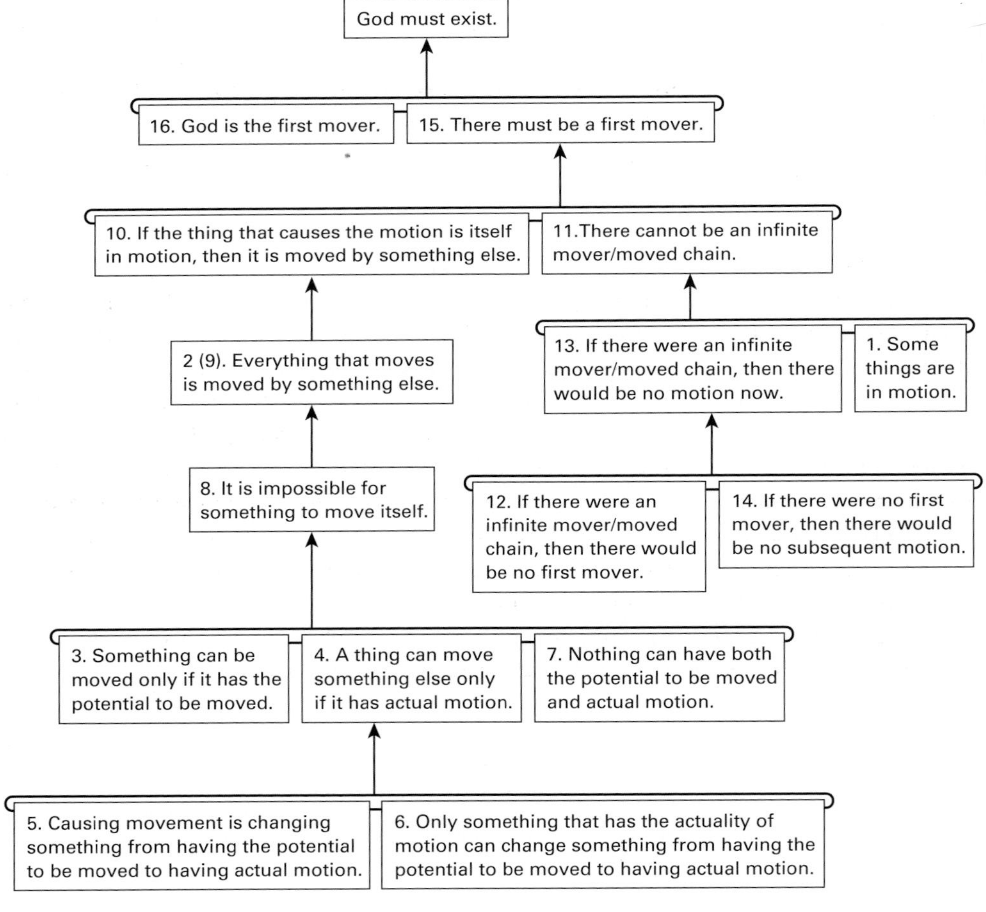

Now that we're clear about what the premises of Aquinas's argument are, and how the premises are supposed to work together to support the conclusion, we can begin to evaluate the argument. Remember that in evaluation we are interested in the soundness (or cogency) of the argument. This means we are interested in whether (a) the premises are true, and (b) whether the premises actually support the conclusion. In terms of the argument diagram, this means we are interested in the content of the boxes and the plausibility and strength of the arrows.

Against Aquinas's first proof for the existence of God, we can consider four major objections:

1. Modern physics tells us that objects do not need a force to put or keep them in motion.
2. The main conclusion—that God exists—does not follow from the combination of premises (13) and (14).
3. Subconclusion (15) does not follow from the combination of premises (10) and (11).
4. It is not obviously true that there can be no infinite mover/moved chain.

Let's take each objection in turn, considering the objection from the point of view of the argument diagram.

First Objection

Aquinas learned his physics from Aristotle's great works. Aristotle's views about motion are much the same as our ordinary commonsense views. That is, Aristotle held that an object's "natural" state is to be at rest. Thus, for an object to move, it needs a force to cause it to move; and for an object to stay in motion, it needs a constant force, or else it will eventually come back to rest.

This view of motion is in sharp contrast to Newtonian physics, which holds that the "natural" state of any object is to be moving with a constant velocity.[3] Thus, an object can be naturally at rest (velocity = 0) or moving with a constant speed in a constant direction. The upshot of this is that Newtonian physics tells us that the motion of an object does not need to be explained at all. Thus, we do not have to assume that if an object is in motion, there was another object or force that put it in motion.

Of course, Aquinas could meet this objection by substituting "acceleration" for "motion." Then there would be a kind of motion that does need to be explained.

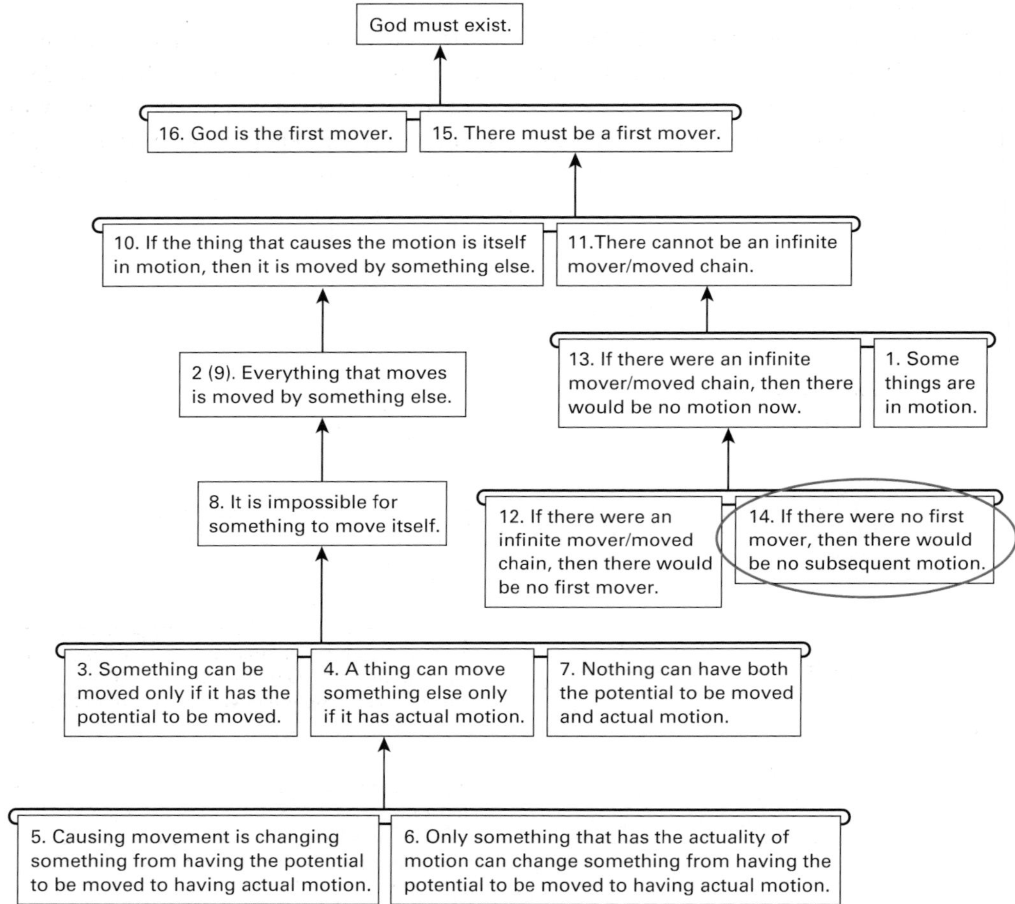
God must exist.
16. God is the first mover.
15. There must be a first mover.
10. If the thing that causes the motion is itself in motion, then it is moved by something else.
11.There cannot be an infinite mover/moved chain.
2 (9). Everything that moves is moved by something else.
13. If there were an infinite mover/moved chain, then there would be no motion now.
1. Some things are in motion.
8. It is impossible for something to move itself.
12. If there were an infinite mover/moved chain, then there would be no first mover.
14. If there were no first mover, then there would be no subsequent motion.
3. Something can be moved only if it has the potential to be moved.
4. A thing can move something else only if it has actual motion.
7. Nothing can have both the potential to be moved and actual motion.
5. Causing movement is changing something from having the potential to be moved to having actual motion.
6. Only something that has the actuality of motion can change something from having the potential to be moved to having actual motion.

Second Objection

Aquinas himself realized that even if (15) and (16) are true, their combination does not guarantee that the conclusion is true. This is because (15) only postulates a being that is a "first mover," while the conception of God to which Aquinas refers is the Christian God, who presumably is understood to have many more attributes—omnipotence, omniscience, and omnibenevolence, for example. In other words, Aquinas is equating the first mover of the Aristotelian kind with the Christian God, when the first mover could in fact be any kind of being at all.

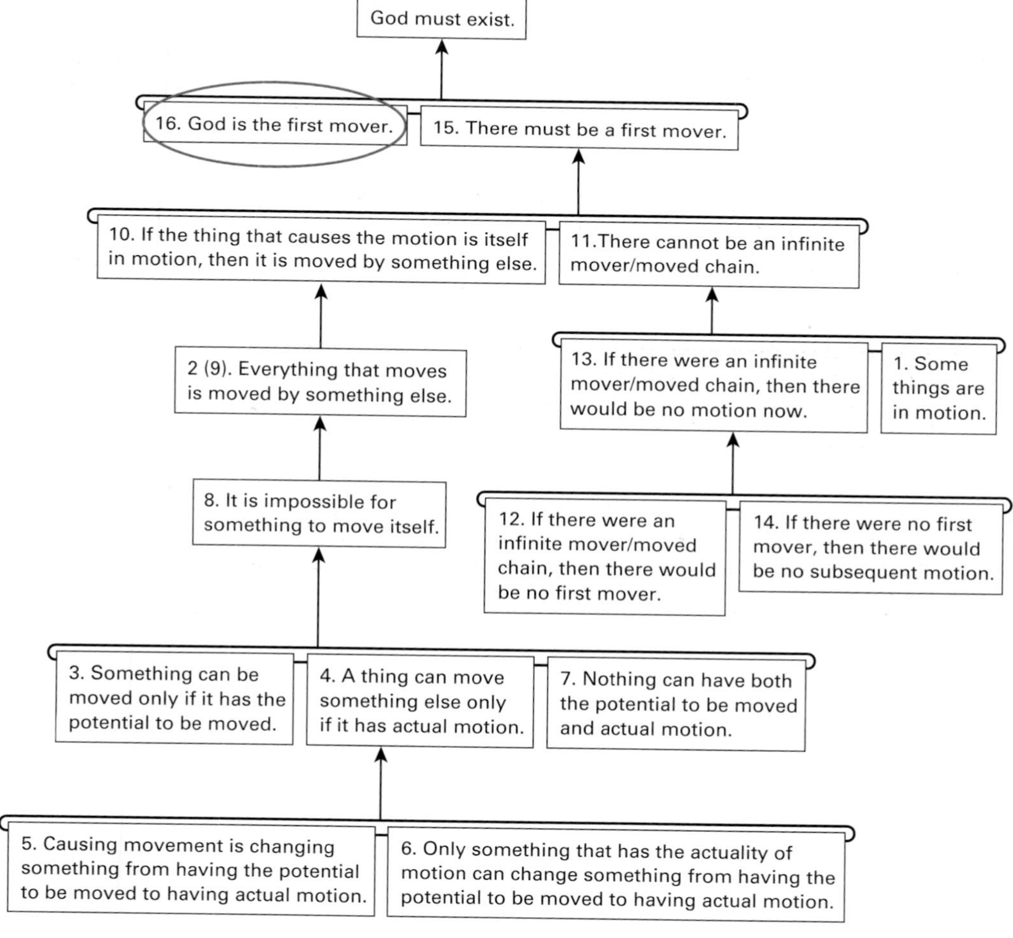

Third Objection

Aquinas claims that what follows from the combination of premises (10) and (11) is that there must be a first mover. When we look more closely, however, it is clear that what actually follows from these premises is more complicated. Aquinas assumes that if there cannot be an infinite mover/moved chain, then there must be a finite mover/moved chain. But all that really follows is that there *could* be a finite mover/moved chain. Aquinas says nothing that suggests that there couldn't also be many finite mover/moved chains or, for that matter, a circular chain.

Let's explore these suggestions. First, consider the following sequences:

(a) $M_1 \rightarrow M_2 \rightarrow \ldots \rightarrow M_{n-1} \rightarrow M_n$
(b) $M_1 \rightarrow M_2 \rightarrow \ldots \rightarrow M_n \rightarrow M_1$

In both diagrams, M_x stands for "mover x," which is just a generic label for any thing that moves; for example, the hand that moves the staff in Aquinas's argument could have the specific label Mn. In each diagram, M_1 is one mover, and the arrows indicate that M_1 moves M_2, M_2 moves M_3, and so on. Diagram (a) represents a chain with one beginning, and diagram (b) represents a circular chain. Each diagram is consistent with the claim that there is not an infinite mover/moved chain.

Second, consider the following sequences:

(a) $M_1 \rightarrow M_2 \rightarrow \ldots \rightarrow M_{n-1} \rightarrow M_n$
(c) $M_{1a} \rightarrow M_{2a} \rightarrow \ldots \rightarrow M_{n-1} \rightarrow M_n$
$M_{1b} \rightarrow M_{2b} \rightarrow \ldots \rightarrow M_{m-1} \rightarrow M_m$
$M_{1c} \rightarrow M_{2c} \rightarrow \ldots \rightarrow M_{k-1} \rightarrow M_k$
$M_{1d} \rightarrow M_{2d} \rightarrow \ldots \rightarrow M_{j-1} \rightarrow M_j$

In diagram (c), M_{1a}, M_{1b}, $M1_c$, and M_{1d} are all "first movers" in the sense that they can put things in motion but do not need anything to move themselves. Now, if M_n (e.g., the hand holding the staff) is the thing whose motion we need to explain, either (a) or (b) would work equally well.

In fact, this second interpretation of the argument is an example of a well-known fallacy: the *quantifier switch* fallacy. To understand this fallacy, consider the following two statements:

(1) Everyone will receive some grade in this class.
(2) There is some grade that everyone in this class will receive.

These statements are clearly very different. The first one describes the usual situation in academic classes: at the end of the class, the instructor assigns you an individual grade based on your performance in the class. The second one however, describes a very unusual situation: one in which everyone in class receives the same grade.

The quantifier switch fallacy occurs when a statement like the second is inferred from a statement like the first. And this seems to be exactly what is happening in Aquinas's argument. Premises (10) and (11) allow us to conclude that:

Every thing that is in motion must be connected by a chain of movement back to some first mover.

But instead, Aquinas concludes something very different:

There is some first mover to which everything that is in motion is connected by a chain of movement.

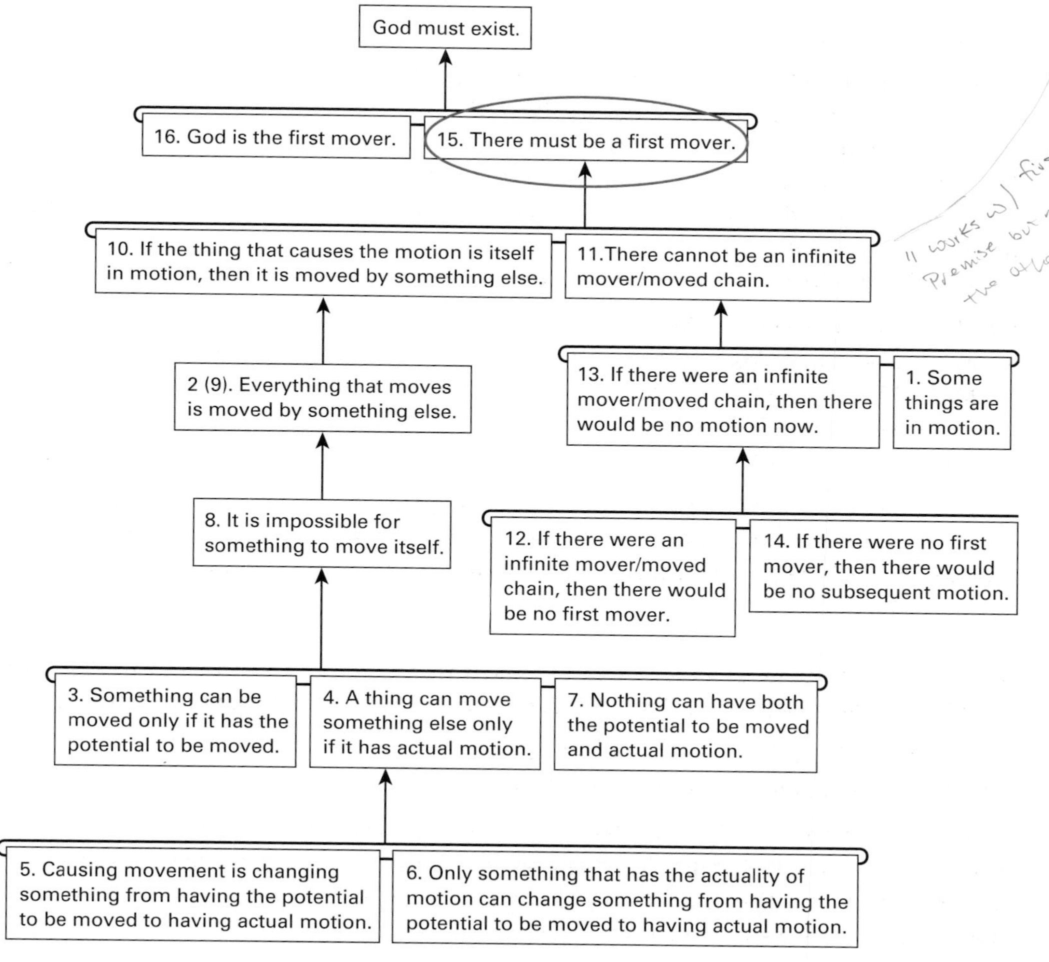

Fourth Objection

Aquinas claims that there can't be a chain of movers that extends infinitely far back into the past. But it's not immediately obvious why this would be impossible; after all, Aquinas doesn't give us any reason to believe that the chain of movers will not extend infinitely far into the *future*—in fact he most likely believed that it would. So why would the past be different? Aquinas's reason is the subargument he gives to support this claim. Aquinas argues, in effect, that causal chains can flow in only one direction, and if the chain has no first member (the first mover), then there can be no chain at all. But why couldn't there be a chain? Aquinas seems to think that the general principle "Every event has a cause" or "Every thing moved has a mover" implies that there must be a first cause. But this principle is consistent with the alternate claim that the causal chain extends infinitely far back into the past.

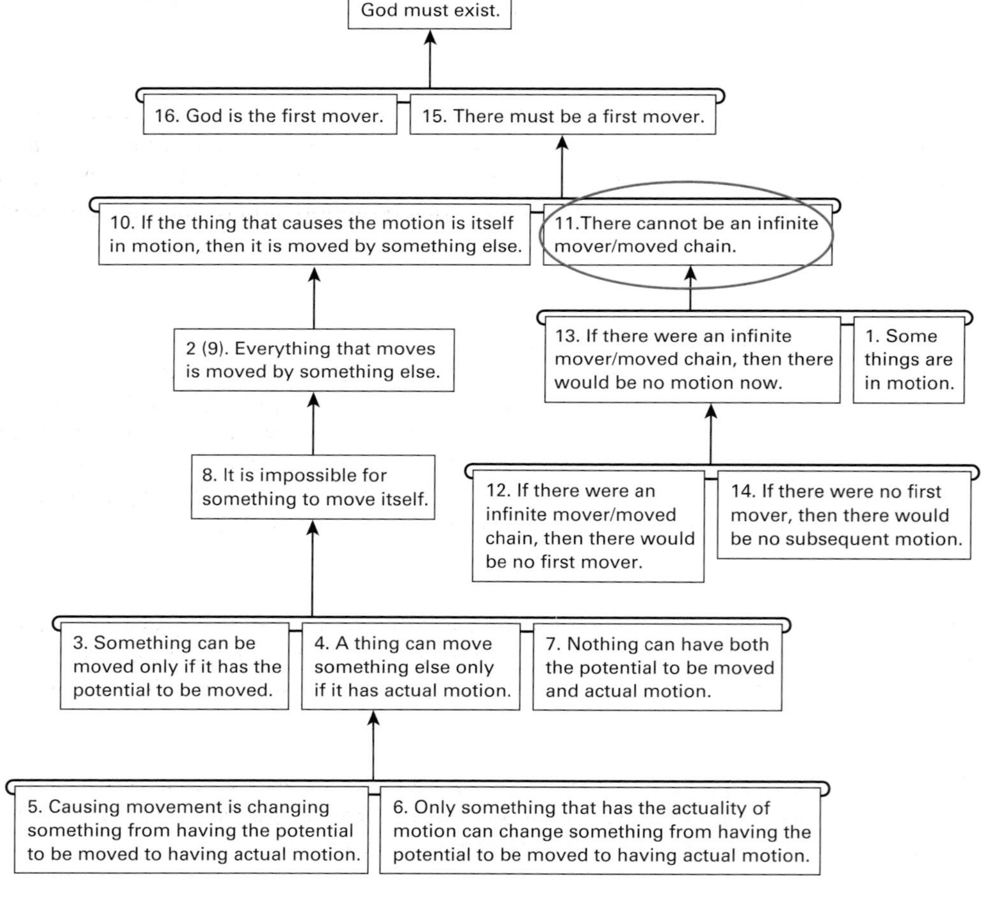

So it seems there are some interesting problems with Aquinas's argument. But, as we saw with Anselm's argument, we have not shown that God does not exist. What we've shown is not that the conclusion of the argument is false, but rather that *this* argument does not give us adequate reasons to believe the conclusion. In fact, one or more of Aquinas's other arguments may provide very good reasons for believing the conclusion (you'll have to analyze them to find out). And even if none of Aquinas's arguments is good, there may be other arguments—maybe even ones you create yourself—that are good. Remember that in order to show that the conclusion is false, one would have to provide good reasons for thinking that God does not exist, that is, an argument against God's existence.

4.3 In-Class Exercises

An asterisk (*) indicates a more challenging exercise.

Exercises 1–5

In the first part of this chapter, we analyzed in detail the argument in chapter 2 of Anselm's *Proslogion*. The following are chapters 3 and 4. For each argument, (a) diagram the argument; (b) determine whether the argument is deductive or nondeductive (and if nondeductive, which kind) and whether the argument is a priori or a posteriori; and (c) identify any potential objections to the argument.

Exercise 1

Chapter 3: That God Cannot Be Thought Not to Exist

In fact, it so undoubtedly exists that it cannot be thought of as not existing. For one can think there exists something that cannot be thought of as not existing, and that would be greater than something which can be thought of as not existing. For if that greater than which cannot be thought can be thought of as not existing, then that greater than which cannot be thought is not that greater than which cannot be thought, which does not make sense. Thus that than which nothing greater can be thought so undoubtedly exists that it cannot even be thought of as not existing.

Exercise 2

And you, Lord God, are this being. You exist so undoubtedly, my Lord God, that you cannot even be thought of as not existing. And deservedly, for if some mind could think of something greater than you, that creature would rise above the creator and could pass judgment on the creator, which is absurd.

Exercise 3

And indeed whatever exists except you alone can be thought of as not existing. You alone of all things most truly exists and thus enjoy existence to the fullest degree of all things, because nothing else exists so undoubtedly, and thus everything else enjoys being in a lesser degree.

Exercise 4

Chapter 4: How the Fool Managed to Say in His Heart That Which Cannot Be Thought

How in the world could he have said in his heart what he could not think? Or how indeed could he not have thought what he said in his heart, since saying it in his heart is the same as thinking it? But if he really thought it because he said it in his heart, and did not say it in his heart because he could not possibly have thought it—and that seems to be precisely what happened—then there must be more than one way in which something can be said in one's heart or thought.

**Exercise 5*

For a thing is thought in one way when the words signifying it are thought, and it is thought in quite another way when the thing signified is understood. God can be thought not to exist in the first way but not in the second. For no one who understands what God is can think that he does not exist. Even though he may say those words in his heart he will give them some other meaning or no meaning at all. For God is that greater than [that] which cannot be thought. Whoever understands this also understands that God exists in such a way that one cannot even think of him as not existing.

Exercises 6–8

The following is a selection of text from Gaunilo's "On Behalf of the Fool." His example of the perfect island is at the very end. For each section of the text, (a) diagram the argument; (b) determine whether the argument is deductive or nondeductive (and if nondeductive, which kind) and whether the argument is a priori or a posteriori; and (c) identify any potential objections to the argument.

Exercise 6

Section 1 [Restatement of Anselm's Argument]

To one who questions whether (or simply denies that) there exists something of such a nature that nothing greater can be imagined, it is said that its existence is proved in the first place by the fact that anyone denying it already has it in his thought, since upon hearing it said he understands what is said; and in the second place by the fact that what he understands necessarily exists not only in the mind but in reality as well. Thus its existence is proved, because it is a greater thing to exist in reality as well than to exist in the mind alone, and if it exists only in the mind, then what exists in reality as well will be greater, and thus that which is greater than all else will be less than something else and not greater than all else, which is nonsense. Thus what is greater than all else must necessarily exist, not only in the mind (which has already been acknowledged to be the case), [but] in reality as well, or else it could not be greater than all else.

**Exercise 7*

Section 5

But through this alone it can hardly be said to attain existence in reality. I will not concede that much to it unless convinced by some indubitable argument. For whoever says that it must exist because otherwise that which is greater than all other beings will not be greater than all other beings, that person isn't paying careful enough attention to what he says. For I do not yet grant, in fact I deny it or at least question it, that the thing existing in my mind is greater than any real thing. Nor do I concede that it exists in any way except this: the sort of existence (if you can call it such) a thing has when the mind attempts to form some image of a thing unknown to it on the basis of nothing more than some words the person has heard. How then is it demonstrated to me that the thing exists in reality merely because it is said to be greater than everything else? For I continue to deny and doubt that this is established, since I continue to question whether this greater thing is in my mind or thought even in the way that many doubtful or unreal things are.

**Exercise 8*

Focus on the argument in quotation marks:

It would first have to be proved to me that this greater thing really exists somewhere. Only then will we be able to infer from the fact that it is greater than everything else that it also subsists in itself.

Section 6

For example, they say there is in the ocean somewhere an island which, due to the difficulty (or rather the impossibility) of finding what does not actually exist, is called "the lost island." And they say that this island has all manner of riches and delights, even more of them than the Isles of the Blest, and having no owner or inhabitant it is superior in the abundance of its riches to all other lands which are inhabited by men. If someone should tell me that such is the case, I will find it easy to understand what he says, since there is nothing difficult about it. But suppose he then adds, as if he were stating a logical consequence,

"Well then, you can no longer doubt that this island more excellent than all other lands really exists somewhere, since you do not doubt that it is in your mind; and since it is more excellent to exist not only in the mind but in reality as well, this island must necessarily exist, because if it didn't, any other island really existing would be more excellent than it, and thus that island now thought of by you as more excellent will not be such."

If, I say, someone tries to convince me through this argument that the island really exists and there should be no more doubt about it, I will either think he is joking or I will have a hard time deciding who is the bigger fool, me if I believe him or him if he thinks he has proved its existence without having first convinced me that this excellence is something undoubtedly existing in reality and not just something false or uncertain existing in my mind.

Exercises 9–12

The following is the rest of the text that we analyzed in the previous section from Aquinas. For each of the remaining ways of proving God exists, (a) diagram the argument; (b) determine whether the argument is deductive or nondeductive (and if nondeductive, which kind) and whether the argument is a priori or a posteriori; and (c) identify any potential objections to the argument. (The translation of this part is from *Quest for Truth*.)

**Exercise 9*

The second way [to prove that God exists] is taken from the idea of the Efficient Cause. For we find that there is among material things a regular order of efficient causes.

a. But we do not find, nor indeed is it possible, that anything is the efficient cause of itself, for in that case it would be prior to itself, which is impossible.
*b. Now it is not possible to proceed to infinity in efficient causes. For if we arrange in order all efficient causes, the first is the cause of the intermediate, and the intermediate is the cause of the last, whether the intermediate may be many or only one. But if we remove a cause the effect is removed; therefore, if there is no *first* among efficient causes, neither will there be a last or an intermediate. But if we proceed to infinity in efficient causes there will be no first efficient cause, and thus there will be no ultimate effect, nor any intermediate efficient causes, which is clearly false.
c. [For we find that there is among material things a regular order of efficient causes.] [Now it is not possible to proceed to infinity in efficient causes.] Therefore it is necessary to suppose the existence of some first efficient cause, and this men call God.

*Exercise 10

The third way [to prove that God exists] rests on the idea of the "contingent" and the "necessary" and is as follows.

a. Now we find that there are certain things in the universe that are capable of existing and not existing, for we find that some things are brought into existence and then destroyed, and consequently, are capable of being or not being.
*b. But it is impossible for all things which exist to be of this kind, because anything that is capable of not existing at sometime or other does not exist. If, therefore, all things are capable of not existing, then there was a time when nothing existed in the universe. But if this is true, there would also be nothing in existence now, because anything that does not exist cannot begin to exist except by the agency of something which has existence. If, therefore, there was once nothing that existed, it would have been impossible for anything to begin to exist, and so nothing would exist now. This is clearly false.
c. Therefore, all things are not contingent, and there must be something which is necessary in the universe. But everything which is necessary either has or has not the cause of its necessity from an outside source. Now it is not possible to proceed to infinity in necessary things which have a cause of their necessity, as has been proved in the case of efficient causes. Therefore it is necessary to suppose the existence of something which is necessary in itself, not having the cause of its necessity from any outside source, but which is the cause of necessity in others. And this "something" we call God.

Exercise 11

The fourth way [to prove that God exists] is taken from the degrees which are found in things.

a. For, among different things we find that one is more or less good, true, noble; and likewise in the case of other things of this kind. But the words "more" or "less" are used of different things in proportion as approximate in their different ways to something which has the particular quality in the highest degree—e.g., we call a thing hotter when it approximates more nearly to that which is hot in the highest degree. There is, therefore, something which is true in the highest degree, good in the highest degree and noble in the highest degree;
b. ... and consequently there must be also something which has being in the highest degree (see Aristotle, Metaphysics 2). But anything which has a certain quality of any kind in the highest degree is also the cause of all the things of that kind, as, for example, fire which is hot in the highest degree is the cause of

all hot things (as is said in the same book). Therefore there exists something which is the cause of being, and goodness, and of every perfection in all existing things; and this we call God.

Exercise 12

The fifth way [to prove that God exists] is taken from the way in which nature is governed.

a. For we observe that certain things which lack [intelligence], such as natural bodies, work for an End. This is obvious because they always, or at any rate very frequently, operate in the same way so as to attain the best possible result. Hence it is clear that they do not arrive at their goal by chance, but by purpose.
b. But those things which have no [intelligence] do not move towards a goal unless they are guided by someone or something which does possess knowledge and intelligence—e.g., an arrow by an archer. Therefore, there does exist something which possesses intelligence by which all natural things are directed to their goal; and this we call God.

Exercises 13–18

The following exercises are intended to ensure your understanding of both Anselm's and Aquinas' texts, and to help you further explore the ideas presented in this chapter.

Exercise 13: Now that you have read my textual analysis of Anselm's argument, summarize it in your own words.
Exercise 14: Summarize, in your own words, each of Anselm's arguments in exercises 1–5 above.
Exercise 15: Summarize, in your own words, each of Gaunilo's arguments in exercises 6–8 above.
Exercise 16: Now that you have read my textual analysis of Aquinas' argument, summarize it in your own words.
Exercise 17: Summarize, in your own words, each of Aquinas's arguments in exercises 9–12 (the second through fifth ways to prove that God exists).
Exercise 18: In convincing another person to believe a proposition, do you think an a priori argument or an a posteriori argument is better? Why? If it depends on the circumstances, what are those circumstances, and how does it depend on them?

5 Deductive Arguments against the Existence of God

5.1 Michael Martin, "Three Reasons for Nonbelief"
5.2 John Mackie, "Evil and Omnipotence"
5.3 In-Class Exercises
5.4 Reading Questions

5.1 Michael Martin, "Three Reasons for Nonbelief"

Michael Martin (1932–) is an American philosopher at Boston University. He attended Arizona State University as an undergraduate and University of Arizona for his Master's and Harvard University for his PhD. He earned his PhD in 1962, and took a job immediately at the University of Colorado. He left Colorado for Boston University, where he is still an emeritus member of the faculty. Known primarily as a philosopher of religion, he has also worked in philosophy of social science and philosophy of law.

Martin has published several books in the philosophy of religion, the most recent of which are *The Myth of Afterlife* (2012), *The Cambridge Companion to Atheism* (2006), *The Improbability of God* (2006), *The Impossibility of God* (2003), *Atheism, Morality, and Meaning* (2002), and *Theism vs. Atheism: The Internet Debate* (2000). The selection we will be analyzing below is "Three Arguments for Nonbelief," an article Martin published in 2001 in the journal *Free Inquiry*.

We consider Martin's argument for a couple of reasons. First, most of the arguments we have studied so far have been linked arguments, but Martin's gives us a very good example of a convergent argument. Second, Martin's argument is a combination of a deductive and nondeductive argument. The convergent part of the argument is nondeductive—it seems to be a kind of argument by inductive enumeration. It seems that Martin intends the rest of the argument to be a deductive argument.

Let's look at Martin's text in more detail. Specifically, we will analyze and diagram the argument, and then discuss criticisms.

From "Three Arguments for Nonbelief."[1]

New Thoughts on an Old Subject

In this essay I will present three fresh arguments to justify nonbelief in the theistic God usually associated with Christianity and Judaism. First, the Argument from Incoherence shows that the concept of God is like the concept of a round square or a four-sided triangle. Round squares or four-sided triangles cannot exist; neither can God. Second, the Argument from Nonbelief was originally presented by contemporary American philosopher Theodore Drange. Especially relevant to evangelical Christianity and Orthodox Judaism, it maintains that the large amount of nonbelief in the world makes the existence of God improbable. Third is a new Moral Argument for Nonbelief constructed by contemporary Canadian philosopher Raymond Bradley. It turns on the conflict between the view that God would not cause or condone immoral acts and biblical statements in which God does precisely this.

...

The Argument from Incoherence

One good reason[A] not to believe that God exists is that the very concept of God is incoherent,[1] in the same way as is the concept of a round square or the "largest number." In accordance with our two perspectives, philosophical and biblical, this argument can be made in two ways:

First,[B] some properties attributed to God in the Bible are inconsistent.[2] For example, God is said to be invisible (Col. 1:15, 1 Tim. 1:17, 6:16), a being that has never been seen (John 1:18, 1 John 4:12).[3] Yet[C] several people in the Bible, among them Moses (Exod. 33:11, 23), Abraham, Isaac, and Jacob (Gen. 12:7, 26:2; Exod. 6:3) report having seen God.[4] God is supposed to have said, "You cannot see my face, for no one can see me and live" (Gen. 32:30).[5] However,[D] Jacob saw God and lived (Gen. 32:30).[6] In some places God is described as merciful[7] [Psalms 86:5, 100:5, 103:8, 106:1, 136:2, 148:8–9; Joel 2:13; Mic. 7:18; James 5:11], in others as lacking mercy[8] [Deut. 7:2, 16, 20:16–17; Josh. 6:21, 10:11, 19, 40, 11:6–20; Isa. 6, 19, 15:3; Nah. 1:2; Jer. 13:14; Matt. 8:12, 13:42, 50, 25:30, 41, 46; Mark 3:29; 2 Thes. 1:8–9; Rev. 14:9–11, 21:8], in some places a being who repents and changes his mind,[9] in others as a being who never repents and changes his mind,[10] in some places as a being who deceives and causes confusion and evil,[11] and in others as a being who never does,[12] in some places as someone who punishes children for their parents' wrongdoing,[13] and in others as one who never does.[14] So[E] if one takes what the Bible says seriously, God cannot exist.[15]

In the introduction and the conclusion, Martin tells us that he wants to provide three (types of) arguments against the existence of God.

The first argument that Martin gives is the *argument from incoherence*. The "one good reason" (A) to believe that the conclusion is true is that the concept of God is incoherent (1). He says that we can demonstrate this incoherence in two ways (we will leave the second way for the exercises at the end).

The first way, indicated by (B), is to show that some descriptions of God, in various places in the Bible, contradict each other (2). Each pair of these descriptions can be seen as a different, independent reason to believe the conclusion. In other words, Martin is giving us a convergent argument for this subconclusion.

The first example is that in some places God is said to be invisible (3), "yet" (C) in others, he is said to be visible (4):

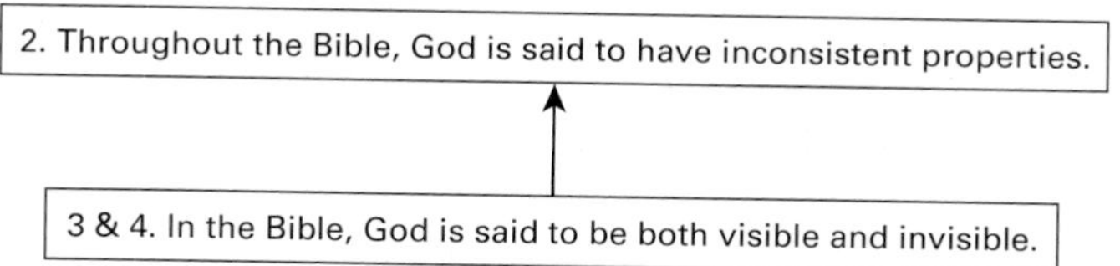

The second example is that in some places it is said that no one can see God and live (5); "however" (D), in others it is said that people saw God and lived (6):

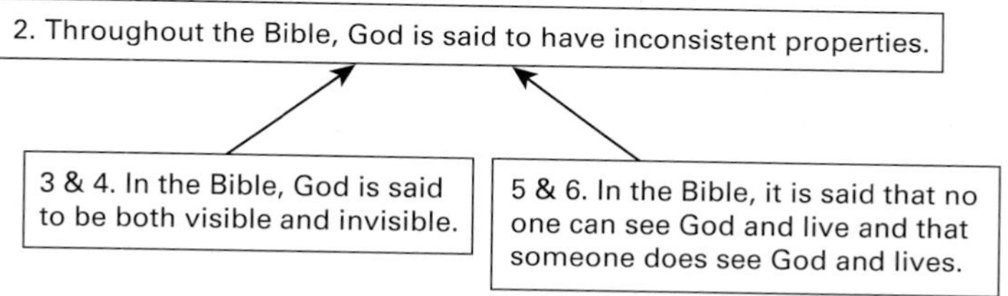

The next example is that in some places God is described as merciful (7) and in others as merciless (8):

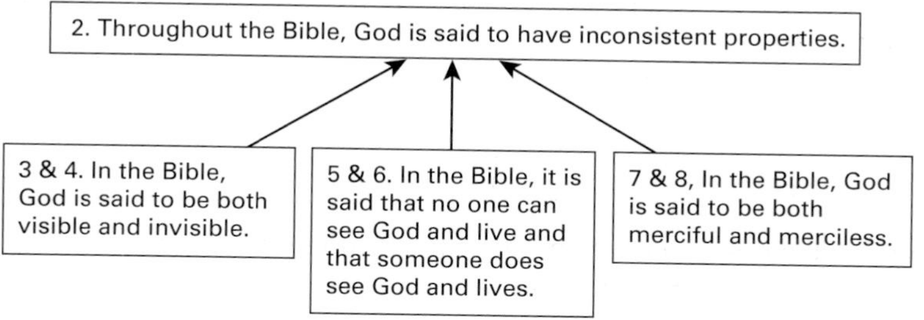

A further example is that in some places God is said to be a being who both repents and changes his mind (9) and does not (10):

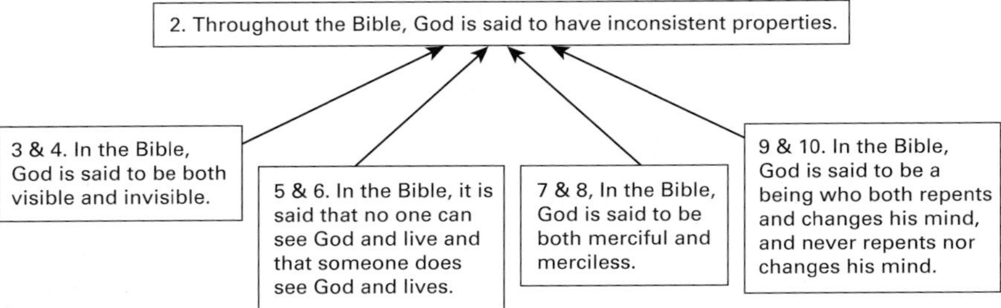

In addition, in some places God is said to be a being who both deceives and causes confusion and evil (11) and does not (12):

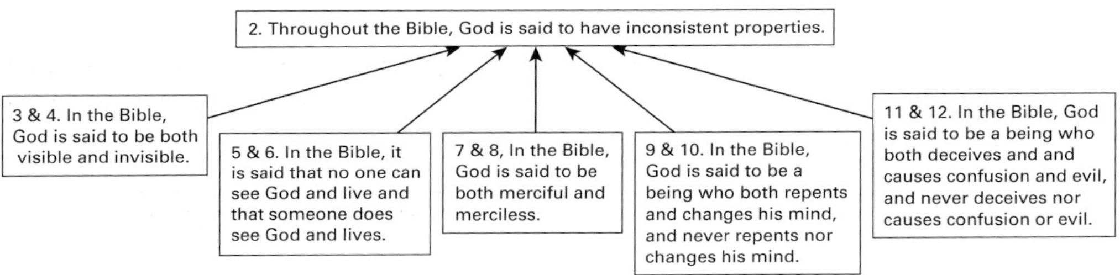

And finally, in some places God is said to be a being who both punishes children for their parents' wrongdoing (13) and does not (14):

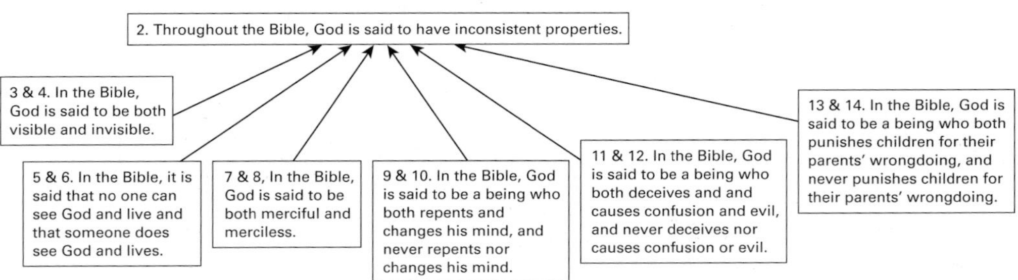

Recall that Martin's argument is an example of a combination of a deductive and a nondeductive argument. We have here, then, reconstructed the nondeductive part, which is the convergent argument above. But, overall, the argument is supposed to be deductive. To see this, we have to fit this in with the rest of Martin's argument. So, finally, we have the argument that supports Martin's first claim that the very concept of God is incoherent (1), which in turn supports the last claim that if one takes the Bible seriously, then God does not exist (15):

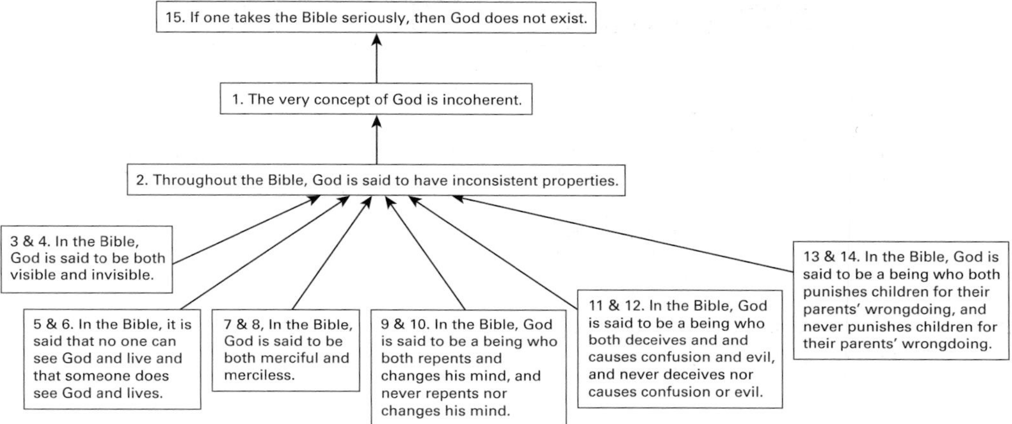

But, of course, this form of the argument isn't obviously deductive. What's missing are the implicit premises linking (2) to (1), and (1) to (15). If we put in reasonable candidates for these implicit premises, we have the following:

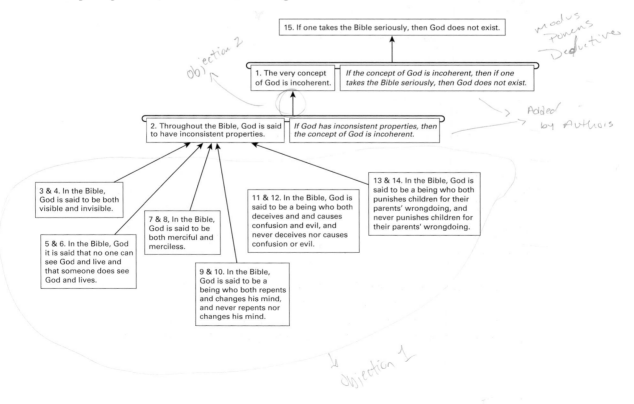

15. If one takes the Bible seriously, then God does not exist.

1. The very concept of God is incoherent. | *If the concept of God is incoherent, then if one takes the Bible seriously, then God does not exist.*

2. Throughout the Bible, God is said to have inconsistent properties. | *If God has inconsistent properties, then the concept of God is incoherent.*

3 & 4. In the Bible, God is said to be both visible and invisible.

5 & 6. In the Bible, God it is said that no one can see God and live and that someone does see God and lives.

7 & 8, In the Bible, God is said to be both merciful and merciless.

9 & 10. In the Bible, God is said to be a being who both repents and changes his mind, and never repents nor changes his mind.

11 & 12. In the Bible, God is said to be a being who both deceives and and causes confusion and evil, and never deceives nor causes confusion or evil.

13 & 14. In the Bible, God is said to be a being who both punishes children for their parents' wrongdoing, and never punishes children for their parents' wrongdoing.

Now that we're clear about what the premises of Martin's argument are, and how the premises are supposed to work together to support the conclusion, we can begin to evaluate the argument. Remember that in evaluation we are interested in the soundness (or cogency) of the argument. This means we are interested in (a) whether the premises are true and (b) whether the premises actually support the conclusion. In terms of the argument diagram, this means we are interested in the content of the boxes and the plausibility and strength of the arrows.

Against Martin's argument against the existence of God, we can consider at least two objections.

1. There could be several objections to the claims that support premise (2). Here, we will consider one such objection: in the Bible, God is not actually said to be both visible and invisible—premise (3 & 4) is false.
2. Martin's argument does not show that the concept of God is incoherent, only that the biblical conception of God is incoherent.

I will take each objection in turn, considering the objection from the point of view of the argument diagram.

First Objection

This objection questions the truth of the claim that "in the Bible, God is said to be both visible and invisible."

In particular, the objection is that Martin is assuming that the various cases of God being both visible and invisible refer to the same sense of "seeing." First, consider the passages from the Old Testament that seem to imply that God can be seen.

Then, consider the passages from the New Testament that seem to imply that either God is invisible or God has never been seen.

As noted, the first set of passages is from the Old Testament, while the second is from the New Testament. This matters because it could be the case that the language of the Old Testament is just a bit different from that of the New, and so they really aren't contradictory.

Some theologians explain the discrepancy as follows. For something to be visible, in one sense, it must be a corporeal body that can reflect light into the eyes of the person who sees the object. So, God is invisible in the sense that he is not corporeal, and so cannot reflect light in this way.

On the other hand, we sometimes talk about things being visible if we can see their effects. In physics, for example, we can't see fundamental particles in the sense that they reflect light into our eyes; rather, we see, for example, tracks made by these particles in bubble chambers. In the same way, God can be "seen" in the manifestation of his influence on both living and nonliving things in the world, as well as in the visions of prophets and the hearts of people.

Thus, the argument goes, God is technically invisible in the way that is described in the New Testament. However, God can be seen in various ways, and these are the kinds of situations described, though perhaps not very precisely, in the Old Testament.

More objections along these lines could be produced for each of the other parts of Martin's convergent argument.

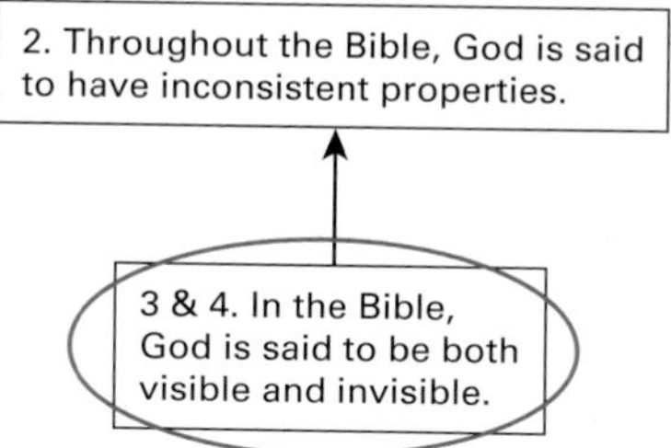

From the New International Version:

The LORD would speak to Moses face to face, as a man speaks with his friend. Then Moses would return to the camp, but his young aide Joshua son of Nun did not leave the tent. (Exod. 33:11)

"Then I will remove my hand and you will see my back; but my face must not be seen." (Exod. 33:23)

And

He is the image of the invisible God, the firstborn of all creation. (Col. 1:15)

Now to the King eternal, immortal, invisible, the only God, be honor and glory forever and ever. Amen. (1 Tim. 1:17)

... who alone is immortal and who lives in unapproachable light, whom no one has seen or can see. To him be honor and might forever. Amen. (1 Tim 6:16)

No one has ever seen God, but God the One and Only, who is at the Father's side, has made him known. (John 1:18)

No one has ever seen God; but if we love one another, God lives in us and his love is made complete in us. (1 John 4:12)

Second Objection

In the beginning of Martin's first argument he says that he will show that "the very concept of God is incoherent, in the same way as is the concept of a round square or the largest number." His reason for this is that throughout the Bible, God is said to have inconsistent properties.

According to the principle of charity, we inserted an implicit premise above to make this subargument valid. But, the premise inserted to make the argument valid isn't obviously true. Martin is explicitly focusing on an argument against biblical literalism, and so is only really concerned with the God of the Christian Bible.

So, to truly make the implied premise be consistent with premise (2), it would have to be something like "If throughout the Bible, God is said to have inconsistent properties, then the concept of God is incoherent." But this way of phrasing the implied premise shows what is wrong with the argument. Surely it is not the case that if the Christian God has inconsistent properties, then the concept of *any* God whatsoever is incoherent. The concept of the God of Judaism or Hinduism could be coherent, even if the concept of the Christian God is not.

Thus, premise (2) does not support statement (1) as written; at most it supports a statement like "The concept of God in the Christian Bible is incoherent." And this is not as absolute a statement as saying that the concept of a round square is incoherent. The latter applies to any square at all, whereas Martin's claim applies only to one conception of God.

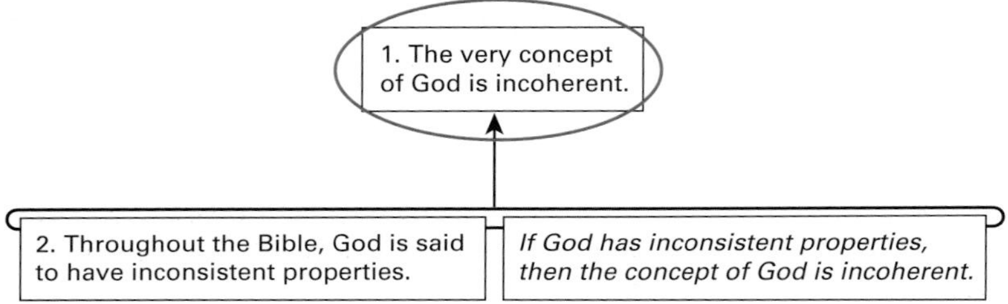

In this article, Martin has two more main arguments against the existence of God. These arguments and further objections will be explored in the exercises below. First, though, we will consider another kind of argument against God's existence.

5.2 John Mackie, "Evil and Omnipotence"

John Mackie (1917–1981) was an Australian philosopher, who graduated from the University of Sydney before taking a fellowship at Oxford in 1940. His first faculty position was at the University of Otago in New Zealand; he then moved to a faculty position at the University of Sydney in 1959. In 1963, he became chair of philosophy at the University of York, and 1967 he was elected university fellow at University College, Oxford.

Mackie contributed to many areas besides philosophy of religion, such as philosophy of science, metaphysics, and ethics. He published six books in his lifetime covering all of these topics: *Truth, Probability, and Paradox* (1973), *The Cement of the Universe: A Study of Causation* (1974), *Problems from Locke* (1976), *Ethics: Inventing Right and Wrong* (1977), *Hume's Moral Theory* (1980), and *The Miracle of Theism: Arguments For and Against the Existence of God* (1982). The selection we will be analyzing below is "Evil and Omnipotence," an article Mackie published in 1955 in the journal *Mind*.

Mackie's argument is a deductive argument against the existence of God. It is interesting not least because it is a very good example of a reductio ad absurdum argument. Let's look at Mackie's text in more detail. Specifically, we will analyze and diagram the argument and then discuss criticisms.

From "Evil and Omnipotence."[2]

I think, however, that a more telling criticism [against theists] can be made by way of the traditional problem of evil. Here it can be shown,[A] not that religious beliefs lack rational support, but that they are positively irrational, that the several parts of the essential theological doctrine are inconsistent with one another,[1] so that[B] the theologian can maintain his position as a whole only by a much more extreme rejection of reason than in the former case.[2] He must now be prepared to believe, not merely what cannot be proved, but what can be disproved from other beliefs that he also holds.[3]

The problem of evil, in the sense in which I shall be using the phrase, is a problem only for someone who believes that there is a God who is both omnipotent and wholly good. And it is a logical problem, the problem of clarifying and reconciling a number of beliefs …

In its simplest form the problem is this: God is omnipotent; God is wholly good;[4] and yet[C] evil exists.[5] There seems to be some contradiction between these three propositions,[6] so that if any two of them were true the third would be false. But at the same time all three are essential parts of most theological positions:[7] the theologian, it seems, at once *must* adhere and *cannot consistently* adhere to all three. (The problem does not arise only for theists, but I shall discuss it in the form in which it presents itself for ordinary theism.)

However, the contradiction does not arise immediately; to show it we need some additional premises,[D] or perhaps some quasi-logical rules connecting the terms 'good', 'evil', and omnipotent'. These additional principles are that[E] good is opposed to evil, in such a way that a good thing always eliminates evil as far as it can,[8] and that[F] there are no limits to what an omnipotent thing can do.[9] From these it follows that[G] a good omnipotent thing eliminates evil completely,[10] and then[H] the propositions that a good omnipotent thing exists, and that evil exists, are incompatible.[11]

In the first paragraph of "Evil and Omnipotence," Mackie tells us that the dedicated theist—a person who believes in the traditional Christian God—may not be swayed from the belief in God even if he or she admits that there are no rational proofs of God's existence. Thus, Mackie wants to go beyond the argument that belief in God lacks rational support to provide a further sound, deductive argument that belief in God is actually *irrational*.

The first indicator phrase (A) lets us know that that the main conclusion follows. After this main conclusion is the first part of Mackie's argument. The first premise of this part of the argument is that there are certain important tenets that the theist holds that are inconsistent with each other (1), meaning that they cannot all be true at the same time—for example, one of them must be false if the others are true. As indicated by (B), this leads to the subconclusion represented by (2) and (3).

The argument seems to proceed like this: parts of the theist's doctrine are inconsistent (1); so in order to keep his whole doctrine, the theist must be prepared to believe what can be disproved from his or her other beliefs (3). The implication here is that knowingly having inconsistent beliefs is an extreme rejection of reason. Thus, ultimately, the theist can keep his whole doctrine only with an extreme rejection of reason (2); so, his beliefs are irrational.

We can represent this chain of reasoning, with the addition of the implicit premise, like this:

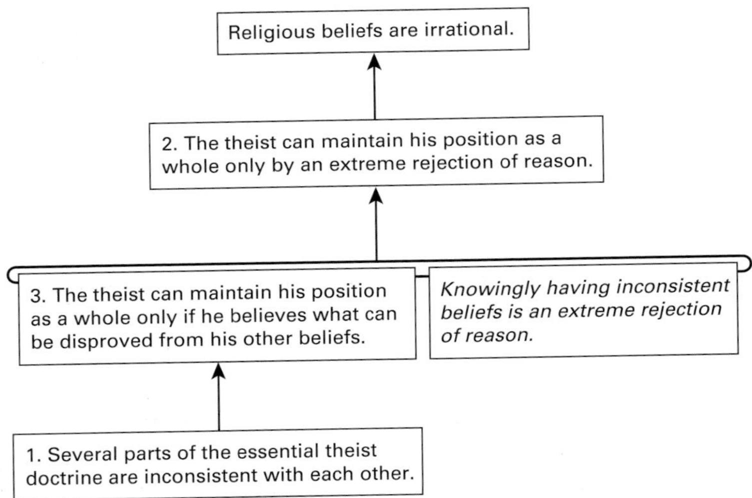

Mackie then provides a further argument to support his claim that the various parts of the doctrine are inconsistent, indicated by the two parts of (C). The two important parts of the theist's doctrine are that God is good and omnipotent (4) and that evil exists (5). Mackie gets more specific in (6) than he does above in statement (1)—that, in particular, (4) and (5) are inconsistent. The inconsistency wouldn't be a problem, but they are all essential parts of the doctrine (7). Thus, several *essential* parts of the doctrine are inconsistent (1).

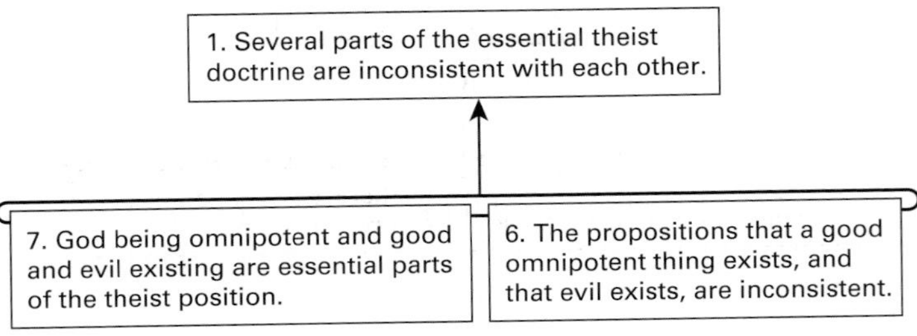

But how are they are inconsistent? This comprises the second part of the argument that Mackie presents, as indicated by (D) and (E). The first additional premise is that something that is good (which God is supposed to be) always eliminates evil as far as it can (8). This premise, as indicated by (F), is combined with the additional premise that something that is omnipotent (as God is also supposed to be) can do anything (9). As indicated by (G), these premises support the claim that something that is both good and omnipotent would eliminate evil completely (10):

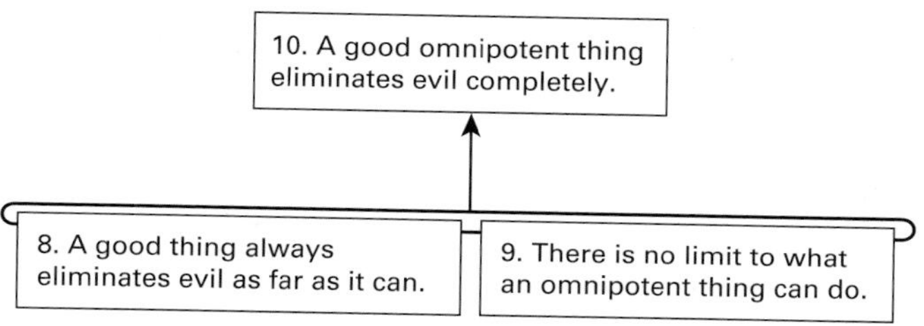

What follows from this subargument is that two propositions—that a good omnipotent thing exists and that evil exists—are incompatible (11). To see how this inference is supposed to work, it will be helpful to add in some of the implied subconclusions that connect (8) and (9) to (10). First, from (10), we can infer the conditional statement: If a good omnipotent thing exists, then there is no evil. The argument can be represented like this:

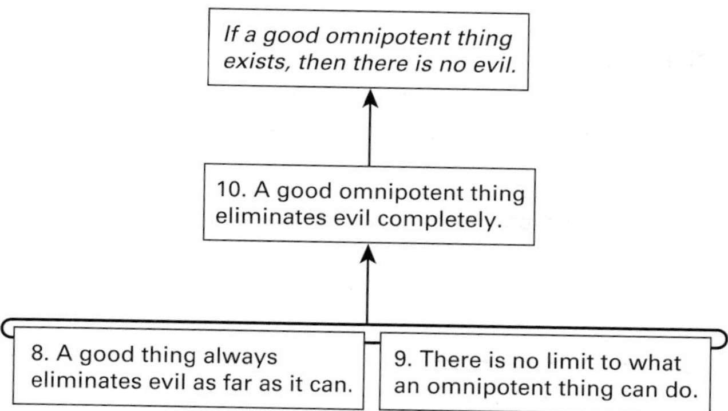

But of course, one of the essential parts of the theist's doctrine is that evil does exist (5). Thus, we get an implied subconclusion: No good omnipotent thing exists:

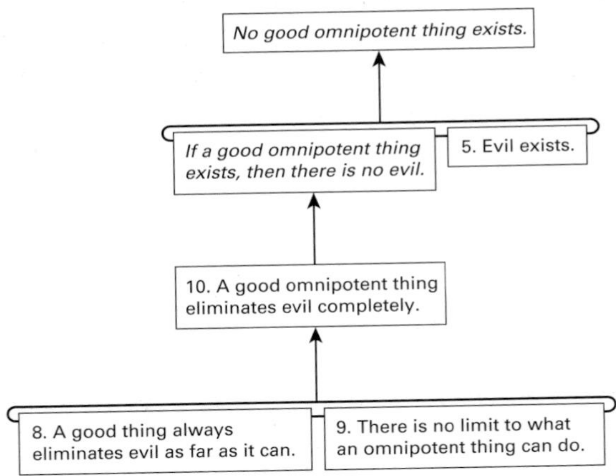

The other essential part of the theist's doctrine, though, is that God exists, and God is both good and omnipotent (4). So we have two claims: that a good omnipotent thing exists, and that no good omnipotent thing exists. These claims oppose each other, so he concludes that these claims are inconsistent (6):

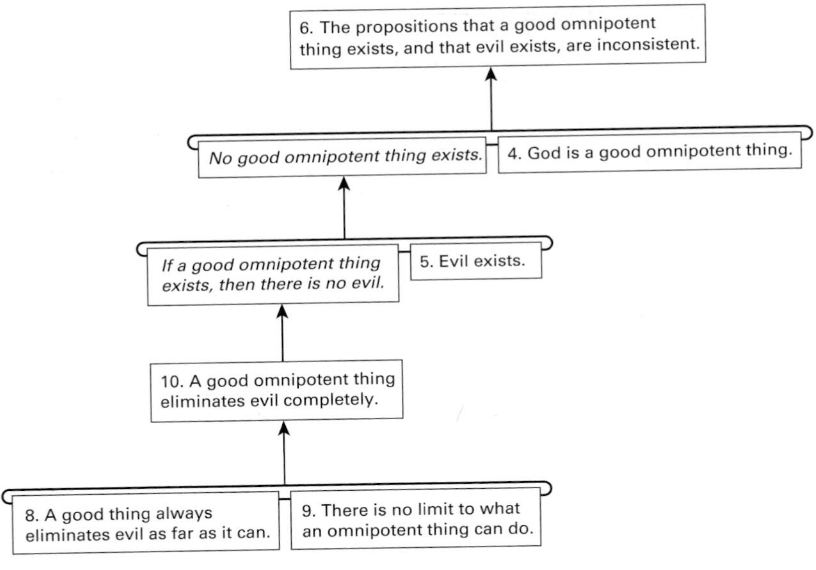

This argument is, in fact, an example of a reductio ad absurdum argument. (Recall the form of a reductio that we discussed in chapter 2, section 2.4.) Here, we start with the assumption that a good omnipotent thing exists. Then we derive the contrary claim that no good omnipotent thing exists. When we combine these two claims, we get a contradiction. The main principle of a reductio argument is that if, based on an assumption, we can derive a contradiction, then the assumption must be false. Thus, instead of merely concluding that some central tenets of the theist's doctrine are inconsistent, we could conclude that (the traditional Christian version of) God does not exist:

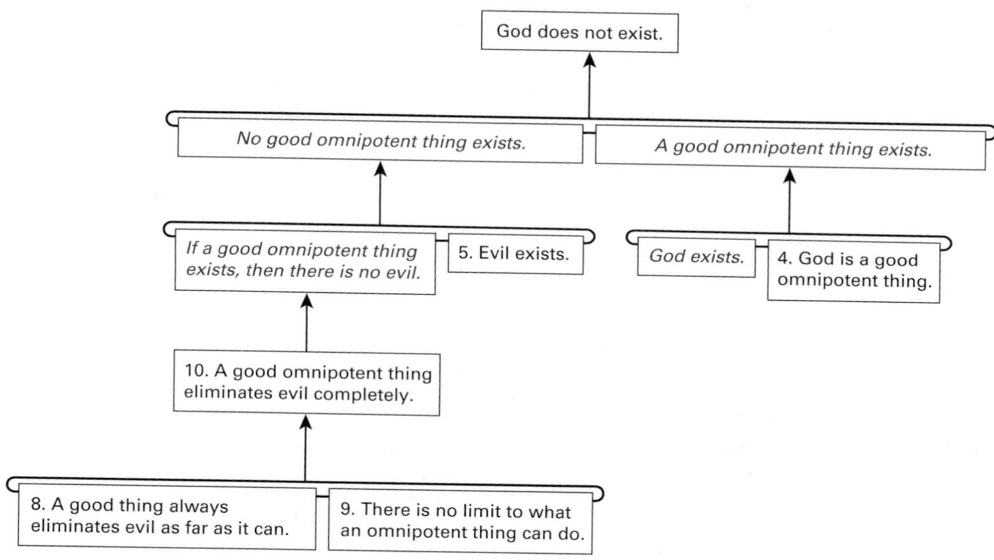

After establishing the basic argument from evil, Mackie considers objections to this argument. First, Mackie acknowledges one way that the theist can deny the conclusion of this argument, that is, one way that the theist can avoid being irrational. All he has to do is deny one of the assumptions:

- God is wholly good (4).
- God is omnipotent (4).
- Evil exists (5).
- Good is opposed to the evil that exists (8).
- There is no limit to what an omnipotent thing can do (9).

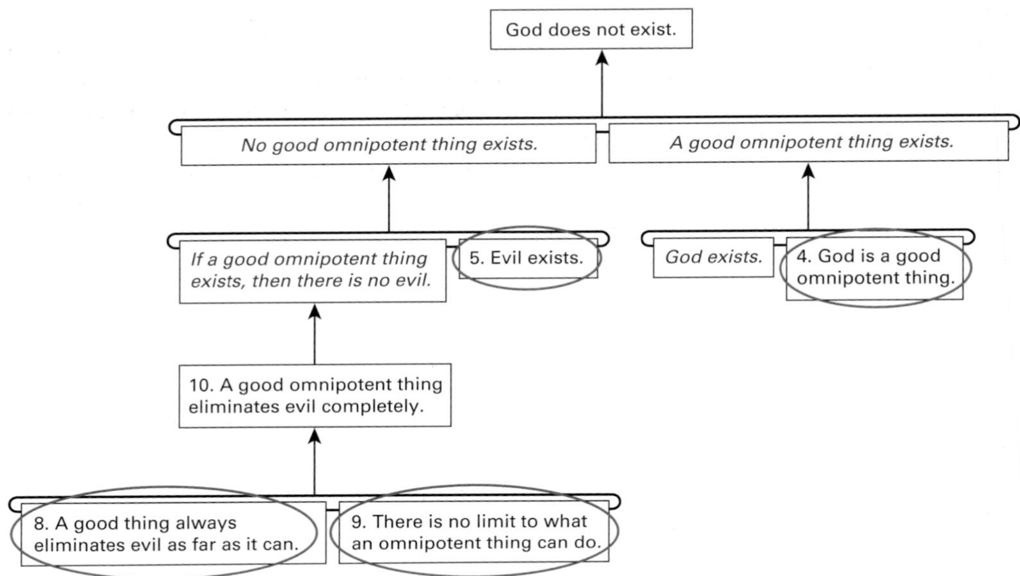

If any of these assumptions is false, the argument does not go through.

First, one could change the definition of "omnipotent" so that there are in fact things that an omnipotent being cannot do.

Second, one could deny that there is evil in the world by claiming that what we call evil isn't real evil.

But of course, the denial of any one of these assumptions seems to be contrary to traditional Christian doctrine. And what one cannot do, Mackie says, is reject one of these assumptions at the outset, but accept it in other contexts.

Further solutions, along with Mackie's replies, are left for the exercises.

5.3 In-Class Exercises

An asterisk (*) indicates a more challenging exercise.

Exercises 1–6

In the first part of this chapter, we analyzed in detail an argument given by Michael Martin in "Three Arguments for Nonbelief." The following passages contain other arguments from this article. For each selection, (a) diagram the argument; (b) determine whether the argument is deductive or nondeductive (and if nondeductive, which kind) and whether the argument is a priori or a posteriori; and (c) identify any potential objections to the argument.

Exercise 1

To say that God is all-knowing, then, is to say that God has all propositional knowledge, all procedural knowledge, and all knowledge by acquaintance. This has implications for the existence of God that usually have not been noticed. First, God's omniscience conflicts with His disembodiedness. If God were omniscient, then God would have all knowledge, including, for example, knowledge of how to swim. Yet only a being with a body can have such procedural knowledge—that is, actually possess the skill of swimming—and by definition God does not have a body. Therefore, God's attribute of being disembodied and His attribute of being omniscient are in conflict. Thus, if God is both omniscient and disembodied, God does not exist. Since God is both omniscient and disembodied, therefore He does not exist.

**Exercise 2*

A second reason for disbelieving in God is the large number of nonbelievers in the world. The Argument from Nonbelief is especially telling against evangelical Christianity although it has some force against other religions, for example, Orthodox Judaism. Evangelical Christianity asserts that

1. God is merciful and all-loving, compassionate and caring towards humanity;
2. The Bible, and only the Bible, is the source of God's word;
3. God wants all humans to be saved;
4. A necessary condition for being saved is becoming aware of the word of God and accepting it.

Supposing for the sake of the argument that evangelical Christianity is true, it is difficult to understand why there are nearly one billion nonbelievers in the world. How can a merciful God, a God who wants all humans to be saved, not provide clear and unambiguous information about His word to humans when having this information is necessary for salvation? Yet, as we know, countless millions of people down through history have not been exposed to the teaching of the Bible. Those who have been were often exposed in superficial and cursory ways that were not conducive to acceptance. Even today there are millions of people who, through no fault of their own, either remain ignorant of the Christian message or, because of shortcomings in their religious education, reject it. One would expect that, if God were rational, He would have arranged things in such a way that there would be more believers.

**Exercise 3*

Bradley presents a moral argument for the nonexistence of God by showing that four basic claims associated with the Bible are in conflict.

1. Any act that God commits, causes, commands, or condones is morally permissible.
2. The Bible reveals to us many of the acts that God commits, causes, commands, or condones.
3. It is morally impermissible for God to commit, cause, command, or condone acts that violate our moral principles.
4. The Bible tells us that God does in fact commit, cause, command, or condone acts that violate our moral principles.

Exercise 4

There are great difficulties standing in the way of anyone who wishes to deny any of these claims, yet since they are in conflict, at least one of them must be denied. To deny the first claim—that any act that

God commits, commands, and so on is morally permissible—would be to admit that God is immoral or even evil. But this would mean that He is not worthy of worship.

Exercise 5

To deny the second claim—that the Bible reveals to us many of the acts that God commits, commands, and so on—would be to give up the foundation of religious and moral epistemology. If this claim is false, then how can we know what we ought or ought not to do? The Bible, according to theists, is the major source of our knowledge of ethical principles.

Exercise 6

To deny the third claim—that it is morally impermissible for God to commit, command, and so on acts that violate our moral principles—would mean that it is morally permissible to perform acts such as deliberately slaughtering innocent men, women, and children; making people cannibalize their friends and family; practicing human sacrifice; or torturing people endlessly for their beliefs. It would be to align God with moral monsters such as Hitler, Stalin, and Pol Pot. No theist who believes the Ten Commandments or the Sermon on the Mount could deny that this third claim is true.

Exercises 7–9

In the second part of this chapter, we analyzed in detail an argument given by John Mackie in "Evil and Omnipotence." The following passages contain other arguments from this article. For each selection, (a) diagram the argument; (b) determine whether the argument is deductive or nondeductive (and if nondeductive, which kind) and whether the argument is a priori or a posteriori; and (c) identify any potential objections to the argument.

Exercise 7

It is sometimes suggested that evil is necessary as a counterpart to good, that if there were no evil there could be no good either, and that this solves the problem of evil. It is true that it points to an answer to the question "Why should there be evil?" But it does so only by qualifying some of the propositions that constitute the problem.

First, it sets a limit to what God can do, saying that God *cannot* create good without simultaneously creating evil, and this means either that God is not omnipotent or that there are *some* limits to what an omnipotent thing can do.

**Exercise 8*

Much more important is a solution which at first seems to be a mere variant of the previous one, that evil may contribute to the goodness of a whole in which it is found, so that the universe as a whole is better as it is, with some evil in it, than it would be if there were no evil. … This solution usually starts from the assumption that the evil whose existence gives rise to the problem of evil is primarily what is called physical evil, that is to say, pain. In Hume's rather half-hearted presentation of the problem of evil, the evils that he stresses are pain and disease, and those who reply to him argue that the existence of pain and disease makes possible the existence of sympathy, benevolence, heroism, and the gradually successful struggle of doctors and reformers to overcome these evils. ... Let us call pain and misery "first order evil" or "evil (1)." What contrasts with this, namely, pleasure and happiness, will be called 'first order good' or "good (1)." Distinct from this is "second order good" or "good (2)" which somehow emerges in a complex situation in which evil (1) is a necessary component—logically, not merely causally, necessary. ... It is also being assumed that second order good is more important than first order good or evil, in particular that it more than outweighs the first order evil it involves.

Exercise 9

There might, however, be several objections to this solution. ... But, thirdly, the fatal objection is this. Our analysis shows clearly the possibility of the existence of a *second* order evil, an evil (2) contrasting with good (2) as evil (1) contrasts with good (1). This would include malevolence, cruelty, callousness, cowardice, and states in which good (1) is decreasing and evil (1) increasing. And just as good (2) is held to be the important kind of good, the kind that God is concerned to promote, so evil (2) will, by analogy, be the important kind of evil, the kind which God, if he were wholly good and omnipotent, would eliminate. And yet evil (2) plainly exists, and indeed most theists (in other contexts) stress its existence more than that of evil (1). We should, therefore, state the problem of evil in terms of second order evil, and against this form of the problem the present solution is useless.

**Exercise 10*

Another highly influential philosopher has offered a different argument for solution (3) above. Gottfried Leibniz, in *Theodicy*,[3] argues that the problem of evil is solved by the existence of humans' free will. For the selection below, (a) diagram the argument; (b) determine whether the argument is deductive or nondeductive (and if nondeductive, which kind) and whether the argument is a priori or a posteriori; and (c) identify any potential objections to the argument.

[T]he best course is not always that one which tends towards avoiding evil, since it is possible that the evil may be accompanied by a greater good. For example, the general of an army will prefer a great victory with a slight wound to a state of affairs without wound and without victory. I have proved this in further detail in this work by pointing out, through instances taken from mathematics and elsewhere, that an imperfection in the part may be required for a greater perfection in the whole. I have followed therein the opinion of St. Augustine, who said a hundred times that God permitted evil in order to derive from it a good, that is to say, a greater good. ... For the better understanding of the matter I added, following the example of many good authors, that it was consistent with order and the general good for God to grant to certain of his creatures the opportunity to exercise their freedom, even when he foresaw that they would turn to evil: for God could easily correct the evil, [but] it was not fitting that in order to prevent sin he should always act in an extraordinary way. It will therefore sufficiently refute the objection to show that a world with evil may be better than a world without evil.

Exercises 11–15

The following exercises are intended to ensure your understanding of both Martin's and Mackie's texts, and to help you further explore the ideas presented in this chapter.

Exercise 11: Now that you have read my textual analysis of Martin's argument, summarize it in your own words.

Exercise 12: Summarize, in your own words, each of Martin's arguments in exercises 1–6 above.

Exercise 13: Now that you have read my textual analysis of Mackie's argument, summarize it in your own words.

Exercise 14: Summarize, in your own words, each of Mackie's arguments in exercises 7–9 above.

Exercise 15: Summarize, in your own words, Leibniz's argument in exercise 10 above. Does his argument adequately address the problem of evil? Why or why not?

5.3 Reading Questions

1. Martin assumes that for people to believe in the Christian God, the Bible must not describe God inconsistently. Do you agree? Why or why not?
2. Martin also seems to assume that God himself should be consistent, if we are to be justified in believing in him. Do you agree? Why or why not?
3. Explain the paradox of omnipotence.
4. Is it possible, as Mackie says, that God could have created people who freely choose to do good always?
5. Is finite evil okay if there is infinite good after death?
6. Could what we perceive as evil actually be good in the eyes of God?
7. Is it necessary for evil to exist for good to exist?

6 Nondeductive Arguments for the Existence of God

6.1 David Hume, *Dialogues Concerning Natural Religion*
6.2 William Paley, *Natural Theology*
6.3 In-Class Exercises
6.4 Reading Questions

6.1 David Hume, *Dialogues Concerning Natural Religion*

Born in 1711 in Edinburgh, Scotland, David Hume was one of the most influential philosophers of the Enlightenment and was highly regarded as a historian and essayist as well. As a young man, Hume moved to Paris to study the French philosophers. It was there that he drafted his first major philosophical work, *A Treatise of Human Nature* (published in multiple volumes in 1739–1740). In 1737, Hume returned to England to publish. It was not, however, received as well as Hume had expected; he said that "it fell still-born from the press, without reaching such distinction as even to excite a murmur among the zealots."[1] He then published *Essays, Moral and Political*, in two volumes (1741 and 1742). Hume took a governmental post and traveled to Italy where he began reworking his ideas from the *Treatise*; this produced two new volumes: *An Enquiry Concerning Human Understanding* (1748) and *An Enquiry Concerning the Principles of Morals* (1751). By this time he'd developed a reputation as an atheist and skeptic and was never able to become a professor at a university. In 1755, Hume was ready to publish his *Dialogues Concerning Natural Religion*, as well as a number of essays. His publisher, however, was threatened with a lawsuit from a theologian who did not like Hume's perspective. Thus, he arranged to have it published after his death in 1779.

Hume's works have had an enormous influence on both philosophers and scientists ever since. In 1783, Immanuel Kant wrote: "I freely admit: it was David Hume's remark that first, many years ago, interrupted my dogmatic slumber and gave a completely different direction to my enquiries in the field of speculative philosophy."[2] In 1776, Jeremy Bentham wrote: "For my own part, I well remember, no sooner had I read that part of the work [*A Treatise of Human Nature*] which touches on this subject, than I felt as if scales had fallen from my eyes."[3] Charles Darwin said that Hume influenced him greatly, and contemporary philosophers regard him as the world's first cognitive scientist.

Hume's *Dialogues* is a fictional tale in which the narrator, Pamphilus, recounts to a friend a conversation he witnessed between Cleanthes, Demea, and Philo. Hume has Cleanthes provide an argument for the existence of God to the two others, Philo and Demea. The particular kind of argument he gives is a posteriori, but it is also explicitly an argument by analogy. Thus, Cleanthes intends the argument to be a cogent, nondeductive argument, the conclusion of which is that that an intelligent deity (God) exists.

Let's look at Hume's text in more detail. Specifically, we will analyze and diagram the argument, and then discuss criticisms of it.

From *Dialogues Concerning Natural Religion*.[4]

I shan't beat about the bush, said Cleanthes, addressing himself to Demea. Still less shall I reply to Philo's pious speeches. What I shall do is to explain briefly how I conceive this matter. Look round the world, contemplating the whole and every part of it; you'll find it to be nothing but one big machine, subdivided into an infinite number of smaller ones, which in their turn could be subdivided to a degree beyond what human senses and faculties can trace and explain.[1] All these various machines, and even their most minute parts, are adjusted to each other so precisely that everyone who has ever contemplated them is filled with wonder.[2] The intricate fitting of means to ends throughout all nature is just like (though more wonderful than) the fittings of means to ends in things that have been produced by us[3]—...

... products of human designs, thought, wisdom, and intelligence.[4] Since,[A] [therefore][B] the effects resemble each other,[5] we are led to infer by all the rules of analogy,[6] that[C] the causes are also alike;[7] ...

... and that[D] the author of nature is somewhat similar to the mind of man, though he has much larger faculties to go with the grandeur of the work he has carried out.[8] ...

... By this argument a posteriori, and by this argument alone, do we prove both that[E] there is a God, and that he resembles human mind and intelligence.

This conclusion that God exists is at the end of the selection. Cleanthes' first claim is that if you look at the natural world you will see that it is a great machine made up of other machines (1) and that these machines are adjusted to each other with an incredible accuracy (2).

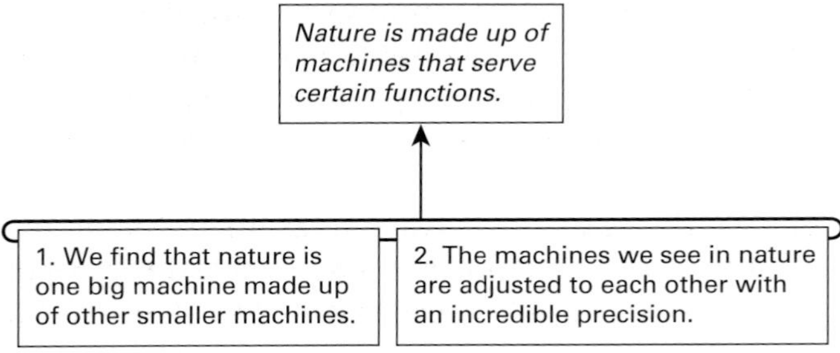

The next claim, (3), actually contains a number of points. First, by saying "the intricate fitting of means to ends," Cleanthes is claiming not only that nature is a great machine made up of other machines, but also that these machines are so constructed (the means) to serve certain purposes (the ends). One interpretation is that we can tell these machines in nature do have particular purposes because they are "adjusted to each other so precisely." Thus, I represent this statement as the unstated conclusion of statements (1) and (2).

Cleanthes then claims that the machines found in nature resemble the machines made by people (3). The implication seems to be that the resemblance is due to the fact that machines made by people also are adjusted to serve certain purposes.

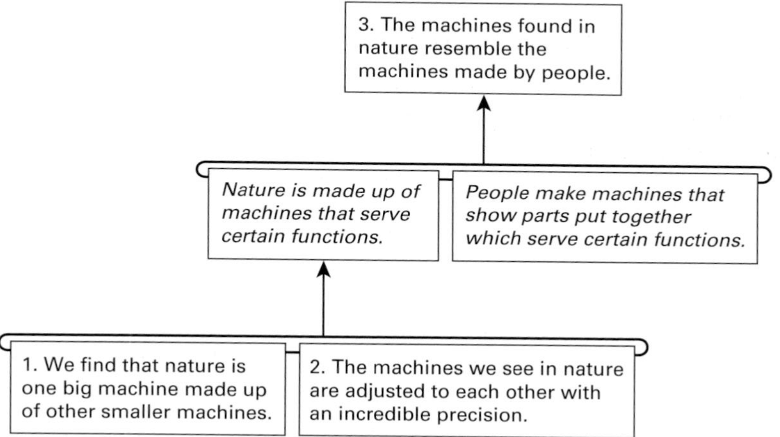

The second part of the statement about the resemblance claims that machines constructed by humans—"human contrivances"—are products of "human design, thought, wisdom and intelligence" (4). But, let us set aside this claim for now.

The "since" (A) and "therefore" (B) indicate that what follows is a subconclusion that will be used later as a premise in another argument. The next claim, that the machines of nature and the machines of humans are both effects of some cause that resemble each other (5), will be a part of this inference. The "we are lead to infer … that" (C) indicates that (3) and (5) are to be combined with the "rules of analogy" (6) to support the claim that the cause of machines in nature must resemble the cause of machines made by people (7).

Recall the discussion of an *argument by analogy* from Part I. The main principle can be described as follows: if X causes A, and A is analogous (similar in appropriate respects) to B, then X causes B. Thus, I rewrite claim (6) as: Effects that resemble each other have causes that resemble each other.

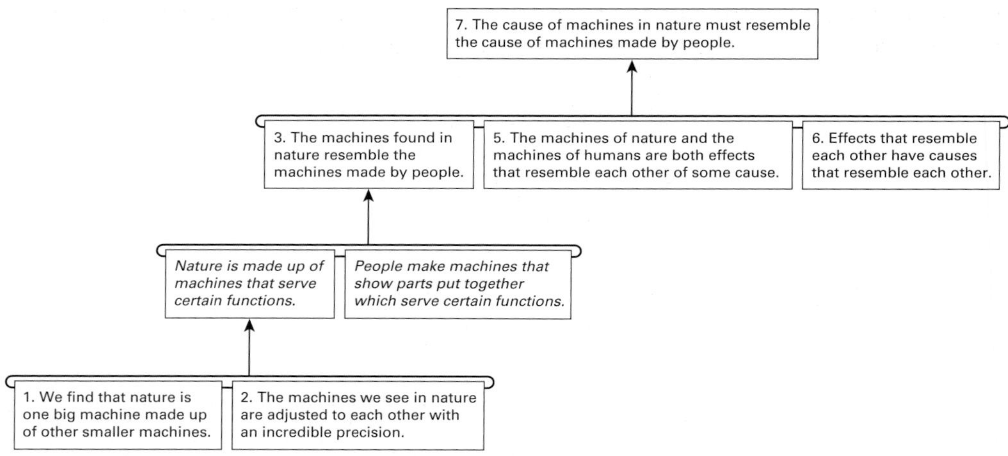

The "and that" (D) indicates that a further conclusion to be drawn is that the Author of Nature is somewhat similar to the mind of man, but better (8). It is here that we need claim (4) from above. This is because Cleanthes is not trying to show that "the cause of machines of nature" resembles just any aspect of human beings; he wants to show that the cause of machines is an intelligent designer. So, we need to add the fact that machines in nature resemble human-made machines *because* both kinds of machines are made for a purpose, and so made by creative, intelligent minds.

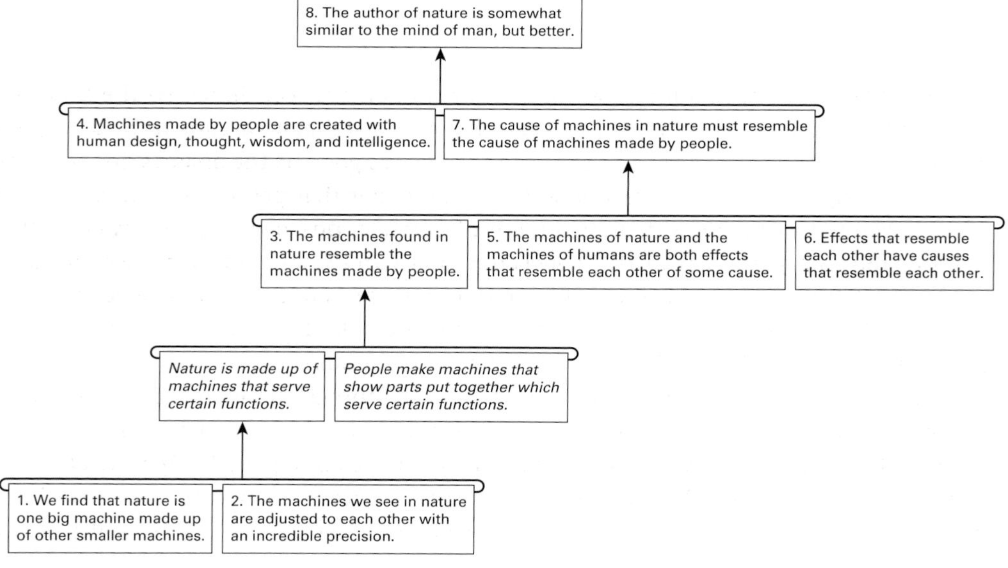

And finally, the phrase "By this argument a posteriori, and by this argument alone, do we prove at once" (E) indicates that we have arrived at the final conclusion.

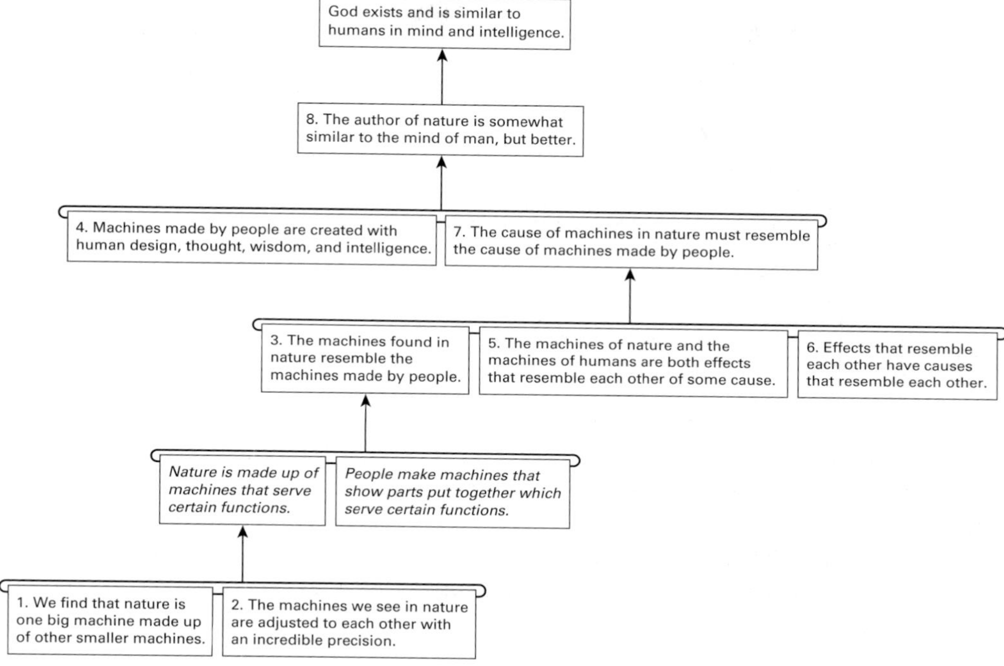

Objections

After Cleanthes gives the argument by analogy for God's existence, Hume has the character named Philo respond. In this first paragraph, Philo explains that an argument by analogy is not a deductive argument, and that its strength is only as good as the analogy between the two things being compared. For example, Philo points out that people are similar enough to each other to conclude that the circulation of blood in one person is the same as that in another. But the analogy is weaker between humans and frogs, and thus the conclusion that the circulation of blood in frogs is like that in humans is not as well justified. And still less justified is the conclusion that sap circulates in vegetables like blood circulates through humans, as humans and vegetables are hardly analogous at all.

In the next paragraph, Philo tries to reconstruct Cleanthes' argument. First, he points out that the existence of parts working together is not a priori proof of design, but that our experience is that machines and other things that are made up of parts finely tuned to work together are the products of human design. Not just any arrangement of pieces of steel will produce a watch, and not just any arrangement of stone, mortar, and wood will produce a house. Thus, the argument depends on there being parts of the universe that resemble human machines, *and* that in our experience working machines are the product of design and not chance.

In other words, Philo is contending that the basic argument by analogy looks like this:

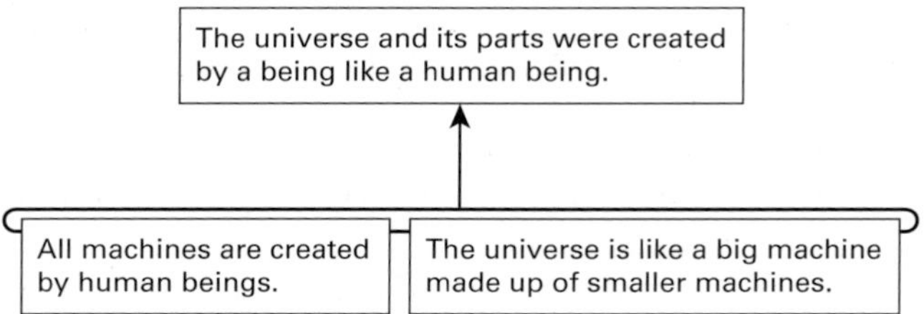

But, of course, this conclusion isn't enough, because there are many ways that a being could "be like" a human. For example, human beings make mistakes. But Cleanthes doesn't want this argument:

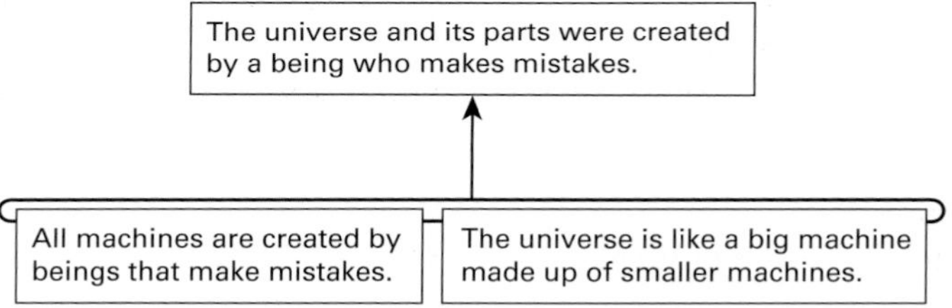

Instead, the argument is specifically supposed to show that the universe was created by an intelligent designer. So, Cleanthes really wants this kind of argument:

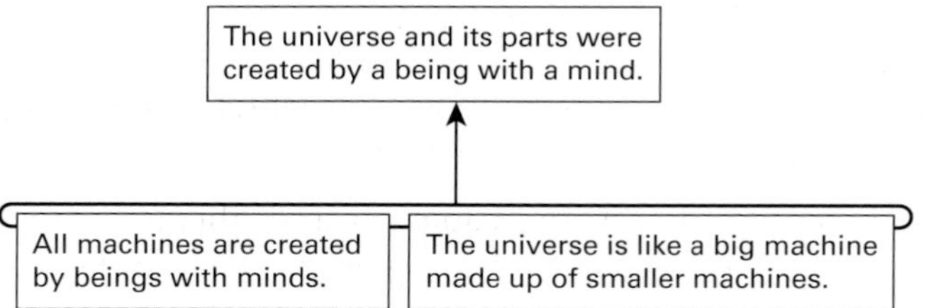

But, to get this kind of argument (and not the argument that concludes that universe was created by a being who makes mistakes), he needs something stronger that says that all human-made machines are goal-directed *because* they were created by intelligent designers. What Cleanthes really needs is this argument:

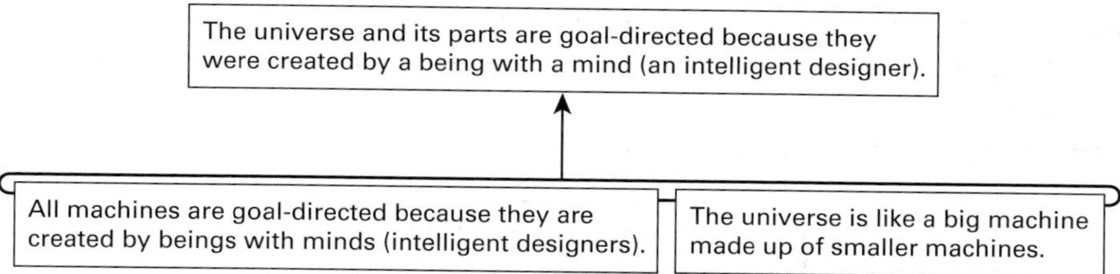

Next, Philo raises his objections to Cleanthes' argument, emphasizing again that an argument by analogy is only as strong as the analogy itself. The more different the two things being compared, the weaker the argument.

In fact, each of Philo's objections to Cleanthes' argument contains some reason to doubt that the great machine of the world is appropriately analogous to things made by humans. Philo shows this by extending the analogy to what he sees as its logical consequences, and these consequences undermine the traditional view of God's attributes. The three attributes Philo considers here are infinity, perfection, and unity; that is, God is supposed to be infinite (not limited in any way), perfect (having no defects and making no mistakes), and singular (there is one and only one God).

The analysis of the four specific objections Philo raises is left for the exercises at the end of the chapter.

Overall Objection

In a word, Cleanthes, someone who follows your hypothesis can perhaps assert or conjecture that: "The universe at some time arose from something like design."[14] But[F] beyond that he can't make a case for any further details, and is left to fill in his theology by wildly imagining or guessing the rest.[15]

. . .

You rightly give signs of horror, Demea, at these strange suppositions; but these—and a thousand more like them—are Cleanthes' suppositions, not mine. As soon as the attributes of God are supposed to be finite, [imperfect, and multiple] all these suppositions [of alternative theologies] get a foot-hold.[16] Speaking for myself, I can't see that having such a wild and unsettled a system of theology is in any way preferable to having none at all—that is, being an atheist.

Ultimately, Philo combines all of these objections to cast doubt on the strength of Cleanthes' argument by analogy for God's existence. The argument, Philo contends, allows us to conclude that the world was designed and created according to those designs (14). It does not, however, allow us to conclude anything further about the creator that is not just a guess (15), so it does not allow us to conclude that God—the traditional Christian God—exists. In fact, the objections above show that it is possible, according to Cleanthes' reasoning, that God is finite, imperfect, and multiple. If this is possible, in contradiction to traditional Christianity, then there is room for any number of alternative theologies (16)—which is exactly the opposite of what Cleanthes was trying to show.

Thus, the overall objection looks like this:

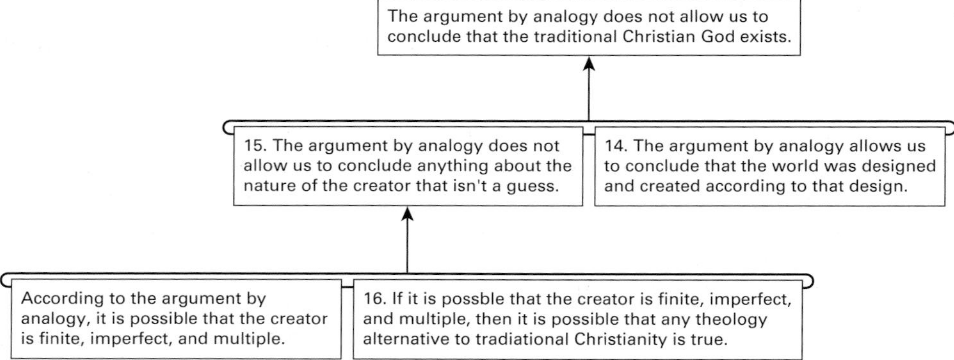

There is another avenue for using the apparent design in nature to prove the existence of God that Hume does not consider here. We will see this alternative in the next section.

6.2 William Paley, *Natural Theology*

Like Hume, William Paley (1743–1805) was an enormously influential philosopher during the Enlightenment. Born in Peterborough, England, Paley graduated from Christ's College (Cambridge University) in 1763. He subsequently became a tutor there, teaching moral philosophy, in 1768. His lectures in this course became the basis for his most influential book, *The Principles of Moral and Political Philosophy*, published in 1785. This book eventually became required reading for all undergraduates at Cambridge, and was read by Charles Darwin a century later. Darwin was much more influenced, however, by Paley's other book (which was not required reading): *Natural Theology: Or, Evidences of the Existence and Attributes of the Deity*.

Like Aquinas and Anselm, Paley was engaged in natural theology, and was concerned with providing a "proof" for God's existence. He believed that people do not have to depend on personal revelation to come to believe that there is a God, but rather can use their reasoning abilities to argue that God exists. Paley did not invent the argument from design (as we saw in chapter 5 with Aquinas), but he is famous for the "watchmaker" analogy, which we will see below in the first chapter of his text.

Most philosophers interpret Paley's argument as an argument by analogy, similar to Hume's. Below, I will make the case that Paley's argument is best understood as a combination of an argument by analogy and an abductive argument (inference to the best explanation). To do this, I'll need to jump around in the text a bit. We start with one of Paley's arguments by analogy. We will then consider Paley's "Surprise Principle," and end with Paley's famous watch analogy.

Now, let's look at Paley's text in more detail, starting with the second paragraph and then moving to the first. Specifically, we will analyze and diagram each of the arguments given and then discuss criticisms.

From *Natural Theology*.[5]

I know no better method of introducing so large a subject, than that of comparing a single thing with a single thing; an eye, for example, with a telescope.[1] As far as the examination of the instrument goes, there is precisely the same proof that[A] the eye was made for vision, as there is that the telescope was made for assisting it.[2] They are made upon the same principles;[3] both being adjusted to the laws by which the transmission and refraction of rays of light are regulated.[4] I speak not of the origin of the laws themselves; but, such laws being fixed, the construction, in both cases, is adapted to them. For instance; these laws require, in order to produce the same effect, that the rays of light, in passing from water into the eye, should be refracted by a more convex surface, than when it passes out of air into the eye. Accordingly we find, that the eye of a fish, in that part of it called the crystalline lense, is much rounder than the eye of terrestrial animals.

Ultimately, the conclusion for which Paley wants to argue is that something in nature (i.e., something not constructed by humans) was designed by some intelligence for a purpose. Here, he begins the analogy by telling us that he is going to compare the eye and the telescope (1); in other words, he is claiming that the eye is like the telescope in relevant ways. Then he claims that he can prove that the eye was made for vision (his main conclusion in this section) by combining (1) with the known fact that the telescope was made for assisting vision (2).

To make a strong argument by analogy, though, you have to show that the two things you are comparing really are analogous in the relevant ways. His support for the claim that the eye is like the telescope is that they are constructed according to the same physical principles (3). And his support for (3) is that the particular physical principles that guide the design of both are the laws that govern the transmission and refraction of light (4).

We can represent this part of the argument as follows:

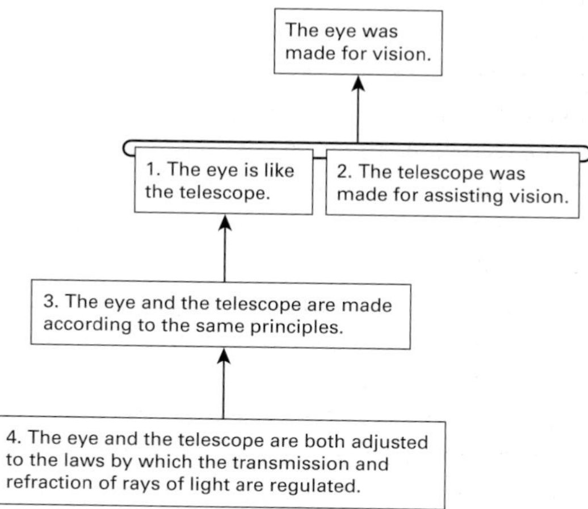

It may seem like this is the same kind of argument presented by the character Cleanthes in Hume's *Dialogues Concerning Natural Religion*, but the important difference is that Paley is not comparing the entire universe to a machine; rather, he is comparing individual natural objects to individual artificial objects. The difference is subtle but important. The structure of Paley's argument, as we will see below, depends on being able to make parallel arguments for both individual artificial objects (like telescopes) and individual natural objects (like eyes).

In crossing a heath, suppose I pitched my foot against a stone, and were asked how the stone came to be there; I might possibly answer, that, for any thing I knew to the contrary, it had lain there for ever: nor would it perhaps be very easy to show the absurdity of this answer. But suppose I had found a watch upon the ground, and it should be inquired how the watch happened to be in that place; I should hardly think of the answer which I had before given, that, for any thing I knew, the watch might have always been there. Yet why should not this answer serve for the watch as well as for the stone? Why is it not as admissible in the second case, as in the first?[5] For this reason, and for no other, viz. that,[B] when we come to inspect the watch, we perceive (what we could not discover in the stone) that its several parts are framed and put together for a purpose,[6] e.g. that they are so formed and adjusted as to produce motion, and that motion so regulated as to point out the hour of the day; that, if the different parts had been differently shaped from what they are, of a different size from what they are, or placed after any other manner, or in any other order, than that in which they are placed, either no motion at all would have been carried on in the machine, or none which would have answered the use that is now served by it.[7] To reckon up a few of the plainest of these parts, and of their offices, all tending to one result:—We see a cylindrical box containing a coiled elastic spring, which, by its endeavour to relax itself, turns round the box. We next observe a flexible chain (artificially wrought for the sake of flexure), communicating the action of the spring from the box to the fusee. We then find a series of wheels, the teeth of which catch in, and apply to, each other, conducting the motion from the fusee to the balance, and from the balance to the pointer; and at the same time, by the size and shape of those wheels, so regulating that motion, as to terminate in causing an index, by an equable and measured progression, to pass over a given space in a given time. We take notice that the wheels are made of brass in order to keep them from rust; the springs of steel, no other metal being so elastic; that over the face of the watch there is placed a glass, a material employed in no other part of the work, but in the room of which, if there had been any other than a transparent substance, the hour could not be seen without opening the case. This mechanism being observed (it requires indeed an examination of the instrument, and perhaps some previous knowledge of the subject, to perceive and understand it; but being once, as we have said, observed and understood), the inference, we think, is inevitable, that[B] the watch must have had a maker:[8] that there must have existed, at some time, and at some place or other, an artificer or artificers who formed it for the purpose which we find it actually to answer; who comprehended its construction, and designed its use.

Now that we've seen the basic argument from analogy, let's go back to the beginning and take a look at Paley's watch example. Here, the watch serves a similar purpose as the telescope in the previous example—it is a human-made artifact that was designed by some intelligence for a purpose.

If we rewrite the rhetorical question, the conclusion of this subargument is: "When asked how a watch came to be on a path, it is not admissible to say that for all I know it could have been there forever" (5). The indicator phrase (B) tells us that the reasons for this conclusion are that we see that the parts of the watch were put together for a purpose (6) and that if the parts were differently shaped, sized, placed or ordered, the watch could not fulfill its purpose (7).

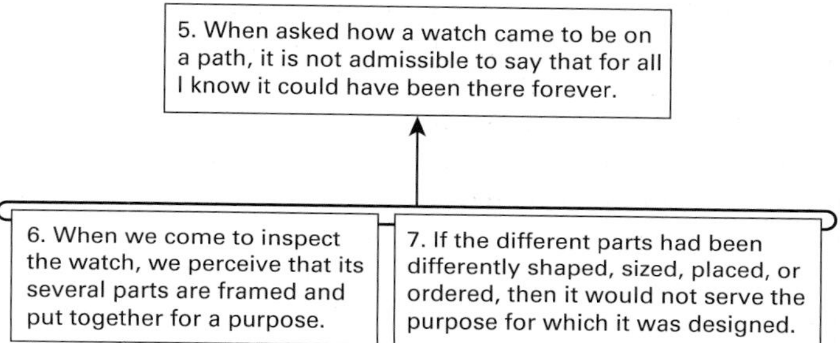

But there is an intermediate step, which Paley gets to after his long description of the actual parts of a watch. This is that the perceived purpose of the watch and the precision of its parts lead to the conclusion that the watch must have had a maker who designed it for that purpose (8). And this, then, is why the answer for the watch cannot be the same as that for the stone.

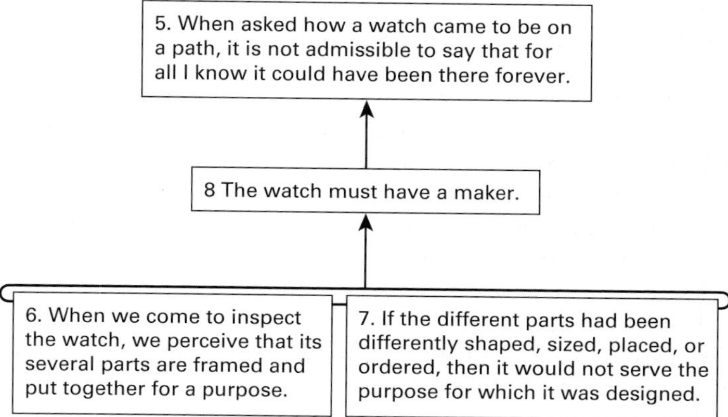

Here, then, we are introduced to Paley's "Surprise Principle" for explanations, which is one way of understanding an abductive argument. First, Paley observes the object (the stone or the rock) lying in the path; then he tries to come up with an explanation for this observation. He seems to consider two possible explanations:

1. that the object exists as a random accident, and
2. that the object exists as a product of an intelligent designer.

One explanation makes the observation less surprising than the other. For the stone, since it does not seem to have a purpose, the explanation that it was formed and placed in the path by random acts of nature—for example, wind and rain—is not surprising, and so that explanation is perfectly reasonable. On the other hand, we would be very surprised to learn that the watch was formed and placed on the path by random acts of nature; but we would not be surprised at all to learn that someone had designed and created the watch, and someone (perhaps the same person, perhaps not) left it on the path for some reason.

The argument scheme is thus:

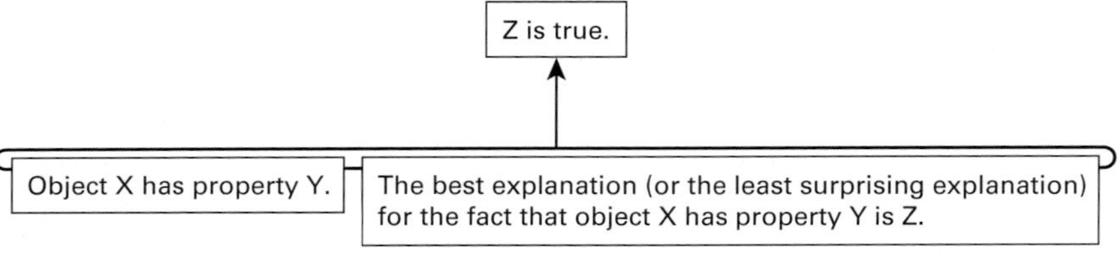

And Paley's argument for the watch is:

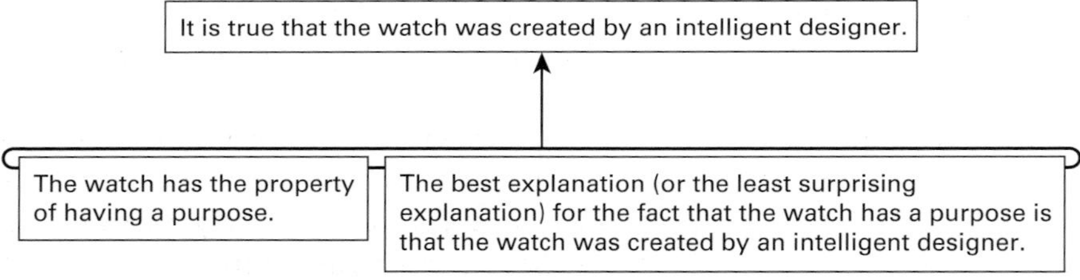

We can more precisely characterize Paley's Surprise Principle like this:

For two hypotheses H_1 and H_2, observation O favors H_2 over H_1 if and only if

- If H_1 were true, you wouldn't expect O.
  - O would be surprising.
- And, if H_2 were true, you would expect O.
  - O would be unsurprising.

Notice that the use of Paley's Surprise Principle is not novel; rather, it is a normal part of scientific practice. Consider the case of Gregor Mendel: in his monastery's garden, Mendel carried out breeding experiments with pea plants. He crossed tall pea plants with short ones and noted the proportion of tall and short plants among the offspring. He also did this with plants with smooth peas and those with wrinkled peas. He noticed that the offspring of these plants had characteristics of their parents in very definite proportions. This led him to make an interesting observation.

Observation: Experimental crosses in pea plants of certain sorts lead their offspring to exhibit characteristics in very definite proportions.

Seeing this, he wondered why this happens. This led him to invent a story:

Suppose each plant contains particles (Mendel called them "differentiating characters"; we call them "genes") that control the observed characteristics of tall and short, wrinkled and smooth, in certain specific ways.

He hypothesized that each parent contributes half its genes to the offspring and the process occurs in accordance with definite rules.

Hypothesis: There are "differentiating characters" in pea plants, and they obey certain laws.

The point is that if this hypothesis were true, then it would explain the observation. But notice that Mendel never saw a gene (this happened much later), so he made an inference about something that couldn't be observed directly. Mendel clearly did not use deduction (his hypothesis could have been wrong). Neither did Mendel use induction; induction would only say that, from his sample experience (observations), in general breeding plants will lead to the same proportions of characteristics that he saw (whether in America or Europe). Finally, Mendel did not argue by analogy; he didn't claim that peas were like something else that was already known to have genes. Rather, he argued for his hypothesis by claiming that it was the best explanation for the observations.

So, now we have the abductive argument for the claim that the watch has an intelligent designer. What's next? Here is where the argument by analogy comes in. Paley claims that the watch (or the telescope) is analogous to the eye in one especially relevant way: Upon examination, the eye, like the watch, clearly has a purpose, and if the parts were differently shaped, sized, placed, or ordered, the eye could not fulfill its purpose.

So the argument by analogy goes like this:

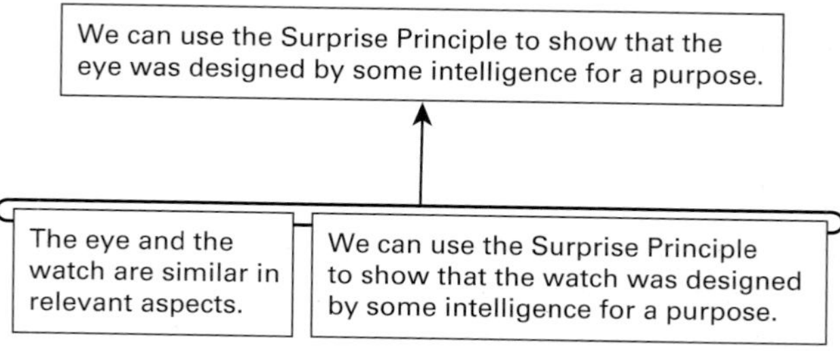

Or, as he did in the first selection we read, by comparing the eye to the telescope:

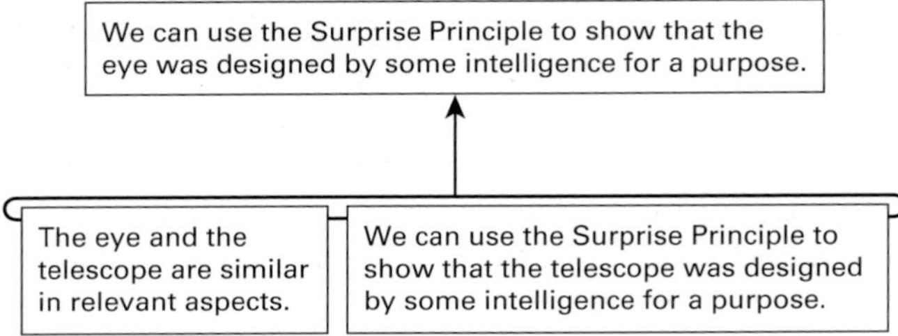

Overall, then, the argument looks like this:

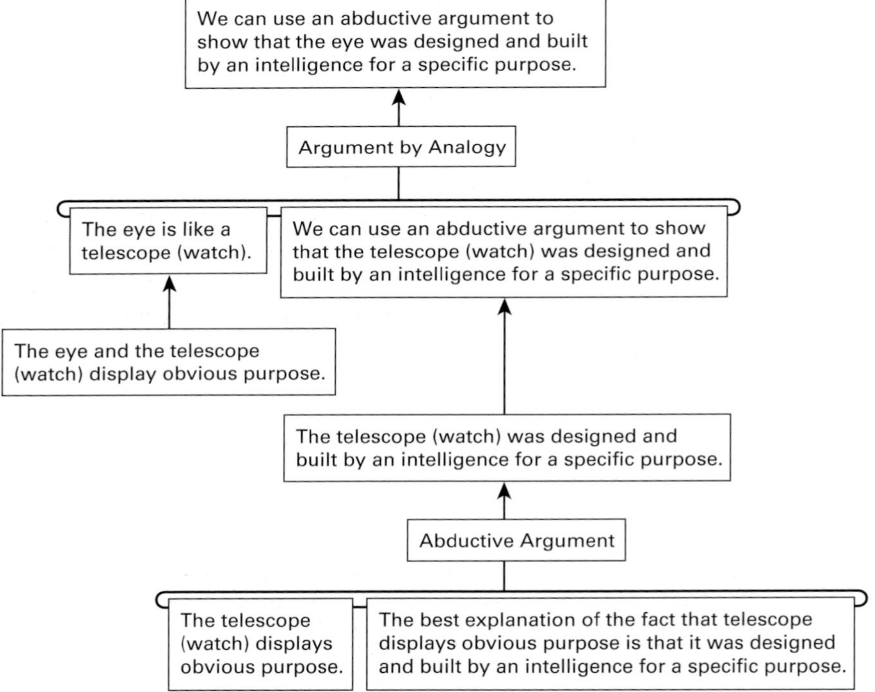

Objections

In *Natural Theology*, Paley actually raises and responds to several possible objections to his own argument. These will be considered in the exercises below. We will consider two main objections here.

First Objection

The first question about Paley's argument is: Doesn't Paley's argument suffer from the same defects as the argument Hume presented? I think not, and here's why. Recall that we criticized the argument Cleanthes presented on the basis of the seemingly bad analogy between a machine and the universe. Philo argues that there are too many ways in which the universe is not like a machine for us to be able to base any conclusions about the universe from characteristics of human-made machines. Paley makes an analogy too, between the eye and the telescope (or watch). But Paley's argument by analogy is quite different from Hume's. Recall that Hume's argument looks like this:

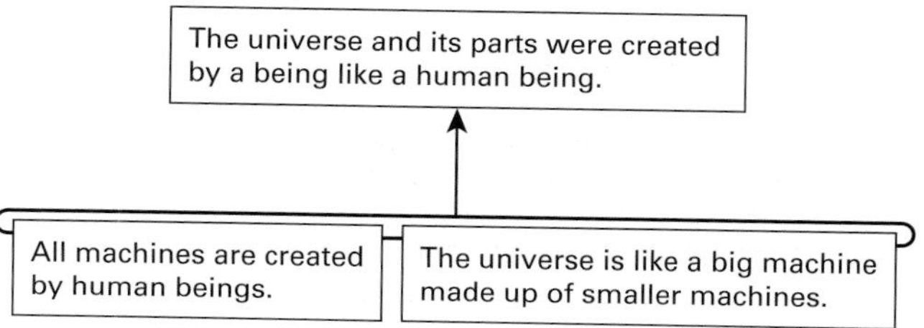

The problem with this is that we can use the same argument scheme to argue, for example, that the universe was created by a being who makes mistakes. In general, this argument is vulnerable because machines have other properties besides being created by human beings. Cleanthes, in presenting this argument, has not specified enough which are the relevant ways in which the universe is like a machine, and so multiple conclusions can be drawn. Paley's argument, on the other hand, looks like this:

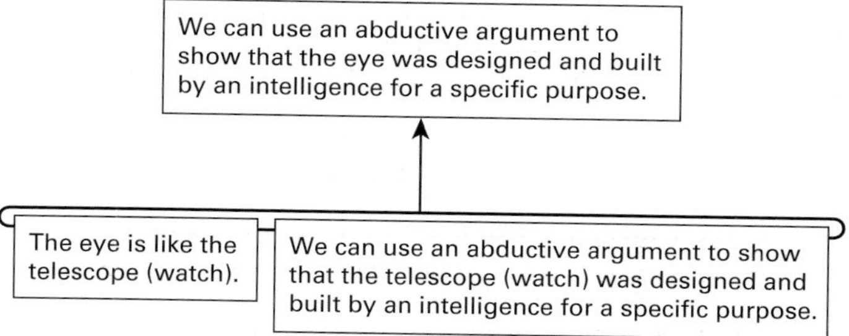

Paley's argument is not vulnerable in the same way, because for his argument to work, the eye and the telescope (or watch) only have to be similar in one particular way—that upon inspection, they clearly have a purpose. It doesn't matter that there are ways in which the eye and telescope are different. The only relevant similarity is that they both exhibit purpose, because that's the only thing that is needed for the abductive argument to work.

Second Objection

Just as an argument by analogy is only as good as the analogy, an abductive argument is only as good as the alternative explanations that are considered. Recall the explanation of Paley's Surprise Principle from above:

For two hypotheses H_1 and H_2, observation O favors H_2 over H_1 if and only if

- If H_1 were true, you wouldn't expect O.
  - O would be surprising.
- And, if H_2 were true, you would expect O.
  - O would be unsurprising.

This is fine if there are only two hypotheses being considered for the "best explanation." And this is what Paley does; he considers only two hypotheses as explanations for the goal-directedness observed in things like the eye: random occurrence and intelligent design. But what about a third possible hypothesis: evolution by natural selection? Obviously, Paley did not know about this hypothesis, so he can hardly be blamed for not considering it. But Paley's design argument is still popular in current debates about intelligent design, so let's take a look.

To draw the same conclusion as Paley, we would have to be able to show that the intelligent design hypothesis is less surprising, given the observations, than both the randomness hypothesis and the natural selection hypothesis. If we concentrate only on observations of things like the eye, then it may seem plausible that the design hypothesis would be the least surprising.

However, there is another aspect of the Surprise Principle that we must consider. Just as the argument is only as strong as the alternative explanations that are considered, the abductive argument is only as strong as the variety of observations considered to need explanation. The objection here is that observations of things like the eye are not the only observations that should be considered.

Stephen Jay Gould (1941–2002) was a Harvard University Professor of Geology and the Curator of Invertebrate Paleontology at the Museum of Comparative Zoology. In addition to his academic career, he was a prolific popular science writer. Two of his most influential popular pieces are *Ever Since Darwin: Reflections on Natural History* (1977) and *The Panda's Thumb: More Reflections on Natural History* (1980).[6] In *The Panda's Thumb*, Gould argues that there are two important kinds of observations that should be considered.

From *The Panda's Thumb: More Reflections on Natural History*

Giant pandas are peculiar bears, members of the order Carnivora. Conventional bears are the most omnivorous representatives of their order, but pandas have restricted this catholicity of taste in the other direction—they belie the name of their order by subsisting almost entirely on bamboo. They live in dense forests of bamboo at high elevations in the mountains of western China. There they sit, largely unthreatened by predators, munching bamboo ten to twelve hours each day.

continues

… They sat upright and manipulated the stalks with their forepaws, shedding the leaves and consuming only the shoots.

I was amazed by their dexterity and wondered how the scion of a stock adapted for running could use its hands so adroitly. They held the stalks of bamboo in their paws and stripped off the leaves by passing the stalks between an apparently flexible thumb and the remaining fingers. This puzzled me. I had learned that a dexterous, opposable thumb stood among the hallmarks of human success. We had maintained, even exaggerated, this important flexibility of our primate forebears, while most mammals had sacrificed it in specializing their digits. Carnivores run, stab, and scratch. My cat may manipulate me psychologically, but he'll never type or play the piano.

So I counted the panda's other digits and received an even greater surprise: there were five, not four. Was the "thumb" a separately evolved sixth finger? Fortunately the giant panda has its bible, a monograph by D. Dwight Davis, late curator of vertebrate anatomy at Chicago's Field Museum of Natural History. It is probably the greatest work of modern evolutionary comparative anatomy, and it contains more than anyone would ever want to know about pandas. Davis had the answer, of course.

The panda's "thumb" is not, anatomically, a finger at all. It is constructed from a bone called the radial sesamoid, normally a small component of the wrist. In pandas, the radial sesamoid is greatly enlarged and elongated until it "almost" equals the metapodial bones of the true digits in length. The radial sesamoid underlies a pad on the panda's forepaw; the five digits form the framework of another pad, the palmar. A shallow furrow separates the two pads and serves as a channelway for bamboo stalks.

The panda's thumb comes equipped not only with a bone to give it strength but also with muscles to sustain its agility. These muscles, like the radial sesamoid bone itself, did not arise *de novo*. Like the parts of Darwin's orchids they are familiar bits of anatomy remodeled for a new function. The abductor of the radial sesamoid (the muscle that pulls it away from the true digits) bears the formidable name *abductor pollicis longus* ("the long abductor of the thumb"—*pollicis* is the genitive of *pollex*, Latin for "thumb"). Its name is a giveaway. In other carnivores, this muscle attaches to the first digit, or true thumb. Two shorter muscles run between the radial sesamoid and the pollex. They pull the sesamoid "thumb" towards the true digits. …

The panda's thumb provides an elegant zoological counterpart to Darwin's orchids. An engineer's best solution is debarred by history. The panda's true thumb is committed to another role, too specialized for a different function to become an opposable, manipulating digit. So the panda must use parts on hand and settle for an enlarged wrist bone and a somewhat clumsy, but quite workable, solution. The sesamoid thumb wins no prize in an engineer's derby. It is, to use Michael Ghiselin's phrase, a contraption, not a lovely contrivance …

This is the problem that Darwin faced, for his creationist opponents did view each species as unaltered from its initial formation. How did Darwin prove that modern species are the products of history? We might suppose that he looked toward the most impressive results of evolution, the complex and perfected adaptations of organisms to their environments: the butterfly passing for a dead leaf, the bittern for a branch, the superb engineering of a gull aloft or a tuna in the sea.

continues

> *continued*
>
> Paradoxically, he did just the opposite. He searched for oddities and imperfections. The gull may be a marvel of design; if one believes in evolution beforehand, then the engineering of its wing reflects the shaping power of natural selection. But you cannot demonstrate evolution with perfection because perfection need not have a history. After all, perfection of organic design has long been the favorite argument of creationists, who saw in consummate engineering the direct hand of a divine architect. A bird's wing, as an aerodynamic marvel, might have been created exactly as we find it today.
>
> But, Darwin reasoned, if organisms have a history, then ancestral stages should leave remnants behind. Remnants of the past that don't make sense in present terms—the useless, the odd, the peculiar, the incongruous—are the signs of history. They supply proof that the world was not made in its present form. When history perfects, it covers its own tracks. …
>
> And why should the fetus of a whale make teeth in its mother's womb only to resorb them later and live a life sifting krill on a whalebone filter, unless its ancestors had functional teeth and these teeth survive as a remnant during a stage when they do no harm?

The first kind of observation Gould makes is many organisms have features that are imperfect, and sometimes just barely functional. For example, as Gould explains, giant pandas have a spur of bone that sticks out like a thumb and muscles that adapted to shift that bone. This allows pandas to eat bamboo, but it's a really clumsy tool for pandas.

Applying the Surprise Principle, we can argue that evolution by natural selection is more plausible than intelligent design. The observation is that many organisms have "contraptions" that are cobbled together from parts that do not seem intended for that purpose. First, if evolution is true, this observation would be expected and would not be surprising, because the theory says that existent structures of organisms will change as the need for them changes. Second, if the design hypothesis is true, this observation would be surprising. An intelligent designer could have designed things much better, if it had been making beings perfectly adapted to its environment.

The second kind of observation Gould says should be considered is that many organisms have features that serve no purpose. One example of this is human vestigial organs like the appendix. In addition, human embryos have some organs, like gills, that they later lose. These suggest that humans evolved from something that actually used these things, and they have remained because they did not interfere with the fitness of humans.

There are countless other examples in other organisms that Gould describes throughout this book. Whale embryos develop teeth only to lose them before birth. Whales also have vestigial leg and pelvis bones. Many flightless beetles have the remnants of wings underneath their fused wing covers. Dandelions have the capability to sexually reproduce, but they don't—they reproduce asexually.

Again applying the Surprise Principle, we can argue that evolution by natural selection is more plausible than the intelligent design hypothesis. The observation is that organisms have traces of organs, bones, and other structures that they do not use. First, if evolution is true, this observation would be expected and would not be surprising, because the theory says that these organs were useful in the past but no longer are. Second, if the design hypothesis is true, this observation would be surprising. An intelligent designer could have designed and created organisms perfectly without giving them such useless and strange structures.

We should note that Paley did not advocate perfect design. He just claimed that there must have been an intelligent designer. So he argued for a much more minimal hypothesis. Let's call it the *minimal theory of intelligent design*. This theory holds that an intelligent designer is responsible for the creation of each species, but it is silent about in what way they were designed, perfect or otherwise.

The problem with the minimal theory of intelligent design is that it predicts nothing. It doesn't tell you what to expect when you look at organisms, so the theory cannot be confirmed or denied; there is no evidence that stands in its favor or against it. Thus, we cannot test it as an explanation of observations. As a result, the justification of Paley's intelligent design claim is no longer abductive.

But we can consider a more modern version of Paley's intelligent design theory. We'll take the following as a fairly representative version of the contemporary thesis. According to the *(nearly) perfectionist theory of intelligent design*, a designer separately created each species and made each of them (nearly) perfectly adapted to their environment.

Unlike the minimal theory, this theory does make two predictions about what we should find in our observations:

1. Linear speciation: there are no ancestral connections between different species (i.e., no two species have a common ancestor) and organisms appear abruptly, are unrelated, and linked only by their designer.
2. (Near) perfect adaptation: each species is (nearly) perfectly adapted to its environment (scorpions are suited to the desert, polar bears suited to the arctic); the designer knows what each species needs and so provides for it.

What do predictions have to do with abduction? The way Paley used the abductive argument, he was explaining observations that he had already made. Predictions, though, are anticipated observations. But determining the predictions a theory makes tells us what that theory is able to explain.

Does this mean that the theory of intelligent design is false? No; all we have done here is draw attention to problems with Paley's abductive argument, as well as some potential problems with contemporary abductive arguments. But remember that even a bad argument can have a true conclusion.

6.3 In-Class Exercises

An asterisk (*) indicates a more challenging exercise.

Exercises 1–6

In the first part of this chapter, we analyzed in detail an argument given by Cleanthes in Hume's *Dialogues Concerning Natural Religion*. The following selections contain other arguments from Hume's *Dialogues*. For each selection, (a) diagram the argument; (b) determine whether the argument is deductive or nondeductive (and if nondeductive, which kind) and whether the argument is a priori or a posteriori; and (c) identify any potential objections to the argument.

Exercise 1

For this argument, you will diagram it in two parts. The first (part a) is the overall argument, and the second is the subargument (part b) that occurs where the ellipses are in the first part of the argument (part a).

a. The argument that I would insist on, replied Demea, is the common one: Whatever exists must have a cause or reason for its existence, as it is absolutely impossible for anything to produce itself, or be the cause of its own existence. In working back, therefore, from effects to causes, we must either (1) go on tracing causes to infinity, without any ultimate cause at all, or (2) at last have recourse to some ultimate cause that is necessarily existent [and therefore doesn't need an external cause]. Supposition (1) is absurd, as I now prove: ... So we must [adopt supposition (2), and] have recourse to a necessarily existent being, who carries the reason of his existence in himself and cannot be supposed not to exist without an express contradiction. So there is such a being; that is, there is a God.

*b. (Hint: This argument can be viewed as a reductio ad absurdum.)
In the [supposed] infinite chain or series of causes and effects, each single effect is made to exist by the power and efficacy of the cause that immediately preceded it; but the whole eternal chain or series, considered as a whole, is not caused by anything; and yet it obviously requires a cause or reason, as much as any particular thing that begins to exist in time. We are entitled to ask why this particular series of causes existed from eternity, and not some other series, or no series at all. If there is no necessarily existent being, all the suppositions we can make about this are equally possible; and there is no more absurdity in nothing's having existed from eternity than there is in the series of causes that constitutes the universe. What was it, then, that made something exist rather than nothing, and gave existence to one particular possibility as against any of the others? External causes? We are supposing that there aren't any. Chance? That's a word without a meaning. Was it Nothing? But that can never produce anything.

Exercise 2

For this argument, you will diagram it in two parts.

a. And is it possible, Cleanthes, said Philo, that after all these reflections, and countless others that might be suggested, you still stick to your anthropomorphism, and assert that the moral attributes of God—his justice, benevolence, mercy, and uprightness—are of the same nature as these virtues in human creatures? We grant that his power is infinite: whatever he wills to happen does happen. But neither man nor any other animal is happy; therefore God doesn't will their happiness. His knowledge is infinite: he is never mistaken in his choice of means to any end. But the course of nature doesn't lead to human or animal happiness; therefore nature isn't established for that purpose. Through the whole range of human knowledge, there are no inferences more certain and infallible than these. Well, then, in what respect do his benevolence and mercy resemble the benevolence and mercy of men?

*b. You ascribe, Cleanthes (and I believe justly), a purpose and intention to Nature. But what, I beseech you, is the object of that curious artifice and machinery, which she has displayed in all animals? The preservation alone of individuals, and propagation of the species. It seems enough for her purpose, if such a rank be barely upheld in the universe, without any care or concern for the happiness of the members that compose it. No resource for this purpose: no machinery, in order merely to give pleasure or ease: no fund of pure joy and contentment: no indulgence, without some want or necessity accompanying it. At least, the few phenomena of this nature are overbalanced by opposite phenomena of still greater importance.

Our sense of music, harmony, and indeed beauty of all kinds, gives satisfaction, without being absolutely necessary to the preservation and propagation of the species. But what racking pains, on the other hand, arise from gouts, gravels, megrims, toothaches, rheumatisms, where the injury to the animal machinery is either small or incurable? Mirth, laughter, play, frolic, seems gratuitous satisfactions, which have no further tendency: spleen, melancholy, discontent, superstition, are pains of the same nature. How then does the Divine benevolence display itself, in the sense of you Anthropomorphites? None but we Mystics, as you were pleased to call us, can account for this strange mixture of phenomena, by deriving it from attributes, infinitely perfect, but incomprehensible.

Exercise 3

Now, Cleanthes, said Philo, pouncing with an air of triumph, note the consequences!

First, by this method of reasoning, you give up all claim to infinity in any of the attributes of God. For, as the cause ought to be proportioned to the effect, and the effect—so far as we know—is not infinite; what right have we (on your theory) to ascribe infinity to God? You will still have to say that when we remove him so far from similarity to human creatures, we give in to the most arbitrary hypothesis, and at the same time weaken all proofs of his existence.

Exercise 4

Secondly, your theory gives you no reason to ascribe perfection to the God even in his capacity as a finite being, or to suppose him to be free from every error, mistake, or incoherence, in his activities. Consider the many inexplicable difficulties in the works of nature—[illnesses, earthquakes, floods, volcanoes, and so on]. If we think we can prove *á priori* that the world has a perfect creator, all these calamities become unproblematic: we can say that they only seem to us to be difficulties because we with our limited intellects can't follow all the infinitely complex details of which they are a part. But according to your line of reasoning these difficulties are real; indeed they might be emphasized as new instances of the world's likeness to the products of human skill and contrivance! You must, at least, admit that we with our limited knowledge can't possibly tell, whether this system contains any great faults, or deserves any considerable praise, when compared to other possible, and perhaps even when compared to real ones. If the *Æneid* were read to a peasant, could he judge it to be absolutely faultless? Could he even give it its proper place in the ranking of the productions of human intelligence—he who had never seen any of the others?

Exercise 5
Even if this world were a perfect product, we still couldn't be sure whether all the excellences of the work can justly be ascribed to the workman. When we survey a ship, we may get an exalted idea of the ingenuity of the carpenter who built such a complicated, useful, and beautiful machine. But then we shall be surprised to find that the carpenter is a stupid tradesman who imitated others, and followed a trade which has gradually improved down the centuries, after multiplied trials, mistakes, corrections, deliberations, and controversies. Perhaps our world is like that ship. It may be that many worlds were botched and bungled, throughout an eternity, before our present system was built; much labour lost, many useless trials made, and a slow but continued improvement carried on during infinite ages in the world-making trade. In subjects such as this, who can determine what is true—who indeed can even guess what is probable—when so many hypotheses can be put forward, and even more can be imagined?

Exercise 6
And what shadow of an argument, continued Philo, can you produce, from your hypothesis, to prove that God is one being? A great many men join together to build a house or ship, to found and develop a city, to create a commonwealth; why couldn't several gods combine in designing and making a world? This would only serve to make divine activities more like human ones [for] by sharing the work among several gods we can reduce still further the attributes of each one of them; we can get rid of the extensive power and knowledge that we have to suppose the one God to possess (if there is only one)—the extent of power and knowledge which, according to you, serves merely to weaken the argument for God's existence.

Exercises 7–14
After explaining the watch argument at the beginning of chapter 1, Paley introduces several potential objections to his argument, along with his replies to these objections. Recall that the watch argument is:

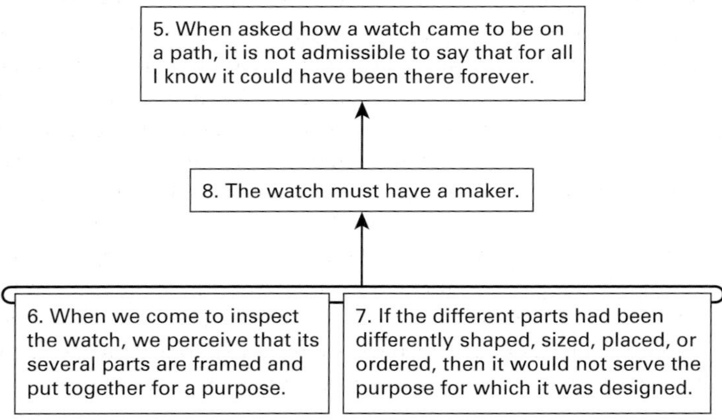

The task in these exercises is to determine which part of the argument the objection and its reply are directed to, and to diagram the argument and the objection and reply, for each of Paley's potential objections given below. For a refresher on diagramming objections and replies, review section 3.4 in chapter 3.

Exercise 7

I. Nor would it, I apprehend, weaken the conclusion, that we had never seen a watch made; that we had never known an artist capable of making one; that we were altogether incapable of executing such a piece of workmanship ourselves, or of understanding in what manner it was performed; all this being no more than what is true of some exquisite remains of ancient art, of some lost arts, and, to the generality of mankind, of the more curious productions of modern manufacture. Does one man in a million know how oval frames are turned? Ignorance of this kind exalts our opinion of the unseen and unknown artist's skill, if he be unseen and unknown, but raises no doubt in our minds of the existence and agency of such an artist, at some former time, and in some place or other. Nor can I perceive that it varies at all the inference, whether the question arise concerning a human agent, or concerning an agent of a different species, or an agent possessing, in some respects, a different nature.

Exercise 8

II. Neither, secondly, would it invalidate our conclusion, that the watch sometimes went wrong, or that it seldom went exactly right. The purpose of the machinery, the design, and the designer, might be evident, and in the case supposed would be evident, in whatever way we accounted for the irregularity of the movement, or whether we could account for it or not. It is not necessary that a machine be perfect, in order to show with what design it was made: still less necessary, where the only question is, whether it were made with any design at all.

Exercise 9

III. Nor, thirdly, would it bring any uncertainty into the argument, if there were a few parts of the watch, concerning which we could not discover, or had not yet discovered, in what manner they conduced to the general effect; or even some parts, concerning which we could not ascertain, whether they conduced to that effect in any manner whatever. For, as to the first branch of the case; if by the loss, or disorder, or decay of the parts in question, the movement of the watch were found in fact to be stopped, or disturbed, or retarded, no doubt would remain in our minds as to the utility or intention of these parts, although we should be unable to investigate the manner according to which, or the connexion by which, the ultimate effect depended upon their action or assistance; and the more complex is the machine, the more likely is this obscurity to arise. Then, as to the second thing supposed, namely, that there were parts which might be spared, without prejudice to the movement of the watch, and that we had proved this by experiment,—these superfluous parts, even if we were completely assured that they were such, would not vacate the reasoning which we had instituted concerning other parts. The indication of contrivance remained, with respect to them, nearly as it was before.

Exercise 10

IV. Nor, fourthly, would any man in his senses think the existence of the watch, with its various machinery, accounted for, by being told that it was one out of possible combinations of material forms; that whatever he had found in the place where he found the watch, must have contained some internal configuration or other; and that this configuration might be the structure now exhibited, viz. of the works of a watch, as well as a different structure.

Exercise 11

V. Nor, fifthly, would it yield his inquiry more satisfaction to be answered, that there existed in things a principle of order, which had disposed the parts of the watch into their present form and situation. He never knew a watch made by the principle of order; nor can he even form to himself an idea of what is meant by a principle of order, distinct from the intelligence of the watch-maker.

Exercise 12

VI. Sixthly, he would be surprised to hear that the mechanism of the watch was no proof of contrivance, only a motive to induce the mind to think so.

Exercise 13

VII. And not less surprised to be informed, that the watch in his hand was nothing more than the result of the laws of metallic nature. It is a perversion of language to assign any law, as the efficient, operative cause of any thing. A law presupposes an agent; for it is only the mode, according to which an agent proceeds: it implies a power; for it is the order, according to which that power acts. Without this agent, without this power, which are both distinct from itself, the law does nothing; is nothing. The expression, "the law of metallic nature," may sound strange and harsh to a philosophic ear; but it seems quite as justifiable as some others which are more familiar to him, such as "the law of vegetable nature," "the law of animal nature," or indeed as "the law of nature" in general, when assigned as the cause of phænomena, in exclusion of agency and power; or when it is substituted into the place of these.

Exercise 14

VIII. Neither, lastly, would our observer be driven out of his conclusion, or from his confidence in its truth, by being told that he knew nothing at all about the matter. He knows enough for his argument: he knows the utility of the end: he knows the subserviency and adaptation of the means to the end. These points being known, his ignorance of other points, his doubts concerning other points, affect not the certainty of his reasoning. The consciousness of knowing little, need not beget a distrust of that which he does know.

Exercises 15–18

The following exercises are intended to ensure your understanding of both Hume's and Paley's texts, and to help you further explore the ideas presented in this chapter.

Exercise 15: Now that you have read my textual analysis of Hume's argument, summarize it in your own words.

Exercise 16: Summarize, in your own words, each of Hume's arguments in exercises 1–6 above.
Exercise 17: Now that you have read my textual analysis of Paley's argument, summarize it in your own words.
Exercise 18: Summarize, in your own words, each of Paley's replies in exercises 7–14 above.

6.4 Reading Questions

1. Hume conjectured that the dispute between those who believe in God and those who do not is "merely" a verbal dispute. That is, he thought that perhaps they really only disagree about who or what is the source of the order in the universe. They both agree, he contends, that there is definite order in the universe, and that the order must be something entirely different from what human creativity and ingenuity could create. Do you agree that this disagreement could be just a verbal disagreement? Why or why not?
2. In contesting Cleanthes' initial argument for the existence of God, Philo asserts that Cleanthes is mistakenly extending the strength of an inductive argument (as defined in chapter 2) to all arguments by analogy. How does Philo make this argument? Is it a good argument? Why or why not?
3. If you'd never seen a particular object before, how would you decide whether it was designed for some purpose or "just came like that"? What is the justification of your criterion for deciding?
4. *What does Paley think we* will infer about a found watch that we would not infer about a found stone? Why would we infer this? Do you agree that we would? Why or why not?
5. What are the similarities between Paley's argument and Aquinas's fifth way (chapter 4, In-Class Exercise 12)?

III Epistemology

Introduction

Next on our agenda is epistemology, and in particular arguments about the definition and sources of knowledge. I think a case can be made for epistemology as the true core of philosophy, because what we ultimately want is to have knowledge in all of the other areas of philosophy. For example:

- We want to know whether God exists, as well as whether we can prove that God exists.
- We want to know what the difference is, if any, between the mind and the body (or the brain).
- We want to know whether we have free will.
- We want to know what the difference is between right and wrong.
- We want to know what actions we are morally responsible for, if any.

These are, of course, only a few of the things we would like to know, but I think the idea is clear.

Another reason for turning to epistemology at this time is that many of the theories of knowledge we will encounter in this part will help us understand the theories of mind, free will, and morality we will analyze later on. For example, Hume (whom we met in chapter 6) makes an argument (which we will encounter in Part V) that we live in a deterministic world and that we have free will. This is quite a difficult position to defend, as we shall see, and we can't understand Hume's argument unless we first understand Hume's theory of causation. In addition, René Descartes makes an argument (which we will encounter in Part IV) that one's mind is something very different from one's body or brain. Again, this is a difficult position to defend, and we can't understand Descartes's argument unless we first understand his theory of knowledge.

Recall that epistemology covers the following types of questions:

- What is knowledge?
- What can I know?
- What do I know?

Also recall that in one of his arguments against the existence of God, John Mackie (chapter 5, sec. 5.2) explained that we ordinarily recognize three different types of knowledge:

- "Knowledge how" (skill knowledge)
  - To swim, to ride a bike, shoot a basketball
- "Knowledge of" (knowledge by acquaintance)
  - A person, a city
- "Knowledge that"
  - Propositional knowledge
    - I know that I have free will.
    - I know that "Other people have minds" is true.

The first two don't address our questions about free will or mind–body duality, and we also have limited space, so we will concentrate on propositional knowledge in Part III.

Learning Objectives for Part III

At the end of Part III, you will be able to:

- Describe:
  - The traditional definition of knowledge and one prominent challenge to that definition
  - Cartesian radical doubt
  - The problem of induction
- Discuss:
  - Alternatives to the traditional account of knowledge
  - The strengths and weaknesses of Plato's and Gettier's arguments concerning the definition of knowledge
  - The strengths and weaknesses of Descartes's arguments
  - The strengths and weaknesses of Hume's, Reichenbach's and Popper's attempts to solve the problem of induction
  - Goodman's new problem of induction
- Define:
  - Conceptual analysis
  - Cartesian radical doubt
  - The problem of induction
  - Falsificationism

Preliminary Questions for Part III

1. What is knowledge? Can we define it?
2. Do we have knowledge? If so, what do we know? What can we know?
3. Can we only know what we can prove to be true?

4. How are my beliefs formed?
5. Can I trust my senses?
6. Do I have innate knowledge?
7. Are my beliefs justified? If so, how are they justified?
8. How does science work?
9. Are scientific beliefs justified?
10. We have been wrong about so many things in the past, so why should I believe that our current theories are true?
11. Do we get knowledge from science?
12. Is science the best way to obtain knowledge?

Definition of Knowledge

When we try to come up with a definition of knowledge, we may be tempted to list all the things we know, as individuals or as a society. As Plato has taught us, though, a good definition does not simply list things that satisfy the definition; rather, a good definition provides necessary and sufficient conditions for something's meeting that definition. So let's look more closely at this idea of necessary and sufficient conditions.

Example
Let's say that in one of your courses, the syllabus says that earning As on all your assignments is a necessary and sufficient condition for getting an A in the class. What does this mean? Well, it certainly means that if you get As on all your assignments, then you get an A in the class. But this conditional explains only a sufficient condition—after all, if it only said "You get an A in the class if you earn As on all your assignments" (which is another way of expressing the same conditional), you may well think that there are other ways to get an A in the class (such as acing the exam, washing your professors car, etc.). If this were the case, then earning As on all of your assignments would be sufficient for getting an A in the class, but not necessary.

So what makes the condition necessary? Well, if earning As on all your assignments is necessary for getting an A in the class, then you can't get an A without doing that. Thus, we express the necessity by saying "You get an A in the class only if you earn As on all your assignments." This makes it clear that the very least you have to do is earn As on all your assignments to get an A in the class, although if this were the only statement in the syllabus, you may think that there are other things you need to do as well.

So, what we need for necessary and sufficient conditions is both of these conditional statements. We can express these two conditional statements as one by saying: "You get an A in the course if and only if you earn As on all your assignments."

Similarly, then, a definition of something should express the necessary and sufficient conditions for being that thing. Consider the definition of a bachelor: A bachelor is an unmarried adult male. That is, we can say: a person is a bachelor if and only if that person is: (a) unmarried, (b) an adult, and (c) a male. This states the sufficient condition that if someone is (a), (b), and (c), then that person is a bachelor, and the necessary condition that if someone is a bachelor, then that person is (a), (b), and (c) (alternately, someone is (a), (b), and (c) only if that person is a bachelor).

Back to the definition of knowledge. As we will see in chapter 7, ever since Plato wrote about knowledge in the fourth century BC, philosophers have generally agreed on the following definition of propositional knowledge:

S (the subject) knows that P (the proposition) if and only if

- P is true,
- S believes P, and
- S is justified in believing P.

This definition of knowledge reigned supreme until Edmund Gettier published a very short but very influential paper in 1963. We will discuss Gettier's argument about the inadequacies of this definition in chapter 7 as well.

Justification and Certainty

Above we learned that, for centuries, philosophers have understood knowledge to be justified true belief. While we will explore the drawbacks of this definition of knowledge raised by Gettier, philosophers still believe that it is necessary for a belief to be justified if it is to count as knowledge, even if it is not sufficient. Gettier just used our intuitions about what makes a belief justified, but Plato gave us an explicit claim about what it might mean for a belief to be justified; he postulated in Theaetetus that a justified belief is one that is accompanied by a reason.

But, of course, "accompanied by a reason" is a little too vague to be a useful definition of justification. Let us consider, then, the actual example Plato uses in his argument—a trial in which lawyers are trying to convince a jury of some fact. Let's imagine that this fact is that Euclid stabbed Terpsion (these are the two characters at the very beginning of the dialogue). In the dialogue, both Socrates and Theaetetus agree that the belief that "It is true that Euclid stabbed Terpsion" would count as knowledge if the juror had been an eye witness, but that the same belief is not knowledge if the juror is merely being persuaded by a lawyer.

Thus, at least one kind of justification for a belief is sensing it for oneself—either seeing it, hearing it, feeling it, or the like, depending on what the belief is. Let us call these perceptual beliefs, as they are beliefs that we form based on our perceptions of the world around us. In chapter 8, we will see that seventeenth-century philosopher René Descartes questions whether sensing something—seeing someone cross the street, for example—is enough of a justification to make the belief that it happened count as knowledge that it happened.

Why does he question this? Because our senses often produce false beliefs—if the action happened too quickly, or we were too far away to see what really happened, for example. Descartes is worried because our perceptual beliefs are not certain; we cannot be 100 percent certain that any perceptual belief we have is true. This is a problem for Descartes because his view is that for a belief to count as knowledge, it not only has to be true, it has to be certain. So, we could characterize Descartes's position as follows: knowledge is justified true belief, and our beliefs are justified only if they are certain. Descartes solves his problem by offering a reason to accept many of our perceptual beliefs as certainly true.

Ultimately, then, Descartes is looking for a method or process of obtaining perceptual beliefs that would guarantee that they are true, and this involves the postulation of innate ideas—ideas that we have independently of our experiences. In the second reading of chapter 8, seventeenth-century English philosopher John Locke argues that Descartes is wrong, and that people are not born with any innate ideas.

The eighteenth-century philosopher David Hume, in the reading that follows Locke's, is not so much concerned with the justification of our immediate perceptual beliefs. He believes that these can be certain if we use both our senses and our reason. What he is concerned with, though, is our beliefs that are based on our perceptual beliefs. In particular, he is worried about our beliefs in scientific laws and the predictions they entail. This has come to be known as the problem of induction.

The Problem of Induction

Induction has often been described as an inference to a generalization from a collection of specific instances, or an inference to an event in the future from a collection of past instances. Thus, Hume's concern about the justification of each of these two inferences has been called Hume's problem of induction or just the problem of induction. This problem is, I think it is fair to say, one of the most important that philosophers have been tackling in the years since Hume so eloquently articulated it, partially because Hume offered a less-than-satisfactory solution.

In chapter 9, we encounter several twentieth-century attempts to solve Hume's problem of induction. First, Hans Reichenbach offers a kind of solution based on his theory of probability. He argues, in effect, that while we can't be certain that induction will produce the truth, it's our best choice of methods to make predictions. That is, if anything can produce the truth, induction can; and induction is more reliable than any of the other possible methods.

In the second reading of chapter 9, Karl Popper proposes a different kind of solution to Hume's problem of induction. He says that it doesn't matter whether we can be certain that induction leads us to the truth, because science is not actually based on induction. He argues that, instead, scientists are falsificationists, and offers a defense of this approach to science.

In the final reading, Nelson Goodman looks beyond Hume's problem of induction to propose a new difficulty, namely, the conceptual problem of how we pick out the data that go into our inductive inferences in the first place.

Whether Descartes, Hume, Reichenbach, Popper, and Goodman adequately solve their respective problems is still a topic of much debate.

7 The Definition of Knowledge

7.1 Plato, *Theaetetus*
7.2 Edmund L. Gettier, "Is Justified True Belief Knowledge?"
7.3 In-Class Exercises
7.4 Reading Questions

7.1 Plato, *Theaetetus*

Recall that we briefly encountered Plato in chapter 1. *Apology*, which we read there, was written before *Republic*, in which Plato explains in detail many of his philosophical positions. Contact with followers of Pythagoras and Heraclitus influenced his ideas about mathematics and immortality of the soul, as well as a world that is in constant flux. He developed the theory of the Forms that are eternal and independent of the earthly world; earthly objects or acts are what they are by virtue of their relationship to or "participation" in a Form. Thus, there is, for example, a Form of "horse," and horses in our world are horses (and not cows or pigs) because they have a special relationship to the Form "horse." Similarly, an action by a person is just if and only if the action has a special relationship with the eternal Form of "justice." Plato's theory of the Forms is developed in the most detail in his *Republic*.

Just as there is a Form of "justice," there is also a Form of "knowledge." Plato's position is that we have two cognitive faculties: (a) knowledge of the real (the eternal unchanging Forms) and (b), belief in appearances (beliefs about earthly objects and actions). Knowledge of the Forms must be infallible—that is, it must be absolutely certain, incapable of being false. But beliefs can be either true or false, and are of the way earthly things seem to be. All of Plato's dialogues are, in one way or another, concerned with obtaining knowledge of the Forms—justice, virtue, the good, and so on.

How do we obtain this knowledge? For Plato, knowledge of something at least includes a set of necessary and sufficient conditions—so that knowledge of "virtue" would include the set of necessary and sufficient conditions an action must fulfill in order to be "virtuous." Plato's theory is that our souls are immortal and know all about all the Forms. When we are born, our soul is transferred to a new body, and we forget everything we knew. As we live our lives, then, learning then is a process of "remembering" what our souls knew before birth. And our memories are stimulated by dialogue. In *Theaetetus*, Socrates compares his role to that of a midwife—he does not produce, or give birth to, knowledge; rather, he aids others in the production of their own knowledge. Socrates' constant questioning is his method of getting others to remember what they once knew.

The topic of *Theaetetus* is the question: What is knowledge? In a dialogue in three parts, Socrates and Theaetetus explore three answers to this question. First, Theaetetus suggests that we know what we perceive; knowledge is perception. Socrates points out that this would mean that knowledge is relative to the perceiver. Because knowledge must be the same for everyone, they both agree that perception is not a good definition. The passage we will now explore picks up in the second part of the dialogue, after Theaetetus suggests that knowledge is true belief.

Let's look at Plato's text in more detail. Specifically, we will analyze and diagram the argument, and then in the next section, we will discuss an important criticism of it.

From *Theaetetus*.[1]

Socrates: Then tell me, what definition [of knowledge] can we give with the least risk of contradicting ourselves? …

Theaetetus: That true belief is knowledge. Surely there can at least be no mistake in believing what is true and the consequences are always satisfactory. …

Socrates: Well, we need not go far to see this much. You will find a whole profession to prove that true belief is not knowledge.

Theaetetus: How so? What profession?

Socrates: The profession of those paragons of intellect known as orators and lawyers. There you have men who use their skill to produce conviction, not by instruction, but by making people believe whatever they want them to believe. You can hardly imagine teachers so clever as to be able, in the short time allowed by the clock to instruct their hearers thoroughly in the true facts of a case of robbery or other violence which those hearers had not witnessed.[1]

Theaetetus: No, I cannot imagine that, but they can convince them.

Socrates: And[A] by convincing you mean making them believe something.[2]

Theaetetus: Of course.

Socrates: And when a jury is rightly convinced of facts which can be known only by an eyewitness, then, judging by hearsay and accepting a true belief, they are judging without knowledge,[3] although,[B] if they find the right verdict, their conviction is correct?[4]

Theaetetus: Certainly.

Socrates: But[C] if true belief and knowledge were the same thing, the best of jurymen could never have a correct belief without knowledge.[5] It now appears that[D] they must be different things.[6]

In this part of the dialogue, Socrates convinces Theaetetus that knowledge is not just true belief. He explains that all you need to understand this is to consider lawyers in action in a courtroom. Here Socrates makes a distinction between instruction and convincing. Instruction, on his account, is leading someone to learn the truth, while convincing someone is merely leading someone to believe something that may be true or false.

First, Theaetetus agrees that the short time allowed for oral arguments in a courtroom is not enough for a lawyer to *teach* the jury the truth (1), but there is plenty of time for a lawyer to make the jury believe the truth (2).

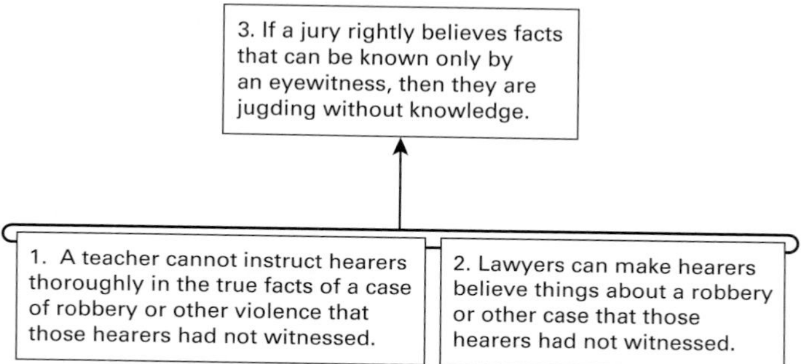

These claims combine according to (A) to support the conclusion that, even if the jury's belief is correct, they do not actually know the facts (3).

Then, as indicated by "although" (B), (3) combines with the claim that if the jury's belief is correct then they have true belief (4), to support the implied claim that if the jury believes the correct facts, then they have true belief without having knowledge.

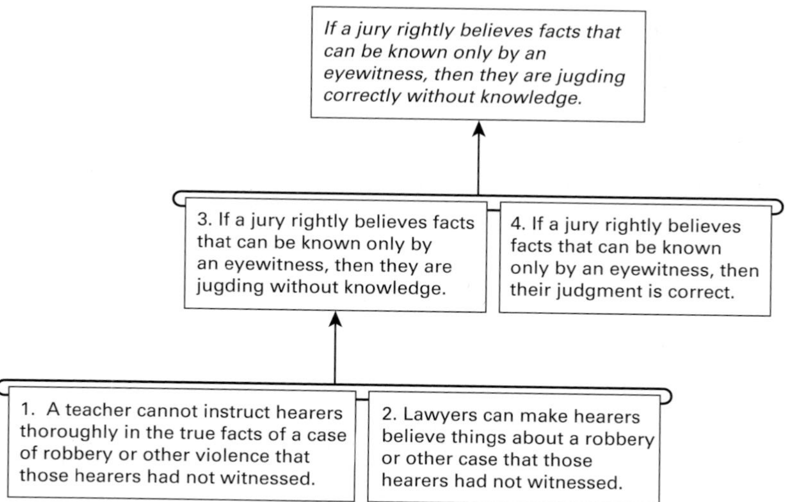

As indicated by "but" (C) and "in now appears that" (D), this implied claim combines with claim (5) to support (6). Claim (5) is a rather complicated conditional statement. Here Socrates is saying:

If true belief and knowledge were the same thing, *then* (if the jury believes the correct facts, then the jury would have true belief and knowledge).

The consequent of the italicized conditional is itself a conditional statement that is refuted by the implied statement.

Thus, by *modus tollens*, we have that the antecedent is false, and true belief and knowledge are not the same thing (6).

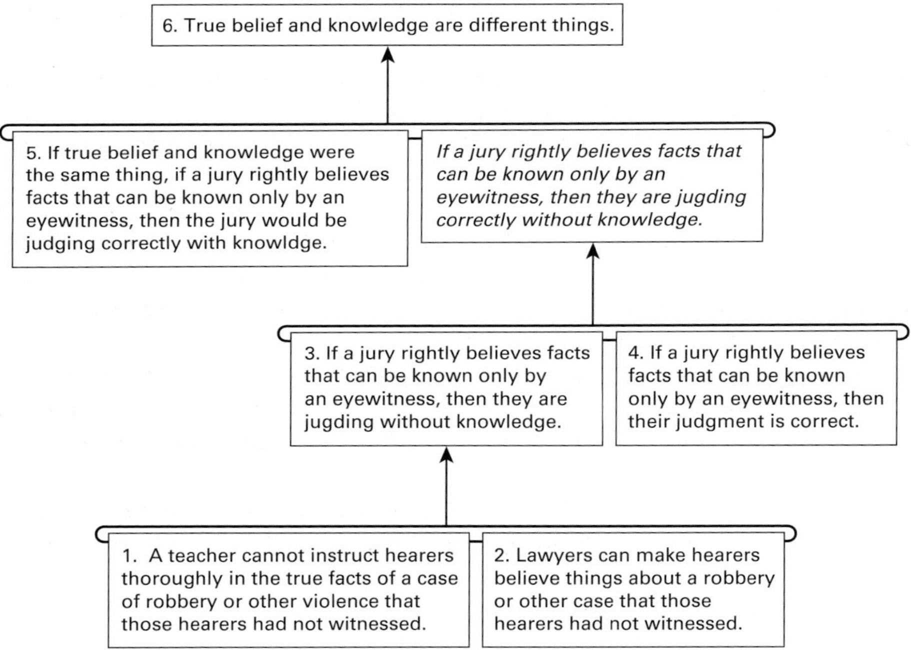

Finally, Socrates and Theaetetus entertain the third possibility for a definition of knowledge: that knowledge is true belief with an account. In the rest of the dialogue, they struggle to determine what "with an account" might mean. These arguments are left for the exercises.

Ultimately, Plato's legacy is that philosophers for the next 2,000 years would take the definition of knowledge to be "justified true belief," where the problem is determining what "justification" is. That is, until 1963, when Edmund Gettier published the article to which we turn next.

7.2 Edmund L. Gettier, "Is Justified True Belief Knowledge?"

Edmund L. Gettier is an American philosopher who is currently an emeritus professor at the University of Massachusetts, Amherst. He was born in Baltimore, Maryland, and earned his doctorate at Cornell. His first teaching position was at Wayne State University in Detroit, Michigan. It was during his time at Wayne State that Gettier published one of the most famous (and shortest!) philosophical papers of the twentieth century. He first published "Is Justified True Belief Knowledge?" in a South American journal because he wasn't sure what the American reception would be. Shortly after, though, it was published in its original English in the journal *Analysis*.

Gettier never published another article, but instead turned to training students in modal logic—in particular, finding counterexamples and simplifying semantics. But, his legacy lives on in the fact that every epistemologist since has to wrestle with what are now referred to as *the Gettier problem in justification*.

In this article, Gettier presents a challenge to the conception of knowledge as justified true belief that philosophers had generally assumed since Plato. In it, Gettier does not offer an alternative definition of justification, but rather relies on our intuitions about the justification of a few very ordinary kinds of statements.

Let's call the proposed necessary and sufficient conditions for knowledge described in the introduction to this chapter the "JTB" (justified true belief) account. Put simply, Gettier argues that the JTB conditions are not a sufficient condition for the truth of S knows that P, and that this leads us to the fact that someone could have a justified true belief about something but still not have knowledge of that thing.

The argument uses the method of *conceptual analysis*—analyzing what we mean when we use a particular concept in a specified context—to show that there are conceivable cases in which a person has a justified true belief in which we are hesitant to say that this person actually knows.

Gettier's argument in "Is Justified True Belief Knowledge?" is an example of a *reductio ad absurdum* of Plato's definition of knowledge. Let's look at his criticism of Plato more closely.

From "Is Justified True Belief Knowledge?"[2]

Various attempts have been made in recent years to state necessary and sufficient conditions for someone's knowing a given proposition. The attempts have often been such that they can be stated in a form similar to the following:

(a) S knows that P IFF (i.e., if and only if): (i) P is true, (ii) S believes that P, and (iii) S is justified in believing that P.

...

I shall argue that[A] (a) is false in that the conditions stated therein do not constitute a sufficient condition for the truth of the proposition that S knows that P. ...

I shall begin by noting two points. First,[B] in that sense of "justified" in which S's being justified in believing P is a necessary condition of S's knowing that P, it is possible for a person to be justified in believing a proposition that is in fact false.[1] Secondly,[C] for any proposition P, if S is justified in believing P, and P entails Q, and S deduces Q from P and accepts Q as a result of this deduction, then S is justified in believing Q.[2] Keeping these two points in mind, I shall now present two cases in which the conditions stated in (a) are true for some proposition, though it is at the same time false that the person in question knows that proposition.[3]

... In our example, then, all of the following are true: (i) (e) is true, (ii) Smith believes that (e) is true, and (iii) Smith is justified in believing that (e) is true.[4] ...

But it is equally clear that[D] Smith does not KNOW that (e) is true;[5] for[E] (e) is true in virtue of the number of coins in Smith's pocket,[6] while[F] Smith does not know how many coins are in Smith's pocket,[7] and[G] bases his belief in (e) on a count of the coins in Jones's pocket, whom he falsely believes to be the man who will get the job.[8]

First, Gettier reminds us of the standard definition of knowledge that we saw in the introduction to this section. His basic argument, indicated by (A), is that this definition identifies certain kinds of cases as knowledge that, intuitively, we wouldn't consider to be knowledge (3). This is represented as:

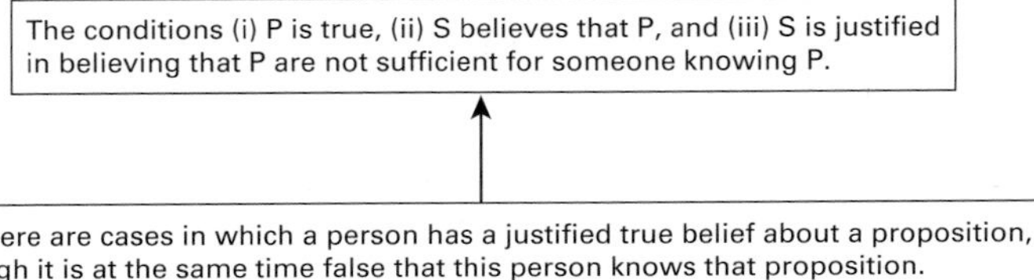
The conditions (i) P is true, (ii) S believes that P, and (iii) S is justified in believing that P are not sufficient for someone knowing P.
3. There are cases in which a person has a justified true belief about a proposition, though it is at the same time false that this person knows that proposition.

Next, Gettier gives us two principles that are supposed to hold in general for any kind of propositional beliefs. First, it is possible to be justified in holding a false belief (1). This seems true—I may be quite justified in my belief that it is going to rain tomorrow if I have seen forecasts in the paper, on the news, and from the national weather service. Nonetheless, it may not rain, and so my belief was false, even though it was justified.

Second, Gettier proposes a bit of logic: if I am justified in believing proposition P ("It's going to rain tomorrow"), and I can deduce proposition Q ("If I don't have an umbrella tomorrow, I will get wet on my walk to work") from P, then I am justified in believing Q (2). This also seems to be intuitively correct.

Then, we are invited to consider the first case. It is stipulated that Smith is justified in believing the following two propositions: (d_1) Jones will get the job and (d_2) Jones has ten coins in his pocket. From this, Smith deduces that (e) the person who will get the job has ten coins in his pocket.

By proposition (1), it's possible for Smith to believe that Jones will get the job, even if this is not true. And from proposition (2), if Smith is justified in believing the first two propositions (d_1 and d_2), then he is justified in believing the third (e). So, it is possible that in a case like this, (e) could be true, Smith could believe (e), and Smith could be justified in believing (e) (4).

Thus, in this case Smith would have a justified true belief of (e):

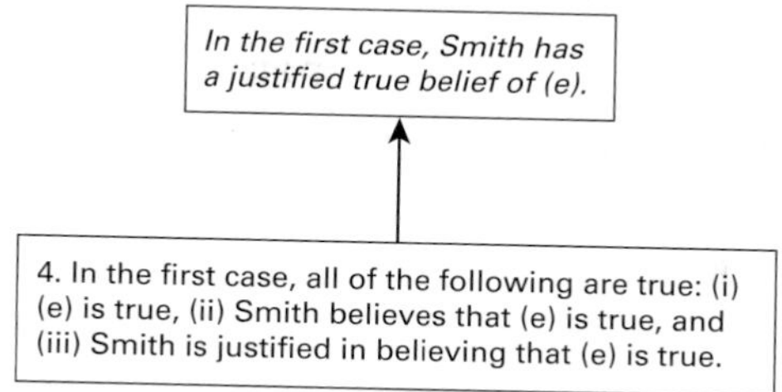
In the first case, Smith has a justified true belief of (e).
4. In the first case, all of the following are true: (i) (e) is true, (ii) Smith believes that (e) is true, and (iii) Smith is justified in believing that (e) is true.

It turns out, though, that (d_1) is false, but (e) is still true, because Smith unknowingly has ten coins in his pocket (7) and Smith is the one who gets the job (6), so he bases his belief on a falsehood (8). So Smith is still justified in believing (e), even though it seems wrong, as indicated by (D), to say that Smith *knows* (e) (5). That (6), (7), and (8) combine to support (5) is indicated by (E), (F), and (G).

The whole argument from this first case can be represented as:

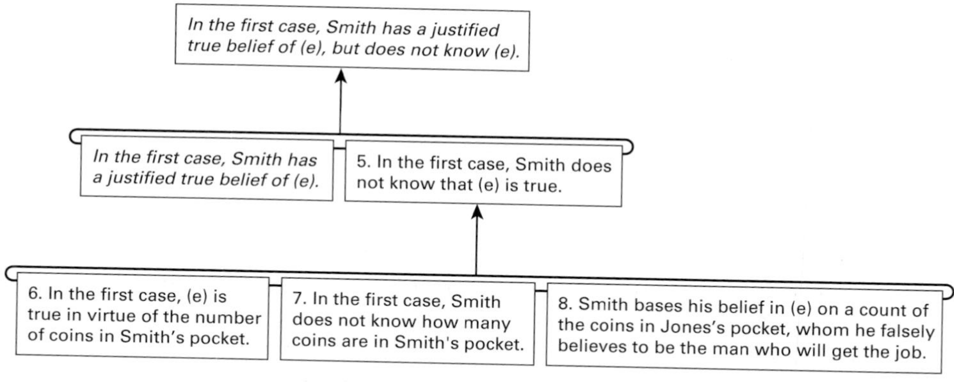
In the first case, Smith has a justified true belief of (e), but does not know (e).
In the first case, Smith has a justified true belief of (e).
5. In the first case, Smith does not know that (e) is true.
6. In the first case, (e) is true in virtue of the number of coins in Smith's pocket.
7. In the first case, Smith does not know how many coins are in Smith's pocket.
8. Smith bases his belief in (e) on a count of the coins in Jones's pocket, whom he falsely believes to be the man who will get the job.

Now, let's turn to the second case:

... If these two conditions hold, then Smith does not KNOW that (h) is true,[9] even though[H]

(i) (h) is true,

(ii) Smith does believe that (h) is true, and

(iii) Smith is justified in believing that (h) is true.[10]

These two examples show that[I] definition (a) does not state a sufficient condition for someone's knowing a given proposition. The same cases, with appropriate changes, will suffice to show that neither definition (b) nor definition (c) do so either.

This case is similar to the first in that it is stipulated that Smith is justified in believing (f). Now, from any proposition P, one can deduce the disjunction "either P or T." For example, if it is true that Pittsburgh is in Pennsylvania, then it is true that either Pittsburgh is in Pennsylvania or Cleveland is in Pennsylvania. The reason is that a disjunction is true if at least one of its disjuncts is true. So, again, by principles (1) and (2), Smith is justified in believing "either (f) or [any proposition]."

In the second case, it is stipulated that Smith is justified in believing that (f) Jones owns a Ford. Smith also has a friend, Brown, whose whereabouts are unknown to Smith. Smith randomly picks a city from a map, and forms the belief that (h) either Jones owns a Ford, or Brown is in Barcelona.

Again, unbeknownst to Smith, (f) is actually false, but (h) is true, because Brown really is in Barcelona. So, Smith has a justified true belief in (h) (10), even though it seems wrong to say that Smith *knows* (h) (9), because he believes it for the wrong reasons.

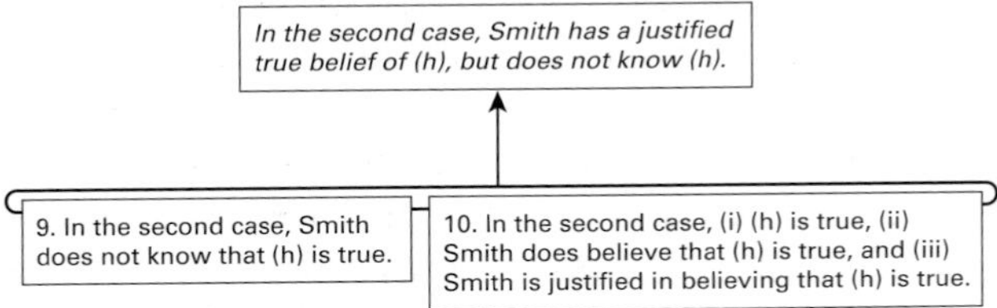
In the second case, Smith has a justified true belief of (h), but does not know (h).
9. In the second case, Smith does not know that (h) is true.
10. In the second case, (i) (h) is true, (ii) Smith does believe that (h) is true, and (iii) Smith is justified in believing that (h) is true.

Just as Gettier indicated in the beginning of the article, we have cases in which a person has a justified true belief about a proposition but does not know that proposition (3). Therefore, he concludes, the standard JTB conditions are not actually sufficient for knowledge.

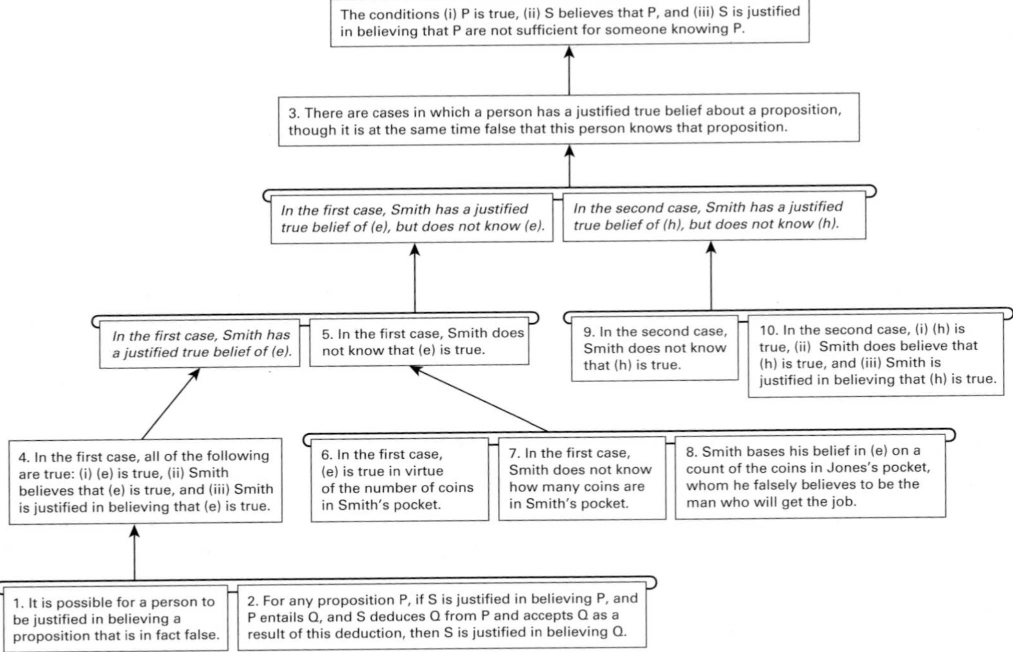
The conditions (i) P is true, (ii) S believes that P, and (iii) S is justified in believing that P are not sufficient for someone knowing P.
3. There are cases in which a person has a justified true belief about a proposition, though it is at the same time false that this person knows that proposition.
In the first case, Smith has a justified true belief of (e), but does not know (e).
In the second case, Smith has a justified true belief of (h), but does not know (h).
In the first case, Smith has a justified true belief of (e).
5. In the first case, Smith does not know that (e) is true.
9. In the second case, Smith does not know that (h) is true.
10. In the second case, (i) (h) is true, (ii) Smith does believe that (h) is true, and (iii) Smith is justified in believing that (h) is true.
4. In the first case, all of the following are true: (i) (e) is true, (ii) Smith believes that (e) is true, and (iii) Smith is justified in believing that (e) is true.
6. In the first case, (e) is true in virtue of the number of coins in Smith's pocket.
7. In the first case, Smith does not know how many coins are in Smith's pocket.
8. Smith bases his belief in (e) on a count of the coins in Jones's pocket, whom he falsely believes to be the man who will get the job.
1. It is possible for a person to be justified in believing a proposition that is in fact false.
2. For any proposition P, if S is justified in believing P, and P entails Q, and S deduces Q from P and accepts Q as a result of this deduction, then S is justified in believing Q.

Now let's consider an objection to Gettier's argument.

Objection

Consider the first part of the diagram we constructed for Gettier's argument. We can make the case that the two "points" that Gettier said to keep in mind are some of the general principles that support (4), along with the particular facts. For our purposes, then, we can represent that subargument in the diagram on the right.

The second principle Gettier proposes, given in statement (2), is that if you are justified in believing proposition P, and you deduce Q from P, then you are justified in believing Q. This is often called the *transitivity of justification*. In both cases, Smith has a true belief that is logically deduced from a false belief. By the transitivity of justification, if Smith was justified in believing the false premise, then Smith is justified in believing the true premise that he deduced from the false one.

But, statement (2) is given here with no argument—what if it's not entirely true? The objection here is that Gettier's examples are defective because in neither case is Smith actually justified in believing the statement in question. The justification of the statement relies on the principle that false propositions can justify one's belief in other propositions. But this principle might be false. If so, then we would not really have a case of justified true belief that is not knowledge.

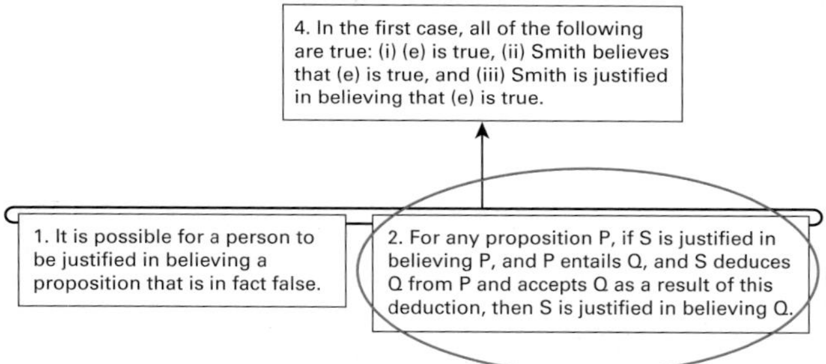
4. In the first case, all of the following are true: (i) (e) is true, (ii) Smith believes that (e) is true, and (iii) Smith is justified in believing that (e) is true.
1. It is possible for a person to be justified in believing a proposition that is in fact false.
2. For any proposition P, if S is justified in believing P, and P entails Q, and S deduces Q from P and accepts Q as a result of this deduction, then S is justified in believing Q.

It is precisely the fact that Smith deduced the true belief from a false belief that makes us hesitant to say that Smith knows in either case. Thus, the solution might be to modify the standard account as follows.

S knows that P if and only if:

(i) P is true,
(ii) S believes that P,
(iii) S is justified in believing that P, and
(iv) the justification of S's belief that P does not depend on the justification of a false belief S has.

In the exercises below, we will explore a particular response to this objection.

7.3 In-Class Exercises

An asterisk (*) indicates a more challenging exercise.

Exercises 1–4

In the first section of this chapter, we analyzed in detail an argument given by Plato in *Theaetetus*. The following selections contain other arguments from this dialogue. For each selection, (a) diagram the argument, and (b) identify any potential objections to the argument.

Exercise 1

Socrates: … So when a man gets hold of the true notion of something without an account, his mind does think truly of it, but he does not know it, for if one cannot give and receive an account of a thing, one has no knowledge of that thing. But when he has also got hold of an account, all this becomes possible to him and he is fully equipped with knowledge.

Does that version represent the dream as you heard it, or not?

Theaetetus: Perfectly.

Socrates: So this dream finds favor and you hold that a true notion with the addition of an account is knowledge?

Exercise 2

Socrates: Well then, what is this term "account" intended to convey to us? I think it must mean one of three things.

Theaetetus: What are they?

Socrates: The first will be giving overt expression to one's thought by means of vocal sound with names and verbs, casting an image of one's notion on the stream that flows through the lips, like a reflection in a mirror or in water. Do you agree that expression of that sort is an "account"?

Theaetetus: I do. We certainly call that expressing ourselves in speech.

Socrates: On the other hand, that is a thing that anyone can do more or less readily. If a man is not born deaf or dumb, he can signify what he thinks on any subject. So in this sense anyone whatever who has a correct notion evidently will have it "with an account" and there will be no place left anywhere for a correct notion apart from knowledge.

Theaetetus: True.

Exercise 3

Socrates: Then we must not be too ready to charge the author of the definition of knowledge now before us with talking nonsense. Perhaps that is not what he meant. He may have meant being able to reply to the question, what any given thing is, by enumerating its elements.

…

Socrates: Tell me if you approve, my friend, and whether you accept the view that the complete enumeration of elements is an account of any given thing, whereas description in terms of syllables or of any larger unit still leaves it unaccounted for. Then we can look into the matter further.

Theaetetus: Well, I do accept that.

Socrates: Do you think, then, that anyone has knowledge of whatever it may be, when he thinks that one and the same thing is a part sometimes of one thing, sometimes of a different thing, or again when he believes now one and now another thing to be part of one and the same thing?

Theaetetus: Certainly not.

Socrates: Have you forgotten, then, that when you first began learning to read and write, that was what you and your schoolfellows did?

Theaetetus: Do you mean, when we thought that now one letter and now another was part of the same syllable, and when we put the same letter sometimes into the proper syllable, sometimes into another?

Socrates: That is what I mean.

Theaetetus: Then I have certainly not forgotten, and I do not think that one has reached knowledge so long as one is in that condition.

Socrates: Well then, if at that stage you are writing "Theaetetus" and you think you ought to write T and H and E and do so, and again when you are trying to write "Theodorus," you think you ought to write T and H and E and do so, can we say that you know the first syllable of your two names?

Theaetetus: No, we have just agreed that one has not knowledge so long as one is in that condition.

Socrates: And there is no reason why a person should not be in the same condition with respect to the second, third, and fourth syllables as well?

Theaetetus: None whatever.

Socrates: Can we, then, say that whenever in writing "Theaetetus" he puts down all the letters in order, then he is in possession of the complete catalogue of elements together with correct belief?

Theaetetus: Obviously.

Socrates: Being still, as we agree, without knowledge, though his beliefs are correct?

Theaetetus: Yes.

Socrates: Although he possesses the "account" in addition to right belief. For when he wrote he was in possession of the catalogue of the elements which we agreed was the "account."

Theaetetus: True.

Socrates: So, my friend, there is such a thing as right belief together with an account, which is not yet entitled to be called knowledge.

*Exercise 4

Theaetetus: A good reminder. There is still one meaning [of "account"] left. The first was what might be called the image of thought in spoken sound, and the one we have just discussed was going all through the elements to arrive at the whole. What is the third?

Socrates: The meaning most people would give—being able to name some mark by which the thing one is asked about differs from everything else.

...

Socrates: And if, besides a right notion about a thing, whatever it may be, you grasp its difference from all other things, you will have arrived at knowledge of what, till then, you had only a notion of.

...

Socrates: I will explain, if I can. Suppose I have a correct notion about you; if I add to that the account of you, then, we are to understand, I know you. Otherwise I have only a notion.

Theaetetus: Yes.

Socrates: And "account" means putting your differences into words.

Theaetetus: Yes.

Socrates: So, at the time when I had only a notion, my mind did not grasp any of the points in which you differ from others?

Theaetetus: Apparently not.

Socrates: Then I must have had before my mind one of those common things will belong to another person as much as to you.

Theaetetus: That follows.

Socrates: But look here! If that was so, how could I possibly be having a notion you rather than of anyone else? Suppose I was thinking, Theaetetus is one who is a man and has a nose and eyes and a mouth and so forth, enumerating every part of the body. Will thinking in that way result in my thinking of Theaetetus rather than of Theodorus, or, as they say, of the man in the street?

Theaetetus: How should it?

Socrates: Well, now suppose I think not merely of a man with a nose and eyes, but of one with a snub nose and prominent eyes. Once more shall I be having a notion of you any more than of myself or anyone else of that description?

Theaetetus: No.

Socrates: In fact, there will be no notion of Theaetetus in my mind, I suppose, until this particular snubness has stamped and registered within me a record distinct from all the other cases of snubness that I have seen, and so with every other part of you. Then, if I meet you tomorrow, that trait will revive my memory and give me a correct notion about you.

Theaetetus: Quite true.

Socrates: If that is so, the correct notion of anything must itself include the differentness of that thing.

Theaetetus: Evidently.

Socrates: Then what meaning is left for getting hold of an "account" in addition to the correct notion? If, on the one hand, it means adding the notion of how a thing differs from other things, such an injunction is simply absurd.

Theaetetus: How so?

Socrates: When we have a correct notion of the way in which certain things differ from other things, it tells us to add a correct notion of the way in which they differ from other things. On this showing, the most vicious of circles would be nothing to this injunction. It might better deserve to be called the sort of direction a blind man might give. To tell us to get hold of something we already have, in order to get to know something we are already thinking of, suggests a state of the most absolute darkness.

Theaetetus: Whereas, if … ? The supposition you made just now implied that you would state some alternative. What was it?

Socrates: If the direction to add an "account" means that we are to get to know the differentness, as opposed to merely having a notion of it, this most admirable of all definitions of knowledge will be a pretty business, because "getting to know" means acquiring knowledge, doesn't it?

Theaetetus: Yes.

Socrates: So, apparently, to the question, "What is knowledge?" our definition will reply, "Correct belief together with knowledge of a differentness," for, according to it, "adding an account" will come to that.

Theaetetus: So it seems.

Socrates: Yes, and when we are inquiring after the nature of knowledge, nothing could be sillier than to say that it is correct belief together with a *knowledge* of differentness or of anything whatever. So, Theaetetus, neither perception, nor true belief, nor the addition of an "account" to true belief can be knowledge.

Exercise 5

In the second section of this chapter, we analyzed in detail an argument given by Edmund Gettier in "Is Justified True Belief Knowledge?" After our analysis, we considered a possible objection to Gettier's argument. The following selection contains a response by Richard Feldman to that objection.[3] For this selection, (a) diagram Feldman's argument, and (b) identify any potential objections to the argument.

… I think, though, that there are examples very much like Gettier's that do not rely on this allegedly false principle. To see this, let us first consider one example in the form in which Meyers and Stern discuss it, and then consider a slight modification of it.

Suppose Mr. Nogot tells Smith that he owns a Ford and even shows him a certificate to that effect. Suppose, further, that up till now Nogot has always been reliable and honest in his dealings with Smith. Let us call the conjunction of all this evidence (m). Smith is thus justified in believing that Mr. Nogot who is in his office owns a Ford (r) and, consequently, is justified in believing that someone in his office owns a Ford (h). As it turns out, though, (m) and (h) are true but (r) is false. So, the Gettier example runs. Smith has a justified true belief in (h), but he clearly does not know (h).

What is supposed to justify (h) in this example is (r). But since (r) is false, the example runs afoul of the disputed principle. Since (r) is false, it justifies nothing. Hence, if the principle is false, the counter-example fails.

We can alter the example slightly, however, so that what justifies (h) for Smith is true and he knows that it is. Suppose he deduces from (m) its existential generalization:

(n) There is someone in the office who told Smith that he owns a Ford and even showed him a certificate to that effect, and who up till now has always been reliable and honest in his dealings with Smith.

(n), we should note, is true and Smith knows that it is, since he has correctly deduced it from (m), which he knows to be true. On the basis of (n) Smith believes (h)—someone in the office owns a Ford. Just as the Nogot evidence, (m), justified (r)—Nogot owns a Ford—in the original example, (n) justifies (h) in this example. Thus Smith has a justified true belief in (h), knows his evidence to be true, but still does not know (h). I conclude that even if a proposition can be justified for a person only if his evidence is true, or only if he knows it to be true, there are still counter-examples to the justified true belief analysis of knowledge of the Gettier sort. In the above example, Smith reasoned from the proposition (m), which he knew to be true, to the proposition (n), which he also knew, to the truth of (h); yet he still did not know (h). So some examples, similar to Gettier's, do not "turn on the principle that someone can be justified in accepting a certain proposition ... even though (his evidence) ... is false."

Exercises 6–9

The following questions are intended to ensure your understanding of both Plato's and Gettier's texts, and to help you further explore the ideas presented in this chapter.

Exercise 6: Now that you have read my textual analysis of Plato's argument, summarize it in your own words.
Exercise 7: Summarize, in your own words, each of the arguments Socrates presents in exercises 1–4 above.
Exercise 8: Now that you have read my textual analysis of Gettier's argument, summarize it in your own words.
Exercise 9: Summarize, in your own words, Feldman's response in exercise 5 above to the objection we raised to Gettier's argument.

7.4 Reading Questions

1. In the beginning of the selection of Plato's *Theaetetus*, Socrates says to his companion: "You are generous indeed, my dear Theaetetus—so openhanded that, when you are asked for one simple thing, you offer a whole variety." What did Socrates mean here? Is he being serious in his compliment to Theaetetus—that he is being generous—or is he being playful? How does Socrates use his explanation of this comment to tell Theaetetus what a good definition of knowledge would be?
2. A little later in the dialogue, Theaetetus reasserts an earlier suggestion that knowledge is true belief. Socrates, however, claims: "You will find a whole profession to prove that true belief is not knowledge." What is this profession? How do people of this profession prove that true belief is not knowledge? Is it their intention to offer this proof, or is Socrates making some deeper connections?
3. Near the end of the selection, Socrates recalls a dream and then makes the following argument: "So when a man gets hold of the true notion of something without an account,

his mind does think truly of it, but he does not know it, for if one cannot give and receive an account of a thing, one has no knowledge of that thing." What does Socrates mean? How can a person have a true belief but not knowledge? What does it mean to give and receive an account of something? What role does this giving and receiving of an account have in knowledge?

4. Socrates seems to end his discussion with the declaration that knowledge is not true belief with an "account." Are there other kinds of "accounts" that he has not thought of? What kind of account do you think is necessary for a true belief to count as knowledge?

5. After he explains some common definitions of "S knows that P," Gettier makes the following claim: "The conditions stated therein do not constitute a sufficient condition for the truth of the proposition that S knows that P." What does he mean when he says that these conditions are not sufficient? Does that imply that they are not necessary, either? Why or why not?

6. At the end of his article, Gettier claims: "These two examples show that definition (a) does not state a sufficient condition for someone's knowing a given proposition." Directly after, he makes the further claim: "The same cases, with appropriate changes, will suffice to show that neither definition (b) nor definition (c) do so either." What are definitions (b) and (c)? How would these cases need to be changed to support this second claim?

7. Some philosophers claim that JTB needs a simple additional condition: whatever facts are taken to justify a belief in a proposition must be causes of the truth of that proposition. Does this proposal avoid Gettier's example? If so, can you think of other examples that present difficulties for the proposal?

8. Consider the "Lottery Paradox." Let's say you buy a ticket in a fair lottery (meaning each ticket has an equal chance of winning). You do it for charity because you believe your ticket will not win. This seems like a justified belief, since there are more than a million tickets. The next week the drawing occurs and it turns out you were right; your ticket is not a winner. So you had a justified true belief. But did you have knowledge? That is, did you know you would not win? Why or why not?

9. Consider the "Surprise Test Paradox," by Roy Sorensen:[4] A teacher announces that there will be a surprise test next week. A student objects that this is impossible: "The class meets on Monday, Wednesday, and Friday. If the test is given on Friday, then on Thursday I would be able to predict that the test is on Friday. It would not be a surprise. Can the test be given on Wednesday? No, because on Tuesday I would know that the test will not be on Friday (thanks to the previous reasoning) and know that the test was not on Monday (thanks to memory). Therefore, on Tuesday I could foresee that the test will be on Wednesday. A test on Wednesday would not be a surprise. Could the surprise test be on Monday? On Sunday, the previous two eliminations would be available to me. Consequently, I would know that the test must be on Monday. So a Monday test would also fail to be a surprise. Therefore, it is impossible for there to be a surprise test." Can the teacher fulfill this announcement?

8 Justification and Certainty

8.1 René Descartes, *Meditations on First Philosophy*
8.2 John Locke, *An Essay Concerning Human Understanding*
8.3 David Hume, *An Enquiry Concerning Human Understanding*
8.4 In-Class Exercises
8.5 Reading Questions

8.1 René Descartes, *Meditations on First Philosophy*

Born in La Haye en Touraine,[1] a town in central France, René Descartes (1596–1650) was both a philosopher and a mathematician, generally acknowledged as the first philosopher of the "modern" period. He was schooled in the Aristotelian tradition and earned a law degree, but he spent most of his time on mathematics. *Meditations on First Philosophy* was not published until 1641, but, according to Descartes, the philosophical journey that culminated in this work began in southern Germany on November 10, 1619. Descartes's goal was to find a philosophical foundation for the sciences, taking mathematics as the paradigm of human understanding.

Descartes wrote the *Meditations* as a sort of dialogue he is having with himself, but each meditation is ultimately an argument for some specific conclusion that he will use as a premise in *Mediation VI*, in his main argument. The problem Descartes confronts in *Meditation I* is finding a foundation for all of his scientific knowledge. What he is seeking are *basic beliefs*—beliefs that cannot possibly be false and so are automatically justified—that can support all of his other beliefs. His reasoning is that, because the basic beliefs are justified, any belief based on them will be justified as well. However, the conclusion of Descartes's argument in this passage is that all of his beliefs are doubtful, which leads him to wonder whether he knows anything at all.

Descartes's argument offers one of the most powerful and profound thought experiments in all of philosophy. Let's look at his text in more detail. Specifically, we will analyze and diagram the argument and then discuss criticisms of it.

In the first passage of *Meditation I*, Descartes explains what motivated him to engage in this project. Descartes lived during the scientific revolution, in which natural philosophers (the scientists of his time) were breaking new ground by doing experiments on the world around them, rather than using Aristotle's ancient method of mere observation coupled with rational deduction. But, Descartes worried, the only way experimental science can work is if the world and the objects in it are in reality roughly the way they appear to be to us. And the way that objects appear to be to us depends on our senses (sight, touch, etc.). But, he argues, our senses can sometimes fool us.

So the project Descartes begins in the *Meditations* is to determine the justification of the beliefs we acquire from the information received by our senses. I may have the belief that the sky is blue because this is the signal my brain is receiving from the light entering my eyes. But how do I know that my belief is correct? What justifies my taking this belief to be true?

To answer this question, Descartes describes a new method of philosophical inquiry: radical doubt. He wants to set aside any belief he has that he is not absolutely sure is correct to try to find the ones of which he is certain. But he says this doesn't mean that he has to sort through every belief. Why not? Because he thinks that beliefs are like bricks in a wall: the beliefs at the top are supported by the beliefs directly underneath them, and those are supported by the ones directly beneath them, and so on, until we come to the bottom of the wall. The bricks at the bottom are the foundation for all the other beliefs. Thus, if he can show that any of these foundational beliefs are uncertain, then he can set aside any belief that traces its support back to that belief.

In *Meditation I*, then, Descartes argues that all his beliefs are uncertain or doubtful, because his foundational beliefs are all doubtful. The basic structure of Descartes's argument looks like this:

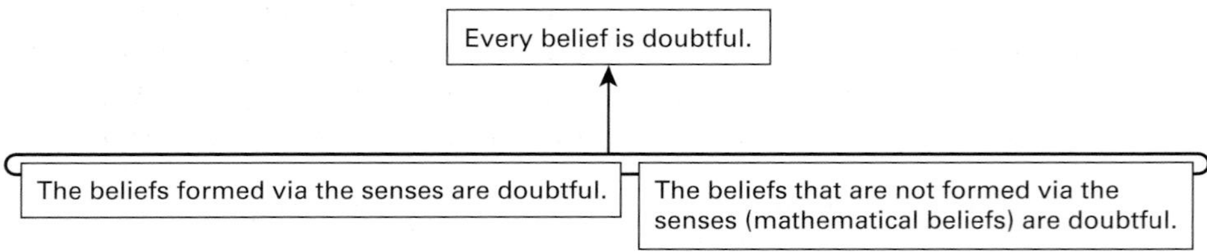

Each of the premises for this conclusion has a subargument supporting it. Let's look first at the argument for the premise that the beliefs formed via the senses are doubtful.

From *Meditations on First Philosophy: Meditation I*.[2]

Whatever I have accepted until now as most true has come to me through my senses.[1] But[A] occasionally I have found that they have deceived me,[2] and[B] it is unwise to trust completely those who have deceived us even once.[3]

[The next paragraph presents a series of considerations back and forth. It is set out here as a discussion between two people, but that isn't how Descartes presented it.—Trans.]

Hopeful: Yet[C] although the senses sometimes deceive us about objects which are very small or distant, that doesn't apply to my belief that I am here, sitting by the fire, wearing a winter dressing-gown, holding this piece of paper in my hands, and so on. It seems to be quite impossible to doubt beliefs like these, which come from the senses.[4] Another example: how can I doubt that these hands or this whole body are mine?[*] To doubt such things I would have to liken myself to brain-damaged madmen who are convinced they are kings when really they are paupers, or say they are dressed in purple when they are naked, or that they are pumpkins, or made of glass.[5] But[D] such people are insane, and I would be thought equally mad if I modeled myself on them.[6]

Doubtful (sarcastically): What a brilliant piece of reasoning! As if I were not a man who sleeps at night, and often has all the same experiences while asleep as madmen do when awake[7]—indeed sometimes even more improbable ones. Often in my dreams I am convinced of just such familiar events—that I am sitting by the fire in my dressing-gown—when in fact I am lying undressed in bed![#]

Descartes begins his search for indubitable beliefs by starting with one class of beliefs—the ones that come from his senses. As indicated by the "But" (A) and the "and" (B), claims (1), (2), and (3) work together to support the implied conclusion that he should not trust his senses and that beliefs based on his senses can be doubted.

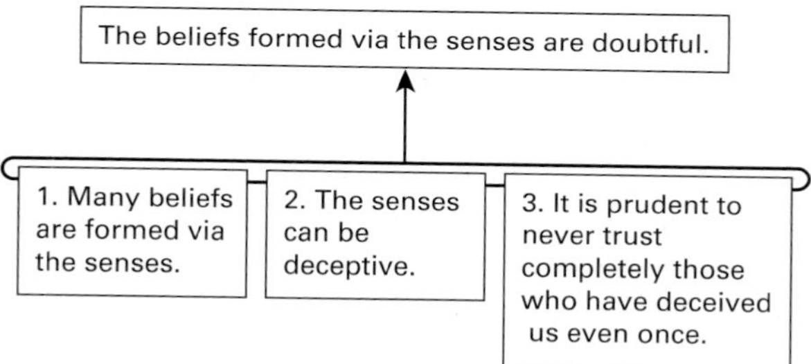

But, as indicated by the "Yet" (C), Descartes raises an objection to his line of reasoning: "there are many other beliefs [besides those about objects that are small or far away] about which doubt is quite impossible" (4). But then he responds to this objection by admitting that people who are insane are often wrong about things of which they claim to be absolutely sure.

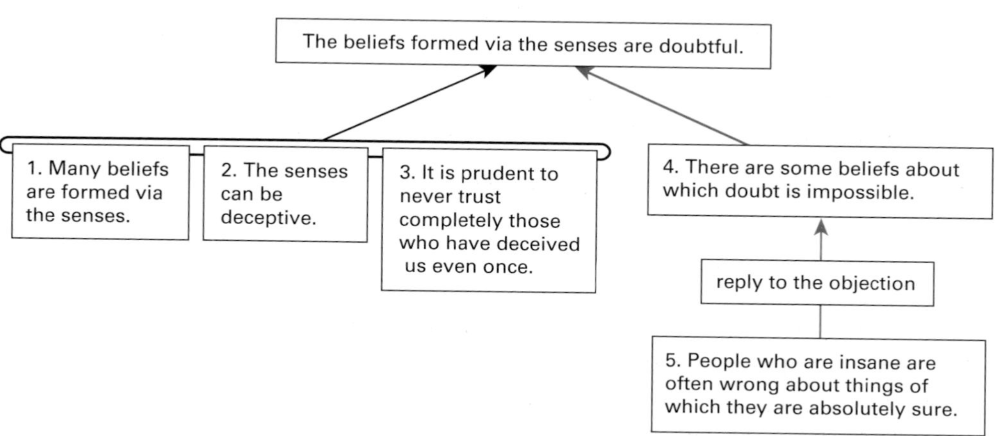

Descartes objects to this reply as well, as indicated by the "But" (D), with the claim that he would be considered insane himself if he used the beliefs of insane people to judge his own (6). He responds to this objection by noting that he is a "man who sleeps at night, and regularly has all the same experiences while asleep as madmen do when awake" (7) and giving the example of dreaming that he is sitting by the fire (#).

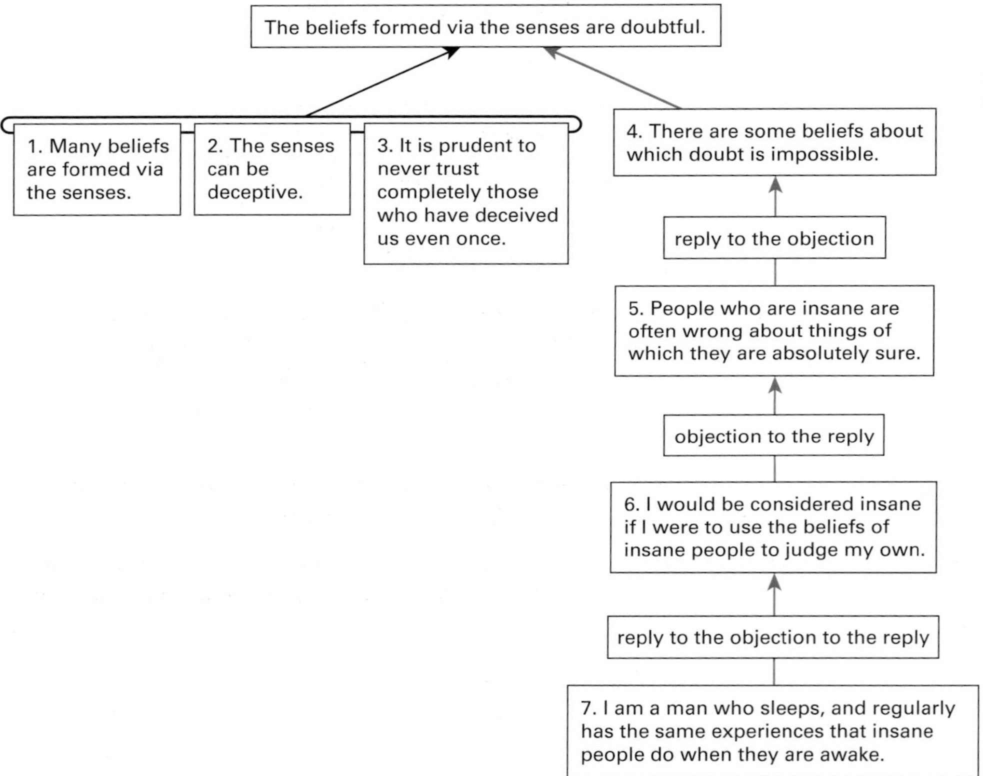

Hopeful: Yet[E] right now my eyes are certainly wide open when I look at this piece of paper; I shake my head and it isn't asleep; when I rub one hand against the other, I do it deliberately, and know what I am doing.[8] This wouldn't all happen with such clarity to someone asleep.

Doubtful: Indeed! As if I didn't remember other occasions when I have been tricked by exactly similar thoughts while asleep![9] As I think about this more carefully, I realize that there is never any reliable way of distinguishing being awake from being asleep.[10] This discovery makes me dizzy, [joke—Trans.] which itself reinforces the notion that I may be asleep!

As indicated by the "Yet" (E), Descartes responds that he is sure right now that he is not asleep (8), but then admits that on other occasions he has been sure that he was not asleep when he in fact was (9). Ultimately, he realizes that "there are never any sure signs by means of which being awake can be distinguished from being asleep" (10).

If we collapse all the objection/reply back-and-forth in this section of *Meditation I,* then the argument can fruitfully be represented by the following diagram:

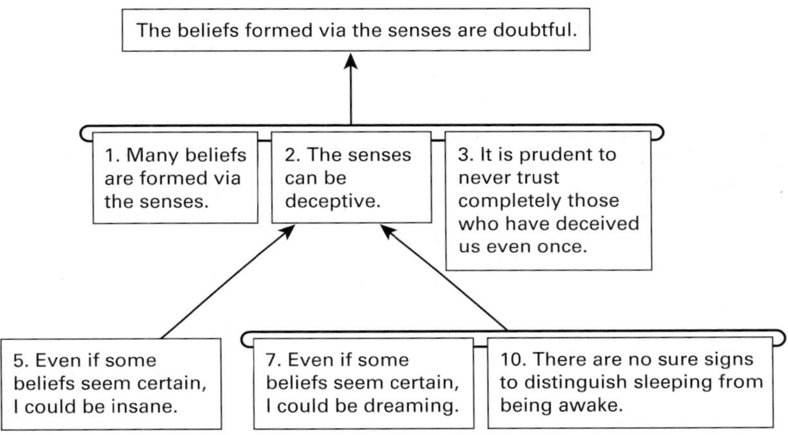

Having finished with this first subargument—that beliefs formed via the senses are doubtful—Descartes considers his beliefs that aren't formed by the senses.

> Suppose then that I am dreaming—it isn't true that I, with my eyes are open, am moving my head and stretching out my hands. Suppose, indeed, that I do not even *have* hands or any body at all. Still, it has to be admitted that the visions that come in sleep are like paintings: they must have been made as copies of real things,[11] so[F] at least these general kinds of things—eyes, head, hands and the body as a whole—must be real and not imaginary.[12] For[G] even when painters try to depict sirens and satyrs with the most extraordinary bodies, they simply jumble up the limbs of different animals,[14] rather than inventing natures that are entirely new.[13] Or[H] if they do succeed in thinking up something completely fictitious and unreal—not remotely like anything ever seen before—at least the colors used in the picture must be real.[15] These are the elements out of which we make all our mental images of things—the true and also the false ones.

In this passage, he first notes that, even if he is sleeping, the things he dreams about have some kind of basis in reality (11). The reason is, as indicated by the "For" (G), that even when painters paint things that aren't real, they must use elements of things that are real, "rather than inventing natures that entirely new" (13),[3] because they just "jumble up the limbs of different animals" (14), or at least use real colors to make new things (15). As indicated by the "Or" (H), claims (14) and (15) seem to be separate reasons to believe (13), since Descartes is implying that even if (14) isn't true, (15) still supports (13). Then, as indicated by the "so"

(F), claim (11), itself supported by claim (13), supports the claim that some general kinds of things, like eyes, heads, and bodies, must be real (12).

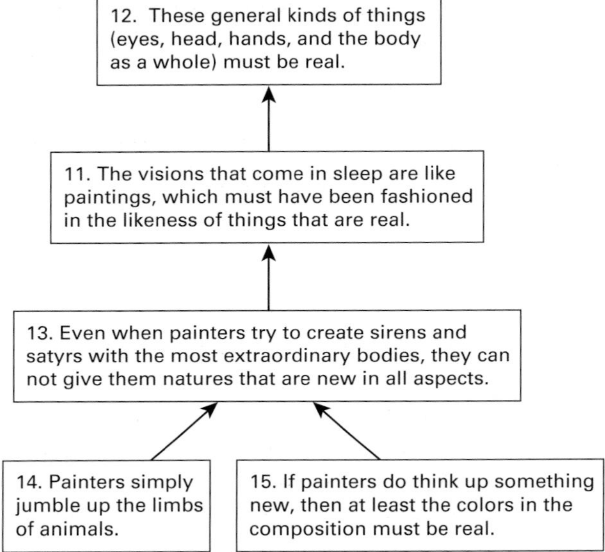

Descartes then moves to an argument that is more abstract than one just about paintings.

By similar reasoning,[I] although these general kinds of things—eyes, head, hands and so on—could be imaginary, it must at least be admitted that[J] certain other even simpler and more universal things are real.[16] These are as it were the real colors from which we form all the images of things, whether true or false, that occur in our thought. These simpler and more universal kinds include *body*, and *extension*; the *shape* of extended things; their *quantity, size* and *number*; the *places* things can be in, the *time* through which they can last, and so on.

So it seems reasonable to conclude that[K] physics, astronomy, medicine, and all other sciences dealing with things that have complex structures are doubtful; while arithmetic, geometry and other studies of the simplest and most general things—whether they really exist in nature or not—contain something certain and indubitable.[17] For whether I am awake or asleep, two plus three makes five, and a square has only four sides.[S] It seems impossible to suspect that such obvious truths might be false.

However,[L] I have for many years been sure that there is an all-powerful God who made me to be the sort of creature that I am.[18] How do I know that he hasn't brought it about that there is no earth, no sky, nothing that takes up space, no shape, no size, no place, while making sure that all these things appear to me to exist?[19] Anyway, I sometimes think that others go wrong even when they think they have the most perfect knowledge; so how do I know that I myself don't go wrong every time I add two and three or count the sides of a square?[20]

As indicated by the phrases "By similar reasoning" (I) and "it must at least be admitted that" (J), this more abstract conclusion is that there are some simple, universal things that must be real (16). And by (K), Descartes takes this to support the claim that disciplines that deal with the simple and universal contain beliefs that are indubitable (17). To illustrate what he means, he gives us the example of 2 plus 3 equaling 5 or a square having four sides, no matter whether he is awake or dreaming (§).

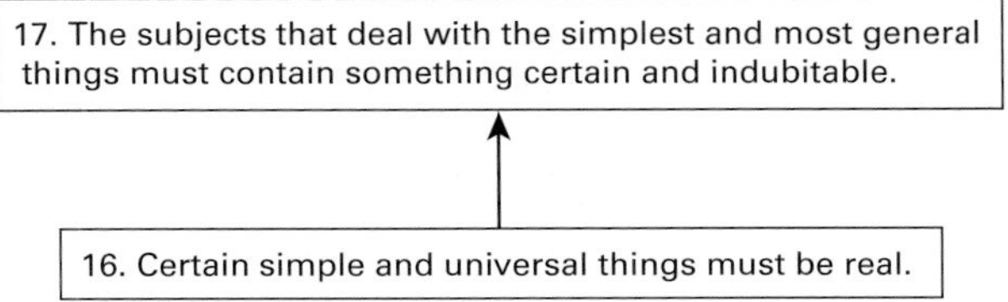

As indicated by "However" (L), though, Descartes doubts his reasoning, and objects to (17) by noting that God could be deceiving him about 2 plus 3 equaling 5 or a square having four sides. He first asserts God's existence and omnipotence (18) and then notes that, seemingly because of this omnipotence, God could have made it the case that nothing is the way it appears to be (19). And because God could have done this, God could have made it the case that 2 plus 3 does not actually equal 5 or that there are not four sides to a square (20).

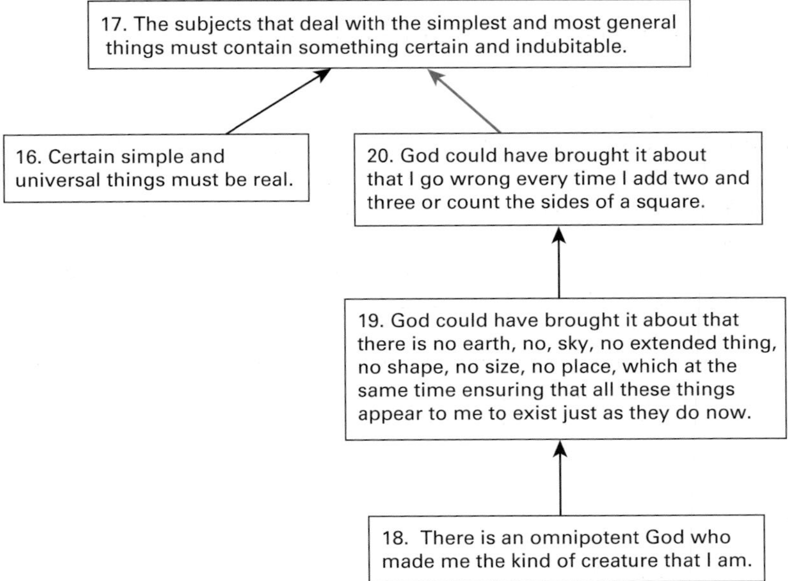

In response to this line of reasoning, Descartes begins his dialogue with himself again:

Well, [you might say],[M] God would not let me be deceived like that,[21] because[N] he is said to be supremely good.[22] But,[O] [I reply], if God's goodness would stop him from letting me be deceived all the time, you would expect it to stop him from allowing me to be deceived even occasionally;[23] yet[P] clearly I sometimes am deceived.[24]

Some people would deny the existence of such a powerful God rather than believe that everything else is uncertain. Let us grant them—for purposes of argument—that there is no God, and theology is fiction. On their view, then, I am a product of fate or chance or a long chain of causes and effects. But the *less* powerful they make my original cause, the *more* likely it is that I am so imperfect as to be deceived all the time—because deception and error seem to be imperfections. Having no answer to these arguments, I am driven back to the position that[Q] *doubts can properly be raised about any of my former beliefs*. I don't reach this conclusion in a flippant or casual manner, but on the basis of powerful and well thought-out reasons. So in future, if I want to discover any certainty, I must withhold my assent from these former beliefs just as carefully as I withhold it from obvious falsehoods.

As indicated by the "Well, [you might say]" (M), Descartes raises an objection to claim (20) based on God's benevolence: God is supremely good (22) and so he would not let Descartes be wrong about arithmetic and geometry (21).

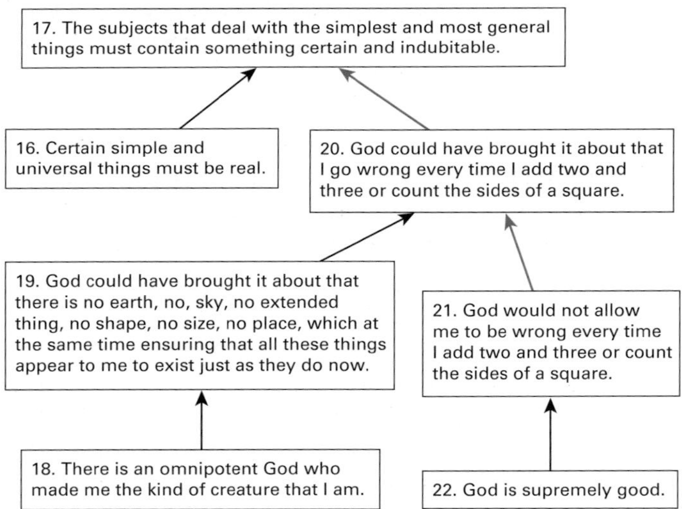

Descartes reasons that if God's goodness somehow prevented him from deceiving Descartes all the time, then his goodness should prevent him from deceiving Descartes some of the time, as well (23). But Descartes is deceived sometimes (24), as he noted at the beginning of this passage. As indicated by the "yet" (P), claims (23) and (24) are meant to be combined to provide an objection to (21).

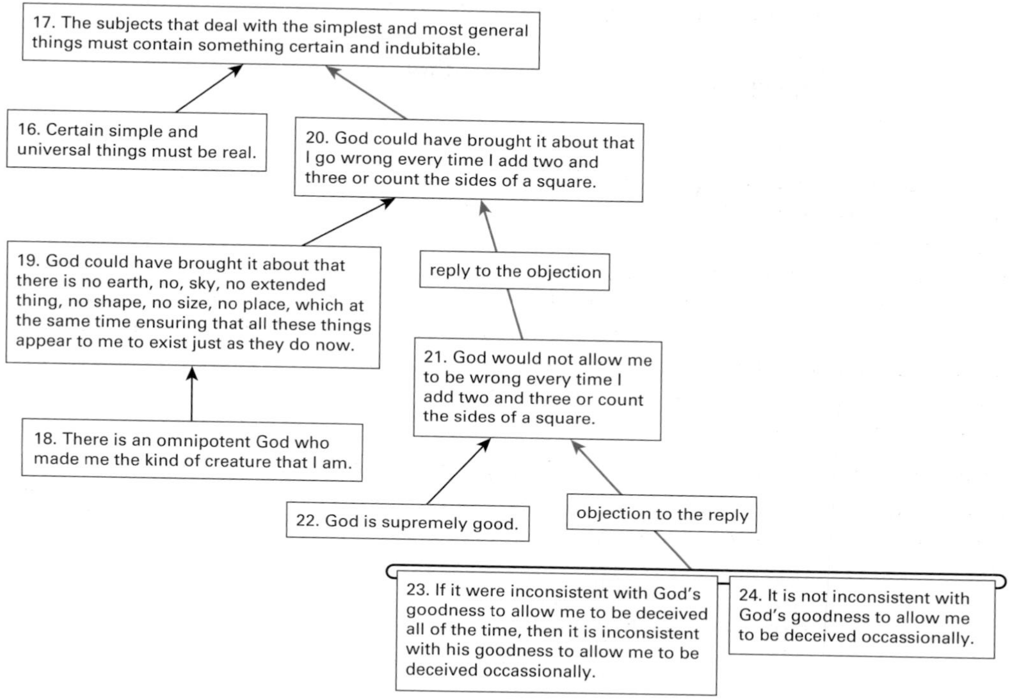

Ultimately, Descartes cannot find a reply to this last objection, and so he is forced to reject claim (17). Then, if we combine this rejection with the first part of the argument and note that, as indicated by his saying that he is "driven back to the position" (Q), his conclusion is that all of his beliefs are doubtful, we can see the two prongs of his argument.

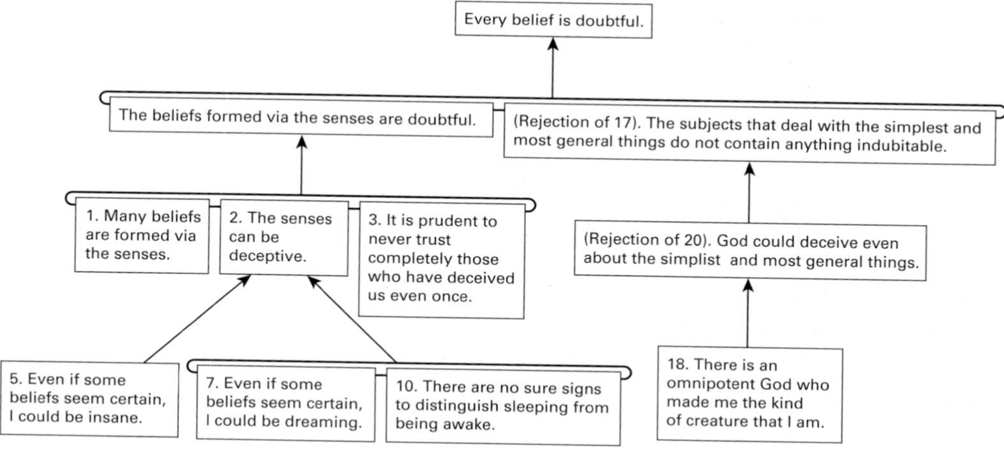

The underlying assumption here is that there are only two sources of beliefs: the senses and the mind. That is, we can sense things about the external world, and we can reason about mathematics. Thus, if we can possibly doubt the beliefs from these two sources, then *all* our beliefs are doubtful.

One objection, then, might be that Descartes hasn't thought of all the possible kinds of belief. Perhaps there are more kinds of beliefs than sensory or mathematical. So he supposes, at the end of the first Meditation, that there is some kind of intelligent being whose purpose is to deceive Descartes about everything he believes. This has come to be known as the *Cartesian evil demon* and is seen as the heart of the method of radical doubt that Descartes employs to establish a basis for his beliefs about the natural world.

The problem now is that Descartes has no basis whatsoever for his beliefs. In *Meditation II*, he again takes up the question of whether there are any beliefs at all that are certain. Let's take a look at that now.

From *Meditations on First Philosophy: Meditation II*.[4]

I will suppose, then, that everything I see is fictitious.[1] I will believe that my memory tells me nothing but lies. I have no senses. Body, shape, extension, movement and place are illusions. So what remains true? Perhaps just the one fact that nothing is certain!

Hopeful: Still, how do I know that there isn't something—not on that list—about which there is no room for even the slightest doubt? Isn't there a God (call him what you will) who gives me the thoughts I am now having?

Doubtful: But why do I think this, since I might myself be the author of these thoughts?

Hopeful: But then doesn't it follow that I am, at least, *something*?

Doubtful: This is very confusing, because I have just said that I have no senses and no body, and I am so bound up with a body and with senses that one would think that I can't exist without them. Now that I have convinced myself that there is nothing in the world—no sky, no earth, no minds, no bodies—does it follow that I don't exist either?[2]

Hopeful: No it does not follow; for[A] if I *convinced myself of something* then I *certainly existed*.[3]

Doubtful: But there is a supremely powerful and cunning deceiver who deliberately deceives me all the time![4]

Hopeful: Even then, if he is deceiving me I undoubtedly exist:[5] let him deceive me all he can, he will never bring it about that *I am nothing* while *I think I am something*. So after thoroughly thinking the matter through I conclude that this proposition,[B] *I am, I exist*, must be true whenever I assert it or think it.[6]

As I have analyzed the argument in *Meditation II*, there are four main parts. The first is the question of the doubtfulness of Descartes's own existence. He comes to the conclusion that he can be certain that he exists, even if he cannot be certain about anything else.

This first argument proceeds as follows. After recounting the events of *Meditation I*, Descartes begins this discussion with the conclusion he previously drew—that he is being deceived about everything and there is nothing in the world (1). He then asks whether, if nothing in the world exists, that means that he does not exist (2). These statements can be seen as working together to support the conclusion that "I do not exist," but, in keeping with Descartes's tendency to write as though he is having a conversation with himself, I represent it here as being an objection to the claim "I exist."

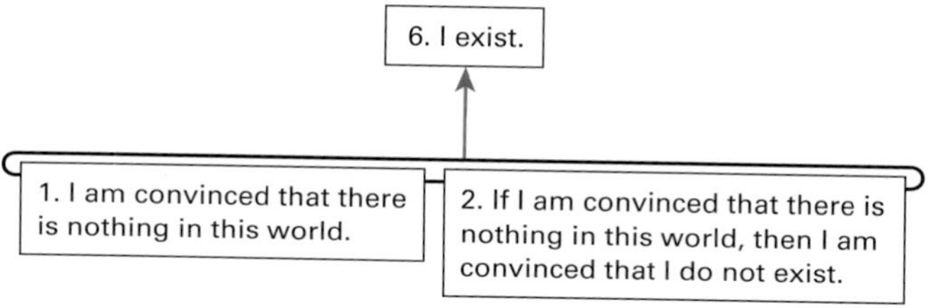

He then replies to his own objection, indicated by (A), that if he is convinced of something, anything, then he must exist, since (and this seems to be only implied) there must be an "I" who is performing the cognitive act of "being convinced of something."

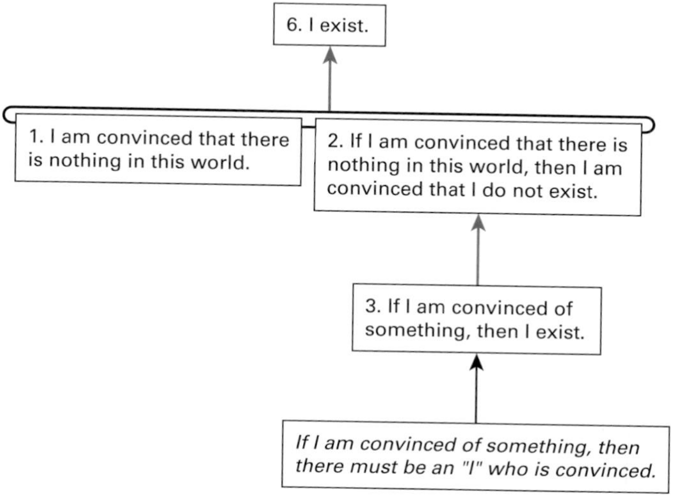

Still, Descartes doubts that he exists, because of his supposition that there is an evil demon deceiving him about everything (4). He counters himself again, though, by pointing out that even if he is being deceived by the evil demon, there still must be an "I" on whom the deception is perpetrated. Thus, this is another reason to believe, even in spite of the possibility of the deceptive evil demon, that he does in fact exist.

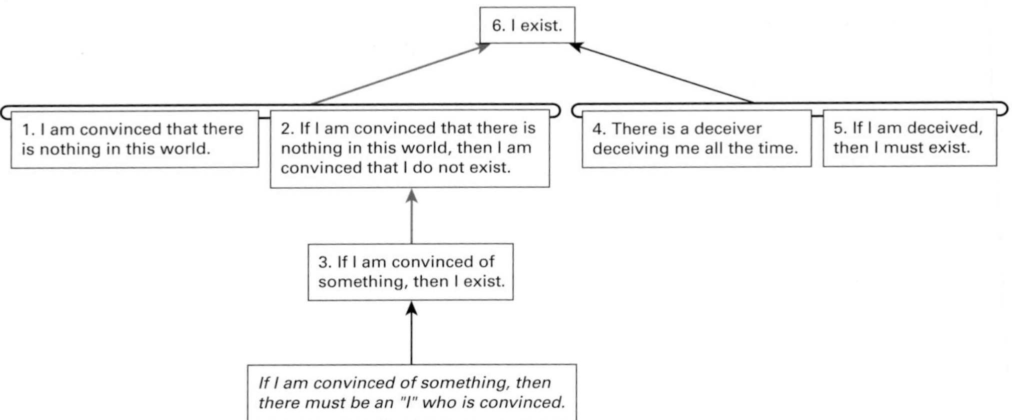

Now that Descartes can be certain that he does exist, the second part of the overall argument is an exploration of what the "I" is that is doing the existing:

But now that I am supposing there is a supremely powerful and malicious deceiver who has set out to trick me in every way he can—*now* what shall I say that I am? Can I *now* claim to have any of the features that I used to think belong to a body? When I think about them really carefully, I find that they are all open to doubt. ... Thinking? At last I have discovered it—thought! This is the one thing that can't be separated from me.[7] I am, I exist—that is certain. But for how long? For as long as I am thinking. But perhaps no longer than that; for it *might* be that if I stopped thinking I would stop existing; and [I have to treat that possibility as though it were actual, because] my present policy is to reject everything that isn't necessarily true. Strictly speaking, then, I am simply a thing that thinks[8]—a mind, or intelligence, or intellect, or reason, these being words whose meaning I have only just come to know. Still, I am a real, existing thing. What kind of a thing? I have answered that: a thinking thing.[9]

What else am I? I will use my imagination to see if I am anything more. I am not that structure of limbs and organs that is called a human body;[10] nor am I a thin vapor that permeates the limbs[11]—a wind, fire, air, breath, or whatever I imagine; for[C] I have supposed all these things to be nothing[12] [because[D] I have supposed all bodies to be nothing].[13] ... I know that I exist, and I am asking: what is this *I* that I know? My knowledge of it can't depend on things of whose existence I am still unaware; so it can't depend on anything that I invent in my imagination. The word "invent" points to what is wrong with relying on my imagination in this matter: if I used imagination to show that I was something or other, that would be mere invention, mere story-telling;[14] for[E] imagining is simply contemplating the shape or image of a bodily thing.[15] That makes imagination suspect,[16] for[F] while I know for sure that I exist, I know that everything relating to the nature of body [including imagination] could be mere dreams;[17] so it would be silly for me to say "I will use my imagination to get a clearer understanding of what I am"—as silly, indeed, as to say "I am now awake, and see some truth; but I shall deliberately fall asleep so as to see even more, and more truly, in my dreams"! If my mind is to get a clear understanding of its own nature, it had better not look to the imagination for it.

Well, then, what am I? A thing that thinks. What is that? A thing that doubts, understands, affirms, denies, wants, refuses, and also imagines and senses.

That is a long list of attributes for me to have—and it really is I who have them all. Why should it not be? Isn't it one and the same "I" who now

doubts almost everything,

understands some things,

affirms this one thing—namely, that I exist and think,

denies everything else,

wants to know more,

refuses to be deceived,

imagines many things involuntarily, and

is aware of others that seem to come from the senses?[#]

Isn't all this just as true as the fact that I exist, even if I am in a perpetual dream, and even if my creator is doing his best to deceive me? These activities are all aspects of my thinking,[18] and[G] are all inseparable from myself.[19] The fact that it is I who doubt and understand and want is so obvious that I can't see how to make it any clearer.

In the above passage, Descartes considers various options for what the "I" is—a body, the vital force, and sense perception. He rejects these because he is still supposing that he is being deceived about having a body, and both the vital force and sense perception depend on having a body.

The answer he accepts is that he is a thing that thinks (8) because it is certain that thinking is the one thing that cannot be separated from the "I" that exists (7). He repeats this claim that he is a thinking thing in (9).

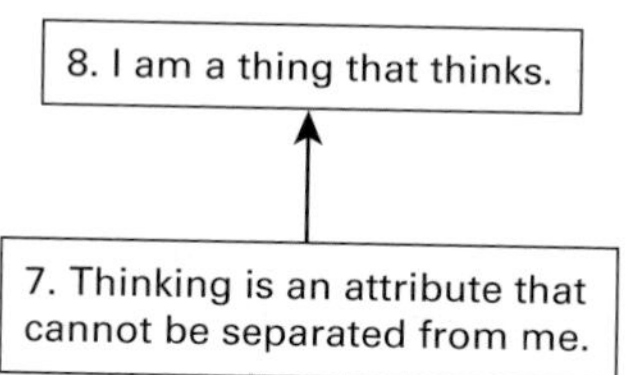

Why does he believe that thinking is something that he cannot separate from himself? He lists examples of all of the cognitive activities of the "I" that exists: doubting, understanding, affirming, denying, wanting, refusing, imagining, and sensing (#). He claims, then, that all of these cognitive activities are part of the more general activity of thinking (16). And, just as in the first subargument, he can be certain he exists when he engages in any of these activities.

Thus, it is these kinds of activities that cannot be separated from him (17). So, the second part of Descartes's argument looks like this:

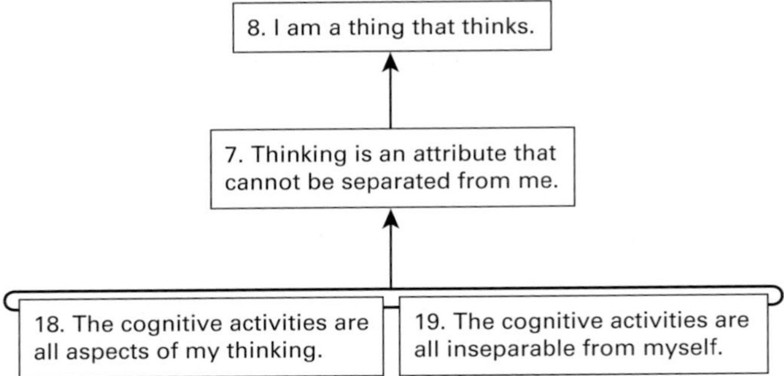

The third part of Descartes's argument comes in between the first two and last two statements in the argument above. Now Descartes wants to show not only that he is a thing that thinks (8), but also that that is all he is—he is nothing other than a thing that thinks. In other words, he wants to show that thinking is the only attribute that cannot be separated from himself. So, he goes back to his original suggestions—body, vital force, and imagination.

He argues that he is neither a body (10) nor a vital force (11). His reasoning begins with the fact that he is supposing that there are no bodies at all (13). This claim supports (10) directly and (11) indirectly because it is implied that one needs a body to have a vital force, and so he is supposing that no vital forces exist (12).

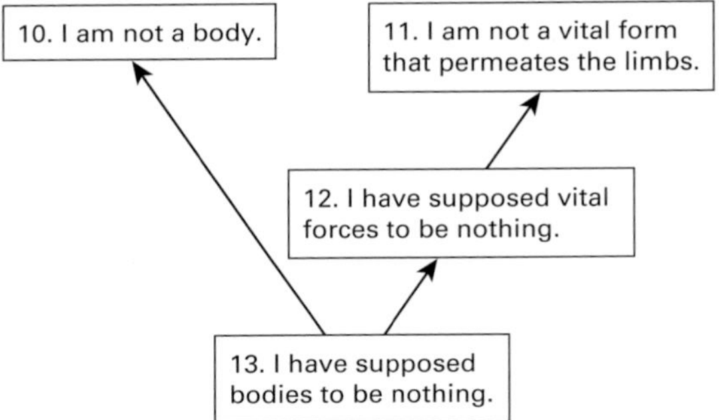

He also, though, wonders if the "I" is not just a thinking thing but also something else that he can show using his imagination. He rejects this too because one can imagine only shapes, colors, and so on—all attributes of bodies. As indicated by the "for" (E), the claim that if he used his imagination, he would only be inventing falsehoods (14) is supported by the claim that when one imagines, one can contemplate only the shape or image of a bodily thing. The next "for" (F) indicates that the claim that he is not something else that he can show in his imagination (16) is supported by what he just said plus the fact that he is supposing that bodily things do not exist.

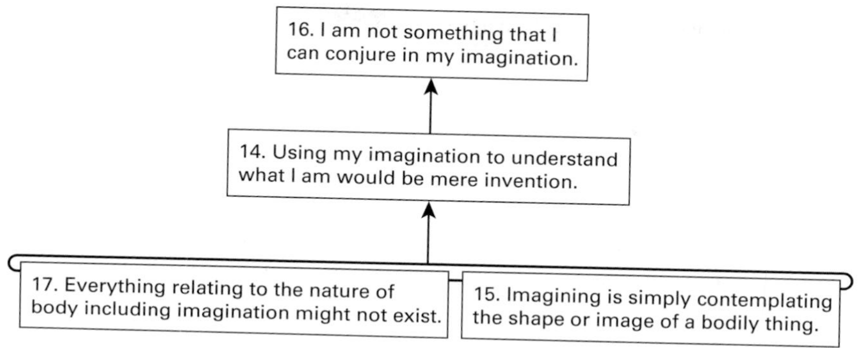

These three subconclusions—(10), (11), and (16)—combine to support the implied claim that Descartes is nothing else other than a thing that thinks.

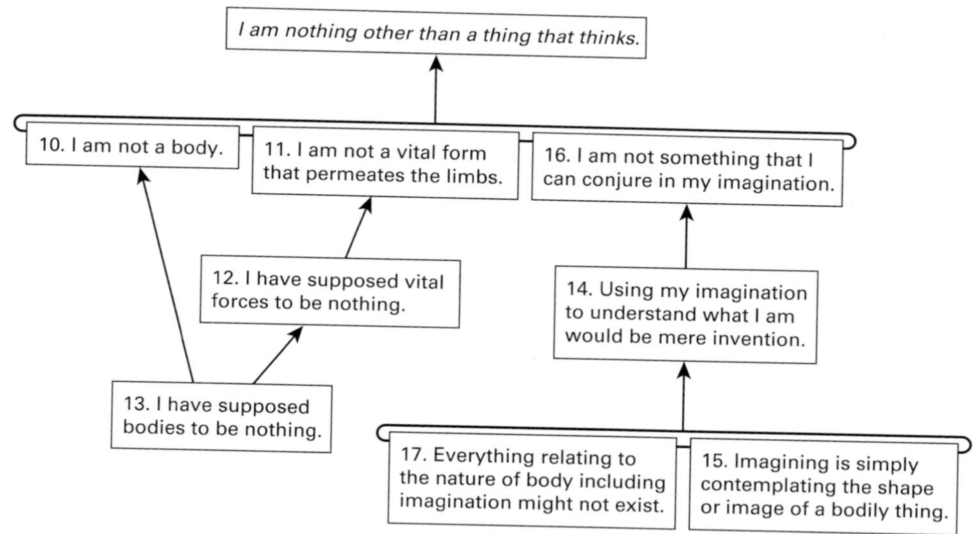

The final part of Descartes's argument amounts to assuring himself that the conclusion that he has drawn—that he is nothing but a thing that thinks—cannot be doubted, unlike all of his other beliefs. In keeping with his style, he presents this last part as a back-and-forth exchange with himself:

All this is starting to give me a better understanding of what I am. But[H] I still can't help thinking that bodies—of which I form mental images and which the senses investigate—are much more clearly known to me than is this puzzling "I" that can't be pictured in the imagination.[20] It would be surprising if this were right, though; for it would be surprising if I had a clearer grasp of things that I realize are doubtful, unknown and foreign to me—[namely, bodies]—than I have of what is true and known—namely my own self. ...

But what am I to say about this mind, or about myself? (So far, remember, I don't admit that there is anything to me *except* a mind.) What, I ask, is this 'I' that seems to perceive the wax so clearly? Surely, I am aware of my own self in a truer and more certain way than I am of the wax, and also in a much more distinct and evident way.[21] What leads me to think that the wax exists—namely, that I see it—leads much more obviously to the conclusion that I exist.[22] What I see might not really be the wax; perhaps I don't even have eyes with which to see anything. But when *I see* or *think I see* (I am not here distinguishing the two), it is simply not possible that I who am now thinking am not *something*.[23] Similarly, that *I exist* follows from the other bases for judging that *the wax exists*—that I touch it, that I imagine it, or any other basis, and similarly for my bases for judging that anything else exists outside me.[24] As I came to perceive the wax more distinctly by applying not just sight and touch but other considerations, all this too contributed to my knowing myself even more distinctly,[25] because[I] whatever goes into my perception of the wax or of any other body must do even more to establish the nature of my own mind.[26] What comes to my mind from bodies, therefore,[J] helps me to know my mind distinctly;[27] yet[K] all of that pales into insignificance—it is hardly worth mentioning—when compared with what my mind contains *within itself* that enables me to know it distinctly.[28]

See! With no effort I have reached the place where I wanted to be! I now know that[L] even bodies are perceived not by the senses or by imagination but by the intellect alone, not through their being touched or seen but through their being understood;[29] and this helps me to understand that[M] I can perceive my own mind more easily and clearly than I can anything else.[30] Since the grip of old opinions is hard to shake off, however, I want to pause and meditate for a while on this new knowledge of mine, fixing it more deeply in my memory.

In spite of his previous subargument, as indicated by (H), he claims that it still seems that it is easier to know what physical objects (corporeal things) really are than to know who the "I" really is (20).

20. Corporeal things are known much more distinctly than that obscure part of me which does not come under the imagination.

He wants to provide a compelling response to this statement, and this is the impetus for launching into the example of the wax. Ultimately, the wax example is supposed to have two purposes. First, Descartes wants to demonstrate that real knowledge of the wax (which is a corporeal thing) is gained not through the senses or the imagination, but only by pure reason. Second, the wax is supposed to be analogous to the "I" that Descartes is trying to understand, so that if he does really understand the wax through pure reason, then if he understands the "I," it will be through pure reason alone.

First, Descartes claims that he has a better understanding of the "I" than he has of the wax (21). The reason he gives is that even if the wax doesn't exist, the fact that he senses it proves that he exists (23). The reasons for this and that seeing the wax is a cognitive activity, which proves that he exists (22), and touching and imagining the wax are also cognitive activities, which prove that he exists (24).

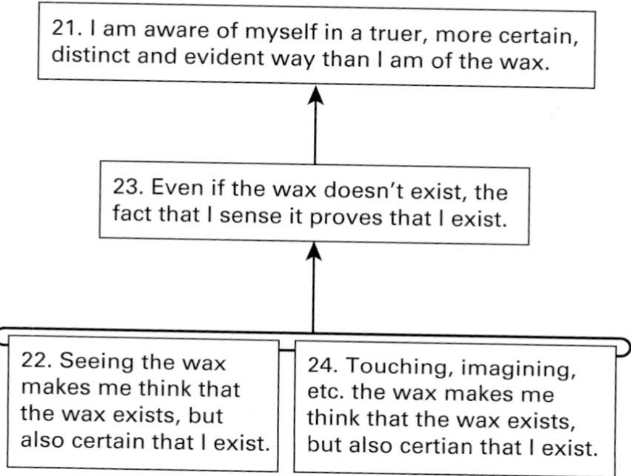

21. I am aware of myself in a truer, more certain, distinct and evident way than I am of the wax.
23. Even if the wax doesn't exist, the fact that I sense it proves that I exist.
22. Seeing the wax makes me think that the wax exists, but also certain that I exist.
24. Touching, imagining, etc. the wax makes me think that the wax exists, but also certian that I exist.

Next, he considers the previous claim that he comes to truly know the wax not through the senses, but through pure reason. He then claims that the pure reason that enables him to know the wax contributes to his ability to know his own mind (25). Indicated by the "because" (I), the reason he gives is that whatever he does to understand the wax establishes the nature of his own mind (26). As indicated by the "therefore" (J), these claims support the further claim that his understanding of corporeal bodies, in general, helps him to understand his own mind (27).

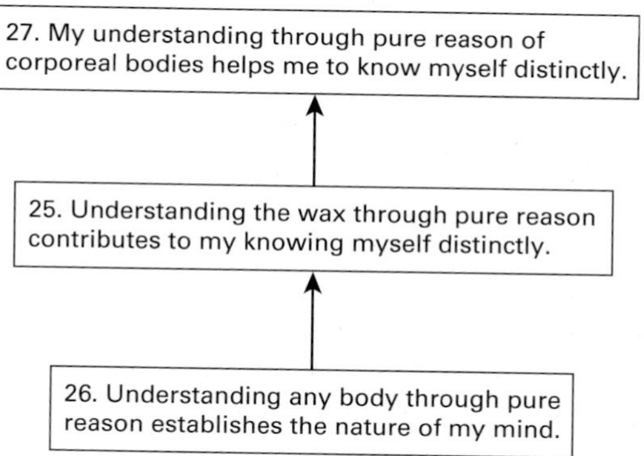

The upshot of Descartes's argument in this passage is that both his sense perception and his understanding through pure reason of the wax enable him to know that he exists.

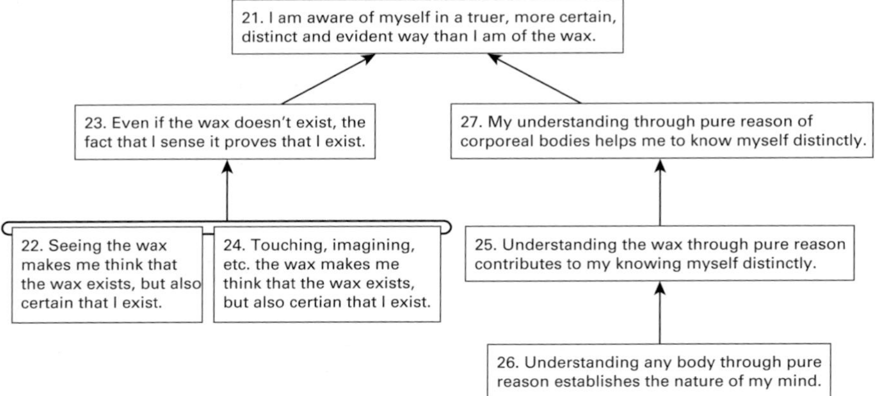

On the other hand, as indicated by the "yet" (K), he says that within his mind is a far greater ability to understand itself than is afforded by his perception and understanding of the wax (28). Here Descartes is relying on the analogy between his mind and the wax. Even without contemplating any corporeal bodies, if he goes through the same steps he went through to understand the wax but this time to understand his mind, he can come to know the "I" that certainly exists clearly and distinctly. This is the argument that he lays out in the last paragraph. As indicated by (L), the example of the wax supports the claim that corporeal bodies are truly understood through pure reason alone (29). This fact, along with the considerations of the previous paragraph, supports his claim, as indicated by (M), that there is nothing easier for Descartes to know than his own mind (30).

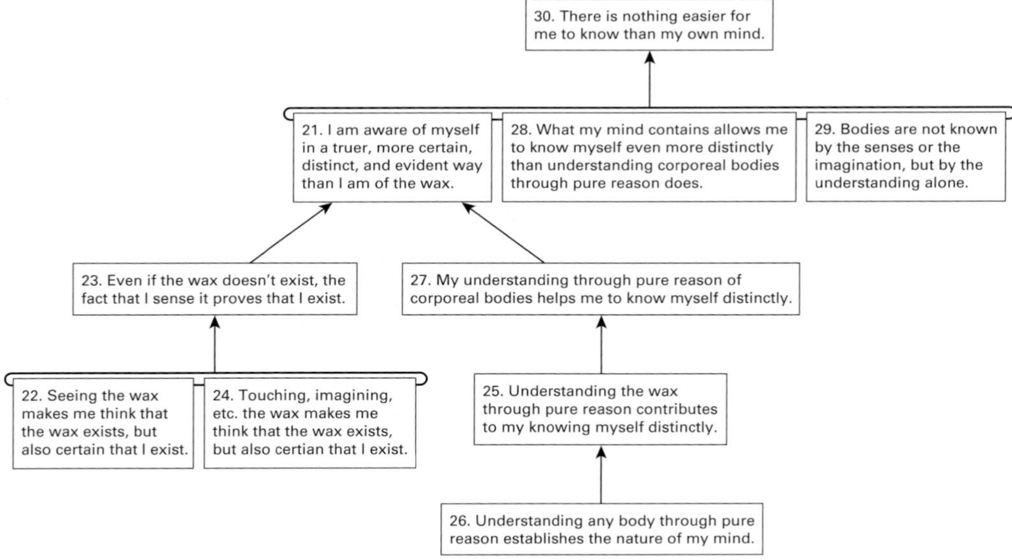

This, then, is the response to claim (20) that Descartes set out to find, which ultimately means that he cannot be wrong about his claim that he is nothing but a thing that thinks. This is because (20) was originally posed as a possible objection to the claim that he can't be wrong.

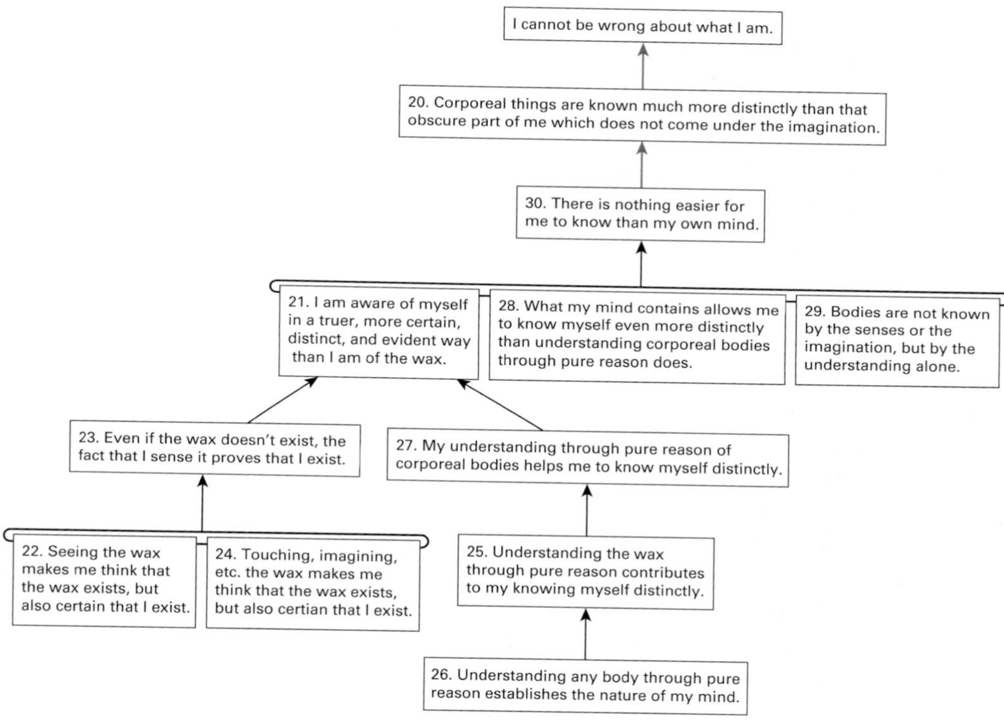
I cannot be wrong about what I am.
20. Corporeal things are known much more distinctly than that obscure part of me which does not come under the imagination.
30. There is nothing easier for me to know than my own mind.
21. I am aware of myself in a truer, more certain, distinct, and evident way than I am of the wax.
28. What my mind contains allows me to know myself even more distinctly than understanding corporeal bodies through pure reason does.
29. Bodies are not known by the senses or the imagination, but by the understanding alone.
23. Even if the wax doesn't exist, the fact that I sense it proves that I exist.
27. My understanding through pure reason of corporeal bodies helps me to know myself distinctly.
22. Seeing the wax makes me think that the wax exists, but also certain that I exist.
24. Touching, imagining, etc. the wax makes me think that the wax exists, but also certian that I exist.
25. Understanding the wax through pure reason contributes to my knowing myself distinctly.
26. Understanding any body through pure reason establishes the nature of my mind.

So where do we stand now? Let's put all four parts of Descartes's argument in *Mediation II* together:

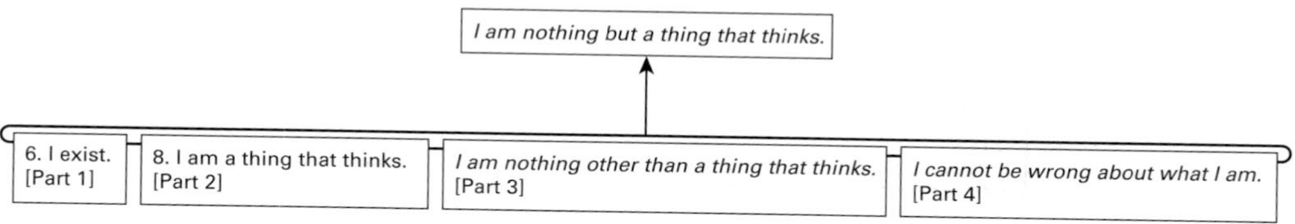
I am nothing but a thing that thinks.
6. I exist. [Part 1]
8. I am a thing that thinks. [Part 2]
I am nothing other than a thing that thinks. [Part 3]
I cannot be wrong about what I am. [Part 4]

More of Descartes's arguments in the *Meditations* are explored in the exercises.

8.2 John Locke, *An Essay Concerning Human Understanding*

John Locke (1632–1704) was born in England, near Bristol, to Puritan parents. His father was a lawyer and served in the Parliamentary forces during the English Civil War, which eventually contributed to Locke's views in political philosophy, as did his close association with Anthony Ashley Cooper. Locke trained in both philosophy and medicine at Oxford, and was awarded degrees in both. His most famous philosophical works are *An Essay Concerning Human Understanding* and *Two Treatises on Government*, both published in 1690. These works distinguished him as the first of the great English empiricists and the father of classical liberalism, respectively.

Locke's interactions with the great scientists of his time (although they were called *natural philosophers* back then)—Robert Boyle, Thomas Willis, and Robert Hooke—also influenced him greatly. In his *Essay*, Locke argues against philosophers like Descartes who believe that knowledge of reality is fundamentally grounded in our reason and innate ideas; instead, he argues that it is experience that provides the grounding for this knowledge. In *Meditation III*, for example, Descartes uses the claim that people have an innate idea of God as a premise in his argument that God would not allow us to be constantly deceived by the evil demon. In the following section of the *Essay*, Locke argues that people do not have innate ideas, although he uses the example of some logical principles instead of the idea of God.

Let's look at Locke's argument against the innatists (those who believe that we are born with innate ideas) in more detail. Specifically, we will analyze and diagram the argument found in Book I, chapter 2, sections 1–5 of the *Essay*. Arguments that Locke provides later in the *Essay* for his positive theory of the origins of knowledge will be explored in the exercises.

From *An Essay Concerning Human Understanding*.[5]

1. … I shall present the reasons that made me *doubt the truth of the innateness doctrine*. That will be my excuse for my mistake, if that's what it is. Whether it is a mistake can be decided by those who are willing, as I am, to welcome truth wherever they find it.

2. Nothing is more commonly taken for granted than that[A] certain principles, both speculative [= "having to do with what is the case"] and practical [= "having to do with morality, or what *ought to be* the case"] are accepted by all mankind.[1] Some people have argued that because[B] these principles are (they think) universally accepted,[2] they must have been stamped onto the souls of men from the outset.[3]

3. This argument from universal consent has a defect in it.[C] Even if it were in fact true that all mankind agreed in accepting certain truths, that wouldn't prove them to be innate if universal agreement could be explained in some other way;[4] and[D] I think it can.[5]

4. Worse still,[E] this *argument from universal acceptance* which is used to prove that there are innate principles can be turned into a proof that there are none;[6] because[F] there aren't any principles to which all mankind give universal assent.[7] I shall begin with speculative principles, taking as my example those much vaunted logical principles "Whatever is, is" and "It is impossible for the same thing to be and not to be," which are the most widely thought to be innate. They are so firmly and generally believed to be accepted by everyone in the world that it may be thought strange that anyone should question this. Yet

I am willing to say that these propositions, far from being accepted by everyone, have never even been heard of by a great part of mankind.[8]

First Locke explains the most common argument for innate principles. In this argument, as indicated by (A), it is stipulated that certain principles are universally accepted (1). That is, there are certain principles that every human being acknowledges to be true. This claim is repeated in (2), when it is then taken, as indicated by (B), to support the claim that these principles are innate (3). Locke likens this innateness to the image of certain principles being imprinted on the soul, or the mind, before a person is born. Here is this basic "argument from universal acceptance":

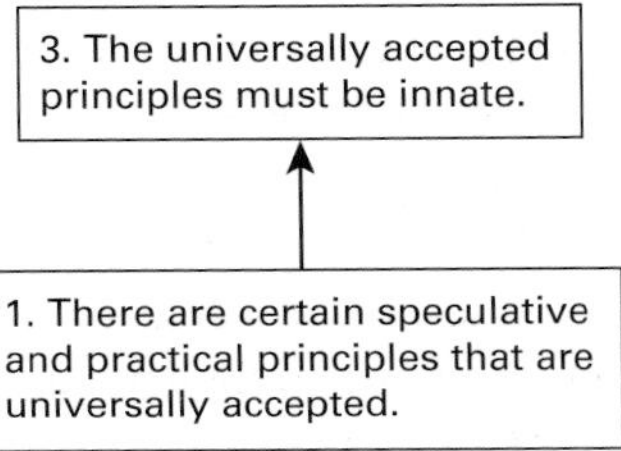

Locke wants to argue that this is a bad argument, and he proposes two ways to do this. First, one could argue that even if the premise were true, it doesn't support the conclusion. Here Locke seems to be implying that the argument from universal acceptance is an *abductive* argument—an inference to the best explanation. That is, proponents of the argument think that the best explanation of the fact that there are principles that everyone accepts is that everyone is born knowing them.

So, Locke argues, if there is a better explanation of this fact, then there would be no good reason to think that the principles are innate. This avenue for criticizing the argument from universal acceptance is indicated by (C). The first claim is that if universal agreement could be explained in some other way, then it would not prove innateness (4). As indicated by (D), this claim is to be combined with the claim that, in fact, Locke can explain it in another way (5), to object to the conclusion drawn in the argument:

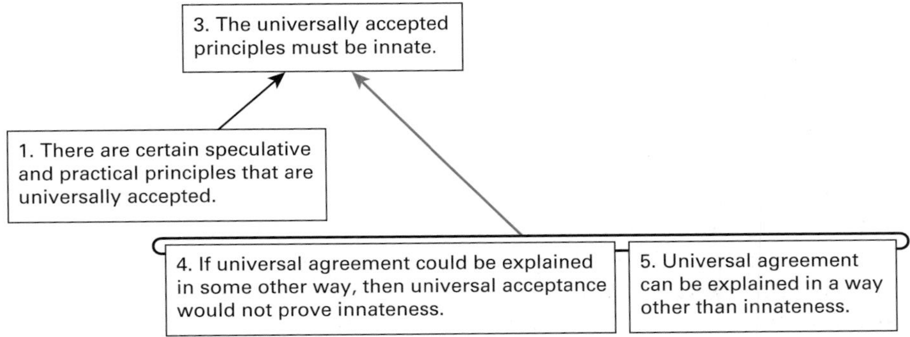

Before telling us what this alternative explanation is, Locke explores a second way one could show that this argument is defective, as indicated by (E). Here, Locke says that regardless of whether the premise supports the conclusion, the argument is bad, as indicated by (F), because the premise is false—there aren't any principles that are universally accepted (7).

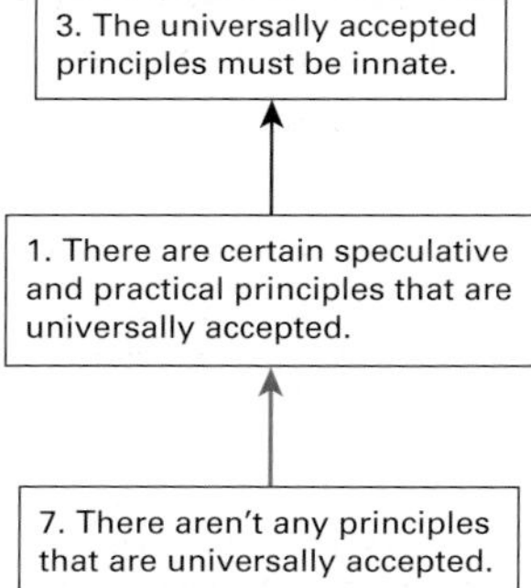

Locke's reason for believing that they not universally accepted is that a lot of people have never even contemplated these principles (8)—children and idiots,[6] for example (9).

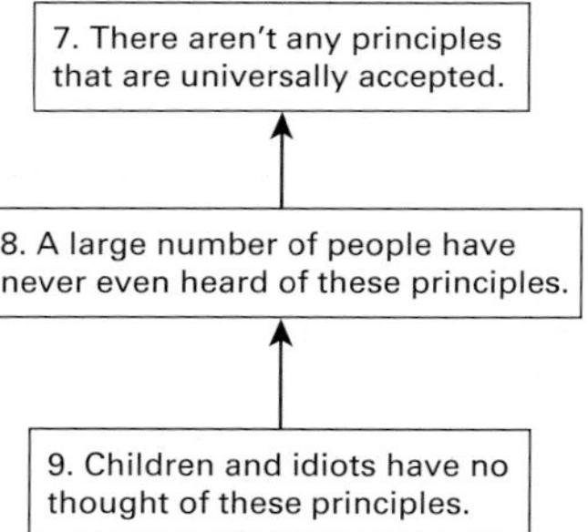

7. There aren't any principles that are universally accepted.
8. A large number of people have never even heard of these principles.
9. Children and idiots have no thought of these principles.

Locke then gives us an argument that since there are some people who don't know anything of these principles, they cannot be innate or "imprinted on the soul":

> 5. Children and idiots have no thought—not an inkling—of these principles,[9] and that fact alone is enough to destroy the universal assent that there would have to be for any truth that was genuinely innate. For[G] it seems to me nearly a contradiction to say that there are truths imprinted on the soul that it doesn't perceive or understand[10]—because[H] if "imprinting" means anything it means making something be perceived:[11] to imprint anything on the mind without the mind's perceiving it seems to me hardly intelligible.[12] So[I] if children and idiots have souls, minds, with those principles imprinted on them, they can't help perceiving them and assenting to them.[13] Since[J] they don't do that,[14] it is evident that[K] the principles are not innately impressed upon their minds.[15]

As indicated by (G), this argument begins with the claim that it is a contradiction to say that there are truths imprinted on the soul that the soul doesn't perceive or understand (10). As indicated by (H), this is supported by the fact that "imprinting" just means "making something be perceived" (11). So, talking about imprinting without perceiving is unintelligible (12), which is a restatement of (10).

As indicated by (I), this subargument supports the claim that if children and idiots had souls with these principles imprinted on them, then they would perceive and assent to them (13). As indicated by (J), this premise combines with the fact that children do not perceive and assent to these principles (14), which is a restatement of (9), to support the claim that these principles are not imprinted on the souls of children and idiots (15). Thus, the principles are not universally accepted.

This final argument in this section can be diagrammed as:

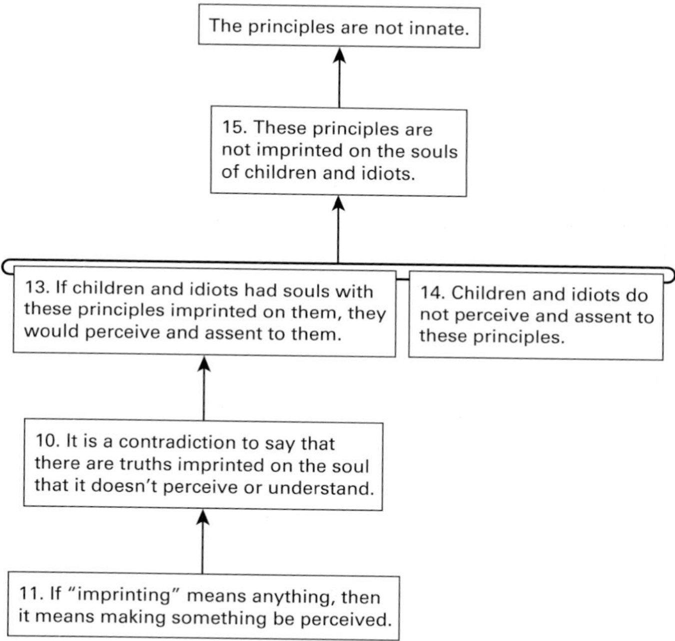

At the beginning of Book II of the *Essay* (chapter 1, section 1), Locke goes back to his first line of argument, attempting to show that there is another explanation of the fact that so many people have the same ideas:

Chapter 1: Ideas in General, and Their Origin

…

5. … When we have taken a full survey of the ideas we get from these sources, and of their various modes, combinations, and relations, we shall find they are our whole stock of ideas;[1] and [so][A] we have nothing in our minds that didn't come in one of these two ways.[2]

6. If you look carefully at the state of a new-born child, you will find little reason to think that he is well stocked with ideas that are to be the matter of his future knowledge.[3] He gets ideas gradually;[4]

and though the ideas of obvious and familiar qualities imprint themselves before the memory begins to keep a record of when or how, ideas of unusual qualities are different. Some of them come so late that most people can remember when they first had them.[5] And[B] if we had reason to, we could arrange for a child to be brought up in such a way as to have very few ideas, even ordinary ones, until he had grown to manhood.[6] In actuality children are born into the world surrounded by bodies that perpetually affect them so as to imprint on their minds a variety of ideas: light and colours are busy everywhere, as long as the eyes are open; sounds and some tangible qualities engage the senses appropriate to them, and force an entrance into the mind. But I think it will be readily admitted that[C] if a child were kept in a place where he never saw any other but black and white till he was a man, he would have no ideas of scarlet or green[7]—any more than a person has an idea of the taste of oysters or of pineapples if he has never actually tasted either.

In the sections 2–4 of Book II, chapter 1, Locke proposes his theory of the mind as a blank slate (*tabula rasa*) at birth—here he calls it "white paper." Our minds do get imprinted with ideas, but only after we begin to have sensations and reflections. The sensations are our direct perceptual experiences like color, texture, temperature, softness, and so on. The reflections are the result of the operation of our minds on our sensations, and here we get the ideas of perception, thinking, willing, and the like. Thus, all of our ideas come from *observation*—either of the external world (sensation) or of the internal world of our minds (reflection).

But why should we believe his theory, rather than the theory of the innatists? The main argument comes in two parts in sections 5 and 6. In the first part, Locke says that we can tell just by reflecting on our own ideas that they all come from sensation or reflection (1), and so there isn't anything in our minds that doesn't come from sensation or reflection (2). As indicated by (A), statement (1) supports statement (2).

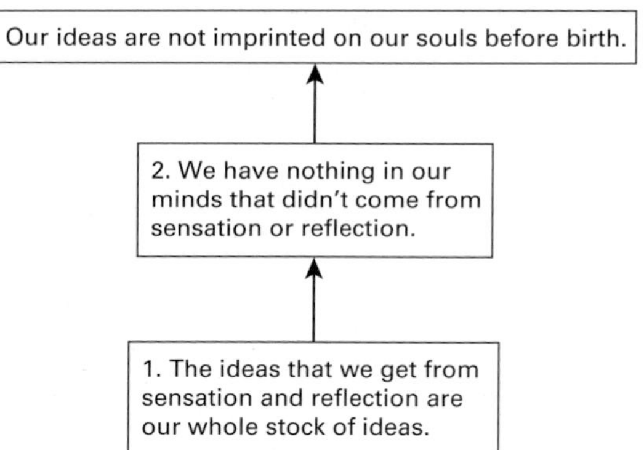

The second part of the argument comes from considering the development of a child from birth to adulthood. First, children get their ideas gradually (4). Second, some ideas of unusual qualities come so late in life that most people can remember when they first had them (5). Finally, we could arrange it so that a child could get even usual ideas, like color, late in life as well (6). The reason, Locke says, for (6) is that it is obvious that if a child were kept in a place where he did not see any colors but black and white until he was grown, then he would have no ideas of colors like scarlet or green (7).

As indicated by (B), and the fact that these three statements are about three different kinds of situations, (4), (5), and (6) are three separate reasons to believe (3), which in turn supports the previous claim that our ideas are not imprinted on our souls before birth.

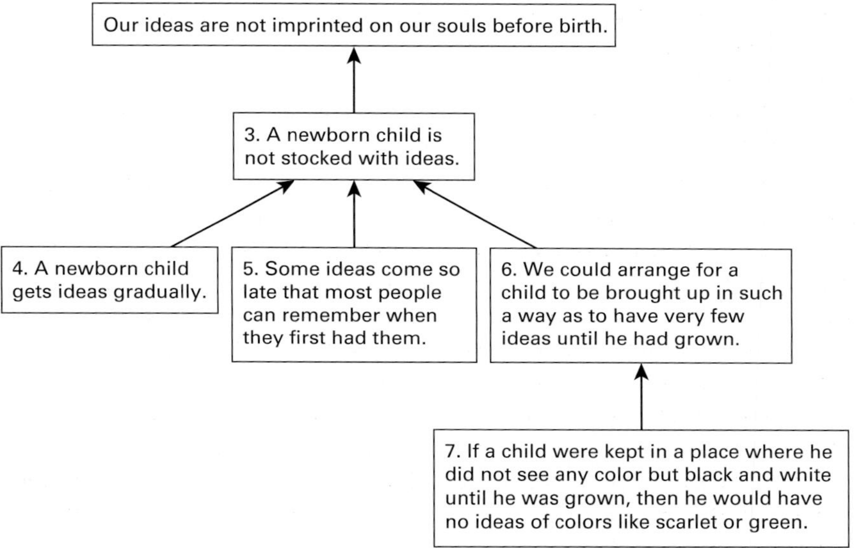

The whole argument in this section looks like this:

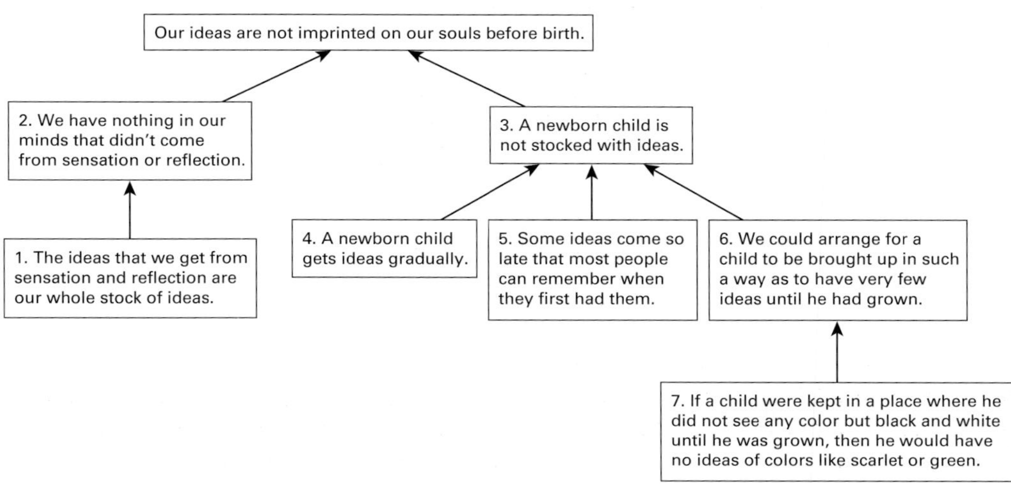

In the next sections of his *Essay*, Locke explains what the innatists might say in reply to the arguments in sections 1–5. These arguments are explored in the exercises.

8.3 David Hume, *An Enquiry Concerning Human Understanding*

We are familiar with David Hume from chapter 6. Here we will be considering one of his greatest philosophical works: *An Enquiry Concerning Human Understanding* (1748). As a young man, Hume moved to France and studied the famous French philosophers Descartes and Malebranche, among others. Over the course of four years, Hume wrote his first major philosophical work, *A Treatise on Human Nature*. It was a comprehensive tome, covering everything from ethics to epistemology. Hume moved back to England in 1737 to publish it, editing out many sections to please his benefactor, Bishop Butler. After it was published (in three volumes, 1739–1740), Hume was very disappointed with its reception among English intellectuals. Nevertheless the publication of the *Treatise* cemented Hume's reputation as an atheist and skeptic.

A decade later, Hume wrote a second comprehensive philosophical essay, reworking some of the material from the *Treatise* and adding more. He published this work in two volumes: *An Enquiry Concerning Human Understanding* (1748) and *An Enquiry Concerning the Principles of Morals* (1751). In the former, Hume describes what has become known as the *problem of induction*. He couches this problem in terms of knowledge of causes, but it can be broadly understood as presenting a problem for any kind of empirical inquiry. Here, we will be concerned with section 4, parts 1 and 2, of *An Enquiry Concerning Human Understanding*.

Both Descartes and Hume are skeptics—they are questioning the justification of our beliefs, especially scientific beliefs. Hume, though, wanted to distinguish his own form of skepticism from Descartes's; he labeled Descartes's attitude *antecedent skepticism* and his own *consequent skepticism*. Descartes was concerned to doubt every belief (including those formed from our senses) that does not have antecedent infallibility (i.e., is not a priori certain). Once Descartes convinced himself that certain of his sense beliefs were reliable, he was happy to conclude that scientific beliefs are justified. Hume, on the other hand, believes that we need not be skeptical of the beliefs formed by our senses, for we can correct them through reason. Rather, Hume is skeptical about what we can do with those beliefs—what we are justified in believing based on those beliefs. Hume, then, is still worried about our scientific beliefs, especially those that are generalizations (e.g., "All objects fall to the earth at a rate of 9.8 m/s2") or are used to predict what will happen in the future (e.g., "The next solar eclipse visible from the United States mainland will happen on August 21, 2017).

Let's look at Hume's text in more detail. Specifically, we will analyze and diagram the argument, and then discuss criticisms of it.

From *An Enquiry Concerning Human Understanding.*[7]

Sceptical Doubts Part I

I venture to assert, as true without exception, that *knowledge about causes is never acquired through a priori reasoning, and always comes from our experience of finding that particular objects are constantly associated with one other*. [When Hume is discussing cause and effect, his word "object" often covers *events* as well as *things*.] ...

If you are not yet convinced that absolutely[A] all the laws of nature and operations of bodies can be known only by experience,[1] consider the following. If we are asked to say what the effects will be of some object, without consulting past experience of it, how can the mind go about doing this? It must invent or imagine some event as being the object's effect;[2] and[B] clearly this invention must be entirely arbitrary.[3] The mind can't possibly find the effect in the supposed cause,[4] however carefully we examine it, for[C] the effect is totally different from the cause[5] and therefore[D] can never be discovered in it.[6]

First, Hume argues that causal knowledge is always a posteriori knowledge, and his main conclusion in this section is that "knowledge of cause and effect is obtained by the experience of constant conjunction." The constant conjunction Hume is talking about here is the experience we have of a cause always and necessarily being accompanied by or followed by its effect.

As indicated by (A), the main reason Hume gives in support of this main conclusion is that we can come to know the laws of nature (especially laws of causes and effect) only through our experiences (1). The reasons given are that, without consulting any of our past experiences, we would only be able to guess what the effect of a cause is (2), and (B) this guess would just be completely arbitrary (3).

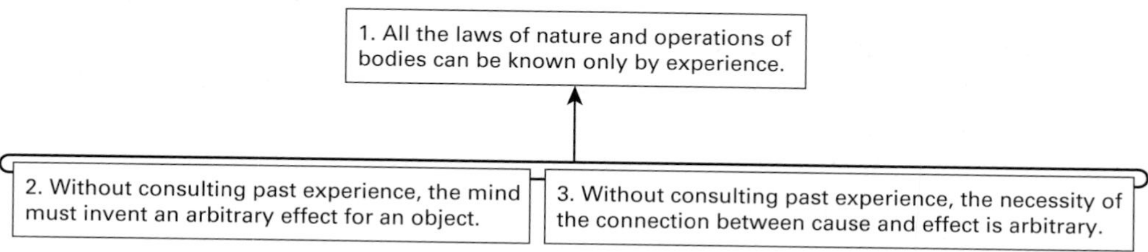

The reason given for (2) is that we can't just inspect an object (the cause) and figure out what its effect is going to be without consulting past experience (4), because effects are totally different from their causes (5). For example, if we have an object like a baseball, we can't know that it will break a window without having had experience with objects breaking glass in the past. For all we know, baseballs interact with windows like foam balls do. The conclusion from (5), that the effect can't be discovered in the cause (6), is a restatement of (4).

So, this part of the argument is about trying to figure out what might follow the cause, and we can represent it as:

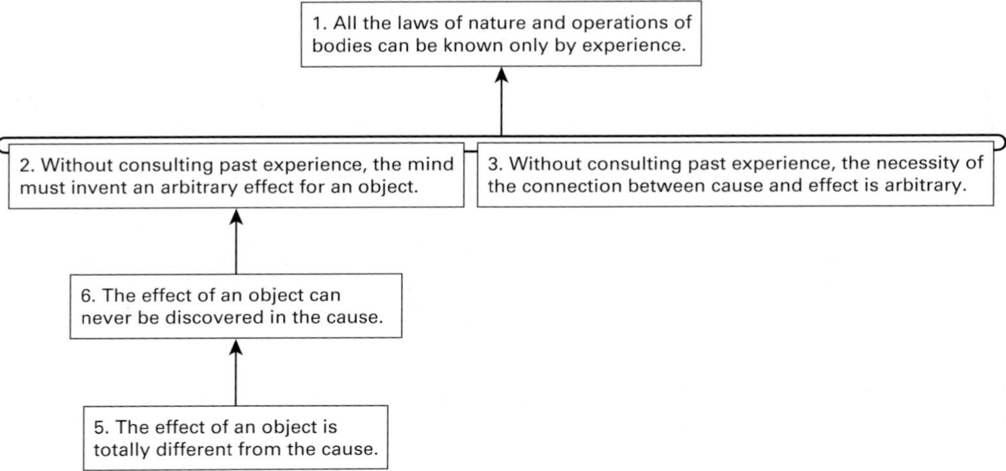

The other part of the argument is about discovering a necessary link between a cause and its effect:

> Just as the first imagining or inventing of a particular effect is arbitrary if it isn't based on experience, the same holds for the supposed tie or connection between cause and effect—the tie that binds them together and makes it impossible for that cause to have any effect but that one.[7] Suppose for example that I see one billiard ball moving in a straight line towards another: even if the contact between them should happen to suggest to me the idea of motion in the second ball, aren't there a hundred different events that I can conceive might follow from that cause? May not both balls remain still? May not the first bounce straight back the way it came, or bounce off in some other direction? All these suppositions are consistent and conceivable. Why then should we prefer just one, which is no more consistent or conceivable than the rest?[#] Our a priori reasonings will never reveal any basis for this preference.[8]

In particular, event 1 might be followed by event 2, but how do we know whether event 1 caused event 2? For example, the barometer reading going down is followed by a storm; but does the barometer cause storms? No, the dropping ambient pressure causes the barometer to drop, and causes the storm to develop. So, there's no necessary connection between barometers and storms—if your barometer is broken and never drops, that doesn't mean that storms will never form. This causal connection is the necessity that Hume is considering.

Hume claims that even if we had a potential effect to consider, without consulting past experience, we can't be sure that there is a necessary connection between the cause and that effect; that is, we can't be sure that the effect will be *that* one, as opposed to another one (7).

After the example with the billiard balls (#), Hume claims that the reason we can't do this without consulting experience is that a priori reasoning won't work (8).

We can represent this part of the argument as:

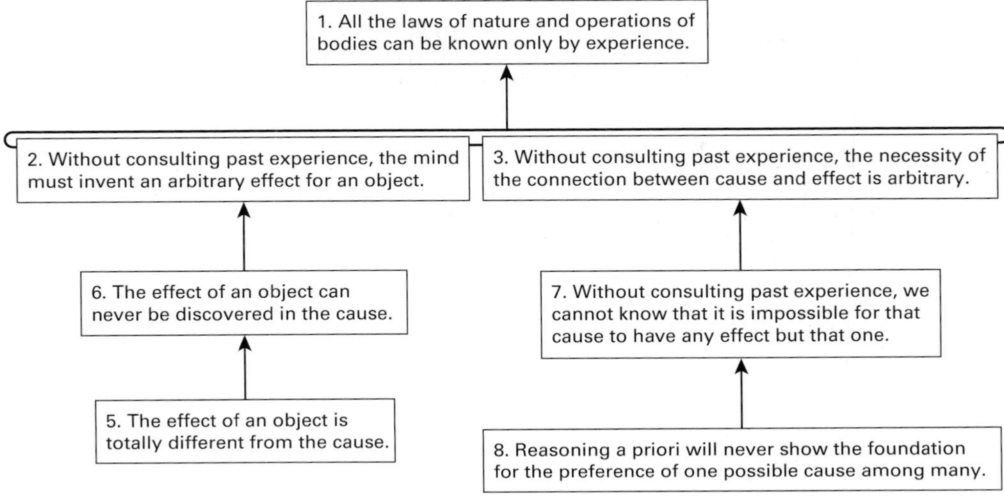

And then the whole argument looks like this:

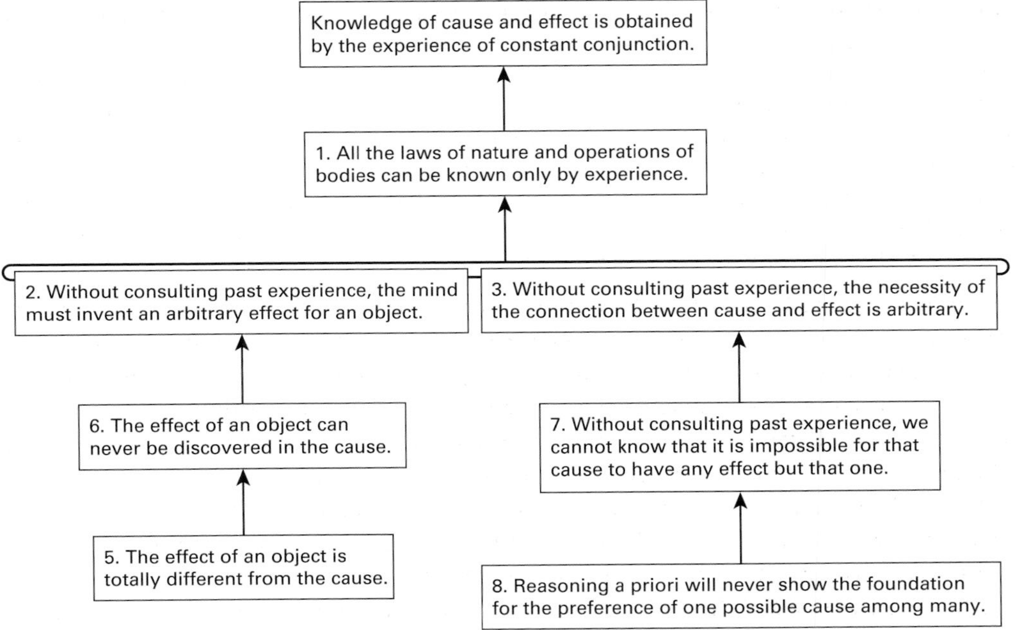

Now, Hume takes the conclusion of the argument in the previous section to argue for his ultimate conclusion: that our knowledge of cause and effect is unjustified. The reason is that our knowledge of cause and effect is obtained by the experience of constant conjunction, but our conclusions based on constant conjunction are not founded on reason:

Sceptical Doubts Part II

In this section I shall settle for something easy, offering only a negative answer to the question I have raised about what inferences from experience are based on. It is this: even after we have experience of the operations of cause and effect, *the conclusions we draw from that experience are not based on reasoning or on any process of the understanding*. I shall try to explain and defend this answer.

It must be granted that nature has kept us at a distance from all its secrets, and has allowed us to know only a few superficial qualities of objects, concealing from us the powers and energies on which the influence of the objects entirely depends. Our senses tell us about the color, weight and consistency of bread; but neither the senses nor reason can ever tell us about the qualities that enable bread to nourish a human body. Sight or touch gives us an idea of the *motion* of bodies; but as for the amazing *force* that keeps a body moving for ever unless it collides with other bodies—we cannot have the remotest conception of that. Despite this ignorance of natural powers and principles, however, we always assume that the same sensible qualities [= "qualities that can be seen or felt or heard, etc."] will have the same secret powers,[1] and[A] we expect them to have the same effects that we have found them to have in our past experience.[2] If we are given some stuff with the color and consistency of bread that we have eaten in the past, we don't hesitate to repeat the experiment of eating it, confidently expecting it to nourish and support us. That is what we do every morning at the breakfast table: confidently experimenting with bread-like stuff by eating it! ... The bread that I formerly ate nourished me; that is, a body with such and such sensible qualities did at that time have such and such secret powers. But does it follow that other bread must also nourish me at other times, and that the same perceptible qualities must always be accompanied by the same secret powers? It does not seem to follow necessarily. Anyway, it must be admitted that in such a case as this the mind draws a conclusion; it takes a certain step, goes through a process of thought or inference, which needs to be explained. These two propositions are far from being the same:

I have found that such and such an object has always had such and such an effect.

I foresee that other objects which appear similar will have similar effects.

The second proposition is always inferred from the first;[3] and if you wish I shall grant that it is rightly inferred. But if you insist that the inference is made by a chain of reasoning, I challenge you to produce the reasoning. The connection between these propositions is not intuitive[4] [that is, the second does not self-evidently and immediately follow from the first].[5] If the inference is to be conducted through reason alone, it must be with help from some intermediate step. But when I try to think what that intermediate step might be, I am defeated. Those who assert that it really exists and is the origin of all our conclusions about matters of fact owe us an account of what it is. ...

All reasonings fall into two kinds: (1) demonstrative reasoning, or that concerning relations of ideas, and (2) factual reasoning, or that concerning matters of fact and existence. That no demonstrative arguments are involved in this inference seems evident;[6] since[B] there is no outright contradiction in supposing that the course of nature will change so that an object that seems like ones we have experienced will have different or contrary effects from theirs.[7] Can't I clearly and distinctly conceive that snowy stuff falling from the clouds might taste salty or feel hot? Is there anything unintelligible about supposing that all the trees will flourish in December and lose their leaves in June? Now, if something is intelligible and can be distinctly conceived, it implies no contradiction and can never be proved false by any demonstrative argument or abstract *a priori* reasoning.

So[C] if there are arguments to justify us in trusting past experience and making it the standard of our future judgment, these arguments can only be probable [inductive];[8] that is, they must be of the kind (2) that concern matters of fact and real existence, to put it in terms of the classification I have given. But[D] probable [inductive] reasoning, if I have described it accurately, can't provide us with the argument we are looking for.[9] According to my account,[E] all arguments about existence [matters of fact] are based on the relation of cause and effect;[10] our knowledge of that relation is derived entirely from experience;[11] and[F] in drawing conclusions from experience we assume that the future will be like the past.[12] So[G] if we try to prove this assumption by probable arguments, i.e. arguments regarding existence, we shall obviously be going in a circle, taking for granted the very point that is in question.[13]

In this section, Hume explains explicitly what we infer from constant conjunction. Consider the two statements in italics: we experience constant conjunction (*"I have found that such and such an object has always had such and such an effect"*) and make the inference that *"other objects which appear similar will have similar effects"*:

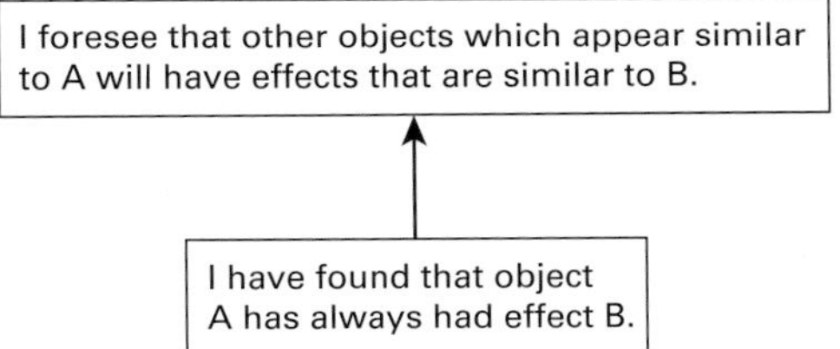

Hume claims that making the inference is so natural that we always do it.

First, we have experience of one kind of event always being followed by another. We assume that the first kind of event will always have the same causal powers it has had in the past (1), and we expect that in the future causes will have the same effects that they have had in the past (2). Thus, he concludes after explaining the bread example, we always make this inference (3).

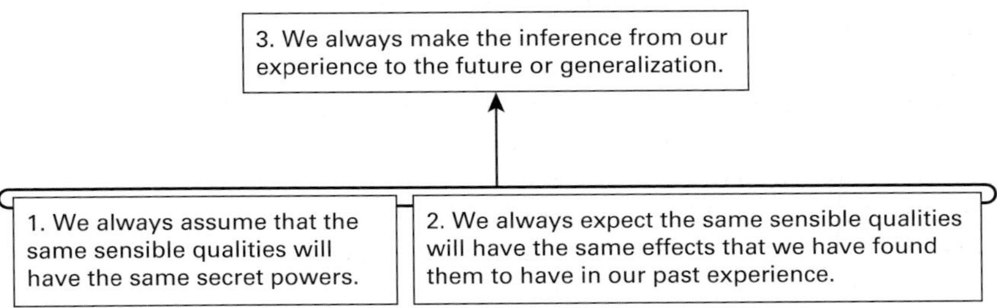

So, Hume asks, what justifies this inference? We make this inference, but why should we think that it is a good inference to make? First, he asks whether the inference is intuitive—meaning whether we can look at this inference and see immediately that it is a valid inference to make. He concludes that it is not intuitive (4), because (as he argued in the previous section) the second italicized statement does not obviously follow from the first italicized statement (5).

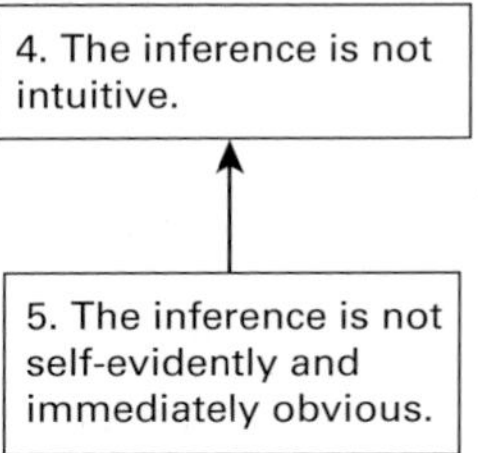

Next, he asks whether the inference is demonstrative—whether the inference is actually a series of valid logical steps, so that the argument is actually valid, even if its validity is not immediately obvious. But here too he concludes that the inference is not demonstrative (6), because it would be no contradiction if the first statement were true and the second statement false (7). Recall that in a valid argument, the truth of the premise guarantees the truth of the conclusion, so this can't be a valid argument.

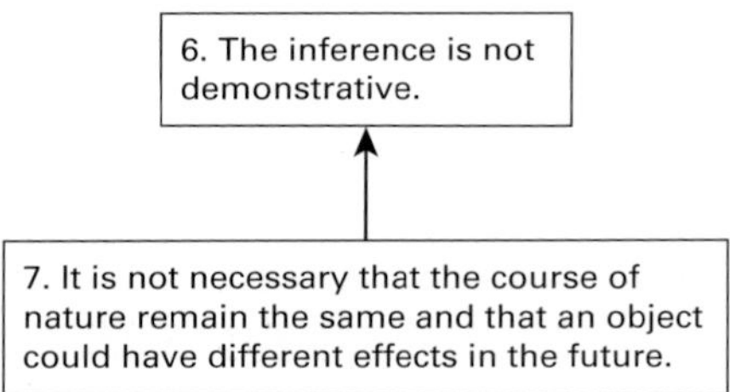

So what do we conclude from these two points? Recall that we divided arguments into two kinds: deductive and nondeductive. Using our language, then, Hume has argued that the inference is not deductive. Thus, the inference, if justified, must be nondeductive. This is what he's saying in statement (8). (For Hume, nondeductive = inductive.)

This second part of the argument can be diagrammed as:

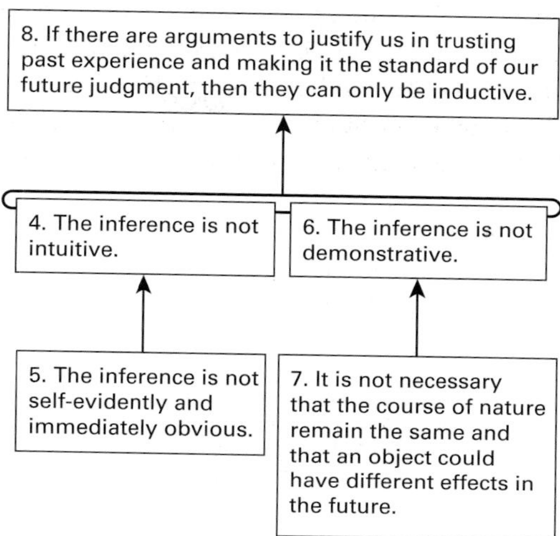

Hume then argues that the inference cannot be justified if it is inductive (9), because that would be arguing in a circle (13). We will look at this argument in detail below, but for now, Hume argues that everything we know about the world beyond our immediate senses is based on our knowledge of cause and effect (10), *and* everything we know about cause and effect is based on past experience (11), *and* whenever we base conclusions on past experience, we are assuming that our future experience will be like that past experience (12). This is also known as the *principle of the uniformity of nature*.

This part of the argument can be represented as:

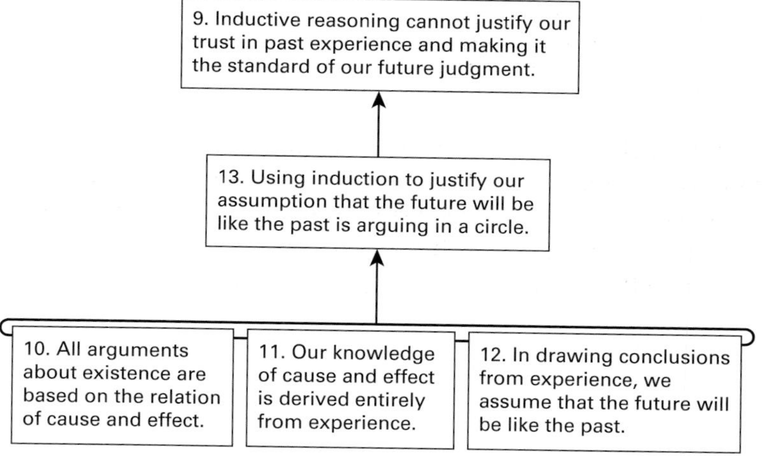

Then, the overall argument looks like this:

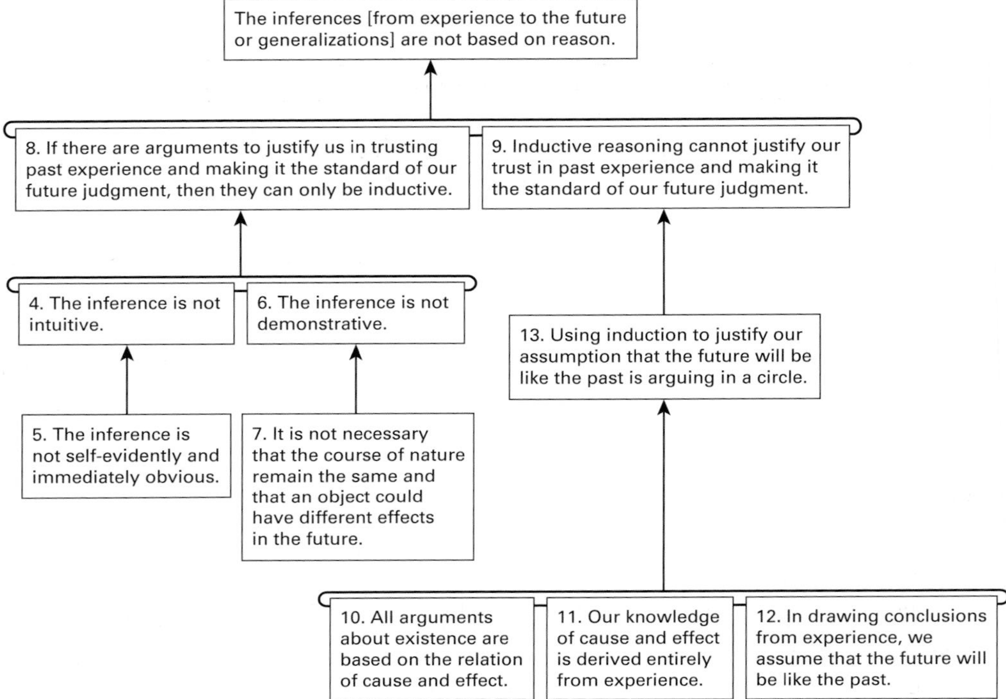

Now, let's go back to Hume's circularity argument. Consider some causal claims: low air pressure causes storms, exercise causes weight loss, aspirin causes headaches to disappear. Causal claims, as Hume notes, are more than just claims about things that co-occur. It's not just that low air pressure and storms happen to occur at the same time; it's not just that increased exercise and increased weight loss happen at the same time; it's not that taking an aspirin and your headache disappearing occur together. The causal claim is that there is a necessary connection between low air pressure and storms, etc., such that we can predict future storms based on our knowledge of current air pressure.

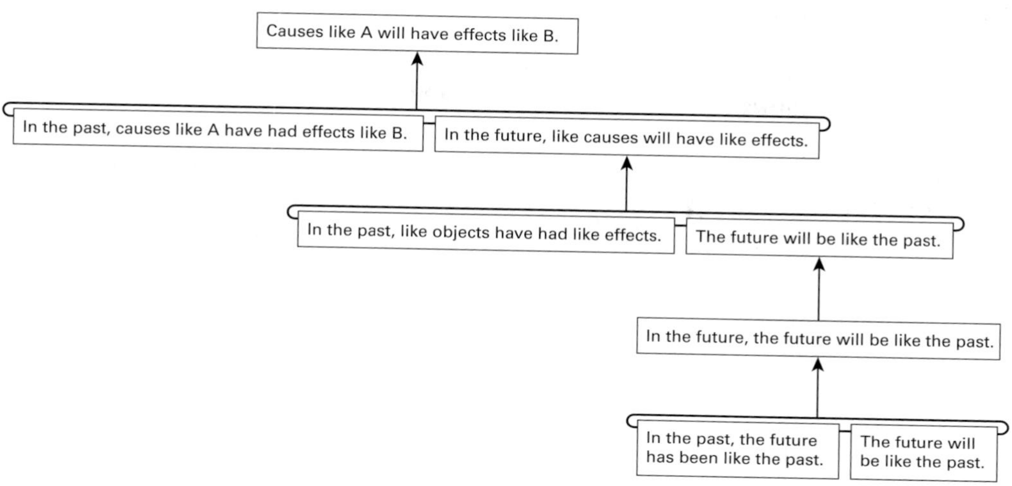

So, the upshot is that Hume believes:

1. Science relies on induction to formulate laws and make predictions.
2. Induction is not rationally justified.
3. So, scientific "knowledge" isn't knowledge at all, because it is not rationally justified.

Now what? In the next section of the *Enquiry*, Hume presents his "Sceptical Solution." We will explore this solution in the exercises, but note here that although most philosophers accepted Hume's argument about induction, they were not enamored with his solution. Immanuel Kant's work in epistemology, for example, was based on a response to this problem posed by Hume. In the next chapter we will explore other, more recent responses.

8.4 In-Class Exercises

An asterisk (*) indicates a more challenging exercise.

Exercises 1–5

In the first part of this chapter, we analyzed in detail the argument given by Descartes in *Meditation I*. Then, we followed with the argument in *Meditation II*. The following selections contain arguments from *Meditation III*. For each selection, (a) diagram the argument and (b) identify any potential objections to the argument.

Exercise 1

That lists everything that I truly know, or at least everything I have, up to now, discovered that I know. Now I will look more carefully to see whether I have overlooked other facts about myself. *I am certain that I am a thinking thing*. Doesn't that tell me what it takes for me to be certain about anything? In this first item of knowledge there is simply a clear and distinct perception of what I am asserting; this wouldn't be enough to make me certain of its truth if it could ever turn out that something that I perceived so clearly and distinctly was false. So I now seem to be able to lay it down as a general rule that *whatever I perceive very clearly and distinctly is true*.

Exercise 2

Now it is obvious by the natural light that the total cause of something must contain at least as much reality as does the effect. For where could the effect get its reality from if not from the cause? And how could the cause give reality to the effect unless it first had that reality itself? Two things follow from this: that something can't arise from nothing, and that what is more perfect—that is, contains in itself more reality—can't arise from what is less perfect. And this is plainly true not only for "actual" or "intrinsic" reality (as philosophers call it) but also for the *representative* reality of ideas—that is, the reality that a idea represents.

Exercise 3

The longer and more carefully I examine all these points, the more clearly and distinctly I recognize their truth. But what is my conclusion to be? If I find that some idea of mine has so much representative reality that I am sure the same reality doesn't reside in *me*, either straightforwardly or in a higher form, and hence that I myself can't be the cause of the idea, then [because everything must have *some* cause], it will necessarily follow that I am not alone in the world: there exists some other thing that is the cause of that idea.

If no such idea is to be found in me, I shall have no argument to show that anything exists apart from myself; for, despite a most careful and wide-ranging survey, this is the only argument I have so far been able to find.

Exercise 4

So there remains only the idea of God: is there anything in *that* which couldn't have originated in myself? By the word "God" I understand a substance that is infinite, eternal, unchangeable, independent, supremely intelligent, supremely powerful, which created myself and anything else that may exist. The more carefully I concentrate on these attributes, the less possible it seems that *any* of them could have originated from me alone. So this whole discussion implies that God necessarily exists.

Exercise 5

The core of the argument is this: I couldn't exist with the nature that I have—that is, containing within me the idea of God—if God didn't really exist. By "God" I mean the very being the idea of whom is within me—the one that has no defects and has all those perfections that I can't *grasp* but can somehow *touch* with my thought. This shows clearly that it is not possible for him to be a deceiver, since the natural light makes it clear that all fraud and deception depend on some defect.

Exercises 6–7

The following selections contain arguments from *Meditation IV*. For each selection, (a) diagram the argument and (b) identify any potential objections to the argument.

Exercise 6

To begin with, I see that it is impossible that God should ever deceive me. Only someone who has something wrong with him will engage in trickery or deception. That someone is able to deceive others may be a sign of his skill or power, but his wanting to deceive them is a sign of his malice or weakness; and those are not to be found in God.

Exercise 7

Next, I know from experience that I have a faculty of judgment; and this, like everything else I have, was given to me by God. Since God doesn't want to deceive me, I am sure that he didn't give me a faculty of judgment that would lead me into error while I was using it correctly.

Exercises 8–11

In the second part of this chapter, we analyzed in detail the argument given by Locke in *An Essay Concerning Human Understanding*. The following selections contain arguments from the same selection. In the sections directly following the ones analyzed above, Locke explains what the innatists might say in reply to the arguments in sections 1–5:

Book I—Innate Notions

Chapter 2: No innate [speculative] principles in the mind

…

6. To avoid this conclusion, it is usually answered that all men know and assent to these truths when they come to the use of reason, and this is enough to prove the truths innate. I answer as follows.

7. People who are in the grip of a prejudice don't bother to look carefully at what they say; and so they will say things that are suspect—indeed almost meaningless—and pass them off as clear reasons. The foregoing claim that innateness is proved by assent-when-reason-is-reached, if it is to be turned into something clear and applied to our present question, must mean either (1) that as soon as men come to the use of reason these supposedly innate truths come to be known and observed by them, or (2) that the use and exercise of men's reason assists them in the discovery of these truths, making them known with certainty.

Below are Locke's arguments concerning each possible interpretation of the claim. For each selection, (a) diagram the argument and (b) identify any potential objections to the argument.

*Exercise 8

8. If they mean (2) that by the use of reason men may discover these principles, and that this is sufficient to prove them innate, they must be arguing for this conclusion:

Whatever truths reason can enable us to know for certain, and make us firmly assent to, are all innate, that is, naturally imprinted on the mind; on the grounds that universal assent proves innateness, and that all we mean by something's being "universally assented to" in this context is merely that we can come to know it for sure, and be brought to assent to it, by the use of reason.

This line of thought wipes out the distinction between the *maxims* [= "basic axioms"] of the mathematicians and the *theorems* they deduce from them; all must equally count as innate because they can all be known for certain through the use of reason.

Exercise 9

9. How can people who take this view think that we need to use *reason* to discover principles that are supposedly innate? ...We may as well think that the use of reason is necessary to make our *eyes discover visible objects* as that we need to have (or to use) reason to make the *understanding see what is originally engraved* on it and cannot be in the understanding before being noticed by it. "Reason shows us those truths that have been imprinted"—this amounts to saying that the use of reason enables a man to learn what he already knew.

Exercise 10

10. In reply to my final remark in section 8, it may be said that maxims and other innate truths *are*, whereas mathematical demonstrations and other non-innate truths *are not*, assented to as soon as the question is put. ... I freely acknowledge that maxims differ from mathematical demonstrations in this way: we grasp and assent to the latter only with the help of reason, using proofs, whereas the former—the basic maxims—are embraced and assented to as soon as they are understood, without the least reasoning. But so much the worse for the view that reason is needed for the discovery of these general truths [= maxims], since it must be admitted that reasoning plays no part in *their* discovery. And I think those who take this view that innate truths are known by reason will hesitate to assert that the knowledge of the maxim that *it is impossible for the same thing to be and not to be* is a deduction of our reason. For by making our knowledge of such a principle depend on the labour of our thoughts they would be destroying that bounty of nature they seem so fond of. In all reasoning we search and flail around, having to take pains and stick to the problem. What sense does it make to suppose that all *this* is needed to discover something that was imprinted on us by nature?
11. ... It is therefore utterly false that reason assists us in the knowledge of these maxims; and as I have also been arguing, if it were true it would prove that they are *not* innate!

Exercise 11

12. Of the two interpretations mentioned in section 7, I now come to the one labeled (1). If by "knowing and assenting to them when we come to the use of reason" the innatists mean that this is *when* the mind comes to notice them, and that *as soon as* children acquire the use of reason they come also to know and assent to these maxims, this also is false and frivolous. It is false because these maxims are

obviously not in the mind as early as the use of reason. We observe ever so many instances of the use of reason in children long before they have any knowledge of the maxim that *it is impossible for the same thing to be and not to be*. Similarly with illiterate people and savages. ...

Exercises 12–13

In the third part of this chapter, we analyzed in detail the argument given by Hume in *An Enquiry Concerning Human Understanding, Part IV*. The following selections contain arguments from the same selection. For each selection, (a) diagram the argument and (b) identify any potential objections to the argument.

Exercise 12

Here, Hume recaps the argument we first analyzed.

In short, every effect is a distinct even from its cause. So it can't be discovered *in* the cause, and the first invention or conception of it *a priori* must be wholly arbitrary. Furthermore, even after it has been suggested, the linking it with the cause must still appear as arbitrary, because plenty of other possible effects must seem just as consistent and natural from reason's point of view. So there isn't the slightest hope of reaching any conclusions about causes and effect without the help of experience.

**Exercise 13*

When a man says

"I have found in all past instances such and such sensible qualities conjoined with such and such secret powers,"

and then goes on to say

"Similar sensible qualities will always be combined with similar secret powers,"

he isn't guilty of merely repeating himself; these propositions are in no way the same. "The second proposition is inferred from the first," you may say; but you must admit that the inference isn't intuitive [= "can't be seen at a glance to be valid"], and it isn't demonstrative either [= "can't be carried through by a series of steps each of which can be seen at a glance to be valid"]. What kind of inference is it, then? To call it "experiential" is to assume the point that is in question. For all inferences from experience are based on the assumption that the future will resemble the past, and that similar powers will be combined with similar sensible qualities. As soon as the suspicion is planted that the course of nature may change, so that the past stops being a guide to the future, all experience becomes useless and can't support any inference or conclusion. So no arguments from experience can *support* this resemblance of the past to the future, because all such arguments are *based on* the assumption of that resemblance. ...

It is certain that the most ignorant and stupid peasants, even infants, indeed even brute beasts, improve by experience and learn the qualities of natural objects by observing their effects. When a child has felt pain from touching the flame of a candle, he will be careful not to put his hand near any candle, and will expect a similar effect from any cause that is similar in its appearance. If you assert that the child's understanding comes to this conclusion through a process of argument, it is fair for me to demand that you produce that argument, and you have no excuse for refusing to comply.

Exercises 14–16

In Part V of *An Enquiry Concerning Human Understanding*, Hume offers his solution to the problem of induction. The following selections contain arguments from this section. For each selection, (a) diagram the argument, and (b) identify any potential objections to the argument.

Exercise 14

Suppose that a highly intelligent and thoughtful person were suddenly brought into this world; he would immediately observe one event following another, but that is all he could discover. He would not be able by any reasoning to reach the idea of cause and effect, because (firstly) the particular powers by which all [causal] operations are performed are never perceived through the senses, and (secondly) there is no *reason* to conclude that one event causes another merely because it precedes it. Their occurring together may be arbitrary and casual, with no causal connection between them. In short, until such a person had more experience he could never reason about any matter of fact, or be sure of anything beyond what was immediately present to his memory and senses.

Exercise 15

Now suppose that our person gains more experience, and lives long enough in the world to observe similar objects or events occurring together constantly; *now* what conclusion does he draw from this experience? He immediately infers the existence of one object from the appearance of the other! Yet all his experience has not given him any idea or knowledge of the secret power by which one object produces another; nor can any process of reasoning have led him to draw this inference. But he finds that he *can't help* drawing it: and he will not be swayed from this even if he becomes convinced that there is no intellectual support for the inference. Something else is at work, compelling him to go through with it. It is *custom* or *habit*. When we are inclined to behave or think in some way, not because it can be justified by reasoning or some process of the understanding but just because we have behaved or thought like that so often in the past, we always say that this inclination is the effect of "custom."

Exercise 16

In using that word ["custom"] we don't claim to give the basic reason for the inclination. All we are doing is to point out a fundamental feature of human nature which everyone agrees is there, and which is well known by its effects. Perhaps that is as far as we can go. Perhaps, that is, we can't discover the cause of this cause, and must rest content with it as the deepest we can go in explaining our conclusions from experience. Our ability to go that far should satisfy us; we oughtn't to complain about the narrowness of our faculties because they won't take us any further. We do at least have here a very intelligible proposition and perhaps a true one: *After the constant conjunction of two objects—heat and flame, for instance, or weight and solidity—sheer habit makes us expect the one when we experience the other.* Indeed, this hypothesis seems to be the only one that could explain why we draw from a thousand instances an inference which we can't draw from a single one that is exactly like each of the thousand. Reason isn't like that. The conclusions it draws from considering one circle are the same as it would form after surveying all the circles in the universe. But no man, having seen only one body move after being pushed by another, could infer that every other body will move after a similar collision. All inferences from experience, therefore, are effects of custom and not of reasoning.

Exercises 17–22

The following exercises are intended to ensure your understanding of Descartes's, Locke's, and Hume's texts, and to help you further explore the ideas presented in this chapter.

Exercise 17: Now that you have read my textual analysis of Descartes's argument, summarize it in your own words.

Exercise 18: Summarize, in your own words, each of the arguments in exercises 1–7 above.

Exercise 19: Now that you have read my textual analysis of Locke's argument, summarize it in your own words.

Exercise 20: Summarize, in your own words, each of the arguments in exercises 8–11 above.

Exercise 21: Now that you have read my textual analysis of Hume's arguments, summarize it in your own words.

Exercise 22: Summarize, in your own words, each of the arguments in exercises 12–16 above.

8.5 Reading Questions

1. In *Meditations I* and *II*, what does Descartes identify as a primary source of human error? Do you agree? Why or why not?
2. In the section about the piece of wax in *Meditation II*, Descartes describes what people often say about their "knowledge" of the wax and argues that some of the ways they claim to "know" are reasonable candidates for knowledge of the wax and some aren't. Give your own account of his views about which of our claims to know the wax deserve being called knowledge and which don't. Do you think Descartes is right about this? Why or why not?
3. In his *Essay Concerning Human Understanding*, Locke seems to think that an "idea" must be a conscious, single thought, and that by arguing against innate ideas in that sense he has defeated the claim that we are born with a priori understanding. Contemporary cognitive psychologists tend to talk of "concepts" rather than ideas, and they regard concepts as capacities for identifying and distinguishing kinds of things and circumstances. How might a cognitive psychologist who thinks that there are innate concepts reply to Locke's argument?
4. In Book II, chapter 1 of the *Essay*, Locke gives and argues for a theory of the sources of all human ideas. His theory is very different from that of Descartes. In your own words, give Locke's account of the source of our ideas, at least one of the arguments he gives in favor of his views, and say how Locke's view of the sources of our ideas agrees with and differs from Descartes's view.
5. In your own words, what does Hume mean when he claims that through the relation of cause and effect "alone, we go beyond the evidence of our memory and sense"? Do you agree? Why or why not?

9 The Problem of Induction

9.1 Hans Reichenbach, *Experience and Prediction*
9.2 Karl Popper, "Science: Conjectures and Refutations"
9.3 Nelson Goodman, *Fact, Fiction, and Forecast*
9.4 In-Class Exercises
9.5 Reading Questions

9.1 Hans Reichenbach, *Experience and Prediction*

Hans Reichenbach (1891–1953) was born in Hamburg, Germany, to a half-Jewish father and non-Jewish mother. Early on, he studied civil engineering at Technische Hochschule, but he mingled with the preeminent physicists of his time at their universities throughout Germany: Ernst Cassirer, Max Planck, Arnold Sommerfeld, David Hilbert, and, later, Albert Einstein. In 1915, Reichenbach received his degree in philosophy, with a dissertation on probability theory, from the University at Erlangen. In 1920, he was hired as a professor at Polytechnic at Stuttgart, and in 1926, he took a professorship at the University of Berlin. When Hitler came to power in 1933, Reichenbach was fired from the University of Berlin because he was considered to be Jewish. Almost immediately, he moved to Turkey to teach at the University of Istanbul, and in 1938, he secured a position at UCLA.

Reichenbach's work focused mainly on what he called "scientific philosophy," what we now would call "philosophy of physics." In particular, he was interested in scientific methodology and the justification of our belief in what physics tells us about the world. In addition to founding the journal *Erkenntnis* with Rudolf Carnap, Reichenbach published many books and articles. His books include *Axiomatization of the Theory of Relativity* (1924), *From Copernicus to Einstein* (1927), *The Philosophy of Space and Time* (1928), *The Theory of Probability* (1935), *Experience and Prediction: An Analysis of the Foundations and the Structure of Knowledge* (1938), *Philosophic Foundations of Quantum Mechanics* (1944), *Elements of Symbolic Logic* (1947), and *The Rise of Scientific Philosophy* (1951).

The selection we will analyze is from his 1938 book, *Experience and Prediction*. Here he argues that, despite Hume's skeptical argument against the justification of induction, we do have good reason to believe the results of scientific induction. You may have wondered, after reading the section on Hume in the previous chapter, what all the fuss is about. Surely, you may have thought, even if we can't say that the results of an inductive inference are certainly true, we can at least say that they are *probably* true. This is exactly what Reichenbach thought.

Recall that Hume's objection to the principle of induction is that, for induction to succeed, we need to assume that future will be like the past—that is, that the principle of the uniformity of nature (PUN) is true. This is a problem because the only justification we have of PUN is inductive. Thus, Hume says, the justification of induction is circular.

For Reichenbach, success means producing the truth about the future. Hume, he says, assumes that proving that induction must be successful is both necessary and sufficient for being justified in using induction. This means that Reichenbach contends that Hume thought that one can be justified in using induction *if and only if* one can prove that induction will always lead to the truth. Reichenbach objects to this characterization of justification, and says that being able to prove that induction leads to the truth is *sufficient* for using it, but that such a proof is not *necessary* for being justified in using it. That is, Reichenbach thinks that there are other ways that one can be justified in in using induction.

In this selection, Reichenbach says:

> If we cannot realize the sufficient conditions of success, we shall at least realize the necessary conditions. If we were able to show that the inductive inference is a necessary condition of success, it would be justified; such a proof would satisfy any demands which may be raised about the justification of induction.
>
> Now obviously there is a great difference between our example and induction. The reasoning of the physician presupposes inductions; his knowledge about an operation as the only possible means of saving a life is based on inductive generalizations, just as are all other statements of empirical character. But we wanted only to illustrate the logical structure of our reasoning. If we want to regard such a reasoning as a justification of the principle of induction, the character of induction as a necessary condition of success must be demonstrated in a way which does not presuppose induction. Such a proof, however, can be given.

To understand this, recall the discussion of necessary and sufficient conditions in the introduction to Part III. We can represent "A is *sufficient* for B" as "if A, then B." And, we can represent "A is *necessary* for B" as "if B, then A." The former means that A's being true, by itself, can make B true, but also that there are other conditions, perhaps, that could also make B true. The latter means that whatever else is needed to make B true, A's being true must be included.

Now, he says, Hume was right about the fact that we can't prove that induction will always be successful at granting us knowledge of the world. So, we can't show that using induction is sufficient for success. What he wants to do, however, is show that being able to use induction is necessary for success. He asks us to consider the following dilemma: either PUN is true or it is false. If it is false, then no method is going to reliably lead us to the truth about the future. If PUN is true, however, then induction *will* reliably lead us to the truth, even if there are also other methods that would do so as well. Thus, he says, induction being applicable is a necessary condition for success.

But this is not quite enough. What about the other possible methods? How can we be justified in using induction, if there is another method that may be better? This, then, is Reichenbach's task: we can provide a justification of the principle of induction if we can show that it is the best method available for gathering predictive knowledge. Let's see how he does this.

From *Experience and Prediction*.[1]

If we want to construct this proof, we must begin with a determination of the aim of induction. It is usually said that we perform inductions with the aim of foreseeing the future. This determination is vague; let us replace it by a formulation more precise in character:

The aim of induction is to find series of events whose frequency of occurrence converges toward a limit. [1] …

Now it is obvious that[A] we have no guaranty that this aim is at all attainable.[2] The world may be so disorderly that it is impossible for us to construct series with a limit.[3] Let us introduce the term "predictable" for a world which is sufficiently ordered to enable us to construct series with a limit.[4] We must admit, then, that[B] we do not know whether the world is predictable.[5]

But, if the world is predictable, let us ask what the logical function of the principle of induction will be. For this purpose, we must consider the definition of limit. The frequency h^n has a limit at p, if for any given $\in$ there is an n such that h^n is within $p \pm \in$ and remains within this interval for all the rest of the series.[6] Comparing our formulation of the principle of induction (§38) with this, we may infer from the definition of the limit that,[C] if there is a limit, there is an element of the series from which the principle of induction leads to the true value of the limit.[7] In this sense the principle of induction is a necessary condition for the determination of a limit.[8] …

It is in the analysis expounded that we see the solution of Hume's problem. Hume demanded too much when he wanted for a justification of the inductive inference a proof that its conclusion is true. What his objections demonstrate is only that such a proof cannot be given. We do not perform, however, an inductive inference with the pretension of obtaining a true statement. What we obtain is a wager;[9] and[D] it is the best wager we can lay[10] because[E] it corresponds to a procedure the applicability of which is the necessary condition of the possibility of predictions.[11] To fulfill the conditions sufficient for the attainment of true predictions does not lie in our power; let us be glad that we are able to fulfill at least the conditions necessary for the realization of this intrinsic aim of science

Reichenbach's argument begins with his more precise formulation of the principle of induction (1). Suppose we flip a *weighted* coin to determine the probability of getting heads. Consider the ratio:

the number of times I have flipped the coin and it has come up heads, divided by the number of times I have flipped the coin.

This ratio is "the observed frequency of heads," and let's say that after 100 flips, this frequency is 2/3. We might be tempted to say that the weighting causes this bias, and the long-run frequency of getting heads with this coin will always be 2/3.

Hume says that we use induction to infer from the fact that the ratio has been 2/3 in the past to the prediction that it will be 2/3 in the future, but this inference is not justified because we don't know that nature is uniform. So, nature being uniform, according to Reichenbach, just means that there is, in fact—whether we know it or not—a limit to this ratio in the long run. Thus, we use induction to try to find the correct limit of the frequency of occurrences of the events in which we are interested.

As indicated by (A), the first argument here is Reichenbach's concession to Hume: we have no guarantee that we can attain this aim (2). Why? Because nature may not be uniform; that is, nature may be so disorderly that the series we construct does not converge to a limit at all (3). If we combine this with the definition of "predictable" (3), we can infer, as indicated by (B), that we don't know if the world is predictable (4).

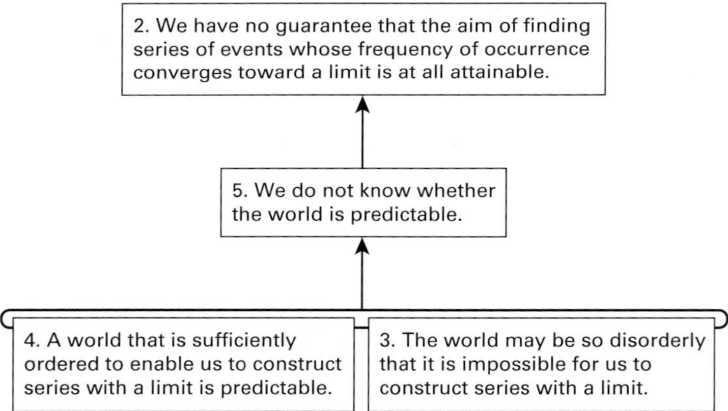

But what if the world is predictable? What can we say about the efficacy of induction then? Reichenbach gives us the definition of a "limit" (6). Then, as indicated by (C), he says that (1) and (6) can be combined to support the claim that *if there is a limit*, then using induction will lead us to that limit (7). This in turn supports his contention that the principle of induction is a necessary condition for the determination of a limit (8). This means that if a limit can be determined at all, induction can determine it. So, the ability to use induction to find the limit is necessary for there being a limit at all.

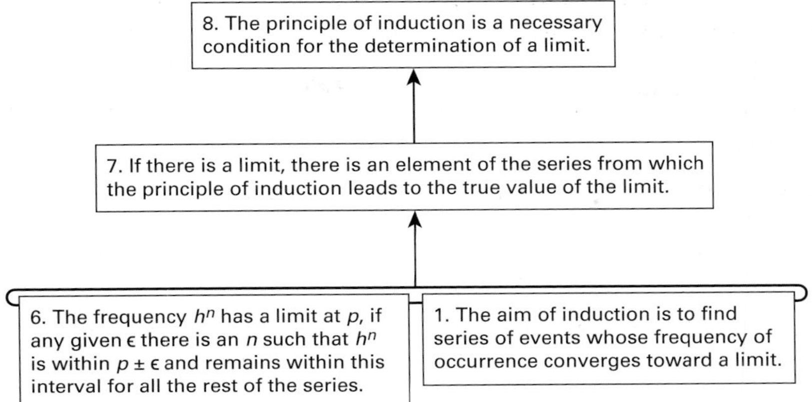

This then is what solves Hume's problem (9); that is, this is what justifies our use of induction: When we use induction, we get a guess about the future—a guess that we would be willing to place a bet on (10). What's more, the product of using induction gives us the best guess possible (11). The reason is, as indicated by (E), that the applicability of induction is the necessary condition of the possibility of predictions (12), which is really a restatement of (8). This means that we don't know whether predictions are possible, but we do know that if they are, induction will make the best predictions.

As indicated by (D), we can combine (10) and (11) to support the claim that the use of induction is justified (9).

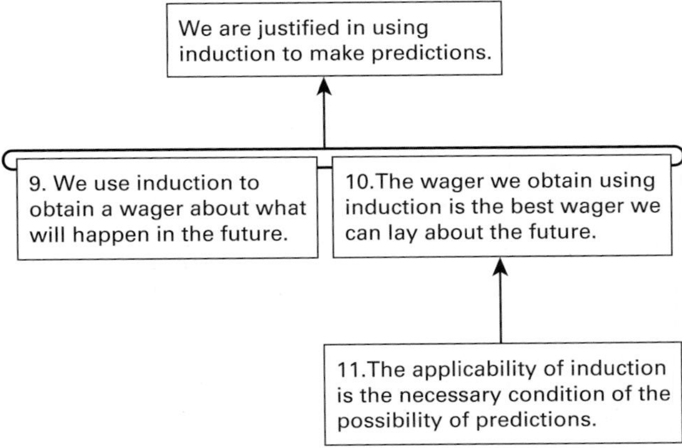

So, Reichenbach's solution to the problem of induction is a conditional one: *if* the world is such that the future is predictable, *then* induction is the best method to use to make predictions. If, on the other hand, the world is not predictable, then no method will work. Thus, we are justified in using induction.

This may not seem like much of a solution, but remember that Reichenbach did admit that using Hume's assumptions, Hume's argument is perfectly sound. Thus, the only way to justify induction is to change the assumptions.

In the next section, we will see another attempt to do just that, made by Karl Popper.

9.2 Karl Popper, "Science: Conjectures and Refutations"

Karl Raimund Popper (1902–1994) was born in Vienna, Austria, where he earned his PhD in philosophy at the age of twenty-four. He spent a brief time teaching at Canterbury University College in New Zealand, but from 1945 until his death, he taught at the London School of Economics.

While Popper was a noted political philosopher, he is most remembered for being one of the greatest philosophers of science in the twentieth century. One reason is that Popper's work actually made a significant impact outside the philosophical community—a great many scientists in the second half of the twentieth century knew of and respected Popper's work.

While Popper was at school, the local philosophical scene was centered on what we now call the *Vienna Circle*. Moritz Schlick had been appointed as chair of Natural Philosophy at the University of Vienna in 1922, and he surrounded himself with similarly scientifically minded scholars. Their aim was to unify science and purge it of all its (as they saw it) "metaphysical nonsense." They drew their inspiration from Ludwig Wittgenstein's *Tractatus*, and so, since Popper and Wittgenstein did not get along, Popper was never invited to be a member of the group.

The Vienna Circle was the birthplace of the philosophical movement called *logical positivism*, and Popper's first book, *Logik der Forschung* (1934), was mainly concerned with criticizing this new philosophy. In 1937, he left Austria for a post at the University of Canterbury in New Zealand. It was during his time at Canterbury that Popper published his first political book, *The Open Society and Its Enemies*, in 1945. The next year he moved to England to a post at the London School of Economics.

In 1959, *Logik der Forschung* was published in English under the title *The Logic of Scientific Discovery*, and it solidified Popper's reputation as one of the most influential twentieth-century philosophers of science. The article we are going to analyze in this section is the transcript of a lecture he gave in 1953, which largely anticipated the content of this book. He has several aims in this lecture:

1. the criterion of demarcation for science
2. a criticism of logical positivism
3. a defense of his work from logical positivist critics
4. a solution to Hume's problem of induction

The criterion of demarcation is what separates science from nonscience. If we could find the correct criterion, then we could apply it to any intellectual endeavor and figure out which ones are scientific (like physics and biology) and which are not (like Marxist history and Freudian psychology). Here, we will only consider the part of the lecture that deals with Hume's problem of induction, but we will have to return to the problem of demarcation to understand Popper's solution. Now, let's look at Popper's text in more detail. Specifically, we will analyze and diagram the argument and then discuss criticisms of it.

From *Conjectures and Refutations.*[2]

This apparently psychological criticism has a purely logical basis which may be summed up in the following simple argument. (It happens to be the one from which I originally started my criticism.) The kind of repetition envisaged by Hume can never be perfect; the cases he has in mind cannot be cases of perfect sameness; they can only be cases of similarity.[1] Thus[A] *they are repetitions only from a certain point of view.*[2] (What has the effect upon me of a repetition may not have this effect upon a spider.) But this means that, for logical reasons,[B] there must always be a point of view—such as a system of expectations, anticipations, assumptions, or *interests—before* there can be any repetition;[3] which point of view, consequently,[C] cannot be merely the result of repetition.[4]

We must thus[D] replace, for the purposes of a psychological theory of the origin of our beliefs, the naive idea of events which *are* similar by the idea of events to which we react by *interpreting* them as being similar.[5] But if this is so (and I can see no escape from it) then[E] Hume's psychological theory of induction leads to an infinite regress, precisely analogous to that other infinite regress which was discovered by Hume himself, and used by him to explode the logical theory of induction. For[F] what do we wish to explain?

First, Popper argues that Hume's psychological solution to the problem of induction is not logically viable, because it leads to an infinite regress.

Popper's argument is a chain of reasoning, beginning with claim (1). The idea here is that no matter how similar two events or situations are, they can never be exactly the same, if only because they take place at different times. This leads to claim (2), that Hume's "repetitions," which are supposed to be the basis of our scientific knowledge, are only repetitions from a certain point of view.

For example, let's say that we are measuring the acceleration due to gravity on various days in September. We can make many of the conditions of the experiment the same for each run; but every day the weather (humidity, temperature, air pressure, etc.) is different, as is the experimenter's affect (mood, tiredness, etc.), the time of day, and a whole host of other things. You might say that those differences don't matter; we need only the apparatus and measuring instruments to be the same. But that's precisely the point. We are concerned with the experiment, so the experiments are repetitions for *us*. A spider, however, may not recognize these events as repetitions, because it is greatly affected by the weather.

From this, Popper concludes that there must always be a point of view before can be any repetition (3). A point of view, he says, is constituted by expectations and assumptions. Thus, the point of view cannot be a result of experiencing similar events or situations (4).

So, Popper concludes, we have to replace, in Hume's theory, the idea of "similar events" simpliciter with the idea of "events that we interpret to be similar" (5). This argument can be represented as:

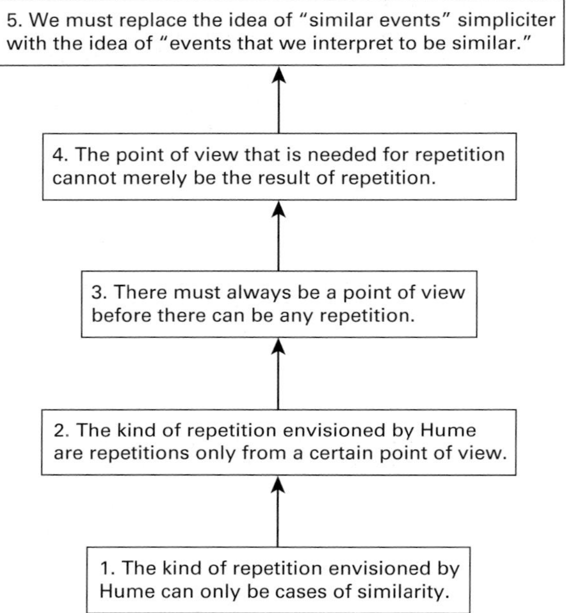

This leads to Popper's main conclusion in this section: Hume's psychological theory of induction leads to an infinite regress. But, as indicated by "for" (F), it seems that Popper draws this conclusion based on claim (5) *and* another argument to follow. Let's consider that further argument.

In the example of the puppies we wish to explain behaviour which may be described as *recognizing or interpreting* a situation as a repetition of another.[6] Clearly, we cannot hope to explain this by an appeal to earlier repetitions,[7] once we realize that the earlier repetitions must also have been repetitions-for-them,[8] so that precisely the same problem arises again: that of *recognizing or interpreting* a situation as a repetition of another.[9]

First he says that what we want to explain is the fact that we (as well as other creatures) interpret some situations as repetitions and not others (6). But we can't explain this by saying it is the result of an inference from earlier repetitions (7), because earlier repetitions must have also been cases of recognizing a situation as a repetition (8). The unstated premise that helps (8) support (7) is, I believe, something like: We would have to explain the earlier behavior of recognizing a situation as a repetition by an appeal to even earlier repetitions. And this is the sense in which Popper believes this series of explanations leads to an infinite regress.

Claims (6) and (7) combine to support the claim that if we do what is called for in claim (5), then we can't explain our interpretation of a situation as a repetition without falling into an infinite regress (9).

This argument can be represented as:

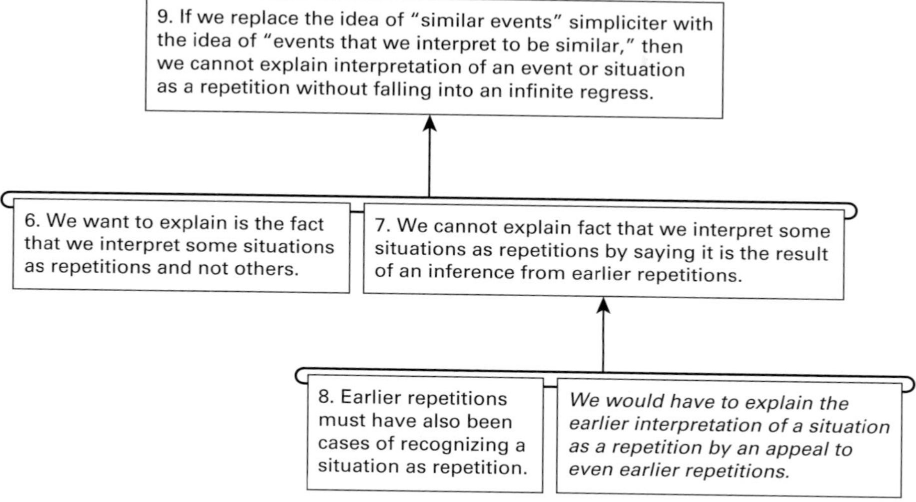

Then, (5) and (9) combine to support the main conclusion:

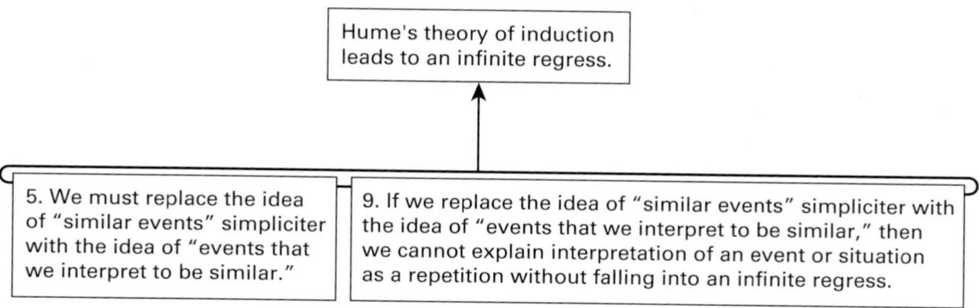

Now that Popper has shown that even Hume's weak solution is no good, he turns to giving a solution of his own.

Hume, I felt, had never accepted the full force of his own logical analysis. Having refuted the logical idea of induction he was faced with the following problem: how do we actually obtain our knowledge, as a matter of psychological fact, if induction is a procedure which is logically invalid and rationally unjustifiable? There are two possible answers: (1) We obtain our knowledge by a non-inductive procedure. This answer would have allowed Hume to retain a form of rationalism. (2) We obtain our knowledge by repetition and induction,[16] and therefore[K] by a logically invalid and rationally unjustifiable procedure,[17] so that[L] all apparent knowledge is merely a kind of belief—belief based on habit.[18] This answer would imply that[M] even scientific knowledge is irrational,[19] so that[N] rationalism is absurd, and must be given up.[20]

First, Popper reconstructs the argument that leads to the problematic conclusion that scientific "knowledge" is not knowledge at all, but irrational belief. There are two ways to obtain our knowledge, according to Hume (and Popper does not challenge this). Either we obtain our knowledge by a noninductive procedure, or we obtain it by repetition and induction (16).

He notes that the first option would have allowed Hume to be a rationalist. *Rationalism* for Popper is the philosophical position that all knowledge is belief justified using facts and our ability to reason. Thus, our knowledge is *rationally* justified.

The unstated premise is that we do not obtain our knowledge by a noninductive procedure, which implies that we do obtain our knowledge by repetition and induction. But, as Hume argued, induction is logically invalid and rationally unjustifiable. So, we obtain our knowledge by a logically invalid and rationally unjustifiable procedure (17). This means, in turn, that all apparent knowledge (meaning everything we thought was knowledge) is merely belief based on habit (18). From this we conclude that scientific knowledge is irrational (19), and then we further conclude that rationalism is absurd (20).

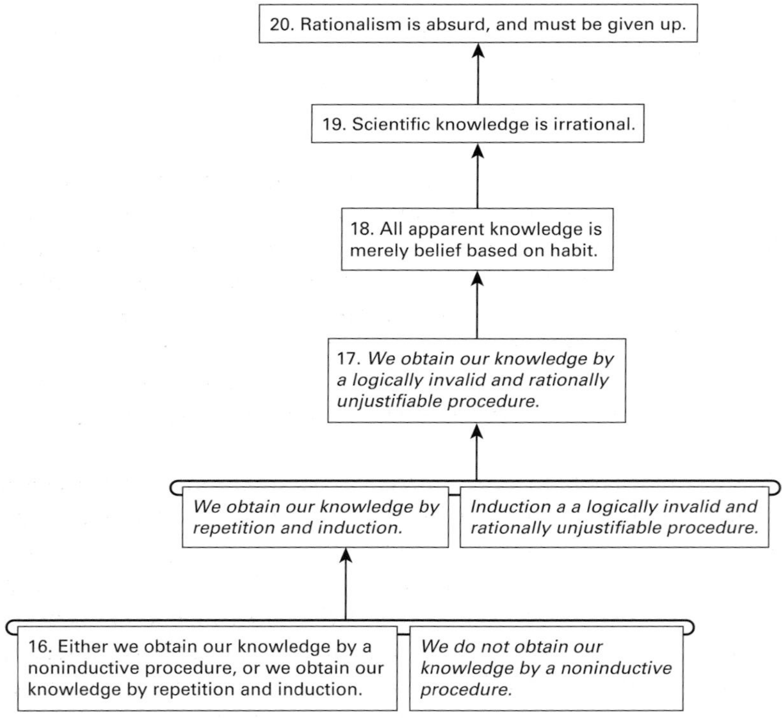

What Popper wants to do is reject the implicit premise that we do not obtain our knowledge by a noninductive procedure:

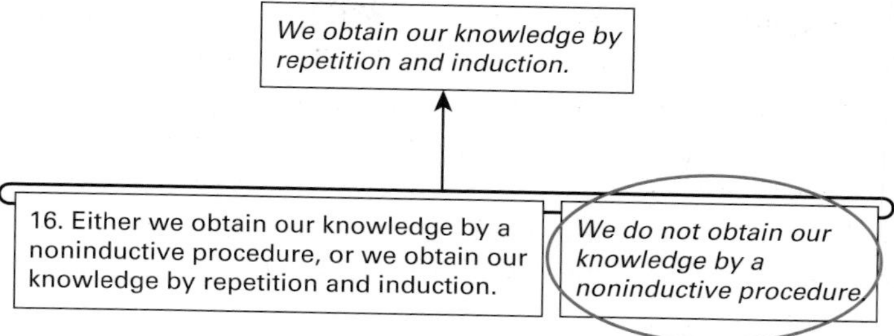

Rather, Popper rejects the claim that we obtain our knowledge by induction, and comes to the conclusion that we obtain our knowledge by a noninductive procedure:

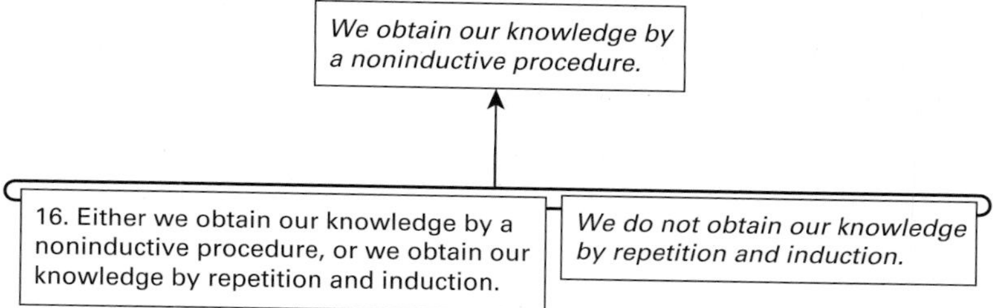

This noninductive procedure is what Popper calls "conjectures and refutations." First, we make up theories (conjectures). These theories can come from anywhere—they may arise from expectations we have upon being born, they may originate from our dreams or myths, or they may arise from previous theories—and then we test them against our observations. In fact, Popper believes that we are born with the propensity to impose regularities on the world around us. So, theory-postulating comes naturally to us. If our observations contradict the theory, then we reject the theory (refutations) and look for a new one. And Popper's claim is that we do this in both our ordinary, everyday lives, from cradle to grave, *and* in scientific practice.

Ultimately, Popper's theory of scientific practice rests on the difference between two kinds of arguments. Let *T* represent a scientific theory, and let *E* represent an event that *T* predicts will be the outcome of an experiment or observation. We can represent this prediction by saying that "If *T* is true, then *E* is (or will be) true," or as "If *T*, then *E*." One argument proceeds as follows: "We know that if *T* is true, then *E* should be true. It turns out that *E* is true. Therefore, *T* must be true." Popper calls this argument "the logic of confirmation." That is, if *T* predicts *E*, then discovering that *E* is true confirms that *T* is true. The second argument, which Popper calls "the logic of refutation," proceeds as follows: "We know that if *T* is true, then *E* should be true. It turns out that *E* is false. Therefore, *T* must be false." That is, if *T* predicts *E*, then discovering that *E* is false refutes *T*.

These two arguments can be represented as:

Confirmation:

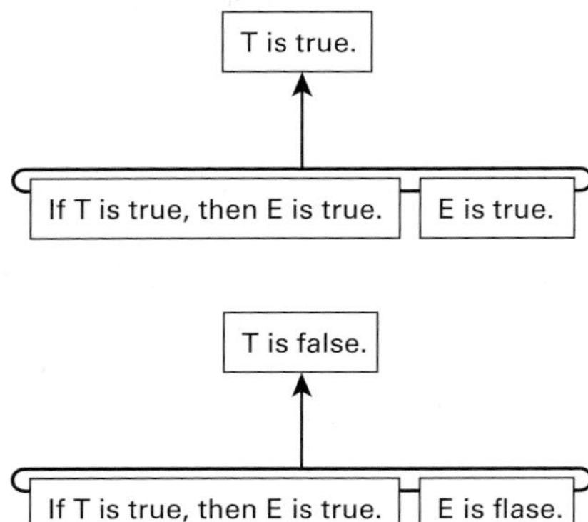

Refutation:

Alert readers will recognize from chapter 2 that the argument on the top is an instance of the fallacy of affirming the consequent, and so is invalid; while the argument on the bottom is an instance of a modus tollens argument, and so is valid. Popper says that the logic of confirmation is flawed, and so we can never be sure, even if all the evidence is consistent with it, that a scientific theory is true. However, since the logic of refutation is valid, we can be certain, based on experiments and/or observations, that a scientific theory is false.

Now, let's consider two objections to Popper's theory of scientific practice.

First Objection

It is never the case that one can derive a prediction of a theory based on just the theory alone. No one can make a prediction based on a scientific theory without specifying the specific conditions under which the prediction will be made. For example, consider the ability to predict what the current will be through a battery/wire circuit using Ohm's law. This prediction will depend on the voltage of the battery and the resistance of the wire. An accurate prediction will be produced only if we are right about the theory *and* the voltage *and* the resistance. In this kind of setup, the theory is the *main hypothesis*, and the value of the voltage and the value of the resistance are *auxiliary hypotheses*.

Thus, the statement "If *T* is true, then *E* is true" should really be "If *T* and *V* and *R* are all true, then *E* is true." But then if *E* turns out to be false, all we can know for certain is that either *T* or *V* or *R* or some combination of those is false; we can't know for certain which one is false. Thus, the logic of refutation isn't as simple as Popper makes it appear here, and the prescription for how science ought to be done is not clear.

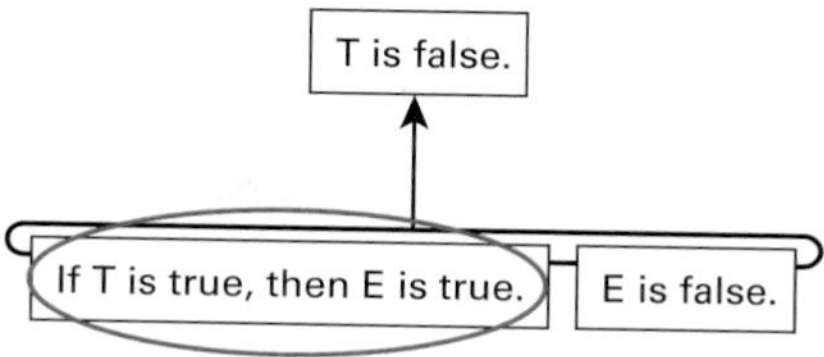

Second Objection

Furthermore, since there are always auxiliary hypotheses involved in making a prediction, one is never really compelled to give up the main hypothesis when a prediction based on that hypothesis is wrong. Rather, one can always blame the wrong prediction on one of the auxiliary hypotheses. Thus, even as a mere description of actual scientific practice, Popper's theory falls short since it does not explain why sometimes a wrong prediction leads to the rejection of the main hypothesis, and sometimes it does not.

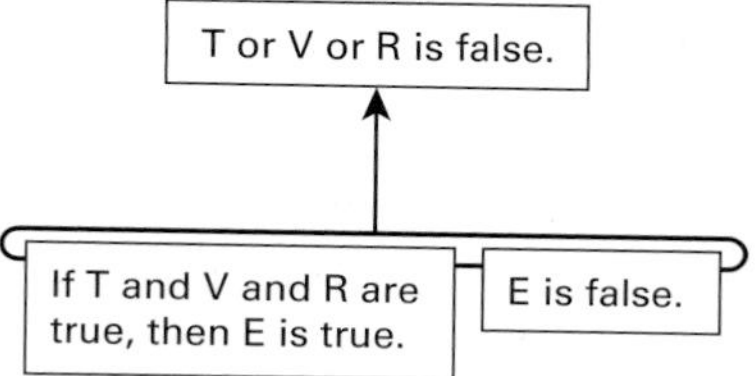

In the last section of this chapter we encounter not only a different solution to Hume's problem, but also a new problem that is similar to the old.

9.3 Nelson Goodman, *Fact, Fiction, and Forecast*

Nelson Goodman (1906–1998) was an American philosopher who was concerned with a wide range of philosophical problems, including mathematics, science, metaphysics, and aesthetics. Harvard University bookmarked his academic career at both ends. He received his bachelor's degree in 1928 and his PhD in philosophy in 1941, both from Harvard. He ended his career as a full professor of philosophy at Harvard from 1967 to 1977, when he retired. In between, he taught at Tufts University, the University of Pennsylvania, and Brandeis.

Goodman is perhaps best known for his work on Hume's problem of induction, which began with his work on confirmation of scientific theories and cumulated in his "new" problem of induction. Here we will read a presentation of this new problem from the third chapter of his 1955 book, *Fact, Fiction, and Forecast.*

First, Goodman briefly explains Hume's problem of induction and surveys a few attempted solutions. He argues that the most promising route to a solution is to ask why deduction and induction are treated differently. After all, the only reason we say that good deductive arguments are valid is that the rules of inference accord with our beliefs about good argumentation. So, why can't we just do the same with induction? That is, we should say that good inductive arguments are valid (or, at least, justified) when they use rules of inference that accord with our beliefs about good argumentation. The task then is to develop these rules of inductive inference.

The problem, however, is that developing these rules is quite difficult. Goodman argues that it is, at its core, the same problem as is confronted by those who try to describe scientific method—when does a piece of evidence provide confirmation for a theory? It is here that he introduces what he calls the "new riddle of induction."

Let's look at Goodman's text in more detail. Specifically, we will analyze and diagram the argument, but first we need to understand the content of the claims that Goodman makes before his argument begins.

From *Fact, Fiction, and Forecast.*[3]

3. The Constructive Task of Confirmation Theory

...

Does not induction proceed in just the opposite direction from deduction? Surely some of the evidence statements that inductively support a general hypothesis are consequences of it. Since the consequence relation is already well defined by deductive logic, will we not be on firm ground in saying that confirmation embraces the converse relation? The laws of deduction in reverse will then be among the laws of induction.

Let's see where this leads us. We naturally assume further that whatever confirms a given statement confirms also whatever follows from that statement. But if we combine this assumption with our proposed principle, we get the embarrassing result that every statement confirms every other.

Surprising as it may be that such innocent beginnings lead to such an intolerable conclusion, the proof is very easy. Start with any statement S_1. It is a consequence of,[1] and[A] so[B] by our present criterion[2] confirms, the conjunction of S_1 and any statement whatsoever[3]—call it S_2. But[C] the confirmed conjunction, $S_1 \cdot S_2$, of course has S_2 as a consequence.[4] Thus[D] every statement confirms all statements.

What given evidence confirms is not what we arrive at by generalizing from separate items of it, but—roughly speaking—what we arrive at by generalizing from the total stated evidence. The central idea for an improved definition is that, within certain limitations, what is asserted to be true for the narrow universe of the evidence statements is confirmed for the whole universe of discourse. Thus if our evidence is E_1 and E_2, neither the hypothesis that all things are black nor the hypothesis that all things are non-black is confirmed; for neither is true for the evidence-universe consisting of *b* and *c*.

First, let's start with a concrete example. Suppose I am entertaining the hypothesis (H) that all cats are mammals. One piece of evidence for this hypothesis is the evidence statement (S_1) that my own cat, Fluffy, is a mammal. Of course, this piece of evidence does not prove that H is true; but right now Goodman wants to classify evidence statements as either confirming the hypothesis or disconfirming the hypothesis. So, within this dichotomy, we want a definition that tells us that S_1 confirms H.

Given this, Goodman proposes a simple definition of confirmation: An evidence statement, S, confirms a hypothesis, H, just in case H entails S. We represent this entailment as $H \rightarrow S$.

Beyond this, Goodman says it is reasonable to suppose that if $H \rightarrow I$, for example, then if S confirms H, then S will confirm I as well. For example, if it's the case that all cats are mammals (H), then it is also the case that all cats are animals (I). So, if the fact that my cat is a mammal confirms H, then it will also confirm I.

The problem with this, Goodman, says, is that every statement confirms all statements. If we have two statements, S_1 and S_2, then we represent their conjunction as $(S_1 \cdot S_2)$. Then Goodman points about that $(S_1 \cdot S_2) \rightarrow S_1$ (1). As indicated by (A), this is to be combined with our confirmation criterion that if $H \rightarrow S$, then S confirms H (2). As indicated by (B), the combination supports the claim that $S1$ confirms $(S_1 \cdot S_2)$.

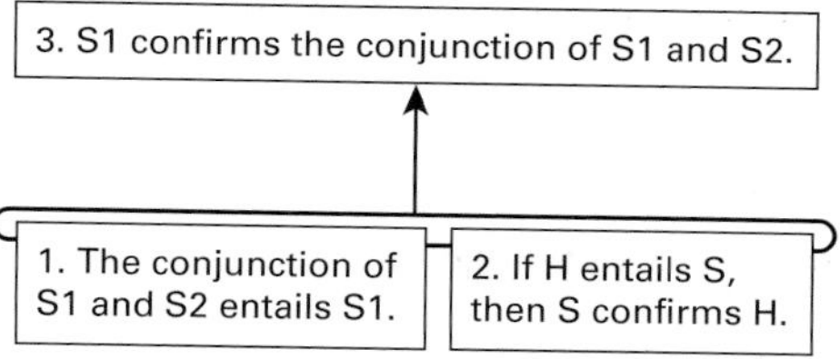

As indicated by (C), this conclusion is to be combined with the observation that $(S_1 \cdot S_2)$ *also* entails S_2 (4). Then, as indicated by (D), this combination supports the conclusion that every statement confirms every other statement.

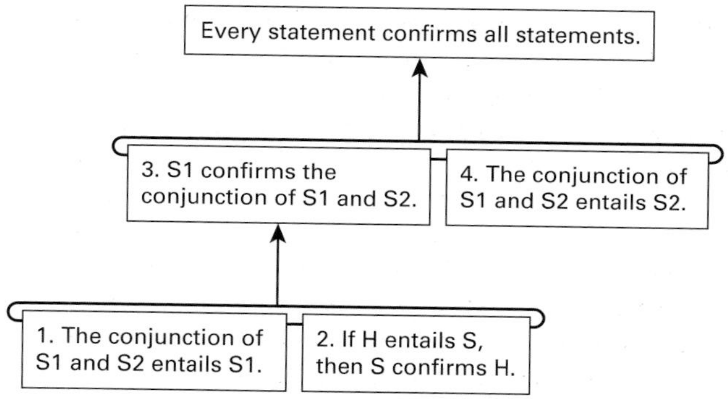

That paragraph goes a little too quickly, though. How do (3) and (4) support the conclusion that every statement confirms all statements? Let's take it more slowly. First, consider a hypothesis that is the conjunction of all the statements you can imagine, whether or not they are true. So, $H = S_1 \cdot S_2 \cdot S_3 \cdot S_4 \cdot S_5 \cdot S_6 \cdot S_7 \cdot \ldots$. As an example, let's say that the statements include the following:

S_1: My cat is a mammal.
S_2: This lizard is a reptile.
S_3: That car is red.

S_4: The Earth is flat.
S_5: My watch is broken.
S_6: My father likes chocolate.
S_7: My mother is a doctor.
…

So my hypothesis, H, is: "My cat is a mammal *and* this lizard is a reptile *and* that car is red *and* the earth is flat *and* my watch is broken *and* my father likes chocolate *and* my mother is a doctor *and* … ."

But consider that if H is true, then each of these statements is true. So, H entails each of these statements—for example: $H \rightarrow S_5$. Recall that if $H \rightarrow S$, then S confirms H. But we also said that if $H \rightarrow I$, then if S confirms H, then S will confirm I as well. So, on this definition of confirmation, S_1 confirms H, and $H \rightarrow S_5$, so S_1 confirms S_5. But that doesn't seem right; the fact that my cat is a mammal shouldn't confirm the fact that my watch is broken. That's not what we have in mind when we're talking about confirmation.

So, Goodman says we need a better definition of confirmation. He says:

> … a hypothesis is genuinely confirmed only by a statement that is an instance of it in the special sense of entailing not the hypothesis itself but its relativization or restriction to the class of entities mentioned by that statement.

Thus, the new definition is that S confirms H just in case H entails S and the entities in H are the same as the entities in S. So, we have the good consequence that the fact that my cat is a mammal confirms the hypothesis that all cats are mammals, but we don't have the bad consequence that the fact that my cat is a mammal confirms the fact that my watch is broken.

The problem, Goodman says, is that this definition won't work either. This leads us to the next section of his article.

4. The New Riddle of Induction

…

Suppose that[A] all emeralds examined before a certain time *t* are green.[1] At time *t*, then,[B] our observations support the hypothesis that all emeralds are green;[2] and[C] this is in accord with our definition of confirmation.[3] Our evidence statements assert that emerald *a* is green, that emerald *b* is green, and so on;[4] and each confirms the general hypothesis that all emeralds are green.[5] So far, so good.

Now let me introduce another predicate less familiar than "green." It is the predicate "grue" and it applies to all things examined before *t* just in case they are green but to other things just in case they are blue.[6]

Then[D] at time *t* we have, for each evidence statement asserting that a given emerald is green, a parallel evidence statement asserting that that emerald is grue.[7] And[E] the statements that emerald *a* is grue, that emerald *b* is grue, and so on, will each confirm the general hypothesis that all emeralds are grue.[8]

Thus[F] according to our definition, the prediction that all emeralds subsequently examined will be green and the prediction that all will be grue are alike confirmed by evidence statements describing the same observations.[9] But[G] if an emerald subsequently examined is grue, it is blue[10] and hence[H] not green.[11] Thus although we are well aware which of the two incompatible predictions is genuinely confirmed, they are equally well confirmed according to our present definition.[12

As indicated by (A), Goodman asks us to imagine a scenario in which all emeralds that have been examined (by any person) before a certain time, say January 1, 2020, are green (1). This is fine, because it fits perfectly well with our actual experience. Let's say, then that our hypothesis is that all emeralds are green (regardless of whether they have ever been, or will ever be, examined by a person). Our fixed-up definition of confirmation is that *S* confirms *H* just in case *H* entails *S* *and* the entities in *H* are the same as the entities in *S* (3). As indicated by (C) and (B), (1) and (2) combine to support the claim that our observation in (1) confirms our hypothesis (3).

Goodman then reiterates this argument—our evidence is that each of a whole bunch of emeralds has been observed to be green (4), and that each of these evidence statements confirms our hypothesis (5).

Although he doesn't say so explicitly here, Goodman believes that if a hypothesis entails an evidence statement, $H \rightarrow S$, then *S* not only confirms *H* when it is observed, but also confirms that *H* predicts that *S* will be observed, if it hasn't been already. Thus, if at time *t* our observations confirm the hypothesis that all emeralds are green (2), then they also confirm the prediction that any particular emerald examined after time *t* will be green.

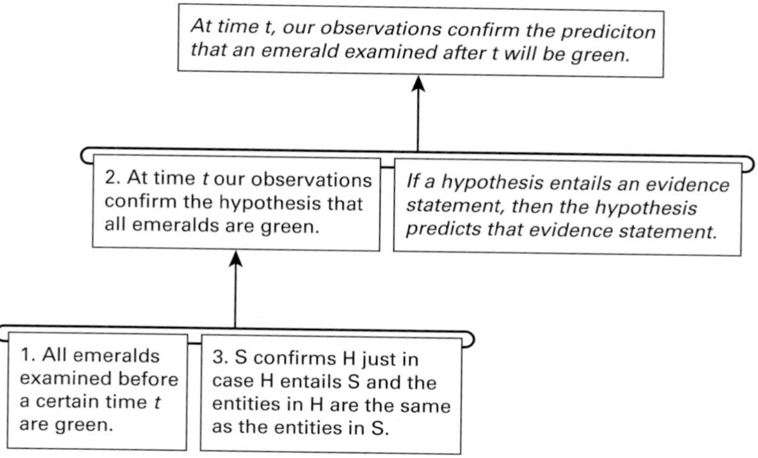

Goodman describes "green" as a "predicate," meaning that "green" can be applied to something like "emeralds." Now, Goodman asks us to consider a different predicate, which he calls "grue." Something is "grue" just in case it is examined before *t* and found to be green or it is examined after *t* and found to be blue (6).

What does this mean? Consider the time we used above: January 1, 2020. If something is observed (examined) to be green by a person before this time, then we say that it is grue.

Additionally, if something is observed to be blue by a person for the first time *after* that time, then we also say that it is grue. It's not that things change color—it just depends on when the thing is *first* observed. Something first observed to be green after this time is *not* grue. (It's "bleen," but more on that later.)

As indicated by (D), statement (6) supports the claim that at time t we have, for each evidence statement asserting that a given emerald is green, a parallel evidence statement asserting that that emerald is grue (7). Thus we can conclude that all emeralds examined before a certain time t are grue.

As indicated by (E), using our definition of confirmation (3), this supports the claim that at time *t* our observations confirm the hypothesis that all emeralds are grue (8). This, together with the observations about prediction, supports the claim that at time *t* our observations confirm the prediction that an emerald examined after *t* will be grue.

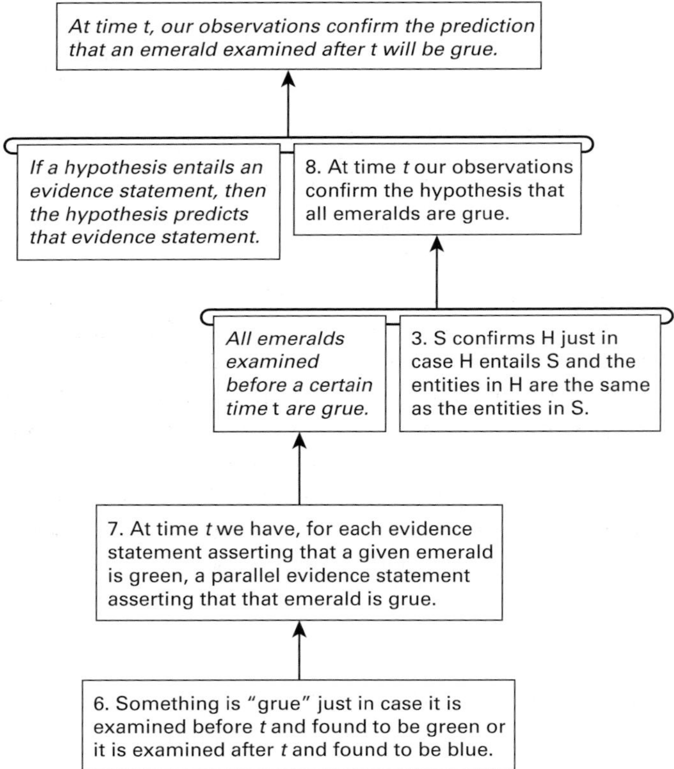

As indicated by (F), these two subconclusions support the claim that the prediction that all emeralds examined after time *t* will be green and the prediction that all will be grue are alike confirmed by the same observations (9). According to our definition of "grue," if a grue emerald is examined after *t*, then it is blue (10). This supports, as indicated by (H), the claim that if a grue emerald is examined after *t*, then it is not green (11). Then, as indicated by (G), (9) and (11) combine to support the claim that two incompatible predictions are equally well-confirmed (12).

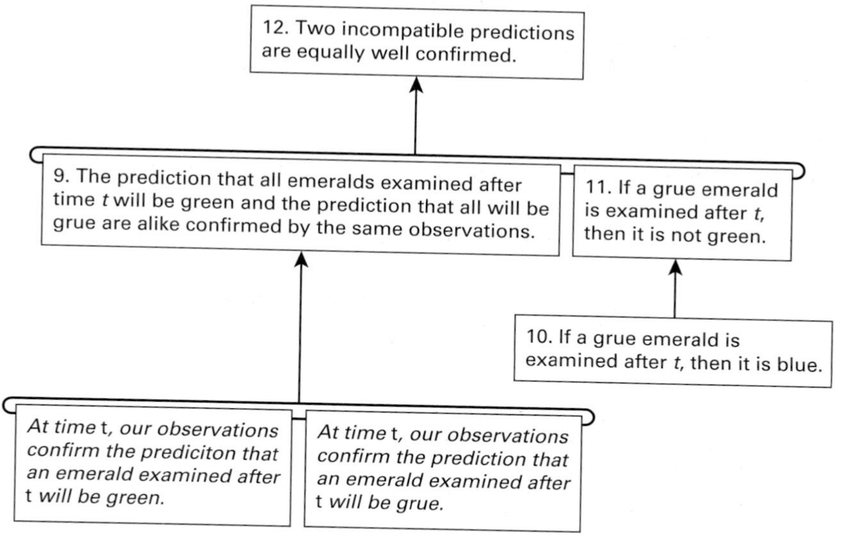

According to Goodman, two incompatible predictions are equally well-confirmed because the fact that all the emeralds that have been examined before time *t* are green supports both (a) the prediction that the next emerald examined after time *t* will be green *and* (b) the prediction that the next emerald examined after time *t* will be blue. Thus, the argument is that there is something wrong with our modified definition of confirmation, because a good definition of confirmation shouldn't allow this to happen.

Of course, you are probably saying right now that this hypothetical predicate "grue" is crazy, and no one would use such a definition of color in her hypothesis. Goodman's response to this kind of objection will be explored in the exercises.

9.4 In-Class Exercises

An asterisk (*) indicates a more challenging exercise.

Exercises 1–6

In the first part of this chapter, we analyzed in detail Reichenbach's criticism of Hume's solution to the problem of induction. Reichenbach then offers a solution of his own. The following selections contain further arguments from Reichenbach's article. For each selection, (a) diagram the argument and (b) identify any potential objections to the argument.

Exercise 1

Now it is obvious that a system of wagers of the more general type may have advantages. The "correction" c_n may be determined in such a way that the resulting wager furnishes even at an early stage of the series a good approximation of the limit p. The prophecies of a good clairvoyant would be of this type. On the other hand, it may happen also that c_n is badly determined, i.e., that the convergence is delayed by the correction. If the term c_n is arbitrarily formulated, we know nothing about the two possibilities. The value $c_n = 0$—i.e., the inductive principle—is therefore the value of the smallest risk; any other determination may worsen the convergence. This is a practical reason for preferring the inductive principle.

Exercise 2

These considerations lead, however, to a more precise formulation of the logical structure of the inductive inference. We must say that, if there is any method which leads to the limit of the frequency, the inductive principle will do the same; if there is a limit of the frequency, the inductive principle is a sufficient condition to find it. If we omit now the premise that there is a limit of the frequency, we cannot say that the inductive principle is the necessary condition of finding it because there are other methods using a correction c_n. There is a set of equivalent conditions such that the choice of one of the members of the set is necessary if we want to find the limit; and, if there is a limit, each of the members of the set is an appropriate method for finding it. We may say, therefore, that the *applicability* of the inductive principle is a necessary condition of the existence of a limit of the frequency.

Exercise 3

Our analysis of the problem of induction is based on our definition of the aim of induction as the evaluation of a limit of the frequency. Certain objections may be raised as to this statement of the aim of induction.

The first objection is based on the idea that our formulation demands too much, that the postulate of the existence of the limit of the frequency is too strong a postulate. It is argued that the world might be predictable even if there are no limits of frequencies, that our definition of predictability would restrict this concept too narrowly, excluding other types of structure which might perhaps be accessible to predictions without involving series of events with limits of their frequencies. Applied to our theory of induction, this objection would shake the cogency of our justification; by keeping strictly to the principle of induction, the man of science might exclude other possibilities of foreseeing the future which might work even if the inductive inference should fail.

Exercise 4

To this we must reply that our postulate does not demand the existence of a limit of the frequency for all series of events. It is sufficient if there is a certain number of series of this kind; by means of these we should then be able to determine the other series. We may imagine series which oscillate between two numerical values of the frequency; it can be shown that the description of series of this type is reducible to the indication of determinable subseries having a limit of the frequency. Let us introduce the term *reducible series* for series which are reducible to other series having a limit of their frequency; our definition of predictability then states only that the world is constituted by reducible series. The inductive procedure, the method of anticipation and later correction, will lead automatically to distinguishing series having a limit from other series and to the description of these others by means of the series having a limit. We cannot enter here into the mathematical details of this problem; for an elaboration of this we must refer to another publication.

Exercise 5

To elude our defense, the objection might be continued by the construction of a world in which there is no series having a limit. In such a world, so our adversary might argue, there might be a clairvoyant who knows every event of a series individually, who could foretell precisely what would happen from event to event—is not this "foreseeing the future" without having a limit of a frequency at one's disposal?

Exercise 6

We cannot admit this. Let us call *C* the case in which the prediction of the clairvoyant corresponds to the event observed later, non-*C* the opposite case. Now if the clairvoyant should have the faculty supposed, the series of events of the type *C* and not-*C* would define a series with a limit of the frequency. If the man should be a perfect prophet, this limit would be the number 1; however we may admit less perfect prophets with a lower limit. Anyway, we have constructed here a series with a limit. We must have such a series if we want to control the prophet; our control would consist in nothing but the application of the principle of induction to the series of events *C* and not-*C*, i.e., in an inductive inference as to the reliability of the prophet, based on his successes. Only if the reduction to such a series with a limit is possible can we know whether or not the man is a good prophet because only this reduction gives us the means of control.

Exercise 7

In the second part of this chapter, we analyzed in detail Popper's criticism of Hume's solution to the problem of induction. The following selection contains Popper's restatement of this argument. For this selection, (a) diagram the argument, and (b) identify any potential objections to the argument.

To put it more concisely, similarity-for-us is the product of a response involving interpretations (which may be inadequate) and anticipations or expectations (which may never be fulfilled). It is therefore impossible to explain anticipations, or expectations, as resulting from many repetitions, as suggested by Hume. For even the first repetition-for-us must be based upon similarity-for-us, and therefore upon expectations—precisely the kind of thing we wished to explain. This shows that there is an infinite regress involved in Hume's psychological theory.

Exercises 8–9

The following exercises refer to selections or ideas from the rest of Popper's *Conjectures and Refutations*.

Exercise 8

Consider the example of the puppies that Popper cites (reproduced below). Given his solution to the problem of induction, what would Popper's explanation be?

"A lighted cigarette was held near the noses of the young puppies," reports F. Bäge. "They sniffed at it once, turned tail, and nothing would induce them to come back to the source of the smell and to sniff again. A few days later, they reacted to the mere sight of a cigarette or even of a rolled piece of white paper, by bounding away, and sneezing." If we try to explain cases like this by postulating a vast number of long repetitive sequences at a still earlier age we are not only romancing, but forgetting that in the clever puppies' short lives there must be room not only for repetition but also for a great deal of novelty, and consequently of non-repetition.

Exercise 9

Research the discovery of the planet Neptune. (a) Why were people searching for a new planet (Neptune)? (b) Does this search and discovery sequence follow Popper's description of the scientific method? Why or why not?

Exercises 10–13

In the third part of this chapter, we analyzed in detail Goodman's "new riddle of induction." The following selections contain further arguments from Goodman's article. For each selection, (a) diagram the argument and (b) identify any potential objections to the argument.

Exercise 10

This passage picks up directly after the passage analyzed in the previous section.

Moreover, it is clear that if we simply choose an appropriate predicate, then on the basis of these same observations we shall have equal confirmation, by our definition, for any prediction whatever about other emeralds—or indeed about anything else. As in our earlier example, only the predictions subsumed under lawlike hypotheses are genuinely confirmed; but we have no criterion as yet for determining lawlikeness. And now we see that without some such criterion, our definition not merely includes a few unwanted cases, but is so completely ineffectual that it virtually excludes nothing. We are left once again with the intolerable result that anything confirms anything. This difficulty cannot be set aside as an annoying detail to be taken care of in due course. It has to be met before our definition will work at all.

Exercise 11

This statement will not go unprotested. "Consider," it will be argued, "the predicates 'blue' and 'green' and the predicate 'grue' introduced earlier, and also the predicate 'bleen' that applies to emeralds examined before time *t* just in case they are blue and to other emeralds just in case they are green. Surely it is clear," the argument runs, "that the first two are purely qualitative and the second two are not; for the meaning of each of the latter two plainly involves reference to a specific temporal position."

Exercise 12

To this I reply that indeed I do recognize the first two as well-behaved predicates admissible in lawlike hypotheses, and the second two as ill-behaved predicates. But the argument that the former but not the latter are purely qualitative seems to me quite unsound. True enough, if we start with "blue" and "green," then "grue" and "bleen" will be explained in terms of "blue" and "green" and a temporal term. But equally truly, if we start with "grue" and "bleen," then "blue" and "green" will be explained in terms of "grue" and "bleen" and a temporal term; "green," for example, applies to emeralds examined before time *t* just in case they are grue, and to other emeralds just in case they are bleen. Thus qualitativeness is an entirely relative matter and does not by itself establish any dichotomy of predicates. This relativity seems to be completely overlooked by those who contend that the qualitative character of a predicate is a criterion for its good behavior.

Exercise 13

Of course, one may ask why we need worry about such unfamiliar predicates as "grue" or about accidental hypotheses in general, since we are unlikely to use them in making predictions. If our definition works for such hypotheses as are normally employed, isn't that all we need? In a sense, yes; but only in the sense that we need no definition, no theory of induction, and no philosophy of knowledge at all. We get along well enough without them in daily life and in scientific research. But if we seek a theory at all, we cannot excuse gross anomalies resulting from a proposed theory by pleading that we can avoid them in practice. The odd cases we have been considering are clinically pure cases that, though seldom encountered in practice, nevertheless display to best advantage the symptoms of a widespread and destructive malady.

Exercises 14–19

The following exercises are intended to ensure your understanding of Reichenbach's, Popper's, and Goodman's texts, and to help you further explore the ideas presented in this chapter.

Exercise 14: Now that you have read my textual analysis of Reichenbach's argument, summarize it in your own words.

Exercise 15: Now that you have read my textual analysis of Popper's argument, summarize it in your own words.

Exercise 16: Now that you have read my textual analysis of Goodman's argument, summarize it in your own words.

Exercise 17: Summarize, in your own words, each of the arguments in exercises 1–6 above.

Exercise 18: Summarize, in your own words, the argument in exercise 7 above.

Exercise 19: Summarize, in your own words, each of the arguments in exercises 10–13 above.

9.5 Reading Questions

1. Reichenbach says: "But I should say a philosopher who is to put aside his principles any time he steers a motorcar is a bad philosopher." What does he mean?
2. What is Reichenbach's example of the clairvoyant supposed to show? Why wouldn't clairvoyance, if it were real, be a better method of prediction than induction?
3. What does Popper think that Hume got right about the problem of induction? What does Popper think he got wrong?
4. What is rationalism, according to Popper? Why must we give it up?
5. Popper's "solution" to the problem of induction is not really a solution as Hume conceived it. Popper has not shown a way for knowledge obtained by induction to be justified. Rather, he thinks Hume made an airtight argument that induction can't be rationally justified. So why does Popper call it a "solution"?
6. What does Popper mean in the following passage?

> The demand for rational proofs in science indicates a failure to keep distinct the broad realm of rationality and the narrow realm of rational certainty: it is an untenable, an unreasonable demand. Nevertheless, the role of logical argument, of deductive logical reasoning, remains all-important for the critical approach; not because it allows us to prove our theories, or to infer them from observation statements, but because only by purely deductive reasoning is it possible for us to discover what our theories imply, and thus to criticize them effectively.

7. Goodman speaks of defining a "valid inductive inference." What do you think he means by that? What problem is it supposed to solve?
8. When defending his notions of "grue" and "bleen," Goodman says: "But equally truly, if we start with 'grue' and 'bleen,' then 'blue' and 'green' will be explained in terms of 'grue' and 'bleen' and a temporal term." What does this mean? Why does he point this out?

IV Theory of Mind

Introduction

Recall in the first chapter we separated philosophy into four broad categories:

- Epistemology
- Metaphysics
- Value theory
- Logic

And recall that metaphysics is the study of what there is. In Part II we tackled two metaphysical questions: (1) Does God exist? And (2) Why is there evil in the world? In this part and the next, we tackle a few more metaphysical problems. For now we will be concerned with questions about the nature of the mind.

Learning Objectives for Part IV

At the end of Part IV, you will be able to:

- Describe:
  - The difference between dualism and materialism
  - The difference between the varieties of materialism
- Discuss:
  - The strengths and weaknesses of the arguments for and against dualism
  - The strengths and weaknesses of the arguments for and against materialism
- Define:
  - Category mistake
  - Qualia
  - Dualism
  - Materialism
  - Logical behaviorism
  - Identity theory
  - Functionalism

Preliminary Questions for Part IV

1. How do you know if other people have minds?
2. Can the mind survive the death of the body?
3. Are there only physical or material substances in the world?
4. Is the mind the same as the brain?
5. If not, how does the mind interact with the brain?
6. What are the causes of our actions?
7. What is consciousness?
8. Are only humans conscious?
9. How can we tell if someone or something is conscious?
10. Can two different people have the same conscious experiences? How would we know?
11. Could a computer be conscious?
12. Could a computer think or be intelligent?

Nature of the Mind

Broadly speaking, there are two main kinds of philosophical theories about the mind: *dualism* and *materialism* (or *physicalism*). Dualists generally believe that there are two kinds of substances in the world: mental and physical. Minds are made of the mental substance and brains and bodies are made of the physical substance. Materialists, on the other hand, believe that there is only one kind of substance in the world, and that minds and brains are both made of a material substance.

These two theories can be further divided into different categories. The two mains kinds of dualism are called *Cartesian* (named for René Descartes) and *popular*. Cartesian dualists hold that the mind is not only made of a different substance than the body, but also that it has no mass, extension, or location. Popular dualists, on the other hand, agree that the mind is made of a different substance, but generally think that it is spatially located (usually in the head). In chapter 10, we will reconsider Descartes's arguments in *Meditations on First Philosophy: Meditation VI* for the view that the mind and body are separate and distinct.

In contrast, there are several different kinds of materialism. The first is *property dualism*, which holds that there is only one type of substance in the world—material or physical substance—but that physical matter can have two types of properties: physical properties and mental properties. On this theory, the mind is the collection of the mental properties, or states, of the brain, while the collection of physical properties is just referred to as the brain. Drilling down even further, there are at least two types of property dualism, according to how one thinks that the mind interacts with the brain. *Epiphenomenalists* believe that mental states are caused by brain states, but that mental states have no causal powers themselves, while *interactionists* believe that mental states are caused by physical states and vice versa.

The second type of materialist theory of the mind is *logical behaviorism*. This is the view that mental states (like being in pain, or seeing red, or hearing a song) are nothing more than collections of dispositions to behave. That is, "having pain in my left pinky toe" is just the collection of the dispositions I have to act in certain ways: saying "ouch," nursing my toe, avoiding the table leg in the future, and so on. In this way, a mental state is like a family—a family is just the collection of certain people, and a mental state is just a collection of certain behaviors. And just as it would be a category mistake to say that I have parents, grandparents, siblings, and a family, as if "family" were in the same category as "sister," it is also a *category mistake* to say that I have a mind and a brain, as if "mind" were in the same category as "brain." In chapter 10, we will also read a selection by Gilbert Ryle, a twentieth-century logical behaviorist who criticizes Descartes's dualism.

The third type is *identity theory*. This is the view that mental states are the same thing as particular brain states. That is, my brain is composed of neurons, chemicals, and so on, and at any given moment some neurons are firing and some chemicals are being exchanged, and so on. We can say that a brain state is a certain pattern of neuronal firing and distribution of chemicals, and so on, so that when I stub my left pinky toe on the table leg, a signal is sent to my brain and my brain changes from the state it was in to a new state. And part of this new brain state is identical to my mental state of having pain in my toe.

The fourth, and arguably the most prominent, type of materialist theory is *functionalism*. Functionalism is similar to identity theory in that mental states—thoughts, pains, and so on—are the same thing as physical states. But functionalism is different in that physical states are defined not as particular (human) brain states but rather by their functional roles in producing other internal states and outputs. In other words, functionalism holds that the defining feature of any mental state is the set of causal relations it bears to the environment, other mental states, and behavior. Thus, one does not even have to have a human brain to have a mental state; one needs only a complex enough system to have physical states that fulfill the same function as brain states do. In chapter 11, we will consider J. J. C. Smart's arguments for the identity theory and Jerry Fodor's arguments for functionalism.

Phenomenology

As mentioned above, there is a debate among materialists about whether the mind and mental states can be purely physical properties of our brains. One of the criticisms of logical behaviorism, for example, is that there seems to be much more to "pain in my left pinky toe" than just the different kinds of ways I am disposed to behave. Logical behaviorism seems to leave out the most important aspect of pain—the fact that it hurts! That is, there is a certain *quality* to pain—what it feels like—that materialism fails to capture.

Property dualists point out that we have many other phenomenal experiences besides the feel of pain: what an apple tastes like, what it is like to see the color red. These qualitative experiences are sometimes referred to as *qualia*, and the "problem of qualia" is that theories of mind that only recognize physical properties of brains seem unable to account for qualia. In chapter 12, we will analyze arguments given by both Thomas Nagel and Frank Jackson that purely physicalist theories leave out qualia.

Intelligent Computers

In 1936, British mathematician Alan Turing (1912–1954) produced a definition of computation, developed the idea of a "Turing machine," and determined the absolute limit on what could be done with computation. This work formed the basis of modern computer science. Turing had given his interpretation of computability in terms of "states of mind," and later equated building a computer to "building a brain." After his work as a code breaker in World War II, Turing moved to Manchester University and in 1950 published an article in the philosophical journal *Mind* titled "Computing Machinery and Intelligence."[1] It was in this paper that he first considered the possibility of an intelligent computer. In it he first considers and rejects various reasons for thinking that computers could never think, then describes the basic idea of a computer program, and finally proposes a behavioral test for determining whether a machine is thinking. This has come to be known as the "Turing test."

Turing argued that "the question, 'Can machines think?' should be replaced by 'Are there imaginable digital computers which would do well in the imitation game?'" In chapter 13, we will analyze an argument by John Searle that even if a computer could pass the Turing test, that is not enough to allow us to say that it is intelligent, and a reply to this argument by Dan Dennett.

10 Dualism

10.1 René Descartes, *Meditations on First Philosophy*
10.2 Gilbert Ryle, "Descartes' Myth"
10.3 In-Class Exercises
10.4 Reading Questions

10.1 René Descartes, *Meditations on First Philosophy*

Recall our discussion of Descartes from chapter 8. There I said that the first five meditations in his *Meditations on First Philosophy* are supposed to provide the premises for Descartes's overall argument in the sixth, and final, meditation. We saw that in *Meditation I*, Descartes argues that all his beliefs can be doubted. But in *Meditation II*, we saw that Descartes argues that there is, in fact, one thing he believes that cannot be doubted: the fact that he exists. In *Meditation III*, Descartes uses the fact that he exists and the fact that he has an idea of God to argue that God exists. In *Meditation IV*, Descartes uses the fact that God exists to argue that God would not make it so that he is constantly deceived; rather, God has made it so that everything he perceives "clearly and distinctly" is true. That is, if Descartes is very careful in his investigations, then he can actually trust his senses and his reasoning.

One problem with Descartes's overall argument is what philosophers call the *Cartesian circle*. The argument in *Meditation III* depends on the premise that everything that Descartes perceives clearly and distinctly is true to show that God exists. But then in *Meditation IV*, he uses the fact that God exists to show that everything he perceives "clearly and distinctly" is true.

This circularity in Descartes's argument is not what concerns us here, however. What is important in this meditation for us is Descartes's argument that his mind and his body are two different things. Descartes gave some of this argument in *Meditation III*, but here in *Meditation VI* is where he presents his dualism most clearly.

Let's look at his text in more detail. Specifically, we will analyze and diagram the argument and then discuss criticisms of it.

From *Meditations on First Philosophy: Meditation VI.*[2]

(3) But now, when I am beginning to know myself and my maker better, although I don't think I should recklessly accept everything I seem to have got from the senses, neither do I think it should all be called into doubt.

First, I know that[A] if I have a clear and distinct thought of something, God could have created it in a way that exactly corresponds to my thought.[1] So[B] the fact that[C] I can clearly and distinctly think of one thing apart from another[2] assures me that[D] the two things are distinct from one another[3]—[that is, that they are *two*]—since[E] they can be separated by God.[4] Never mind *how* they could be separated; that does not affect the judgment that they are distinct. I know that I exist and that nothing else belongs to my nature or essence except that I am a thinking thing; from this it follows that my essence consists solely in my being a thinking thing, even though there may be a body that is very closely joined to me. I have a clear and distinct idea of myself as something that thinks and isn't extended,[5] and[F] one of body as something that is extended and does not think.[6] So[G] it is certain that I am really distinct from my body and can exist without it.

In section 3 of *Meditation VI,* Descartes gives us two arguments that his mind and his body are two separate and distinct things. The indicator (A) tells us that the first argument is starting here. Descartes's first premise is what he claims to have established in *Meditation IV*: that God has made it such that everything he perceives clearly and distinctly is true (1). Next we have the statement: "I can clearly and distinctly think of one thing apart from another" (2). Which things is he talking about? Since Descartes wants to make an argument about two specific things below, here he is just inviting us to imagine a very general situation in which he clearly and distinctly perceives two things as being separate from each other. As indicated by (D), this supports his contention that these two things really are separate from each other (3).

But, Descartes thinks that (2) cannot support (3) alone—it needs an element from the first very general statement he made (1). That is, (1) supports the claim that the two things he clearly and distinctly perceives as being separate can be separated by God (4). And now we have the following argument construction: (1), so, (2); therefore (3), since (4); which means that (1) supports (4), which is linked with (2) to provide support for (3):

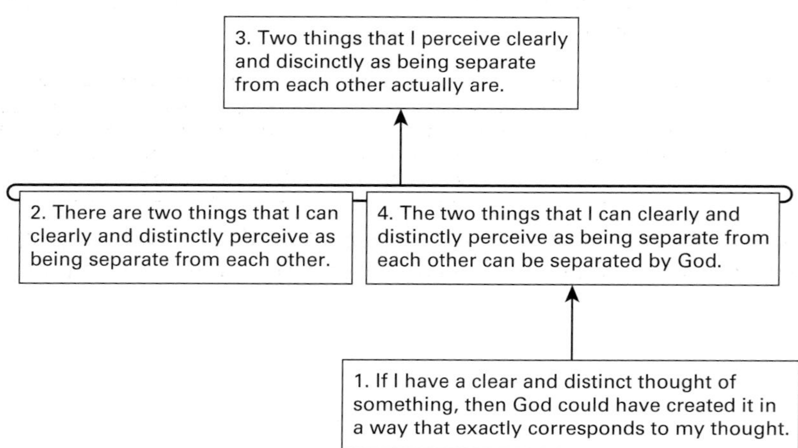
3. Two things that I perceive clearly and discinctly as being separate from each other actually are.
2. There are two things that I can clearly and distinctly perceive as being separate from each other.
4. The two things that I can clearly and distinctly perceive as being separate from each other can be separated by God.
1. If I have a clear and distinct thought of something, then God could have created it in a way that exactly corresponds to my thought.

Descartes then uses this conclusion to support an argument in which the two things he perceives are his mind and his body. He says that he clearly and distinctly perceives himself as something that thinks and is not extended (5). He also says that he clearly and distinctly perceives his body as something that does not think and is extended (6). By (F) and (G), we know that these statements are supposed be combined with each other to support the main conclusion that Descartes's mind is separate from his body.

Thus, we have Descartes's first argument:

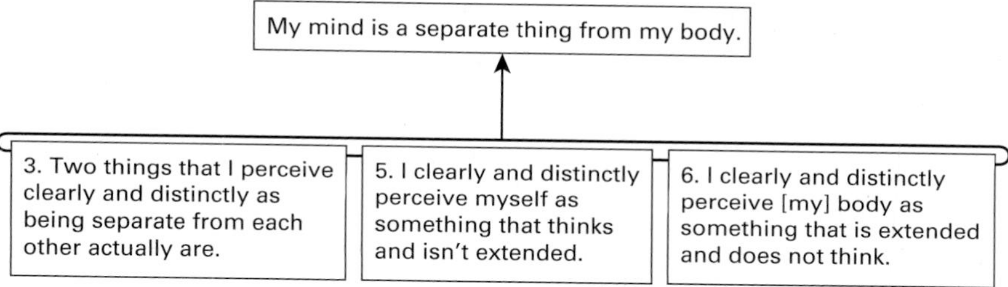

His second argument is presented as follows:

Besides this, I find that[H] I am capable of certain special kinds of thinking [= "mental activity"], namely imagination and sensory perception.[7] Now,[I] I can clearly and distinctly understand myself as a whole without these faculties;[8] but[J] I can't understand them without me, that is, without an intellectual substance for them to belong to.[9] A faculty or capacity essentially involves *acts*,[10] so[K] it involves some *thing* that acts;[11] so I see that[L] I differ from my faculties as a thing differs from its properties.[12]

As indicated by (H), Descartes has another argument for the same conclusion. He first says he can tell (probably via introspection) that he is capable of certain kinds of mental faculties like imagination and sensory perception (7). Then he says that he can clearly and distinctly understand himself as a whole without these specific faculties (8). As indicated by (I), these two are meant to be combined. Then he says that he cannot understand these specific capacities without an intellectual substance for them to belong to (9). As indicated by (J), this is meant to be combined with the first two statements.

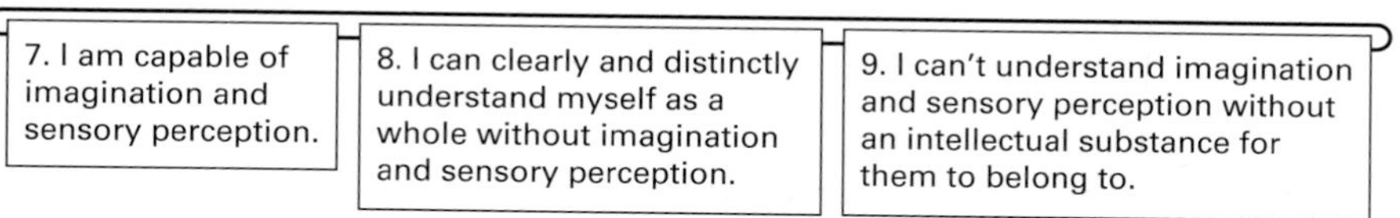

Next, though, Descartes takes the time to explain why (9) is true. According to (K), the fact that a faculty essentially involves acts (10) supports the claim that the faculty involves a thing that acts (11). So now we have:

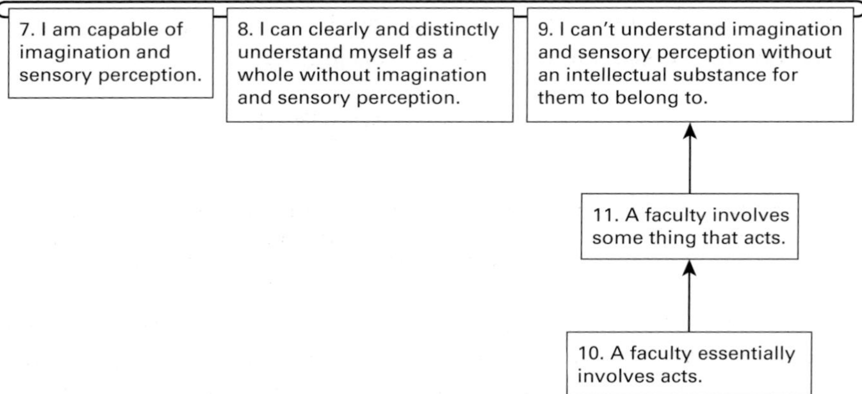

As indicated by (L), this in turn supports Descartes's claim that he is not the same as his faculties, just like a ball is not the same as its color (12).

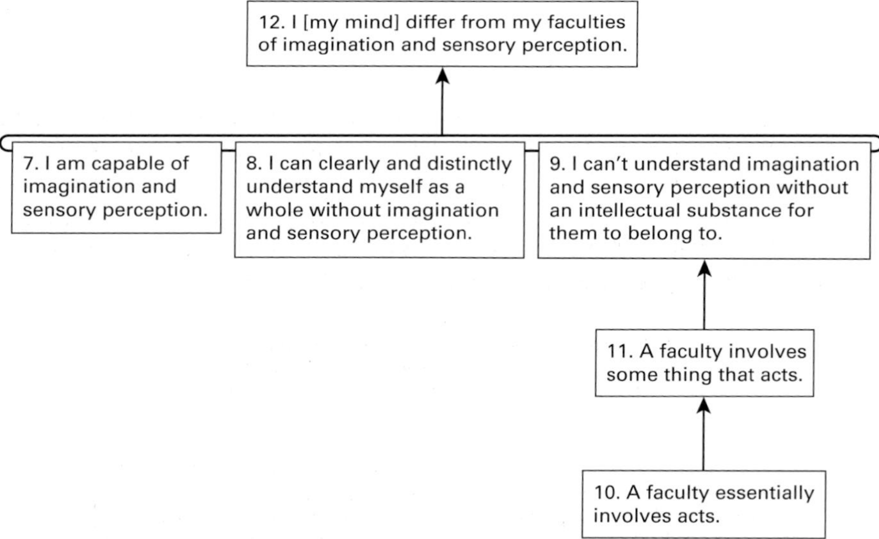

In this argument and the next, Descartes uses a logical principle called *Leibniz's law*, after Gottfried Wilhelm von Leibniz, seventeenth-century philosopher and mathematician. In general, Leibniz's law says that if two things, say A and B, are identical, then A and B must both have the same properties. That is, if A has a particular property, then B must have the same property. And conversely, if A doesn't have some other particular property, then B can't have that property either. This, of course, makes complete sense. Suppose my sister thinks that I am wearing *her* shirt. I can rebut her claim by showing her that the shirt I'm actually wearing has different properties than the one she thinks I'm wearing. For example, I could show her that the shirt I'm wearing has my name written on the tag (since this kind of thing happens with her all the time), and her shirt does not have my name on it.

We can represent an argument using Leibniz's law like this:

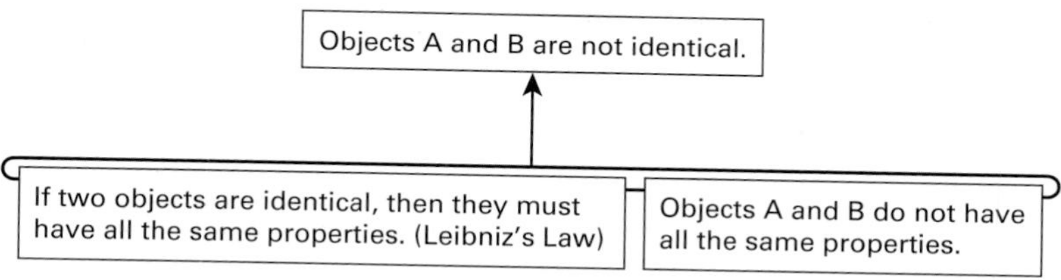

The conclusion of the previous argument is that Descartes' mind is different from his faculties of imagination and sensory perception. But recall, the entire sentence (12): "I differ from my faculties as a thing differs from its properties." So, in essence, Descartes is saying that his mind has some properties, like imagination and sensory perception.

In the next part, Descartes turns to the properties that his *body* has.

Of course[M] there are other faculties—such as those of moving around, changing shape, and so on—which also need a substance to belong to;[13] but[N] it must be a bodily or extended substance and not a thinking one,[14] because[O] those faculties essentially involve extension but not thought.[15]

As indicated by (M), Descartes continues the argument from above. Here he lists other faculties that need to belong to a substance (13). These faculties need to belong to an extended substance, not a thinking one (14). As indicated by (O), the fact that these faculties essentially involve extension but not thought (15) supports the previous claim (14). As indicated by (N), (13) and (14) combine to support a conclusion that Descartes does not explicitly state: that these faculties belong to a substance different from him (his mind).

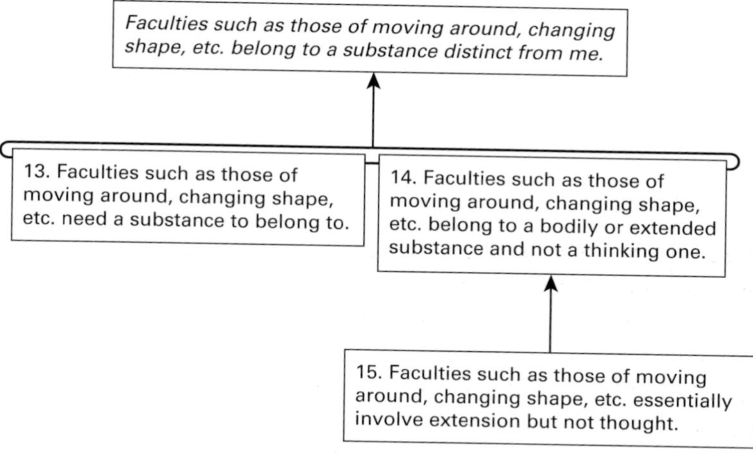

Ultimately, then, Descartes wants to make the argument that since his mind has one set of properties and his body has another, his mind and his body have different properties:

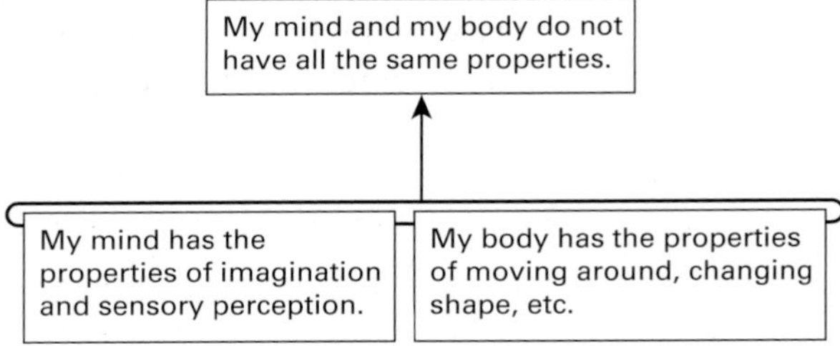

He can then use this, along with Leibniz's law, to show that his mind is distinct from his body:

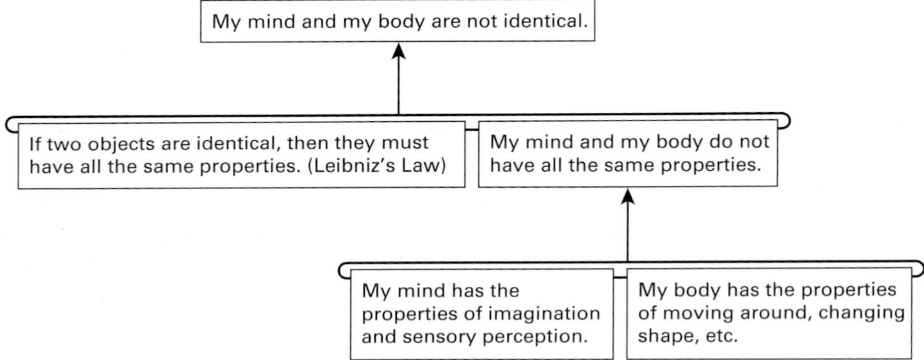

This is an example of Descartes's *interactionist dualism*:

- The mind and the body are made of different substances (dualism).
  - The body is made of a physical substance, meaning:
    - it has a location in time and space,
    - it has extension and shape,
    - it does not think,
    - it is made up of parts (it is divisible), and
    - it has the kinds of properties that physical substances have.
  - The mind is made of some kind of mental substance, meaning:
    - it has a location in time but not in space,
    - it has neither extension nor shape,
    - it thinks,
    - it is indivisible, and
    - is has the kinds of properties that mental substances have.
- The mind and body exert causal influences on each other (interactionism).

Let's turn now to some objections to Descartes's argument in *Meditation VI*.

First Objection

The most common objection to dualism is that it can't make sense of the connection between mind and body. It seems clear that there is a connection. A change in my body often causes a change in my mind; for example, damage to my body causes pain. And a change in my mind often causes a change in my body; for example, if I become thirsty, I will get up to get a drink of water.

But if the mind is made up of a different substance than the body, how do the two interact with each other? Descartes explained his own theory in his book, *The Passions of the Soul*:[3]

> Although the soul is joined to the whole body, there's a certain part of the body where it exercises its functions more particularly than in all the others. It's commonly thought that this part is the brain, because of its relation to the sense-organs, or the heart, because it feels to us as though that's where our passions are. But on looking into this very carefully I think I can clearly see that the part of the body in which the soul directly does its work is … a certain very small gland deep inside the brain, in a position such that … the slightest movements by it can greatly alter the course of the nearby spirits passing through the brain, and conversely any little change in the course of those spirits can greatly alter the movements of the gland.

But there are a few problems with this explanation. First, if the mind has no spatial location, how is it that there is a precise spatial location at which it interacts with the body? Furthermore, this only purports to explain *where* the mind and the body interact, not *how* they do it. If an object changes position with no physical cause, then the laws of physics—for example, conservation of energy—are violated. But that is exactly what Descartes is suggesting: that something nonphysical (i.e., mental) can cause a change in something physical.

Second Objection

A second major objection to Descartes's argument is his use of Leibniz's law. Certain kinds of properties follow Leibniz's Law, but others do not. For example, consider the following arguments:

Argument 1:

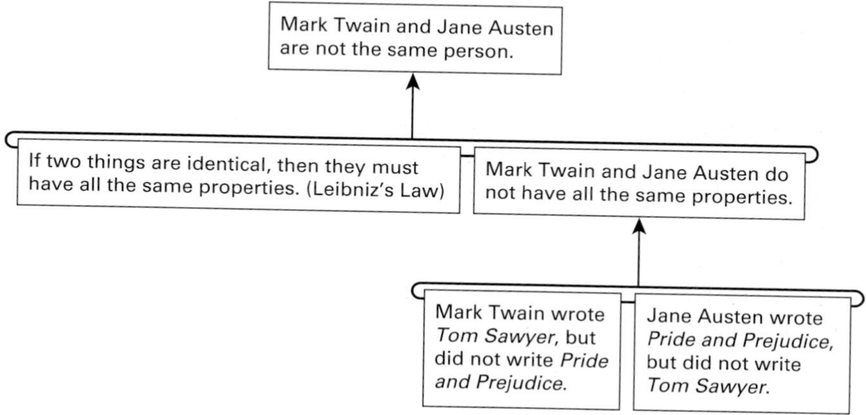

and
Argument 2:

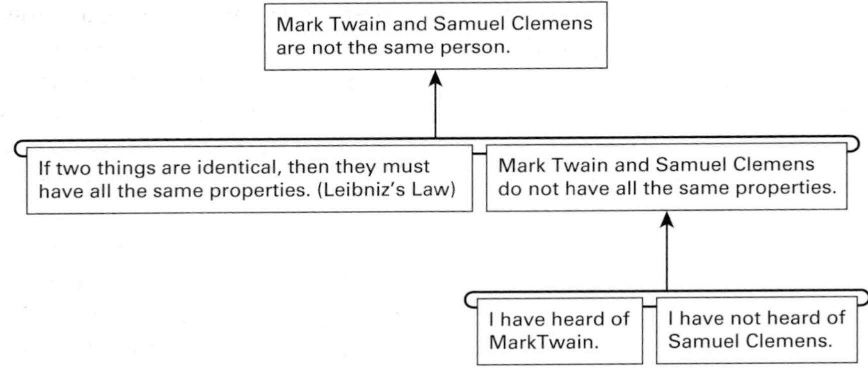

Argument 1 seems good—the premises are all true, and they lead to a true conclusion. But there's something wrong with Argument 2. Let's say the premises were all true (that I had not ever heard of Samuel Clemens). They seem to lead logically to the conclusion, but the conclusion is false. What went wrong? The problem is that the properties that appear in Argument 1 are of a different kind from those that appear in Argument 2. The properties in Argument 1—writing *Tom Sawyer*, for example—are properties of the *people* (objects) in question—Mark Twain and Jane Austin. But the properties that appear in Argument 2—having heard of Mark Twain, for example—are not properties of the things in question; they are properties of *me*.

Looking closely at Descartes's arguments, we see that his reasons for believing that his mind and body have different properties have to do with his *perceptions*. He says that he perceives "clearly and distinctly" that his mind has one set of properties and his body has another. From his argument in *Meditation IV*, Descartes believes that everything he perceives "clearly and distinctly" is true, and not subject to doubt. But, as I explained in the introduction to this part, Descartes reached this conclusion using circular reasoning.

So, if Descartes has not given us a good reason to believe that everything he perceives clearly and distinctly is in fact true, then he is reporting properties of himself—what he perceives about his mind and his body—rather than real properties of his mind and body. Thus we have no good reason to believe that his mind and his body really have different properties, and thus are not identical.

Finally, in the next section we explore an objection that Gilbert Ryle raises to Descartes's arguments.

10.2 Gilbert Ryle, "Descartes' Myth"

Born in Brighton, England, Gilbert Ryle (1900–1976) was one of the foremost "ordinary language" philosophers of the twentieth century. Ryle attended Brighton College, and then studied philosophy at Queen's College, Oxford. After graduating in 1924, he was appointed to the faculty at Christ Church College, Oxford, where he remained until his retirement in 1968.

Inspired by German philosopher Ludwig Wittgenstein, Ryle was of the opinion that all philosophical problems only seemed like problems because the terms of the debate were not sufficiently clear. Once the vagueness and ambiguities have been eliminated, he believed, the philosophical problems would just disappear.

Ryle's most famous philosophical work, *The Concept of Mind*, has been interpreted as proving definitively that Cartesian dualism is false and also as promoting the theory of philosophical behaviorism. While he may not have actually been a philosophical behaviorist himself, he did emphasize the aspects of the doctrine that have survived into the twenty-first century—the view that a person's behavior is relevant to the characterization of his or her mind.

In the first chapter of *The Concept of Mind* Ryle presents his famous argument against what he termed Descartes's "ghost in the machine." He really has two goals in this chapter. The first is to argue against dualism, and the second is to argue against the related doctrine of mentalism—the view that mental states are "inner" causes of behavior. Here, though, we will just be concerned with his argument against dualism.

Ryle offers a historically novel argument against Cartesian dualism. First, he explains what he calls the "official doctrine." This is the doctrine that people have both bodies and minds but that minds are radically different from bodies. Then, Ryle explains how this doctrine leads to various philosophical problems including the "problem of free will" (which we will discuss in Part V). The argument he then presents is not really about these particular philosophical problems, but about the underlying assumptions that lead to these problems. Let's look at his text in more detail. Specifically, we will analyze and diagram the argument and then discuss criticisms of it.

As the title of the second section in Ryle's chapter says, he wants to show that the official doctrine—Descartes's theory of the mind—is absurd, hence false. Ryle provides several arguments for this conclusion, but I want here to concentrate on one that he gives in section 3.

First, Ryle argues that Descartes posited the official doctrine as a way to reconcile mechanical science with the fact of free will (we will explore this argument in the exercises). Ryle argues that the *para-mechanical hypothesis*—the reconciliation that minds are also centers of causal processes—is an assumption of the official doctrine, since philosophers immediately recognized that the causal interaction between minds and bodies is a problem for the official doctrine.

Next, Ryle explains how the official doctrine has been taken to lead to the problem of free will: on the one hand, the difference between people and machines seems to be that humans behave as if they have free will; but on the other, if minds are just "spectral machines," then there seems to be no room for free will. Ultimately, he calls the argument that the official doctrine leads to the problem of free will "broken-backed" because, as he wants to show, the explanation for the fact that we can all tell the difference between a human and a robot itself presupposes that we cannot tell the difference between a human and a robot.

From *The Concept of the Mind.*[4]

It is an historical curiosity that it was not noticed that[A] the entire argument was broken-backed. Theorists correctly assumed that[B] any sane man could already recognise the differences between, say, rational and non-rational utterances or between purposive and automatic behaviour.[1] Else there would have been nothing requiring to be salved from mechanism.[2]

Yet[C] the explanation given presupposed that one person could in principle never recognise the difference between the rational and the irrational utterances issuing from other human bodies,[3] since[D] he could never get access to the postulated immaterial causes of some of their utterances.[4] Save for the doubtful exception of himself, he could never tell the difference between a man and a Robot.[5] It would have to be conceded, for example, that, for all that we can tell, the inner lives of persons who are classed as idiots or lunatics are as rational as those of anyone else. Perhaps only their overt behaviour is disappointing; that is to say, perhaps "idiots" are not really idiotic, or "lunatics" lunatic. Perhaps, too, some of those who are classed as sane are really idiots.

According to the theory, external observers could never know how the overt behaviour of others is correlated with their mental powers and processes[6] and so[E] they could never know or even plausibly conjecture whether their applications of mental-conduct concepts to these other people were correct or incorrect.[7] It would then[F] be hazardous or impossible for a man to claim sanity or logical consistency even for himself,[8] since[G] he would be debarred from comparing his own performances with those of others.[9]

In short, our characterisations of persons and their performances as intelligent, prudent and virtuous or as stupid, hypocritical and cowardly could never have been made,[10] so[H] the problem of providing a special causal hypothesis to serve as the basis of such diagnoses would never have arisen.[11] The question, 'How do persons differ from machines?' arose just because everyone already knew how to apply mental-conduct concepts before the new causal hypothesis was introduced.[12] This causal hypothesis could not therefore[I] be the source of the criteria used in those applications.[13] Nor, of course, has the causal hypothesis in any degree improved our handling of those criteria. We still distinguish good from bad arithmetic, politic from impolitic conduct and fertile from infertile imaginations in the ways in which Descartes himself distinguished them before and after he speculated how the applicability of these criteria was compatible with the principle of mechanical causation.

First, as indicated by (B), Ryle gives an argument that he thinks is perfectly reasonable. The claim that any sane person can recognize the differences between intelligent and unintelligent behavior or between purposive and automatic behavior (1) is essentially the claim that sane people can tell the difference between a person and a robot. This is supported by the claim that if this weren't true, there wouldn't be anything to explain (2), that is, there wouldn't be any problem of free will. In other words, the fact that people can tell the difference between a person and a robot is what gives rise to the problem of free will. So, the implication is that there is, in fact, something to explain, and this combines with (2) to support (1).

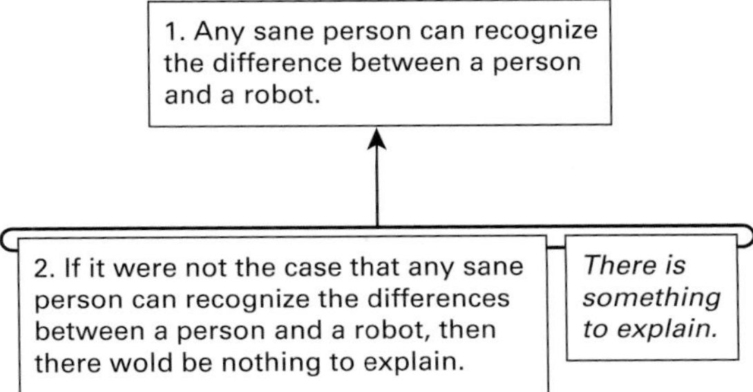

The problem, according to Ryle, is that if the "official" doctrine were really true, there wouldn't be anything to explain because people wouldn't be able to tell the difference between a person and a robot. To see this, let's start from the beginning. The "official doctrine" is the *double-life theory*, that everyone has an "outer" life that is accessible to everyone and an "inner" life that is accessible to no one except that person, along with the *causal hypothesis*, that the mind is governed by nonmechanical causal laws, just like the physical world is governed by mechanical causal laws.

The claim he makes here is that this explanation presupposes that someone could never recognize the difference between rational and irrational speech (3). As indicated by (D), the reason is that one person can never get access to the "inner" life of another that is the cause of his behavior (4). And this leads to the conclusion that if the official doctrine were true, then no one would ever be able to tell the difference between a person and a robot (5). So, the implication is that if the official doctrine were true, then there would be nothing to explain! This, then supports the conclusion that the argument that the official doctrine leads to the problem of free will is broken-backed.

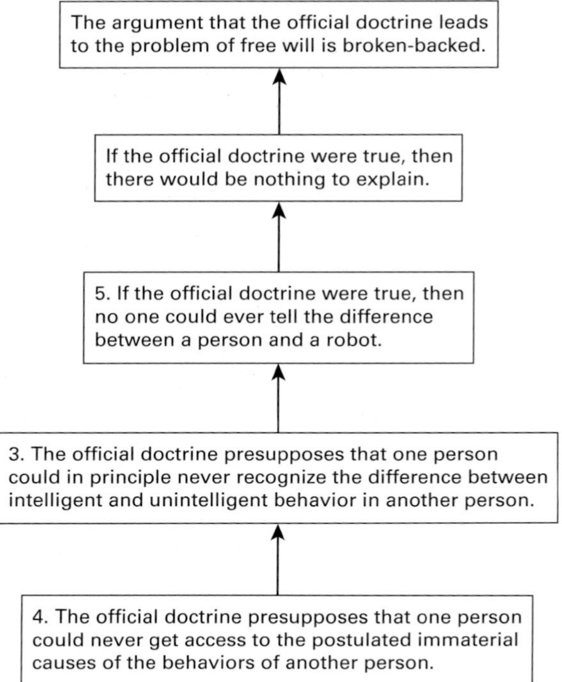

After giving some examples, Ryle elaborates on the reasons he has for the claim that if the official doctrine is true, then no one could ever recognize the difference between rational and irrational speech (3).

First, he claims that if the official doctrine were true, then a person could never know how the observable behavior of others is correlated with their mental powers and processes (6). As indicated by (E), this supports the claim that if the official doctrine were true, then a person could never know whether his applications of mental-conduct concepts to these other people were correct or incorrect (7).

As indicated by (G), the claim that if the official doctrine were true, then no person could compare his own performances with those of others (9) supports the claim that if the official doctrine were true, then no person could claim sanity or logical consistency even for himself (8). And, and indicated by (F), the subargument containing (8) and (9) is supported by the subargument containing (6) and (7).

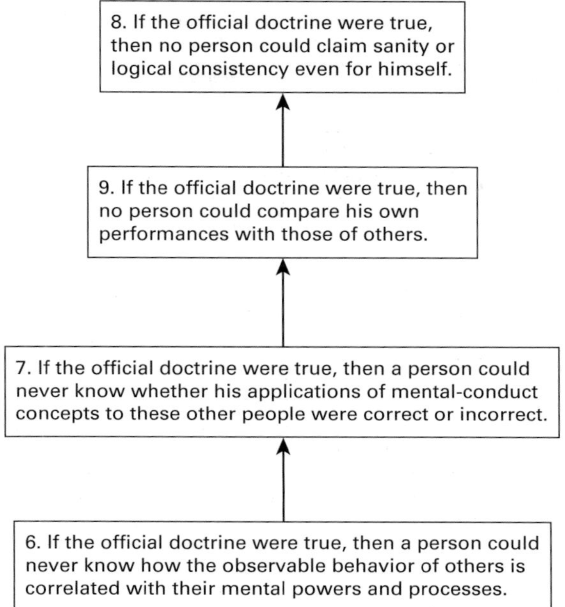
8. If the official doctrine were true, then no person could claim sanity or logical consistency even for himself.
9. If the official doctrine were true, then no person could compare his own performances with those of others.
7. If the official doctrine were true, then a person could never know whether his applications of mental-conduct concepts to these other people were correct or incorrect.
6. If the official doctrine were true, then a person could never know how the observable behavior of others is correlated with their mental powers and processes.

In this next part, Ryle says not only that (7) supports (8), but also that (7) supports the claim if the official doctrine were true, then no person could evaluate the behavior of anyone else (10). (7) is really just a special instance of (10). As indicated by (H), (10) then supports the claim that if the official doctrine were true, then the problem of providing a special causal hypothesis to serve as the basis of our evaluations would never have arisen (11). Why not? His answer is that the question of how people differ from machines arose just because everyone already knew how to apply mental-conduct concepts before the new causal hypothesis was introduced (12). So, as indicated by (I), (11) and (12) combine to support the claim that the causal hypothesis of the official doctrine cannot be the source of the criteria used in applying mental-conduct concepts (13).

Thus, we return to the original claim that the official doctrine, which contains the causal hypothesis, does not lead to the problem of free will.

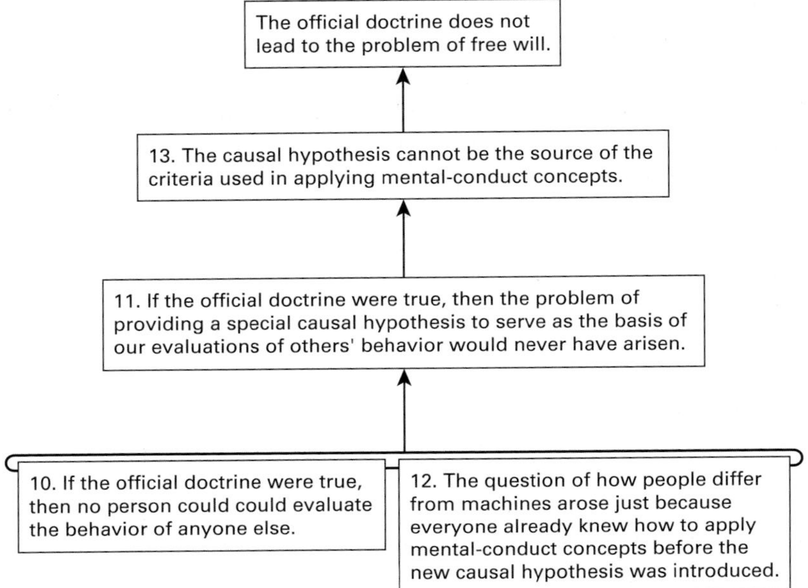

We can see now how Ryle's argument supports the behaviorist theory of mind. Ryle considers Cartesian dualism to be a kind of "mentalism," which is the general view that mental states (states of the mind) are inner causes of behavior. Ryle argues that mentalism is false as follows:

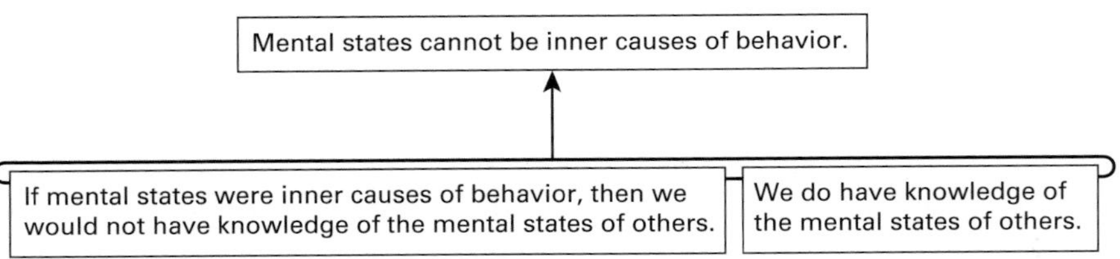

So, if mental states are not inner causes of behavior, then what are they? Behaviorism says that mental states are nothing other than dispositions to behave. And this is why, ultimately, mental states cannot be in the same category as physical states; because mental states are just collections of dispositions of our physical states to change. For example, suppose I stub my left pinky toe on the coffee table. The behaviorist says that my mental state of "pain" is nothing more than the collection of behaviors, such as saying "I am in pain," screaming, withdrawing my toe, nursing the injury, taking pain medicine, and so on.

Let's consider some objections to this view.

First Objection

The behaviorist's analysis of my pain seems to ignore or deny an important aspect of my experience. That is, pain hurts! No matter what my behavior is, there is a certain qualitative experience that I have when I stub my left pinky toe. In fact, it seems reasonable to suppose that there can be pain without any "pain behavior." An extreme example is that of "anesthetic awareness," a situation in which a patient is undergoing a specific kind of surgery that requires a paralytic (like eye surgery), but not enough anesthesia has been administered. The patient feels the pain of the operation but cannot perform any behaviors that would signal to the operating staff that she is in pain.[5] Thus, the behaviorist's account of mental states seems incomplete.

Second Objection

Another objection to the behaviorist's account of mental states is that a person will only have certain dispositions to behave if he or she has particular beliefs and desires. For example, consider again the pain in my left pinky toe: I would only have the disposition to scream if I *believe* that someone will hear me; I would only have the disposition to say "I am in pain" if I *want* to tell the truth; I will only have the disposition to take pain medicine if I *believe* it will relieve the pain and I *want* to relieve the pain. Thus, to define pain with a complete list of dispositions to behave, the behaviorist has to bring in descriptions of other mental states. This means, however, that the behaviorist will no longer be defining the mental state solely by referring to observable behaviors. Thus, the behaviorist's project seems doomed from the start.

This second objection gives us a glimpse of the theories of mental states we will explore in the next chapter.

10.3 In-Class Exercises

An asterisk (*) indicates a more challenging exercise.

Exercises 1–2

In the first part of this chapter, we analyzed in detail the argument Descartes gives in *Meditation VI*. The following selections contain arguments from that same chapter. For each selection, (a) diagram the argument and (b) identify any potential objections to the argument.

Exercise 1

Of course there are other faculties—such as those of moving around, changing shape, and so on—which also need a substance to belong to; but it must be a bodily or extended substance and not a thinking one, because those faculties essentially involve extension but not thought. Now, I have a *passive* faculty of sensory perception, that is, an ability to *receive* and recognize ideas of perceptible objects; but I would have no use for this unless something—myself or something else—had an *active* faculty for *producing* those ideas in the first place. But this faculty can't be in me, since clearly it does not presuppose any thought on my part, and sensory ideas are produced without my cooperation and often even against my will. So sensory ideas must be produced by some substance other than me—a substance that actually *has* (either in a straightforward way or in a higher form) all the reality that is *represented* in the ideas that it produces.

Exercise 2

Either (a) this substance is a body, in which case it will straightforwardly contain everything that is represented in the ideas; or else (b) it is God, or some creature more noble than a body, in which case it will contain in a higher form whatever is to be found in the ideas. I can reject (b), and be confident that God does not transmit sensory ideas to me either directly from himself or through some creature that does not straightforwardly contain what is represented in the ideas. God has given me no way of recognizing any such "higher form" source for these ideas; on the contrary, he has strongly inclined me to believe that bodies produce them. So if the ideas were transmitted from a source other than corporeal things, God would be a deceiver; and he is not. So bodies exist. They may not all correspond exactly with my sensory intake of them, for much of what comes in through the senses is obscure and confused. But at least bodies have all the properties that I clearly and distinctly understand, that is, all that fall within the province of pure mathematics.

Exercise 3

The following selection contains an argument from Descartes's *Passions of the Soul*.[6] For this selection, (a) diagram the argument and (b) identify any potential objections to the argument.

We need to recognize that the soul is really joined to the whole body, and that we cannot properly say that it exists in any one part of the body to the exclusion of the others. For the body is a unity which is in a sense indivisible because of the arrangement of its organs, these being so related to one another that the removal of any one of them renders the whole body defective. And the soul is of such a nature that it has no relation to extension, or to the dimensions or other properties of the matter of which the body is composed: it is related solely to the whole assemblage of the body's organs. This is obvious from our inability to conceive of a half or a third of a soul, or of the extension which a soul occupies. Nor does the soul become any smaller if we cut off some part of the body, but it becomes completely separate from the body when we break up the assemblage of the body's organs.

Exercises 4–5

In the second part of this chapter, we analyzed in detail an argument Ryle gives in *Descartes' Myth*. The following selections contain arguments from that same chapter. For each selection, (a) diagram the argument and (b) identify any potential objections to the argument.

Exercise 4

One of the chief intellectual origins of what I have yet to prove to be the Cartesian category-mistake seems to be this. When Galileo showed that his methods of scientific discovery were competent to provide a mechanical theory which should cover every occupant of space, Descartes found in himself two conflicting motives. As a man of scientific genius he could not but endorse the claims of mechanics, yet as a religious and moral man he could not accept, as Hobbes accepted, the discouraging rider to those claims, namely that human nature differs only in degree of complexity from clockwork. The mental could not be just a variety of the mechanical.

Exercise 5

He [Descartes] and subsequent philosophers naturally but erroneously availed themselves of the following escape-route. Since mental-conduct words are not to be construed as signifying the occurrence of mechanical processes, they must be construed as signifying the occurrence of non-mechanical processes; since mechanical laws explain movements in space, as the effects of other movements in space, other laws must explain some of the non-spatial workings of minds as the effects of other non-spatial workings of minds. The difference between the human behaviours which we describe as intelligent and those which we describe as unintelligent must be a difference in their causation; so, while some movements of human tongues and limbs are the effects of mechanical causes, others must be the effects of non-mechanical causes, i.e. some issue from movements of particles of matter, others from workings of the mind.

Exercises 6–9

The following exercises are intended to ensure your understanding of Descartes's and Ryle's texts, and to help you further explore the ideas presented in this chapter.

Exercise 6: Now that you have read my textual analysis of Descartes's argument in *Meditation VI*, summarize it in your own words.
Exercise 7: Summarize, in your own words, each of the arguments in exercises 1–3 above.
Exercise 8: Now that you have read my textual analysis of Ryle's argument, summarize it in your own words.
Exercise 9: Summarize, in your own words, each of the arguments in exercises 4 and 5 above.

10.4 Reading Questions

1. How "clearly and distinctly" does Descartes understand the relationship between the mind and body? How clearly do you understand this relationship?
2. How can a completely nonphysical thing interact with a completely physical thing?
3. Is there a way to salvage Descartes's argument that the mind and body are distinct?
4. Ryle claims that the "official doctrine" is one that not only philosophers but also the public in general believe. Do you agree? Why or why not?
5. Ryle explains why philosophers since Descartes have believed that the "official doctrine" leads to the problem of free will. Explain Ryle's reasoning in your own words.
6. Do you agree with Ryle that Descartes has committed a category mistake? Why or why not?
7. How would Ryle explain that we know about the mental states of other people?

11 Materialism

11.1 J. J. C. Smart, "Sensations and Brain Processes"
11.2 Jerry Fodor, "The Mind–Body Problem"
11.3 In-Class Exercises
11.4 Reading Questions

11.1 J. J. C. Smart, "Sensations and Brain Processes"

John Jamieson Carswell "Jack" Smart (1920–2012) was born in Cambridge to Scottish parents. His parents returned to Scotland with the children after his father moved from Cambridge University to the University of Glasgow. Smart earned an MA at Glasgow (in Scotland, an MA is an undergraduate degree in liberal arts) in 1946, and then a BPhil (which is a graduate degree) from Oxford University in 1948. His first position was at Corpus Christi College at Oxford, but in 1950, Smart took a position at the University of Adelaide in Australia. He moved to La Trobe University in 1972, the Australian National University in 1976, and Monash University in 1985, after his retirement.

Smart's main interests in philosophy were metaphysics and ethics. He was a utilitarian, defending act utilitarianism over rule utilitarianism in "Extreme and Restricted Utilitarianism" in 1956, *An Outline of a System of Utilitarian Ethics* in 1961, and *Utilitarianism: For and Against* in 1973. He was also interested in the philosophy of time, defending the view that the passage of time is an illusion. He wrote several books in philosophy of science: *Philosophy and Scientific Realism* in 1963, *Problems of Space and Time* in 1964, and *Between Science and Philosophy: An Introduction to the Philosophy of Science* in 1968.

But Smart was probably best known for his work in the philosophy of mind. He was one of the first philosophers to defend the view that the mind is identical to the brain. This defense first came in his article titled "Sensations and Brain Processes," which revolutionized the discipline. It is this article that is excerpted below. Although not apparent in this groundbreaking work, Smart was especially interested in the nature of color sensations and the problem of the inverted spectrum. (We will see this problem in the next section of this chapter.) Now, let's look at Smart's text in more detail. Specifically, we will analyze and diagram the main argument, as well as one of the objections he considers.

From "Sensations and Brain Processes."[1]

[I]t is the object of this paper to show that[A] there are no philosophical arguments which compel us to be dualists.[1] …

The issue between the brain-process theory and epiphenomenalism seems to be of the above sort. (Assuming that a behavioristic reduction of introspective reports is not possible.) If it be agreed that[B] there are no cogent philosophical arguments which force us into accepting dualism,[2] and if[C] the brain-process theory and dualism are equally consistent with the facts,[3] then[D] the principles of parsimony and simplicity[4] seem to me to decide overwhelmingly[E] in favor of the brain-process theory.[5] As I pointed out earlier,[F] dualism involves a large number of irreducible psychophysical laws (whereby the "nomological danglers" dangle) of a queer sort, that just have to be taken on trust, and are just as difficult to swallow as the irreducible facts about the paleontology of the earth with which we are faced on Philip Gosse's theory.[6]

Early in his article, as indicated by (A), Smart says the project is to show that there are no good arguments *for* dualism (1). But why does he do this? How would this relate to physicalism and the brain-process theory? Smart answers these questions in the last paragraph.

Here, as indicated by (B), (C), (D), and (E), he gives a long "if, then" statement that contains his main argument. The form of the statement is: if X is true and Y is true, then it is true that Z leads to W. Here, X is the claim that there are no good arguments for dualism (2), which is a restatement of (1), Y is the claim that the brain-process theory and dualism are equally consistent with the facts (3), Z is Occam's razor (4), and W is the claim that the brain-process theory is true (5).

Notice that I have equated Smart's "principles of parsimony and simplicity" with *Occam's razor*. That is because he cites Occam's razor near the beginning of the article as the reason why he prefers the brain-process theory, and because Occam's razor *is* a principle of parsimony. There are a few different ways to state this principle, which may have slightly different meanings. The first is: if two theories are equally consistent with the facts, we should prefer the simpler theory. The second is: if multiple theories are equally consistent with the facts, the simplest theory is most likely the true theory. I believe that Smart is endorsing the second variation, and so I shall use that.

If we transform the long "if, then" statement into an argument, we can represent it as:

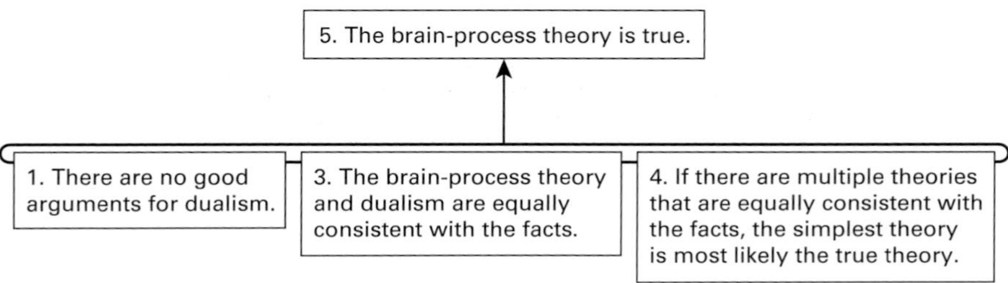

As indicated by (A), the bulk of Smart's article is supposed to be devoted to supporting premise (1). But, if we look back, the bulk of the article is actually devoted to considering objections to the brain-process theory. How are these two goals related? For each objection, the argument Smart presents can be seen as either an objection to brain-process theory, *or* an argument for dualism. Let's look at Objection 1:

Objection 1. Any illiterate peasant can talk perfectly well about his after-images, or how things look or feel to him, or about his aches and pains, and yet he may know nothing whatever about neurophysiology.[7] A man may, like Aristotle, believe that the brain is an organ for cooling the body without any impairment of his ability to make true statements about his sensations. Hence[G] the things we are talking about when we describe our sensations cannot be processes in the brain.[8]

Reply. ... Consider lightning. Modern physical science tells us that lightning is a certain kind of electrical discharge due to ionization of clouds of water-vapor in the atmosphere. This, it is now believed, is what the true nature of lightning is. Note that there are not two things: a flash of lightning and an electrical discharge. There is one thing, a flash of lightning, which is described scientifically as an electrical discharge to the earth from a cloud of ionized water-molecules. The case is not at all like that of explaining a footprint by reference to a burglar. We say that what lightning really is, what its true nature as revealed by science is, is an electric discharge. (It is not the true nature of a footprint to be a burglar.)

To forestall irrelevant objections, I should like to make it clear that by "lightning" I mean the publicly observable physical object, lightning, not a visual sense-datum of lightning. I say that the publicly observable physical object lightning is in fact the electric discharge, not just a correlate of it. The sense-datum, or at least the having of the sense-datum, the "look" of lightning, may well in my view be a correlate of the electric discharge. For in my view it is a brain state *caused* by the lightning. But we should no more confuse sensations of lightning with lightning than we confuse sensations of a table with the table.

In short, the reply to Objection 1 is that there can be contingent statements of the form "A is identical with B," and a person may well know that something is an A without knowing that it is a B.[9] An illiterate peasant might well be able to talk about his sensations without knowing about his brain processes, just as he can talk about lightning though he knows nothing of electricity.

The first claim is that any person can talk perfectly well about his sensations without knowing anything about neurophysiology (7). According to (G), this supports the conclusion that the things we talk about when we describe our sensations cannot be brain processes (8).

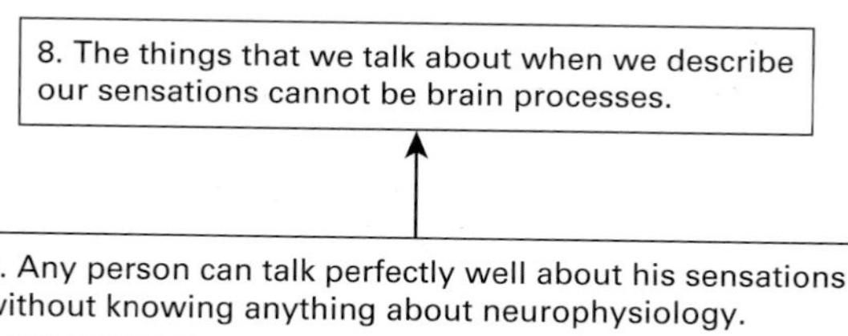
8. The things that we talk about when we describe our sensations cannot be brain processes.
7. Any person can talk perfectly well about his sensations without knowing anything about neurophysiology.

The first part of the reply is to point out that the objection must contain an unstated assumption in order for it to work:

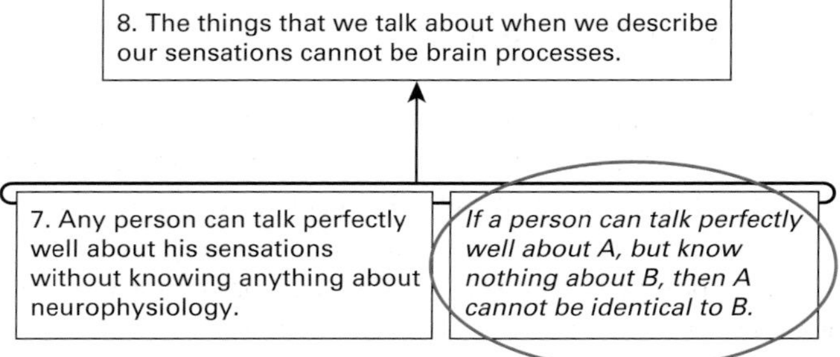
8. The things that we talk about when we describe our sensations cannot be brain processes.
7. Any person can talk perfectly well about his sensations without knowing anything about neurophysiology.
If a person can talk perfectly well about A, but know nothing about B, then A cannot be identical to B.

The next step is to show why this unstated assumption is false. By using it in another argument, we can see that it is plainly problematic:

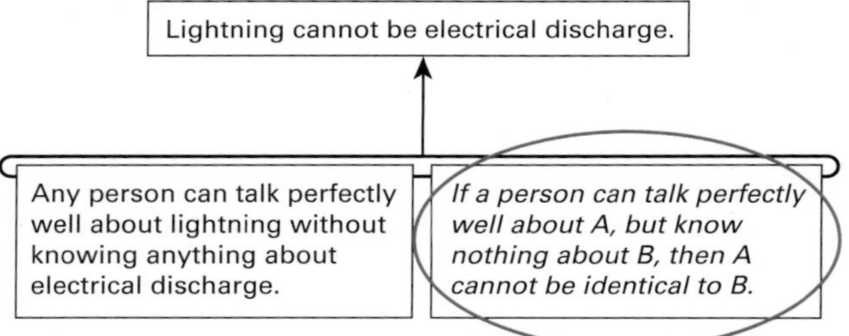
Lightning cannot be electrical discharge.
Any person can talk perfectly well about lightning without knowing anything about electrical discharge.
If a person can talk perfectly well about A, but know nothing about B, then A cannot be identical to B.

Since this conclusion is false, there must be something wrong with one of the premises. We know that the first premise is true—just ask any toddler, or Smart's illiterate peasant. So, it must be the unstated assumption that is false, and a person may well know that something is an A without knowing that it is a B, even though it is contingently true that A is identical to B (9).

The reply can then be represented as:

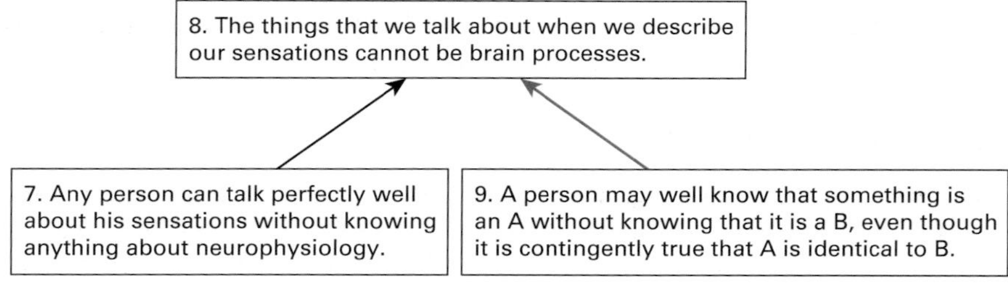
8. The things that we talk about when we describe our sensations cannot be brain processes.
7. Any person can talk perfectly well about his sensations without knowing anything about neurophysiology.
9. A person may well know that something is an A without knowing that it is a B, even though it is contingently true that A is identical to B.

We will explore the rest of the objections that Smart considers in the exercises. In the next section, we will encounter a criticism of Smart's mind–brain identity theory.

11.2 Jerry Fodor, "The Mind–Body Problem"

Jerry Alan Fodor was born in 1935 in New York City. He received his undergraduate degree from Columbia University in 1956, and his PhD in philosophy from Princeton in 1960. Fodor began his career at MIT, moved to the City University of New York in 1986, and then to Rutgers University in 1988, where he is the State of New Jersey Professor of Philosophy and Cognitive Science. Fodor has written numerous books in philosophy of mind, philosophy of language, and cognitive science. Here is a list of just a few:

Psychological Explanation (1968)
The Language of Thought (1975)
Representations: Philosophical Essays on the Foundations of Cognitive Science (1979)
The Modularity of Mind: An Essay on Faculty Psychology (1983)
Psychosemantics: The Problem of Meaning in the Philosophy of Mind (1987)
A Theory of Content and Other Essays (1990)
The Elm and the Expert: Mentalese and Its Semantics (1994)
Concepts: Where Cognitive Science Went Wrong (1998)
In Critical Condition (1998)
The Mind Doesn't Work That Way: The Scope and Limits of Computational Psychology (2000)

In the early part of his career, Fodor, along with several other prominent philosophers, was concerned that neither of the current (at the time) views of the relationship between the mind and the body were tenable. Logical behaviorists (e.g., Ryle from the previous chapter) ignored the causal connections between mental states, while identity theorists (e.g., Smart from the previous section) ignored the intuition that things other than biological humans could have mental states. The best position, he argued, is functionalism, although he claimed to have reservations about that too.

In 1981, Fodor wrote an article for *Scientific American* titled "The Mind–Body Problem," explaining dualism, behaviorism, identity theory, and functionalism. In it he lays out the reasons to be skeptical of the first three and in favor of the last. In addition, Fodor offers both detailed descriptions of the various theories of mind and an argument that one of them stands above the rest. Let's look at his text in more detail.

From "The Mind–Body Problem."[2]

All of this emerged ten or fifteen years ago as a nasty dilemma for the materialist program in the philosophy of mind. On the one hand[A] the identity theorist (and not the logical behaviorist) had got right the causal character of the interactions of mind and body.[1] On the other[B] the logical behaviorist (and not the identity theorist) had got right the relational character of mental properties.[2] Functionalism has apparently been able to resolve the dilemma.[3] By stressing the distinction computer science draws between hardware and software the functionalist can make sense of both the causal and the relational character of the mental.[4] …

Functionalism construes the concept of causal role in such a way that a mental state can be defined by its causal relations to other mental states.[5] …

Since functionalism recognizes that mental particulars may be physical, it is compatible with the idea that mental causation is a species of physical causation. In other words, functionalism tolerates the materialist solution to the mind–body problem provided by the central-state identity theory. It is possible for the functionalist to assert both that mental properties are typically defined in terms of their relations and that interactions of mind and body are typically causal in however robust a notion of causality is required by psychological explanations.[6] The logical behaviorist can endorse only the first assertion[7] and[C] the type physicalist only the second.[8] As a result[D] functionalism seems to capture the best features of the materialist alternatives to dualism.[9] It is no wonder that functionalism has become increasingly popular.

After Fodor explains the differences between dualism, behaviorism, identity theory, and functionalism, he argues that functionalism is the best of the lot. In fact, he gives roughly the same argument in two different places.

The first version of the argument comes when Fodor is first introducing functionalism. From the previous explanations he has given, Fodor has two claims, indicated by (A) and (B), that highlight the good parts of behaviorism and identity theory. The first is that the identity theorist is able to make sense of the causal character of the interactions of mind and body (1). The second is that the logical behaviorist can make sense of the relational character of mental properties (2). The conclusion is that functionalism has been able to resolve the dilemma between logical behaviorism and identity theory (3). Why has it been able to do so? Because functionalism can make sense of *both* the causal and the relational character of the mental (4).

This argument can be represented as:

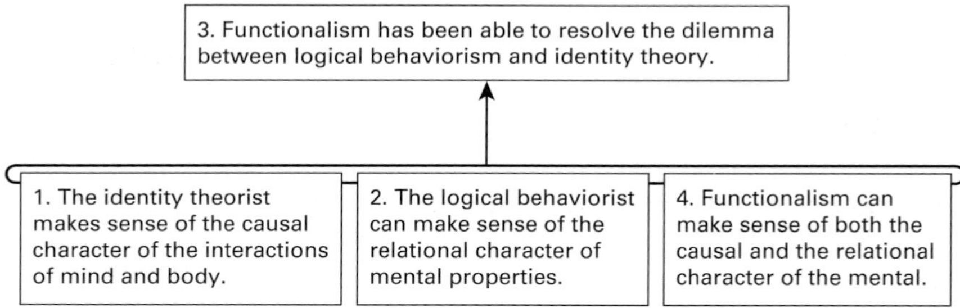

A few paragraphs later, it seems that Fodor is giving the same argument, only in a little more detail. First, he says that functionalism construes the concept of causal role in such a way that a mental state can be defined by its causal relations to other mental states (5). This, obviously, incorporates both "causal" and "relational," and so supports the claim that it is possible for the functionalist to assert both that mental properties are typically defined in terms of their relations and that interactions of mind and body are typically causal (6).

To get to the conclusion that functionalism is better than behaviorism or identity theory, Fodor must remind us of the limitations of these two. First, he claims that the logical behaviorist can endorse only the assertion that mental properties are typically defined in terms of their relations (7), and second, he claims that the type physicalist (meaning the identity theorist) can endorse only the assertion that interactions of mind and body are typically causal (8). If we combine these, as indicated by (C), they support the conclusion, as indicated by (D), that functionalism captures the best features of the materialist alternatives to dualism (9).

This argument can be represented as:

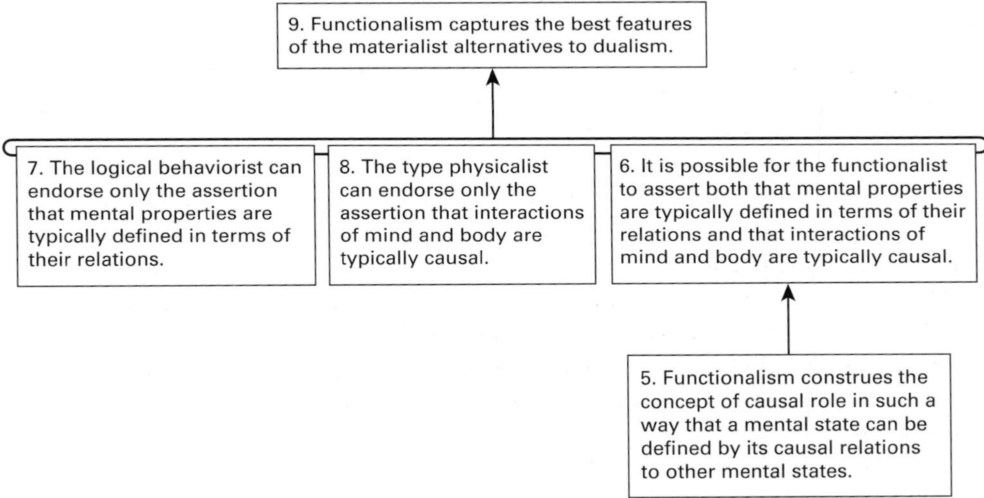

We will explore one of the most famous criticisms of functionalism in the exercises.

11.3 In-Class Exercises

An asterisk (*) indicates a more challenging exercise.

Exercises 1–5

In the first section of this chapter, we analyzed in detail the argument and one objection given by Smart in "Sensations and Brain Processes." The following selections contain the rest of the objections to the brain-process theory. For each selection, (a) diagram the argument in the objection and (b) diagram the reply.

Exercise 1

Objection 2. It is only a contingent fact (if it is a fact) that when we have a certain kind of sensation there is a certain kind of process in our brain. Indeed it is possible, though perhaps in the highest degree unlikely, that our present physiological theories will be as out of date as the ancient theory connecting mental processes with goings on in the heart. It follows that when we report a sensation we are not reporting a brain-process.

Reply. The objection certainly proves that when we say "I have an after-image" we cannot *mean* something of the form "I have such and such a brain-process." But this does not show that what we report (having an after-image) is not *in fact* a brain process. "I see lightning" does not *mean* "I see an electric discharge." Indeed, it is logically possible (though highly unlikely) that the electrical discharge account of lightning might one day be given up. Again, "I see the Evening Star" does not *mean* the same as "I see the Morning Star," and yet "the Evening Star and the Morning Star are one and the same thing" is a contingent proposition. Possibly Objection 2 derives some of its apparent strength from a "Fido"-Fido theory of meaning. If the meaning of an expression were what the expression named, then of course it *would* follow from the fact that "sensation" and "brain-process" have different meanings that they cannot name one and the same thing.

Exercise 2

Objection 4. The after-image is not in physical space. The brain-process is. So the after-image is not a brain-process.

Reply. This is an ignoratio elenchi. I am not arguing that the after-image is a brain-process, but that the experience of having an after-image is a brain-process. It is the experience which is reported in the introspective report. Similarly, if it is objected that the after-image is yellowy-orange but that a surgeon looking into your brain would see nothing yellowy-orange, my reply is that it is the experience of seeing yellowy-orange that is being described, and this experience is not a yellowy-orange something. So to say that a brain-process cannot be yellowy-orange is not to say that a brain-process cannot in fact be the experience of having a yellowy-orange after-image. There is, in a sense, no such thing as an after-image or a sense-datum, though there is such a thing as the experience of having an image, and this experience is described indirectly in material object language, not in phenomenal language, for there is no such thing. We describe the experience by saying, in effect, that it is like the experience we have when, for example, we really see a yellowy-orange patch on the wall. Trees and wallpaper can be green, but not the experience of seeing or imagining a tree or wallpaper. (Or if they are described as green or yellow this can only be in a derived sense.)

Exercise 3

Objection 5. It would make sense to say of a molecular movement in the brain that it is swift or slow, straight or circular, but it makes no sense to say this of the experience of seeing something yellow.

Reply. So far we have not given sense to talk of experiences as swift or slow, straight or circular. But I am not claiming that "experience" and "brain-process" mean the same or even that they have the same logic. "Somebody" and "the doctor" do not have the same logic, but this does not lead us to suppose that talking about somebody telephoning is talking about someone over and above, say, the doctor. The ordinary man when he reports an experience is reporting that something is going on, but he leaves it open as to what sort of thing is going on, whether in a material solid medium, or perhaps in some sort of gaseous medium, or even perhaps in some sort of nonspatial medium (if this makes sense). All that I am saying is that "experience" and "brain-process" may in fact refer to the same thing, and if so we may easily adopt a convention (which is not a change in our present rules for the use of experience words but an addition to them) whereby it would make sense to talk of an experience in terms appropriate to physical processes.

Exercise 4

Objection 6. Sensations are private, brain processes are *public*. If I sincerely say, "I see a yellowish-orange after-image" and I am not making a verbal mistake, then I cannot be wrong. But I can be wrong about a brain-process. The scientist looking into my brain might be having an illusion. Moreover, it makes sense to say that two or more people are observing the same brain-process but not that two or more people are reporting the same inner experience.

Reply. This shows that the language of introspective reports has a different logic from the language of material processes. It is obvious that until the brain-process theory is much improved and widely accepted there will be no *criteria* for saying "Smith has an experience of such-and-such a sort" *except* Smith's introspective reports. So we have adopted a rule of language that (normally) what Smith says goes.

**Exercise 5*

Objection 7. I can imagine myself turned to stone and yet having images, aches, pains, and so on.

Reply. I can imagine that the electrical theory of lightning is false, that lightning is some sort of purely optical phenomenon. I can imagine that lightning is not an electrical discharge. I can imagine that the Evening Star is not the Morning Star. But it is. All the objection shows is that "experience" and "brain-process" do not have the same meaning. It does not show that an experience is not in fact a brain process.

This objection is perhaps much the same as one which can be summed up by the slogan: "What can be composed of nothing cannot be composed of anything." The argument goes as follows: on the brain-process thesis the identity between the brain-process and the experience is a contingent one. So it is logically possible that there should be no brain-process, and no process of any other sort, either (no heart process, no kidney process, no liver process). There would be the experience but no "corresponding" physiological process with which we might be able to identify it empirically.

I suspect that the objector is thinking of the experience as a ghostly entity. So it is composed of something, not of nothing, after all. On his view it is composed of ghost stuff, and on mine it is composed of brain stuff. Perhaps the counter-reply will be that the experience is simple and uncompounded, and so it is not composed of anything after all. This seems to be a quibble, for, if it were taken seriously, the remark "What can be composed of nothing cannot be composed of anything" could be recast as an a priori argument against Democritus and atomism and for Descartes and infinite divisibility. And it seems odd that a question of this sort could be settled a priori. We must therefore construe the word "composed" in a very weak sense, which would allow us to say that even an indivisible atom is composed of something (namely, itself). The dualist cannot really say that an experience can be composed of nothing. For he holds that experiences are something over and above material processes, that is, that they are a sort of ghost stuff. (Or perhaps ripples in an underlying ghost stuff.) I say that the dualist's hypothesis is a perfectly intelligible one. But I say that experiences are not to be identified with ghost stuff but with brain stuff. This is another hypothesis, and in my view a very plausible one. The present argument cannot knock it down a priori.

Exercises 6–9

In the second section of this chapter, we analyzed two versions of the main argument in Fodor's "The Mind–Body Problem." The following are arguments from the selection *against* dualism, behaviorism, and identity theory. For each, (a) diagram the argument and (b) identify any potential objections to the argument.

**Exercise 6*

The chief drawback of dualism is its failure to account adequately for mental causation. If the mind is nonphysical, it has no position in physical space. How, then, can a mental cause give rise to a behavioral effect that has a position in space? To put it another way, how can the nonphysical give rise to the physical without violating the laws of the conservation of mass, of energy and of momentum?

Exercise 7

The strongest argument against behaviorism is that psychology has not turned out this way; the opposite has happened. As psychology has matured, the framework of mental states and processes that is apparently needed to account for experimental observations has grown all the more elaborate. Particularly in the case of human behavior psychological theories satisfying the methodological tenets of radical behaviorism have proved largely sterile, as would be expected if the postulated mental processes are real and causally effective.

**Exercise 8*

Event-event causation actually seems to be quite common in the realm of the mental. Mental causes typically give rise to behavioral effects by virtue of their interaction with other mental causes. For example, having a headache causes a disposition to take aspirin only if one also has the desire to get rid of the headache, the belief that aspirin exists, the belief that taking aspirin reduces headaches and so on. Since mental states interact in generating behavior, it will be necessary to find a construal of psychological explanations that posits mental processes: causal sequences of mental events. It is this construal that logical behaviorism fails to provide.

Such considerations bring out a fundamental way in which logical behaviorism is quite similar to radical behaviorism. It is true that the logical behaviorist, unlike the radical behaviorist, acknowledges the existence of mental states. Yet since the underlying tenet of logical behaviorism is that references to mental states can be translated out of psychological explanations by employing behavioral hypotheticals, all talk of mental states and processes is in a sense heuristic. The only facts to which the behaviorist is actually committed are facts about relations between stimuli and responses. In this respect logical behaviorism is just radical behaviorism in a semantic form. Although the former theory offers a construal of mental causation, the construal is Pickwickian. What does not really exist cannot cause anything, and the logical behaviorist, like the radical behaviorist, believes deep down that mental causes do not exist.

Exercise 9

Type physicalism is not a plausible doctrine about mental properties even if token physicalism is right about mental particulars. The problem with type physicalism is that the psychological constitution of a system seems to depend not on its hardware, or physical composition, but on its software, or program. Why should the philosopher dismiss the possibility that silicon-based Martians have pains, assuming that the silicon is properly organized? And why should the philosopher rule out the possibility of machines having beliefs, assuming that the machines are correctly programmed? If it is logically possible that Martians and machines could have mental properties, then mental properties and neurophysiological processes cannot be identical, however much they may prove to be coextensive.

*Exercise 10

In 1978, Ned Block, now a philosopher at New York University, published an article titled "Troubles with Functionalism."[3] In it, he argues that functionalism cannot be the right theory of mind because of what he calls "the absent qualia argument." The following is a selection from that article. Here, (a) diagram the argument and (b) identify any potential objections to the argument.

In this section I shall describe a class of devices that embarrass all versions of functionalism in that they indicate functionalism is guilty of liberalism—classifying systems that lack mentality as having mentality. ...

Suppose we convert the government of China to functionalism, and we convince its officials that it would enormously enhance their international prestige to realize a human mind for an hour. We provide each of the billion people in China (I chose China because it has a billion inhabitants) with a specially designed two-way radio that connects them in the appropriate way to other persons and to the artificial body mentioned in the previous example. We replace the little men with a radio transmitter and receiver connected to the input and output neurons. Instead of a bulletin board, we arrange to have letters displayed on a series of satellites placed so that they can be seen from anywhere in China. Surely such a system is not physically impossible. It could be functionally equivalent to you for a short time, say an hour.

... Any system that has a set of inputs, outputs, and states related in the way described realizes that machine table, even if it exists for only an instant. For the hour the Chinese system is "on," it *does* have a set of inputs, outputs, and states of which such conditionals are true. Whatever the initial state, the system will respond in whatever way the machine table directs. This is how *any* computer realizes the machine table it realizes. ...

What makes the homunculi-headed system (count the two systems as variants of a single system) just described a prima facie counter example to (machine) functionalism is that there is prima facie doubt whether it has any mental states at all—especially whether it has what philosophers have variously called "qualitative states," "raw feels," or "immediate phenomenological qualities."...

The force of the prima facie counterexample can be made clearer as follows: Machine functionalism says that each mental state is identical to a machine-table state. For example, a particular qualitative state, Q, is identical to a machine-table state, S_q. But if there is nothing it is like to be the homunculi-headed system, it cannot be in Q even when it is in S_q. Thus, if there is prima facie doubt about the homunculi-headed system's mentality, there is prima facie doubt that $Q = S_q$, i.e., doubt that the kind of functionalism under consideration is true. Call this argument the Absent Qualia Argument.

Exercises 11–14

The following exercises are intended to ensure your understanding of Smart's and Fodor's texts, and to help you further explore the ideas presented in this chapter.

Exercise 11: Now that you have read my textual analysis of Smart's argument in "Sensations and Brain Processes," summarize it in your own words.
Exercise 12: Summarize, in your own words, each of the arguments in exercises 1–5 above.
Exercise 13: Now that you have read my textual analysis of Fodor's argument in "The Mind–Body Problem," summarize it in your own words.
Exercise 14: Summarize, in your own words, each of the arguments in exercises 6–10 above.

11.4 Reading Questions

1. According to Smart, what is the brain-process theory? How does it differ from dualism?
2. When Smart writes that mental states are identical with brain processes, what does he mean by "identical"? What does he explicitly not mean?
3. In fact, although Smart doesn't explain it this way, the first example he considers is an instance of a misuse of Leibniz's law. (Recall the discussion of Descartes's misuse of Leibniz's law in the previous chapter.) Explain the misuse.
4. In Fodor's view, what is the difference between "radical behaviorism" and "logical behaviorism"? Why does Fodor think they are unsuccessful?
5. What is "central-state identity theory"? How does it compare to behaviorism, according to Fodor?
6. Explain the problem of the inverted spectrum and how it presents a difficulty for functionalism.

12 Antimaterialism

12.1 Thomas Nagel, "What Is It Like to Be a Bat?"
12.2 Frank Jackson, "Epiphenomenal Qualia"
12.3 Paul Churchland, "Knowing Qualia: A Reply to Jackson"
12.4 In-Class Exercises
12.5 Reading Questions

12.1 Thomas Nagel, "What Is It Like to Be a Bat?"

Thomas Nagel was born in Belgrade, Yugoslavia (now Serbia) in 1937. He graduated from Cornell University with a BA in 1958, from Oxford with a BPhil in 1960, and from Harvard University with a PhD in 1963. His first academic position was at University of California, Berkeley, in 1963, and then in 1966, he moved to Princeton University. In 1980 Nagel moved to New York University, where is currently University Professor of Philosophy and Law.

Nagel has published numerous books on philosophy of mind, ethics, and political philosophy. His publications include:

The Possibility of Altruism, 1970
Philosophy, Morality, and International Affairs: Essays Edited for the Society for Philosophy and Public Affairs, 1974
The View from Nowhere, 1986
What Does It All Mean? A Very Short Introduction to Philosophy, 1987
Mortal Questions, 1991
Equality and Partiality, 1991
The Last Word, 1997
Mind and Cosmos: Why the Materialist Neo-Darwinian Conception of Nature Is Almost Certainly False, 2012

Perhaps, though, Nagel's most famous written work is his 1974 article titled "What Is It Like to Be a Bat?" In this text, Nagel's purpose is to question the kinds of physicalist (or materialist) theories of mind that we encountered in the previous chapter. The main concept with which Nagel is concerned is "reduction"—specifically the reduction of one kind of phenomenon to another. The history of science has seen many successful instances of reduction: the fact that temperature is really mean molecular kinetic energy means that we have *reduced* this aspect of thermodynamics to classical mechanics. In the case of the mind–body problem, physicalists like J. J. C. Smart want to reduce the mental to the physical. This means that they want to provide a theory that shows mental states (e.g., pain) are just, or *are reducible to*, physical states (e.g., a particular neurophysical pattern in the brain).

Nagel's argument in "What Is It Like to Be a Bat?" offers one of the most famous thought experiments in the philosophy of mind. Let's look at his text in more detail.

From "What Is it Like to Be a Bat?"[1]

The most important and characteristic feature of conscious mental phenomena is very poorly understood. Most reductionist theories do not even try to explain it. And careful examination will show that[A] no currently available concept of reduction is applicable to it. Perhaps a new theoretical form can be devised for the purpose, but such a solution, if it exists, lies in the distant intellectual future. …

… [The relation between facts on the one hand and conceptual schemes or systems of representation on the other] enables us to make a general observation about the subjective character of experience. Whatever may be the status of facts about what it is like to be a human being, or a bat, or a Martian, these appear to be facts that embody a particular point of view.[1] …

This bears directly on the mind–body problem. For if the facts of experience—facts about what it is like *for* the experiencing organism—are accessible only from one point of view, then it is a mystery how the true character of experiences could be revealed in the physical operation of that organism.[2] The latter is a domain of objective facts *par excellence*—the kind that can be observed and understood from many points of view and by individuals with differing perceptual systems.[3] …

In the case of experience, on the other hand, the connection with a particular point of view seems much closer. It is difficult to understand what could be meant by the *objective* character of an experience, apart from the particular point of view from which its subject apprehends it. After all, what would be left of what it was like to be a bat if one removed the viewpoint of the bat? But if experience does not have, in addition to its subjective character, an objective nature that can be apprehended from many different points of view, then how can it be supposed that a Martian investigating my brain might be observing physical processes which were my mental processes (as he might observe physical processes which were bolts of lightning), only from a different point of view?[4] How, for that matter, could a human physiologist observe them from another point of view?

In the second paragraph of his article, as indicated by the phrase "careful examination will show" (A), Nagel tells us that what he wants to show is that no currently available concept of reduction (like functionalism or identity theory) is applicable to conscious phenomena.

First, Nagel asks us to consider not what it would be like for us to experience behaving like a bat, but rather what it is like for a bat to behave like a bat. He claims that we cannot imagine what it is like to be a bat because our perceptual apparatuses are so different. Nevertheless, he says, if a bat has conscious experiences (like pain or fear), then there is something that it is like to be a bat, even if we can't know what that is. The point of this example is to provide a basis for his claim that facts about "what it is like to be a human" (or a bat, or anything) are facts that embody a particular point of view (1).

The physical operations of an organism, however, are objective facts. That is, facts about which neurons are being stimulated by which other neurons and so on are things that can be observed and understood from many points of view (3). So objective facts are those that can be understood from many points of view. This supports Nagel's claim that if the facts about what it is like to be a human are accessible from only one point of view, then the true character of experiences cannot be objective (2).

If we combine statements (1) and (2), we can draw Nagel's unstated conclusion that the true character of experiences cannot be objective. This argument can be represented as:

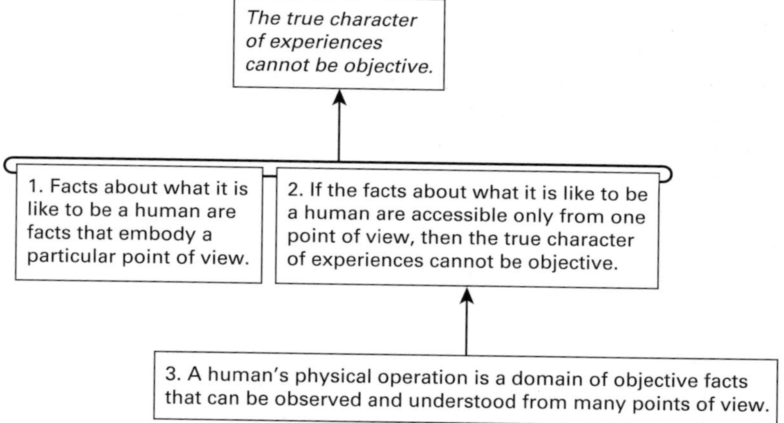

Nagel next claims that if experience cannot be objective, then my brain's physical processes cannot be my mental processes only from a different point of view (4). If we combine this with the conclusion from the argument above, then we can draw Nagel's second unstated conclusion that my brain's physical processes cannot be my mental processes.

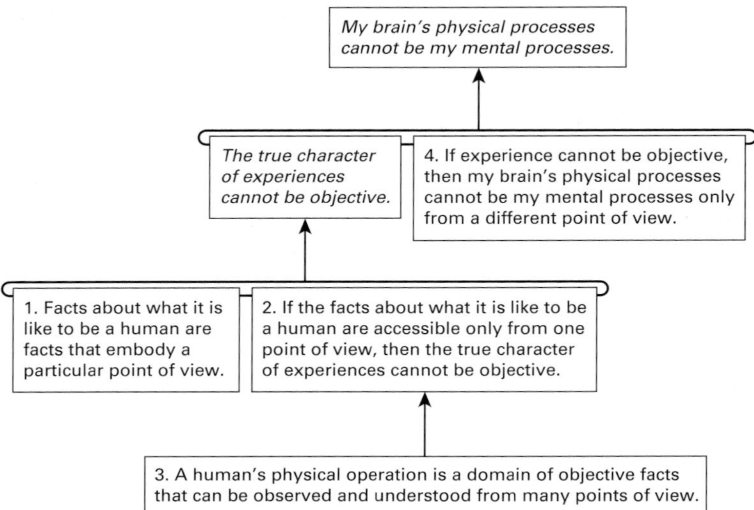

But identifying mind and brain is exactly what the current physicalist theories want to do, according to Nagel; they want to explain how my brain's physical processes can be identical to my brain's mental processes. Thus, we can draw Nagel's main conclusion that no currently available concept of reduction is applicable to conscious mental phenomena.

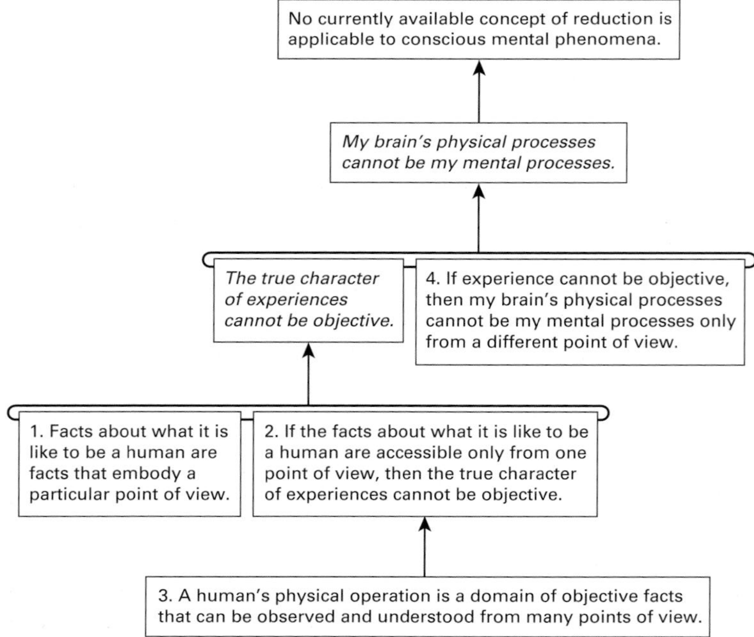

In the next section, Frank Jackson offers an argument for a similar thesis, but also criticizes Nagel's argument. Let's look at Jackson's arguments now.

12.2 Frank Jackson, "Epiphenomenal Qualia"

Frank Jackson was born in Australia in 1943. He graduated from the University of Melbourne with an undergraduate degree in philosophy and mathematics, and graduated from La Trobe University with a PhD in philosophy. Jackson's first academic appointment was a year-long position at the University of Adelaide in 1967. He then moved to Monash University and in 1986 finally settled at Australian National University, where he became professor of philosophy and head of the philosophy program. Currently, Jackson splits his time between ANU and Princeton University.

Jackson has published several books in philosophy of mind, as well as epistemology, metaphysics and metaethics. His books include:

Perception: A Representative Theory, 1977
Conditionals, 1987
The Philosophy of Mind and Cognition, 1996
From Metaphysics to Ethics: A Defense of Conceptual Analysis, 1997
Mind, Method, and Conditionals: Selected Essays, 1998

Perhaps Jackson's most famous contribution to philosophy is the "Mary argument," first given in "Epiphenomenal Qualia." In this article, Jackson, like Nagel, is concerned to show that any theory that says that the mind is nothing but the brain must be false. He uses the term "qualia" to denote those special subjective experiences Nagel wrote about in "What Is It Like to Be a Bat?" We have qualia, for example, when we see colors, feel pain, taste sugar, and so on. We can explain (or we could, with a sufficiently advanced neuroscience) all the physical processes that happen in our bodies and brains when we feel pain. But, Jackson says, there's something else besides these processes—the fact that pain hurts. There is a qualitative experience of feeling pain such that no one who has never had that experience can know what it is like to feel pain. Jackson says it's this experience that physicalism cannot explain.

Jackson's argument may seem to be just a version of Nagel's argument, but Jackson adamantly denies this. Let's look at his text in more detail. In section I of "Epiphenomenal Qualia," Jackson gives us his famous "Mary argument" to show that physicalism is false.

From "Epiphenomenal Qualia."[2]

… The same point can be made with normal people and familiar colours. Mary is a brilliant scientist who is, for whatever reason, forced to investigate the world from a black and white room *via* a black and white television monitor. She specialises in the neurophysiology of vision and acquires, let us suppose, all the physical information there is to obtain about what goes on when we see ripe tomatoes, or the sky, and use terms like "red," "blue," and so on.[1] She discovers, for example, just which wave-length combinations from the sky stimulate the retina, and exactly how this produces via the central nervous system the contraction of the vocal chords and expulsion of air from the lungs that results in the uttering of the sentence "The sky is blue." (It can hardly be denied that it is in principle possible to obtain all this physical information from black and white television, otherwise the Open University would of *necessity* need to use colour television.)

What will happen when Mary is released from her black and white room or is given a colour television monitor? Will she *learn* anything or not? It seems just obvious that[A] she will learn something about the world and our visual experience of it.[2] But then it is inescapable that[B] her previous knowledge was incomplete.[3] But[C] she had *all* the physical information.[4] *Ergo*[D] there is more to have than that,[5] and[E] Physicalism is false.

To begin the thought experiment about Mary, Jackson stipulates that Mary knows everything there is to know about neuroscience, so the claim is that Mary has all the physical information about what goes on when we see color and use color terms (1). But, he says, when Mary is released she will learn something new about our visual experiences (2). He claims that this is obvious (A), but the reason for (2) that Jackson has given elsewhere is that when Mary is released she will learn *what it is like to see red*. In her black and white room, Mary knew all there is to know about how the brain works, but she had never seen the color red, so she doesn't know what it is like to see red. But when she is released and sees something red for the first time, she has a new piece of knowledge: the knowledge of what it is like to see red.

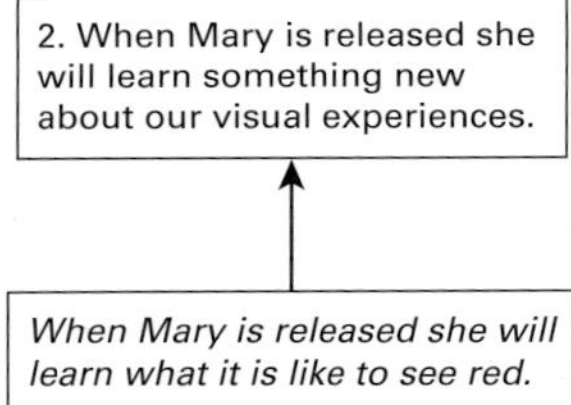

Then, Jackson claims, since she learns something new, as indicated by (B), Mary's total knowledge of our visual experiences was incomplete prior to her release (3).

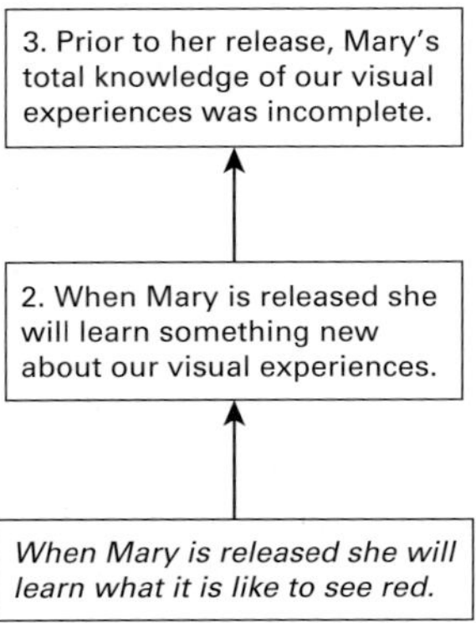

But remember that Mary knew everything about neuroscience. This supports the claim that prior to her release, Mary's knowledge of the *physical* aspects of our visual experiences was complete (4).

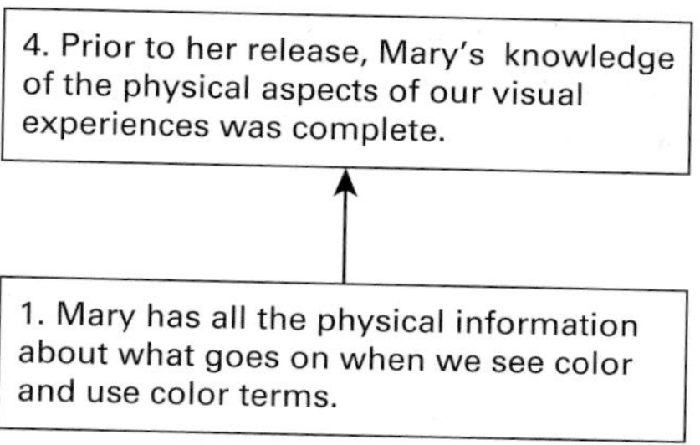

As indicated by (C) and (D), statements (3) and (4) then combine to support Jackson's claim that there is more information about our visual experiences than the physical information (5).

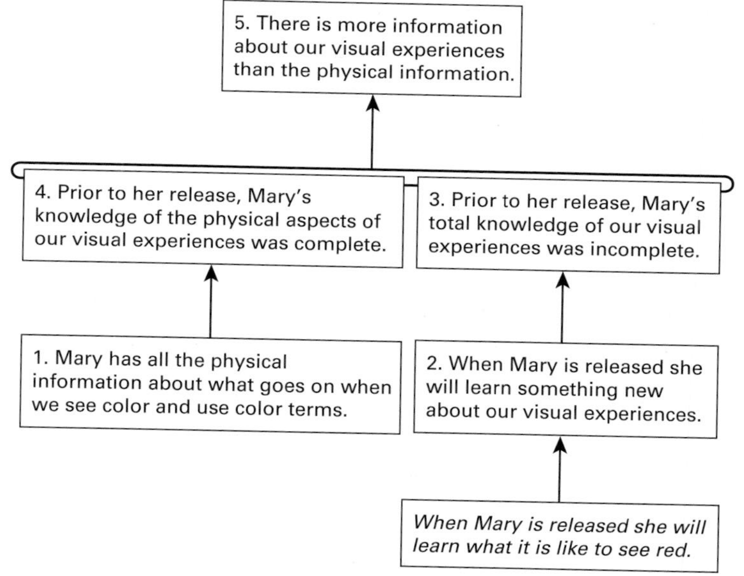

To get to the final conclusion, Jackson implicitly uses the definition of physicalism. Physicalism says that all information about our visual experiences is physical information. As indicated by (E), this definition combines with (5) to support the claim that physicalism is false.

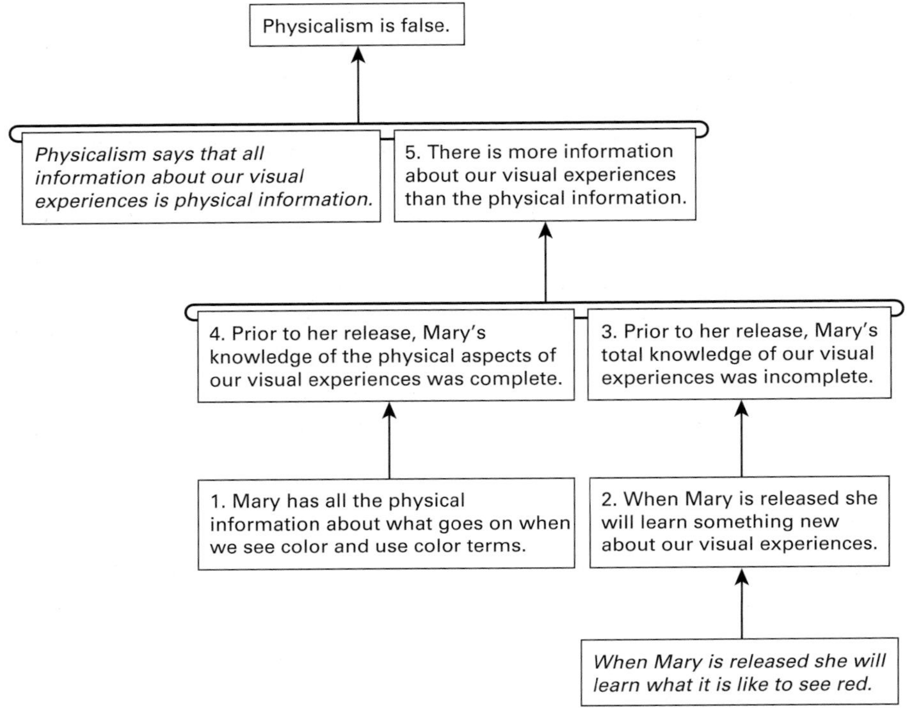

In the next section, we will read a critique of Jackson's argument from Paul Churchland.

12.3 Paul Churchland, "Knowing Qualia: A Reply to Jackson"

Paul Churchland was born in Vancouver, British Columbia, Canada, in 1942. He graduated in 1964 with a BA in philosophy, physics, and mathematics from the University of British Columbia, and in 1969 with a PhD in philosophy from the University of Pittsburgh. While still in graduate school, Churchland lectured at the University of Pittsburgh at Greensburg and the University of Toronto. His first academic appointment was at the University of Manitoba in 1969, and he moved to the University of California, San Diego, in 1984. Churchland was the philosophy department chair at UCSD from 1986 to 1990, and held the Valtz Chair of Philosophy from 2003 until his retirement in 2010. He is now professor emeritus at UCSD.

Churchland has published extensively in philosophy of science, the philosophy of mind, artificial intelligence and cognitive neurobiology, epistemology, and perception. Here is a selection of his books:

Scientific Realism and the Plasticity of Mind, 1979
Matter and Consciousness, 1984

Images of Science: Scientific Realism versus Constructive Empiricism, 1985
A Neurocomputational Perspective: The Nature of Mind and the Structure of Science, 1989
The Engine of Reason, The Seat of the Soul: A Philosophical Journey into the Brain, 1995
The Churchlands and Their Critics, 1996
On the Contrary: Critical Essays, 1987–1997 (with Patricia Smith Churchland), 1998
Neurophilosophy at Work, 2007
Plato's Camera: How the Physical Brain Captures a Landscape of Abstract Universals, 2012

Churchland has been the most prominent defender of physicalism and critic of Nagel and Jackson. In fact, Churchland and Jackson each have a history of publishing objections and replies to each other. Churchland criticized Jackson's "Epiphenomenal Qualia" in an article titled "Reduction, Qualia, and the Direct Introspection of Brain States." Jackson responded to this criticism in an article titled "What Mary Didn't Know," and Churchland replied back in a chapter of *A Neurocomputational Perspective* titled "Knowing Qualia: A Reply to Jackson," which contains the argument analyzed below.

From *A Neurocomputational Perspective*.[3]

Jackson concedes the criticism I leveled at my own statement of his argument—specifically, that it involves an equivocation on "knows about"—but he insists that my reconstruction does not represent the argument he wishes to defend. I accept his instruction, and turn my attention to the summary of the argument he provides at the bottom of page 293. Mary, you will recall, has been raised in innocence of any color experience, but has an exhaustive command of neuroscience.

(1 Mary (before her release) knows everything physical there is to know about other people.[1]
(2) Mary (before her release) does not know everything there is to know about other people[2a] (because[A] she *learns* something about them on her release).[2b]
∴[B] (3)There are truths about other people (and herself) which escape the physicalist story.[3]

...

Specifically, premise (1) is plausibly true, within Jackson's story about Mary's color-free upbringing, only on the interpretation of "knows about" that casts the object of knowledge as something propositional,[4] as something adequately expressible in an English sentence. Mary, to put it briefly, gets 100 percent on every written and oral exam; she can pronounce on the truth of any given sentence about the physical characteristics of persons, especially the states of their brains. Her "knowledge by description" of physical facts about persons is without lacunae.

Premise (2), however, is plausibly true only on the interpretation of "knows about" that casts the object of knowledge as something non-propositional,[5] as something inarticulable, as something that is non-truth-valuable. What Mary is missing is some form of "knowledge by acquaintance," acquaintance with a sensory character, prototype, or universal, perhaps.

Given this[C] prima facie difference in the sense of "knows about," or the kind of knowledge appearing in each premise,[6] we are still looking at a prima facie case of an argument invalid by reason of[D] equivocation on a critical term.[7] Replace either of the "*K*"s above with a distinct letter, as acknowledgment of the ambiguity demands, and the inference to (3) evaporates.

In his reply, Churchland argues that Jackson's argument is invalid. First, Churchland gives Jackson's own reconstruction of the Mary argument. Clearly, statements (1) and (2), as Churchland labels them, are the premises and (3) is the conclusion. Notice, however, that statement (2) is actually a subargument. As indicated by (A), (2a) is supported by (2b). And, as indicated by (B), which is the mathematical representation of "therefore," (3) is the conclusion. So, we can represent the argument like this:

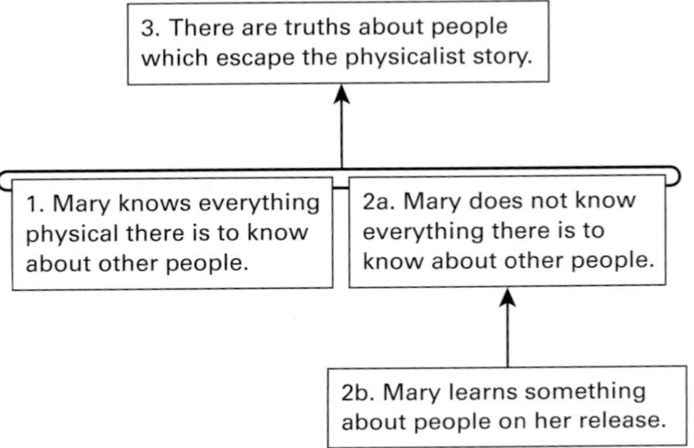

Next, Churchland gives his own argument that Jackson's argument is invalid. First, Churchland claims that the first premise is true only if "knows about" means "knows propositionally about" (4). What does this mean? Propositions are the things that statements convey, so propositions are things that can be true or false and are generally expressible in some language. Propositions about color vision might include, for example, "When a person with normal vision sees a red apple, the red-green cones in her retina are excited."

So when we say that Mary has, through research, come to know all there is to know about people, what we mean is that she can articulate all of the true statements about humans' brains. We can rewrite premise (1) as "Mary knows everything propositional there is to know about other people." If we label propositional knowledge as "knowledge$_P$," then we can write the premise as "Mary knows$_P$ everything there is to know$_P$ about people."

Next, Churchland claims that premise (2) is true only if "knows about" means "knows non-propositionally about" (5). Having this kind of knowledge, Churchland explains later, is like knowing how to properly swing a golf club, or knowing how to tell the difference between male and female faces, or knowing how to whistle through one's teeth. These are skills that people may have even if they can't articulate in words how to do these things.

So Mary may know all of the true propositions about people's brains, but she does not have the skill of discriminating red objects from other colored objects. She does not know how to discriminate red objects. If we label non-propositional knowledge as "knowledge$_{NP}$" then we can rewrite premise (2a) as "Mary does not know$_{NP}$ everything there is to know$_{NP}$ about people." And the reason is that upon her release, Mary learns something new—she now knows$_{NP}$ what red looks like.

Jackson's argument can now, according to Churchland, be represented as:

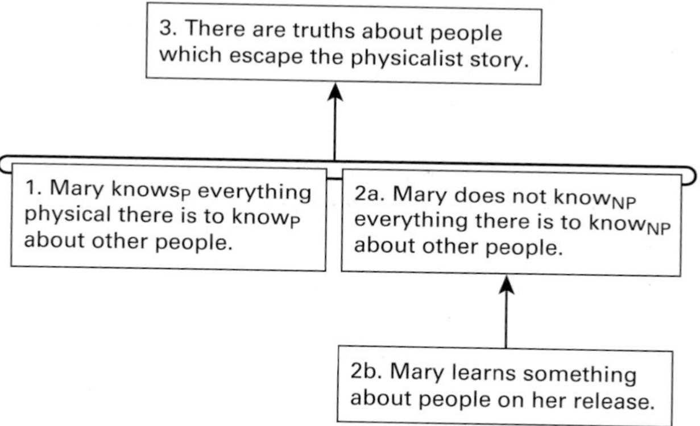

Now, we can see the thrust of Churchland's argument. First, Jackson's first premise is true only if "knows about" means "knows propositionally about" (4). Second, Jackson's second premise is true only if "knows about" means "knows non-propositionally about" (5). Thus, the meaning of the term "knows" is not the same in these two premises (6).

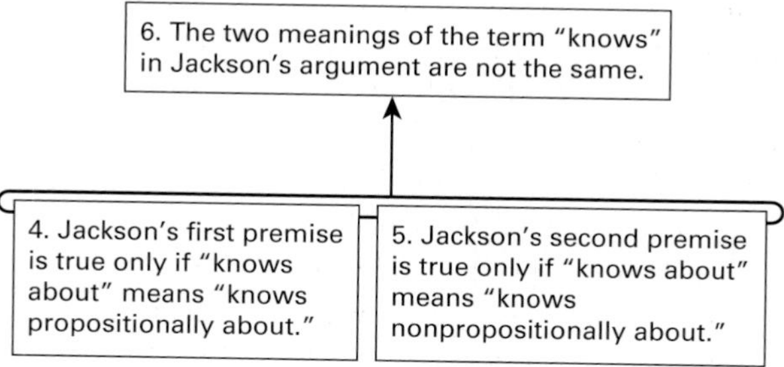

According to (C) and (D), statement (6) provides support for the main conclusion through supporting (7). Then (7) is to be combined with unstated premise that arguments that equivocate on a critical term are invalid to support the main conclusion.

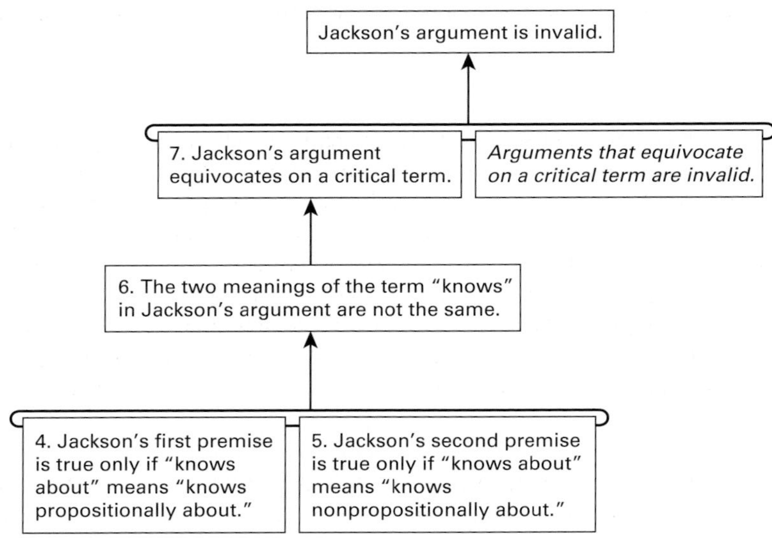

We will explore more of the arguments in Churchland's text in the exercises.

12.4 In-Class Exercises

An asterisk (*) indicates a more challenging exercise.

Exercises 1–3

In the first part of this chapter, we analyzed in detail the argument given by Nagel in "What Is it Like to Be a Bat?" The following selections contain arguments from that same article. For each selection, (a) diagram the argument and (b) identify any potential objections to the argument.

Exercise 1

We appear to be faced with a general difficulty about psychophysical reduction. In other areas the process of reduction is a move in the direction of greater objectivity, toward a more accurate view of the real nature of things. This is accomplished by reducing our dependence on individual or species—specific points of view toward the object of investigation. We describe it not in terms of the impressions it makes on our senses, but in terms of its more general effects and of properties detectable by means other than the human senses. The less it depends on a specifically human viewpoint, the more objective is our description. It is possible to follow this path because although the concepts and ideas we employ in thinking about the external world are initially applied from a point of view that involves our perceptual apparatus, they are used by us to refer to things beyond themselves toward which we *have* the phenomenal point of view. Therefore we can abandon it in favor of another, and still be thinking about the same things.

Exercise 2

Experience itself, however, does not seem to fit the pattern. The idea of moving from appearance to reality seems to make no sense here. What is the analogue in this case to pursuing a more objective understanding of the same phenomena by abandoning the initial subjective viewpoint toward them in favor of another that is more objective but concerns the same thing? Certainly it *appears* unlikely that we will get closer to the real nature of human experience by leaving behind the particularity of our human point of view and striving for a description in terms accessible to beings that could not imagine what it was like to be us. If the subjective character of experience is fully comprehensible only from one point of view, then any shift to greater objectivity—that is, less attachment to a specific viewpoint—does not take us nearer to the real nature of the phenomenon: it takes us farther away from it.

Exercise 3

But while we are right to leave this point of view aside in seeking a fuller understanding of the external world, we cannot ignore it permanently, since it is the essence of the internal world, and not merely a point of view on it. Most of the neobehaviorism of recent philosophical psychology results from the effort to substitute an objective concept of mind for the real thing, in order to have nothing left over which cannot be reduced. If we acknowledge that a physical theory of mind must account for the subjective character of experience, we must admit that no presently available conception gives us a clue how this could be done. The problem is unique. If mental processes are indeed physical processes, then there is something it is like, intrinsically, to undergo certain physical processes. What it is for such a thing to be the case remains a mystery.

*Exercise 4

The following selection contains an argument from Paul Churchland's "Reduction, Qualia, and the Direct Introspection of Brain States"[4] against Nagel's argument in "What Is it Like to Be a Bat?" For this selection, (a) diagram the argument and (b) identify any potential objections to the argument.

A second argument urges the point that the intrinsic character of experiences, the qualia of sensations, are essentially accessible from only a single point of view, the subjective point of view of the experiencing subject. The properties of physical brain states, by contrast, are accessible from a variety of entirely objective points of view. We cannot hope adequately to account for the former, therefore, in terms of properties appropriate to the latter domain (cf. Nagel, 442–444).

This somewhat diffuse argument appears to be an instance of the following argument:

(1) The qualia of my sensations are directly known by me, by introspection, as elements of my conscious self.

(2) The properties of my brain states are not directly known by me, by introspection, as elements of my conscious self.

∴ (3) The qualia of my sensations ≠ the properties of my brain states.

And perhaps there is a second argument here as well, a complement to the first:

(1) The properties of my brain states are known-by-the-various-external-senses, as having such-and-such physical properties.
(2) The qualia of my sensations are *not* known-by-the-various-external-senses, as having such-and-such physical properties.
∴ (3) The qualia of my sensations ≠ the properties of my brain states.

... The problem with all these arguments is that the "property" ascribed in premise 1 and withheld in premise 2 consists only in the subject item's being *recognized, perceived,* or *known* as something, *under some specific description or other*. Such apprehension is not a genuine feature of the item itself, fit for divining identities, since one and the same subject may be successfully recognized under one description (e.g., "qualia of my mental state"), and yet fail to be recognized under another, equally accurate, co-referential description (e.g., "property of my brain state").

Exercises 5–9

In the second part of this chapter, we analyzed in detail the argument given by Jackson in "Epiphenomenal Qualia." The following selections contain more arguments from that same article. For each selection, (a) diagram the argument and (b) identify any potential objections to the argument.

Exercise 5

By the Modal Argument I mean an argument of the following style. Sceptics about other minds are not making a mistake in deductive logic, whatever else may be wrong with their position. No amount of physical information about another *logically entails* that he or she is conscious or feels anything at all. Consequently there is a possible world with organisms exactly like us in every physical respect (and remember that includes functional states, physical history, *et al.*) but which differ from us profoundly in that they have no conscious mental life at all. But then what is it that we have and they lack? Not anything physical *ex hypothesi*. In all physical regards we and they are exactly alike. Consequently there is more to us than the purely physical. Thus Physicalism is false. ... The trouble rather with the Modal argument is that it rests on a disputable modal intuition. Disputable because it is disputed. Some sincerely deny that there can be physical replicas of us in other possible worlds which nevertheless lack consciousness. Moreover, at least one person who once had the intuition now has doubts.

Exercise 6

This is perfectly true; but is no objection to qualia, for it rests on an overly optimistic view of the human animal, and its powers. We are the products of Evolution. We understand and sense what we need to understand and sense in order to survive. Epiphenomenal qualia are totally irrelevant to survival. At no stage of our evolution did natural selection favour those who could make sense of how they are caused and the laws governing them, or in fact why they exist at all. And that is why we can't.

Exercise 7

Three reasons are standardly given for holding that a quale like the hurtfulness of a pain must be causally efficacious in the physical world, and so, for instance, that its instantiation must sometimes make a difference to what happens in the brain. None, I will argue, has any real force.

(i) It is supposed to be just obvious that the hurtfulness of pain is partly responsible for the subject seeking to avoid pain, saying "It hurts" and so on. But, to reverse Hume, anything can fail to cause anything. No matter how often *B* follows *A*, and no matter how initially obvious the causality of the connection seems, the hypothesis that *A* causes *B* can be overturned by an over-arching theory which shows the two as distinct effects of a common underlying causal process.

To the untutored the image on the screen of Lee Marvin's fist moving from left to right immediately followed by the image of John Wayne's head moving in the same general direction looks as causal as anything. And of course throughout countless Westerns images similar to the first are followed by images similar to the second. All this counts for precisely nothing when we know the over-arching theory concerning how the relevant images are both effects of an underlying causal process involving the projector and the film. The epiphenomenalist can say exactly the same about the connection between, for example, hurtfulness and behaviour. It is simply a consequence of the fact that certain happenings in the brain cause both.

Exercise 8

(ii) The second objection relates to Darwin's Theory of Evolution. According to natural selection the traits that evolve over time are those conducive to physical survival. We may assume that qualia evolved over time—we have them, the earliest forms of life do not—and so we should expect qualia to be conducive to survival. The objection is that they could hardly help us to survive if they do nothing to the physical world.

The appeal of this argument is undeniable, but there is a good reply to it. Polar bears have particularly thick, warm coats. The Theory of Evolution explains this (we suppose) by pointing out that having a thick, warm coat is conducive to survival in the Arctic. But having a thick coat goes along with having a heavy coat, and having a heavy coat is *not* conducive to survival. It slows the animal down.

Does this mean that we have refuted Darwin because we have found an evolved trait—having a heavy coat—which is not conducive to survival? Clearly not. Having a heavy coat is an unavoidable concomitant of having a warm coat (in the context, modern insulation was not available), and the advantages for survival of having a warm coat outweighed the disadvantages of having a heavy one. The point is that all we can extract from Darwin's theory is that we should expect any evolved characteristic to be *either* conducive to survival *or* a by-product of one that is so conducive. The epiphenomenalist holds that qualia fall into the latter category. They are a by-product of certain brain processes that are highly conducive to survival.

Exercise 9

(iii) The third objection is based on a point about how we come to know about other minds. We know about other minds by knowing about other behaviour, at least in part. The nature of the inference is a matter of some controversy, but it is not a matter of controversy that it proceeds from behaviour. That is why we think that stones do not feel and dogs do feel. But, runs the objection, how can a person's behaviour provide any reason for believing he has qualia like mine, or indeed any qualia at all, unless this behaviour can be regarded as the *outcome* of the qualia. Man Friday's footprint was evidence of Man Friday because footprints are causal outcomes of feet attached to people. And an epiphenomenalist cannot regard behaviour, or indeed anything physical, as an outcome of qualia.

But consider my reading in *The Times* that Spurs won. This provides excellent evidence that *The Telegraph* has also reported that Spurs won, despite the fact that (I trust) *The Telegraph* does not get the results from *The Times*. They each send their own reporters to the game. *The Telegraph*'s report is in no sense an outcome of *The Times*', but the latter provides good evidence for the former nevertheless.

The reasoning involved can be reconstructed thus. I read in *The Times* that Spurs won. This gives me reason to think that Spurs won because I know that Spurs' winning is the most likely candidate to be what caused the report in *The Times*. But I also know that Spurs' winning would have had many effects, including almost certainly a report in *The Telegraph*.

Exercises 10–11

In the third part of this chapter, we analyzed in detail the argument given by Churchland in "Knowing Qualia: A Reply to Jackson." The following selections contain more arguments from that same article. For each selection, (a) diagram the argument and (b) identify any potential objections to the argument.

*Exercise 10

This distributed representation is not remotely propositional or discursive, but it is entirely real. All trichromatic animals have one, even those without any linguistic capacity. It apparently makes possible the many abilities we expect from color-competent creatures: discrimination, recognition, imagination, and so on. Such a representation is presumably what a person with Mary's upbringing would lack, or possess only in stunted or incomplete form. Her representational space within the relevant area of neurons would contain only the subspace for black, white, and the intervening shades of gray, for the visual examples that have shaped her synaptic configuration were limited to these. There is thus more than just a clutch of abilities missing in Mary: there is a complex representation—a processing framework that deserves to be called "cognitive"—that she either lacks or has in reduced form. There is indeed something she "does not know." Jackson's premise (2), we may assume, is thus true on these wholly materialist assumptions.

These same assumptions are entirely consistent with the further assumption that elsewhere in Mary's brain—in the language areas, for example—she has stored a detailed and even exhaustive set of discursive, propositional, truth-valuable representations of what goes on in people's brains during the experience of color, a set she has brought into being by the exhaustive reading of authoritative texts in a completed cognitive neuroscience. She may even be able to explain her own representational deficit, as sketched above, in complete neurophysical detail. Jackson's premise (1), we may thus assume, is also true on these wholly materialist assumptions.

The view sketched above is a live candidate for the correct story of sensory coding and sensory recognition. But whether or not it is true, it is at least a logical possibility. Accordingly, what we have sketched here is a consistent but entirely *physical* model (i.e., a model in which Jackson's conclusion is false) in which both of Jackson's premises are true under the appropriate interpretation. They can hardly entail a conclusion, then, that is inconsistent with physicalism.

Exercise 11

My final objection to Jackson was aimed more at breaking the grip of the ideology behind his argument than at the argument itself. That ideology includes a domain of properties—the qualia of subjective experience—that are held to be metaphysically distinct from the objective physical properties addressed by orthodox science. It is not a surprise, then, on this view, that one might know all physical facts, and yet be ignorant of some domain of these nonphysical qualia. The contrast between what is known and what is not known simply reflects an antecedent metaphysical division in the furniture of the world.

But there is another way to look at the situation, one that finds no such division. Our capacity for recognizing a range of (currently) inarticulable features in our subjective experience is easily explained on materialist principles. … Our discursive inarticulation of those features is no surprise either, and signifies nothing about their metaphysical status. … Indeed, that veil of inarticulation may itself be swept aside by suitable learning. What we are now able spontaneously to report about our internal states and cognitive activities need not define the limit on what we might be able to report, spontaneously and accurately, if we were taught a more appropriate conceptual scheme in which to express our discriminations. In closing, let me again urge on Jackson this exciting possibility.

Exercises 12–17

The following exercises are intended to ensure your understanding of Nagel's, Jackson's, and Churchland's texts and to help you further explore the ideas presented in this chapter.

Exercise 12: Now that you have read my textual analysis of Nagel's argument in "What Is It Like to Be a Bat?," summarize it in your own words.
Exercise 13: Summarize, in your own words, each of the arguments in exercises 1–4 above.
Exercise 14: Now that you have read my textual analysis of Jackson's argument in "Epiphenomenal Qualia," summarize it in your own words.
Exercise 15: Summarize, in your own words, each of the arguments in exercises 5–9 above.
Exercise 16: Now that you have read my textual analysis of Churchland's argument in "Knowing Qualia: A Reply to Jackson," summarize it in your own words.
Exercise 17: Summarize, in your own words, each of the arguments in exercises 10 and 11 above.

12.5 Reading Questions

1. Why does Nagel use a bat as an example in his article, instead of some other kind of animal?
2. According to Nagel, what is the difference between subjective experience and objective experience? Why does he think one cannot be reduced to the other?
3. What is Jackson's reply to Nagel's argument? How does he use "Fred" in this reply?

4. Both Nagel and Jackson use the phrase "what it is like to …," as in "What it is like to be a bat" or "What it is like to see red." What do these kinds of phrases mean? To what do they refer? Do you think there is something that is what it's like to see red? Why or why not?
5. Do you think Churchland is representing Jackson's argument fairly? Why or why not?
6. Churchland says that Jackson's argument has a heavy burden. What is this burden, and why is it important?

13 Consciousness

13.1 John Searle, "Can Computers Think?"
13.2 Dan Dennett, "Consciousness Imagined"
13.3 In-Class Exercises
13.4 Reading Questions

13.1 John Searle, "Can Computers Think?"

John Searle (1932–) was born in Denver, Colorado, and earned his undergraduate degree at the University of Wisconsin. Subsequently, as a Rhodes Scholar, he earned his doctorate in philosophy at Oxford University. Searle began his career at the University of California at Berkeley in 1959, and was a member of the free speech movement. He still teaches at Berkeley and is currently the Slusser Professor Emeritus of the Philosophy of Mind and Language.

Searle has published numerous books on a wide range of philosophical topics. His publications include:

Speech Acts: An Essay in the Philosophy of Language, 1969
Intentionality: An Essay in the Philosophy of Mind, 1983
Minds, Brains, and Science: The 1984 Reith Lectures, 1984
Foundations of Illocutionary Logic (with Daniel Vanderveken), 1985
John Searle and His Critics, 1991
The Rediscovery of the Mind, 1992
The Construction of Social Reality, 1995
Rationality in Action, 2001
Making the Social World: The Structure of Human Civilization, 2010

Perhaps, though, Searle's most famous written work is chapter 2 of his *Minds, Brains, and Science*, titled "Can Computers Think?" In this text, Searle's purpose is to argue, against Turing, that passing the Turing Test is not a sufficient condition for a computer to be said to be intelligent, and that the whole project of "Strong AI" is wrongheaded. In this argument,

Searle offers another of the most famous thought experiments in philosophy. Let's look at his text in more detail.

From *Minds, Brains, and Science.*[1]

But this feature of programs, that they are defined purely formally or syntactically, is fatal to the view that mental processes and program processes are identical. ...

Now the point of the story is simply this: by virtue of implementing a formal computer program from the point of view of an outside observer, you behave exactly as if you understood Chinese,[1] but all the same[A] you don't understand a word of Chinese.[2] But[B] if going through the appropriate computer program for understanding Chinese is not enough to give you an understanding of Chinese, then it is not enough to give *any other digital computer* an understanding of Chinese.[3] And again, the reason for this can be stated quite simply.[C] If you don't understand Chinese, then no other computer could understand Chinese[4] because[D] no digital computer, just by virtue of running a program, has anything that you don't have.[5] All that the computer has, as you have, is a formal program for manipulating uninterpreted Chinese symbols.[6]

In "Can Computers Think?" Searle invites us to consider a particular thought experiment, and then builds an argument from the result. His ultimate goal is to show that a digital computer executing a program could not possibly be said to think.

After describing the thought experiment, Searle explains the results: you (as stipulated) behave exactly as if you understand Chinese (1), but you don't actually understand Chinese (2). Let us set these statements aside for the moment.

The heart of the argument is the next claim: if executing the appropriate computer program is insufficient for giving you an understanding of Chinese, then executing the appropriate computer program is insufficient for giving any other digital computer an understanding of Chinese (3). As indicated by (C), the statement that supports this claim is that if you don't understand Chinese (in this scenario), then no other computer could understand Chinese (4). We can represent this as:

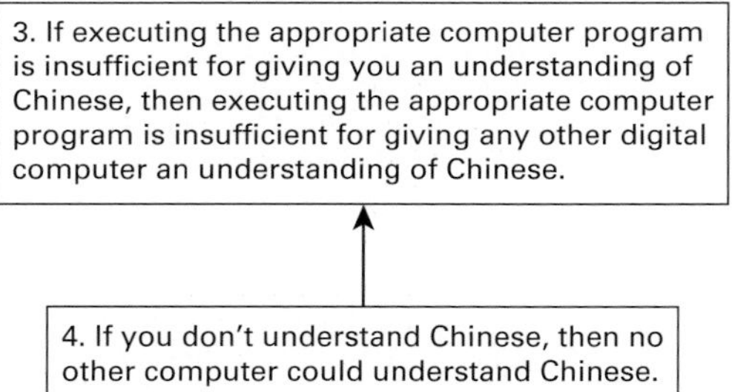
3. If executing the appropriate computer program is insufficient for giving you an understanding of Chinese, then executing the appropriate computer program is insufficient for giving any other digital computer an understanding of Chinese.
4. If you don't understand Chinese, then no other computer could understand Chinese.

Next, as indicated by (D), (4) is then supported by the claim that no digital computer, just by virtue of running a program, has anything that you don't have (5). And (5) in turn is supported by the claim that all that you and the computer have is a formal program for manipulating uninterpreted Chinese symbols (6). We can represent this whole chain of argumentation as:

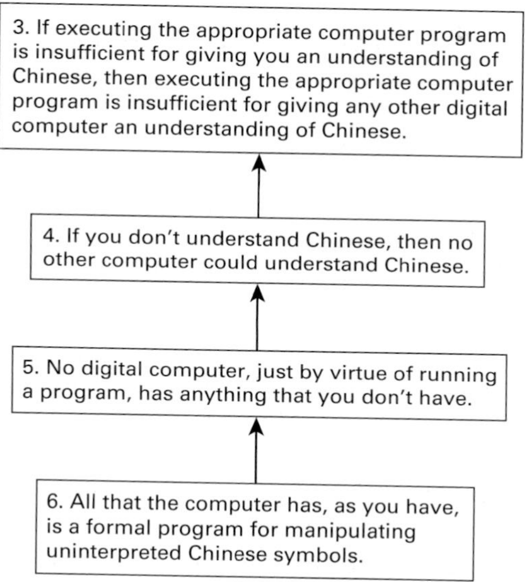
3. If executing the appropriate computer program is insufficient for giving you an understanding of Chinese, then executing the appropriate computer program is insufficient for giving any other digital computer an understanding of Chinese.
4. If you don't understand Chinese, then no other computer could understand Chinese.
5. No digital computer, just by virtue of running a program, has anything that you don't have.
6. All that the computer has, as you have, is a formal program for manipulating uninterpreted Chinese symbols.

Now we have a conditional statement as the subconclusion of this argument, which, as indicated by (B), is supposed to be combined with (1) and (2). I think it is more useful, however, to represent (1) and (2) as combining to support the unstated subconclusion that executing the appropriate computer program is insufficient for giving you an understanding of Chinese:

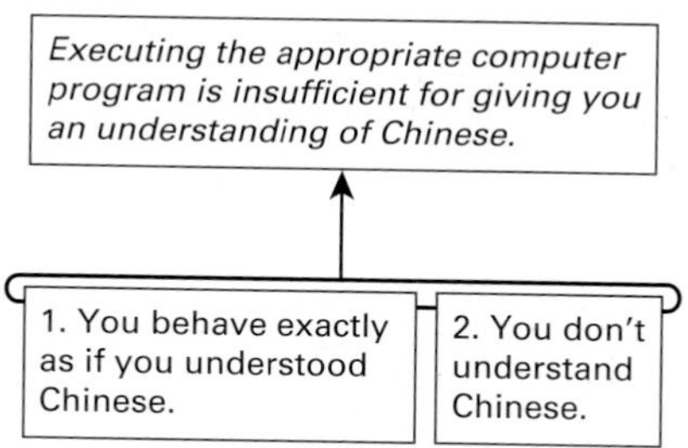
Executing the appropriate computer program is insufficient for giving you an understanding of Chinese.
1. You behave exactly as if you understood Chinese.
2. You don't understand Chinese.

We can then combine this subconclusion with (3) to conclude that executing the appropriate computer program is insufficient for giving any other digital computer an understanding of Chinese, and thus that mental processes cannot be identical to program processes:

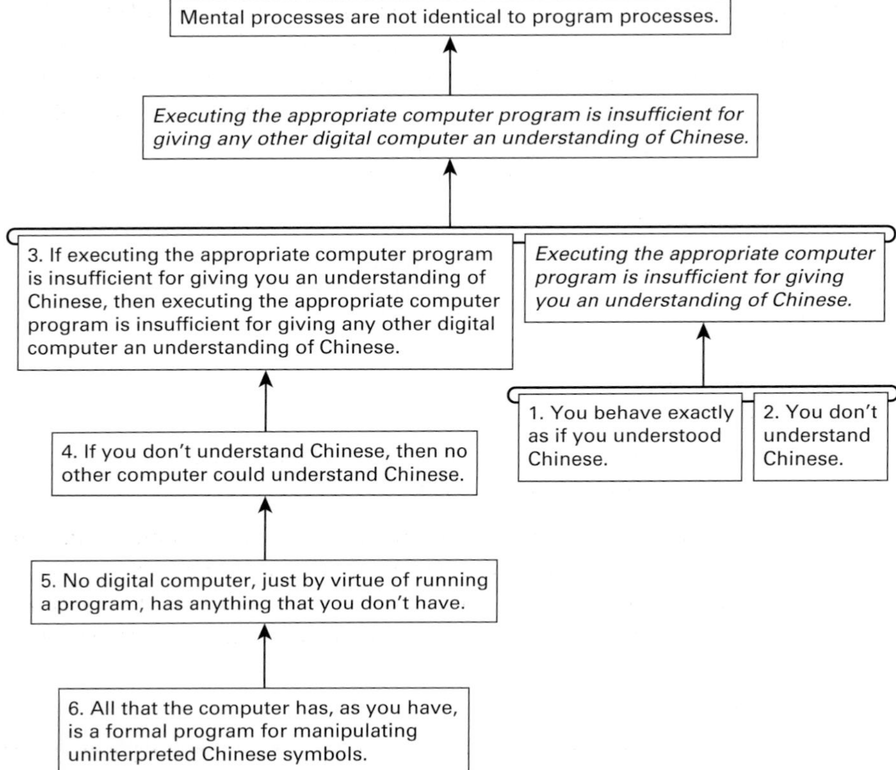
Mental processes are not identical to program processes.
Executing the appropriate computer program is insufficient for giving any other digital computer an understanding of Chinese.
3. If executing the appropriate computer program is insufficient for giving you an understanding of Chinese, then executing the appropriate computer program is insufficient for giving any other digital computer an understanding of Chinese.
Executing the appropriate computer program is insufficient for giving you an understanding of Chinese.
1. You behave exactly as if you understood Chinese.
2. You don't understand Chinese.
4. If you don't understand Chinese, then no other computer could understand Chinese.
5. No digital computer, just by virtue of running a program, has anything that you don't have.
6. All that the computer has, as you have, is a formal program for manipulating uninterpreted Chinese symbols.

By virtue of Searle's thought experiment, we can substitute any kind of thinking or understanding into this argument in place of the Chinese language. Thus, we have the more general conclusion that executing the appropriate computer program is insufficient for giving any digital computer the ability to think or understand. And so, mental processes cannot be the same as program processes. Humans think and understand not because we are digital computers, but because we are more than digital computers; just being a digital computer is not enough.

Searle draws some further conclusions, which we will explore in the exercises. Now, we turn to a philosopher who raises objections to Searle's argument.

13.2 Dan Dennett, "Consciousness Imagined"

Daniel Dennett was born in 1942 in Boston, Massachusetts. He earned his undergraduate degree in philosophy from Harvard University in 1963, and his doctorate degree in philosophy from Oxford University in 1965. His first academic appointment was at the University of California at Irvine until 1971, when he moved to Tufts University, where he has taught ever since. He is now University Professor, Fletcher Professor of Philosophy, and the codirector of the Center for Cognitive Studies; and he specializes in philosophy of mind, philosophy of science, philosophy of biology, and cognitive science.

Dennett has published many books on various philosophical topics, including:

Content and Consciousness, 1969
Brainstorms, 1978
Elbow Room, 1984
The Intentional Stance, 1987
Consciousness Explained, 1991
Darwin's Dangerous Idea, 1995
Kinds of Minds, 1996
Sweet Dreams: Philosophical Obstacles to a Science of Consciousness, 2005
Intuition Pumps and Other Tools for Thinking, 2013

One of Dennett's most straightforward replies to Searle's "Chinese room" argument above is in chapter 14 of *Consciousness Explained*, titled "Consciousness Imagined." Here, Dennett argues that Searle can draw the "obvious" conclusion from his thought experiment only because he is not taking his own setup seriously. Let's look at Dennett's text in more detail.

From *Consciousness Explained.*[2]

There has been a huge outpouring of reaction to Searle's many versions of this thought experiment over the last decade, and ... it is undeniable that its "conclusion" continues to seem "obvious" to many people. Why? Because people don't actually imagine the case in the detail that it requires.

... [S]ince[A] Searle stipulates that the program passes the Turing test,[1] and since[B] this level of conversational sophistication would surely be within its powers,[2] unless we try to imagine the complexities of a program capable of generating this sort of conversation, we are not following directions.[3] ...

That fact is that[C] any program that could actually hold up its end in the conversation depicted would have to be an extraordinarily supple, sophisticated, and multilayered system, brimming with "world knowledge" and meta-knowledge and meta-meta-knowledge about its own responses, the likely responses of its interlocutor, its own "motivations" and the motivations of its interlocutor, and much, much more.[4] Searle does not deny that programs can have all this structure, of course. He simply discourages us from attending to it. But[D] if we are to do a good job imagining the case, we are not only entitled but obliged to imagine that the program Searle is hand-simulating has all this structure[5]—and more, if only we can imagine it. But[E] then it is no longer obvious, I trust, that there is no genuine understanding of the joke going on. …

Dennett argues that Searle's claim—that no digital computer, by virtue of executing an appropriate program, could ever be said to understand Chinese—is not justified. That is, Searle says that in his thought experiment, it is obvious that the program (of which he is a part) does not understand the conversation; and Dennett argues that this is not at all obvious.

First, Dennett gives us a hypothetical conversation between the "Chinese room" program that Searle imagines himself to be in and a judge of the Turing test. Dennett then points out that, in his thought experiment, Searle stipulates that the program passes the Turing test (1). In addition, Dennett claims that any program that passed the Turing test would be able to have a high level of conversational sophistication (2), along the lines of his example.

As indicated by (A) and (B), these two claims combine to support the claim that if we do not try to imagine the complexities of a program capable of generating a high level of conversational sophistication, then we are not following directions (3). It is useful, here, to state the implicit intermediate step that Searle stipulates that the program would be able to have a high level of conversational sophistication. We can represent this as:

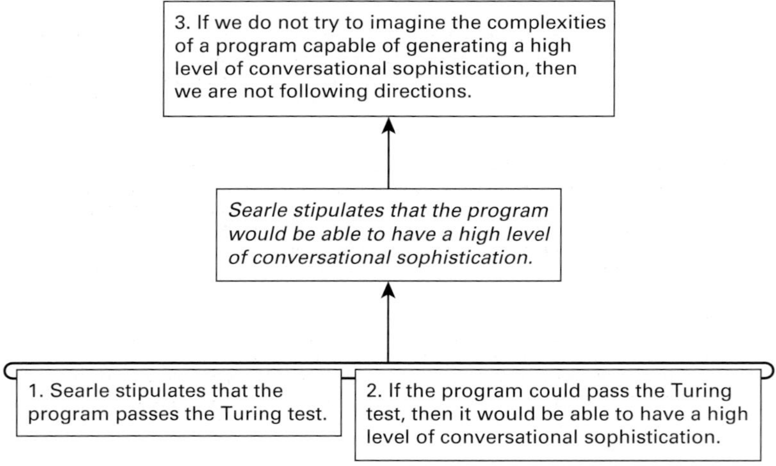

Then, Dennett explains that any program that is capable of generating a high level of conversational sophistication would have a very complex structure (4). So, if we are following directions—that is, doing a good job of imagining the case—we have to imagine that the program has this complex structure. We can represent this as:

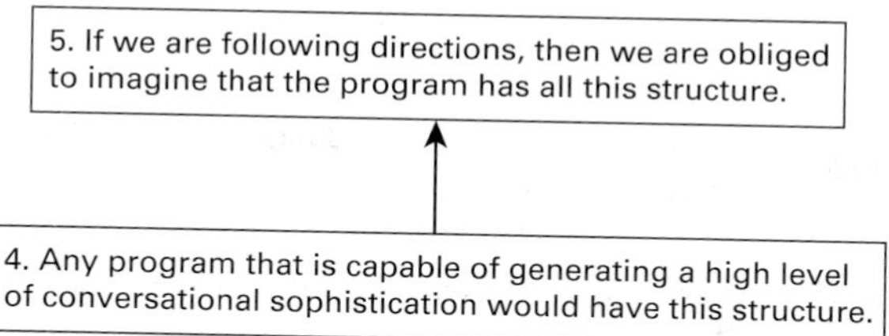

So, the implicit conclusion here is that, in stipulating that the program passes the Turing test, Searle is actually stipulating that the program has this complex structure. Moreover, we have the implicit premise that if the program does have this complex structure, then it is not obvious that the program does not genuinely understand the program. This line of reasoning, then, supports the conclusion that in Searle's thought experiment it is not in fact obvious that the program does not genuinely understand the conversation.

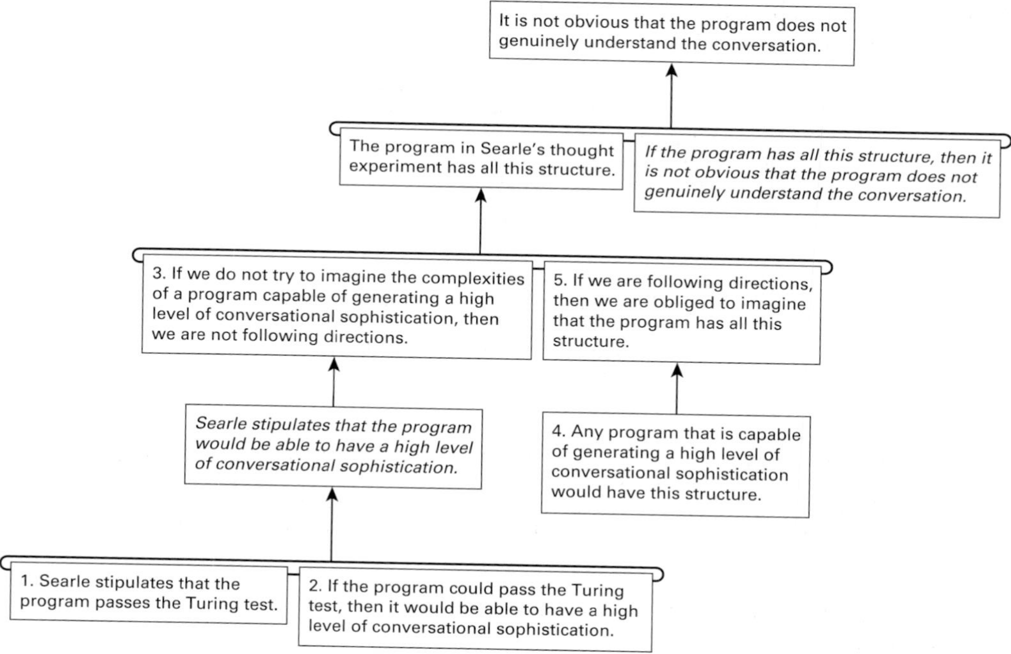

In the exercises, we will explore further aspects of Dennett's argument.

13.3 In-Class Exercises

An asterisk (*) indicates a more challenging exercise.

Exercises 1–4

In the first section of this chapter, we analyzed in detail Searle's argument in "Can Computers Think?" The following selections contain arguments from that same article. For each selection, (a) diagram the argument and (b) identify any potential objections to the argument.

Exercise 1

The argument has a very simple logical structure, so you can see whether it is valid or invalid. The first premise is:

1. *Brains cause minds.*

Now, of course, that is really too crude. What we mean by that is that mental processes that we consider to constitute a mind are caused, entirely caused, by processes going on inside the brain. But let's be crude, let's just abbreviate that as three words—brains cause minds. And that is just a fact about how the world works. Now let's write proposition number two:

2. *Syntax is not sufficient for semantics.*

That proposition is a conceptual truth. It just articulates our distinction between the notion of what is purely formal and what has content. Now, to these two propositions—that brains cause minds and that syntax is not sufficient for semantics—let's add a third and a fourth:

3. *Computer programs are entirely defined by their formal, or syntactical, structure.*

That proposition, I take it, is true by definition; it is part of what we mean by the notion of a computer program.

4. *Minds have mental contents; specifically, they have semantic contents.*

And that, I take it, is just an obvious fact about how our minds work. My thoughts, and beliefs, and desires are about something, or they refer to something, or they concern states of affairs in the world; and they do that because their content directs them at these states of affairs in the world. Now, from these four premises, we can draw our first conclusion; and it follows obviously from premises 2, 3 and 4:

CONCLUSION 1. *No computer program by itself is sufficient to give a system a mind. Programs, in short, are not minds, and they are not by themselves sufficient for having minds.*

Exercise 2

Here is a second conclusion:

CONCLUSION 2. *The way that brain functions cause minds cannot be solely in virtue of running a computer program.*

And this second conclusion follows from conjoining the first premise together with our first conclusion. That is, from the fact that brains cause minds and that programs are not enough to do the job, it follows that the way that brains cause minds can't be solely by running a computer program.

Exercise 3

Now, from our first premise, we can also derive a third conclusion:

Conclusion 3. *Anything else that caused minds would have to have causal powers at least equivalent to those of the brain.*

And this third conclusion is a trivial consequence of our first premise. It is a bit like saying that if my petrol engine drives my car at seventy-five miles an hour, then any diesel engine that was capable of doing that would have to have a power output at least equivalent to that of my petrol engine.

Exercise 4

But now, from our first conclusion, that programs are not enough, and our third conclusion, that any other system would have to have causal powers equal to the brain, conclusion four follows immediately:

Conclusion 4. *For any artifact that we might build which had mental states equivalent to human mental states, the implementation of a computer program would not by itself be sufficient. Rather the artifact would have to have powers equivalent to the powers of the human brain.*

Exercises 5–9

In the second part of this chapter, we analyzed in detail Dennett's response to Searle in "Consciousness Imagined." The following selections contain more arguments from that same article. For each selection, (a) diagram the argument and (b) identify any potential objections to the argument.

Exercise 5

Here is how the misdirection occurs. We see clearly enough that if there were understanding in such a giant system, it would not be Searle's understanding (since he is just a cog in the machinery, oblivious to the context of what he is doing). We also see clearly that there is nothing remotely like genuine understanding in any hunk of programming small enough to imagine readily—whatever it is, it's just a mindless routine for transforming symbol strings into other symbol strings according to some mechanical or syntactical recipe. Then comes the suppressed premise: Surely more of the *same*, no matter how much more, would never add up to genuine understanding. But why should anyone think this was true?

Exercise 6

If … we are materialists who are convinced that one way or another our brains are responsible on their own, without miraculous assistance, for our understanding, we must admit that genuine understanding is somehow achieved by a process composed of interactions between a host of subsystems none of which understand a thing by themselves. … It is hard to imagine how "just more of the same" could add up to understanding, but we have very good reason to believe that it does, so in this case, we should try harder, not give up.

Exercises 7–10

The following exercises are intended to ensure your understanding of Searle's and Dennett's texts, and to help you further explore the ideas presented in this chapter.

Exercise 7: Now that you have read my textual analysis of Searle's argument in "Can Computers Think?," summarize it in your own words.
Exercise 8: Summarize, in your own words, each of the arguments in exercises 1–4 above.
Exercise 9: Now that you have read my textual analysis of Dennett's argument in "Consciousness Imagined," summarize it in your own words.
Exercise 10: Summarize, in your own words, each of the arguments in exercises 5–6 above.

13.4 Reading Questions

1. How would Searle explain the fact that we believe that other people have minds? Why does this explanation not extend to robots?
2. Does Searle's thought experiment have any bearing on the adequacy of the Turing test? Why or why not?
3. Is Searle a materialist or a dualist with respect to minds and brains? On what aspects of the article do you justify your claim?
4. How does Searle use the fact that programs are "multiply realizable" to argue that someone who believes in strong AI must also believe in dualism with respect to the human mind?
5. Searle argues that artificial computers cannot, even in principle, be said to think, but he also claims that people are machines that can think. What do you think about applying the term "machine" to a human brain?
6. Do you think Dennett is representing Searle's argument fairly? Why or why not?
7. What are the differences between how Searle and Dennett view "multiply realizable" programs?
8. How would Searle respond to Dennett's argument?

V Free Will and Determinism

Introduction

Why does it matter so much what our minds are like? Well, one reason it matters is that we are concerned about the causes of our actions. And the causes of our actions matter because we are concerned with whether and when we can be held morally responsible for our actions. In between such questions about the nature of minds and questions about morality is the issue of free will—whether we have it, and if so, how it is possible.

You might be asking why we are questioning whether we have free will. Indeed, you might think that it is perfectly obvious that we do have free will. After all, we make decisions all the time that are completely up to us. For example, you are reading this book right now, and presumably the decision to do so was entirely up to you. Of course, it may be required reading, and so you feel like you must read it, but the decision to read it *right now*, rather than, say, look out the window or watch TV right now, is up to you. You could stop reading at any time if, for example, you decide to take a break and get something to eat.

On the other hand, the more we know about the human brain, the more mysterious this notion of free will becomes. Your brain is a massive network of interconnected neurons that pass electrical signals back and forth to each other. For example, light coming into your eyes sends a signal to your visual cortex, which then sends a signal to various other parts of your brain, and as a result you acquire the belief that it's raining outside. Similarly, activity in one area of the brain stimulates activity in another area, which sends a signal to your muscles to contract in certain ways in order to, for example, grab your umbrella.

If we were just considering a simple circuit board in which electrical signals are sent from one place to another, it seems perfectly reasonable to think that the output of the circuit board is entirely determined by the inputs to the board and the design of the board itself. In other words, it seems clear that the circuit board is deterministic. So how is our brain different from this circuit board? It is certainly much more complicated, and made of biological materials. But why, given the advancement of neuroscience, should we think that the outputs of brain activity, like grabbing an umbrella, aren't determined by the inputs to the brain through the senses plus the design of the brain?

The problem is that if our actions, like grabbing an umbrella, are determined ultimately by something external to us, like the light falling on our retinas constituting our visual sensation of rain, then we are not in control of our actions. And if we are not in control of our actions, then we are not acting out of our own free will. So here's the puzzle: we have good reasons to believe that we do perform actions of our own free will, but we also have good reasons to believe that our actions are determined. In Part V, we will explore various attempts to address this puzzle.

Learning Objectives for Part V

At the end of Part V, you will be able to:

- Describe:
  - Alternative definitions of "free will"
  - The debate about free will and determinism
  - The three most common positions in this debate
- Discuss:
  - The strengths and weaknesses of various definitions of free will
  - The strengths and weaknesses of the arguments for and against the various positions in the free will debate
- Define:
  - Compatibilism
  - Incompatibilism
  - Soft determinism
  - Hard determinism
  - Libertarianism

Preliminary Questions for Part V

1. Do we have control over our actions?
2. If so, how much control do we have, and what kind of control do we have?
3. Does every event have a cause?
4. Is the world deterministic?
5. If the world is deterministic, can people have free will?
6. If our actions are free, do we have reasons for taking them?
7. Could free will be just an illusion?

Free Will versus Determinism

The puzzle we are exploring is how we can have good reasons for both believing we have free will and believing our actions are determined. To do this, though, we first need to delve a bit more into the definitions. First, a *deterministic system* is one in which the combination of the initial conditions (the input) and the laws governing the system (how it is designed) completely determine the final conditions (the output). In other words, given some deterministic system, each set of initial conditions will result in one and only one set of final conditions. And if the system ever has those exact initial conditions again, the result will be exactly the same final conditions. Consider hitting a baseball from a tee with a bat. If everything stays exactly the same—the height and weight of the ball, the force of the swing, the weight of the bat, the movement of the air, and so on—then, when it comes to rest, the baseball will end up in exactly the same spot every time. Thus, hitting a baseball on a tee with a bat is a deterministic process.

Determinism, then, is the view that the world and everything in it, including human beings, are deterministic systems.

Free will, on the other hand, is a little harder to define, and different philosophers have offered quite different definitions. So, let's look at the different kinds of positions philosophers have about the free will puzzle. The first question to ask is whether the philosopher believes that a person can have free will even if her actions are determined. If the answer is yes, then she is a *compatibilist*; she thinks that free will is *compatible* with determinism. If the answer is no, then she is an *incompatibilist*; she thinks that free will is *incompatible* with determinism.

A compatibilist who thinks that we both have free will *and* are determined is called a *soft determinist*. How is this possible? A determinist believes that our actions are determined by a series of events that originate outside of us. Consider the example given above of picking up an umbrella: the light originates outside of you, then enters your eye and causes a series of electrical events in your brain, which ultimately culminates in you picking up your umbrella. This may make humans sound like mere automata, but part of the chain of electric signals can be a deliberation process that takes into account your desire to not get wet and your belief that if you take your umbrella then you won't get wet. The way the compatibilist reconciles this with free will is by saying that you picked up your umbrella of your own free will if it's the case that you could have chosen not to pick it up if you had wanted that instead. So, you exercise your free will as long as there is nothing preventing you from choosing not to pick up the umbrella.

The incompatibilist, on the other hand, finds fault with this definition of free will. For the incompatibilist, it doesn't matter if you could have chosen not to pick up the umbrella if you had wanted to; the issue is whether you could have *wanted* not to pick it up. That is, the compatibilist says that having free will means that you could have chosen to act other than you did *if* you had had different beliefs and desires. The incompatibilist says that this isn't free will if your beliefs and desires themselves were determined by something outside of you; if you could not have had different beliefs and desires, then it doesn't matter what different beliefs and desires would have caused you to do.

The incompatibilist says that having free will means that you could have done otherwise, period. It doesn't mean that you could have done otherwise if you'd wanted to do otherwise; rather, it means you could have done otherwise because you *could* have had different beliefs and desires. If you could have had different beliefs and desires, that means that your beliefs and desires aren't determined, and so, the incompatibilist believes, you can't both have free will and be determined.

As such, there are traditionally two different ways to be an incompatibilist: a *hard determinist* believes that our actions are determined, and so we do not have free will, while a *libertarian* believes that we do have free will, and so our actions aren't determined. Table 14.1 can help keep straight these different positions on free will versus determinism.

Table 14.1

	We do have free will	We don't have free will
Our actions are determined	Soft determinism	Hard determinism
Our actions are not determined	Libertarianism	?

The question mark in the lower right indicates that there is no name for the position that our actions are not determined *and* we don't have free will. It's not hard to imagine, though, what a position like this might look like. You might think that we are not completely determined because the universe contains an element of randomness. This is supported by quantum mechanics, one of the most successful theories in the history of physics. But even if the universe does have an element of chance, randomness or indeterminism does not seem to be what we are looking for when finding a place for free will. Maybe you can come up with a good name for this position.

14 Hard Determinism

14.1 Baron d'Holbach, "Of the System of Man's Free Agency"
14.2 Galen Strawson, "The Impossibility of Moral Responsibility"
14.3 In-Class Exercises
14.4 Reading Questions

14.1 Baron d'Holbach, "Of the System of Man's Free Agency"

Paul Heinrich Dietrich (1723–1789) was born in Edesheim, Germany, but was raised by his uncle, Franz Adam Holbach, in Paris, France. Upon being naturalized as a French citizen, Dietrich changed his name to Paul-Henri Thiry, Baron d'Holbach (by then his uncle had changed his name to François-Adam, Baron d'Holbach). D'Holbach attended Leiden University in the Netherlands from 1744–1748, whereupon he returned to Paris.

Because of his uncle's wealth, d'Holbach largely led a life of leisure and was known for two activities: translating German scientific works into French and hosting parties. His Parisian salon was a meeting place for French intellectuals (plus some British and American), many of whom contributed to the *Encyclopédie* (in English: *Encyclopedia, or A Systematic Dictionary of the Sciences, Arts, and Crafts*), which was a collection of the writings of Enlightenment thinkers. D'Holbach was a well-known atheist and published his philosophical writings either anonymously or under pseudonyms. His most representative works in this vein are *Christianity Unveiled* (1761), *the System of Nature* (1770), and *Common Sense* (1772).

Of these, *The System of Nature* is surely the most famous. D'Holbach published this book in 1770 under the name Jean-Baptiste de Mirabaud. In it, he denies the existence of God and argues that everything in the universe is made of matter that is subject to the same mechanical laws. This applies, he says, not only to the motion of the planets and familiar objects, but also to people and the workings of their minds. Let's look at this text more closely.

From *The System of Nature.*[1]

Chapter XI: Of the System of Man's Free Agency

... Man's life is a line that nature commands him to describe upon the surface of the earth, without his ever being able to swerve from it, even for an instant.[1] He is born without his own consent;[2] his organization does in nowise depend upon himself;[3] his ideas come to him involuntarily;[4] his habits are in the power of those who cause him to contract them;[5] he is unceasingly modified by causes, whether visible or concealed, over which he has no control, which necessarily regulate his mode of existence, give the hue to his way of thinking, and determine his manner of acting.[6] ...

The will, as we have elsewhere said, is a modification of the brain, by which it is disposed to action, or prepared to give play to the organs.[7] This will is necessarily determined by the qualities, good or bad, agreeable or painful, of the object or the motive that acts upon his senses, or of which the idea remains with him, and is resuscitated by his memory.[8] In consequence,[A] he acts necessarily,[9] his action is the result of the impulse he receives either from the motive, from the object, or from the idea which has modified his brain, or disposed his will.[10] When he does not act according to this impulse, it is because there comes some new cause, some new motive, some new idea, which modifies his brain in a different manner, gives him a new impulse, determines his will in another way, by which the action of the former impulse is suspended:[11] thus, the sight of an agreeable object, or its idea, determines his will to set him in action to procure it; but if a new object or a new idea more powerfully attracts him, it gives a new direction to his will, annihilates the effect of the former, and prevents the action by which it was to be procured. This is the mode in which reflection, experience, reason, necessarily arrests or suspends the action of man's will: without this he would of necessity have followed the anterior impulse which carried him towards a then desirable object. In all this he always acts according to necessary laws, from which he has no means of emancipating himself.[12] ...

From all that has been advanced in this chapter, it results, that[B] in no one moment of his existence is man a free agent.

Although d'Holbach states his conclusion at many points throughout this selection, a very powerful statement of it comes at the very end of chapter 11: "From all that has been advanced in this chapter, it results, that in no one moment of his existence is man a free agent." Throughout this chapter, d'Holbach argues that, although some people might *believe* that they are free agents—that they actually have free will and thus the power to make choices at various times in their lives—they are actually never free agents. D'Holbach thinks that these people are under the illusion that they have free will because they aren't always aware of the causes of their actions.

D'Holbach makes this argument in two slightly different ways, which we might call *global* and *local*. In the global argument, d'Holbach invites us to look at a person's life as a whole trajectory in space and time, beginning with birth and ending with death. The reason a person is not a free agent, he says, is that one does not choose this trajectory through life; rather one's trajectory is completely determined by influences over which one has no control (1).

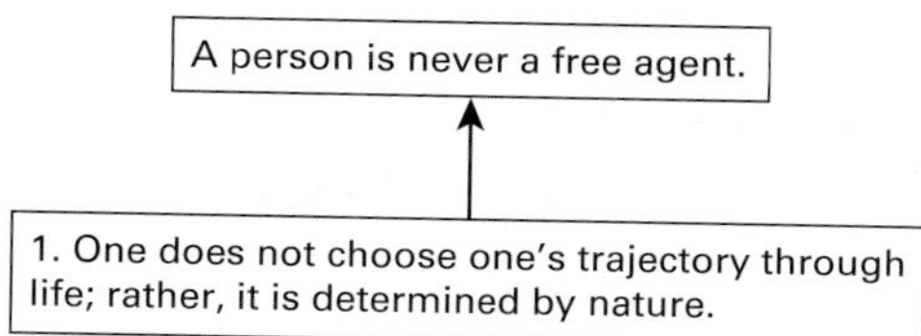

Why does he think this? Well, he says:

- you don't choose to be born (2);
- you don't choose your physiology, that is, how your body (and especially your brain) is constructed (3);
- you don't choose which perceptions, and thus which ideas, to have (4);
- you don't choose your habits—these are chosen by the people who instill those habits in you (e.g., parents and teachers) (5); and
- you don't choose the things that affect you every day (6).

If we take all of these things together, d'Holbach argues, there doesn't seem to be any room for free agency:

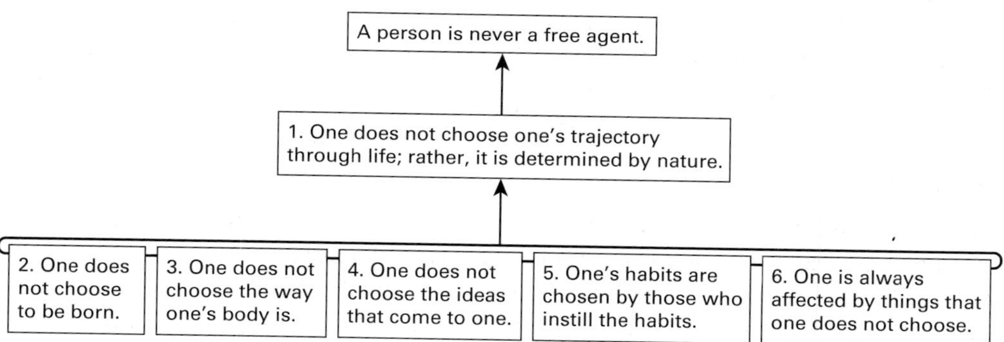

The local argument against free will invites us to think of one particular occasion of action. First, d'Holbach explains what he thinks the will is: a change in one's brain that causes an action (7). Thinking about it in more modern parlance, it is the brain state that causes an impulse to be sent to the muscles that perform the action. And since this brain state had to have been caused by a previous brain state, he refers to the will as this change. This means that the will itself is caused by the thing that changed the brain state—either an external object or perception, or an internal motive (8). As indicated by (A), this supports his contention that one acts necessarily (9), which means that one's actions are necessitated by causes that are ultimately out of one's control.

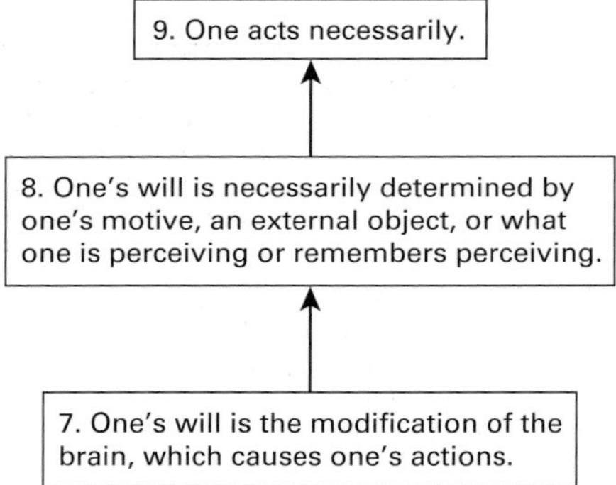

The statements that follow (9) help to fill out this argument. It is generally accepted that one's actions are the result of one's beliefs, desires, and external forces. This means that one's actions are caused either by an external object or perception or by an internal motive (10). If we combine this with (7), we can see that (8) is the result of a kind of syllogism. The will is the change in brain state that causes actions, and actions are the result of an impulse that is caused by motives; therefore, motives determine the will:

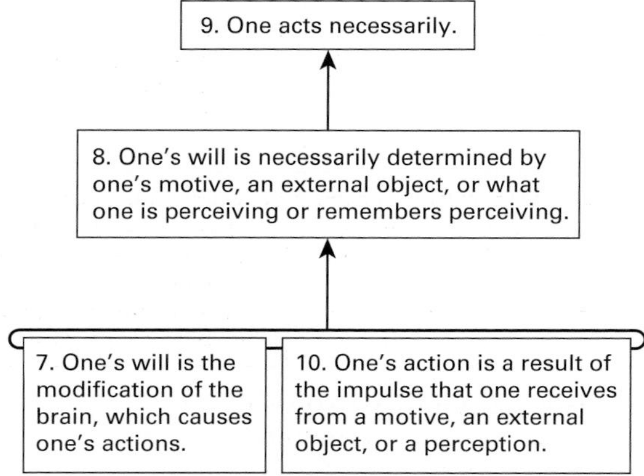

D'Holbach then answers an unstated question: what if my motives dictate one thing, but I end up doing another? His answer is that a new, stronger motive must have come along to override the original motive (11). With this addition, we have an even better case for (9):

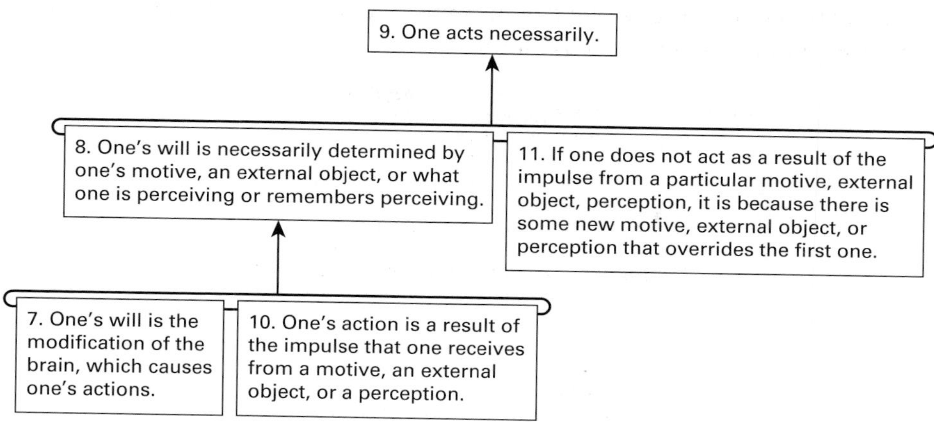

After giving an example of what he means by this overriding motive, d'Holbach makes more explicit what he means by "one acts necessarily." He means that one always acts necessarily according to laws that one cannot escape (12). So, if we substitute this for (9), the overall argument can be represented like this:

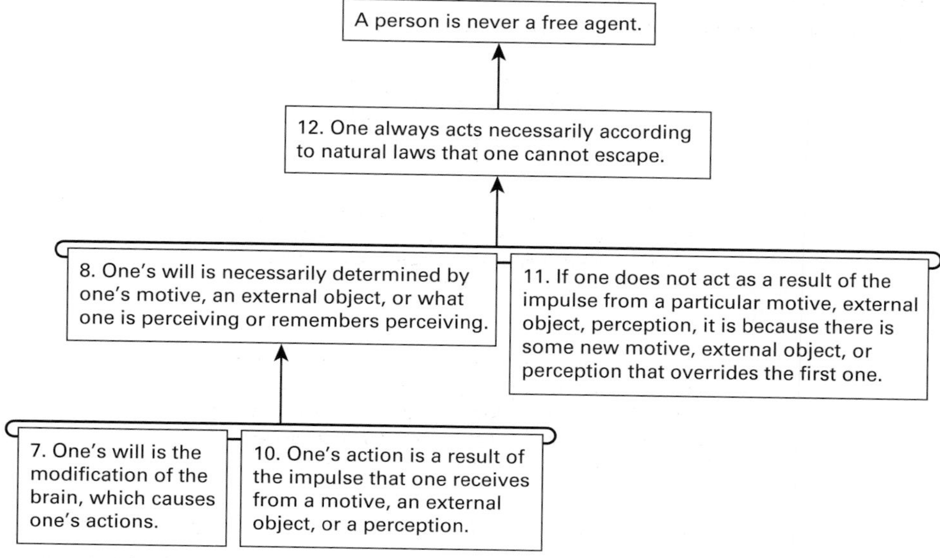

We explore more details of d'Holbach's argument in the exercises. We now turn to a philosopher who is not a hard determinist like d'Holbach, but who presents a similar sort of argument against the claim that anyone can be held morally responsible for his or her actions.

14.2 Galen Strawson, "The Impossibility of Moral Responsibility"

Galen Strawson was born in 1952, in Oxford, England. His father, Peter Strawson (also a well-known philosopher), was a professor at the University of Oxford for most of his career. Galen, though, was educated at the University of Cambridge, receiving his doctorate in philosophy in 1983. He taught at Oxford until 2000, when he moved to the University of Reading. In 2012, Strawson moved to the University of Texas at Austin, where he is professor of philosophy and chair of the philosophy department.

Strawson is known mainly for his work in philosophy of mind and metaphysics, and it is the intersection of these fields that brings him to the issue of free will. He is the author of nearly a dozen books and countless articles, covering topics from Hume and Locke to consciousness and panpsychism.

The following article, "The Impossibility of Moral Responsibility," is surely one of his most famous, for it argues, in effect, that regardless of whether we believe that our behavior is determined, we cannot be held morally responsible for our behavior. This is an excellent example of a causal regress argument (the kind of argument we first saw in chapter 4 with Aquinas), although it has many critics.

Strawson presents several clearly stated versions of the same argument in this article. In what follows, we will examine one of them in detail, leaving the others as exercises.

From "The Impossibility of Moral Responsibility"[2]

A more cumbersome statement of the Basic Argument goes as follows.

(1) Interested in free action, we are particularly interested in actions that are performed for a reason[1] (as opposed to "reflex" actions or mindlessly habitual actions).

(2) When one acts for a reason, what one does is a function of how one is, mentally speaking.[2] (It is also a function of one's height, one's strength, one's place and time, and so on. But the mental factors are crucial when moral responsibility is in question.)

(3) So[A] if one is to be truly responsible for how one acts, one must be truly responsible for how one is, mentally speaking—at least in certain respects.[3]

(4) But[B] to be truly responsible for how one is, mentally speaking, in certain respects, one must have brought it about that one is the way one is, mentally speaking, in certain respects. And it is not merely that one must have caused oneself to be the way one is, mentally speaking. One must have consciously and explicitly chosen to be the way one is, mentally speaking, in certain respects, and one must have succeeded in bringing it about that one is that way.[4]

(5) But[C] one cannot really be said to choose, in a conscious, reasoned, fashion, to be the way one is mentally speaking, in any respect at all, unless one already exists, mentally speaking, already equipped with some principles of choice, "P_1"—preferences, values, pro-attitudes, ideals—in the light of which one chooses how to be.[5]

(6) But[D] then[E] to be truly responsible, on account of having chosen to be the way one is, mentally speaking, in certain respects, one must be truly responsible for one's having the principles of choice P_1 in the light of which one chose how to be.[6]

(7) But[F] for this to be so one must have chosen P_1, in a reasoned, conscious, intentional fashion.[7]
(8) But[G] for this, i.e. (7), to be so one must already have had some principles of choice P_2, in the light of which one chose P_1.[8]
(9) And so on. Here we are setting out on a regress that we cannot stop. True self-determination is impossible[9a] because[H] it requires the actual completion of an infinite series of choices of principles of choice.[9b]
(10) So[I] true moral responsibility is impossible, because[J] it requires true self-determination,[10] as noted in (3).

While Strawson lays out the statements of his argument, the *structure* of the argument is not made clear. He first explains that when it comes to moral responsibility, we are interested only in actions that are performed freely, but this first statement isn't part of the argument; rather, it is just stipulating what kinds of actions we are interested in, *for this particular argument*. The focus is on actions performed for a reason because, it seems, those are the kinds of actions that are most often named as being the result of free will. So we will set the first statement aside.

The next statement begins the argument. Here Strawson describes the causal chain that goes from thinking to acting. If I perform an action for a reason, then there must be, it seems, a direct causal connection from my mind (the way that I mentally am, in Strawson's words) to the action. That is, the action seems to have been caused by my will rather than being accidental or reflexive. So we have the first premise: if one acts for a reason, then one acts because of how one mentally is (2). If we let *M* represent "how one mentally is" and *A* represent one's actions, then the causal chain looks like this:

$$M \rightarrow A$$

But, of course, we are not interested in free actions just for the sake of free actions; we are interested in free actions because free actions are the ones for which we generally assign moral responsibility. There's an unstated premise here: if I am morally responsible for something, then I must be morally responsible for what caused it. Let's add it, because it will show up again and again throughout Strawson's argument. As indicated by (A), the claim that if one is truly responsible for how one acts, then one is responsible for how one mentally is (3) is supported by (2) and this unstated premise.

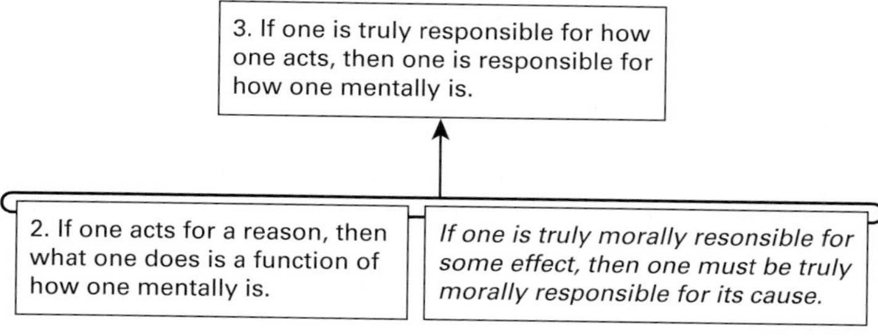

As indicated by (B), this subconclusion is going to be combined with something else, so let us move to another part of the argument. In the next statement, Strawson explains the previous step in the causal chain. The idea is that the way I mentally am now is not the same as how I mentally was in my past. So, how I mentally am now must have been caused by something. But if I am to be responsible for the way I mentally am, then I must be responsible for whatever caused the way I mentally am—which is the unstated premise above. It's not enough, however, to just say that I caused it; I'm only responsible for the cause of the way I mentally am if I caused it for a reason. So, if one is truly responsible for how one mentally is, then one must have consciously and deliberately chosen to be the way one mentally is (4).

The same kind of reasoning applies to choosing how I mentally am; if I am to be responsible for choosing how I mentally am, then I must have done it for a reason. The idea is this: if I could choose the way I mentally am, then there must be at least one other way that I could have mentally been (which would then have caused some possibly different action). Let's represent these two ways I could have mentally been as M_1 and M_2. So, there are two possible causal chains:

$$M_1 \rightarrow A_1$$

$$M_2 \rightarrow A_2$$

If I were able to choose between M_1 and M_2, then I must have had some set of causes for my decision. Strawson calls these causes "principles of choice" and represents the collection of them as P_1. And, I must have had these principles prior to making my decision. So, if I chose M_1 over M_2, then the causal chain would look like this:

$$P_1 \rightarrow M_1 \rightarrow A_1$$

Thus, we have the next statement: if one has consciously and deliberately chosen to be the way one mentally is, then one must be already equipped with principles of choice (5).

As indicated by (C) and (E), (4) and (5) combine to support the claim that if one is truly responsible for how one mentally is, then one is responsible for one's principles of choice (6).

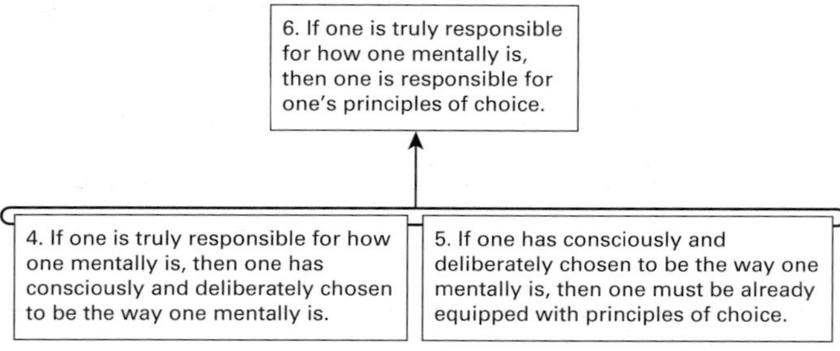
6. If one is truly responsible for how one mentally is, then one is responsible for one's principles of choice.
4. If one is truly responsible for how one mentally is, then one has consciously and deliberately chosen to be the way one mentally is.
5. If one has consciously and deliberately chosen to be the way one mentally is, then one must be already equipped with principles of choice.

But, of course, if one is responsible for P_1, then one must have deliberately chosen P_1 (7), and in order to have chosen P_1, one must have made the choice for a reason, which would involve further principles of choice, P_2 (8). So now the causal chain looks like this:

$$P_2 \rightarrow P_1 \rightarrow M_1 \rightarrow A_1$$

But in order to have chosen P_2, one must have had further principles P_3, and so on, *ad infinitum*. Thus, as indicated by (D), (F), and (G), (6) is to be combined with (7) and (8) to support the claim that if one is truly responsible for how one mentally is, then one must have completed an infinite series of choices of principles of choice (9b).

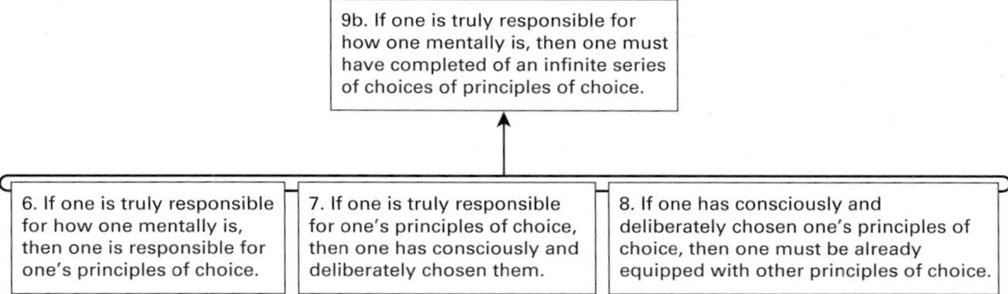
9b. If one is truly responsible for how one mentally is, then one must have completed of an infinite series of choices of principles of choice.
6. If one is truly responsible for how one mentally is, then one is responsible for one's principles of choice.
7. If one is truly responsible for one's principles of choice, then one has consciously and deliberately chosen them.
8. If one has consciously and deliberately chosen one's principles of choice, then one must be already equipped with other principles of choice.

I call this subconclusion (9b) because, as indicated by (H), (9) is actually a subargument, not a single statement, in which (9b) supports the claim that true self-determination is impossible (9a). Keeping the language consistent, and making explicit the unstated premise, we can diagram this part of the argument as:

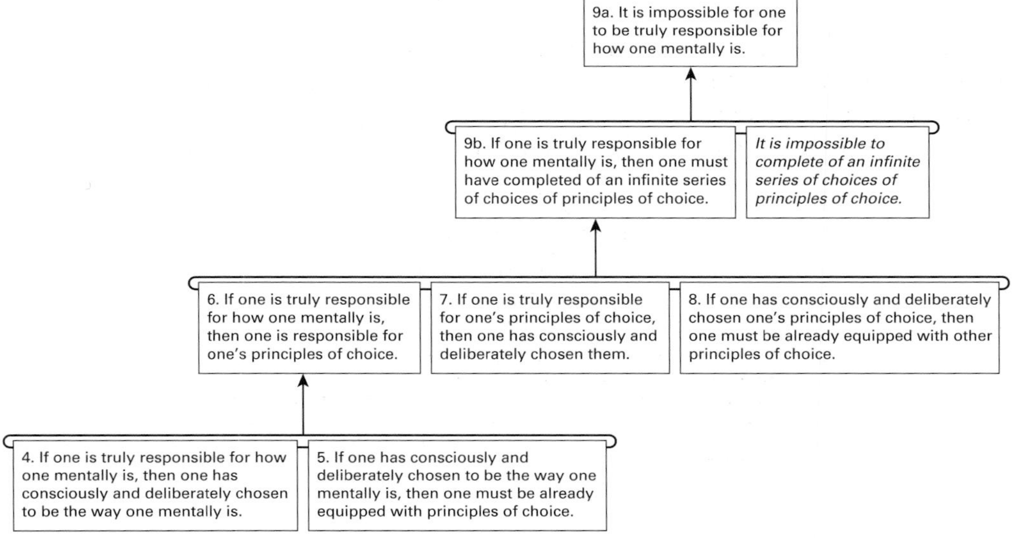
9a. It is impossible for one to be truly responsible for how one mentally is.
9b. If one is truly responsible for how one mentally is, then one must have completed of an infinite series of choices of principles of choice.
It is impossible to complete of an infinite series of choices of principles of choice.
6. If one is truly responsible for how one mentally is, then one is responsible for one's principles of choice.
7. If one is truly responsible for one's principles of choice, then one has consciously and deliberately chosen them.
8. If one has consciously and deliberately chosen one's principles of choice, then one must be already equipped with other principles of choice.
4. If one is truly responsible for how one mentally is, then one has consciously and deliberately chosen to be the way one mentally is.
5. If one has consciously and deliberately chosen to be the way one mentally is, then one must be already equipped with principles of choice.

As indicated by (I), the main conclusion of the argument is that true moral responsibility for any action is impossible. As indicated by (J), this conclusion is supported by the claim that true moral responsibility requires one to be truly responsible for how one acts (10). But how does this connect to the rest of the argument?

To see, let's go back to the beginning of the argument. As indicated by (B), (3) is to be combined the conclusion of this subargument (9a) to support a claim that I think is unstated: that it is impossible for one to be truly responsible for how one acts:

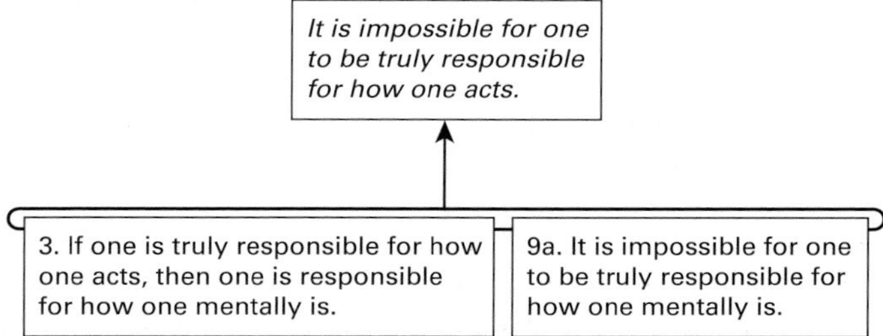

This unstated claim, I think, is to be combined with (10) to support the main conclusion:

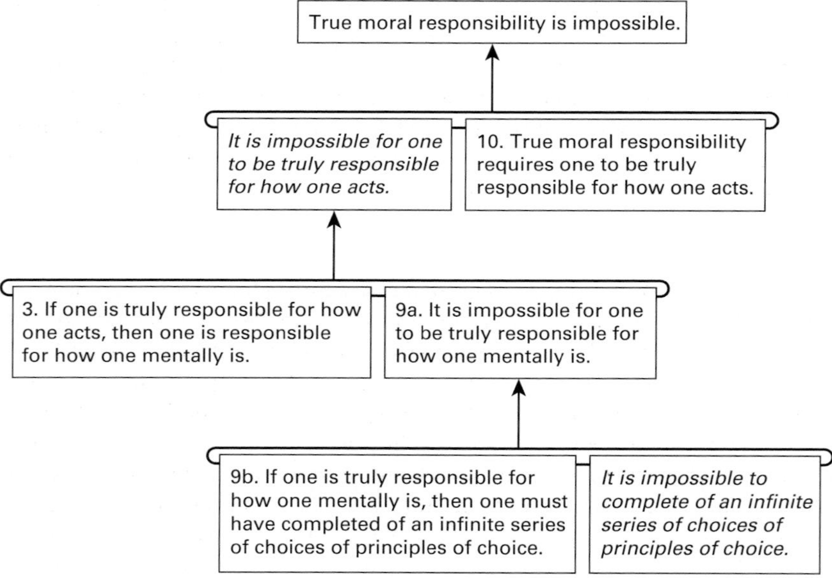

Strawson himself raises several possible objections to this argument, which we will explore in the exercises.

14.3 In-Class Exercises

An asterisk (*) indicates a more challenging exercise.

Exercises 1–2

In the first part of this chapter, we analyzed in detail Baron d'Holbach's argument in *The System of Nature*. The following are more arguments from the selection. For each, (a) diagram the argument and (b) identify any potential objections to the argument.

**Exercise 1*

Man, in his origin, is an imperceptible point, a speck, of which the parts are without form; of which the mobility, the life, escapes his senses; in short, in which he does not perceive any sign of those qualities called *sentiment, feeling, thought, intelligence, force, reason*, &c. Placed in the womb suitable to his expansion, this point unfolds, extends, increases by the continual addition of matter he attracts that is analogous to his being, which consequently assimilates itself with him. Having quitted this womb, so appropriate to conserve his existence, to unfold his qualities, to strengthen his habit; so competent to give, for a season, consistence to the weak rudiments of his frame; he becomes adult: his body has then acquired a considerable extension of bulk, his motion is marked, his action is visible, he is sensible in all his parts; he is a living, an active mass; that is to say, he feels, thinks, and fulfills the functions peculiar to beings of his species. But how has he become sensible? Because he has been by degrees nourished, enlarged, repaired by the continual attraction that takes place within himself of that kind of matter which is pronounced inert, insensible, inanimate; although continually combining itself with his machine, of which it forms an active whole, that is living, that feels, judges, reasons, wills, deliberates, chooses, elects; with a capability of laboring, more or less efficaciously, to his own individual preservation; that is to say, to the maintenance of the harmony of his natural existence.

**Exercise 2*

Thus it will be seen that those who have supposed in man an immaterial substance, distinguished from his body, have not thoroughly understood themselves; indeed they have done nothing more than imagined a negative quality of which they cannot have any correct idea: matter alone is capable of acting on our senses, and without this action nothing would be capable of making itself known to us. They have not seen that a being without extent, is neither in a capacity to move itself, nor has the capability of communicating motion to the body, since such a being, having no parts, has not the faculty of changing its relation, or its distance, relatively to other bodies, nor of exciting motion in the human body, which is itself material. That which is called our soul, moves itself with us; now motion is a property of matter—this soul gives impulse to the arm; the arm, moved by it, makes an impression, a blow, that follows the general law of motion: in this case, the force remaining the same, if the mass was twofold, the blow would be double. This soul again evinces its materiality in the invincible obstacles it encounters on the part of the body. If the arm be moved by its impulse when nothing opposes it, yet this arm can no longer move when it is charged with a weight beyond its strength. Here then is a mass of matter that annihilates the impulse given by a spiritual cause, which spiritual cause having no analogy with matter, ought not to find more difficulty in moving the whole world than in moving a single atom, nor an atom than the universe. From this it is fair to conclude that such a substance is a chimera; a being of the imagination: nevertheless such is the being the metaphysicians have made the contriver and the author of nature!!

Exercises 3–6

In the second section of this chapter, we analyzed in detail one of Strawson's arguments in "The Impossibility of Moral Responsibility." The following are more arguments from the selection. For each, (a) diagram the argument and (b) identify any potential objections to the argument.

Exercise 3

The Basic Argument has various expressions in the literature of free will, and its central idea can be quickly conveyed. (1) Nothing can be *causa sui*—nothing can be the cause of itself. (2) In order to be truly morally responsible for one's actions one would have to be *causa sui*, at least in certain crucial mental respects. (3) Therefore nothing can be truly morally responsible.

Exercise 4

This may seem contrived, but essentially the same argument can be given in a more natural form. (1) It is undeniable that one is the way one is, initially, as a result of heredity and early experience, and it is undeniable that these are things for which one cannot be held to be in any responsible (morally or otherwise). (2) One cannot at any later stage of life hope to accede to true moral responsibility for the way one is by trying to change the way one already is as a result of heredity and previous experience. For (3) both the particular way in which one is moved to try to change oneself, and the degree of one's success in one's attempt at change, will be determined by how one already is as a result of heredity and previous experience. And (4) any further changes that one can bring about only after one has brought about certain initial changes will in turn be determined, via the initial changes, by heredity and previous experience. (5) This may not be the whole story, for it may be that some changes in the way one is are traceable not to heredity and experience but to the influence of indeterministic or random factors. But it is absurd to suppose that indeterministic or random factors, for which one is *ex hypothesi* in no way responsible, can in themselves contribute in any way to one's being truly morally responsible for how one is.

Exercise 5

Let me now restate the Basic Argument in very loose—as it were conversational—terms. New forms of words allow for new forms of objection, but they may be helpful none the less.

(1) You do what you do, in any situation in which you find yourself, because of the way you are.

So

(2) To be truly morally responsible for what you do you must be truly responsible for the way you are—at least in certain crucial mental respects.

Or:

(1) What you intentionally do, given the circumstances in which you (believe you) find yourself, flows necessarily from how you are.

Hence

(2) you have to get to have some responsibility for how you are in order to get to have some responsibility for what you intentionally do, given the circumstances in which you (believe you) find yourself.

Comment. Once again the qualification about "certain mental respects" is one I will take for granted. Obviously one is not responsible for one's sex, one's basic body pattern, one's height, and so on. But if one were not responsible for anything about oneself, how one could be responsible for what one did, given the truth of (1)? This is the fundamental question, and it seems clear that if one is going to be responsible for any aspect of oneself, it had better be some aspect of one's mental nature.

Exercise 6

I take it that (1) is incontrovertible, and that it is (2) that must be resisted. For if (1) and (2) are conceded the case seems lost, because the full argument runs as follows.

(1) You do what you do because of the way you are.

So

(2) To be truly morally responsible for what you do you must be truly responsible for the way are—at least in certain crucial mental respects.

But

(3) You cannot be truly responsible for the way you are, so you cannot be truly responsible for what you do.

Why can't you be truly responsible for the way you are? Because

(4) To be truly responsible for the way you are, you must have intentionally brought it about that you are the way you are, and this is impossible.

Why is it impossible? Well, suppose it is not. Suppose that

(5) You have somehow intentionally brought it about that you are the way you now are, and that you have brought this about in such a way that you can now be said to be truly responsible for being the way you are now.

For this to be true

(6) You must already have had a certain nature N in the light of which you intentionally brought it about that you are as you now are.

But then

(7) For it to be true you and you alone are truly responsible for how you now are, you must be truly responsible for having had the nature N in the light of which you intentionally brought it about that you are the way you now are.

So

(8) You must have intentionally brought it about that you had that nature N, in which case you must have existed already with a prior nature in the light of which you intentionally brought it about that you had the nature N in the light of which you intentionally brought it about that you are the way you now are. …

Exercises 7–10

The following exercises are intended to ensure your understanding of d'Holbach's and Strawson's texts, and to help you further explore the ideas presented in this chapter.

Exercise 7: Now that you have read my textual analysis of d'Holbach's argument, summarize it in your own words.
Exercise 8: Summarize, in your own words, each of the arguments in exercises 1 and 2 above.
Exercise 9: Now that you have read my textual analysis of Strawson's argument, summarize it in your own words.
Exercise 10: Summarize, in your own words, each of the arguments in exercises 3–6 above.

14.4 Reading Questions

1. According to d'Holbach, what is the role that the doctrine of free will plays in religion and in our system of punishment?
2. The example of the poisoned water was intended by libertarians to demonstrate the existence of free will, but d'Holbach disagrees. Explain d'Holbach's response.
3. Libertarians have argued that deliberation demonstrates the existence of free will, but again, d'Holbach disagrees. Explain d'Holbach's view of deliberation.
4. According to d'Holbach, why do people believe that they are free agents?
5. Strawson says that his argument works whether you believe the world is deterministic or indeterministic. Why does he think this? Do you agree? Why or why not?
6. Strawson considers a compatibilist response and argues that a compatibilist position cannot provide true moral responsibility. Do you agree? Why or why not?
7. Strawson considers a libertarian response and argues that indeterminism cannot provide true moral responsibility either. Do you agree? Why or why not?
8. Explain the third option that Strawson considers toward the end of the article. Do you agree with his response to it? Why or why not?

15 Compatibilism

15.1 David Hume, "Of Liberty and Necessity"
15.2 W. T. Stace, "The Problem of Free Will"
15.3 In-Class Exercises
15.4 Reading Questions

15.1 David Hume, "Of Liberty and Necessity"

We are familiar with David Hume from Parts II and III. Here we will be considering another selection from *An Enquiry Concerning Human Understanding* (1748), section 8, parts 1 and 2. Recall from chapter 8 Hume's argument about causation. We say that one event causes another when we infer a necessary connection between the two events. We don't ever observe the causal link; we infer causation from repeated observations of one event following another. And it is by continually using this procedure that we come to have any general knowledge about our world at all.

In section 8, titled "Of Liberty and Necessity," Hume uses his theory of knowledge to argue for a compatibilist view of free will. Recall from the previous chapter that d'Holbach argues that every action a person performs is part of a causal chain of events that ultimately begins outside of his or her control. Thus, he says, a person cannot be said to have free will. Hume, on the other hand, argues that a person's action being a part of a causal chain of events is *required*, along with free will, for him or her to be morally responsible for that action. This argument comes in part 2 of section 8. Before he gets to that argument, however, Hume lays out what he thinks are the most reasonable definitions of determinism (which he refers to as "necessity") in part 1. Let's look at Hume's text from part 1 in more detail. We will analyze and diagram this argument, leaving the argument in part 2 for the exercises.

From *An Enquiry Concerning Human Understanding.*[1]

There is my project, then: to show that all men have always agreed about both necessity and liberty, when those terms are taken in any reasonable sense, and that the whole controversy until now has turned merely upon words. I shall begin by examining the doctrine of necessity.[1] ...

If it turns out that all mankind have always held, without any doubt or hesitation, that these two factors are present in the voluntary actions of men and in the operations of minds—that is, that like is followed by like, and that we are disposed to make inferences on that basis—it follows that all mankind have always agreed in the doctrine of necessity,[2] and have been disputing simply because they did not understand each other.

Here are some points that may satisfy you concerning the constant and regular conjunction of similar events. Everyone acknowledges that there is much uniformity among the actions of men in all nations and ages,[3] and[A] that human nature remains the same in its forces and operations.[4] The same motives always produce the same actions; the same events follow from the same causes. Ambition, avarice, self-love, vanity, friendship, generosity, public spirit—these passions, mixed in various proportions and distributed throughout society, are now (and from the beginning of the world always have been) the source of all the actions and projects that have ever been observed among mankind. Do you want to know the feelings, inclinations, and course of life of the Greeks and Romans? Then study well the character and actions of the French and English: you can't go far wrong in transferring to the former most of your observations regarding the latter. Mankind are so much the same in all times and places that history informs us of nothing new or strange on this topic. The chief use of history is only to reveal the constant and universal principles of human nature by showing men in all kinds of circumstances and situations, and providing us with materials from which we can form our observations and become acquainted with the usual sources of human action and behaviour.[5] These records of wars, intrigues, factions, and revolutions, are so many sets of data that the political theorist or moral philosopher uses to fix the principles of his science; just as the natural scientist learns the nature of plants, minerals, and other external objects by the tests he puts them through. The earth, water, and other elements examined by Aristotle and Hippocrates don't resemble those we find now any more closely than the men described by Polybius and Tacitus resemble those who now govern the world. ...

But[B] if there were no uniformity in human actions, and if the outcomes of all the tests of these matters that we conducted were irregular and did not fit any general patterns, we could not possibly assemble any general observations concerning mankind, and no experience, however thoughtfully pondered, would ever serve any purpose.[6] To revert for a moment to the general point about the need for uniformities if there is to be understanding: Why is the old farmer more skillful in his calling than the young beginner if not because there is a certain uniformity in how the operation of the sun, rain, and earth affects the production of plants, and experience teaches the old practitioner the rules by which this operation is governed and directed? ...

Thus it appears not only that the relation of motives to voluntary actions is as regular and uniform as that of cause to effect in any part of nature, but also that[C] this regular relation has been universally acknowledged among mankind, and has never been the subject of dispute in science or in common life.[7]

Hume acknowledges that if he is going to show that everyone has always agreed on what both necessity and liberty are, then he needs to take them one at a time. So first, he needs to argue that everyone has always agreed about necessity (1). Later on, he switches to showing that everyone has always agreed about liberty (8).

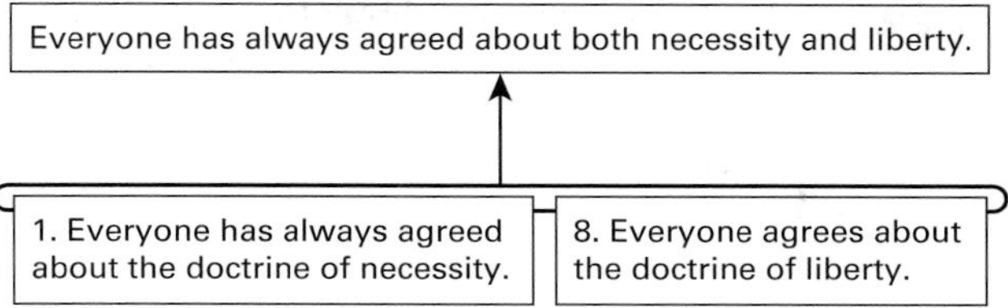

Let's look at the argument about necessity first. Hume claims that if he can show that everyone acknowledges that, in voluntary actions and the operations of the mind, like is followed by like and we are disposed to make inferences on that basis, then he will have shown that everyone has always agreed about the doctrine of necessity (2). He continues by arguing that the antecedent of this conditional statement is true.

The first claim in this argument is that everyone acknowledges that there is uniformity in human actions in all nations and ages (3), and the second is that everyone acknowledges that human nature remains the same in its forces and operations in all nations and ages (4). After these claims, he drops the "everyone acknowledges that" from the statements in his argument, but we can assume that the phrase is implicit in them, since what everyone acknowledges to be true is the aim of the argument.

As indicated by (A), statements (3) and (4) are to be combined to support the claim that we learn about the universal principles of human nature by history and experience (5).

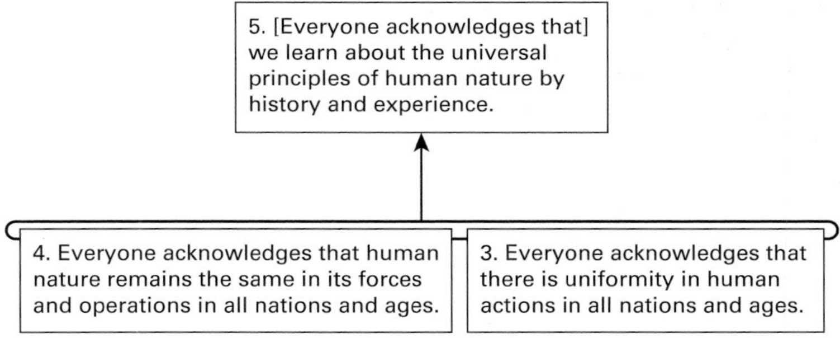

Hume then claims that if there were no uniformity in human actions, then we could not learn anything about human nature from experience (6). As indicated by (B) and (C), this is combined with (5) to support the claim that everyone acknowledges that the relation of motives to voluntary actions is regular and uniform. In other words, if there were no uniformity, then we wouldn't learn from experience (6), but everyone knows that we do learn from experience (5), so everyone knows that there is uniformity.

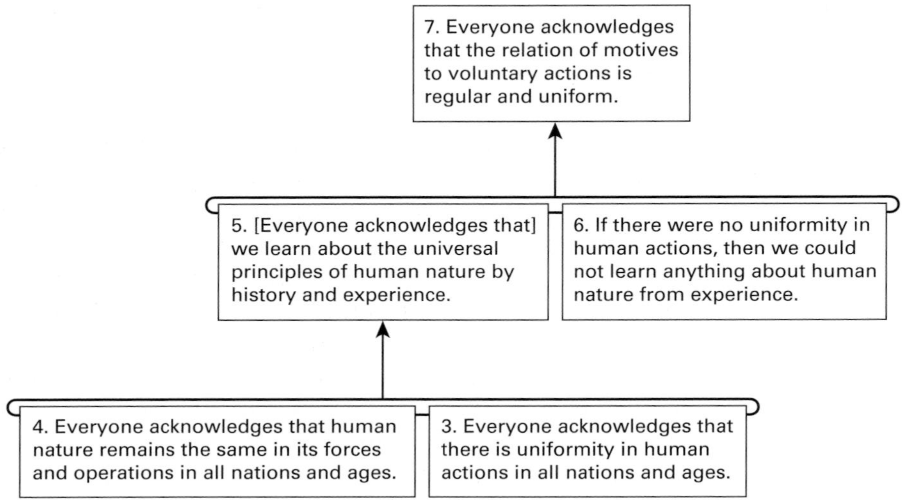

In statement (7), we have the antecedent of statement (2), so these work together to support the conclusion that everyone has always agreed about the doctrine of necessity (1).

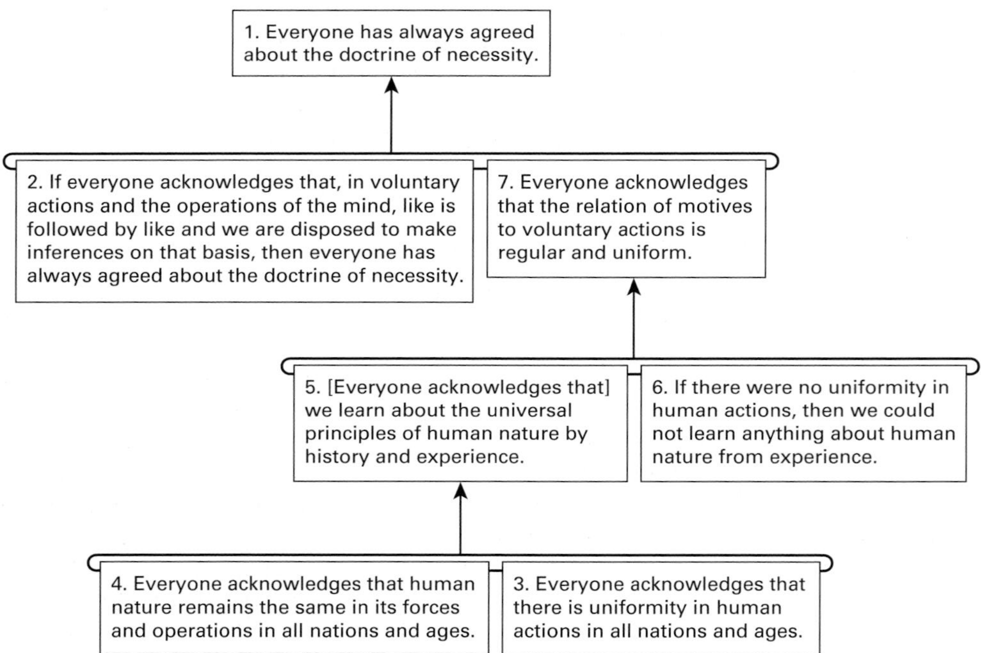

We will consider more of Hume's arguments from this selection in the exercises.

15.2 W. T. Stace, "The Problem of Free Will"

Walter Terence Stace (1886–1967) was a British philosopher who spent the majority of his academic career at Princeton University. Stace was born in London and had intended his studies at Trinity College Dublin to lead to prepare him for a career in the Anglican Church. In school, however, he was introduced to the philosophy of G. F. W. Hegel (1770–1831), a German idealist, and took a degree in philosophy instead. Stace did not enter academia right away, though. He spent the next two decades a British civil servant, and he spent most of that time in Ceylon (now Sri Lanka). After retirement from the civil service, Stace took a position in the philosophy department at Princeton in 1932, where he spent his entire academic career.

During his civil service career, Stace wrote on the history of philosophy, publishing *A Critical History of Greek Philosophy* in 1920 and *The Philosophy of Hegel* in 1924. After arriving at Princeton, he turned more toward British empiricism, strongly influenced by German phenomenalists, writing on epistemology—*The Theory of Knowledge and Existence* (1932) and *Refutation of Realism* (1934)—and then ethics—*The Concept of Morals* (1937). From here he turned to a defense of secularism and an advocation of secular morality in several articles—"Man against Darkness" (1948), "The Need for a Secular Ethic" (1949), and "Mysticism and Human Reason" (1954)—and in his book, *Religion and the Modern Mind* (1952). It is in this last book that, like Hume, Stace argues for a compatibilist view of free will. Let's look at Stace's text from in more detail. We will analyze and diagram this argument, leaving objections to it for the exercises.

From *Religion and the Modern Mind*[2]

I shall show that indeterminism is not what is meant by the phrase "free will" *as it is commonly used.* And I shall attempt to discover the correct definition by inquiring how the phrase is used in ordinary conversation. ...

We have now collected a number of cases of actions which, in the ordinary usage of the English language, would be called cases in which people have acted of their own free will.[1] We should also say in all these cases that they chose to act as they did. We should also say that they could have acted otherwise, if they had chosen.[2] For instance, Mahatma Gandhi was not compelled to fast; he chose to do so. He could have eaten if he had wanted to. When Smith went out to get his lunch, he chose to do so. He could have stayed and done some work, if he had wanted to. We have also collected a number of cases of the opposite kind. They are cases in which men were not able to exercise their free will.[3] They had no choice.[4] They were compelled to do as they did.[5] The man in the desert did not fast of his own free will. He had no choice in the matter. He was compelled to fast because there was nothing for him to eat. And so with the other cases. It ought to be quite easy, by an inspection of these cases, to tell what we ordinarily mean when we say that a man did or did not exercise free will. We ought therefore to be able to extract from them the proper definition of the term. Let us put the cases in a table:

Free Acts	*Unfree Acts*
Gandhi fasting because he wanted to free India.	The man fasting in the desert because there was no food.
Stealing bread because one is hungry.	Stealing because one's employer threatened to beat one.
Signing a confession because one wanted to tell the truth.	Signing because the police beat one.
Leaving the office because one wanted one's lunch.	Leaving because forcibly removed.

It is obvious that[A] to find the correct definition of free acts we must discover what characteristic is common to all the acts in the left-hand column, and is, at the same time, absent from all the acts in the right-hand column.[6] This characteristic which all free acts have, and which no unfree acts have, will be the defining characteristic of free will.[7]

Is being uncaused, or not being determined by causes, the characteristic of which we are in search? It cannot be,[8] because[B] although it is true that all the acts in the right-hand column have causes, such as the beating by the police or the absence of food in the desert, so also do the acts in the left-hand column.[9] Mr. Gandhi's fasting was caused by his desire to free India, the man leaving his office by his hunger, and so on. Moreover[C] there is no reason to doubt that these causes of the free acts were in turn caused by prior conditions, and that these were again the results of causes, and so on back indefinitely into the past.[10] Any physiologist can tell us the causes of hunger. What caused Mr. Gandhi's tremendously powerful desire to free India is no doubt more difficult to discover. But it must have had causes. Some of them may have lain in peculiarities of his glands or brain, others in his past experiences, others in his heredity, others in his education. Defenders of free will have usually tended to deny such facts. But to do so is plainly a case of special pleading, which is unsupported by any scrap of evidence. The only reasonable view is that[C] all human actions, both those which are freely done and those which are not, are either wholly determined by causes, or at least as much determined as other events in nature.[11] It may be true, as the physicists tell us, that nature is not as deterministic as was once thought. But whatever degree of determinism prevails in the world, human actions appear to be as much determined as anything else. And if this is so,[D] it cannot be the case that what distinguishes actions freely chosen from those which are not free is that the latter are determined by causes while the former are not.[12] Therefore,[E] being uncaused or being undetermined by causes, must be an incorrect definition of free will.[13]

What, then, is the difference between acts which are freely done and those which are not? What is the characteristic which is present to all the acts in the left-hand column and absent from all those in the right-hand column? Is it not obvious that,[F] although both sets of actions have causes, the causes of those in the left-hand column are of a *different kind* from the causes of those in the right-hand column?[14] The free acts are all caused by desires, or motives, or by some sort of internal psychological states of the agent's mind.[15] The unfree acts, on the other hand, are all caused by physical forces or physical conditions, outside the agent.[16] Police arrest means physical force exerted from the outside;

the absence of food in the desert is a physical condition of the outside world. We may therefore[G] frame the following rough definitions. *Acts freely done are those whose immediate causes are psychological states in the agent. Acts not freely done are those whose immediate causes are states of affairs external to the agent.*

Stace begins this selection by explaining that he wants to find the correct definition of "free will," which, he thinks, is the way that the phrase is used in ordinary discourse. He gives a number of hypothetical exchanges to use as examples of this ordinary usage. Then, he starts to build his argument. First, as a summary of the examples, he claims that there are cases in which we would say that people have acted of their own free will (1) and that there are cases in which we would say that people have acted not of their own free will (3).

He then offers an explanation of why we say that these acts are either free or unfree. In the cases in which we would say that people have acted of their own free will, the people chose to act as they did and could have acted otherwise, if they had chosen (2). And, in the cases in which we would say that people have acted not of their own free will, the people had no choice but to act as they did (4). And statement (5) is a restatement of (4). But let us set these statements aside for now.

So why is Stace collecting these examples? He tells us after the table: he's going to use these examples as data to figure out what the ordinary usage definition is of free action. What we need to do, he says, is find out what the difference is between free acts and unfree acts. Whatever it is that free acts have and unfree acts don't will be what we are looking for (6). In other words, the defining characteristic of free will will be the characteristic that free acts have and unfree acts don't (7).

Before he presents his argument about what free will *is*, however, Stace argues that free will is *not* indeterminism—that it is not a lack of causation (8). As indicated by (B), the reason is that both free and unfree acts have causes (9). In addition, he claims, the free acts are part of a causal chain that goes back indefinitely to the past (10). As indicated by (B) and (C), these two premises are supposed to be combined to support the claim that all human actions are as determined by causes as are other events in nature (11).

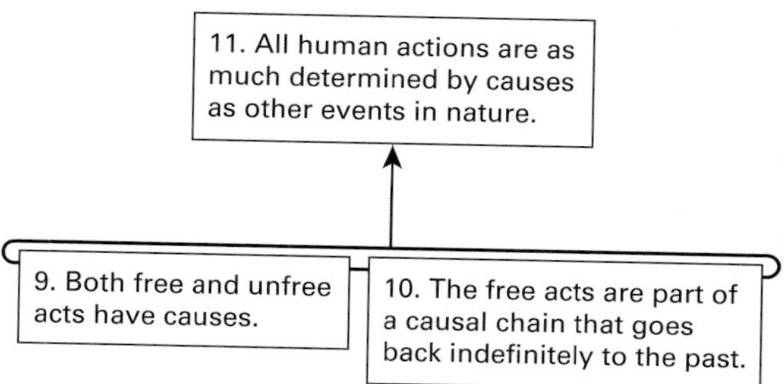

We then combine this conclusion with (7), as indicated by (D), to support the claim that the defining characteristic of free will is not that unfree acts have causes while free acts don't

(12), which is a restatement of (8). And that, as indicated by (E), supports the claim that being uncaused or undetermined is not the definition of free will (13).

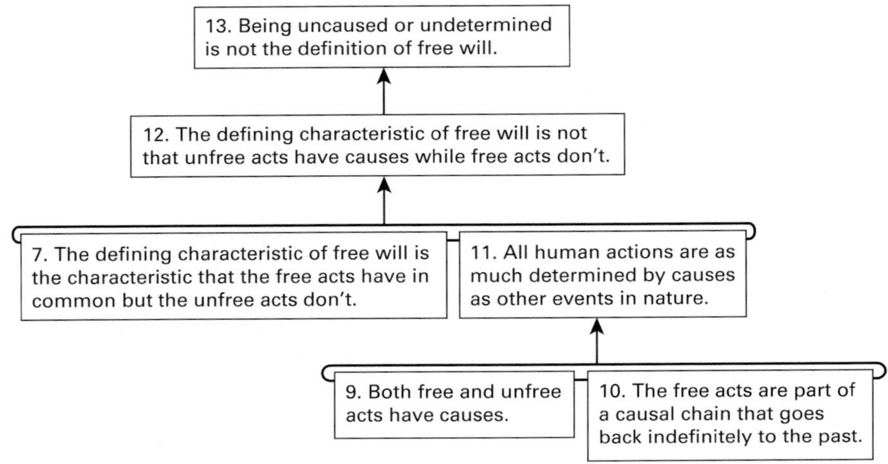

Stace next says that the real difference between free and unfree acts is that they have different *kinds* of causes (14). Why would we think this? Here's where the first four statements of the argument come in. First, there are cases in which we would say that people have acted of their own free will (1), and in these, the people chose to act as they did and could have acted otherwise, if they had chosen (2). These cases can be combined to support the claim that the examples of free acts are caused by internal psychological states of the agent's mind (15).

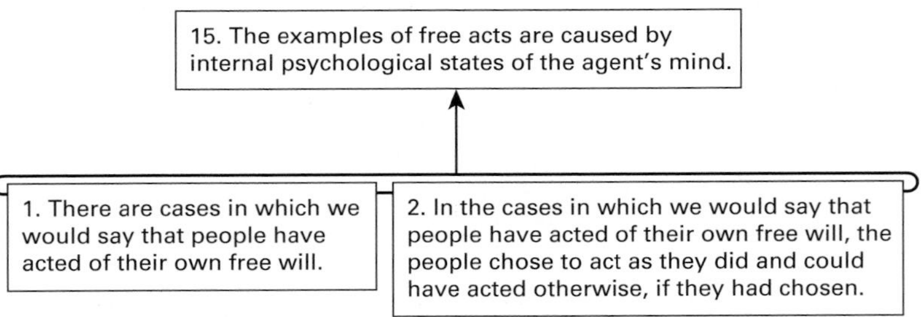

Second, there are cases in which we would say that people have acted not of their own free will (3). And, in these cases, the people had no choice but to act as they did (4). These can be combined to support the claim that the examples of unfree acts are caused by physical forces outside the agent (16).

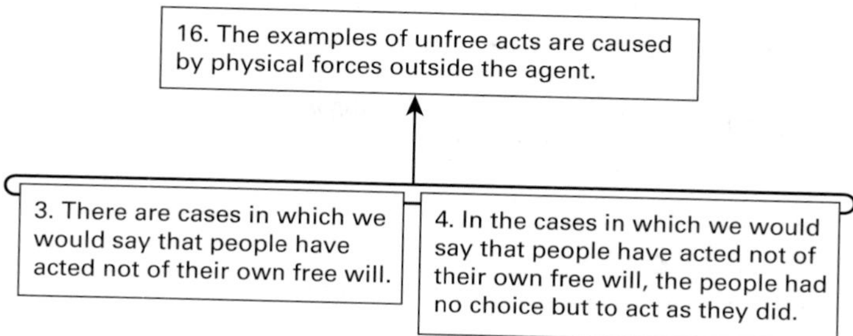

These two subconclusions are essentially all the reasons offered in support of the claim that free acts and unfree acts have different kinds of causes (14). We can combine all this into the overall argument, whose main conclusion, as indicated by (G), is that free acts are those whose immediate causes are the agent's psychological states, while unfree acts are those whose immediate causes are states of affairs external to the agent.

The overall argument, then, looks like this:

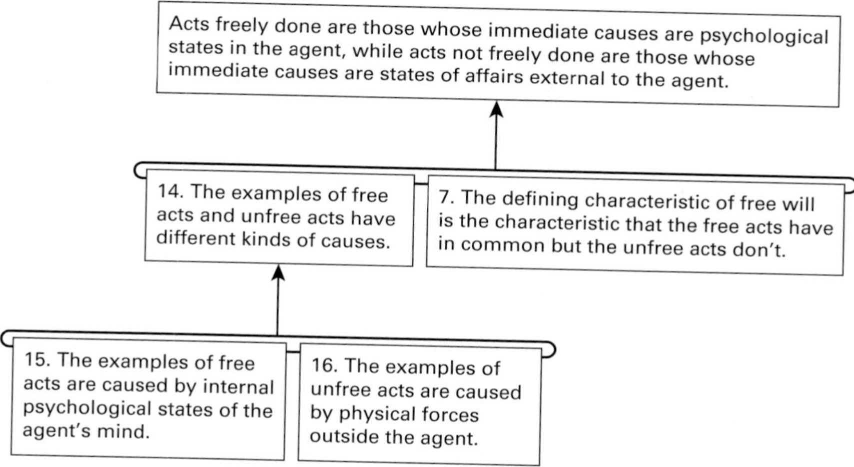

We will consider more of Stace's arguments from this selection, as well as an argument against his definition of *free will* in the exercises.

15.3 In-Class Exercises

An asterisk (*) indicates a more challenging exercise.

Exercises 1–2

In the first section of this chapter, we analyzed in detail one of David Hume's arguments in "On Liberty and Necessity." The following are more arguments from the selection. For each, (a) diagram the argument and (b) identify any potential objections to the argument.

**Exercise 1*

Now, it is from past experience that we draw all our conclusions about the future, and [in these inferences] we conclude that objects that we find to have always been conjoined will always be conjoined in the future; so it may seem superfluous to argue that the experienced uniformity of human actions is a source from which we infer conclusions concerning them. But I shall do so, though briefly, so as to show my over-all position from a different angle.

In all societies people depend so much on one another that hardly any human action is entirely complete in itself, or is performed without some reference to the actions of others that are needed if the action is to produce what the agent intends. The poorest workman, who labours alone, still expects at least the protection of the law to guarantee him the enjoyment of the fruits of his labour. He also expects that when he takes his goods to market, and offers them at a reasonable price, he will find buyers, and will be able through the money he earns to get others to supply him with what he needs for his subsistence. In proportion as a man's dealings with others are wide-ranging and complicated, to that extent his way of life involves a variety of voluntary actions by other people—things people do from their own motives, but which he expects to cooperate with his motives. In arriving at these expectations he goes by past experience, in the same manner as in his reasonings about external objects; and he firmly believes that men, as well as all the kinds of stuff, will continue to behave in the ways that he has found them to do. A manufacturer relies on the labour of his employees for getting a job done, as much as he relies on the tools that he uses, and he would be equally surprised if either the men or the tools disappointed his expectations. In short, this empirical inference and reasoning about the actions of others enters so much into human life that every man is engaged in it at every waking moment. Isn't this a reason to affirm that all mankind have always agreed in the doctrine of necessity, according to my account of it?

Exercise 2

But to continue in this reconciling project regarding the question of liberty and necessity (which is the most contentious question in metaphysics), I shan't need many words to prove that all mankind have always agreed about liberty as well as about necessity, and that the whole dispute about liberty has hitherto been merely verbal. For what is meant by "liberty" when the term is applied to voluntary actions? Surely we can't mean that actions have so little connection with motives, inclinations, and circumstances that the former don't follow with a certain degree of uniformity from the latter, and that motives etc. support no inference by which we can infer actions. For these—[the uniformity and the inference]—are plain and acknowledged matters of fact. By "liberty," then, we can only mean a power of acting or not acting according to the determinations of the will; that is, if we choose to stay still we may do so, and if we choose to move we may do that. This hypothetical liberty—["hypothetical" because it concerns what we may do *if* we so choose]—is universally agreed to belong to everyone who isn't a prisoner and in chains. There is nothing to disagree about here.

Exercises 3–4

In the second section of this chapter, we analyzed in detail one of W. T. Stace's arguments in "The Problem of Free Will." The following are more arguments from the selection. For each, (a) diagram the argument and (b) identify any potential objections to the argument.

Exercise 3

It is plain that if we define free will in this way, then free will certainly exists, and the philosopher's denial of its existence is seen to be what it is—nonsense. For it is obvious that all those actions of men which we should ordinarily attribute to the exercise of their free will, or of which we should say that they freely chose to do them, are in fact actions which have been caused by their own desires, wishes, thoughts, emotions, impulses, or other psychological states.

Exercise 4

Thus we see that moral responsibility is not only consistent with determinism, but requires it. The assumption on which punishment is based is that human behavior is causally determined. If pain could not be a cause of truth-telling there would be no justification at all for punishing lies. If human actions and volitions were uncaused, it would be useless either to punish or reward, or indeed to do anything else to correct people's bad behavior. For nothing that you could do would in any way influence them. Thus moral responsibility would entirely disappear. If there were no determinism of human beings at all, their actions would be completely unpredictable and capricious, and therefore irresponsible. And this is in itself a strong argument against the common view of philosophers that free will means being undetermined by causes.

*Exercise 5

In 1941, a colleague of Stace's at Princeton named Ledger Wood published an article titled "The Free-Will Controversy."[3] In it, he argues that the definition of free will that Hume and Stace are using is nonsense. The following is an argument from the selection. Here, (a) diagram the argument and (b) identify any potential objections to the argument.

Still another introspective fact cited … in support of his doctrine is that the moral agent is in retrospect convinced that he might, *if he had chosen*, have followed a course of action different from that which he actually pursued. The belief that there are genuine alternatives of action and that the choice between them is indeterminate is usually stronger in prospect and in retrospect than at the time of actual decision. The alternatives exist in prospect as imaginatively envisaged possibilities of action and in retrospect as the memory of the state of affairs before the agent had, so to speak, "made up his mind." Especially in retrospect does the agent recall his earlier decision with remorse and repentance, dwelling sorrowfully upon rejected possibilities of action which now loom up as opportunities missed. How frequently one hears the lament: "I regret that decision; I should, and I could, have acted otherwise."

Now the contemplation of alternatives of action with the sentiment of regret produces the illusion of indeterminate choice between alternatives, but a careful analysis of the import of the retrospective judgment, "I could have acted otherwise than I did," will, I believe, disclose it to be an empirically meaningless statement. If I decided in favor of this alternative, rather than that, it can only mean that the circumstances being what they were, and I in the frame of mind I was at the time, no other eventuation was really possible. My statement that I could have acted differently expresses only my memory of an earlier state of suspense, indecision, and uncertainty, intensified by present remorse and the firm determination that if, in the future, I am faced with a similar choice, I shall profit by my earlier mistake. There is, however, in the deliberate situation no evidence of alternatives of action, or the indeterminacy of my choice between them.

Exercises 6–9

The following exercises are intended to ensure your understanding of Hume's and Stace's texts, and to help you further explore the ideas presented in this chapter.

Exercise 6: Now that you have read my textual analysis of Hume's argument, summarize it in your own words.
Exercise 7: Summarize, in your own words, each of the arguments in exercises 1 and 2 above.
Exercise 8: Now that you have read my textual analysis of Stace's argument, summarize it in your own words.
Exercise 9: Summarize, in your own words, each of the arguments in exercises 3–5 above.

15.4 Reading Questions

1. What is Hume's definition of free will? What is Stace's definition? Do you agree with these definitions? Why or why not?
2. Why is it important to determine whether human beings have free will?
3. How does Stace develop his definition of free will? What is the point of the five-legged animal analogy?
4. Hume and Stace are both called "compatibilists." Explain how each thinks that determinism is compatible with free will.
5. Does Wood's argument in exercise 5 above adequately represent and address Stace's argument? Why or why not?

16 Libertarianism

16.1 Roderick M. Chisholm, "Human Freedom and the Self"
16.2 Peter van Inwagen, "The Powers of Rational Beings: Freedom of the Will"
16.3 In-Class Exercises
16.4 Reading Questions

16.1 Roderick M. Chisholm, "Human Freedom and the Self"

Roderick Milton Chisholm was an American philosopher born in North Attleboro, Massachusetts in 1916. He graduated with a BA from Brown University in 1938, and a PhD from Harvard University in 1942. While in graduate school he interacted with, and was subsequently influenced by, a number of great thinkers, including Bertrand Russell, C. I. Lewis, and G. E. Moore. After a stint in the army, Chisholm ended up back at Brown where he spent his entire career. Chisholm died in Providence, Rhode Island, in 1999 at the age of 82.

Chisholm published in a wide variety of philosophical areas during his lifetime. He wrote highly influential works especially in epistemology (*Perceiving: A Philosophical Study*, 1957; *Theory of Knowledge*, 1966; *The Foundations of Knowing*, 1982) and metaphysics and philosophy of language (*Person and Object: A Metaphysical Study*, 1976; *The First Person: An Essay on Reference and Intentionality*, 1981; *On Metaphysics*, 1989; *A Realistic Theory of Categories: An Essay on Ontology*, 1996).

Recall that *libertarianism* is the view that free will and determinism are incompatible, and that humans do in fact have free will. There are many different versions of libertarianism, but one of the most influential is *agent causation*, which Chisholm introduced in his 1964 lecture "Human Freedom and the Self." Let's look at this text in more detail. Specifically, we will analyze and diagram the argument, and then discuss criticisms of it.

From "Human Freedom and the Self."[1]

1. The metaphysical problem of human freedom might be summarized in the following way: Human beings are responsible agents; but this fact appears to conflict with a deterministic view of human action (the view that every event that is involved in an act is caused by some other event); and it *also* appears to conflict with an indeterministic view of human action (the view that the act, or some event that is essential to the act, is not caused at all). To solve the problem, I believe, we must make somewhat far-reaching assumptions about the self or the agent—about the man who performs the act. ...

2. Let us consider some deed, or misdeed, that may be attributed to a responsible agent: one man, say, shot another. If the man was responsible for what he did, then, I would urge, what was to happen at the time of the shooting was something that was entirely up to the man himself. There was a moment at which it was true, both that he could have fired the shot and also that he could have refrained from firing it. And if this is so, then, even though he did fire it, he could have done something else instead. (He didn't find himself firing the shot "against his will," as we say.) I think we can say, more generally, then, that[A] if a man is responsible for a certain event or a certain state of affairs (in our example, the shooting of another man), then that event or state of affairs was brought about by some act of his, and the act was something that was in his power either to perform or not to perform.[1]

But now[B] if the act which he *did* perform was an act that was also in his power *not* to perform, then it could not have been caused or determined by any event that was not itself within his power either to bring about or not to bring about.[2] For example, if what we say he did was really something that was brought about by a second man, one who forced his hand upon the trigger, say, or who, by means of hypnosis, compelled him to perform the act, then since the act was caused by the *second* man it was nothing that was within the power of the *first* man to prevent. And[C] precisely the same thing is true, I think, if instead of referring to a second man who compelled the first one, we speak instead of the *desires* and *beliefs* which the first man happens to have had.[3] For[D] if what we say he did was really something that was brought about by his own beliefs and desires, if these beliefs and desires in the particular situation in which he happened to have found himself caused him to do just what it was that we say he did do, then, since *they* caused it, *he* was unable to do anything other than just what it was that he did do.[4] It makes no difference whether the cause of the deed was internal or external; if the cause was some state or event for which the man himself was not responsible, then he was not responsible for what we have been mistakenly calling his act.[5] If a flood caused the poorly constructed dam to break, then, given the flood and the constitution of the dam, the break, we may say, *had* to occur and nothing could have happened in its place. And if the flood of desire caused the weak-willed man to give in, then he, too, had to do just what it was that he did do and he was no more responsible than was the dam for the results that followed. (It is true, of course, that if the man is responsible for the beliefs and desires that he happens to have, then he may also be responsible for the things they lead him to do. But the question now becomes: *is* he responsible for the beliefs and desires he happens to have? If he is, then there was a time when they were within his power either to acquire or not to acquire, and we are left, therefore, with our general point.)

As indicated by (A), Chisholm says that we can start with an assumption: If a man is responsible for a certain event, then the event was caused by an act of his that he had the power either to perform or not perform (1).

The idea is this: let's say person P causes some event E by performing some action A_1. So we can say that A_1 caused E. Chisholm says that if P is responsible for E, then it was in P's power either to bring about or not to bring about A_1.

Chisholm then says that if a man performs an act and it was in his power not to perform that act, then that act could not have been caused by any event that was not itself within his power either to bring about or not to bring about (2).

Here Chisholm is saying that if A_2 causes A_1, then in order for it to be the case that it was in P's power to perform A_1, it cannot be the case that it was not in P's power to bring about A_2. So Chisholm is saying (1) that if P is responsible for E, then P must have the power to bring about A_1, and (2) that if P has the power to bring about A_1, then P must have the power to bring about A_2.

If we can think of a causal chain of actions/events ultimately leading to E,

$$\ldots A_n \rightarrow A_{n-1} \rightarrow \ldots \rightarrow A_2 \rightarrow A_1 \rightarrow E,$$

then Chisholm is saying that if P is responsible for E, then it had to be in P's power to either bring about or not bring about any event or action in the causal chain leading to E. So, as indicated by (B), (1) and (2) are to be combined to support this implied subconclusion:

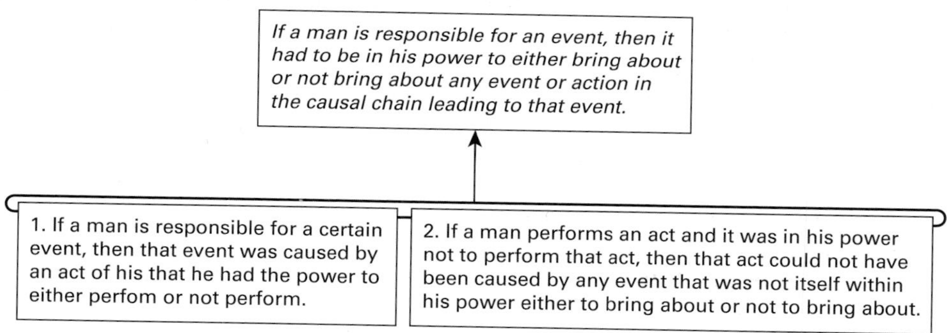
If a man is responsible for an event, then it had to be in his power to either bring about or not bring about any event or action in the causal chain leading to that event.
1. If a man is responsible for a certain event, then that event was caused by an act of his that he had the power to either perfom or not perform.
2. If a man performs an act and it was in his power not to perform that act, then that act could not have been caused by any event that was not itself within his power either to bring about or not to bring about.

Next, Chisholm takes on the point made by the hard determinists and compatibilists—that a person's actions are generally thought to be caused by their beliefs and desires. Unlike hard determinists and compatibilists, though, Chisholm thinks that beliefs and desires are causally no different from an external force (such as another person) that makes someone do something. That is, if a man performs an act and we say that act was caused by his beliefs and desires, then it was not in his power to bring about or not bring about (3).

As indicated by (D), the support for this statement is that if we say a man's act was brought about by his own beliefs and desires, then the man could not have done anything other than what he did (4). Thus, Chisholm believes that a person's beliefs and desires are importantly distinct from that person; that is, if a person's beliefs and desires cause an action, then it was not that person's self that caused that action.

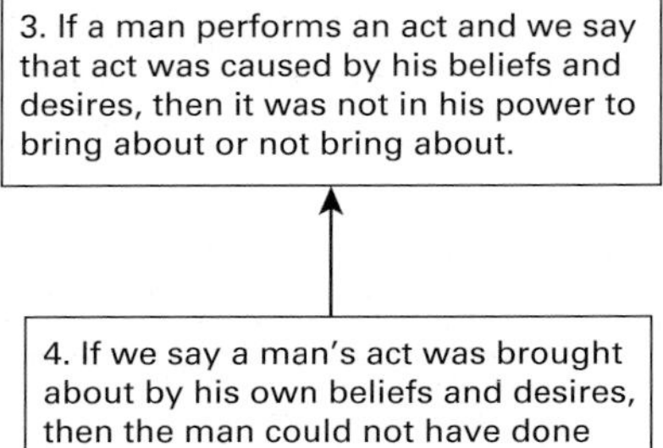

Here, though, "beliefs and desires" are just one instance of something that a person has no control over that causes a person's actions; other examples are reflexive actions, actions forced by another person, and so on. So, we can represent (3) as supporting the more general subconclusion that if we say a man's act was not caused by him, then it was not in his power to bring about or not bring about.

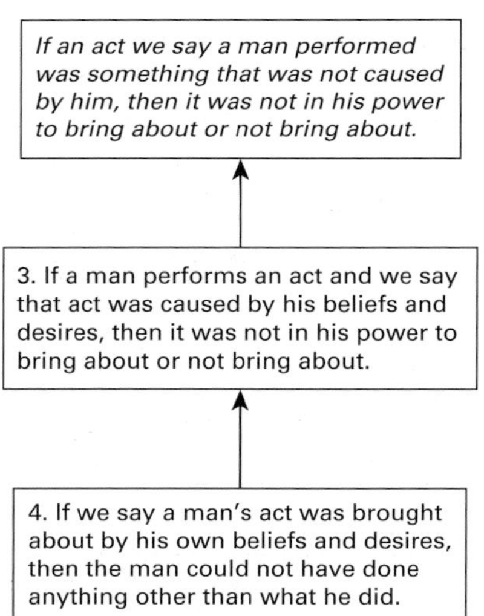

So, if we combine the first implied subconclusion with the new subconclusion, as indicated by (C), then we come to the general conclusion that if the cause of a man's action is something he is not responsible for, then he is not responsible for that action (5).

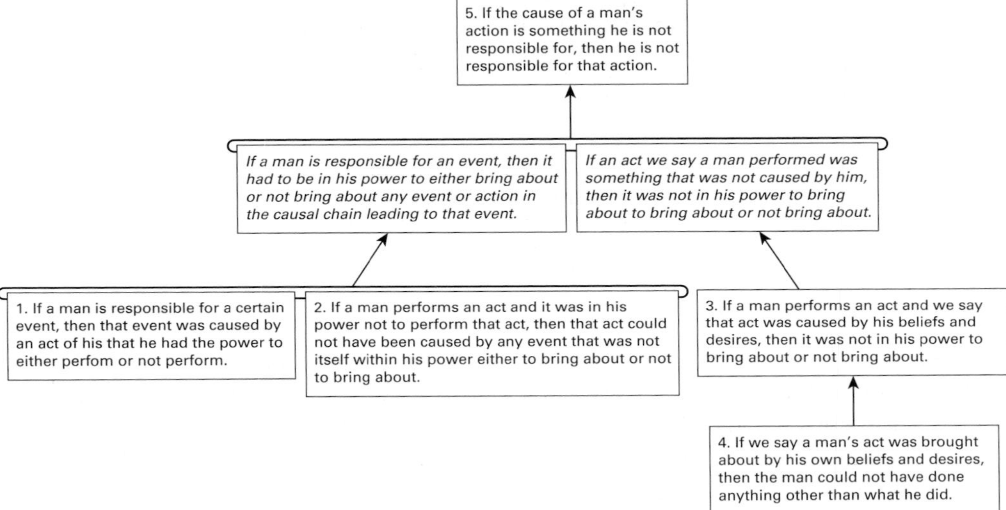
5. If the cause of a man's action is something he is not responsible for, then he is not responsible for that action.
If a man is responsible for an event, then it had to be in his power to either bring about or not bring about any event or action in the causal chain leading to that event.
If an act we say a man performed was something that was not caused by him, then it was not in his power to bring about to bring about or not bring about.
1. If a man is responsible for a certain event, then that event was caused by an act of his that he had the power to either perfom or not perform.
2. If a man performs an act and it was in his power not to perform that act, then that act could not have been caused by any event that was not itself within his power either to bring about or not to bring about.
3. If a man performs an act and we say that act was caused by his beliefs and desires, then it was not in his power to bring about or not bring about.
4. If we say a man's act was brought about by his own beliefs and desires, then the man could not have done anything other than what he did.

But the more interesting result of Chisholm's argument is the specific claim that he seems to be making about actions caused by one's beliefs and desires. If we leave out the second implied subconclusion above, we can see that the more specific conclusion—that is, a more specific version of (5)—is that if a man is responsible for an event, then it cannot be the case that his beliefs and desires caused the act[illegible]nt.

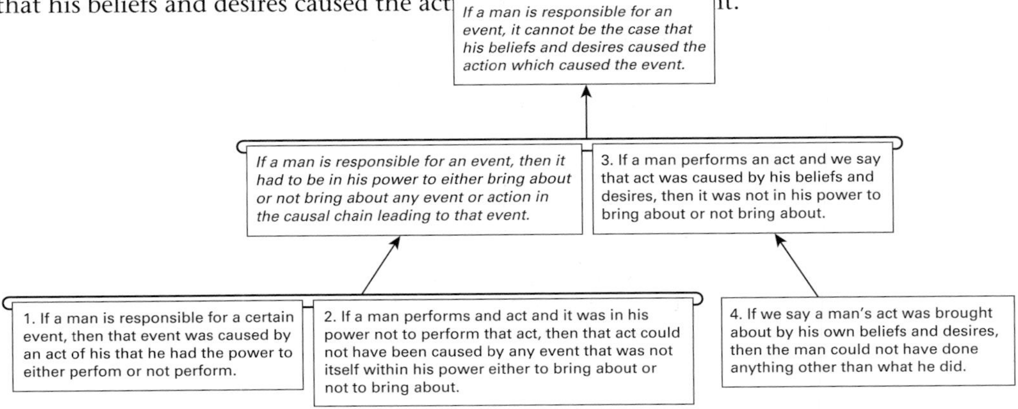
If a man is responsible for an event, it cannot be the case that his beliefs and desires caused the action which caused the event.
If a man is responsible for an event, then it had to be in his power to either bring about or not bring about any event or action in the causal chain leading to that event.
3. If a man performs an act and we say that act was caused by his beliefs and desires, then it was not in his power to bring about or not bring about.
1. If a man is responsible for a certain event, then that event was caused by an act of his that he had the power to either perfom or not perform.
2. If a man performs and act and it was in his power not to perform that act, then that act could not have been caused by any event that was not itself within his power either to bring about or not to bring about.
4. If we say a man's act was brought about by his own beliefs and desires, then the man could not have done anything other than what he did.

This is a very contentions conclusion. Chisholm says explicitly that a person's beliefs and desires (and, presumably, any other mental states that can cause actions, either directly or indirectly) are different from the person's *self*. The obvious question, then, is what is the self? Chisholm does not give us a straightforward answer, but we can get a sense of what he has in mind from the text. It seems as though the self is the agent who causes action, but is not caused to cause that action by anything else. Like Descartes, Chisholm believes that he can know the inner workings of his own mind much better than he can know how the outer world works; and Chisholm says that we take our own agent causation as a given, and as the standard by which we come to know all other kinds of causation.

The mystery of the self, however, is not so easily put to rest. Peter van Inwagen takes this up in the next section.

16.2 Peter van Inwagen, "The Powers of Rational Beings: Freedom of the Will"

Peter van Inwagen is an American philosopher and is currently the John Cardinal O'Hara Professor of Philosophy at the University of Notre Dame. Van Inwagen was born in 1942, received his BS from Rensselaer Polytechnic Institute in 1965, and his PhD in philosophy from the University of Rochester in 1969. His first academic position was at Syracuse University, where he spent twenty-four years. In 1995 he moved to Notre Dame, and has given lectures at universities all over the world.

Van Inwagen has published numerous books in metaphysics, philosophy of religion, and free will: *An Essay on Free Will* (1983), *Material Beings* (1990), *God, Knowledge, and Mystery: Essays in Philosophical Theology* (1995), *The Possibility of Resurrection and Other Essays in Christian Apologetics* (1997), *Ontology, Identity, and Modality* (2001), *The Problem of Evil* (2006), *Metaphysics*, 3rd ed. (2009), and *Existence: Essays in Ontology* (2014). In addition, he has published journal articles in logic and philosophy of language, analytic philosophy, epistemology, and materialism.

Van Inwagen agrees with Chisholm that free will and determinism are incompatible, but he also believes that free will and *in*determinism are incompatible as well. The text that is excerpted below is from chapter 12 of van Inwagen's *Metaphysics*, in which he tries to puzzle out whether there is a third option as Chisholm thinks—not determinism, not indeterminism, but agent causation. He admits that he doesn't really understand what agent causation would be if neither determinism nor indeterminism, and he concludes that the whole debate about free will may be misguided.

We will concentrate on analyzing van Inwagen's argument against the kind of indeterminism Chisholm offers in the first part of this chapter. Prior to the section discussed here, van Inwagen presents an argument against compatibilism—that is, an argument against the proposition that a person can perform actions of her own free will at the same time that her actions are determined. This of course would naturally lead one to explore incompatibilism, of which there are two kinds: hard determinism and libertarianism. In the section here, he argues that the libertarian form of incompatibilism doesn't make sense either. A libertarian has to believe that we have free will, and that our actions are not determined. Thus, van Inwagen wants to consider whether free will is compatible with *in*determinism.

From *Metaphysics*.[2]

We shall see that this supposition leads to a mystery. We shall see that the indeterminism that seems to be required by free will seems also to destroy free will.

Let us look carefully at the consequences of supposing human behavior to be undetermined. Suppose Jane is in an agony of indecision; if her deliberations go one way, she will in a moment speak the words, "John, I lied to you about Alice," and if her deliberations go the other way, she will bite her tongue and remain silent. We have supposed there to be physically possible continuations of the present in which each of these things happens. Given the whole state of the physical world at the present moment, and given the laws of nature, both these things are possible; either might equally well happen.

Each contemplated action will, of course, have antecedents in Jane's cerebral cortex,[1] for[A] it is in that part of Jane (or of her body) that control over her vocal apparatus resides.[2] Let us make a fanciful assumption about these antecedents, since it will make no real difference to our argument what they are. (It will help us to focus our thoughts if we have some sort of mental picture of what goes on inside Jane at the moment of decision.) Let us suppose that[B] a certain current-pulse is proceeding along one of the neural pathways in Jane's brain and that it is about to come to a fork.[3] And let us suppose that[C] if it goes to the left, she will make her confession, and that if it goes to the right, she will remain silent.[4] And let us suppose that[D] it is undetermined which way the pulse will go when it comes to the fork:[5] even an omniscient being with a complete knowledge of the state of Jane's brain and a complete knowledge of the laws of physics and unlimited powers of calculation could say no more than, "The laws and the present state of her brain would allow the pulse to go either way; consequently, no prediction of what the pulse will do when it comes to the fork is possible; it might go to the left, and it might go to the right, and that's all there is to be said."

Now let us ask: Is it *up to Jane* whether the pulse goes to the left or to the right? If we think about this question for a moment, we shall see that[E] it is very hard to see how this could be up to her.[6] Nothing in the way things are at the instant before the pulse makes its "decision" to go one way or the other makes it happen that the pulse goes one way or goes the other.[7] If it goes to the left, that *just happens*.[8] If it goes to the right, *that* just happens.[9] There is no way for Jane to *influence* the pulse.[10] There is no way for her to make it go one way rather than the other.[11] Or, at least,[F] there is no way for her to make it go one way rather than the other and leave the "choice" it makes an undetermined event.[12] If Jane did something to make the pulse go to the left, then, obviously, its going to the left would not be an undetermined event.[13] It is a plausible idea that[G] it is up to an agent what the outcome of a process will be only if the agent is able to arrange things in a way that would make the occurrence of *this* outcome inevitable or in a way that would make the occurrence of *that* outcome inevitable.[14] If this plausible idea is right, there would seem to be no possibility of its being up to Jane (or to anyone else) what the outcome of an *indeterministic* process would be.[15] And it seems to follow that[H] if, when one is trying to decide what to do, it is truly undetermined what the outcome of one's deliberations will be, it cannot be up to one what the outcome of one's deliberations will be.[16] It is, therefore,[I] far from clear whether incompatibilism is a tenable position.[17] The incompatibilist who believes in free will must say this: it is possible, despite the above argument, for it to be up to an agent what the outcome of an indeterministic process will be.[18] But how is the argument to be met?

First, van Inwagen invites us to imagine a very specific scenario in which some hypothetical person, Jane, is deciding between two courses of action. In what follows, it doesn't really matter which actions she is contemplating—he just wants to illustrate a more general point, and it's easier with a concrete example.

With this in mind, he reminds us that an action is caused by something that goes on in the brain, which is, in turn, caused by something else that happens in the brain, and so on. Thus each possible action will have its own chain of causation. This is captured in his claim that each possible action will have antecedents in Jane's brain (1). As indicated by (A), this statement is supported by the claim that control over her vocal apparatus, which causes the public indication of her decision, is located in her brain (2). Thus, we can trace back the cause of Jane's action to an electrical signal that propagates through Jane's neurons. This sentiment is captured by supposing, as indicated by (B), that there is a point at which the brain pulse will either go left or right (3). Statement (4) is just a greater specification of (3), so we will set it aside for now.

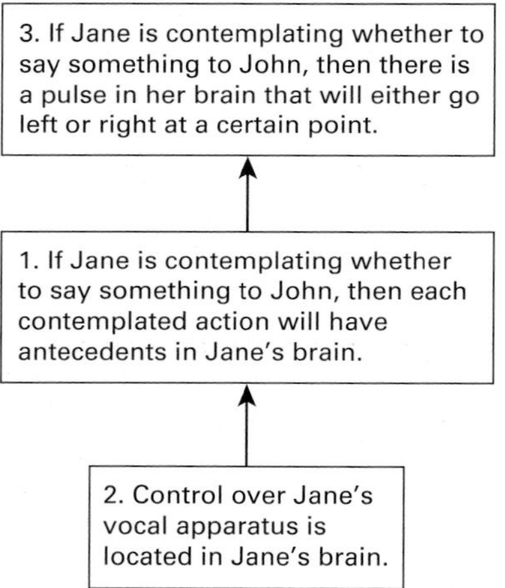
3. If Jane is contemplating whether to say something to John, then there is a pulse in her brain that will either go left or right at a certain point.
1. If Jane is contemplating whether to say something to John, then each contemplated action will have antecedents in Jane's brain.
2. Control over Jane's vocal apparatus is located in Jane's brain.

We also are supposing, as indicated by (D), that it is undetermined whether the pulse will go left or right (5), since it is indeterministic processes that van Inwagen is investigating in this section. As indicated by (E), the combination of these suppositions is going to lead to the conclusion that Jane cannot control whether the pulse goes left or right (6). The argument begins with the claim that nothing in the way things are—the state of the world—when the pulse comes to the fork causes it to go left or right (7). Statements (8) and (9) are specific illustrations of the fact that since nothing causes the pulse to go left or right (7), therefore Jane cannot influence it (10). The statement that there is no way for Jane to make the pulse go left or right (11) is basically a restatement of (10), as is (12), so we will represent the argument like this:

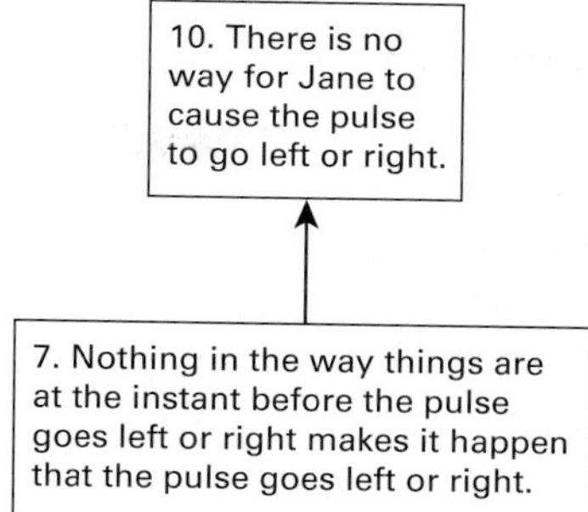
10. There is no way for Jane to cause the pulse to go left or right.
7. Nothing in the way things are at the instant before the pulse goes left or right makes it happen that the pulse goes left or right.

So now we have three statements:

(3) The pulse in Jane's brain is either going left or right.

(5) It is undetermined whether the pulse goes left or right.

(10) Jane cannot cause the pulse to go left or right.

The next claim is that if something (like Jane) did cause the pulse to go left (or right), then the process would not be indeterministic (13). All of these statements together support the claim made earlier: that whether the pulse goes left or right is not under Jane's control (6).

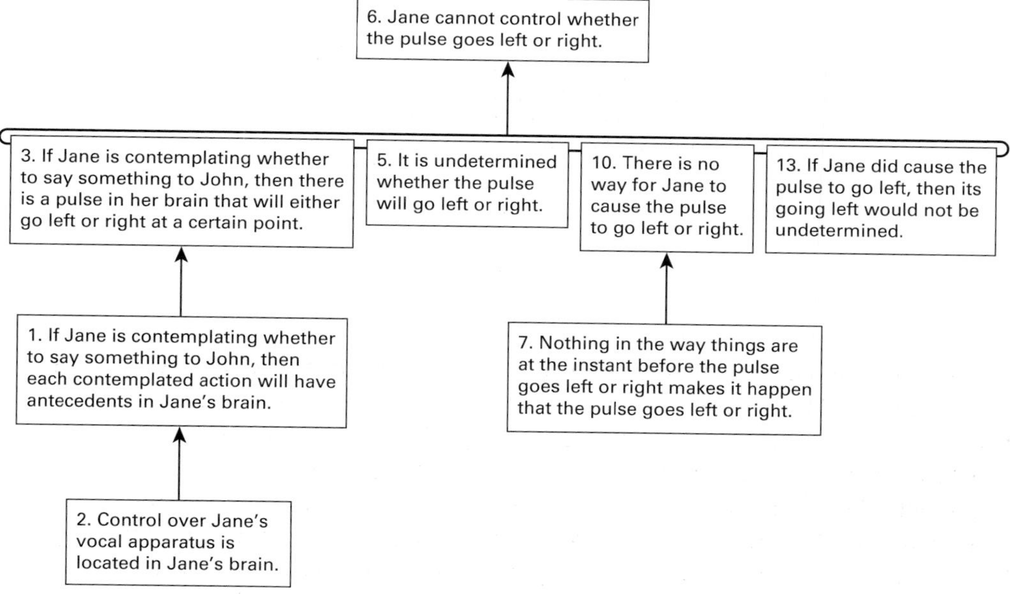
6. Jane cannot control whether the pulse goes left or right.
3. If Jane is contemplating whether to say something to John, then there is a pulse in her brain that will either go left or right at a certain point.
5. It is undetermined whether the pulse will go left or right.
10. There is no way for Jane to cause the pulse to go left or right.
13. If Jane did cause the pulse to go left, then its going left would not be undetermined.
1. If Jane is contemplating whether to say something to John, then each contemplated action will have antecedents in Jane's brain.
7. Nothing in the way things are at the instant before the pulse goes left or right makes it happen that the pulse goes left or right.
2. Control over Jane's vocal apparatus is located in Jane's brain.

Now that we have explored the case of Jane's decision, van Inwagen wants to draw some more general conclusions. Specifically, as indicated by (G), this subargument is supposed to support the general claim that if a person (like Jane) can control the outcome of a process, then he or she can arrange things so that either outcome would be inevitable (14).

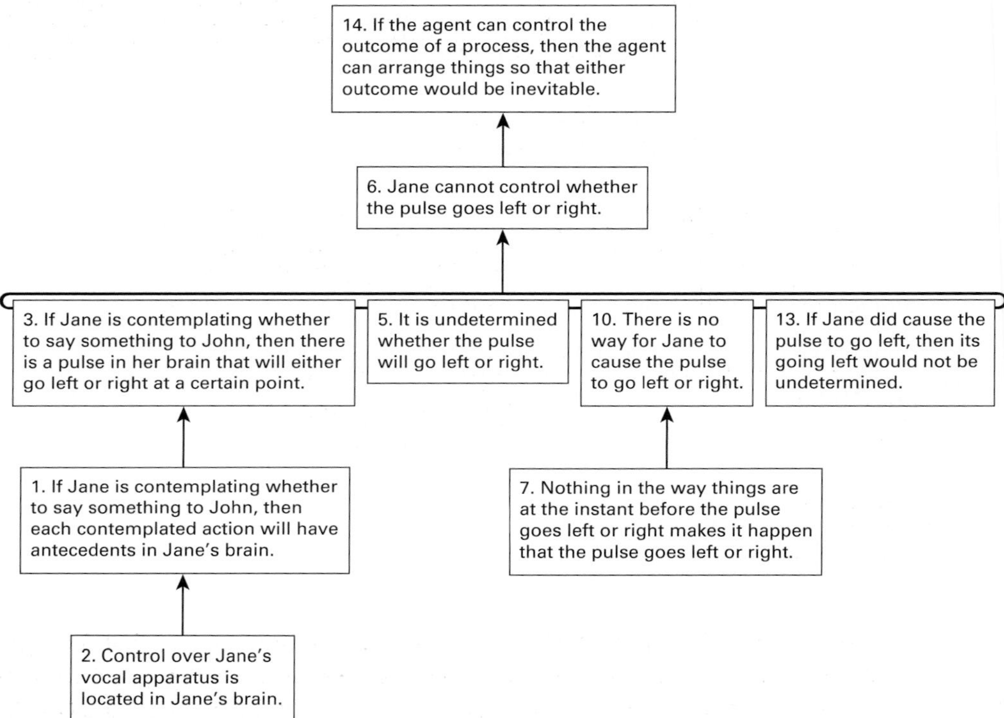
14. If the agent can control the outcome of a process, then the agent can arrange things so that either outcome would be inevitable.
6. Jane cannot control whether the pulse goes left or right.
3. If Jane is contemplating whether to say something to John, then there is a pulse in her brain that will either go left or right at a certain point.
5. It is undetermined whether the pulse will go left or right.
10. There is no way for Jane to cause the pulse to go left or right.
13. If Jane did cause the pulse to go left, then its going left would not be undetermined.
1. If Jane is contemplating whether to say something to John, then each contemplated action will have antecedents in Jane's brain.
7. Nothing in the way things are at the instant before the pulse goes left or right makes it happen that the pulse goes left or right.
2. Control over Jane's vocal apparatus is located in Jane's brain.

And, van Inwagen says, if (14) is true, then the agent (Jane, in this case) can never be said to be in control of the outcome of an indeterministic process (15). As indicated by (H), (14) and (15) combine to support the general claim that if the outcome of one's deliberation process is truly indeterministic, then one cannot control the outcome (16).

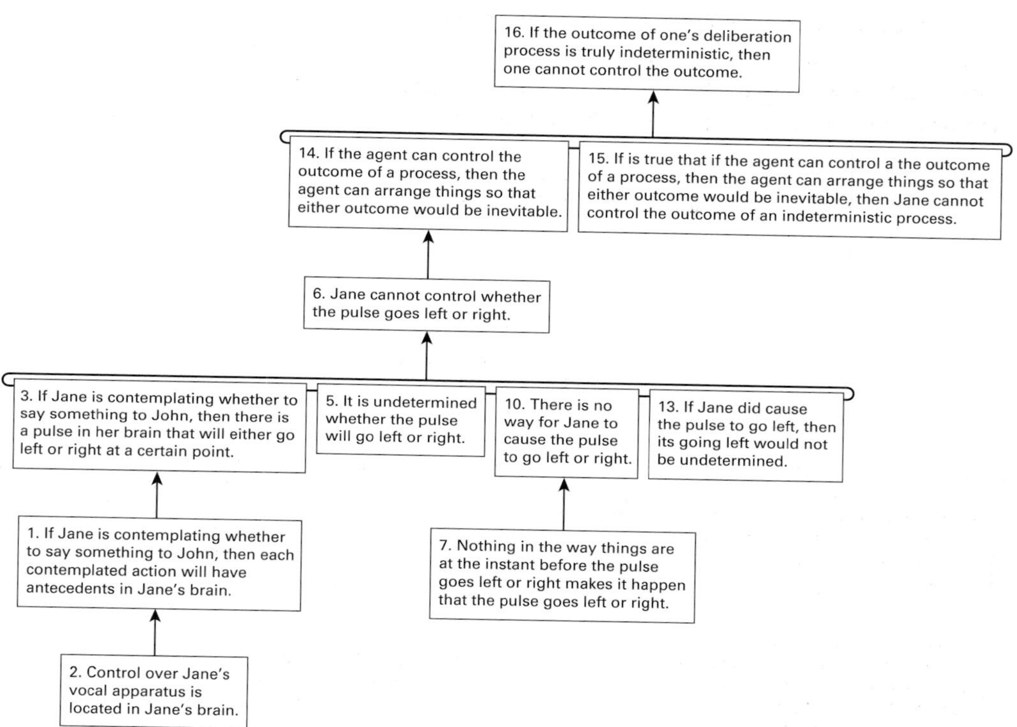
16. If the outcome of one's deliberation process is truly indeterministic, then one cannot control the outcome.
14. If the agent can control the outcome of a process, then the agent can arrange things so that either outcome would be inevitable.
15. If is true that if the agent can control a the outcome of a process, then the agent can arrange things so that either outcome would be inevitable, then Jane cannot control the outcome of an indeterministic process.
6. Jane cannot control whether the pulse goes left or right.
3. If Jane is contemplating whether to say something to John, then there is a pulse in her brain that will either go left or right at a certain point.
5. It is undetermined whether the pulse will go left or right.
10. There is no way for Jane to cause the pulse to go left or right.
13. If Jane did cause the pulse to go left, then its going left would not be undetermined.
1. If Jane is contemplating whether to say something to John, then each contemplated action will have antecedents in Jane's brain.
7. Nothing in the way things are at the instant before the pulse goes left or right makes it happen that the pulse goes left or right.
2. Control over Jane's vocal apparatus is located in Jane's brain.

Then, since libertarians (indeterminists who believe in free will) must believe that the agent can control the outcome of an indeterministic process (18), we can conclude, as indicated by (I) that libertarianism is not a tenable position (17). This in turn supports the main conclusion van Inwagen states at the beginning of this selection: that the indeterminism that seems to be required for free will seems able to destroy free will.

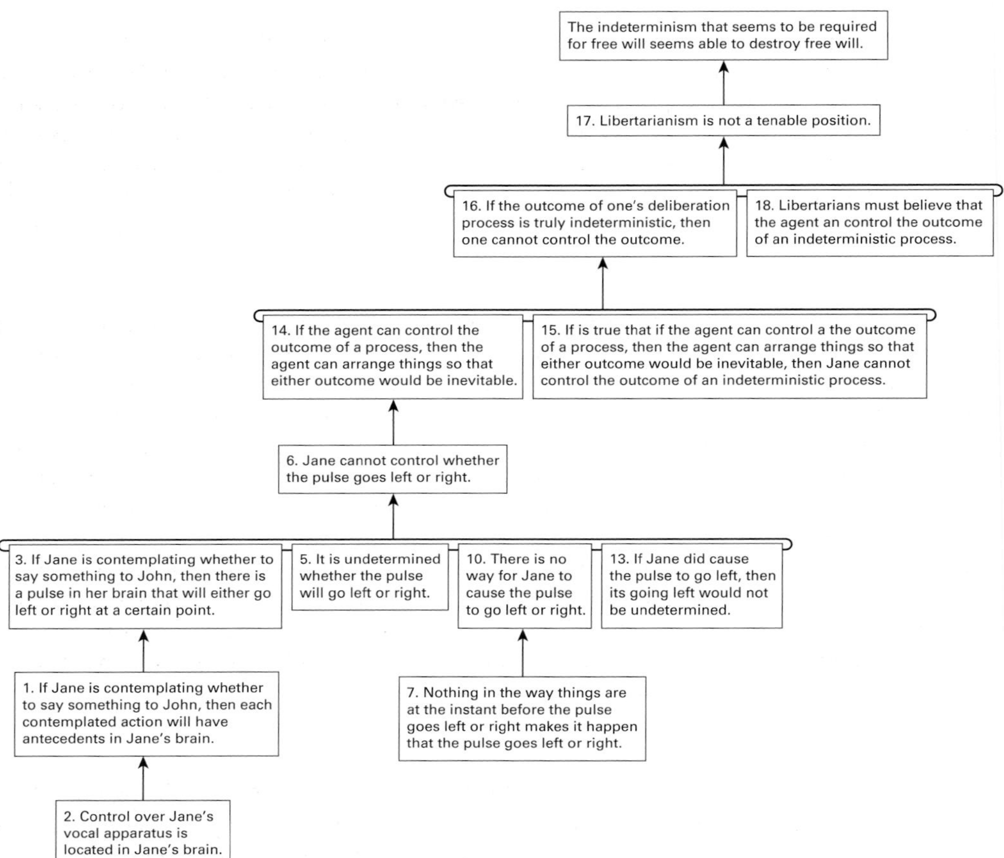
The indeterminism that seems to be required for free will seems able to destroy free will.
17. Libertarianism is not a tenable position.
16. If the outcome of one's deliberation process is truly indeterministic, then one cannot control the outcome.
18. Libertarians must believe that the agent an control the outcome of an indeterministic process.
14. If the agent can control the outcome of a process, then the agent can arrange things so that either outcome would be inevitable.
15. If is true that if the agent can control a the outcome of a process, then the agent can arrange things so that either outcome would be inevitable, then Jane cannot control the outcome of an indeterministic process.
6. Jane cannot control whether the pulse goes left or right.
3. If Jane is contemplating whether to say something to John, then there is a pulse in her brain that will either go left or right at a certain point.
5. It is undetermined whether the pulse will go left or right.
10. There is no way for Jane to cause the pulse to go left or right.
13. If Jane did cause the pulse to go left, then its going left would not be undetermined.
1. If Jane is contemplating whether to say something to John, then each contemplated action will have antecedents in Jane's brain.
7. Nothing in the way things are at the instant before the pulse goes left or right makes it happen that the pulse goes left or right.
2. Control over Jane's vocal apparatus is located in Jane's brain.

Van Inwagen's specific attack on Chisholm's notion of agent causation is explored in the exercises below.

16.3 In-Class Exercises

An asterisk (*) indicates a more challenging exercise.

Exercises 1–2

In the first part of this chapter, we analyzed in detail one of Roderick Chisholm's arguments in "Human Freedom and the Self." The following are more arguments from the selection. For each, (a) diagram the argument and (b) identify any potential objections to the argument.

Exercise 1

5. We must not say that every event involved in the act is caused by some other event; and we must not say that the act is something that is not caused at all. The possibility that remains, therefore, is this: We should say that at least one of the events that are involved in the act is caused, not by any other events, but by something else instead. And this something else can only be the agent—the man. If there is an event that is caused, not by other events, but by the man, then there are some events involved in the act that are not caused by other events. But if the event in question is caused by the man then it *is* caused and we are not committed to saying that there is something involved in the act that is not caused at all.

Exercise 2

8. The second objection is more difficult and concerns the very concept of "immanent causation," or causation by an agent, as this concept is to be interpreted here. The concept is subject to a difficulty which has long been associated with that of the prime mover unmoved. We have said that there must be some event A, presumably some cerebral event, which is caused not by any other event, but by the agent. Since A was not caused by any other event, then the agent himself cannot be said to have undergone any change or produced any other event (such as "an act of will" or the like) which brought A about. But if, when the agent made A happen, there was no event involved other than A itself, no event which could be described as *making* A happen, what did the agent's causation consist of? What, for example, is the difference between A's just happening, and the agent's *causing* A to happen? We cannot attribute the difference to any event that took place within the agent. And so far as the event A itself is concerned, there would seem to be no discernible difference. Thus Aristotle said that the activity of the prime mover is nothing in addition to the motion that it produces, and Suarez said that "the action is in reality nothing but the effect as it flows from the agent."

Exercises 3–5

In the second part of this chapter, we analyzed in detail one of Peter van Inwagen's arguments in "The Powers of Rational Beings." The following is another argument from the selection (exercise 3), objections to that argument (exercise 4), and replies to those objections (exercise 5). For the exercises, (a) diagram the argument in exercise 3, (b) add the objections from exercise 4 to this diagram, and (c) add the replies from exercise 5 to the objections to the diagram.

Exercise 3

Let us now return to the question confronting the incompatibilist who believes in free will: How is it possible for it to be up to an agent what the outcome of an indeterministic process will be? Those incompatibilists who appeal to agent-causation answer this question as follows: "A process's having one outcome rather than one of the other outcomes it might have had is an event. For it to be up to an agent what the outcome of a process will be is for the agent to be able to cause each of the outcomes that process could have. Suppose, for example, that Jane's deciding what to do was an indeterministic process and that this process terminated in her deciding to speak, although, since it was indeterministic, the laws of nature and the way things were when the process was initiated were consistent with its terminating in her remaining silent. But suppose that Jane *caused* the process to terminate in her speaking and that she *once was able* to cause it to terminate in her being silent. Then it was up to her what the outcome was. That is what it is for it to have been up to an agent whether a process would terminate in A or B: to have caused it to terminate in one of these two ways, and to have been *able* to cause it to terminate in the other."

Exercise 4

There are two "standard" objections to this sort of answer. They take the form of questions. The first question is, "But what does one add to the assertion that Jane decided to speak when one says she was the agent-cause of her decision to speak?" The second is, "But what about the event *Jane's becoming the agent-cause of her decision to speak*? According to your position, this event occurred and it was undetermined—for if it were determined by some earlier state of things and the laws of nature, then her decision to speak would have been determined by these same factors. Even if there is such a thing as agent-causation and this event occurred, how could it have been *up to Jane* whether it occurred? And if Jane was the agent-cause of her decision to speak and it was not up to her whether she was the agent-cause of her decision to speak, then it was not up to her whether she would speak or remain silent."

Exercise 5

These two standard objections have standard replies. The first reply is, "I don't know how to answer your question. But that is because causation is a mystery, and not because there is any *special* mystery about *agent*-causation. How would *you* answer the corresponding question about event-causation: What does one add to the assertion that two events occurred in succession when one says the earlier was the *cause* of the later?" The second reply is, "But it *was* up to Jane which of the two events *Jane's becoming the agent-cause of her decision to speak* and *Jane's becoming the agent-cause of her decision to remain silent* would occur. This is because she was the agent-cause of the former and was able to have been the agent-cause of the latter. In any case in which Jane is the agent-cause of an event, she is also the agent-cause of her being the agent-cause of that event, and the agent-cause of her being the agent-cause of her being the agent-cause of that event, and so on 'forever.' Of course, she is no doubt not *aware* of being the agent-cause of all these events, but the doctrine of agent-causation does not entail that agents are aware of all the events of which they are agent-causes."

Exercises 6–9

The following exercises are intended to ensure your understanding of Chisholm's and van Inwagen's texts, and to help you further explore the ideas presented in this chapter.

Exercise 6: Now that you have read my textual analysis of Chisholm's argument, summarize it in your own words.
Exercise 7: Summarize, in your own words, each of the arguments in exercises 1 and 2 above.
Exercise 8: Now that you have read my textual analysis of van Inwagen's argument, summarize it in your own words.
Exercise 9: Summarize, in your own words, each of the arguments in exercises 3–5 above.

16.4 Reading Questions

1. What is the difference, according to Chisholm, between transeunt causation and immanent causation? How does this distinction help his argument?
2. Why, according to Chisholm, is transeunt causation no greater a mystery than immanent causation?
3. What is van Inwagen's No Choice Principle? Do you think it is reasonable? Why or why not?
4. Why, according to van Inwagen, must a compatibilist reject the No Choice Principle? What would it be like to reject that principle?
5. Does van Inwagen accurately represent and assess Chisholm's argument? Why or why not?

VI Ethics

Introduction

It will be useful for us to divide the field of ethics into three categories:

- Meta-ethics
- Normative ethics
- Applied ethics

Broadly construed, meta-ethics asks questions about moral concepts like right and wrong, good and bad, and so on. Normative ethics assumes that there are such things as morally right actions and morally wrong actions and postulates theories that tell us the general differences between them. Finally, applied ethics concentrates on which particular actions are right and wrong, both by applying the normative theories and by appealing to the intuitions that inform these theories. We begin Part VI with meta-ethics.

Learning Objectives for Part VI

At the end of Part VI, you will be able to:

- Discuss the strengths and weakness of:
  - Divine command theory
  - Cultural relativism
- Describe the moral theories of:
  - Virtue ethics
  - Egoism
  - Contractarianism
  - Utilitarianism
  - Deontology
- Define:
  - Subjectivism
  - Conventionalism

- Ethical realism
- Normative
- Descriptive
- Intrinsic value
- Instrumental value

Meta-ethics

In Part II, we asked whether we can prove that God exists. We looked at four different arguments, but ultimately found them all lacking in one way or another. This doesn't mean that God doesn't exist, of course, but now we want to ask: If there is no God, can there be any morality?

Friedrich Nietzsche once famously said, "If God is dead, then everything is permitted." This simple quote captures the widespread view that our morals come from some higher, possibly supernatural, being. This being tells us what is right and wrong, rewards us when we do the right thing, and punishes us when we do the wrong thing. Thus, if there were no higher power—no God, no Allah, and so on—then there wouldn't be anyone to tell us how we ought to behave. In ethics, this position is called *divine command theory*.

However, the central tradition in Western philosophy tries to separate questions of ethics from the issue of what God wants us to do. In our first reading of chapter 17, Plato's *Euthyphro*, we will discover his reason for making this separation. We'll follow this up with an explanation from James Rachels why divine command theory ought to be abandoned. But then what? What are our alternatives if we don't get our morality from God?

I will mention three alternatives here, although we will only explore one of them in any detail (in chapter 19). These alternatives are:

- Subjectivism
- Cultural relativism
- Ethical realism

Each of these theories provides an answer to the questions: Are there ethical facts? And, if so, what makes them true? We know, for example, that there are physical facts: Pike's Peak is over 14,000 feet tall, the Sun is 93 million miles from the Earth, DNA is shaped like a double helix, and so on. And we know what makes those facts true—the way the physical world is. In other words, if I make a claim about the world—say, that the Earth is at the center of the solar system—then that claim is either true or false. More importantly, the truth or falsity of the claim doesn't depend on what I believe to be the case, or what I wish were the case; it depends on the way the world is. If the claim actually corresponds to the way the world is, then the claim is true, and if it doesn't, the claim is false.

But what about moral claims, like "It is wrong to kill an innocent person"? Are they like physical claims—are they true or false depending on whether they correspond to the moral world? Are they true or false regardless of what people may believe about them?

- *Subjectivism*, or *nihilism*, is the view that moral claims are neither true nor false. Rather, these claims merely represent how each person feels about different sorts of actions.
- *Conventionalism*, or *relativism*, is the view that moral claims are either true or false, but the truth or falsity is determined by convention. That is, the truth or falsity is determined by a king, say, or a whole society.
- *Ethical realism*, or *absolutism*, is the view that moral claims are either true or false, and the truth or falsity is determined by the way the objective moral world is, just as the truth or falsity of physical claims are determined by the way the objective physical world is.

We will not explore subjectivism here, but we will explore relativism in chapter 18.

Normative Ethics

Generally, although there are some notable exceptions, Western philosophers have been ethical realists; that is, they have believed that there is some objective fact of the matter about whether a particular moral claim is right or wrong. The task of normative philosophy, then, is to discover the correct moral laws. Here, another analogy with the physical world will help. There are a lot of different physical facts; for example, the planets move in ellipses around the Sun, massive objects fall to the ground at a rate of 9.8 m/s2, and when you throw a ball it follows a parabolic path. In 1687, Isaac Newton published the formula that he argued united all of these facts—the universal law of gravitation. This law explains all the facts we already knew and also helps us predict new facts about the world. A normative theory is similar; it's like a moral law that unites all of the moral facts we know and also tells us what the moral facts will be in novel situations.

There are many different normative ethical theories, including:

- Ethical egoism
- Contractarianism
- Virtue ethics
- Utilitarianism
- Deontological ethics

One of the important distinctions in this section will be between *normative* and *descriptive* accounts of human behavior. Psychological, sociological, and anthropological theories are all examples of descriptive accounts of human behavior. That is, their theories *describe* how human beings actually behave in certain cultures, under specific circumstances, and so on. A normative theory, on the other hand, describes not how people actually behave, but how they *should* or *ought to* behave. For example, one kind of normative theory explains how people should behave if they want to be rational. This kind of theory does not claim that people actually behave rationally, but rather describes the kinds of actions that would be rational.

Normative ethics is concerned with how people ought to behave if they want to be moral—that is, if they want to do the morally right thing as opposed to the morally wrong thing.

Another important distinction will be between *instrumental value* and *intrinsic value*. A thing has instrumental value if we value it for its usefulness in obtaining other things that we value. For example, most people agree that money is instrumentally valuable because we use money to buy what we do value, like food, clothing, and shelter. We can also say that food, clothing, and shelter are instrumentally valuable because they are what we need to be happy, and we value happiness. But notice that it doesn't make sense to ask what having happiness allows us to obtain—happiness is valuable in itself. Thus, we say that happiness is intrinsically valuable. We can see this in a potential exchange between two people:

Helena: I need some money.

Abe: Why do you want money?

Helena: So I can buy something to eat.

Abe: Why do need something to eat?

Helena: Um, 'cause I'm hungry?

Abe: OK, but why do you want to not be hungry?

Helena: I would be much happier if I weren't hungry.

Abe: And why do you want to be happy?

Helena: Um, what? I just do.

Abe: But why?

Helena: Being happy is just good.

It makes sense for Abe to ask Helena why she wants money, food, or not to be hungry because these things are useful to get Helena what she really wants, which is happiness. Thus, we say these things have instrumental value; that is, they are instrumentally good. But Abe's question about why Helena wants to be happy doesn't make sense because, for Helena, happiness isn't a way to get something else. Rather, happiness is the ultimate goal. Thus, we say that happiness is valuable in itself, or has intrinsic value. Keep in mind that there may be things that have purely instrumental value, purely intrinsic value, or both instrumental and intrinsic value.

Virtue Ethics

One of the oldest comprehensive theories of ethics is given by Aristotle around 350 BC in *Nicomachean Ethics*, a book intended for his son, Nicomachus. For Aristotle, the *Ethics* is the study of what is good, and how to become good. First, he believes that a person becomes good, or virtuous, by doing good in the right way. Everyone knows what the good or right thing to do is; the difference is how and why each person acts. The morally weak act on desires to do other than what they know to be right; the morally strong have these desires, but do not act on them; but the virtuous do not even have desires to act contrary to what they know is right.

What are the right actions? Those that lie between extremes (the "golden mean"). Why is this? To understand, recall Aristotle's doctrine of four causes (from the introduction to Part II). Everything, including humans, has a material, efficient, formal, and final cause. What is good and right is what allows human beings to fulfill their purpose. The highest good for Aristotle is that to which all humans aim.

Ethical Egoism

In contrast to always trying to act virtuously, one psychological theory of human behavior makes the following claim: People always act in a way so as to maximize their personal interests. We can call this theory *psychological egoism*. One of the implications of this theory is that there is no true altruism; that is, no one ever acts to promote the interests of others, only his or her own interests. This, of course, is a descriptive theory. Ethical egoism is the normative theory that people *should* always act to maximize their own interests. Ethical egoism often begins with endorsing psychological egoism, and adds to it the view that the morally correct action for a person to perform in any situation is the one that maximizes his or her personal interests.

Contractarianism

Contractarianism shares some features with ethical egoism. Contractarians believe that morality is based on the agreements people make with each other, and that people make these agreements to further their own interests. The idea is that if everyone just pursued his or her own interests, then life would be too chaotic for people to achieve their goals. Thus, people will agree to set aside some of their interests if it means they can freely pursue others that may be more important. If people enter into this agreement with each other, then they have a contract. Contractarianism says that we enter into all kinds of contracts with each other, although some are only implicit, like the *social contract*. The morally correct action to take in any circumstance, then, is the one that honors the (either explicit or implicit) contract.

Utilitarianism

Utilitarianism is often described as saying that the morally correct action in any situation is the one that will produce the greatest good for the greatest number. This makes it a good example of a *consequentialist* moral theory—one that judges the moral worth of an action according to the consequences of the action. In a purely consequentialist theory, the motivations of the person acting are not relevant in deciding whether her actions are right or wrong; it is only the outcome that matters. In this way, utilitarianism is similar to ethical egoism in that they are both consequentialist theories.

Utilitarianism, though, can come in many varieties depending on one's definition of "the good." Actual physical goods like food, water, and shelter could be "the good," and so the correct action in any case would be the one that maximizes these goods for the various people involved. Or, having one's preferences satisfied could what is "good," and so what is right (like the outcome of an election) is the action that satisfies the most number of people. Both Jeremy Bentham and John Stuart Mill (as we will see in chapter 20) subscribe to *hedonistic* utilitarianism, where happiness is the "good" and consists in pleasure and the absence of pain. Thus, on this view, the morally correct action in any circumstance is the one that maximizes pleasure and minimizes pain across all of the people who could be affected by the action.

Deontological Ethics

The word *deontological* comes from the Greek for "study of" (*logos*) and "duty" (*deon*). Deontological theories are best understood in contrast with consequentialist theories. In a deontological theory, the consequences of the action aren't at issue; rather, an action is either morally obligatory (a duty), permissible, or forbidden based on the status of the rule that guided the action, the conformity of the action to a moral norm. Thus, an action is morally correct if it is guided by a rule that is morally correct. The issue, then, is how to determine which are the morally correct rules.

In Immanuel Kant's version of deontological ethics, we can use our uniquely human reasoning to determine which rules are the right ones by imagining what the world would be like if everyone followed some rule without exception.

In chapter 19, we will explore ethical egoism, contractarianism, and virtue ethics; and in chapter 20 we will explore utilitarianism and deontological ethics.

17 Meta-ethics: Divine Command Theory

17.1 Plato, *Euthyphro*
17.2 James Rachels, "Does Morality Depend on Religion?"
17.3 In-Class Exercises
17.4 Reading Questions

17.1 Plato, *Euthyphro*

We first encountered Plato in chapter 1, when we read *Apology*. Another of Plato's dialogues, *Euthyphro*, describes a conversation Socrates has on his way to the trial described in *Apology*. This conversation takes place at the porch of the king archon. The king archon's function is both attorney general and head of religious affairs. This may sound strange to us, but in ancient Greece, all wrongdoings had religious aspects. This meant that what is legal is the same as what is holy or pious. Recall, for example, that one of the charges against Socrates in *Apology* was impiety—a violation of religious standards.

In this dialogue, Euthyphro is there to prosecute his father for the murder of one of Euthyphro's "dependents," which here means either a slave or a hired hand. Since the punishment for Euthyphro's father would be execution, what Euthyphro is doing would be seen as patricide. Killing one's father, in ancient Greek culture, is much worse than killing a slave. But Euthyphro claims he is doing the right thing because it is the pious thing to do. So, Socrates asks Euthyphro to teach him what is pious and cure him of his impiety. Euthyphro agrees, then, to answer the question "What is piety?"

Throughout the dialogue, Euthyphro offers three different definitions of piety. It is the third definition with which we will be concerned here. Euthyphro says, "*The pious is what all the gods love.*" Socrates responds by asking, "Is the pious loved by the gods because it is pious, or is it pious because it is loved by the gods?" Socrates recognizes that there are two ways of understanding this claim in terms of the causal connection between the actions that are pious and the actions that the gods love. Here Socrates is indicating that Euthyphro's claim "the pious is what all the gods love" is ambiguous. On the one hand, you could understand Euthyphro's claim as "an action is pious because it is loved by the gods." On the other hand, you could understand his claim as "an action is loved by the gods because it is pious. This is referred to as *Euthyphro's dilemma.*

Divine command theory says that the first interpretation is the correct one; it says that an action is right (morally correct) because God or the gods command that action. That is, divine command theory says that no actions are intrinsically right or wrong; they only become right or wrong when God commands or forbids them. Thus, sacrificing your only child, for example, would be the right thing to do if God commanded it; or flying planes into buildings full of people would be the right thing to do if God commanded it. In the part of *Euthyphro* that we will be considering below, Socrates attempts to show that this first interpretation is unacceptable. Let's look at Plato's text in more detail. Specifically, we will analyze and diagram one of the main arguments from the second part of the dialogue.

From *Euthyphro.*[1]

Socrates: I shall try to explain more clearly: we speak of something being carried and something carrying, of something being led and something leading, of something being seen and something seeing, and you understand that these things are all different from one another and how they differ?

Euthyphro: I think I do.

Socrates: So there is something being loved and something loving, and the loving is a different thing.

Euthyphro: Of course.

Socrates: Tell me then whether that which is being carried is being carried because someone carries it[1] or for some other reason.

Euthyphro: No, that is the reason.

Socrates: And[A] that which is being led is so because someone leads it,[2] and[B] that which is being seen because someone sees it?[3]

Euthyphro: Certainly.

Socrates: It is not seen by someone because it is being seen but on the contrary it is being seen because someone sees it, nor is it because it is being led that someone leads it but because someone leads it that it is being led; nor does someone carry an object because it is being carried, but it is being carried because someone carries it. Is what I want to say clear, Euthyphro? I want to say this, namely, that if anything comes to be, or is affected, it does not come to be because it is coming to be, but it is coming to be because it comes to be;[4] nor[C] is it affected because it is being affected but because something affects it.[5] Or do you not agree?

Euthyphro: I do.

Socrates: What is being loved is either something that comes to be or something that is affected by something?[6]

Euthyphro: Certainly.

Socrates: So[D] it is in the same case as the things just mentioned; it is not loved by those who love it because it is being loved, but it is being loved because they love it?[7]

Euthyphro: Necessarily.

Socrates: What then[E] do we say about the pious, Euthyphro? Surely that it is loved by all the gods,[8] according to what you say?

Euthyphro: Yes.

Socrates: Is it loved because it is pious,[9] or for some other reason?

Euthyphro: For no other reason.

Socrates: It is loved then[F] because it is pious, but it is not pious because it is loved?[10]

Euthyphro: Apparently.

Socrates: And[G] because it is loved by the gods it is being loved and is dear to the gods?[11]

Euthyphro: Of course.

Socrates: The god-beloved is then[H] not the same as the pious, Euthyphro, nor the pious the same as the god-beloved, as you say it is, but one differs from the other.

Euthyphro: How so, Socrates?

Socrates: Because[I] we agree that the pious is beloved for the reason that it is pious,[12] but[J] it is not pious because it is loved.[13] Is that not so?

Euthyphro: Yes.

Socrates: And[K] that the god-beloved, on the other hand, is so because it is loved by the gods, by the very fact of being loved,[14] but[L] it is not loved because it is god-beloved.[15]

Euthyphro: True.

Socrates: But[M] if the god-beloved and the pious were the same, my dear Euthyphro, and the pious were loved because it was pious, then the god-beloved would be loved because it was god-beloved,[16] and[N] if the god-beloved were god-beloved because it was loved by the gods, then the pious would also be pious because it was loved by the gods;[17] but now you see that[O] they are in opposite cases as being altogether different from each other: the one is of a nature to be loved because it is loved, the other is loved because it is of a nature to be loved.[18] I'm afraid, Euthyphro, that when you were asked what piety is, you did not wish to make its nature clear to me, but you told me an affect or quality of it, that the pious has the quality of being loved by all the gods, but you have not yet told me what the pious is. Now, if you will, do not hide things from me but tell me again from the beginning what piety is, whether loved by the gods or having some other quality—we shall not quarrel about that—but be keen to tell me what the pious and the impious are.

In this part of the dialogue, Socrates is trying to explain to Euthyphro the dilemma of how "the pious" (actions that are pious) is related to "the god-beloved" (actions that the gods love). He begins by listing some more mundane examples of things that will illustrate the difference between something being loved by someone and someone loving something.

Then, Socrates asks Euthyphro which way the causation goes in all of these examples. Say you are carrying a small dog, so the dog has the property of "being carried." Why does it have this property? Socrates says it has this property because someone is carrying it (1). Similarly, if you are walking the dog on a leash, we can say that the dog has the property of "being led" because someone is leading it (2). Or if you are looking at the dog, it has the property of "being seen" because someone sees it (3).

After (3), Socrates reiterates the direction of the causation. You do not see the dog *because* it has the property "being seen." Rather, the dog has the property "being seen" *because* you see it. That is, "being seen" is not some intrinsic property that causes people to look at the dog. Rather, that people are looking at the dog causes it to be seen.

As indicated by (A) and (B), these statements lead Socrates to infer a general rule, given in (4) and (5): If anything has a property (like being seen, coming to be, being affected), then it has that property *because* someone or something is doing something to it (seeing it, making it come to be, affecting it). It is not the case that someone or something does something to an object (seeing it, making it come to be, affecting it) *because* it has a property (being seen, coming to be, being affected). This is represented as:

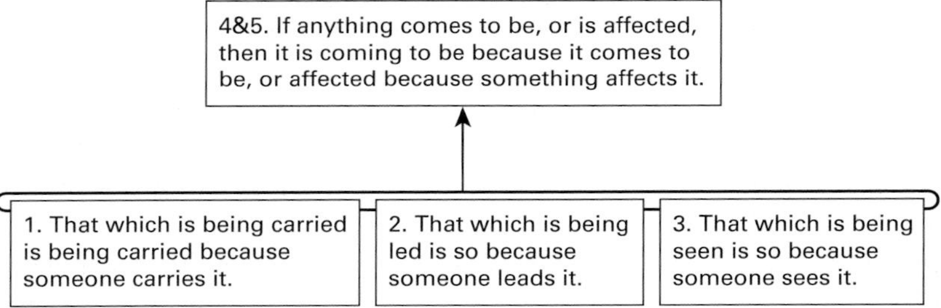

Next, Socrates applies this general principle to the case of something being loved. He first establishes that the property of "being loved" is like the property of "being seen" in that what is loved is either coming to be or being affected (6); thus, "being loved" falls under the general principle. As indicated by (D), Socrates concludes that something has the property "being loved" because someone loves it (7):

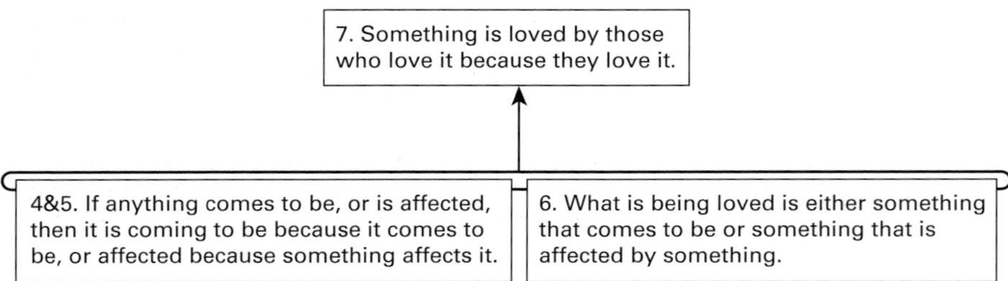

This means that, just as in the example of the dog being seen, if the dog has the property of "being loved," then it is not the case that "being loved" is some kind of intrinsic property of the dog that causes someone to love it. Rather, the fact that someone loves it causes it to have the property "being loved."

As indicated by (E), Socrates moves on to combine (7) with two more observations: "the pious" (which here stands for "any actions which are pious") is loved by all the gods (8) and "the pious" is loved because it is pious (9). As indicated by (F), this leads to the conclusion that "the pious" is not pious because it is loved (10):

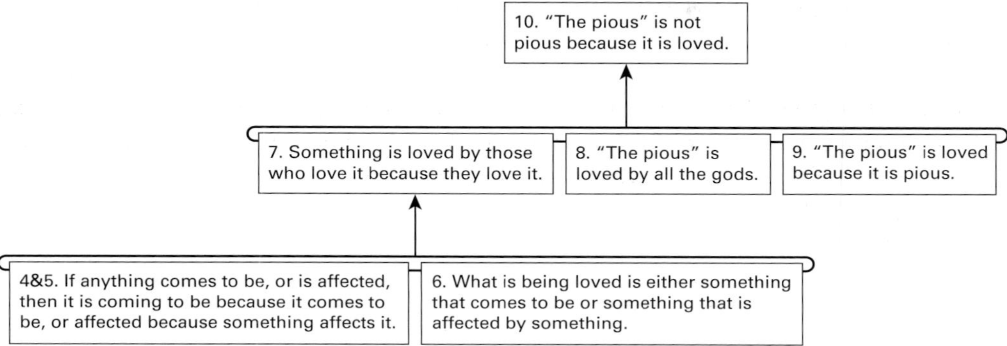

This last claim is the key to the argument presented here. If "the pious" is loved because it is pious, then "being pious" must be an intrinsic property of the actions that are pious. The thrust of Socrates' argument is that "being pious" is an intrinsic property of some actions, but "being god-beloved" is not.

Then, as indicated by (G) and (H), this conclusion is combined with the claim that "the pious" is being loved by the gods because it is loved by the gods (11), to support the main conclusion that "the god-beloved" (which here stands for "the actions that the gods love") is different from "the pious" (as we said above, because the latter property is intrinsic to some actions, while the former is not):

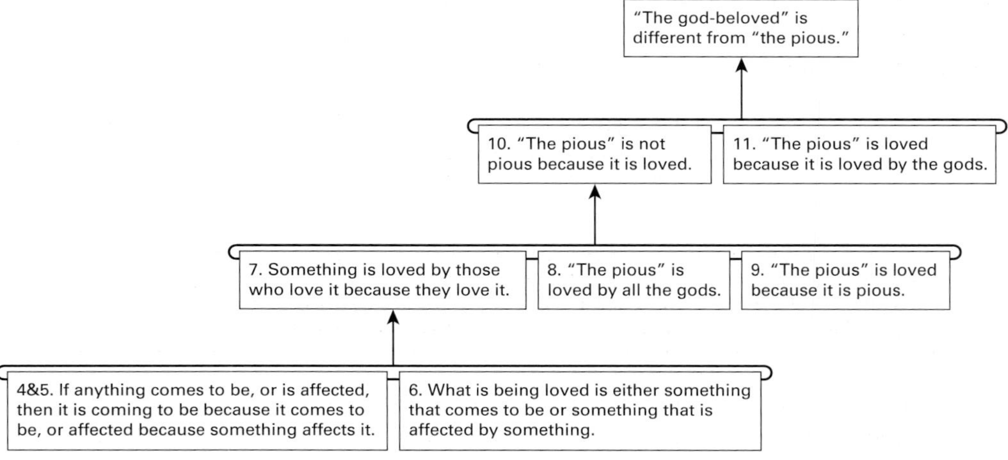

After the statement of the main conclusion, Euthyphro asks Socrates to repeat the argument. Socrates complies, as indicated by (I), by laying out the reasons once more. First, "the pious" is loved because it is pious (12)—a restatement of (9)—and "the pious" is not pious because it is loved (13)—a restatement of 10.

Next, Socrates similarly explains "the god-beloved." It is loved by the gods because the gods are loving it (14), just as the dog is being seen because someone is seeing it; and it is not loved because it has the property of "being god-beloved" (15), just as the dog is not being seen *because* it has the property of "being seen."

Then, Socrates gives us two complex conditional statements. First, he says, if ["the god-beloved" and "the pious" were the same], then [if "the pious" were loved because it was pious, then "the god-beloved" would be loved because it was god-beloved] (16). Then he says, if ["the god-beloved" and "the pious" were the same], then [if "the god-beloved" were god-beloved because it was loved by the gods, then "the pious" would also be pious because it is loved by the gods] (17). Notice that these two statements have the structure: If [A], then [if B, then C]. And, if we can show that C is false, we can show that [if B, then C] is false. By modus tollens, then A would be false. So, what we have are two different ways of getting to the same conclusion, which is a restatement of (18).

Notice again the crucial point, as explained in (18). "The pious" and "the god-beloved" are different because "the god-beloved" has the property of being loved because the gods love it, but the "the pious" has the property of being loved because it is pious. In other words, the fact that the gods love something causes it to be god-beloved, but the fact that something is pious causes the gods to love it.

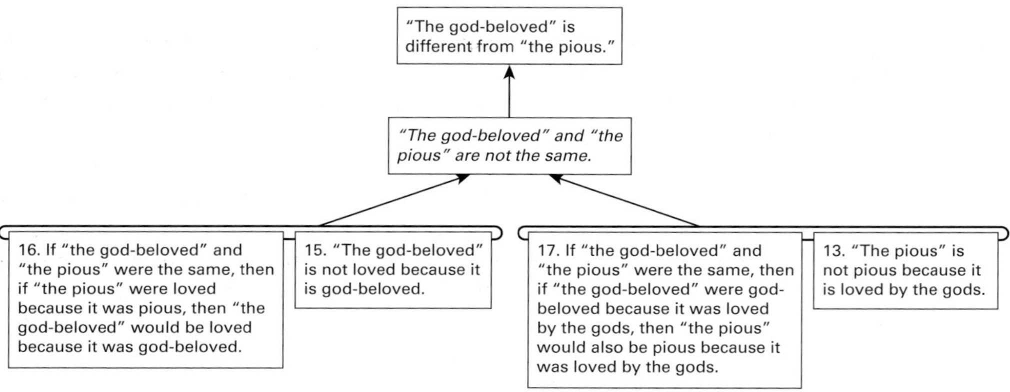

In the next section, we will explore a contemporary version of this argument from James Rachels.

17.2 James Rachels, "Does Morality Depend on Religion?"

James Rachels (1941–2003) was an American philosopher, specializing in applied ethics. He was specifically interested in animal rights and euthanasia. He received his PhD from the University of North Carolina at Chapel Hill in 1967, and taught at a variety of colleges and universities before his final position at the University of Alabama at Birmingham.

Rachels is the author of six books, the most well-known of which is *The Elements of Moral Philosophy*. Below is an excerpt from chapter 4: "Does Morality Depend on Religion?" In the first part of the chapter, Rachels lays out the theological conception of right and wrong: that right actions are those that God commands, and wrong actions are those that God condemns. Then, Rachels reconstructs Socrates' argument from Plato's *Euthyphro*, but more importantly explicitly explains the consequences of divine command theory. Ultimately, he argues that a devout person cannot subscribe to this theory without having to give up many of the important tenets of her religion. Now, let's look at Rachels's text in more detail.

From *The Elements of Moral Philosophy*.[2]

4.2 The Divine Command Theory

... Socrates is skeptical and asks: Is conduct right because the gods command it, or do the gods command it because it is right? This is one of the most famous questions in the history of philosophy. ...

The point is that if we accept the theological conception of right and wrong, we are caught in a dilemma. Socrates' question asks us to clarify what we mean. There are two things we might mean, and both lead to trouble.

1. First, we might mean that *right conduct is right because God commands it.* For example, according to Exodus 20:16, God commands us to be truthful. On this option, the reason we should be truthful is simply that God requires it. Apart from the divine command, truth telling is neither good nor bad. It is God's command that makes truthfulness right.

But this leads to trouble,[1] for[A] it represents God's commands as arbitrary.[2] It means that[B] God could have given different commands just as easily.[3] He could have commanded us to be liars, and then lying, not truthfulness, would be right. (You may be tempted to reply: "But God would never command us to lie." But why not? If he did endorse lying, God would not be commanding us to do wrong, because his command would make it right.) Remember that[C] on this view, honesty was not right before God commanded it.[4] Therefore,[D] he could have had no more reason to command it than its opposite;[5] and so,[E] from a moral point of view, his command is arbitrary.[6]

Another problem is that,[F] on this view, the doctrine of the goodness of God is reduced to nonsense.[7] It is important to religious believers that God is not only all-powerful and all-knowing, but that he is also good;[8] yet[G] if we accept the idea that good and bad are defined by reference to God's will, this notion is deprived of any meaning.[9] What could it mean to say that God's commands are good? If "X is good" means "X is commanded by God" then "God's commands are good" would mean only "God's commands are commanded by God,"[10] an empty truism.[11] ...

Thus[H] if we choose the first of Socrates' two options, we seem to be stuck with consequences that even the most religious people would find unacceptable.[12]

At the beginning of this section, Rachels observes that, of course, atheists will not accept divine command theory. What he wants to show, though, is that theists (religious people) should not accept it either. The reason is that no matter how we interpret the theory, theists have to accept beliefs that are contrary to their religious beliefs.

First Rachels considers the consequences if we interpret divine command theory as meaning that "right conduct is right because God commands it." His first claim is that is interpretation leads to trouble (1), and as indicated by (A), the reason is that this interpretation means that God's commands are arbitrary (2). And, as indicated by (B), the reason that God's commands would be arbitrary is that God could have given different commands from the ones that he did (3):

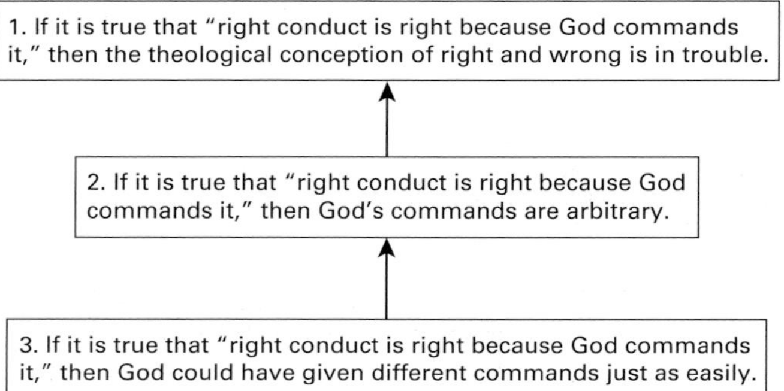
1. If it is true that "right conduct is right because God commands it," then the theological conception of right and wrong is in trouble.
2. If it is true that "right conduct is right because God commands it," then God's commands are arbitrary.
3. If it is true that "right conduct is right because God commands it," then God could have given different commands just as easily.

The reasons Rachels gives for this last claim are that, first, on this interpretation, principles like "Be honest" were not morally correct (or morally incorrect for that matter) before God commanded us to be honest (4), which supports the claim that, on this interpretation, God did not have any reason to command us to be honest rather than commanding us to be dishonest (5).

So, he concludes, on this interpretation, God's commands are arbitrary (6)—which is a restatement of (2):

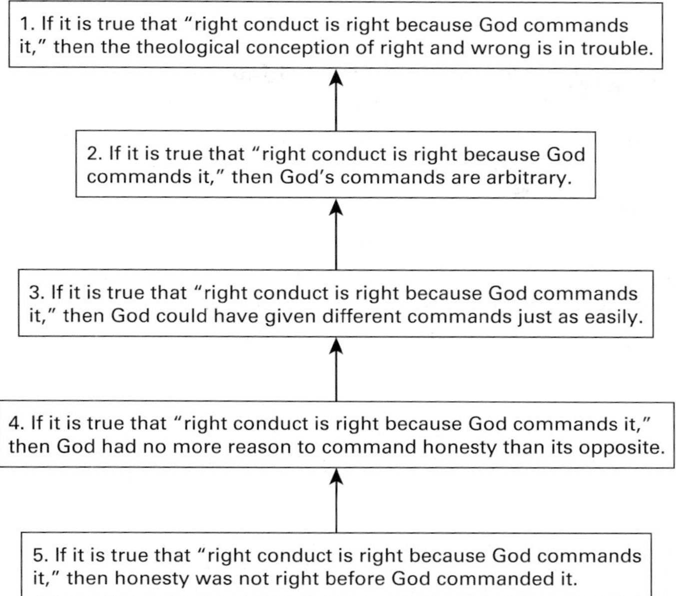
1. If it is true that "right conduct is right because God commands it," then the theological conception of right and wrong is in trouble.
2. If it is true that "right conduct is right because God commands it," then God's commands are arbitrary.
3. If it is true that "right conduct is right because God commands it," then God could have given different commands just as easily.
4. If it is true that "right conduct is right because God commands it," then God had no more reason to command honesty than its opposite.
5. If it is true that "right conduct is right because God commands it," then honesty was not right before God commanded it.

Rachels then offers a second line of reasoning to support claim (1), namely that on this interpretation, "God is good" is nonsense (7). To support this, Rachels says that the doctrine of God's goodness is just as important as the doctrines of his omnipotence and omniscience (8). Here, it seems the best way to interpret what Rachels means by "important" is that if the statement that "God is all good, that is, God's commands are always good" is not meaningful, then the doctrine of God's goodness is nonsense. So, the reason for (7) is, as indicated by (G), both (8) *and* if good and bad are defined by what God wills, then the claim "Good is all good" has no meaning (9). The claim would have no meaning because if "X is good" means that "X is commanded by God," then "God's commands are good would mean only "God's commands are God's commands" (10), and this is obviously but trivially true (11).

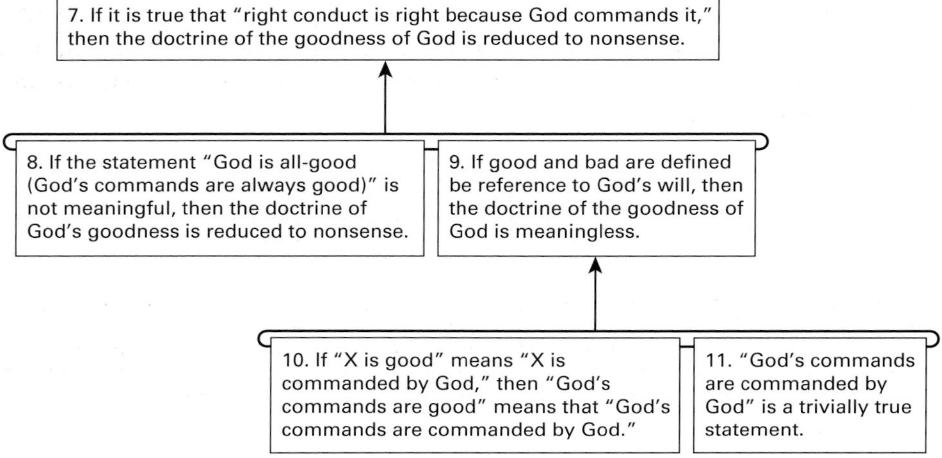
7. If it is true that "right conduct is right because God commands it," then the doctrine of the goodness of God is reduced to nonsense.
8. If the statement "God is all-good (God's commands are always good)" is not meaningful, then the doctrine of God's goodness is reduced to nonsense.
9. If good and bad are defined be reference to God's will, then the doctrine of the goodness of God is meaningless.
10. If "X is good" means "X is commanded by God," then "God's commands are good" means that "God's commands are commanded by God."
11. "God's commands are commanded by God" is a trivially true statement.

Then, as indicated by (H), all of this leads to the same conclusion: that on this first interpretation, we have unacceptable consequences (12), which is a more explicit statement of (1):

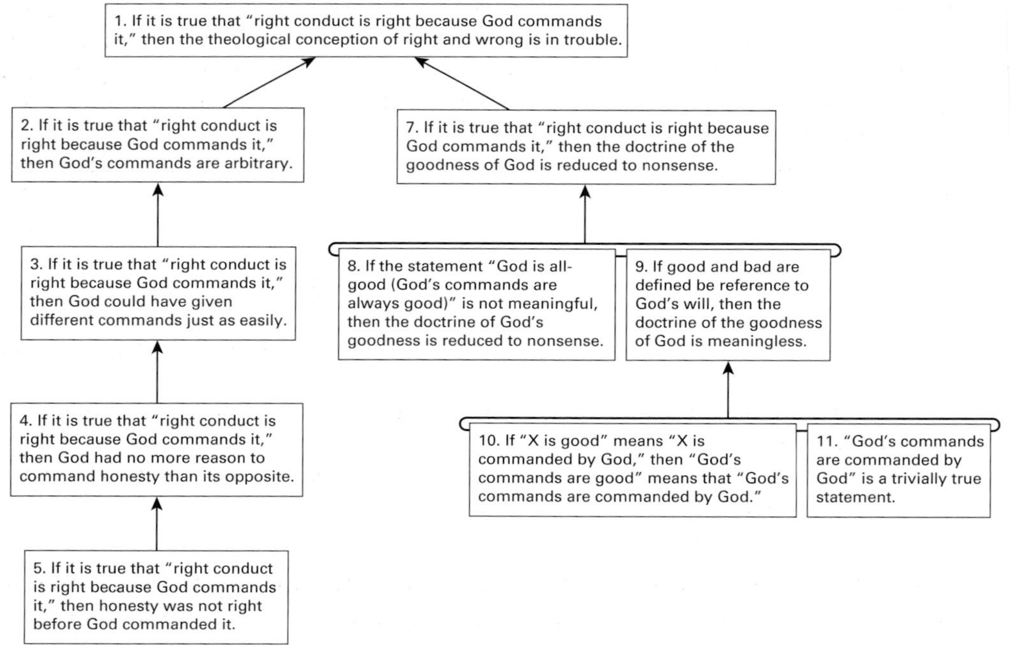
1. If it is true that "right conduct is right because God commands it," then the theological conception of right and wrong is in trouble.
2. If it is true that "right conduct is right because God commands it," then God's commands are arbitrary.
7. If it is true that "right conduct is right because God commands it," then the doctrine of the goodness of God is reduced to nonsense.
3. If it is true that "right conduct is right because God commands it," then God could have given different commands just as easily.
8. If the statement "God is all-good (God's commands are always good)" is not meaningful, then the doctrine of God's goodness is reduced to nonsense.
9. If good and bad are defined be reference to God's will, then the doctrine of the goodness of God is meaningless.
4. If it is true that "right conduct is right because God commands it," then God had no more reason to command honesty than its opposite.
10. If "X is good" means "X is commanded by God," then "God's commands are good" means that "God's commands are commanded by God."
11. "God's commands are commanded by God" is a trivially true statement.
5. If it is true that "right conduct is right because God commands it," then honesty was not right before God commanded it.

So, the general argument looks like this: On this first interpretation, God's commands are arbitrary (2), but religious people believe that God's commands are not arbitrary (implicit). Thus, this first interpretation leads to unacceptable consequences for the devout (12). Additionally, on this first interpretation, the doctrine of God's goodness is meaningless (7), but religious people believe that the doctrine of God's goodness is meaningful (8), and so, presumably, not nonsense. Thus, we have a second reason to believe that the devout would find the first interpretation unacceptable:

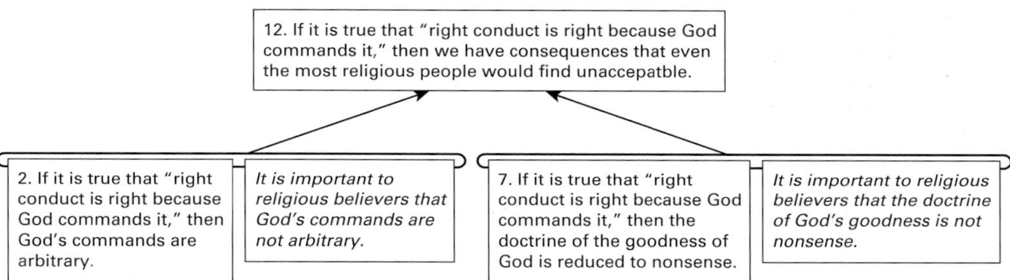
12. If it is true that "right conduct is right because God commands it," then we have consequences that even the most religious people would find unaccepatble.
2. If it is true that "right conduct is right because God commands it," then God's commands are arbitrary.
It is important to religious believers that God's commands are not arbitrary.
7. If it is true that "right conduct is right because God commands it," then the doctrine of the goodness of God is reduced to nonsense.
It is important to religious believers that the doctrine of God's goodness is not nonsense.

2. There is a way to avoid theses troublesome consequences. We can take the second of Socrates' options. We need not say that right conduct is right because God commands it. Instead, we may say that **God commands us to do certain things *because they are right*.** God, who is infinitely wise, realizes that truthfulness is better than deceitfulness, and so he commands us to be truthful; he sees that killing is wrong, and so he commands us not to kill; and so on for all the moral rules. If we take this option, we avoid the troublesome consequences that spoiled the first alternative. God's commands are not arbitrary; they are the result of his wisdom in knowing what is best. And the doctrine of the goodness of God is preserved: To say that his commands are good means that he commands only what, in his perfect wisdom, he sees to be best.

Unfortunately, however, this second option leads to a different problem,[13] which is equally troublesome. In taking this option, we have abandoned the theological conception of right and wrong[14]—when we say that God commands us to be truthful because truthfulness is right, we are acknowledging a standard of right and wrong that is independent of God's will.[15] The rightness exists prior to and independent of God's command, and it is the reason for the command.[16] Thus, if we want to know why we should be truthful, the reply "Because God commands it" does not really tell us, for we may still ask "But why does God command it?" and the answer to *that* question will provide the underlying reason why truthfulness is a good thing. ...

Many religious people believe that they must accept a theological conception of right and wrong because it would be impious not to do so. They feel, somehow, that if they believe in God, they should say that right and wrong are to be defined in terms of his will.[17] But this argument suggests otherwise: It suggests that,[I] on the contrary, the Divine Command Theory itself leads to impious results,[18] so that[J] a devout person should not accept it. ...

What about this second interpretation? Rachels says this leads to trouble as well (13). The reason is that, on this interpretation, we are no longer subscribing to the theological conception of right and wrong (14)—the idea that what is right is what God commands. The reason we are abandoning this notion is that, on this interpretation, if God commands an action because that action is right, then there is a standard of right and wrong independent of what God commands (15). And the reason for this is that, if God commands an action because it is right, then the "rightness" of the action exists before God issues the command (16).

As the example that follows (16) shows, if God commands honesty because honesty is right, then God is merely a messenger telling us that honesty is right. So, God, because of his omniscience, knows perfectly what is right and what is wrong. But, God's command does not cause honesty to be right—God is just passing along the information.

The theological conception is that what is right and wrong depends on God's will. But, on this second interpretation, what is right and wrong is independent of God's will. So, on this interpretation, we are abandoning the theological conception (14):

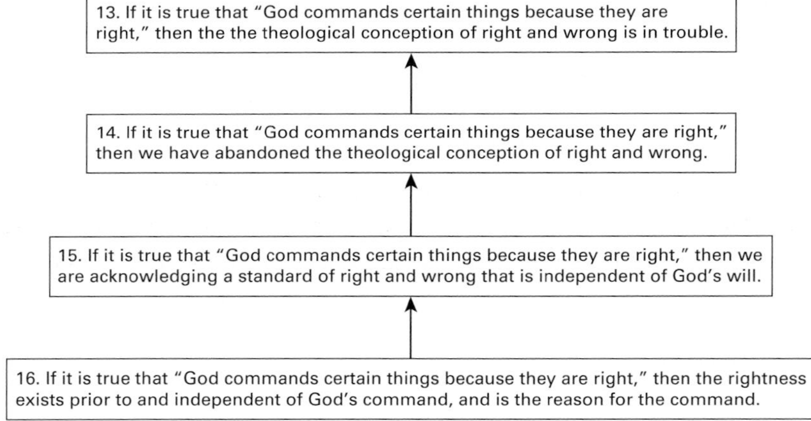

But, as Socrates indicates, it is important for the devout to subscribe to the theological conception of right and wrong (17). If we combine this with (15), we are led to the conclusion that this second interpretation of divine command theory leads to impiety (18):

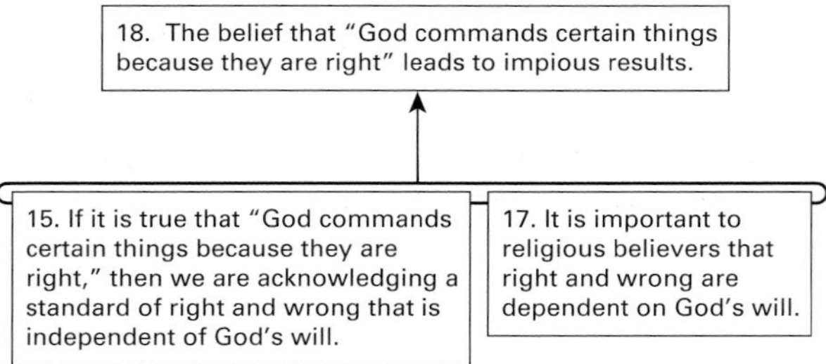

This, then leads to the final conclusion that a devout person should not accept divine command theory. So the whole argument Socrates presents is that both ways of interpreting divine command theory lead to conclusions that a devout person would find unacceptable:

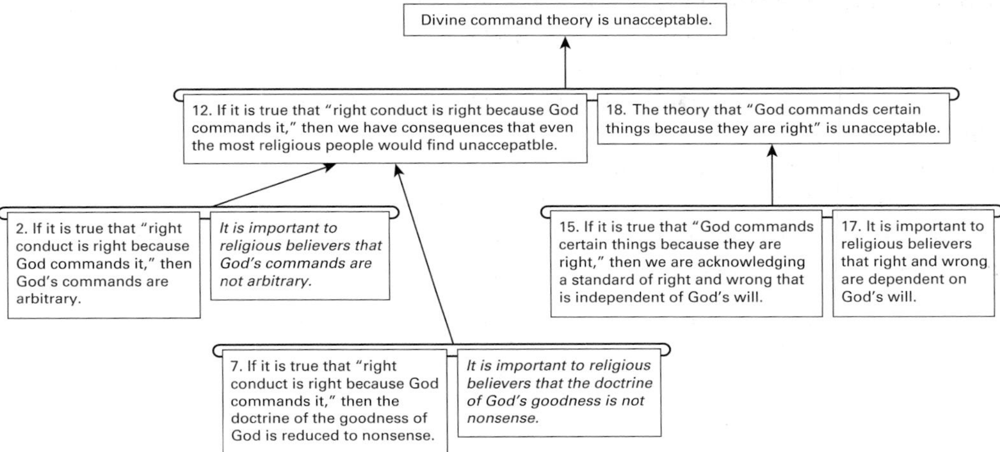
Divine command theory is unacceptable.
12. If it is true that "right conduct is right because God commands it," then we have consequences that even the most religious people would find unaccepatble.
18. The theory that "God commands certain things because they are right" is unacceptable.
2. If it is true that "right conduct is right because God commands it," then God's commands are arbitrary.
It is important to religious believers that God's commands are not arbitrary.
15. If it is true that "God commands certain things because they are right," then we are acknowledging a standard of right and wrong that is independent of God's will.
17. It is important to religious believers that right and wrong are dependent on God's will.
7. If it is true that "right conduct is right because God commands it," then the doctrine of the goodness of God is reduced to nonsense.
It is important to religious believers that the doctrine of God's goodness is not nonsense.

Ultimately, Rachels comes to the same conclusion as Plato—that divine command theory does not make sense, even (or especially) for a devout religious person. So where do we turn? Another popular option, especially among college students, has been cultural relativism. It is this theory to which we turn next.

17.3 In-Class Exercises

An asterisk (*) indicates a more challenging exercise.

Exercises 1–2

In the first part of this chapter, we analyzed in detail an argument given by Plato in *Euthyphro*. The following selections contain another argument from this dialogue. Euthyphro has just told Socrates that what is pious is what is loved by the gods, and Socrates challenges this definition of piety:

Socrates: Come then, let us examine what we mean. An action or a man dear to the gods is pious, but an action or a man hated by the gods is impious. They are not the same, but quite opposite, the pious and the impious. Is that not so? …

Euthyphro: I think so, Socrates.

For each selection, (a) diagram the argument and (b) identify any potential objections to the argument.

Exercise 1

Socrates: We have also stated that the gods are in a state of discord, that they are at odds with each other, Euthyphro, and that they are at enmity with each other. Has that, too, been said?

Euthyphro: It has.

Socrates: What are the subjects of difference that cause hatred and anger? Let us look at it this way. If you and I were to differ about numbers as to which is the greater, would this difference make us enemies and angry with each other, or would we proceed to count and soon resolve our difference about this?

Euthyphro: We would certainly do so.

Socrates: Again, if we differed about the larger and the smaller, we would turn to measurement and soon cease to differ.

Euthyphro: That is so.

Socrates: And about the heavier and the lighter, we would resort to weighing and be reconciled.

Euthyphro: Of course.

Socrates: What subject of difference would make us angry and hostile to each other if we were unable to come to a decision? Perhaps you do not have an answer ready, but examine as I tell you whether these subjects are the just and the unjust, the beautiful and the ugly, the good and the bad. Are these not the subjects of difference about which, when we are unable to come to a satisfactory decision, you and I and other men become hostile to each other whenever we do?

Euthyphro: That is the difference, Socrates, about those subjects.

Socrates: What about the gods, Euthyphro? If indeed they have differences, will it not be about these same subjects?

Euthyphro: It certainly must be so.

Socrates: Then according to your argument, my good Euthyphro, different gods consider different things to be just, beautiful, ugly, good, and bad, for they would not be at odds with one another unless they differed about these subjects, would they?

Euthyphro: You are right.

**Exercise 2:*

Socrates: And they like what each of them considers beautiful, good, and just, and hate the opposites of these?

Euthyphro: Certainly.

Socrates: But you say that the same things are considered just by some gods and unjust by others, and as they dispute about these things they are at odds and at war with each other. Is that not so?

Euthyphro: It is.

Socrates: The same things then are loved by the gods and hated by the gods, and would be both god-loved and god-hated.

Euthyphro: It seems likely.

Socrates: And the same things would be both pious and impious, according to this argument?

Euthyphro: I'm afraid so.

Socrates: So you did not answer my question, you surprising man. I did not ask you what same thing is both pious and impious, and it appears that what is loved by the gods is also hated by them. So it is in no way surprising if your present action, namely punishing your father, may be pleasing to Zeus but displeasing to Kronos and Ouranos, pleasing Hephaestus but displeasing to Hera, and so with any other gods who differ from each other on this subject.

Exercises 3–5

In the second section of this chapter, we analyzed in detail an argument Rachels gives in "Does Morality Depend on Religion?" Exercise 3 contains a summary of the second path of the argument that the devout should not accept divine command theory. Exercises 4 and 5 contain additional arguments Rachels makes against divine command theory in a different edition of his book.[3] For each selection, (a) diagram the argument and (b) identify any potential objections to the argument.

**Exercise 3*

All this may be summarized in the following argument:

1. Suppose God commands us to do what is right. Then either (a) the right actions are right because he commands them or (b) he commands them because they are right.
2. If we take option (a), the God's commands are, from a moral point of view, arbitrary; moreover, the doctrine of the goodness of God is rendered meaningless.
3. If we take option (b), then we will have acknowledged a standard of right and wrong that is independent of God's will. We will have, in effect, given up the theological conception of right and wrong.
4. Therefore, we must either regard God's commands as arbitrary, and give up the doctrine of the goodness of God, or admit that there is a standard of right and wrong that is independent of his will, and give up the theological conception of right and wrong.
5. From a religious point of view, it is unacceptable to regard God's commands as arbitrary or to give up the doctrine of the goodness of God.
6. Therefore, even from a religious point of view, a standard of right and wrong that is independent of God's will must be accepted.

Exercise 4

This idea encounters several difficulties.

1. *This conception of morality is mysterious*. What does it mean to say that God "makes" truthfulness right? It is easy enough to understand how physical objects are made, at least in principle. We have all made something, if only a sand castle or a peanut-butter-and-jelly sandwich. But making truthfulness is not like that; it could not be done by rearranging things in the physical environment. How, then, could it be done? No one knows.

To see this problem, consider some wretched case of child abuse. On the theory we are now considering, God could make *that* instance of child abuse right—not by turning a slap into a friendly pinch of the cheek, but *by commanding that the slap is right*. This proposal defies human understanding. How could merely saying, or commanding, that the slap is right make it right? If true, this conception of morality would be a mystery.

Exercise 5

3. *This conception of morality provides the wrong reasons for moral principles.* There are many things wrong with child abuse: It is malicious; it involves the unnecessary infliction of pain; it can have unwanted long-term psychological effects; and so on. However, the theory we're now considering cannot recognize any of these reasons as important. All it cares about, in the end, is whether child abuse runs counter to God's commands.

There are two ways of confirming that something is wrong here. First, notice something that the theory implies: *If God didn't exist, child abuse wouldn't be wrong.* After all, if God didn't exist, then God wouldn't be around to make child abuse wrong. However, child abuse would still be malicious, so it would still be wrong. Thus, the Divine Command Theory fails. Second, keep in mind that even a religious person might be genuinely in doubt as to what God has commanded. After all, religious texts disagree with each other, and sometimes there seem to be inconsistencies even within a single text. So a person might be in doubt as to what God's will really is. However, a person needn't be in doubt as to whether child abuse is wrong. What God has commanded is one thing; whether hitting children is wrong is another.

Exercises 6–9

The following exercises are intended to ensure your understanding of Plato's and Rachels's texts, and to help you further explore the ideas presented in this chapter.

Exercise 6: Now that you have read my textual analysis of Plato's argument, summarize it in your own words.
Exercise 7: Summarize, in your own words, each of the arguments in exercises 1 and 2 above.
Exercise 8: Now that you have read my textual analysis of Rachels's argument, summarize it in your own words.
Exercise 9: Summarize, in your own words, each of the arguments in exercises 3–5 above.

17.4 Reading Questions

1. In Plato's dialogue, what is the case that Euthyphro is prosecuting? Why would people think it is crazy for him to prosecute it? Why does he do it anyway?
2. Why, according to Rachels, are we generally not surprised when members of the clergy are invited to be ethics advisors? Do you agree that members of the clergy should always be included on ethics advisory boards? Why or why not?
3. What, according to Rachels, is divine command theory? How is his version similar to or different from Plato's version? Were you ever taught a version of divine command theory when you were growing up? If so, how is your version similar to or different from Rachels's and Plato's versions?
4. Rachels claims there are only two ways to interpret the "theological conception of right and wrong." Do you agree, or could there be another way to interpret it? If so, what would that be? If not, why not?
5. What is the theory of natural law? Is this a form of subjectivism, conventionalism, or realism? Justify your answer.

18 Meta-ethics: Relativism

18.1 Ruth Benedict, "Anthropology and the Abnormal"
18.2 James Rachels, "The Challenge of Cultural Relativism"
18.3 In-Class Exercises
18.4 Reading Questions

18.1 Ruth Benedict, "Anthropology and the Abnormal"

Ruth Benedict (1887–1948) was born in New York and graduated from Vassar in 1909. Ten years later, she entered graduate school at Columbia and received her PhD in anthropology in 1923. After graduation, she joined the faculty at Columbia, where she stayed until her untimely death.

Benedict studied and wrote extensively about Native American cultures. She published three major books in the 1930s: *Tales of the Cochiti Indians* (1931), *Zuñi Mythology* (1935), and *Patterns of Culture* (1934). In these works, she compares the practices of seven different tribes, and she argues that we actually see only a small number of different practices across different societies. That is, there seems to be a wide variation, but it's not as varied as we may have thought.

In particular, she was interested in what constitutes "abnormal" behavior in different cultures. For nearly any behavior that is seen as abnormal in one culture, another culture considers that same behavior to be normal. Her conclusion is that morality is defined by culture—"morally right" is equivalent to "normal," and "morally wrong" is equivalent to "abnormal." Thus, what is morally right and morally wrong varies across cultures, and no culture can claim that it has the objectively correct practices, because there are no objectively correct practices.

Ultimately, Benedict is a cultural relativist about morality. She believes that, since what is considered morally correct varies by culture, there is no objective fact of the matter about what is morally correct. If it is morally correct in your society to bury people who die, then if you are a member of that society, there is a fact about what you should do when your father dies. But it's not an *objective* fact—it's a "fact" only relative to your society. Thus, if you were to move to a new society, there might be different facts about what you should do with your father's body.

The following selection is an excerpt from Benedict's article "Anthropology and the Abnormal," which was published in 1934 in the *Journal of General Psychology*. In this section, Benedict's argument is going to be presented in a different way than previous authors'. In the first part of the article, Benedict presents several cases that show how what is "abnormal" varies from culture to culture. Her argument, at the end of the article, depends on her inferences from these cases. Let's look at Benedict's text in more detail. Specifically, we will turn to the last part of the article, which contains Benedict's argument. We will analyze and diagram the argument, but save criticisms of it for the section that follows.

From "Anthropology and the Abnormal."[1]

These illustrations, which it has been possible to indicate only in the briefest manner, force upon us the fact that normality is culturally defined.[1] An adult shaped to the drives and standards of either of these cultures, if he were transported into our civilization, would fall into our categories of abnormality. He would be faced with the psychic dilemmas of the socially unavailable. In his own culture, however, he is the pillar of society, the end result of socially inculcated mores, and the problem of personal instability in his case simply does not arise.

No one civilization can possibly utilize in its mores the whole potential range of human behavior. Just as there are great numbers of possible phonetic articulations, and the possibility of language depends on a selection and standardization of a few of these in order that speech communication may be possible at all, so the possibility of organized behavior of every sort, from the fashions of local dress and houses to the dicta of a people's ethics and religion, depends upon a similar selection among the possible behavior traits.[2] In the field of recognized economic obligations or sex taboos this selection is as nonrational and subconscious a process as it is in the field of phonetics.[3] It is a process which goes on in the group for long periods of time and is historically conditioned by innumerable accidents of isolation or of contact of peoples. In any comprehensive study of psychology, the selection that different cultures have made in the course of history within the great circumference of potential behavior is of great significance.

Every society, beginning with some slight inclination in one direction or another, carries its preference farther and farther, integrating itself more and more completely upon its chosen basis, and discarding those types of behavior that are uncongenial. Most of those organizations of personality that seem to us most uncontrovertibly abnormal have been used by different civilizations in the very foundations of their institutional life.[4] Conversely the most valued traits of our normal individuals have been looked on in differently organized cultures as aberrant.[5] Normality, in short, within a very wide range, is culturally defined.[6] It is primarily a term for the socially elaborated segment of human behavior in any culture; and abnormality, a term for the segment that that particular civilization does not use. The very eyes with which we see the problem are conditioned by the long traditional habits of our own society.

It is a point that has been made more often in relation to ethics than in relation to psychiatry. We do not any longer make the mistake of deriving the morality of our locality and decade directly from the inevitable constitution of human nature.[7] We do not elevate it to the dignity of a first principle. We recognize that morality differs in every society,[8] and is a convenient term for socially approved habits.[9] Mankind has always preferred to say, "It is a moral good," rather than "It is habitual," and the fact of this preference is matter enough for a critical science of ethics. But historically the two phrases are synonymous.[10]

The concept of the normal is properly a variant of the concept of the good.[11] It is that which society has approved.[12] A normal action is one which falls well within the limits of expected behavior for a particular society. Its variability among different peoples is essentially a function of the variability of the behavior patterns that different societies have created for themselves, and can never be wholly divorced from a consideration of culturally institutionalized types of behavior.

After presenting these various cases, Benedict concludes that normality is culturally defined (1). We'll set this claim aside for now.

She then explains the general point of the previous cases—that what is abnormal in our society may be considered perfectly normal in another society. Then, she points out that, as a matter of practical fact, only a portion of possible human behaviors can make up the behaviors that are considered normal in a society. Society selects and standardizes behaviors so it can function (2).

In addition, Benedict explains that society's members don't hold a big meeting to determine these standards. Rather, society and its mores evolve over time. So the standards are not selected by a conscious and rational process (3). The implicit conclusion here, from combining (2) and (3), is that normality is not determined by a conscious and rational process:

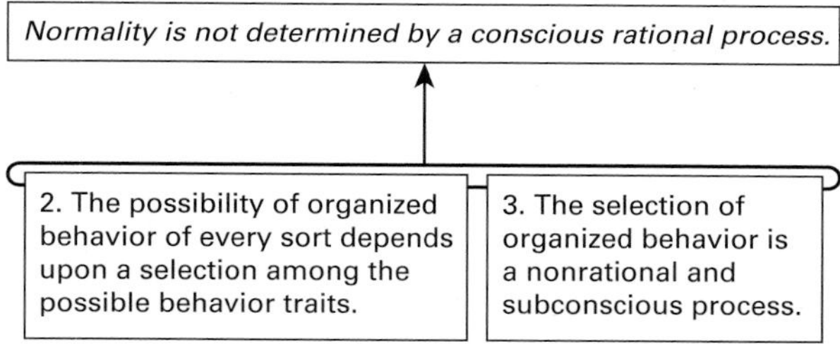

Benedict then summarizes her argument that normality is culturally defined (1). She reiterates the point of the illustrations that many behaviors that our society deems abnormal are considered normal and even respectable in other cultures (4), while behaviors that we consider normal in our culture are regarded as abnormal in others (5). So, normality is culturally defined (6), which is a restatement of (1):

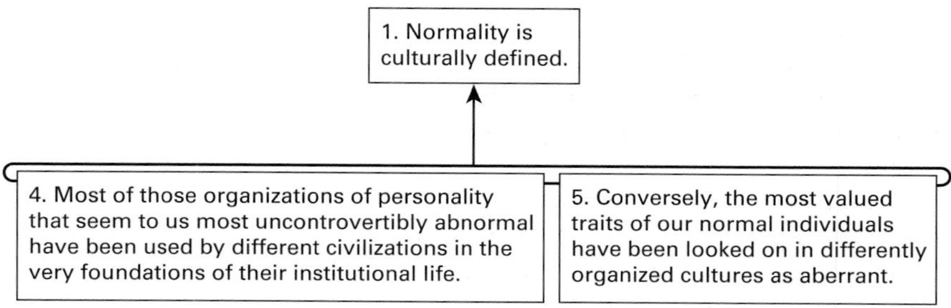

Then Benedict claims that just as "normal" differs by society, "morally correct" differs by society (7), and "morality" is synonymous with "normality" (8). She repeats this second claim in both (9) and (10). How do these relate to the argument above? Further on, Benedict says that "normal" just is what society has approved (11), so what society has approved is culturally defined:

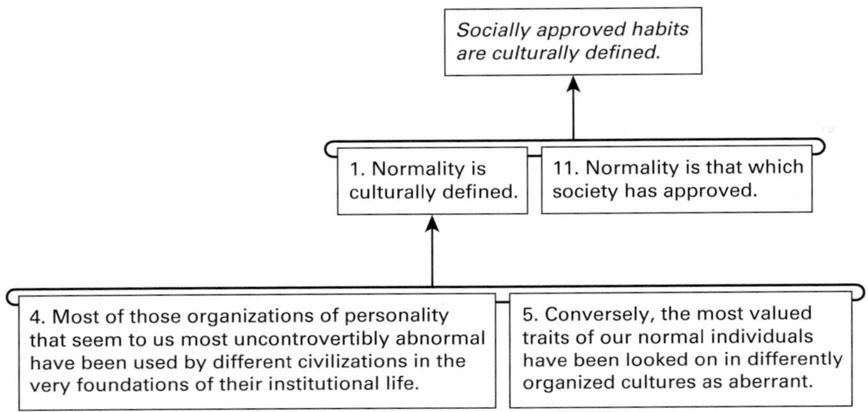

Now that we have the subconclusion that socially approved habits are culturally defined, we can combine this with (8), to support (7):

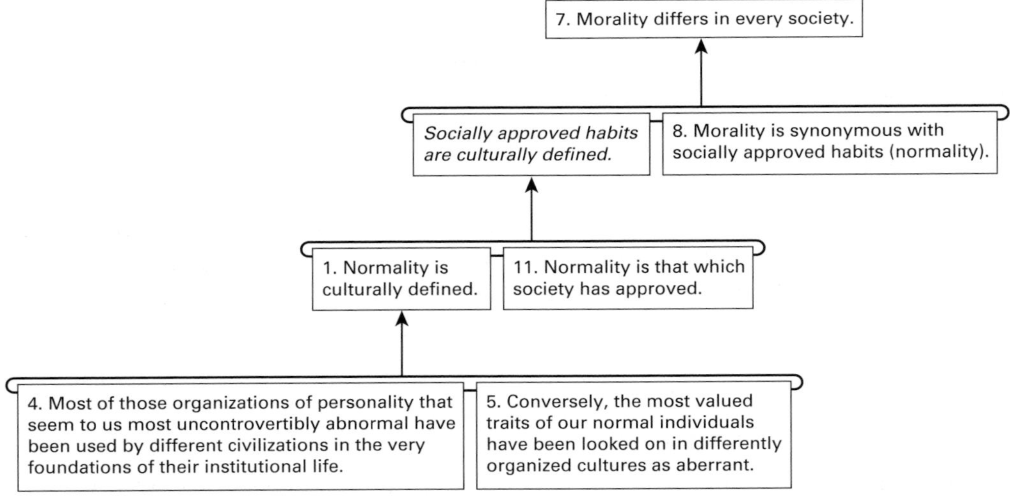

If we go back to the first subargument we discussed, we can see that its subconclusion can be combined with the subconclusion above to support Benedict's main (but implicit) conclusion that there are no objective moral facts. Then the whole argument can be represented as follows:

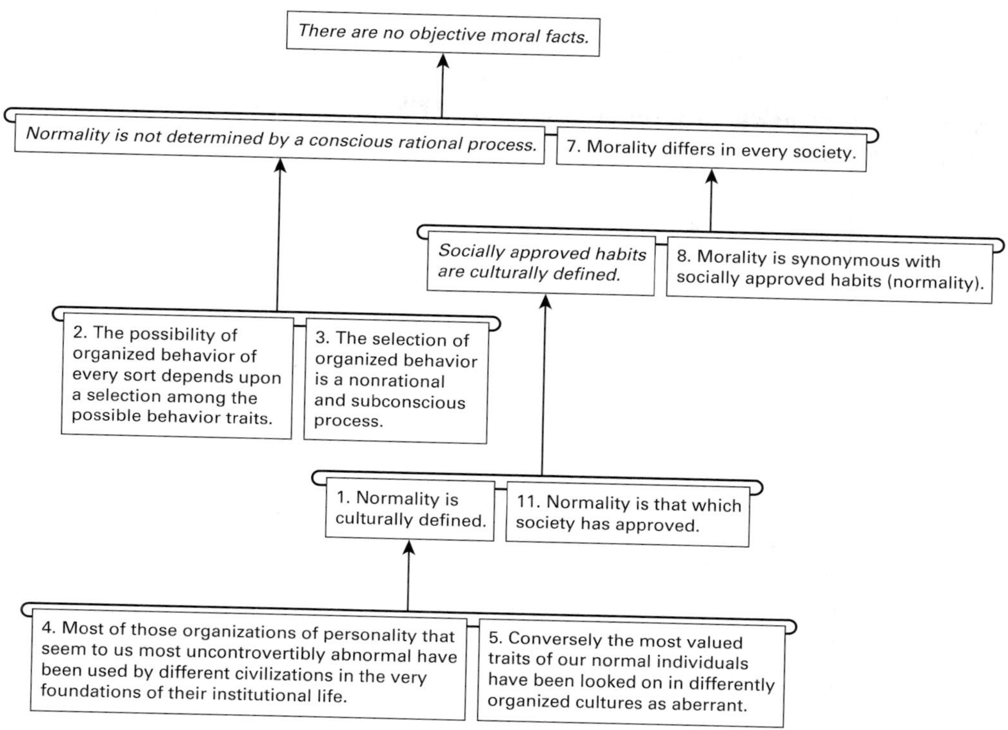

In the next section, we will consider a criticism of this argument, as well as a discussion of the pros and cons of cultural relativism.

18.2 James Rachels, "The Challenge of Cultural Relativism"

Recall that we read a chapter from Rachels's book, *The Elements of Moral Philosophy*, in the previous chapter. Here, we draw again from this book. Below is an excerpt from chapter 2, "The Challenge of Cultural Relativism." First, Rachels gives us two cases, just as Benedict did above, and then he presents his argument. Let's analyze this argument closely.

From *The Elements of Moral Philosophy*.[2]

2.3 The Cultural Differences Argument

Cultural Relativists often employ a certain *form of argument*. They begin with facts about cultures and end up drawing a conclusion about morality. Thus, they invite us to accept this reasoning:

(1) The Greeks believed it was wrong to eat the dead, whereas the Callatians believed it was right to eat the dead.

(2) Therefore, eating the dead is neither objectively right nor objectively wrong. It is merely a matter of opinion, which varies from culture to culture.

Or:

(1) The Eskimos see nothing wrong with infanticide, whereas Americans believe infanticide is immoral.

(2) Therefore, infanticide is neither objectively right nor objectively wrong. It is merely a matter of opinion, which varies from culture to culture.

Clearly, these arguments are variations of one fundamental idea. They are both special cases of a more general argument, which says:

(1) Different cultures have different moral codes.

(2) Therefore, there is no objective "truth" in morality. Right and wrong are only matters of opinion, and opinions vary from culture to culture.

We may call this the Cultural Differences Argument. To many people, it is persuasive. But is it a good argument—is it *sound*?

It is not.[1] For an argument to be sound, its premises must all be true, and the conclusion must follow logically from them. Here, the problem is that[A] the conclusion does not *follow from* the premise[2]—that is, even if the premise is true, the conclusion might still be false. The premise concerns what people *believe*[3]—in some societies, people believe one thing; in other societies, people believe differently. The conclusion, however,[B] concerns *what really is the case*.[4] This sort of conclusion does not follow logically from this sort of premise.[5] In philosophical terms, this means that the argument is invalid [and so unsound—see chapter 2].

Consider again the example of the Greeks and Callatians. The Greeks believed it was wrong to eat the dead; the Callatians believed it was right. Does it follow, from the mere fact that they disagreed, that there is no objective truth in the matter? No, it does not follow; for it could be that the practice was objectively right (or wrong) and that one or the other of them was simply mistaken.

To make the point clearer, consider a different matter. In some societies, people believe the earth is flat. In other societies, such as our own, people believe the earth is a sphere. Does it follow, *from the mere fact that they disagree*, that there is no "objective truth" in geography? Of course not; we would never draw such a conclusion because we realize that[D] the members of some societies might simply be wrong.[6] There is no reason to think that if the world is round everyone must know it.[7] Similarly,[E] there is no reason to think that if there is moral truth everyone must know it.[8] The Cultural Differences Argument tries to derive a substantive conclusion about a subject from the mere fact that people disagree about it. But this is impossible.[9]

This point should not be misunderstood. We are not saying that the conclusion of the argument is false; for all we have said, Cultural Relativism could still be true. The point is that the conclusion does not follow from the premise.[10] This is important, because in order to determine whether the conclusion is true, we need arguments in its support. This means that the Cultural Differences Argument is invalid.[11] Thus the argument fails.

The third set of sentences above are claims that are made in the argument that Rachels is criticizing; we want to diagram this argument, but we don't want to make the mistake of attributing claims to Rachels that he does not actually assert.

The argument that Rachels is criticizing, the cultural differences argument, can be represented like this:

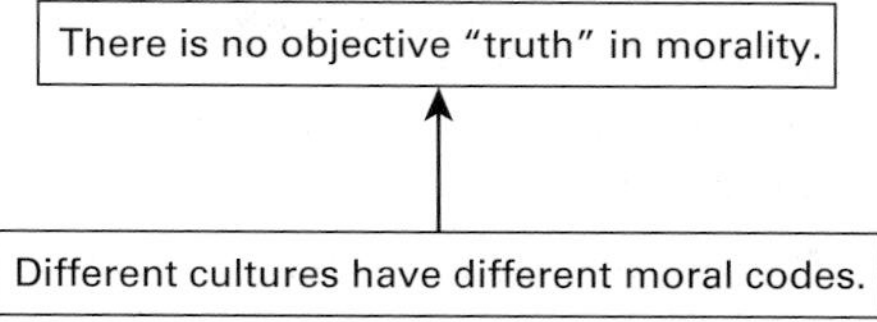

Rachels's argument is that cultural relativism is not plausible. The reason is that the cultural differences argument is not sound (1). Recall that an argument can be unsound in two ways: the premise is false and/or the conclusion does not follow from the premise. The reason that Rachels gives, as indicated by (A), is the latter (2):

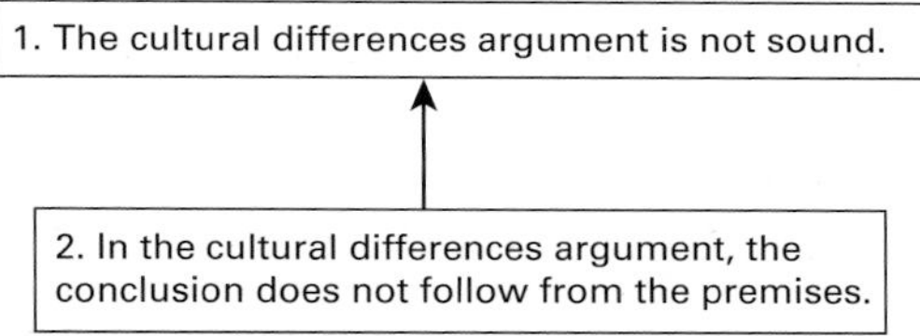

Rachels then explains why the premises don't support the conclusion. First, the premise concerns what people believe (3), and the conclusion concerns what really is the case (4). Second, Rachels claims that a conclusion of this sort does not follow from a premise of this sort. As indicated by (B) and (C), these two claims combine with (5) to support (2).

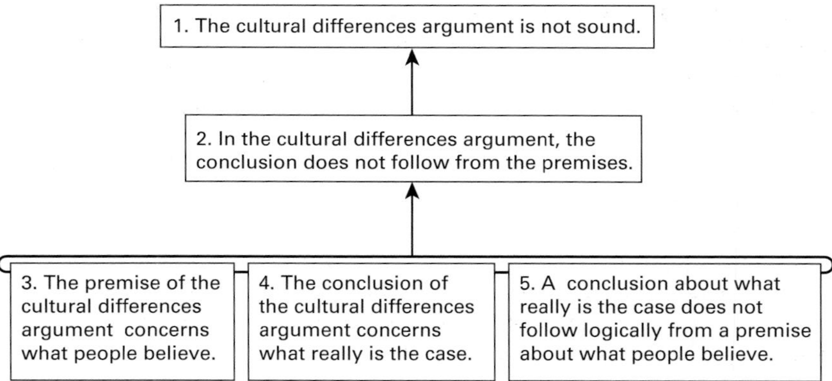

To support (5) Rachels first gives some examples and then draws a general lesson from them, as indicated by (D). First, members of some societies might be wrong about their beliefs about the world (i.e., their physical beliefs) (6). And there is no reason to think that if there is a physical fact, everyone must know it (7).

This is actually an argument by analogy, as indicated by (E), and it contains an implicit claim that it could be the case that moral truths are like physical truths this way. So, (6) and (7) combine with this implicit premise to support the claim that there is no reason to think that if there is a moral fact, everyone must know it (8).

Rachels restates his criticism in (9), which is essentially a restatement of (5), by saying that the mistake in the cultural differences argument is that a conclusion about independent moral facts is inferred from a premise about what people believe (9).

As Rachels reminds us at the end, this criticism of the cultural differences argument does not show that the conclusion of the argument is false, it merely shows that the conclusion doesn't follow from the premise (10), which a restatement of (2). This makes the cultural differences argument invalid (and so unsound) (11), which is a restatement of (1).

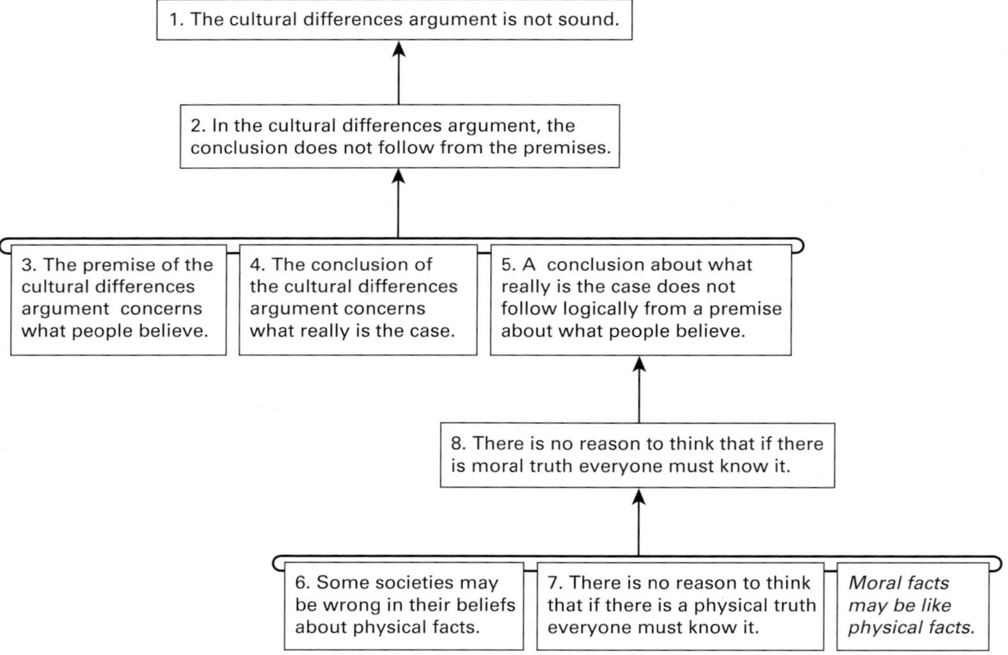

Here, Rachels has simply shown that the conclusion of the argument does not follow. To show that the conclusion of the cultural differences argument about independent moral facts is in fact false, Rachels shows that the conclusion has unacceptable consequences. These arguments are explored in the exercises below.

For the reasons given by Plato and Rachels in this and the previous chapters, most—but not all—moral philosophers have been moral realists. That is, they believe that just as there are physical facts about the world, and science was created to discover them, there are moral facts about the world, and moral philosophy was created to discover them. How do we discover them? This is the topic to which we turn in the next chapter.

18.3 In-Class Exercises

An asterisk (*) indicates a more challenging exercise.

Exercises 1–6

In the second section of this chapter, we analyzed in detail an argument Rachels gives in "The Challenge of Cultural Relativism." Rachels asks a question at the beginning of the next section of that article:

2.4 What Follows From Cultural Relativism

Even if the Cultural Differences Argument is unsound, Cultural Relativism might still be true. What would follow if it were true?

In the passage quoted earlier, William Graham Sumner states the essence of Cultural Relativism. He says that the only measure of right and wrong is the standards of one's society: "The notion of right is in the folkways. It is not outside of them, of independent origin, and brought to test them. In the folkways, whatever is, is right." Suppose we took this seriously. What would be some of the consequences?

The following selections contain other arguments from this article about what the consequences would be. For each selection, (a) diagram the argument and (b) identify any potential objections to the argument.

Exercise 1

1. *We could no longer say that the customs of other societies are morally inferior to our own.* This, of course, is one of the main points stressed by Cultural Relativism. We should never condemn a society merely because it is "different." This attitude seems enlightened, so long as we concentrate on examples like as the funerary practices of the Greeks and Callatians.

However, we would also be barred from criticizing other, less benign practices. For example, the Chinese government has a long history of repressing political dissent within its own borders. At any given time, thousands of political prisoners in China are doing hard labor, and in the Tiananmen Square episode of 1989, Chinese troops slaughtered hundreds, if not thousands, of peaceful protesters. Cultural Relativism would preclude us from saying that Chinese government's policies of oppression are wrong.

Exercise 2

We could not even say that a society that respects free speech is *better* than Chinese society, for that would also imply a universal standard of comparison. The failure to condemn *these* practices does not seem enlightened; on the contrary, political oppression seems wrong *wherever* it occurs. Nevertheless, if we accept Cultural Relativism, we have to regard such practices as immune from criticism.

Exercise 3

2. *We could no longer criticize the code of our own society.* Cultural Relativism suggests a simple test for determining what is right and what is wrong: All we need to do is ask whether the action is in accordance with the code of the society in question. Suppose a resident of India wonders whether her country's caste system—a system of rigid social hierarchy—is morally correct. All she has to do is ask whether this system conforms to her society's moral code. If it does, there is nothing to worry about, at least from a moral point of view.

This implication of Cultural Relativism is disturbing because few of us think that our society's code is perfect—we can think of ways it might be improved. Moreover, we can think of ways in which we might learn from other cultures. Yet Cultural Relativism stops us from criticizing our own society's codes, and it bars us from seeing ways in which other cultures might be better. After all, if right and wrong are relative to culture, this must be true for our own culture, just as it is for all other cultures.

**Exercise 4*

3. *The idea of moral progress is called into doubt.* We think that at least some social changes are for the better. Throughout most of Western history, the place of women in society was narrowly defined. Women could not own property; they could not vote or hold political office; and they were under the almost absolute control of their husbands or fathers. Recently much of this has changed, and most people think of it as progress.

But if Cultural Relativism is correct, can we legitimately think of this as progress? Progress means replacing the old ways with new and improved ways. But by what standard do we judge the new ways as better? If the old ways conformed to the social standards of *their* time, then Cultural Relativism would not judge them by *our* standards. Sexist 19th-century society was a different society from the one we now inhabit. To say that we have made progress implies that present-day society is better—just the sort of transcultural judgment that Cultural Relativism forbids.

**Exercise 5*

Our ideas about social *reform* will also have to be reconsidered. Reformers such as Martin Luther King Jr. have sought to change their societies for the better. But according to Cultural Relativism, there is one way to improve a society: to make it better match its own ideals. After all, the society's ideals are the standard by which reform is assessed. No one, however, may challenge the ideals themselves, for they are by definition correct. According to Cultural Relativism, then, the idea of social reform makes sense only in this limited way.

**Exercise 6*

These three consequences of Cultural Relativism have led many people to reject it. Slavery, we want to say, is wrong wherever it occurs, and one's own society can make fundamental moral progress. Because Cultural Relativism implies that these judgments make no sense, it cannot be right.

Exercises 7–9

The following exercises are intended to ensure your understanding of Benedict's and Rachels's texts, and to help you further explore the ideas presented in this chapter.

Exercise 7: Now that you have read my textual analysis of Benedict's argument, summarize it in your own words.

Exercise 8: Now that you have read my textual analysis of Rachels's argument, summarize it in your own words.

Exercise 9: Summarize, in your own words, each of the arguments in exercises 1–6 above.

18.4 Reading Questions

1. In the beginning of her article, Benedict comments on the "higher" cultures and the "simpler" cultures. Why does she use these terms? Do you think this would have been strange language to use in the 1930s (when she wrote her article)? Would it be strange now? Why or why not?
2. Benedict describes some people in her examples as "abnormals." Why does she use this term? What does she mean by it? Does her use of words like this (along with "higher" and "simpler" cultures) reinforce or undermine the point she is trying to make?
3. What are trance and catalepsy? How does Benedict use these practices to support her argument?
4. After giving several examples, Benedict claims that "normality is culturally defined." What does this mean? What role does this claim play in her argument?
5. According to Rachels, what might lead one to believe that there are no universal moral truths? What is his response to these reasons?
6. Formulate your own version of the cultural differences argument. What does Rachels think is wrong with this kind of argument?
7. What kinds of positions does Rachels think follow from cultural relativism? Why does he think these positions are untenable?
8. Recall the discussion of divine command theory from the previous chapter. Many people think divine command theory is a preferable theory to cultural relativism. Do you agree? Why or why not?
9. Suppose you came across a culture—some group of people basically isolated from the rest of the world—who believes that a baby that is born feet first is a demon, and so must be put to death. You observe a mother give birth to such a child, and the leader of the group is about to kill the baby. Assuming no harm would come to you or anyone else, should you intervene to prevent the killing? Why or why not?

19 Normative Ethics: Virtue Ethics, Egoism, and Contractarianism

19.1 Aristotle, *Nicomachean Ethics*
19.2 James Rachels, "Egoism and Moral Skepticism"
19.3 Thomas Hobbes, *Leviathan*
19.4 In-Class Exercises
19.5 Reading Questions

19.1 Aristotle, *Nicomachean Ethics*

Recall from chapter 1 that Aristotle (384–322 BC) was Plato's most famous student. In the following selection from *Nicomachean Ethics*, Aristotle ultimately argues that the activity of study is the highest good. To do this, he argues that happiness is the highest good and that complete happiness is the activity of study. He has two subarguments for the conclusion that happiness is the highest good, and a separate argument that complete happiness comes with the activity of study. The first subargument depends on the notion that happiness is the most complete goal.

But what does Aristotle mean by "complete"? Here, Aristotle is talking about the difference between *intrinsic value* and *instrumental value*. Recall the discussion of this distinction from the introduction to Part VI. For Aristotle, an end that has intrinsic value is more complete than an end that has merely instrumental value. Let's look at Aristotle's argument more closely.

From *Nicomachean Ethics*.[1]

Though apparently there are many ends, we choose some of them[1]—for instance, wealth, flutes and, in general, instruments because of something else; hence it is clear that[A] not all ends are complete.[2] But[B] the best good is apparently something complete.[3] Hence,[C] if only one end is complete, this will be what we are looking for; and if more than one are complete, the most complete of these will be what we are looking for.[4]

An end pursued in itself, we say, is more complete than an end pursued because of something else;[5] and[D] an end that is never choiceworthy because of something else is more complete than ends that are choiceworthy both in themselves and because of this end;[6] and hence[E] an end that is always [choiceworthy, and also] choiceworthy in itself, never because of something else, is complete without qualification.[7]

[So][F] happiness more than anything else seems complete without qualification,[8] since[G] we always [choose it, and also] choose it because of itself, never because of something else.[9]

Honor, pleasure, understanding and every virtue we certainly choose because of themselves, since we would choose each of them even if it had no further result; but we also choose them for the sake of happiness, supposing that through them we shall be happy. Happiness, by contrast, no one ever chooses for their sake, or for the sake of anything else at all.[10]

The same conclusion [that happiness is complete][11] also appears to follow from[H] self-sufficiency,[12] since[I] the complete good seems to be self-sufficient.[13] … we regard something as self-sufficient when all by itself it makes a life choiceworthy and lacking nothing;[14] and[J] that is what we think happiness does.[15]

Moreover,[K] we think happiness is most choiceworthy of all goods,[16] since[L] it is not counted as one good among many.[17] If it were counted as one among many, then, clearly, we think that the addition of the smallest of goods would make it more choiceworthy;[18] for[M] [the smallest good] that is added becomes an extra quantity of goods[19] [so creating a good larger than the original good], and[N] the larger of two goods is always more choiceworthy.[20] [But[O] we do not think any addition can make happiness more choiceworthy;[21] hence[P] it is most choiceworthy.][22] …

But presumably the remark that the best good is happiness is apparently something [generally] agreed, and what we miss is a clearer statement of what the best good is.

Aristotle presents two arguments that happiness is the highest good. It is important to note here that when Aristotle speaks of "ends" he means "goals," "aims," or "objectives." In (1), he acknowledges that a person may have many goals—someone may have wealth as one of her goals in life—and we choose some subset of them as more important. The fact that there are many goals that we don't choose supports, as indicated by (A), that not all of these goals are complete (2). As indicated by (B), this is combined with the claim that the best good is something complete (3), to support the claim that the goal that is the most complete will be the highest good—the thing we are looking for (4).

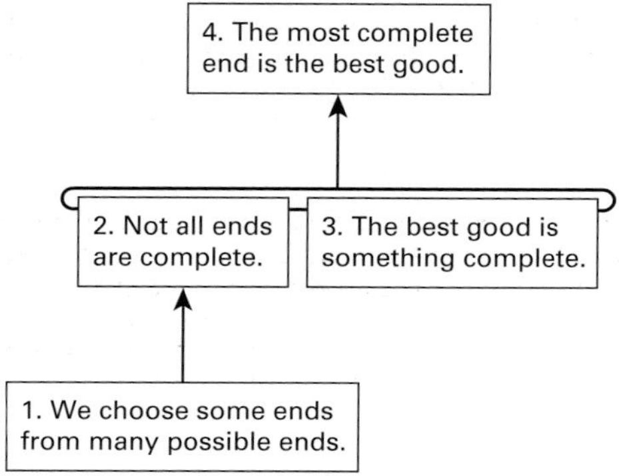

In the next paragraph, Aristotle explains that an end with intrinsic value (i.e., an end that is pursued for itself) is more complete than an end with merely instrumental value (5). He also says that an end with only intrinsic value (never considered choiceworthy because of something external to it) is more complete than an end that has both intrinsic and instrumental value (choiceworthy both in itself and for the sake of something else) (6). As indicated by (D) and (E), these two claims combine to support the claim that and end with only intrinsic value is absolutely complete—complete without qualification (7).

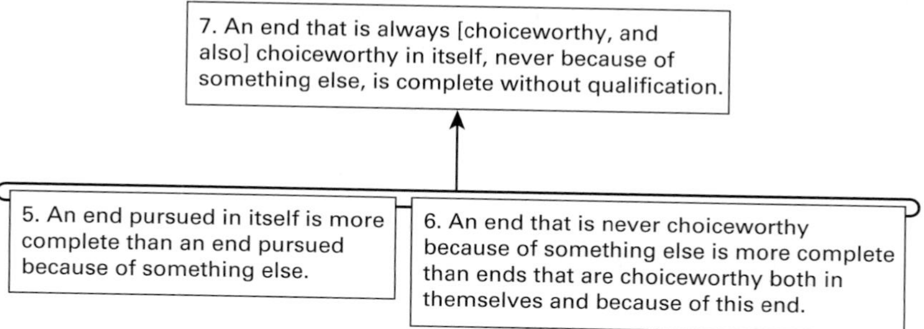

Happiness, Aristotle contends, is something that we value for itself only, and never for the sake of something else (9). That is, happiness has intrinsic value, without having any instrumental value. As indicated by (F) and (G), claim (7), which is a general principle, is combined with a statement about a particular end that fulfills this principle (9), to support the conclusion that happiness is the thing that is complete without qualification (8). Aristotle then gives examples to support his contention that happiness is the only thing that is valued purely for itself—wealth, honor, and the like are all valued because they bring us happiness—and he ends by reiterating claim (9) that we always choose happiness only for itself (10).

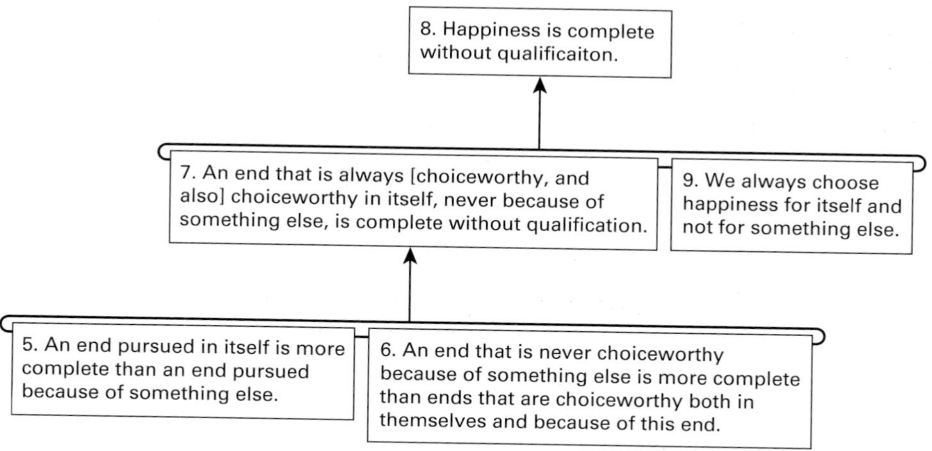

Then, Aristotle presents his second argument for the claim that happiness is complete (11), which is a restatement of (8). Aristotle starts with the general principle that the complete good is self-sufficient (13). As indicated by (H) and (I), this principle combines with the principle of self-sufficiency to support (11).

What is self-sufficiency? He says that something is self-sufficient when it makes a life maximally choiceworthy—we would choose it and we would lack nothing if we choose it (14). Happiness again is the thing that instantiates this principle. We think happiness is what makes a life choiceworthy and lacking nothing (15). As indicated by (J), these two claims combine to support the claim that happiness is self-sufficient (12).

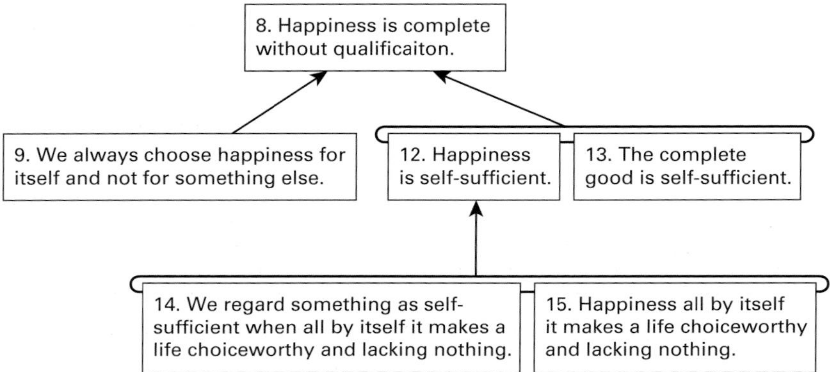

In sum, the basic argument is that happiness is the thing that we value the most (16) because happiness is the most complete (8), and the thing we value the most is the thing that is most complete (4).

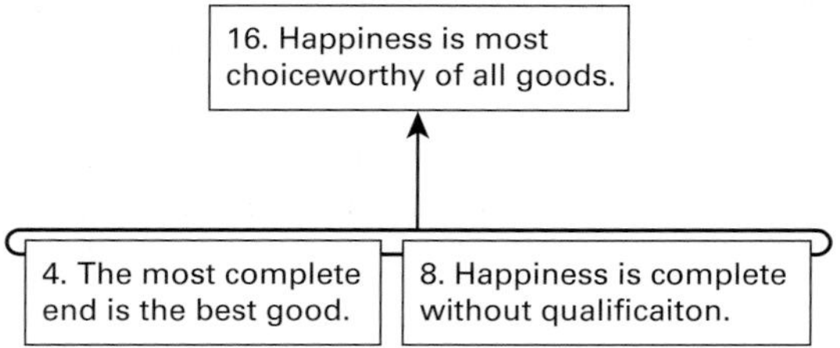

But there is a second, separate line of reasoning that Aristotle gives for the claim that happiness is the thing that we value most (16), as indicated by (K). As indicated by (L), the reason is we don't count happiness as just one good among many. If it were merely one good among many, then we could add something to it to make it better (18). As indicated by (M) and (N), this claim is supported by the claim that if you add something good to something else, then it has more good (19), and the one with more good is better (20). But, contrary to the consequent of (18), we can't add anything to happiness to make it more valuable (21), so, as indicated by (O) and (P), happiness is the most valuable thing, the most choiceworthy (22), which is a restatement of (16).

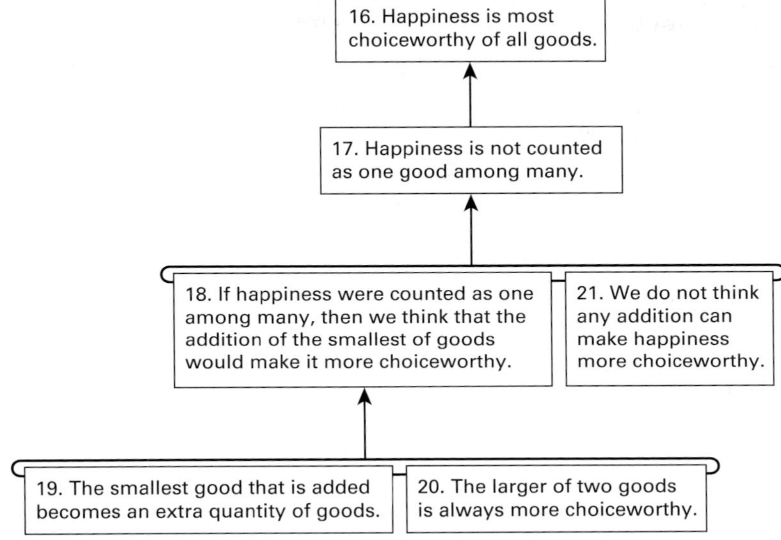

Thus, there are two separate lines of reasoning for this final conclusion:

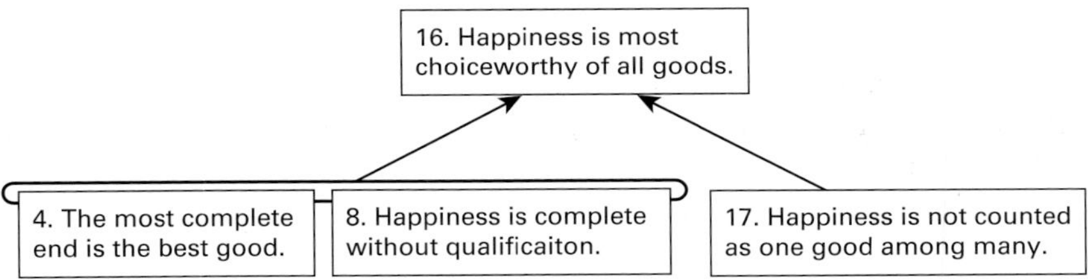

So, Aristotle argues that happiness is the best good; but what does that mean? How do we achieve happiness? This is the subject of the next few arguments Aristotle gives, which we will explore in the exercises.

19.2 James Rachels, "Egoism and Moral Skepticism"

Recall that we read a chapter from Rachels's book, *The Elements of Moral Philosophy*, in both of the previous chapters. Here, we draw again from this book. Below is an excerpt from chapter 5: "Ethical Egoism." Let's consider Rachels's text in more detail. Here we will analyze one of the arguments he presents *for* ethical egoism and one of the arguments he presents *against* it. We will analyze the rest of the arguments in the exercises.

From *The Elements of Moral Philosophy*.[2]

The Argument That Altruism Is Self-Defeating. The first argument has several variations:[A]

- Each of us is intimately familiar with our own individual wants and needs. Moreover, each of us is uniquely placed to pursue those wants and needs effectively. At the same time, we understand the desires and needs of other people only imperfectly,[1] and[B] we are not well situated to pursue them.[2] Therefore,[C] if we try to be "our brother's keeper," we will often bungle the job and end up doing more harm than good.[3]
- At the same time,[D] the policy of "looking out for others" is an offensive intrusion into other people's privacy;[4] it is essentially a policy of minding other people's business.[5]
- Making other people the object of one's "charity" is degrading to them;[6] it robs them of their dignity and self-respect.[7] The offer of charity says, in effect, that they are not competent to care for themselves;[8] and[E] the statement is self-fulfilling.[9] They cease to be self-reliant and become passively dependent on others.[10] That is why the recipients of "charity" are often resentful rather than appreciative.

In each case,[F] the policy of "looking out for others" is said to be self-defeating. If we want to do what is best for people, we should not adopt so-called altruistic policies. On the contrary, if each person looks after his or her own interests, everyone will be better off.

Ethical egoism, as Rachels portrays it here, is essentially a reaction to the untenability of the "ethics of altruism." The ethics of altruism, however, can be spelled out in different ways. Thus, there are variations on the argument against the ethics of altruism, as indicated by (A). So, for each bullet point, Rachels gives a slightly different set of reasons to believe that the ethics of altruism is self-defeating.

First is the claim that we can't understand the desires and needs of other people perfectly (1). As indicated by (B), this combines with the fact that even if we did know them perfectly, we are not well suited to pursuing the desires and needs of others (2). As indicated by (C), the combination supports the claim that if we do try to pursue them, we will often end up doing more harm than good (3). So, the ethics of altruism ends up being not so altruistic.

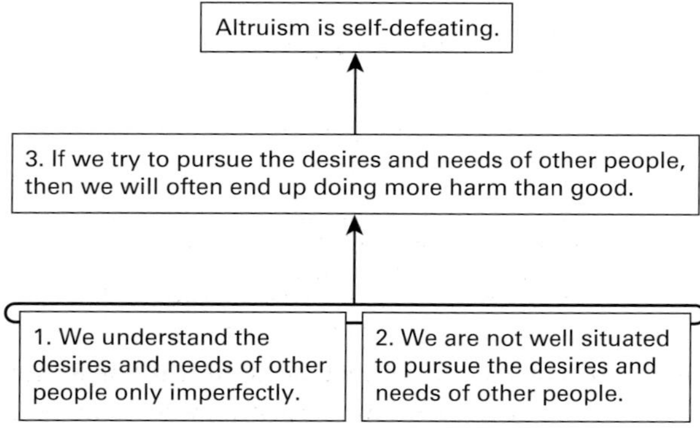

The second argument begins with the claim that looking out for other people is an offensive intrusion into their privacy (4). This is because looking out for other people is the same as "minding other people's business" instead of minding our own (5). Thus, again, the ethics of altruism ends up being not very altruistic.

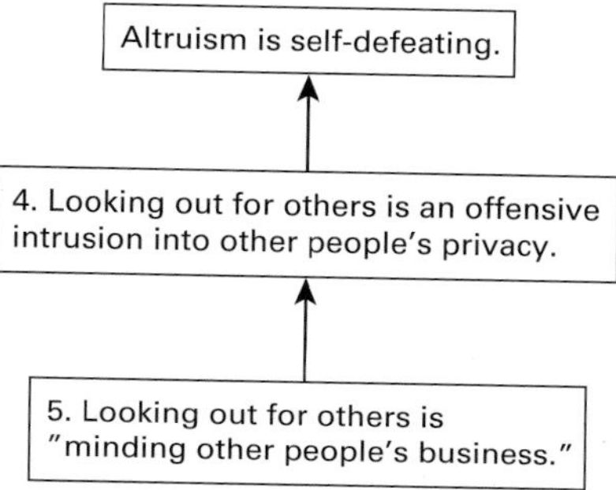

The last argument seems to begin with the implicit assumption that the ethics of altruism is tantamount to charity. The first part of the argument says that making other people the object of one's charity is the same as saying that they are not competent to care for themselves (8). This, then, supports the assertion that making other people the object of one's charity robs them of their dignity and self-respect (7), which, in turn, supports the claim that making other people the object of one's charity is degrading to them (6). Thus, the ethics of altruism is again not very altruistic.

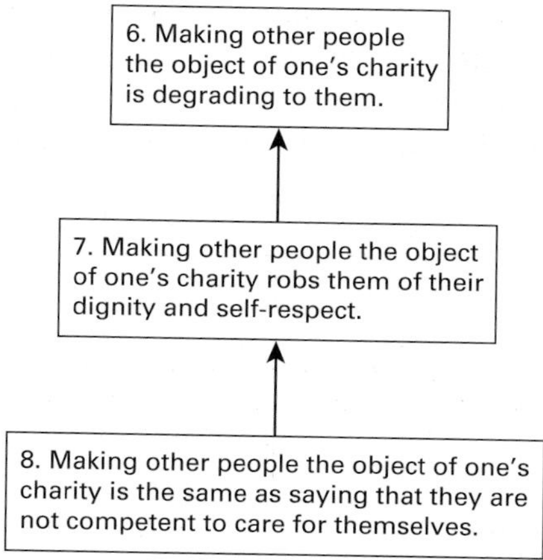

What's more, though, as indicated by (E), we do more than just offend people when we make them the object of our charity; we harm them as well. Making people the object of one's charity makes them become dependent on others (10). This supports the claim that making people the object of one's charity makes it so they are not competent to care for themselves (9). So again, altruism ends up being self-defeating.

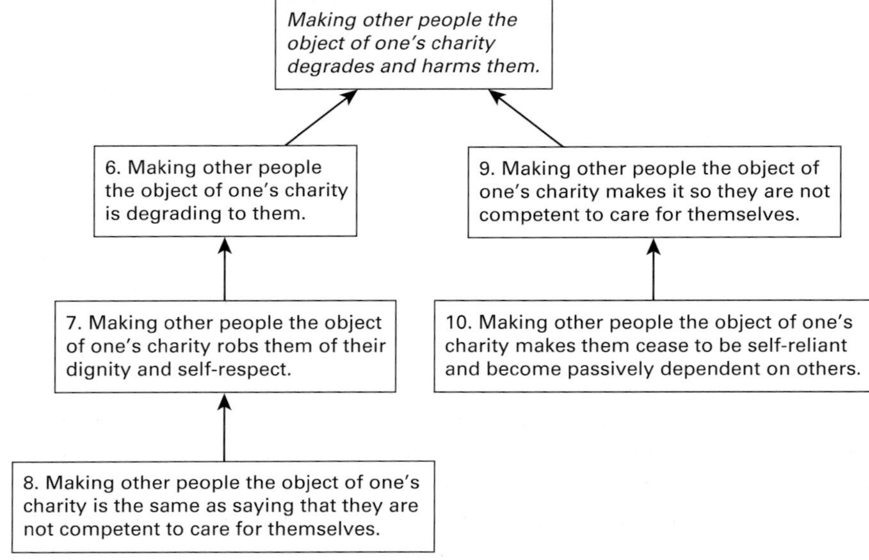

Thus, as indicated by (F), we have three different arguments for the claim that the ethics of altruism is self-defeating.

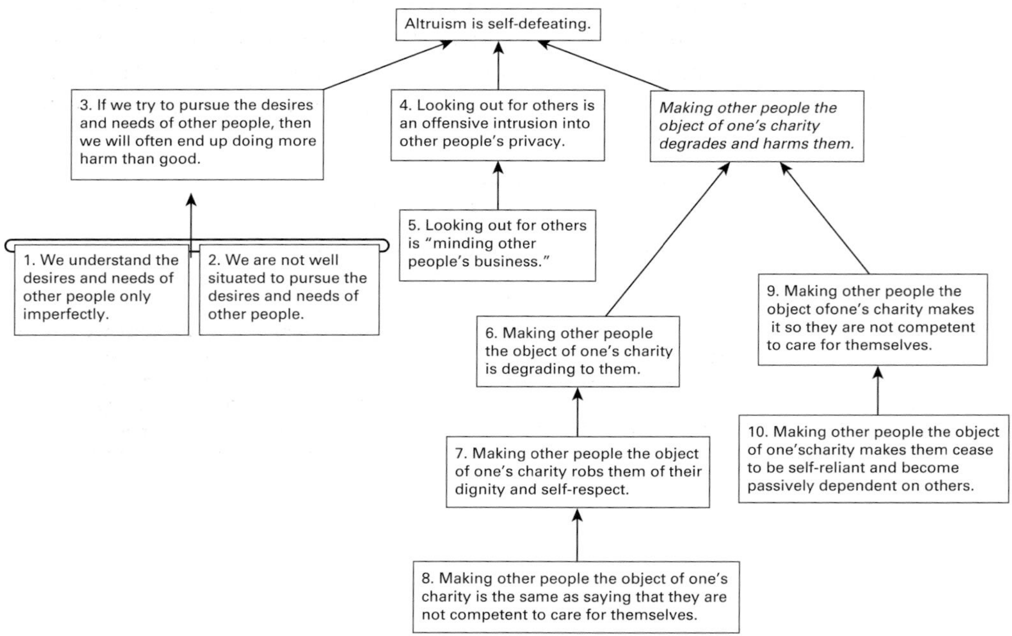

In this chapter of his book, however, Rachels does not actually want to defend ethical egoism. Rather, he is just giving the other side its due. In the second part of the chapter, he gives several arguments *against* ethical egoism. We will analyze one of them here, and explore the rest in the exercises.

The Argument That Ethical Egoism Is Unacceptably Arbitrary.

... There is a general principle that stands in the way of any such justification. Let's call it the Principle of Equal Treatment: *We should treat people in the same way unless there is a good reason not to.*[1] ...

Ethical Egoism is a moral theory of the same type. It advocates dividing the world into two categories of people—ourselves and everyone else[2]—and[A] it urges us to regard the interests of those in the first group as more important than the interests of those in the second group.[3] But[B] each of us can ask, What is the difference between me and everyone else that justifies placing myself in this special category?[4] Am I more intelligent? Are my accomplishments greater? Do I enjoy life more? Are my needs and abilities different from the needs and abilities of others? In short, *what makes me so special?* Failing an answer, it turns out that[C] Ethical Egoism is an arbitrary doctrine,[5] in the same way that racism is arbitrary. Both doctrines violate the Principle of Equal Treatment.[6]

In the first paragraph of this section, Rachels lays out a moral principle that he believes any moral theory ought to accommodate: the *principle of equal treatment* (1). In the next paragraph, Rachels argues that ethical egoism cannot accommodate this principle. First, we have two statements—ethical egoism advocates dividing the world into "ourselves" and "others" (2), and ethical egoism urges us to regard our interests as more important than those of others (3)—and a rhetorical question (4). From this list of examples he gives, it seems as though this question should be interpreted as the statement: There is no difference between me and everyone else that justifies making my interests more important. As indicated by (A) and (B), these three statements are meant to be combined. And, as indicated by (C), they combine to support the claim that ethical egoism is an arbitrary doctrine (5). What does Rachels mean by calling it an "arbitrary" doctrine? He means that it advocates treating other people differently from how we treat ourselves for no good reason.

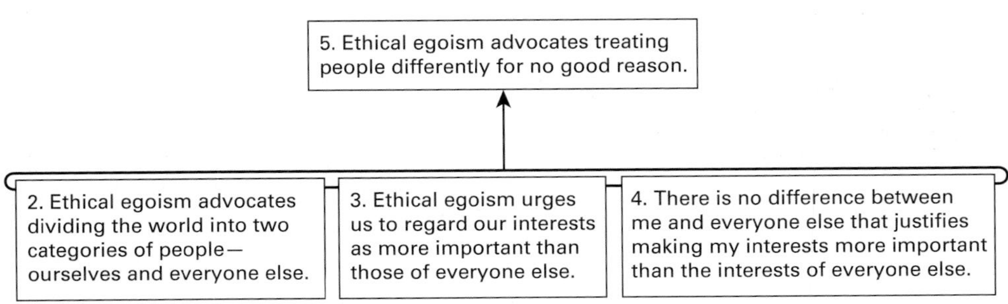

This conclusion (5), then, combined with our moral principle (6), supports Rachels's claim that ethical egoism violates the principle of equal treatment.

This is an example of what philosophers call a *negative* argument—not because of the tone or the words we use, but because it gives us a reason *not* to believe something. Here, this first argument gives us a reason not to believe that ethical egoism is a good moral theory.

A *positive* argument, on the other hand, is one that gives us a good reason *for* a particular belief. It seems that this is what Rachels is doing in the next paragraph. After showing that ethical egoism is an inadequate theory, he needs to convince us what an acceptable moral theory should look like.

Thus,[D] we should care about the interests of other people[7] because[E] their needs and desires are comparable to our own.[8] Consider, one last time, the starving children we could feed by giving up some of our luxuries. Why should we care about them? We care about ourselves, of course—if we were starving we would do almost anything to get food. But what is the difference between us and them? Does hunger affect them any less? Are they less deserving than we are? If we can find no relevant difference between us and them,[9] then we must admit that,[F] if our needs should be met, then so should theirs.[10] This realization—that we are on a par with one another—is the deepest reason why[G] our morality must recognize the needs of others.[11] And that is why, ultimately,[H] Ethical Egoism fails as a moral theory.

An acceptable moral theory should accommodate the principle of equal treatment, so, for the same reasons we should reject ethical egoism, as indicated by (D), we should embrace some moral theory that advocates caring about the interests of other people (7). Rachels goes on in this paragraph, then, to give us a positive argument for this position.

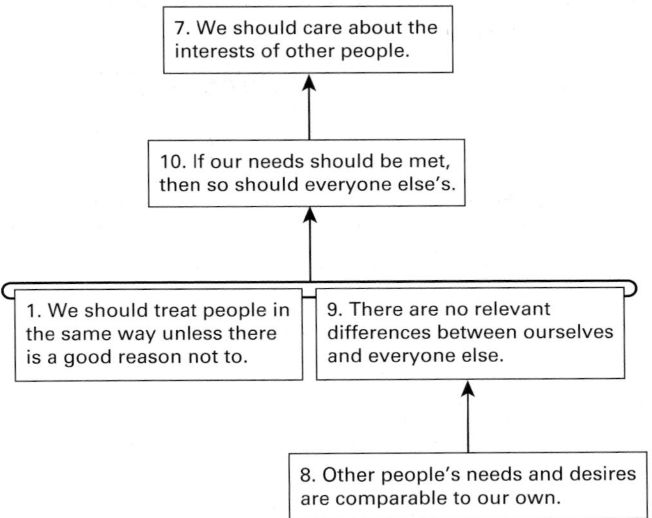

So, ultimately, we have both a positive and a negative argument for the claim that we should care about the needs of other people, and, as indicated by (H), that claim supports Rachels's main conclusion that ethical egoism fails as a moral theory.

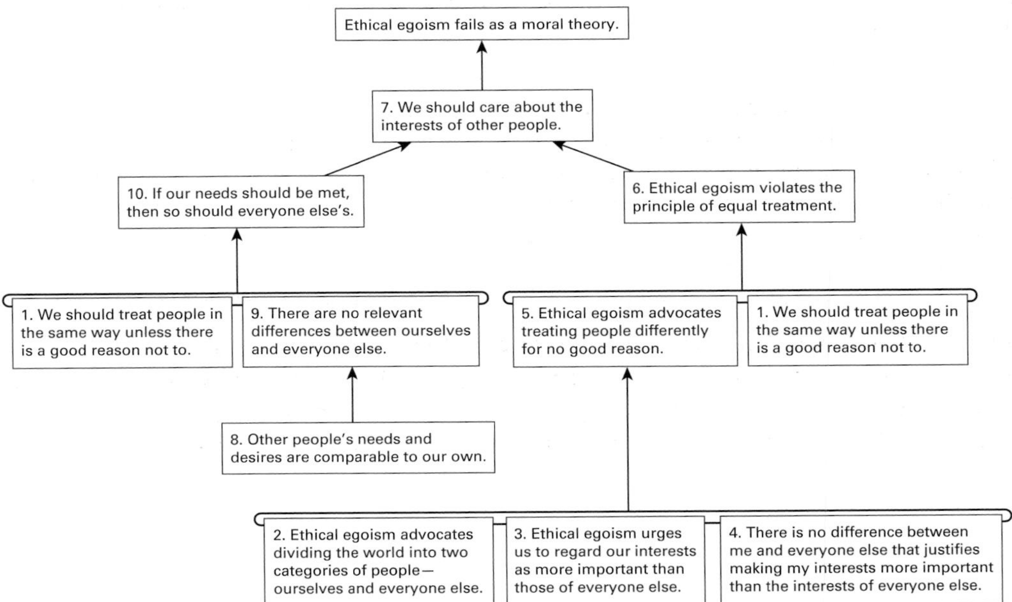

We will explore further arguments from Rachels's chapter in the exercises.

19.3 Thomas Hobbes, *Leviathan*

Thomas Hobbes (1588–1679), perhaps the most influential English philosopher in history, is seen as the founder of modern political philosophy. He was born in the town of Malmesbury, the son of a vicar. In 1602, Hobbes left Malmesbury to study at Oxford, and he graduated in 1608. His first employment after college was as a tutor of a young William Cavendish, and Hobbes continued to work for the family for nearly the rest of his life.

Hobbes was a vocal supporter of the Royalists before the outbreak of the English Civil War. In 1640 he wrote *The Elements of Law, Natural and Politic,* and subsequently left for Paris for fear of retribution from the Parliamentarians. He stayed in Paris while his home country was embroiled in war and King Charles I was executed. In 1651, he wrote *Leviathan*, likely as a response to these events.

In *Leviathan*, Hobbes outlines the foundations of legitimate government, a government not subject to upheavals like civil war. The title of this master work (the full title is *Leviathan or The Matter, Form and Power of a Common Wealth Ecclesiastical and Civil*) refers to a sea creature mentioned in the Old Testament (Psalms 74:13–14; Job 41; Isaiah 27:1). In Hobbes's book, the Leviathan is the sovereign ruler whose power comes from the collective powers given up by the people.

Hobbes's view is that, without government, people live in a constant state of war with each other. Because this is a terrible way to live, people come together to establish a society in which everyone gives up some of their rights so that they can all live in harmony. The only way to ensure compliance, however, is to have a government acting as an enforcer. Hobbes here offers the first modern defense of social contract theory. The "contract" is the agreement all the people make with each other and the government; thus, this view is called *contractarianism*.

But why, you might ask, are we reading Hobbes in the section on ethics? As we shall see below, Hobbes spends a great deal of time describing the "laws of nature." These laws, he argues, are those that people forming a society will naturally endorse as the rules everyone should live by. And, he says, "The true doctrine of the Laws of Nature is the true Moral Philosophy." So contractarianism isn't just a political theory, it is a moral theory too, and we may call it "moral contractarianism."

We read this after the section on ethical egoism, because Hobbes's view shares some features with egoism. For example, Hobbes believes that the reason people would enter into a social contract is to pursue their own interests. However, Hobbes believes that people are rational, and that they will agree *not* to pursue some of their interests if others agree as well, in order to be able to pursue other interests. This is contrary to basic ethical egoism, and it is also the reason contractarianism is not subject to the same criticisms. Let's consider a selection of *Leviathan* in more detail.

From *Leviathan*.[3]

Chapter 13. The natural condition of mankind as concerning their happiness and misery

Nature has made men so equal in their physical and mental capacities[1] that, although sometimes we may find one man who is obviously stronger in body or quicker of mind than another, yet taking all in all the difference between one and another is not so great that one man can claim to have any advantage [of strength or skill or the like] that can't just as well be claimed by some others. As for strength of body:[A] the weakest man is strong enough to kill the strongest, either by a secret plot or by an alliance with others who are in the same danger that he is in.[2]

As for the faculties of the mind:[B] I find that men are even more equal in these than they are in bodily strength. ... Prudence is simply experience;[3] and[C] men will get an equal amount of *that* in an equal period of time spent on things that they equally apply themselves to.[4]

What may make such equality incredible is really just[D] one's vain sense of one's own wisdom, which most men think they have more of than the common herd[5]—that is, more than anyone else except for a few others whom they value because of their fame or because of their agreement with them. It's just a fact about human nature that however much a man may acknowledge many others to be more witty, or more eloquent, or more learned than he is, he won't easily believe that many men are as wise as he is;[6] for[E] he sees his own wisdom close up, and other men's at a distance.[7]

This, however, shows[F] the equality of men rather than their inequality.[8] For[G] ordinarily there is no greater sign that something is equally distributed than that every man is contented with his share![9] ...

So that in the nature of man, we find three principal causes of discord.[10] First competition, secondly distrust, thirdly glory.

The first makes men invade for gain;[11] the second for safety;[12] and the third for reputation.[13] The first use violence to make themselves masters of other men's persons, wives, children, and cattle;[14] the second use it to defend them[selves and their families and property];[15] the third use it for trifles[16]—a word, a smile, a different opinion, and any other sign of a low regard for them personally, if not directly then obliquely through a disrespectful attitude to their family, their friends, their nation, their profession, or their name.

This makes it obvious that[H] for as long as men live without a common power to keep them all in awe, they are in the condition known as "war"; [17] and it is a war of every man against every man. For[I] WAR doesn't consist just in battle or the act of fighting, but in a period of time during which it is well enough known that people are willing to join in battle.[18] So the temporal element in the notion of "when there is war" is like the temporal element in "when there is bad weather." What constitutes bad weather is not a rain-shower or two but an inclination to rain through many days together; similarly, what constitutes war is not actual fighting but a known disposition to fight during a time when there is no assurance to the contrary.[19] All other time is PEACE.

Therefore,[J] whatever results from a time of war, when every man is enemy to every man, also results from a time when men live with no other security but what their own strength and ingenuity provides them with.

At the end of this selection, we can see Hobbes's main conclusion: Whatever results from a state of war also results from a state in which people live in constant fear of each other, with nothing other than their own strength and ingenuity to protect them. How does he get to this claim?

First, Hobbes argues that people in general have the same strength and ingenuity—that they naturally are equal in their physical and mental capacities (1). I think the best way to understand how he supports this claim is by breaking it into two parts, and representing it as implicitly asserting each part separately.

The first part, then, is that people are naturally equal in their physical capacities. As indicated by (A), this is supported by the claim that even the weakest person can kill the strongest under appropriate circumstances (2).

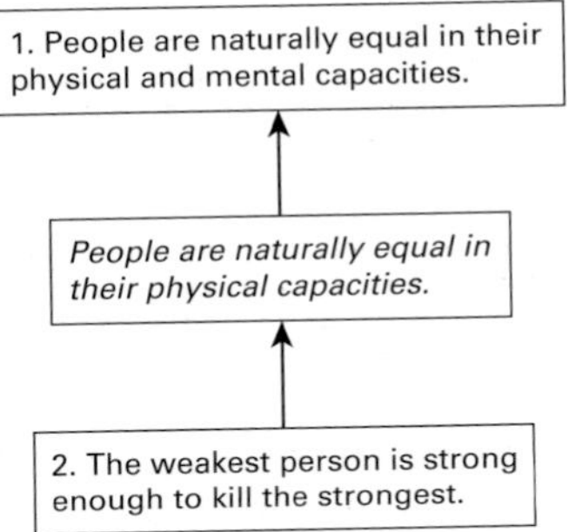

Then, as indicated by (B), he argues that people are naturally equal in their mental capacities. He does this by considering two capacities: prudence and wisdom. Prudence, here, means the capacity to act in one's own interest—to know what one's goals are and to act so as to achieve them. People have the same amount of prudence because prudence is simply experience (3). As indicated by (C), this combines with the claim that people will naturally accrue the same amount of experience by just living and attending to their needs (4).

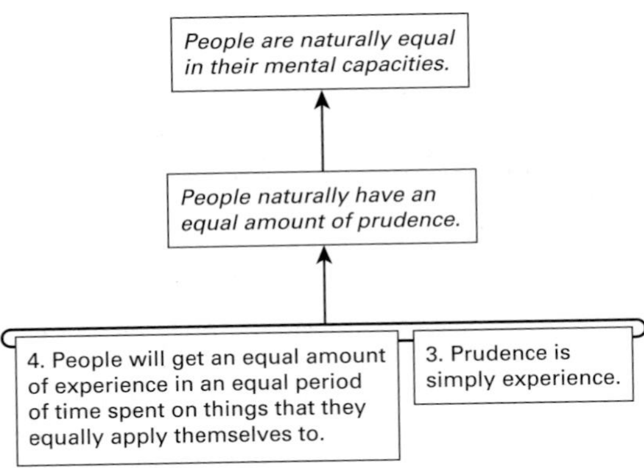

Hobbes turns next to wisdom. He concedes that it may sound incredible that people are naturally equal in their mental capacities (D), but the very reason it sounds incredible makes Hobbes believe it to be true. First, no one will easily believe that many other people are as wise as he (6). As indicated by (E), this is supported by the claim that everyone sees his own wisdom up close, and the wisdom of others only at a distance (7). Then, since no one believes anyone has more wisdom than he, most people believe they actually have *more* wisdom than most other people (5).

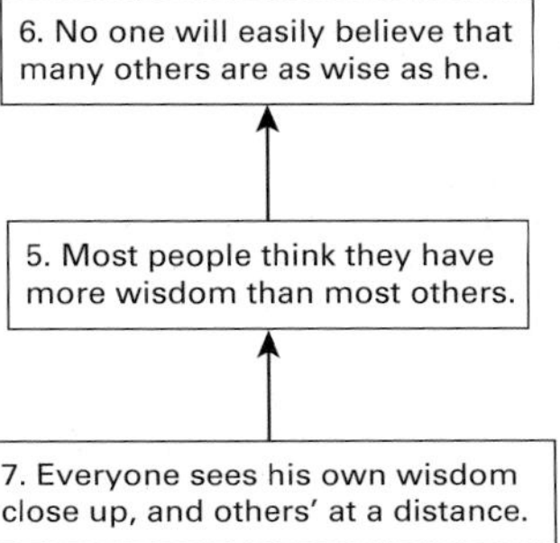

This, Hobbes says, as indicated by (F), shows that people have equal wisdom (8), because, as indicated by (G), everyone being content with what he has is a sure sign that it is distributed equally, combined with the implicit claim that, from the previous subargument, everyone is in fact content with his share of wisdom.

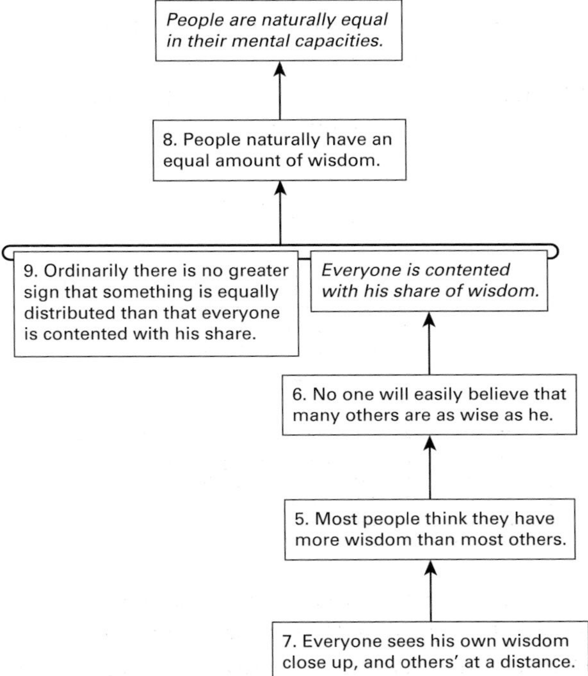

Next, Hobbes turns to the consequences of this equality: competition, distrust, and glory. The three paragraphs (omitted here) seem to be explanations of what each of these three things is, rather than arguments about their nature. The point, however, is that the fact that people are naturally equal in their physical and mental capacities causes competition, distrust, and glory-seeking. The implicit conclusion here seems to be that people are naturally in a state of competition, distrust, and glory-seeking.

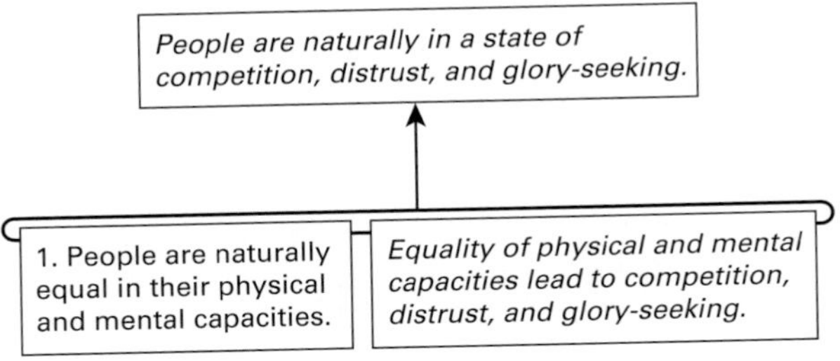

The argument seems to pick up again when Hobbes claims that competition, distrust, and glory are the three principal causes of discord among people (10). The reasons that these cause discord are that they each make people use violence against others: competition makes people use violence to take from others (14), so competition makes people invade for gain (11); distrust makes people use violence to defend themselves (15), so distrust makes people invade for safety; and glory makes people use violence for a host of trivial things (16), so glory makes people invade for reputation (13).

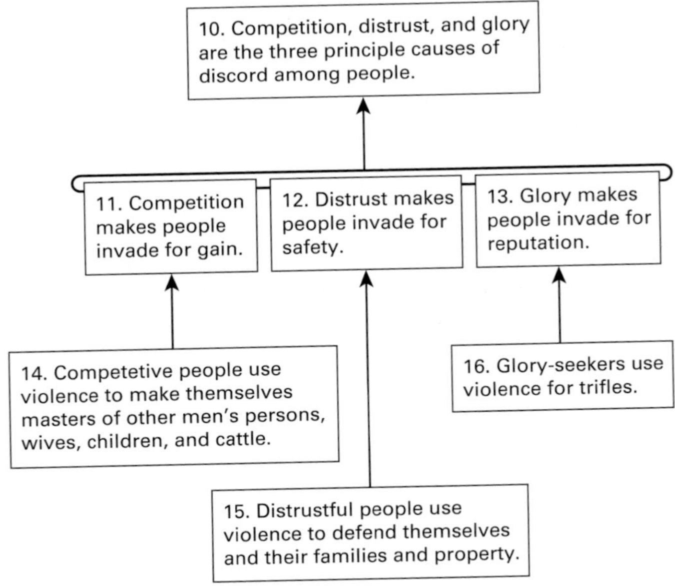

As indicated by (H), Hobbes believes that this discord among people makes it so that if people live together without some power (like a government) to keep them all in awe (afraid of punishment), then they are at war with one another (17). The reason is the discord named above combined with the fact, as indicated by (I), that "war" is not just fighting, but any period in which it is well known that people are willing to begin fighting at any time (18), which is repeated in (19).

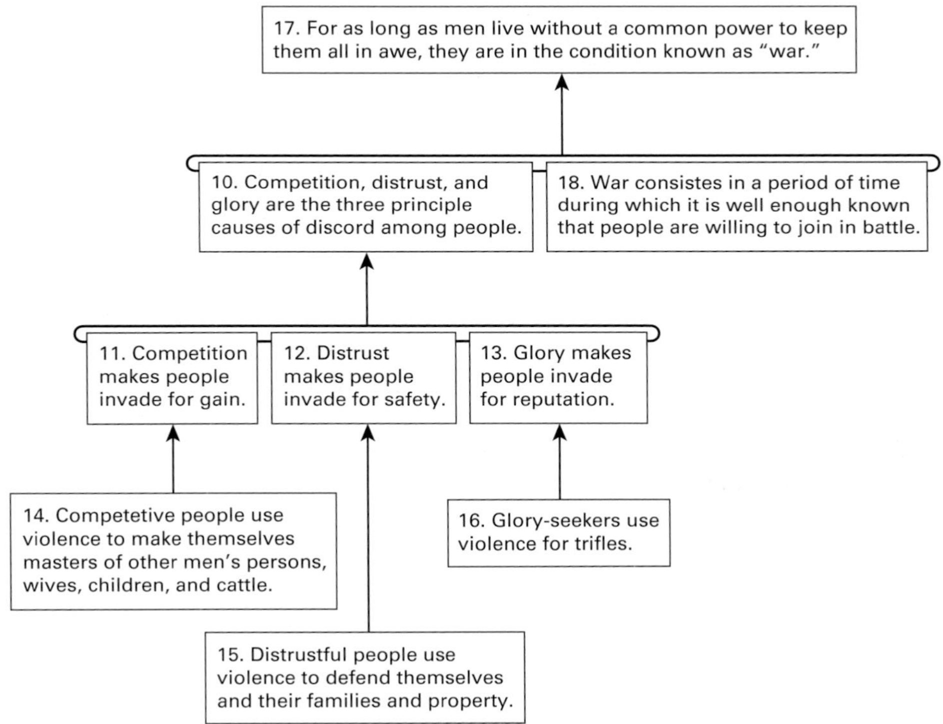

And, so, as indicated by (J), since the State of Nature—the state people are in when there is no government—is a State of War (17), whatever results from a time of war will also result from a time when people live with only their strength and ingenuity to keep them safe.

So, the overall argument in this selection looks like this:

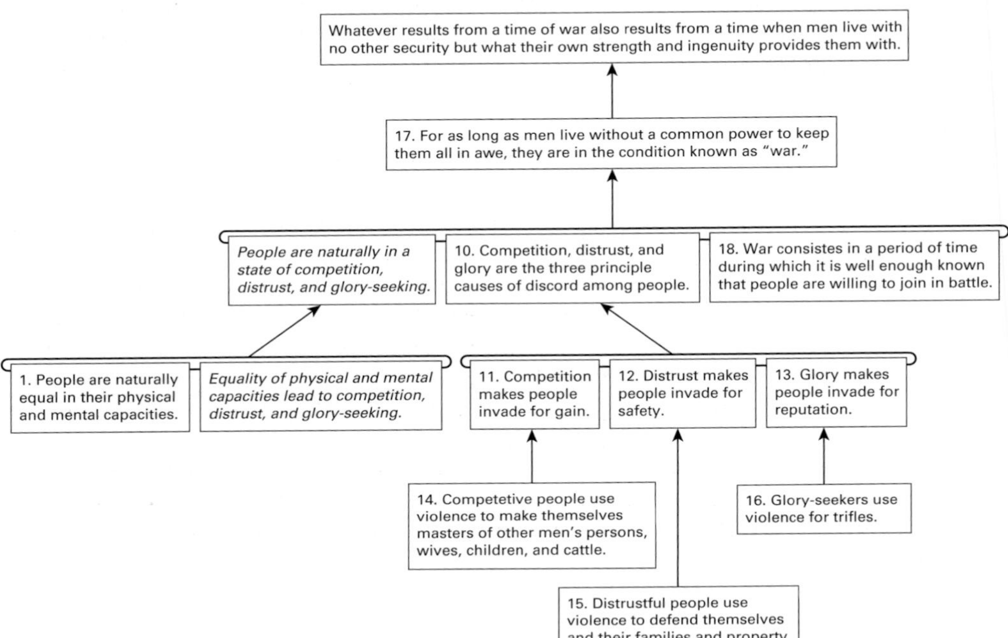

We'll explore more of Hobbes's arguments in the exercises.

19.4 In-Class Exercises

An asterisk (*) indicates a more challenging exercise.

Exercises 1–4

In the first section of this chapter, we analyzed in detail an argument given by Aristotle in *Nicomachean Ethics*. In the following selections, Aristotle gives arguments concerning a human being's proper function. For each, (a) diagram the argument and (b) identify any potential objections to the argument.

Exercise 1

(a) We have found, then, that the human function is the soul's activity that expresses reason [as itself having reason] or requires reason [as obeying reason]. (b) Now the function of F, of a harpist, for instance, is the same in kind, so we say, as the function of an excellent F, an excellent harpist, for instance. (c) The same is true without qualification in every case, when we add to the function the superior achievement that expresses the virtue; for a harpist's function, for instance, is to play the harp, and a good harpist's is to do it well. (d) Now we take the human function to be a certain kind of life, and take this life to be the soul's activity and actions that express reason. (e) [Hence] the excellent man's function is to do this finely and well. (f) Each function is completed well when its completion expresses the proper virtue. (g) Therefore the human good turns out to be the soul's activity that expresses virtue.

Exercise 2

If happiness, then, is activity expressing virtue, it is reasonable for it to express the supreme virtue, which will be the virtue of the best thing.

The best is understanding, or whatever else seems to be the natural ruler and leader, and to understand what is fine and divine, by being itself either divine or the most divine element in us.

Hence complete happiness will be its activity expressing its proper virtue; and we have said that this activity is the activity of study. This seems to agree with what has been said before, and also with the truth.

For this activity is supreme, since understanding is the supreme element in us, and the objects of understanding are the supreme objects of knowledge. …

Hence a human being's complete happiness will be this activity, if it receives a complete span of life, since nothing incomplete is proper to happiness. …

And what we have said previously will also apply now. For what is proper to each thing's nature is supremely best and pleasantest for it; and hence for a human being the life expressing understanding will be supremely best and pleasantest, if understanding above all is the human being. This life, then, will also be happiest.

**Exercise 3*

However, we should examine the principle not only from the conclusion and premises [of a deductive argument], but also from what is said about it; for all the facts harmonize with a true account, whereas the truth soon clashes with a false one.

Goods are divided, then, into three types, some called external, some goods of the soul, others goods of the body; and the goods of the soul are said to be goods to the fullest extent and most of all, and the soul's actions and activities are ascribed to the soul. Hence the account [of the good] is sound, to judge by this belief anyhow—and it is an ancient belief agreed on by philosophers.

Our account is also correct in saying that some sort of actions and activities are the end; for then the end turns out to be a good of the soul, not an external good.

The belief that the happy person lives well and does well in action also agrees with our account, since we have virtually said that the end is a sort of living well and doing well in action.

Further, all the features that people look for in happiness appear to be true of the end described in our account. For to some people it seems to be virtue; to others intelligence; to others some sort of wisdom; to others again it seems to be these, or one of these, involving pleasure or requiring its addition; and others add in external prosperity as well.

Some of these views are traditional, held by many, while others are held by a few reputable men; and it is reasonable for each group to be not entirely in error, but correct on one point at least, or even on most points.

First, our account agrees with those who say happiness is virtue [in general] or some [particular] virtue; for activity expressing virtue is proper to virtue. Presumably, though, it matters quite a bit whether we suppose that the best good consists in possessing or in using, i.e., in a state or in an activity [that actualizes the state]. For while someone may be in a state that achieves no good, if, for instance, he is asleep or inactive in some other way, this cannot be true of the activity; for it will necessarily do actions and do well in them. And just as Olympic prizes are not for the finest and strongest, but for the contestants, since it is only these who win; so also in life [only the fine and good people who act correctly win the prize].

Moreover, the life of these [active people] is also pleasant in itself. For being pleased is a condition of the soul, [hence included in the activity of the soul]. Further, each type of person finds pleasure in whatever he is called a lover of, so that a horse, for instance, pleases the horse-lover, a spectacle the lover of spectacles, and similarly what is just pleases the lover of justice, and in general what expresses virtue pleases the lover of virtue. Hence the things that please most people conflict, because they are not pleasant by nature, whereas the things that please lovers of what is fine are things pleasant by nature; and actions expressing virtue are pleasant in this way; and so they both please lovers of what is fine and are pleasant in themselves.

Hence their life does not need pleasure to be added [to virtuous activity] as some sort of ornament; rather, it has its pleasure within itself. For besides the reasons already given, someone who does not enjoy fine actions is not good; for no one would call him just, for instance, if he did not enjoy doing just actions, or generous if he did not enjoy generous actions, and similarly for the other virtues. If this is so, then actions expressing the virtues are pleasant in themselves.

Moreover, these actions are good and fine as well as pleasant; indeed, they are good, fine and pleasant more than anything else, since on this question the excellent person has good judgment, and his judgment agrees with our conclusions.

Happiness, then, is best, finest and most pleasant, and these three features are not distinguished in the way suggested by the Delian inscription: "What is most just is finest; being healthy is most beneficial; but it is most pleasant to win our heart's desire." For all three features are found in the best activities, and happiness we say is these activities, or [rather] one of them, the best one.

Nonetheless, happiness evidently also needs external goods to be added [to the activity], as we said, since we cannot, or cannot easily, do fine actions if we lack the resources.

For, first of all, in many actions we use friends, wealth and political power just as we use instruments. Further, deprivation of certain [externals]—for instance, good birth, good children, beauty—mars our blessedness; for we do not altogether have the character of happiness if we look utterly repulsive or are ill-born, solitary or childless, and have it even less, presumably, if our children or friends are totally bad, or were good but have died.

And so, as we have said, happiness would seem to need this sort of prosperity added also; that is why some people identify happiness with good fortune, while others [reacting from one extreme to the other] identify it with virtue.

*Exercise 4

Since happiness is an activity of the soul expressing complete virtue, we must examine virtue; for that will perhaps also be a way to study happiness better.

Moreover, the true politician seems to have spent more effort on virtue than on anything else, since he wants to make the citizens good and law-abiding. We find an example of this in the Spartan and Cretan legislators and in any others with their concerns. Since, then, the examination of virtue is proper for political science, the inquiry clearly suits our original decision [to pursue political science].

It is clear that the virtue we must examine is human virtue, since we are also seeking the human good and human happiness. And by human virtue we mean virtue of the soul, not of the body, since we also say that happiness is an activity of the soul. If this is so, then it is clear that the politician must acquire some knowledge about the soul, just as someone setting out to heal the eyes must acquire knowledge about the whole body as well. This is all the more true to the extent that political science is better and more honorable than medicine—and even among doctors the cultivated ones devote a lot of effort to acquiring knowledge about the body. Hence the politician as well [as the student of nature] must study the soul.

But he must study it for the purpose [of inquiring into virtue], as far as suffices for what he seeks; for a more exact treatment would presumably take more effort than his purpose requires. [We] have discussed the soul sufficiently [for our purposes] in [our] popular works as well [as our less popular], and we should use this discussion.

We have said, for instance, that one [part] of the soul is nonrational, while one has reason. Are these distinguished as parts of a body and everything divisible into parts are? Or are they two only in account, and inseparable by nature, as the convex and the concave are in a surface? It does not matter for present purposes.

Consider the nonrational [part]. One [part] of it, i.e., the cause of nutrition and growth, is seemingly plant-like and shared [with other living things]: for we can ascribe this capacity of the soul to everything that is nourished, including embryos, and the same one to complete living things, since this is more reasonable than to ascribe another capacity to them.

Hence the virtue of this capacity is apparently shared, not [specifically] human. For this part and capacity more than others seem to be active in sleep, and here the good and the bad person are least distinct, which is why happy people are said to be no better off than miserable people for half their lives.

And this lack of distinction is not surprising, since sleep is inactivity of the soul insofar as it is called excellent or base, unless to some small extent some movements penetrate [to our awareness], and in this way the decent person comes to have better images [in dreams] than just any random person has. Enough about this, however, and let us leave aside the nutritive part, since by nature It has no share in human virtue.

Another nature in the soul would also seem to be nonrational though in a way it shares in reason.

[Clearly it is nonrational.] For in the continent and the incontinent person we praise their reason, i.e., the [part] of the soul that has reason, because it exhorts them correctly and toward what is best; but they evidently also have in them some other [part] that is by nature something apart from reason, conflicting and struggling with reason.

For just as paralyzed parts of a body, when we decide to move them to the right, do the contrary and move off to the left, the same is true of the soul; for incontinent people have impulses in contrary directions. In bodies, admittedly, we see the part go astray, whereas we do not see it in the soul; nonetheless, presumably, we should suppose that the soul also has something apart from reason, contrary to and countering reason. The [precise] way it is different does not matter.

However, this [part] as well [as the rational part] appears, as we said, to share in reason. At any rate, in the continent person it obeys reason; and in the temperate and the brave person it presumably listens still better to reason, since there it agrees with reason in everything.

The nonrational [part], then, as well [as the whole soul] apparently has two parts. For while the plant-like [part] shares in reason not at all, the [part] with appetites and in general desires shares in reason in a way, insofar as it both listens to reason and obeys it.

It listens in the way in which we are said to "listen to reason" from father or friends, not in the way in which we ["give the reason"] in mathematics.

The nonrational part also [obeys and] is persuaded in some way by reason, as is shown by chastening, and by every sort of reproof and exhortation.

If we ought to say, then, that this [part] also has reason, then the [part] that has reason, as well [as the nonrational part] will have two parts, one that has reason to the full extent by having it within itself, and another [that has it] by listening to reason as to a father.

The division between virtues also reflects this difference. For some virtues are called virtues of thought, others virtues of character; wisdom, comprehension and intelligence are called virtues of thought, generosity and temperance virtues of character.

For when we speak of someone's character we do not say that he is wise or has good comprehension, but that he is gentle or temperate. [Hence these are the virtues of character.] And yet, we also praise the wise person for his state, and the states that are praiseworthy are the ones we call virtues. [Hence wisdom is also a virtue.]

Exercises 5–8

In the second section of this chapter, we analyzed in detail two sets of arguments Rachels gives in "Ethical Egoism." The following selections contain other arguments of his both for and against ethical egoism. For each selection, (a) diagram the argument and (b) identify any potential objections to the argument.

Exercise 5

Ayn Rand's Argument. Ayn Rand (1905–1982) is not read much by philosophers. The ideas associated with her name—that capitalism is a morally superior economic system and that morality demands absolute respect for the rights of individuals—are developed more rigorously by other writers. Nevertheless, she was a charismatic figure who attracted a devoted following during her lifetime. Today, roughly 30 years after her death, the Ayn Rand industry is still going strong. Ethical Egoism is associated with her more than with any other 20th-century writer.

Ayn Rand regarded the "ethics of altruism" as a totally destructive idea, both in society as a whole and in the lives of those taken in by it. Altruism, to her way of thinking, leads to a denial of the value of the individual. It says to a person: Your life is merely some thing to be sacrificed. "If a man accepts the ethics of altruism," she writes, "his first concern is not how to live his life, but how to sacrifice it." Those who promote the ethics of altruism are beneath contempt—they are parasites who, rather than working to build and sustain their own lives, leech off those who do. Rand continues:

> Parasites, moochers, looters, brutes and thugs can be of no value to a human being—nor can he gain any benefit from living in a society geared to *their* needs, demands and protections, a society that treats him as a sacrificial animal and penalizes him for his virtues in order to reward them, for their vices, which means: a society based on the ethics of altruism.

By "sacrificing one's life," Rand does not mean anything so dramatic as dying. A person's life consists, in part, of projects undertaken and goods earned and created, Thus, to demand that a person abandon his projects or give up his goods is to demand that he "sacrifice his life."

Rand also suggests that there is a metaphysical basis for Ethical Egoism. Somehow, it is the only ethic that takes seriously the reality of the individual person. She bemoans "the enormity of the extent to which altruism erodes men's capacity to grasp … the value of an individual life; it reveals a mind in which the reality of a human being has been wiped out."

What, then, of the hungry children? It might be said that Ethical Egoism itself "reveals a mind from which the reality of a human being has been wiped out," namely, the human being who is starving. But Rand quotes with approval the answer given by one of her followers: "Once, when Barbara Brandon was asked by a student: 'What will happen to the poor …?' she answered: 'If *you* want to help them, you will not be stopped.'"

All these remarks are part of one continuous argument that goes something like this:

1. Each person has only one life to live. If we value the individual, then we must agree that this life is of supreme importance. After all, it is all one has, and all one is.
2. The ethics of altruism regards the life of the individual as something that may be sacrificed for the good of others. Therefore the ethics of altruism does not take seriously the value of the individual.
3. Ethical Egoism, which allows each person to view his or her own life as being of ultimate value, does take the individual seriously—it is, in fact, the only philosophy that does.
4. Thus, Ethical Egoism is the philosophy that we ought to accept.

One problem with this argument, as you may have noticed, is that it assumes we have only two options: Either we accept the ethics of altruism, or we accept Ethical Egoism. The choice is then made to look obvious by depicting the ethics of altruism as an insane doctrine that only an idiot would accept. The ethics of altruism is said to be the view that one's own interests have *no* value and that one must be ready to sacrifice oneself *totally* whenever *anyone* asks it. If this is the alternative, then any other view, including Ethical Egoism, will look good by comparison.

But that is hardly a fair picture of the options. What we called the commonsense view stands between the two extremes. It says that one's own interests and the interests of others are both important, and must be balanced against each other. Sometimes, one should act in the interests of others; other times, one should take care of oneself. So, even if we should reject the extreme ethics of altruism, it does not follow that we must accept the other extreme of Ethical Egoism. There is a middle ground.

Exercise 6

Ethical Egoism as Compatible with Commonsense Morality. The third argument takes a different approach. Ethical Egoism usually presented as a *revisionist* moral philosophy, that is, a philosophy that says our commonsense moral views are mistaken. It is possible, however, to interpret Ethical Egoism as a theory that accepts commonsense morality.

This interpretation goes as follows: Ordinary morality consists in obeying certain rules. We must speak the truth, keep our promises, avoid harming others, and so on. At first glance, these duties appear to have little in common—they are just a bunch of discrete rules. Yet there may be a unity to them. Ethical Egoists would say that all these duties are ultimately derived from the one fundamental principle of self-interest.

Understood in this way, Ethical Egoism is not such a radical doctrine. It does not challenge commonsense morality; it only tries to explain and systematize it. And it does a surprisingly good job. It can provide plausible explanations of the duties mentioned above, and more:

- *The duty not to harm others*: If we do things that harm other people, other people will not mind doing things that harm us. We will be shunned and despised; others will not be our friends and will not help us out when we need it. If our offenses are serious enough, we may end up in jail. Thus, it is to our own advantage to avoid harming others.

• *The duty not to lie*: If we lie to other people, we will suffer the ill effects of a bad reputation. People will distrust us and avoid doing business with us. People will be dishonest with us once they realize that we have been dishonest with them. Thus, it is to our own advantage to be truthful.
• *The duty to keep our promises*: It is to our own advantage to enter into mutually beneficial arrangements with other people. To benefit from those arrangements, we need to be able to rely on others to keep their word. But we can hardly expect them to do that if we do not keep our promises to them. Therefore, from the point of view of self-interest, we should keep our promises.

Pursuing this line of reasoning, Thomas Hobbes (1588–1679) suggested that the principle of Ethical Egoism leads to nothing less than the Golden Rule: We should "do unto others" because if we do, others will be more likely to "do unto us."

Does this argument succeed in establishing Ethical Egoism as a viable theory of morality? It may be the best try. However, there are two serious problems with it. First, the argument does not prove as much as it needs to. It shows only that it is mostly to one's advantage to tell the truth, to keep one's promises, and to avoid harming others. But a situation might arise in which you could profit from doing something horrible, like killing someone. In such a case, Ethical Egoism cannot explain why you shouldn't do the horrible thing. Thus, it looks like some of our moral obligations cannot be derived from self-interest.

Second, suppose it is true that giving money to famine relief is somehow to one's own advantage. It doesn't follow that this is the only reason to do so. Another reason might be to help the starving people. Ethical Egoism says that self-interest is the only reason to help others, but nothing in the present argument really supports that.

Exercise 7

The Argument That Ethical Egoism Endorses Wickedness. Consider these wicked actions, taken from various newspaper stories: To make more money, a pharmacist filled prescriptions for cancer patients using watered-down drugs. A paramedic gave emergency patients injections of sterile water rather than morphine, so he could sell the morphine. Parents fed a baby acid so they could fake a lawsuit, claiming the baby's formula was tainted. A nurse raped two patients while they were unconscious. A 73-year-old kept his daughter locked in a cellar for 24 years, and fathered seven children with her, against her will. A 60-year-old man shot his letter carrier seven times because he was $90,000 in debt and thought that being in federal prison would be better than being homeless.

Suppose that someone could actually benefit by doing such things. Wouldn't Ethical Egoism have to approve of such actions? This seems like enough to discredit the doctrine. However, this objection might be unfair to Ethical Egoism, because in saying that these actions are wicked, it assumes a nonegoistic conception of wickedness. Thus, some philosophers have tried to show that there are deeper logical problems with Ethical Egoism. The following argument is typical of such proposals.

Exercise 8

The Argument That Ethical Egoism Is Logically Inconsistent. In his book *The Moral Point of View* (1958), Kurt Baier argues that Ethical Egoism cannot be correct, on purely logical grounds. Baier thinks that the theory leads to contradictions. If this is true, then Ethical Egoism is indeed mistaken, for no theory can be true if it contradicts itself.

Suppose, Baier says, two people are running for president. Let's call them "D" and "R," to stand for "Democrat" and "Republican." Because it would be in D's interest to win, it would be in D's interest to kill R. From this it follows, on Ethical Egoism, that D ought to kill R—it is D's moral duty to do so. But it is also true that it is in R's interest to stay alive. From this it follows that R ought to stop D from killing her—that is R's duty. Now here's the problem. When R protects herself from D, her act is both wrong and not wrong—wrong because it prevents D from doing his duty, and not wrong because it is in R's best interests. But one and the same act cannot be both morally wrong and not morally wrong.

Does this argument refute Ethical Egoism? At first glance, it seems persuasive. However, it is complicated, so we need to set it out with each step individually identified. Then we will be in a position to evaluate it. Spelled out fully, it goes like this:

1. Suppose it is each person's duty to do what is in his own best interest.
2. It is in D's best interest to kill R so that D will win the election.
3. It is in R's best interest to prevent D from killing her.
4. Therefore, D's duty is to kill R, and R's duty is to prevent D from doing it.
5. But it is wrong to prevent someone from doing his duty.
6. Therefore, it is wrong for R to prevent D from killing her.
7. Therefore, it is both wrong and not wrong for R to prevent D from killing her.
8. But no act can be wrong and not wrong; that is a contradiction,
9. Therefore, the assumption with which we started—that it is each person's duty to do what is in his own best interest—cannot be true.

When the argument is set out in this way, we can see its hidden flaw. The logical contradiction—that it is wrong and not wrong for R to prevent D from killing her—does not follow simply from the principle of Ethical Egoism as stated in step (1). It follows from that principle *together with* the premise expressed in step (5), namely that "it is wrong to prevent someone from doing his duty." By putting step (5) in the argument, Baier has added his own assumption.

Thus, we need not reject Ethical Egoism. Instead, we could simply reject this additional premise and thereby avoid the contradiction. That is surely what the Ethical Egoist would do, for the Ethical Egoist would never say, without qualification, that it is always wrong to prevent someone from doing his duty. He would say, instead, that whether one ought to prevent someone from doing his duty depends entirely on whether it would be to one's own advantage to do so. Regardless of whether we like this idea, it is at least what the Ethical Egoist would say, And so, this attempt to convict the egoist of self-contradiction fails.

Exercises 9–13

In the third section of this chapter, we analyzed in detail one of the arguments Hobbes gives in chapter 13 of *Leviathan*. The following selections contain other arguments he presents in that and subsequent chapters. For each selection, (a) diagram the argument and (b) identify any potential objections to the argument.

Exercise 9

In this war of every man against every man nothing can be unjust. The notions of right and wrong, justice and injustice have no place there. Where there is no common power, there is no law; and where there is no law, there is no injustice. In war the two chief virtues are force and fraud. Justice and injustice are not among the faculties [here = "*natural* capacities"] of the body or of the mind. If they were, they could be in a man who was alone in the world, as his senses and passions can. They are qualities that relate to men in society, not in solitude.

Exercise 10

In such conditions there is no place for hard work, because there is no assurance that it will yield results; and consequently no cultivation of the earth, no navigation or use of materials that can be imported by sea, no construction of large buildings, no machines for moving things that require much force, no knowledge of the face of the earth, no account of time, no practical skills, no literature or scholarship, no society; and—worst of all—continual fear and danger of violent death, and the life of man solitary, poor, nasty, brutish, and short.

Exercise 11

From these instances [Jupiter and Coke] one may be apt to infer that

> when the heir apparent of a kingdom kills him who has the throne, even if it is his father, you may call it 'injustice' or anything else you like; but it can't be against reason, seeing that any man's voluntary actions *all* tend to his own benefit, and those actions are most reasonable that conduce most to one's own ends.

This reasoning, though plausible, is nevertheless false.

For this is not a question about mutual promises in the natural condition of men where there is no security of performance on either side—e.g. when there is no civil power governing the people making the promises—for *those* promises are not covenants. Our question is rather this: where one of the parties has performed already, or where there is a power to make him perform, is it against reason for the other party to fail to perform *his* part? I say he acts against reason and most imprudently. My case for this has two parts. When a man does something that tends to his own destruction, so far as one can tell in advance, even if some chance event that he couldn't have expected makes it turn out to his benefit, *that* doesn't make his original action reasonably or wisely done. Secondly, in the natural condition where every man is an enemy to every other man, no-one can live securely without the aid of allies. But who, except by ignorance, will admit into society (which one enters by mutual covenants for the defence of individual members) a man who thinks it rational to break covenants? Who, except through ignorance, will retain him if he has been admitted? So either he will be thrown out of society, and perish, or he will owe his not being thrown out to the ignorance of others who cannot see the danger of their error; and a man cannot reasonably count on such errors by others as the means to his security. Either way, then, what he does is contrary to right reason.

Exercise 12

It's true that certain living creatures, such as bees and ants, live sociably with one another (which is why Aristotle counts them among the 'political' creatures [Greek *politike* = "social"]), although each of them is steered only by its particular judgments and appetites, and they don't have speech through which one might indicate to another what it thinks expedient for the common benefit. You may want to know why mankind can't do the same. My answer to that has six parts.

(1) Men continually compete with one another for honour and dignity, which ants and bees do not; and that leads men, but not those other animals, to envy and hatred and finally war.

(2) Among those lower creatures, the common good of all is the same as the private good of each; and being naturally inclined to their private benefit, in procuring that they also procure the

common benefit. But a man's biggest pleasure in his own goods comes from their being greater than those of others!

(3) Bees and ants etc. don't have the use of reason (as man does), and so they don't see—and don't think they see—any fault in how their common business is organized; whereas very many men think themselves wiser than the rest, and better equipped to govern the public. These men struggle to reform and innovate, one in this way and another in that, thereby bringing the commonwealth into distraction and civil war.

(4) These creatures, though they have some use of voice in making known to one another their desires and other affections, don't have that skill with words through which some men represent good things to others in the guise of evil, and evil in the guise of good, and misrepresent how great various goods and evils are. These activities enable their practitioners to make men discontented, and to disturb their peace, whenever they feel like doing so.

(5) Creatures that lack reason don't have the notion of being insulted or wronged as distinct from being physically damaged; so as long as they are at ease physically they are not offended with their fellows; whereas man is most troublesome when he is most at ease, for that is when he loves to show his wisdom and to control the actions of those who govern the commonwealth.

(6) The agreement of these creatures is natural, whereas men's agreement is by covenant only, which is artificial; so it's no wonder if something besides the covenant is needed to make their agreement constant and lasting, namely a common power to keep them in awe and direct their actions to the common benefit.

Exercise 13

For the laws of nature—enjoining justice, fairness, modesty, mercy, and (in short) treating others as we want them to treat us—are in themselves contrary to our natural passions, unless some power frightens us into observing them. In the absence of such a power, our natural passions carry us to partiality, pride, revenge, and the like. And covenants without the sword are merely words, with no strength to secure a man at all. Every man has obeyed the laws of nature when he has wanted to, which is when he could do it safely; but if there is no power set up, or none that is strong enough for our security, no-one can safely abide by the laws; and in that case every man will and lawfully may rely on his own strength and skill to protect himself against all other men. In all places where men have lived in small families with no larger organized groupings, the trade of robber was so far from being regarded as against the law of nature that it was outright honoured, so that the greater spoils someone gained by robbery, the greater was his honour. The only constraints on robbery came from the laws of honour, which enjoined robbers to abstain from cruelty and to let their victims keep their lives and their farm implements. These days cities and kingdoms (which are only greater families) do what small families used to do back then: for their own security they enlarge their dominions, on the basis of claims that they are in danger and in fear of invasion, or that assistance might be given to invaders by the country they are attacking. They try as hard as they can to subdue or weaken their neighbours, by open force and secret manoeuvres; and if they have no other means for their own security, they do this justly, and are honoured for it in later years.

Exercises 14–19

The following exercises are intended to ensure your understanding of Aristotle's, Rachels's, and Hobbes's texts, and to help you further explore the ideas presented in this chapter.

Exercise 14: Now that you have read my textual analysis of Aristotle's argument, summarize it in your own words.
Exercise 15: Summarize, in your own words, each of the arguments in exercises 1–4 above.
Exercise 16: Now that you have read my textual analysis of Rachels's argument, summarize it in your own words.
Exercise 17: Summarize, in your own words, each of the arguments in exercises 5–8 above.
Exercise 18: Now that you have read my textual analysis of Hobbes's argument, summarize it in your own words.
Exercise 19: Summarize, in your own words, each of the arguments in exercises 9–13 above.

19.5 Reading Questions

1. What does Aristotle mean by "the Good" and "the Highest Good"?
2. What, according to Aristotle, do ordinary people think happiness is? What do the "cultivated" think it is? According to Aristotle, are either of them right? Why or why not?
3. Aristotle says: "An end pursued in itself, we say, is more complete than an end pursued because of something else." What does he mean? What do "in itself" and "because of something else" mean in this context? What does "more complete" mean?
4. According to Aristotle, what is virtue? How do people acquire virtue? What is the difference between virtues of action and virtues of character? What does this difference have to do with Aristotle's view of morality?
5. According to Rachels, what is the difference between psychological egoism and ethical egoism? Why is the difference important?
6. What, according to Rachels, is wrong with the theory of psychological egoism?
7. What, according to Hobbes, is the "State of Nature," the "Right of Nature," and the "Law of Nature"?
8. What is Hobbes's view of human reason? What is it for?
9. Why, according to Hobbes, is the sovereign needed? What powers does the sovereign need to have?
10. How does Hobbes define justice? Do you agree with this definition? Why or why not?
11. According to Hobbes, how can one get rid of a right that one possesses? Are there any rights that one cannot get rid of? Why not? What is the result of getting rid of a right?
12. According to Hobbes, what is the purpose of a law of nature? How does each of the laws he describes contribute to this purpose?

20 Normative Ethics: Utilitarianism and Deontological Ethics

20.1 Jeremy Bentham, *An Introduction to the Principles of Morals and Legislation*
20.2 John Stuart Mill, *Utilitarianism*
20.3 Immanuel Kant, *Groundwork for the Metaphysics of Morals*
20.4 In-Class Exercises
20.5 Reading Questions

20.1 Jeremy Bentham, *An Introduction to the Principles of Morals and Legislation*

Jeremy Bentham (1748–1842) was a child prodigy born to wealthy parents in London, England. He learned to read at age two, and began to study Latin at age three. Bentham graduated from Queen's College at Oxford at age fifteen, and earned a Master's degree at age eighteen. Although he trained to be a lawyer, he never practiced, but was inspired to political activism by the intricacies of English law. Throughout his life, he advocated for the rights of ordinary citizens, including women, to self-governance and economic freedom; he was outspoken against slavery and the death penalty, and in favor of the separation of church and state.

Bentham was great friends with James Mill (father of John Stuart Mill), and together they founded the *Westminster Review* as a publication venue for "philosophical radicals" and an outlet for their promotion of utilitarianism as both a moral and political theory. Bentham wrote prodigiously, publishing more than fifteen books and writing millions of unpublished manuscript pages before he died. He wrote his most famous philosophical work, *An Introduction to the Principles of Morals and Legislation*, in 1780, although it was not published until 1789. In this book, Bentham lays out his most detailed argument for utilitarianism as the foundation for morality as well as good government.

Bentham's motivation for choosing hedonistic utilitarianism over any other kind is the belief that we should not require people to be motivated to act morally in a way that is contrary to human nature. In *An Introduction to the Principles of Morals and Legislation*, Bentham argues that human beings are, in fact, motivated to act only by pleasure and pain. This is a *descriptive* statement of facts about people. To support a moral theory, though, Bentham needs to make an argument about how people *ought* to act; such a claim would be a *normative* statement about how people should be, not how they are. What Bentham argues is that a moral theory should serve the interests of the people it governs. And, since our interests are ultimately pleasure and the avoidance of pain, a moral theory should promote the maximization of pleasure and the minimization of pain for all involved. Let's look at Bentham's argument for utilitarianism. We will explore more of his arguments in the exercises.

From *An Introduction to the Principles of Morals and Legislation*.[1]

Chapter I: Of the Principle of Utility

I. Nature has placed mankind under the governance of two sovereign masters, pain and pleasure.[1] It is for them alone to point out what we ought to do,[2] as well as to determine what we shall do. On the one hand the standard of right and wrong, on the other the chain of causes and effects, are fastened to their throne.[3] They govern us in all we do, in all we say, in all we think: every effort we can make to throw off our subjection, will serve but to demonstrate and confirm it.[4] In [other] words[A] a man may pretend to abjure their empire: but in reality he will remain subject to it all the while.[5] The principle of utility recognizes this subjection, and assumes it for the foundation of that system,[6] the object of which is to rear the fabric of felicity by the hands of reason and of law. Systems which attempt to question it, deal in sounds instead of sense, in caprice instead of reason, in darkness instead of light.

But enough of metaphor and declamation: it is not by such means that moral science is to be improved. …

Chapter II: Of Principles Adverse to That of Utility

I. If the principle of utility be a right principle to be governed by, and that in all cases, it follows from what has been just observed, that whatever principle differs from it in any case must necessarily be a wrong one.

In the first section of this chapter, Bentham argues that the principle of utility (which he doesn't define until the following sections) is the appropriate principle to provide a foundation for a system of moral reasoning. This conclusion isn't stated explicitly, but it seems clear from the context, as we will see. First, Bentham makes the claim that people are governed by pleasure and pain (1). From the next few sentences, it seems that Bentham actually means something stronger than this; he is really claiming that people are governed *only* by pleasure and pain, and not by anything else. This, along with the implicit claim that what governs people is the only thing that can tell us what we do *and* what we ought to do, supports the claim that pleasure and pain tell us what we ought to do (2).

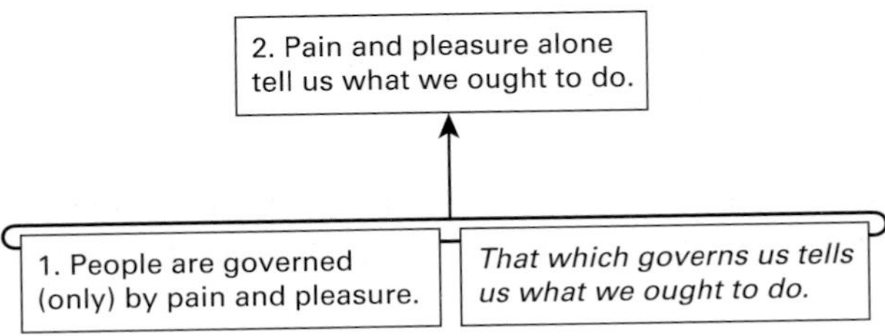

What we ought to do, of course, is what is right, so Bentham combines (2) with this as an implicit premise to conclude that pain and pleasure are the standard of right and wrong (3).

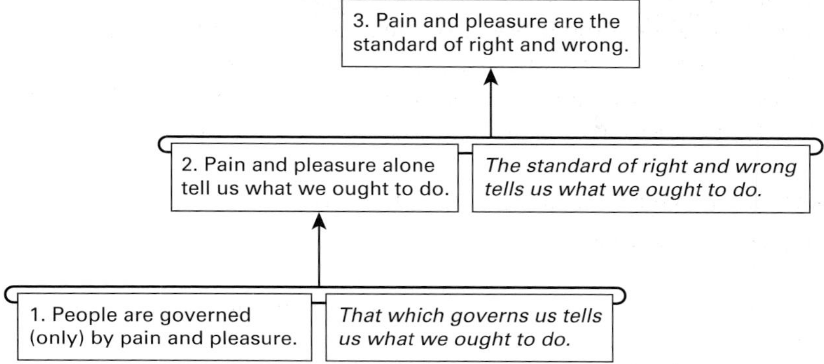

Next, Bentham says that no matter what we do, we will *always* be governed by pleasure and pain (4); that, in fact, if we tried to be governed by something else, it would only be because we *want* to be governed by something else—that being governed by something else would give us pleasure. Thus, trying to be governed by something else only proves that we are governed by pleasure and pain. This seems to be a reason to believe Bentham's first claim—that we are governed only by pleasure and pain (1), which is restated in claim (5), as indicated by (A).

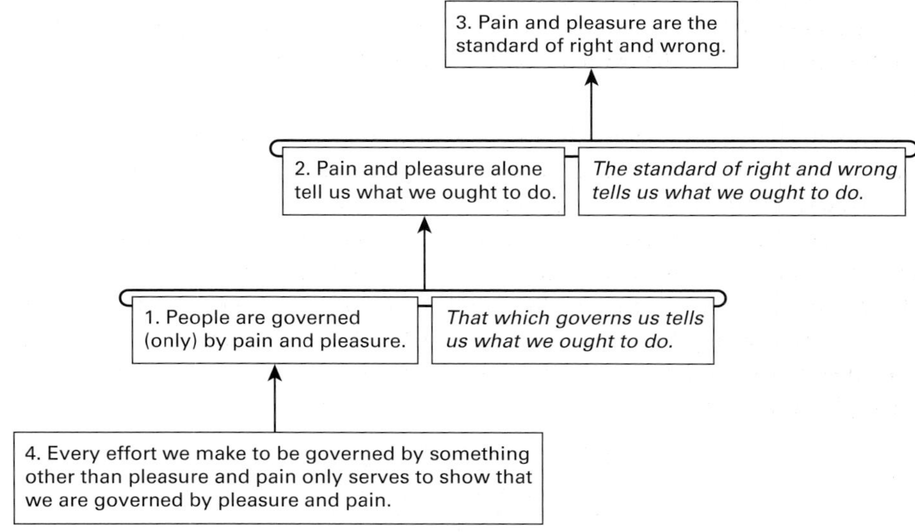

Bentham then claims that the principle of utility recognizes that we are governed only by pleasure and pain, and assumes the conclusion that pleasure and pain are the standard of right and wrong for the foundation of the correct system of moral reasoning (6). The argument, then, is that the principle of utility assumes that pleasure and pain are the standard of right and wrong, *and,* in fact, pleasure and pain *are* the standard of right and wrong, *so* the principle of utility is the appropriate basis for the foundation of moral reasoning.

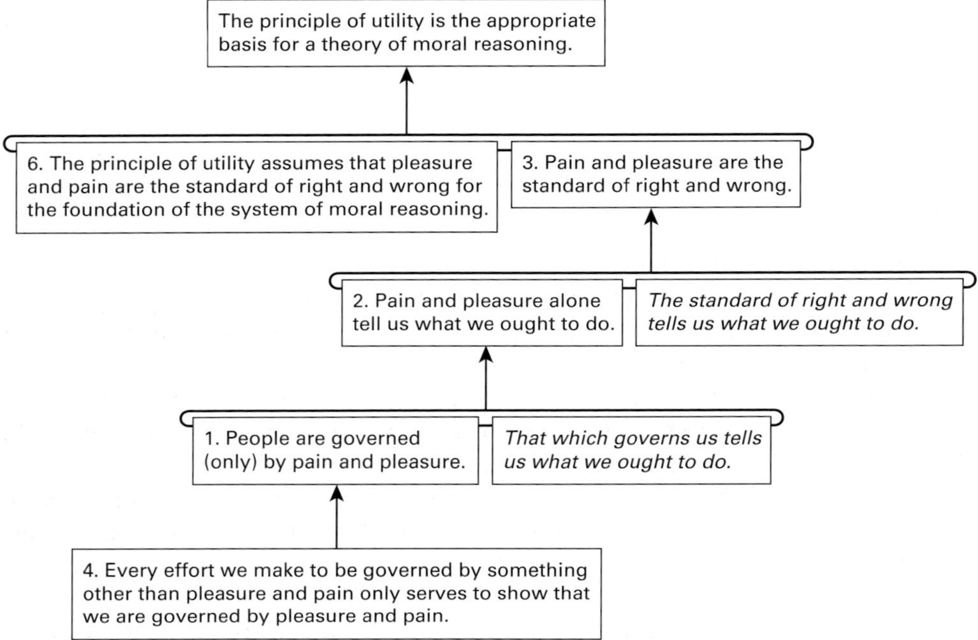

Following this argument, Bentham wants to explain the principle of utility and provide an argument for its scope:

II. The principle of utility is the foundation of the present work: it will be proper therefore at the outset to give an explicit and determinate account of what is meant by it. By the principle of utility is meant that principle which approves or disapproves of every action whatsoever according to the tendency it appears to have to augment or diminish the happiness of the party whose interest is in question:[7] or, what is the same thing in other words to promote or to oppose that happiness. I say of every action whatsoever, and therefore not only of every action of a private individual, but of every measure of government.

III. By utility is meant that property in any object, whereby it tends to produce benefit, advantage, pleasure, good, or happiness, (all this in the present case comes to the same thing) or (what comes again to the same thing)[8] to prevent the happening of mischief, pain, evil, or unhappiness to the party whose interest is considered:[9] if that party be the community in general, then the happiness of the community:[10] if a particular individual, then the happiness of that individual.[11]

IV. The interest of the community is one of the most general expressions that can occur in the phraseology of morals: no wonder that the meaning of it is often lost. When it has a meaning, it is this. The community is a fictitious *body*, composed of the individual persons who are considered as constituting as it were its *members*.[12] The interest of the community then[A] is, what is it?—the sum of the interests of the several members who compose it.[13]

V. It is in vain to talk of the interest of the community, without understanding what is the interest of the individual. A thing is said to promote the interest, or to be for the interest, of an individual, when it tends to add to the sum total of his pleasures: or, what comes to the same thing, to diminish the sum total of his pains.[14]

VI. An action then[B] may be said to be conformable to the principle of utility, or, for shortness sake, to utility, (meaning with respect to the community at large) when the tendency it has to augment the happiness of the community is greater than any it has to diminish it.[15]

In section II, he gives us a statement of the principle: an action is good or bad according to how much it promotes or opposes the happiness of the party whose interest is in question (7).

But a couple of questions arise here—what is utility (or why is this called the "principle of utility"), how does happiness relate to pleasure and pain, and whose happiness counts? In section III, he answers all three of these questions. First, "utility" is the property of something in virtue of which it produces pleasure and prevents pain (9), and second, "happiness" here is the same thing as "pleasure and the absence of pain" (8).

Finally, the "party whose interest is in question" could be the entire community, or it could be just an individual person. In the first case, utility is the property of something in virtue of which it produces happiness for the entire community (10), and in the second, happiness for the individual (11).

Given these commitments, Bentham then considers how to apply the principle of utility when the "party whose interest is in question" is indeed the community. First, he says that the community is nothing more than a collection of individuals (12). As indicated by A, this supports the assertion that the interest of a community is nothing more than the sum of the interests of the individuals who are members of that community (13).

But what are those interests? Bentham claims that something promotes the interest of an individual when it tends to add to the sum total of his pleasures or diminish the sum total of his pains (14). What are we to conclude from this? It seems that (13) and (14) combine to support the implicit conclusion that something promotes the interest of a community when it tends to add to the sum total of the pleasures or diminish the sum total of the pains of the members of the community.

Then, from section III, we know that Bentham believes that for any individual, pleasure is happiness and pain is unhappiness (8), so we can conclude that something promotes the interest of a community when it tends to add to the sum total of the happiness of the members of the community.

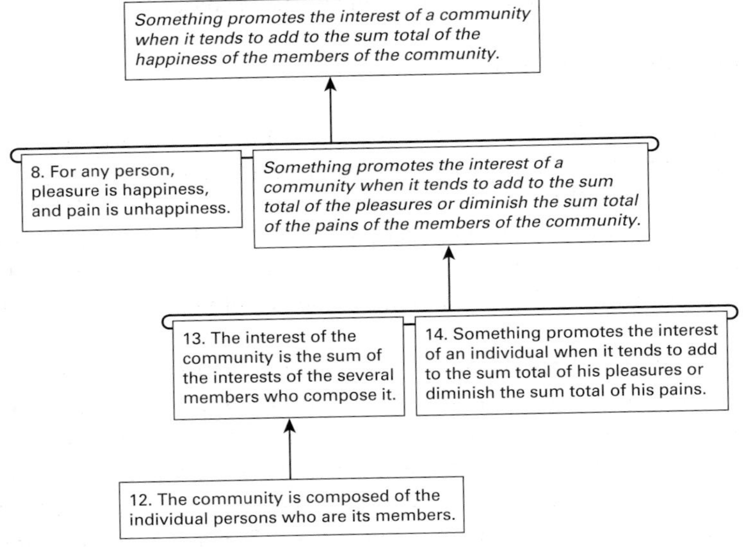

As indicated by (B), this conclusion is to be combined with Bentham's previous claims to support (15).

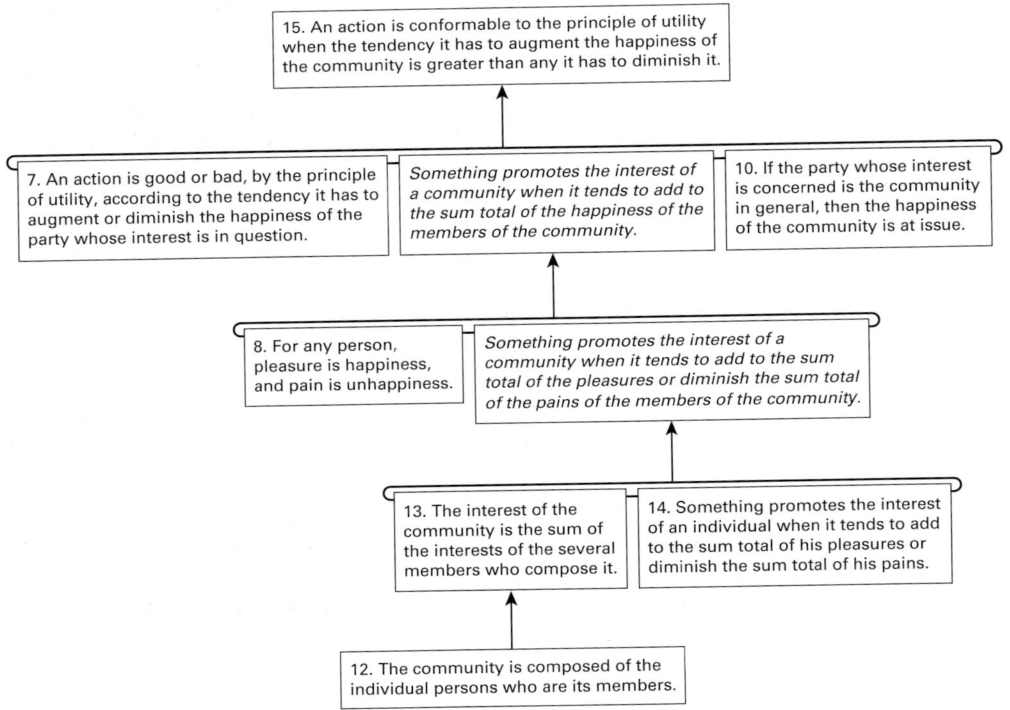

We will explore more of Bentham's arguments in the exercises.

20.2 John Stuart Mill, *Utilitarianism*

John Stuart Mill was born in London 1806 to James Mill, a Scottish historian who worked for the East India Company. James was great friends with Jeremy Bentham (1748–1842), the leading proponent of the ethical doctrine of utilitarianism. It was James's hope that his son would grow up to further the cause of utilitarianism in his own work. John Stuart was a precocious child, and began studying Bentham's work at age fifteen. He succeeded his father at the East India Company, a job that allowed him to pursue philosophy and the liberal politics of James.

Mill's first celebrated work was *A System of Logic*, published in 1843. From there he turned to ethics and political philosophy, publishing *Principles of Political Economy and Some of the Applications to Social Philosophy* in 1848, and, fulfilling the hopes of his father, *Utilitarianism* in 1861. Heavily influenced by Bentham, Mill presents a more sophisticated version of Bentham's moral theory in *Utilitarianism*. From Bentham's work it is clear that he believes that there is only one kind of pleasure and one kind of pain. The pains and pleasures of different people can differ in their intensity, duration, or proximity, but these are really differences in degree, not in kind. Mill, on the other hand, believes that there are different *kinds* of pleasures and pains, with some pleasures being better than others, and some pains being worse than others.

Recall the discussion of *intrinsic* and *instrumental* good from the introduction to Part VI. Mill, like Bentham, believes that pleasure is the only thing that is intrinsically good—that all things that are good are so only because they provide pleasure. Let's look at Mill's argument for happiness as the sole criterion of morality. We will explore more of his arguments in the exercises.

From *Utilitarianism*.[2]

Chapter 4: Of What Sort of Proof the Principle of Utility Is Susceptible

…

2. Questions about ends are, in other words, questions what things are desirable. The utilitarian doctrine is, that happiness is desirable, and the only thing desirable, as an end;[1] all other things being only desirable as means to that end. What ought to be required of this doctrine—what conditions is it requisite that the doctrine should fulfill—to make good its claim to be believed?

3. The only proof capable of being given that an object is visible, is that people actually see it. The only proof that a sound is audible, is that people hear it: and so of the other sources of our experience. In like manner, I apprehend, the sole evidence it is possible to produce that anything is desirable, is that people do actually desire it.[2] If the end which the utilitarian doctrine proposes to itself were not, in theory and in practice, acknowledged to be an end, nothing could ever convince any person that it was so. No reason can be given why the general happiness is desirable,[3] except that[A] each person, so far as

he believes it to be attainable, desires his own happiness.[4] This, however, being a fact, we have not only all the proof which the case admits of, but all which it is possible to require, that[B] happiness is a good:[5] that each person's happiness is a good to that person,[6] and the general happiness, therefore,[C] a good to the aggregate of all persons.[7] Happiness has made out its title as one of the ends of conduct,[8] and consequently[D] one of the criteria of morality.[9]

In chapter 4 of *Utilitarianism*, Mill returns to the question he raised in chapter 1—how can we prove that utilitarianism is the right moral theory? He concedes in the first chapter that a proof in the sense of a sound deductive argument cannot be given; but he explains that the "proof" of which he is speaking here is just a justification for the theory that it would be reasonable to accept.

Recall that the principle of utility, as given by both Bentham and Mill, is that an action is in accordance with the principle when it tends to produce happiness for all involved. Thus, when we say that the principle of utility is the foundation of morality, we are saying that promoting happiness is the morally correct thing to do.

In chapter 4, then, Mill wants to provide a "proof" (in his expanded sense) that happiness is a good—a moral good—and, in fact, the only moral good. This is what he is saying in (1): an "end" for a person here is a goal to which all a person's actions are aimed. So, happiness being desirable as an end means that happiness is the correct thing to designate as the moral good.

For utilitarianism to be correct, it needs to be the case that the general happiness is desirable as an end (3). He begins the argument for this, as indicated by (A), by claiming that the only reason we would have to believe that something is desirable (as an end) is that people actually desire it (2). And, in fact, people do desire their own happiness (4). These together lead to the unstated conclusion that each person's happiness is desirable as an end to that person.

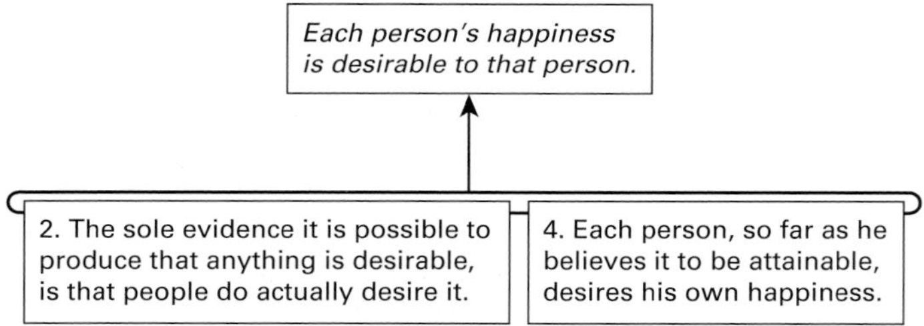

It is then clear that Mill implicitly equates something's being desirable to a person with that thing's being a good to that person. If we combine this implicit premise with the implicit conclusion from above, we can support Mill's claim that each person's happiness is a good to that person (6), which is a more specific version of the claim that happiness is a good (5). As indicated by (C), this in turn supports the claim that the general happiness is a good to the aggregate of all persons (7), which is basically a restatement of (3).

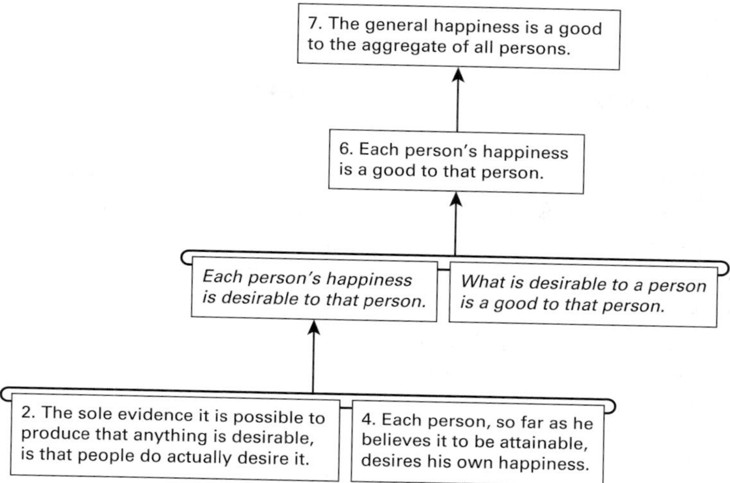

All of this supports Mill's contention that happiness is one of the ends of human conduct (8), which in turn supports, as indicated by (D), the claim that happiness is one of the criteria of morality (9).

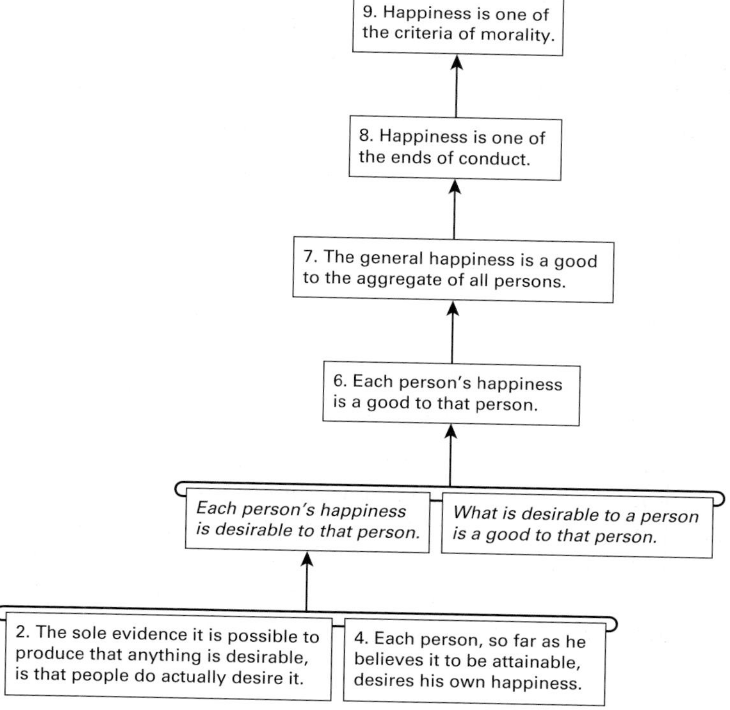

4. But it has not, by this alone, proved itself to be the sole criterion. To do that, it would seem, by the same rule, necessary to show, not only that people desire happiness, but that they never desire anything else.[10] ...

8. It results from the preceding considerations, that[E] there is in reality nothing desired except happiness.[11] Whatever is desired otherwise than as a means to some end beyond itself, and ultimately to happiness, is desired as itself a part of happiness, and is not desired for itself until it has become so.[12] Those who desire virtue for its own sake, desire it either because the consciousness of it is a pleasure, or because the consciousness of being without it is a pain, or for both reasons united; as in truth the pleasure and pain seldom exist separately, but almost always together, the same person feeling pleasure in the degree of virtue attained, and pain in not having attained more. If one of these gave him no pleasure, and the other no pain, he would not love or desire virtue, or would desire it only for the other benefits which it might produce to himself or to persons whom he cared for.

9. We have now, then, an answer to the question, of what sort of proof the principle of utility is susceptible.[F] If the opinion which I have now stated is psychologically true—if human nature is so constituted as to desire nothing which is not either a part of happiness or a means of happiness, we can have no other proof, and we require no other, that these are the only things desirable.[13] If so,[G] happiness is the sole end of human action,[14] and[H] the promotion of it the test by which to judge of all human conduct;[15] from whence it necessarily follows that[I] it must be the criterion of morality.

But, Mill acknowledges, it is not enough to just show that happiness is one of the criteria of morality—he ultimately wants to show that it is the only criterion of morality. To show that, he says, he needs to show not just that people desire happiness, but that they really don't desire anything else (10).

In sections 5–7, Mill gives virtue as an example of something people desire that isn't obviously the same as happiness. For this particular case, Mill shows that virtue is really desired because it is a part of happiness. He returns to this example in section 8, when he concludes, as indicated by (E), that people don't desire anything but happiness (11) based on the generalization that, like virtue, anything that is desired other than as a means to happiness is actually a part of happiness (12).

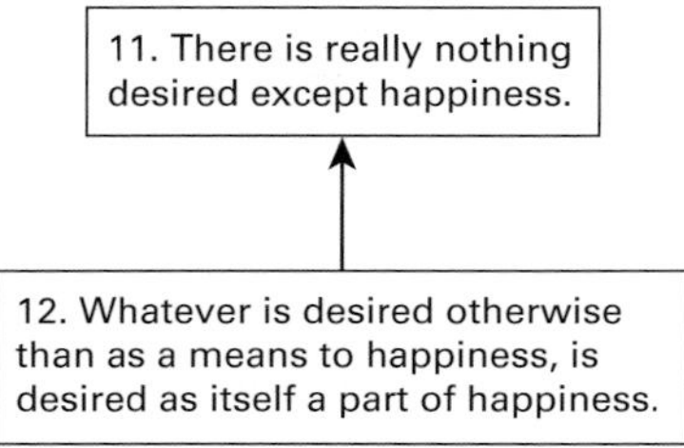

As indicated by (F), we are now brought back to being able to supplement the previous part of the argument. That happiness is the only thing that is desirable in itself (13) is a restatement of (11). Then, as indicated by (G), (11) is combined with the previous results, which I have just represented simply as the implicit claim that happiness is desirable, to support the claim that happiness is the sole end of human action (14).

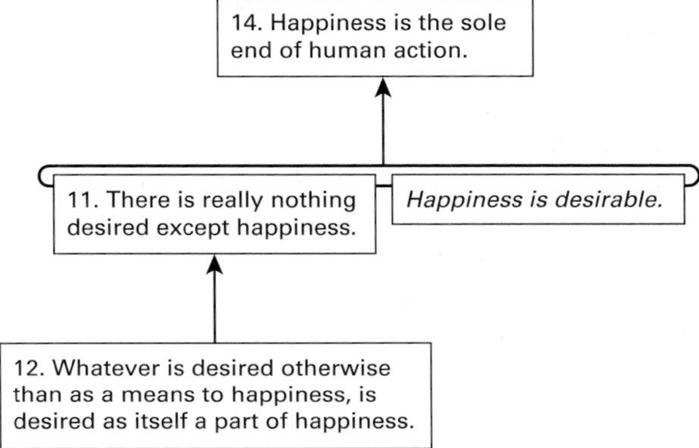

This subconclusion (14), in turn, as indicated by (H), is combined with the general claim that the promotion of the sole end of human action is the test by which we should judge all human conduct (15) to support, as indicated by (I), the final conclusion that happiness must be the one and only criterion of morality.

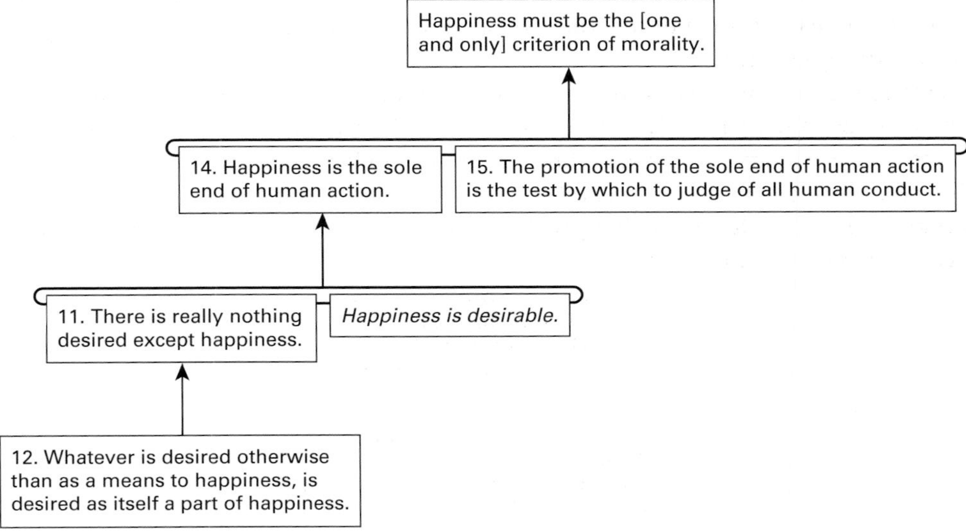

We will explore more of Mill's arguments in the exercises.

20.3 Immanuel Kant, *Groundwork for the Metaphysics of Morals*

Immanuel Kant (1724–1804) was an extraordinarily influential philosopher from a university town called Königsberg, the capitol of East Prussia (now Kaliningrad, Russia). He graduated from the University of Königsberg in 1746 and became a private tutor to young children. Six years later, he joined the faculty at the University and taught there until he retired as age seventy-two.

During Kant's time as a teacher he published several books on a wide variety of topics, including science, logic, history, and philosophy. Most of his early works had little impact, but several of his later works are among the most famous philosophical tomes ever written. In 1781, Kant wrote the *Critique of Pure Reason* (known in philosophy as the *First Critique*). Two years later, Kant wrote *Prolegomena to Any Future Metaphysics* (1783), which, in a conceptual sense, is meant to come *before* the *First Critique*. Kant then revised the *Critique of Pure Reason* (1787), which is so significantly different that scholars typically read both versions (labeled A and B). These two (really, three) works contain Kant's epistemology—his synthesis of the rationalist and empiricist movements of modern philosophy.

In 1785, Kant wrote the *Groundwork of the Metaphysics of Morals*, and then the *Critique of Practical Reason* (known as the *Second Critique)*, three years later. Nine years after that, and after he had retired from the University, he finished the *Metaphysics of Morals*. These works contain Kant's moral theory. The *Groundwork* (as its title suggests) is supposed to lay the foundation for lengthier treatments of his moral theory that came later. Two years after the *Second Critique*, Kant wrote the *Critique of Judgment* (known as the *Third Critique*), which revisits parts of Kant's epistemology, as well as delving into aesthetics.

Here, we are concerned with Kant's moral theory, which is a type of *deontological theory*. Recall that this word comes from the Greek for "study of" (*logos*) and "duty" (*deon*). Deontological theories are best understood in contrast with consequentialist theories, which is why we are reading Kant *after* Mill, even though Kant's *Groundwork* predates Mill's *Utilitarianism* by nearly a century. As we have seen, in a consequentialist theory, an action is judged to be right or wrong based on its consequences, or its outcomes. In a deontological theory, the consequences of the action aren't at issue; rather, an action is either morally obligatory (i.e., is a duty), permissible, or forbidden regardless of the actual results of the action. What makes an action right or wrong is the status of the rule that guided the action, the conformity of the action to a moral norm.

Kant's particular brand of deontological ethics goes further to say that what makes an action right or wrong is not only the status of the rule (or "maxim") that guides it, but also the actor's motivation for following the rule in the first place. For Kant, it is not enough that an action conforms with one's duty; *for the sake of duty* alone must be the reason the action is performed.

Here we will read a selection from the *Groundwork for the Metaphysics of Morals*. Kant has several purposes here. The first is to argue, against an Aristotelian (or anachronistically, a utilitarian like Mill) perhaps, that the highest good is not happiness. Kant thinks that it is not happiness that is the one purely intrinsic good; rather, a *good will* is the only intrinsic good. The second is to explain the concept of a will that is intrinsically good and lay out his principles of morality. Ultimately, Kant believes that (1) ethics is founded on reason, (2) what one's duties are is determined by reason, and (3) it is acting from duty that endows an action with moral value. Let's look at Kant's argument against happiness being the ultimate aim of human beings.

From *Groundwork for the Metaphysics of Morals*.[3]

We take it as an axiom that[A] in the natural constitution of an organized being (i.e. one suitably adapted to life) no organ will be found that isn't perfectly adapted to its purpose, whatever that is.[1] Now suppose that[B] nature's real purpose for you, a being with reason and will, were that you should survive, thrive, and be happy—in that case nature would have hit upon a very poor arrangement in appointing your reason to carry out this purpose![2] For[C] all the actions that you need to perform in order to carry out *this* intention of nature—and indeed the entire regulation of your conduct—would be marked out for you much more exactly and reliably by *instinct* than it ever could be by *reason*.[3] And[D] if nature had favoured you by giving you reason as well as instinct, the role of reason would have been to let you contemplate the happy constitution of your nature, to admire it, to rejoice in it, and to be grateful for it to its beneficent cause;[4] *not* to let you subject your faculty of desire to that weak and delusive guidance and to interfere with nature's purpose. In short, nature would have taken care that reason didn't intrude into *practical morality* and have the presumption, with its weak insight, to think out for itself the plan of happiness and how to get it.[5] Nature would have taken over the choice not only of ends but also of the means to them, and with wise foresight she would have entrusted both to instinct alone.[6]

Kant begins with an axiom, but let's set that aside for now. His argument against the claim that happiness is a human being's ultimate end is a kind of reductio ad absurdum argument. As indicated by (B), Kant invites us to consider what would be true if your happiness were actually your purpose in life. He says that if nature's real purpose for you were your happiness, then nature would not have appointed your reason to carry out the purpose (2). The reason, as indicated by (C), is that if nature's real purpose for you were your happiness, then nature would have appointed instinct rather than inexact and unreliable reason to carry out your purpose. Thus, it seems as though the implicit conclusion here is that your reason is *not* perfectly adapted to carry out your purpose, if that purpose is your happiness.

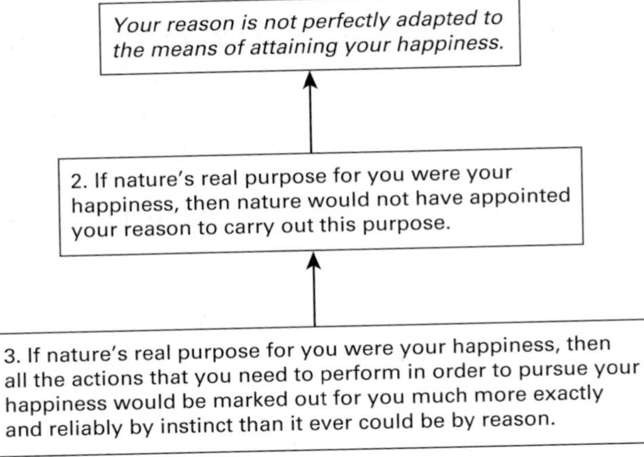

The reason for (3) is that if nature's real purpose for you were your happiness, then nature would have kept your reason away from the identifying and planning of your happiness (5), and just appoint your reason to contemplate your happiness (4). The way it is written here, it seems that (4) and (5) are the reasons to believe (6), but (6) is just a restatement of (3). So we can represent this as:

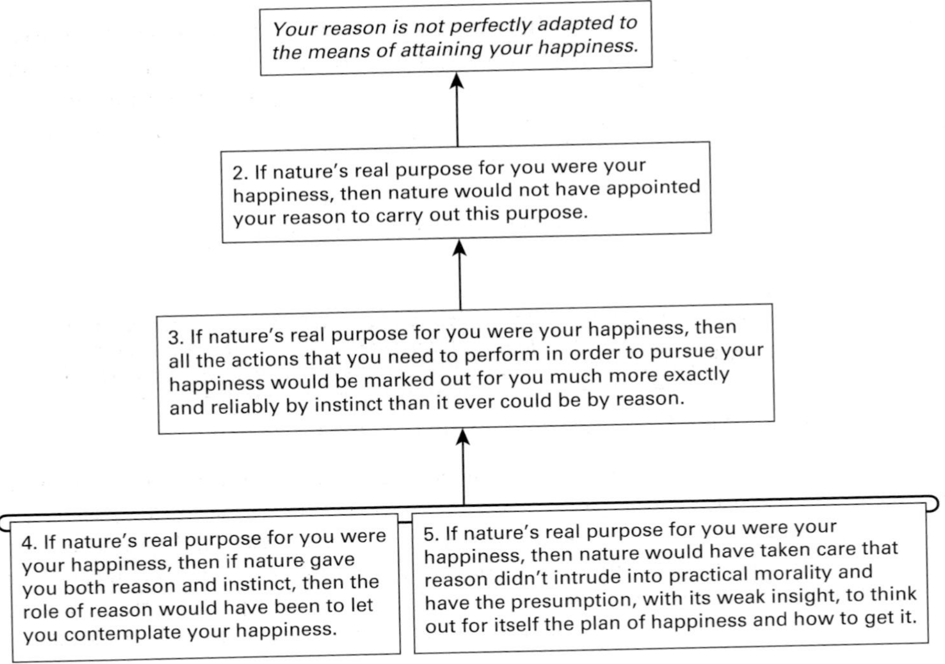

Let's go back to the beginning of this selection. Recall that Kant begins with an *axiom*, which is a premise that Kant believes needs no further support. This premise is that, for any being (like us) that is suitably adapted for living (as we are), that being will have no organs that are not perfectly adapted for their purpose (1). This seems like a scientific statement to our ears, but for Kant, it is actually a religious one—he believed that God made human beings perfectly adapted to their environment and for their ultimate purpose.

There is an underlying assumption here, namely, that your reason is the faculty that is responsible for identifying and attaining your purpose. If we combine this assumption with the axiom, we can support the implicit conclusion that our reason is a faculty that is perfectly adapted to determining an attaining our purpose (we don't think of "reason" as one of our organs, but Kant meant the term much more broadly to include all of our faculties).

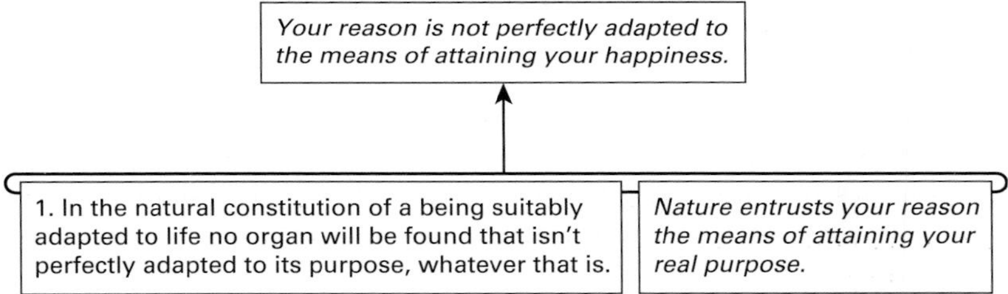

We can see where Kant is going with all of this when we put these two lines of reasoning together; on the one hand, your reason is perfectly adapted to the means of attaining your purpose, and on the other, your reason is not perfectly adapted to the means of attaining your happiness. The clear conclusion, although Kant doesn't say this explicitly, is that nature's real purpose for you is *not* your happiness.

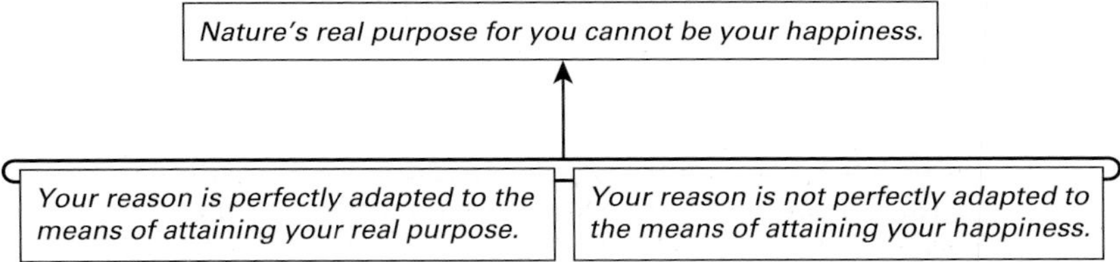

So what is your real purpose? Kant answers this question next.

As for those who play down or outright deny the boastful eulogies that are given of the happiness and contentment that reason can supposedly bring us: the judgment they are making doesn't involve gloom, or ingratitude for how well the world is governed. Rather, it's based on the idea of another and far nobler purpose for their existence. It is for achieving *this* purpose, not happiness, that reason is properly intended; and this purpose is the supreme condition, so that the private purposes of men must for the most part take second place to it. [Its being the supreme or highest condition means that it isn't itself conditional on anything else; it is to be aimed at *no matter what* else is the case; which is why our private plans must stand out of its way.—Trans.]

So[E] reason isn't competent to act as a guide that will lead the will reliably to its objectives and will satisfy all our needs[7] (indeed it *adds* to our needs!); an implanted instinct would do this job much more reliably.[8] Nevertheless,[F] reason is given to us as a *practical* faculty, that is, one that is meant to have an influence on the *will*.[9] Its proper function must be to produce a will that is good *in itself* and not good *as a means*.[10] Why? Because[G]

nature has everywhere distributed capacities suitable to the functions they are to perform,[11]
the means [to good] are, as I have pointed out, better provided for by instinct,[12] and[H]
reason and it alone can produce a will that is good *in itself*.[13]

Here Kant says that there are some people who realize that happiness is not their highest purpose. They don't lament this, though, because they realize that they have a different purpose, one that is nobler than happiness.

To determine our real purpose, we must remember Kant's emphasis on our *will*—the ability to choose our actions—and the fact that we use (or should use) our reason to guide those actions.

In this part, as indicated by (E), Kant first reminds us of the argument from above: Your reason wasn't tasked by nature to guide your will toward your happiness, because your reason isn't competent to guide your will to attain happiness (7); an implanted instinct could guide your will much better (8).

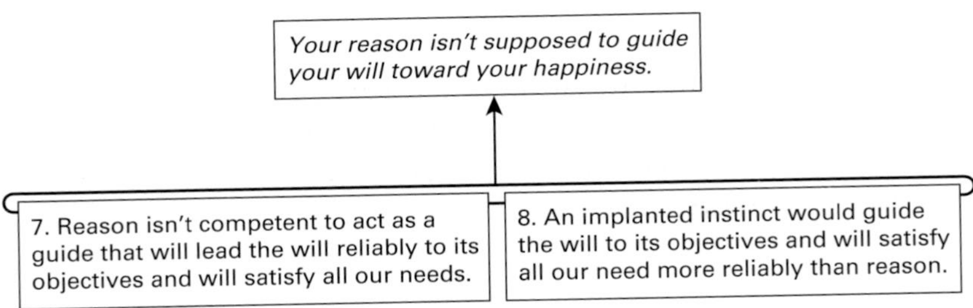

But your reason has been given to you to guide your will (9), so it must be that your reason is guiding your will toward something other than your happiness. This "something other" is a *good will*, a will that is intrinsically good, not merely instrumentally good. As indicated by (F), it seems as though (9) is supposed to be combined with something to support the claim that the proper function of reason must be to produce this good will (10). But, as indicated by (G) and (H), the three last claims seem to be intended to support (10) as well. So, here I have combined (9) with these claims to support (10).

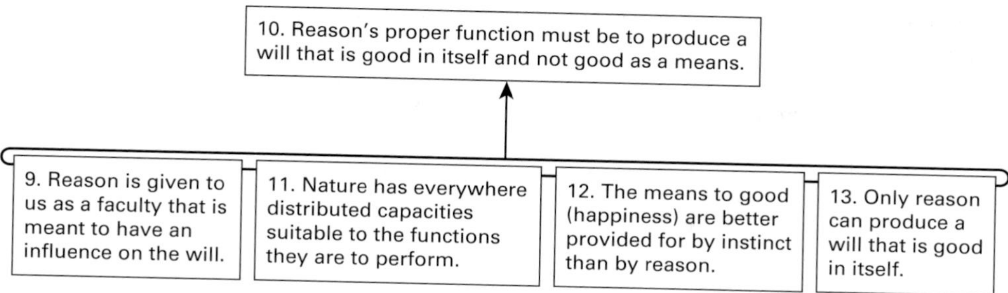

Notice that two of these last three claims seem to be summaries of the arguments from above. First, that our faculties are always suitable to the functions they perform (11) seems to be a restatement of the axiom of adaptation (1). Second, that the means to good (read "happiness") are better provided for by instinct (12) is a restatement of both (8) and (3). And finally, Kant claims that reason is the only faculty we have that could produce a good will (13), so that must be the purpose of having the faculty of reason.

We'll explore more of Kant's arguments in the exercises.

20.4 In-Class Exercises

An asterisk (*) indicates a more challenging exercise.

Exercises 1–2

In the first section of this chapter, we analyzed in detail an argument Bentham gives in *An Introduction to the Principles of Morals and Legislation*. The following selections contain other arguments from the same text. For each selection, (a) diagram the argument and (b) identify any potential objections to the argument.

Exercise 1

By a motive, in the most extensive sense in which the word is ever used with reference to a thinking being, is meant any thing that can contribute to give birth to, or even to prevent, any kind of action. Now the actions of a thinking being is the act either of the body, or only of the mind: and an act of the mind is an act either of the intellectual faculty, or of the will. Acts of the intellectual faculty will sometimes rest in the understanding merely, without exerting any influence in the production of any acts of the will. Motives, which are not of a nature to influence any other acts than those, may be styled purely *speculative* motives, or motives resting in speculation. But as to these acts, neither do they exercise any influence over external acts, or over their consequences, nor consequently over any pain or any pleasure that may be in the number of such consequences. Now it is only on account of their tendency to produce either pain or pleasure, that any acts can be material. With acts, therefore, that rest purely in the understanding, we have not here any concern: nor therefore with any object, if any such there be, which, in the character of a motive, can have no influence on any other acts than those.

Exercise 2

In all this chain of motives, the principal or original link seems to be the last internal motive in prospect: it is to this that all the other motives in prospect owe their materiality: and the immediately acting motive its existence. This motive in prospect, we see, is always some pleasure, or some pain; some pleasure, which the act in question is expected to be a means of continuing or producing: some pain which it is expected to be a means of discontinuing or preventing. A motive is substantially nothing more than pleasure or pain, operating in a certain manner. Now, pleasure is in *itself* a good: nay, even setting aside immunity from pain, the only good: pain is in itself an evil; and, indeed, without exception, the only evil; or else the words good and evil have no meaning. And this is alike true of every sort of pain, and of every sort of pleasure. It follows, therefore, immediately and incontestably, that *there is no such thing as any sort of motive that is in itself a bad one.*

Exercises 3–5

In the second part of this chapter, we analyzed in detail Mill's "proof" of utilitarianism. The following selections contain other arguments from the same text. For each selection, (a) diagram the argument and (b) identify any potential objections to the argument.

Exercise 3

5. If I am asked, what I mean by difference of quality in pleasures, or what makes one pleasure more valuable than another, merely as a pleasure, except its being greater in amount, there is but one possible answer. Of two pleasures, if there be one to which all or almost all who have experience of both give a decided preference, irrespective of any feeling of moral obligation to prefer it, that is the more desirable pleasure. If one of the two is, by those who are competently acquainted with both, placed so far above the other that they prefer it, even though knowing it to be attended with a greater amount of discontent, and would not resign it for any quantity of the other pleasure which their nature is capable of, we are justified in ascribing to the preferred enjoyment a superiority in quality, so far outweighing quantity as to render it, in comparison, of small account.

6. Now it is an unquestionable fact that those who are equally acquainted with, and equally capable of appreciating and enjoying, both, do give a most marked preference to the manner of existence which employs their higher faculties. Few human creatures would consent to be changed into any of the lower animals, for a promise of the fullest allowance of a beast's pleasures; no intelligent human being would consent to be a fool, no instructed person would be an ignoramus, no person of feeling and conscience would be selfish and base, even though they should be persuaded that the fool, the dunce, or the rascal is better satisfied with his lot than they are with theirs. They would not resign what they possess more than he, for the most complete satisfaction of all the desires which they have in common with him. If they ever fancy they would, it is only in cases of unhappiness so extreme, that to escape from it they would exchange their lot for almost any other, however undesirable in their own eyes. A being of higher faculties requires more to make him happy, is capable probably of more acute suffering, and is certainly accessible to it at more points, than one of an inferior type; but in spite of these liabilities, he can never really wish to sink into what he feels to be a lower grade of existence.

Exercise 4

19. The objectors to utilitarianism cannot always be charged with representing it in a discreditable light. On the contrary, those among them who entertain anything like a just idea of its disinterested character, sometimes find fault with its standard as being too high for humanity. They say it is exacting too much to require that people shall always act from the inducement of promoting the general interests of society. But this is to mistake the very meaning of a standard of morals, and to confound the rule of action with the motive of it. It is the business of ethics to tell us what are our duties, or by what test we may know them; but no system of ethics requires that the sole motive of all we do shall be a feeling of duty; on the contrary, ninety-nine hundredths of all our actions are done from other motives, and rightly so done, if the rule of duty does not condemn them.

Exercise 5

Again, defenders of utility often find themselves called upon to reply to such objections as this—that there is not time, previous to action, for calculating and weighing the effects of any line of conduct on the general happiness. This is exactly as if anyone were to say that it is impossible to guide our conduct by Christianity, because there is not time, on every occasion on which anything has to be done, to read through the Old and New Testaments. The answer to the objection is, that there has been ample time, namely, the whole past duration of the human species. During all that time mankind have been learning by experience the tendencies of actions; on which experience all the prudence, as well as all the morality of life, is dependent.

Exercises 6–7

In the last section of this chapter, we analyzed in detail Kant's argument that happiness is not the highest good in *Groundwork for the Metaphysics of Morals*. The following selections contain other arguments from the same text. For each selection, (a) diagram the argument and (b) identify any potential objections to the argument.

Exercise 6

Nothing in the world—*or out of it!*—can possibly be conceived that could be called 'good' without qualification except a GOOD WILL. Mental *talents* such as intelligence, wit, and judgment, and *temperaments* such as courage, resoluteness, and perseverance are doubtless in many ways good and desirable; but they can become extremely bad and harmful if the person's *character* isn't good—i.e. if the *will* that is to make use of these gifts of nature isn't good. Similarly with gifts of fortune. Power, riches, honour, even health, and the over-all well-being and contentment with one's condition that we call "happiness," create pride, often leading to arrogance, if there isn't a good will to correct their influence on the mind. ... Not to mention the fact that the sight of someone who shows no sign of a pure and good will and yet enjoys uninterrupted prosperity will never give pleasure to an impartial rational observer. So it seems that without a good will one can't even be worthy of being happy.

Exercise 7

This good will needn't be the sole and complete good, but it must be the condition of all others, even of the desire for happiness. So we have to consider two purposes: (1) the unconditional purpose of producing a good will, and (2) the conditional purpose of being happy. Of these, (1) requires the cultivation of reason, which—at least in this life—in many ways *limits* and can indeed almost *eliminate* (2) the goal of happiness. This state of affairs is entirely compatible with the wisdom of nature; it doesn't have nature pursuing its goal clumsily; because reason, recognizing that its highest practical calling is to establish a good will, can by achieving that goal get a contentment of its own kind (the kind that comes from attaining a goal set by reason), even though this gets in the way of things that the person merely *prefers*.

***Exercise 8*

Create a diagram for an argument for the claim that "It is morally wrong, when in difficulties, to make a promise I do not intend to keep" that Kant would endorse.

Exercises 9–14

The following exercises are intended to ensure your understanding of Bentham's, Mill's, and Kant's texts, and to help you further explore the ideas presented in this chapter.

Exercise 9: Now that you have read my textual analysis of Bentham's argument, summarize it in your own words.
Exercise 10: Summarize, in your own words, each of the arguments in exercises 1 and 2 above.
Exercise 11: Now that you have read my textual analysis of Mill's argument, summarize it in your own words.
Exercise 12: Summarize, in your own words, each of the arguments in exercises 3–5 above.
Exercise 13: Now that you have read my textual analysis of Kant's argument, summarize it in your own words.
Exercise 14: Summarize, in your own words, each of the arguments in exercises 6 and 7 above.

20.5 Reading Questions

1. Near the end of chapter I, Bentham says: "Has the rectitude of this principle been ever formally contested? It should seem that it had, by those who have not known what they have been meaning. Is it susceptible of any direct proof? it should seem not: for that which is used to prove every thing else, cannot itself be proved: a chain of proofs must have their commencement somewhere. To give such proof is as impossible as it is needless." What does he mean? Why can't a proof be given?
2. How, according to Bentham, are we to decide which of several possible actions is the right one to do? How, in other words, are we supposed to apply the principle of utility when making decisions?

3. In chapter X, Bentham says: "Now, pleasure is in *itself* a good: nay, even setting aside immunity from pain, the only good: pain is in itself an evil; and, indeed, without exception, the only evil; or else the words good and evil have no meaning. And this is alike true of every sort of pain, and of every sort of pleasure." What does he mean when he claims that pleasure is the only good and pain is the only evil? Do you agree? Why or why not?
4. In chapter 2, Mill says: "It is better to be a human being dissatisfied than a pig satisfied; better to be Socrates dissatisfied than a fool satisfied." What does he mean? Do you agree? Why or why not?
5. In chapter 2, Mill says: "The objectors to utilitarianism cannot always be charged with representing it in a discreditable light. On the contrary, those among them who entertain anything like a just idea of its disinterested character, sometimes find fault with its standard as being too high for humanity." How does Mill respond to this criticism?
6. In chapter 2, Mill explains another objection to utilitarianism: "It is often affirmed that utilitarianism renders men cold and unsympathizing; that it chills their moral feelings towards individuals; that it makes them regard only the dry and hard consideration of the consequences of actions, not taking into their moral estimate the qualities from which those actions emanate." How does Mill respond?
7. A common objection to utilitarianism is that while it is true that each person's greatest good is happiness, why should it be the case that ultimately what matters for morality is the sum of everyone's happiness? In other words, why are Bentham and Mill utilitarians, and not egoists?
8. Another common objection to utilitarianism is that only the total happiness matters morally, and not how happiness is distributed. Is this a fair criticism? How would Bentham or Mill respond?
9. Kant says: "Men preserve their lives *according to* duty, but not *from* duty." What does he mean? What is the difference between "according to" duty and "from" duty?
10. Kant says that some rules of conduct ("maxims") have moral content while others do not. Why is this? What is the difference between the two kinds of rules?
11. Kant gives three propositions (or laws) of morality, and he says that the third follows from the first two. Explain what these laws are, and how the third is meant to follow from the first two.
12. What is the difference between a hypothetical imperative and a categorical imperative?
13. In Groundwork for the Metaphysics of Morals, Kant names a number of duties that we have: keeping our promises, telling the truth, developing our talents, and helping people when you can. Can you think of any other duties that Kant would say we have? Why do you think he would agree that those are our duties?

Notes

Preface

1. Jay F. Rosenberg, *The Practice of Philosophy: A Handbook for Beginners*, 3rd ed. (Upper Saddle River, NJ: Prentice Hall, 1996).

2. Plato, *Meno*, trans. G. M. A. Grube, in *Five Dialogues*, 2nd ed., ed. Rev. John M. Cooper (Indianapolis, IN: Hackett, 2002), 89d–100b.

3. René Descartes, *Meditations on First Philosophy*, ed. and trans. E. Haldane and G. R. T. Ross in *The Philosophical Works of Descartes*, Vol. 1 (1641; Cambridge: Cambridge University Press, 1969).

4. P. A. Kirschner, S. J. B. Shum, and C. S. Carr, eds., *Visualizing Argumentation: Software Tools for Collaborative and Educational Sense-Making* (New York: Springer, 2003); C. R. Twardy, "Argument Maps Improve Critical Thinking," *Teaching Philosophy* 27 (2004): 95–116; T. van Gelder, "Enhancing Deliberation through Computer Supported Visualization," in *Visualizing Argumentation*, ed. P.A. Kirschner, S. J. B. Shum, and C. S. Carr, 97–115.

5. M. Harrell, "Argument Diagramming and Critical Thinking in Introductory Philosophy," *Higher Education Research and Development* 30, no. 3 (2011): 371–385; M. Harrell, "No Computer Program Required: Even Pencil-and-Paper Argument Mapping Improves Critical Thinking Skills," *Teaching Philosophy* 31 (2008): 351–374.

6. G. Rowe, F. Macagno, C. Reed, and D. Walton, "Araucaria as a Tool for Diagramming Arguments in Teaching and Studying Philosophy," *Teaching Philosophy* 29 (2006): 111–124.

7. Argutect (Version 3.0) (computer software). Pittsburgh: Knosis, 2002.

8. Athena Standard v. 2.2, © Bertil Rolf and Charlotte Magnusson, http://www.bertilrolf.com/index/Argument_Software.html.

9. Inspiration v. 7.5, © Donald Helfgott and Mona Westhaver, http://www.inspiration.com/.

10. Rationale © Tim van Gelder, http://www.austhinkconsulting.com.

11. M. Harrell, "Using Argument Diagramming Software in the Classroom," *Teaching Philosophy* 28 (2005): 163–177.

12. M. Harrell, "Using Argument Diagramming Software in the Classroom" (2005), paper given at the 2005 North American Computing and Philosophy Conference; M. Harrell, "Using Argument Diagramming Software to Teach Critical Thinking Skills" (2006), paper given at the 2006 North American Computing and Philosophy Conference.

Chapter 1

1. For an elaboration of these questions and answers, see Clark Glymour, *Thinking Things Through*, 2nd ed. (Cambridge, MA: MIT Press, 2015).

2. Bertrand Russell, *The Problems of Philosophy* (Home University Library, 1912). Reprinted by Hackett Publishing, Indianapolis, 1990.

3. Aristotle, *Physics* (Oxford translation), in *The Complete Works of Aristotle*, ed. Jonathan Barnes (Princeton: Princeton University Press, 1984).

4. Aristotle, *Physics*.

Chapter 2

1. Plato, *Meno*, trans. G. M. A. Grube, in *Five Dialogues*, 2nd ed., ed. John M. Cooper (Indianapolis, IN: Hackett, 2002).

Chapter 4

1. St. Anselm, *Proslogion*, trans. David Burr, Department of History, Virginia Tech, Blacksburg, Virginia. http://www.history.vt.edu/Burr/Anselm.html.

2. Thomas Aquinas, *Summa Theologica*, trans. Laurence Shapcote (London: O. P. Benziger Brothers, 1911).

3. This argument does not change even if you consider that quantum mechanics and general relativity have supplanted Newtonian physics. General relativity holds that an object's "natural" state is to move at a constant speed in a straight line, where a straight line may seem to not be straight because of the curvature of spacetime.

Chapter 5

1. Michael Martin, "Three Arguments for Nonbelief," *Free Inquiry*, September 22, 2001.

2. John Mackie, "Evil and Omnipotence" *Mind* 64, no. 254 (1955): 200–212.

3. G. W. Leibniz, *Theodicy: Essays on the Goodness of God the Freedom of Man and the Origin of Evil*, ed. with an introduction by Austin Farrer, trans. E. M. Huggard from C. J. Gerhardt's edition of the *Collected Philosophical Works*, 1875–90 Peru, IL: Open Court, 1985).

Chapter 6

1. David Hume, in *The Life of David Hume, Esq. Written by Himself* (London, 1777).

2. Immanuel Kant, *Prolegomena to Any Future Metaphysics*, rev. ed., ed. and trans. Gary Hatfield (Cambridge: Cambridge University Press, 2004).

3. Jeremy Bentham, *A Fragment on Government; Being an Examination of Whit Is Delivered, on the Subject of Government in General, in the Introduction to Sir William Blackstone's Commentaries* (London, 1776).

4. David Hume, *Dialogues Concerning Natural Religion*, 2nd ed. (London, 1779), trans. Jonathan Bennett, http://www.earlymoderntexts.com/authors/hume. © 2010–2015 Jonathan Bennett.

5. William Paley, *Natural Theology: Or, Evidences of the Existence and Attributes of the Deity*, 12th ed. (London: J. Faulder, 1809).

6. Stephen Jay Gould, *The Panda's Thumb: More Reflections on National History* (New York: W. W. Norton, 1980).

Chapter 7

1. *Theaetetus*, in *The Collected Dialogues of Plato*, trans. F. M. Cornford (Princeton: Princeton University Press, 1958).

2. Edmund L. Gettier, "Is Justified True Belief Knowledge?" *Analysis* 23 (1963): 121–123.

3. Richard Feldman, "An Alleged Defect in Gettier Counter-Examples," *Australasian Journal of Philosophy* 52 (1974): 68–69.

4. Roy Sorensen, "Epistemic Paradoxes," in *The Stanford Encyclopedia of Philosophy* (Spring 2012 ed.), ed. Edward N. Zalta, http://plato.stanford.edu/archives/spr2012/entries/epistemic-paradoxes/.

Chapter 8

1. La Haye en Touraine was renamed La Haye-Descartes in 1802, and then renamed Descartes in 1967.

2. René Descartes, *Meditations on First Philosophy: Meditation I*, trans. Jonathan Bennett, http://www.earlymoderntexts.com/authors/descartes. © 2010–2015 Jonathan Bennett. (Originally published as *Meditationes de prima philosophia, in qua Dei existentia et animae immortalitas demonstrantur* [Paris: Michel Soly, 1641].)

3. I call this statement (13) because it starts before statement (14).

4. René Descartes, *Meditations on First Philosophy: Meditation II*, trans. Jonathan Bennett, http://www.earlymoderntexts.com/authors/descartes. © 2010–2015 Jonathan Bennett.

5. John Locke, *An Essay Concerning Human Understanding* (1690), trans. Jonathan Bennett, http://www.earlymoderntexts.com/authors/locke. © 2010–2015 Jonathan Bennett.

6. This term for the mentally challenged was widely used in Locke's time.

7. David Hume, *An Enquiry Concerning Human Understanding* (1748), trans. Jonathan Bennett, http://www.earlymoderntexts.com/authors/hume. © 2010–2015 Jonathan Bennett.

Chapter 9

1. Hans Reichenbach, *Experience and Prediction: An Analysis of the Foundation and the Structure of Knowledge* (Chicago: University of Chicago Press, 1938).

2. Karl R. Popper, *Conjectures and Refutations: The Growth of Scientific Knowledge* (New York: Basic Books, 1962), pp 33–59.

3. Nelson Goodman, "The New Riddle of Induction," chapter 3 in *Fact, Fiction, and Forecast* (Cambridge, MA: Harvard University Press, 1955).

Chapter 10

1. Alan Turing, "Computing Machinery and Intelligence," *Mind* 59, no. 236 (1950): 433–460.

2. René Descartes, *Meditations on First Philosophy: Meditation VI*, trans. Jonathan Bennett, http://www.earlymoderntexts.com/authors/descartes. © 2010–2015 Jonathan Bennett. (Originally published as *Meditationes de prima philosophia* [Paris: Michel Soly, 1641].)

3. René Descartes, *The Passions of the Soul*, trans. Jonathan Bennett, http://www.earlymoderntexts.com/authors/descartes. © 2010–2015 Jonathan Bennett. (Originally published as *Les passions de l'âme* [Amsterdam: Lodewijk Elsevier, 1649].)

4. Gilbert Ryle, *The Concept of Mind* (New York: Barnes & Noble, 1949).

5. Jeanette M. Liska *Silenced Screams: Surviving Anesthetic Awareness During Surgery: A True Life Account* (Park Ridge, IL: American Association of Nurse Anesthetists, 2002).

6. Descartes, *The Passions of the Soul*.

Chapter 11

1. J. J. C. Smart, "Sensations and Brain Processes," *Philosophical Review* 68, no. 2 (1959): 141–156.

2. Jerry A. Fodor, "The Mind–Body Problem," *Scientific American* 244, no. 1 (1981): 114–123.

3. Ned Block, "Troubles with Functionalism," in *Perception and Cognition: Issues in the Foundations of Psychology*, ed. C. W. Savage (Minneapolis: University of Minnesota Press, 1978), 261–325.

Chapter 12

1. Thomas Nagel, "What Is It Like to Be a Bat?" *Philosophical Review* 83, no. 4 (1974): 435–450.

2. Frank Jackson, "Epiphenomenal Qualia," *Philosophical Quarterly* 32, no. 127 (1982): 127–136.

3. Paul Churchland, *A Neurocomputational Perspective: The Nature of Mind and the Structure of Science* (Cambridge, MA: MIT Press, 1989).

4. Paul Churchland, "Reduction, Qualia, and the Direct Introspection of Brain States," *Journal of Philosophy* 82, no. 1 (1985): 8–28.

Chapter 13

1. John Searle, *Minds, Brains, and Science* (Cambridge, MA: Harvard University Press, 1984).

2. Dan Dennett, *Consciousness Explained* (New York: Little, Brown, 1991).

Chapter 14

1. Baron d'Holbach, *The System of Nature, or The Laws of the Moral and Physical World* (1858), trans. H. D. Robinson, © 2001.

2. Galen Strawson, "The Impossibility of Moral Responsibility," *Philosophical Studies* 75 (1994): 5–24.

Chapter 15

1. David Hume, *An Enquiry Concerning Human Understanding* (1748), ed. Jonathan Bennett, http://www.earlymoderntexts.com/authors/hume. © 2010–2015 Jonathan Bennett.

2. W. T. Stace, *Religion and the Modern Mind* (New York: J. B. Lippincott, 1952).

3. Ledger Wood, "The Free-Will Controversy," *Philosophy* 16, no. 64 (1941): 386–397.

Chapter 16

1. Roderick Chisholm, "Human Freedom and the Self," originally published as "The Lindley Lecture," University of Kansas, 1964, 3–15.

2. Peter van Inwagen, *Metaphysics*, 3rd ed. (Boulder: Westview Press, 2008).

Chapter 17

1. Plato, *The Trial and Death of Socrates*, trans. G. M. A. Grube (Indianapolis: Hackett, 1975).

2. James Rachels, *The Elements of Moral Philosophy*, 4th ed. (New York: McGraw-Hill, 2002).

3. James Rachels and Stuart Rachels, *The Elements of Moral Philosophy*, 7th ed. (New York: McGraw-Hill, 2012).

Chapter 18

1. Ruth Benedict, "Anthropology and the Abnormal," *Journal of General Psychology* 10 (1934): 59–82.

2. James Rachels and Stuart Rachels, *The Elements of Moral Philosophy*, 7th ed. (New York: McGraw-Hill, 2012).

Chapter 19

1. Aristotle, *Nicomachean Ethics*, Book I, sec. 7, in *Introductory Readings*, trans. Terrance Irwin and Gail Fine (Indianapolis: Hackett, 1996).

2. James Rachels and Stuart Rachels, *The Elements of Moral Philosophy*, 7th ed. (New York: McGraw-Hill, 2012).

3. Thomas Hobbes, *Leviathan* (1651), trans. Jonathan Bennett, http://www.earlymoderntexts.com/authors/hobbes. © 2010–2015 Jonathan Bennett.

Chapter 20

1. Jeremy Bentham, *An Introduction to the Principles of Morals and Legislation* (1789), http://utilitarianism.org/jeremy-bentham/index.html.

2. John Stuart Mill, *Utilitarianism*, in *Utilitarianism and On Liberty*, 2nd ed., ed. M. Warnock, (Malden, MA: Blackwell, 2003), 181–235.

3. Immanuel Kant, *Groundwork for the Metaphysics of Morals* (1785), trans. Jonathan Bennett, http://earlymoderntexts.com/authors/kant. © 2010–2015 Jonathan Bennett.

Index

Abduction. *See* Abductive (argument)
Abductive (argument), 29, 89, 90, 91, 144–155, 207
Absent qualia argument, 287–288
Absolutism. *See* Ethical realism
Academy (Plato's school), 7
Aesthetics, 5
Affirming the consequent, 26
Agent causation. *See* Libertarianism (free will)
Altruism, 406–409, 422–423
Analogy, argument from. *See* Argument by analogy
Anselm, 90, 93–100, 113–115, 144
Antecedent, 16, 17
Antecedent skepticism, 212
Anthropology, 389–393. *See also* Cultural relativism
"Anthropology and the Abnormal" (Benedict), 389–393
Antimaterialism, 289–300
Apology (Plato), 8, 13, 373
A posteriori, 27–28, 89, 90, 91, 102
A posteriori deductive argument, 90. *See also* Deductive (argument)
A posteriori nondeductive abductive argument, 90. *See also* Abductive (argument); Nondeductive (argument)
A posteriori nondeductive argument by analogy, 90. *See also* Argument by analogy; Nondeductive (argument)
Applied ethics, 367
A priori, 27, 28, 89–90, 93, 98
A priori deductive argument, 90. *See also* Deductive (argument)
Aquinas, Thomas, 90–91, 101–113, 115–117, 144
Araucaria (software), xii
Argument, 7
  analysis, x, 9, chs. 2–3
  creation, 10
  evaluation, 9–10, ch. 2
Argument by analogy, 28, 89, 90, 92, ch. 6
Argument by induction. *See* Inductive (argument)
Argument diagramming, ch. 3
  benefits of, xii–xiii
  online course for, xiii
  rules of, 37, 41, 65–66
  software for, xii-xiii
  as visualization of argument, x
Argument forms, 24–27
  invalid, 26–27
  valid, 24–25
Argument from analogy. *See* Argument by analogy
Argument from design, 92, ch. 6
Argument from evil, 91, 126–132, 134–135
Argument from incoherence, 91, 120–126
Argument from nonbelief, 120, 133
Argument from religious experience, 91
Argument to the best explanation. *See* Abductive (argument)
Argument visualization. *See* Argument diagramming
Argutect (software), xii
Aristotle, 90, 91–92, 101, 107, 109, 187, 188, 370–371
  four causes, 8, 91–92, 371
  life and works, 8
  Nicomachean Ethics, 401–405, 418–422, 428
  on proof, 7
  on Zeno's paradoxes, 5–6, 9, 12
Artificial intelligence, ch. 13
Athena Standard (software), xii
Augustine, 89, 90, 135
Auxiliary hypothesis, 240–241

Baier, Kurt, 424–425
Basic argument (against moral responsibility), 328–332, 334–335
Basic belief, 187
Bayes, Thomas, 7
Bayes' theorem, 7
Behaviorism. *See* Logical behaviorism
Benedict, Ruth, 389–398
Bentham, Jeremy, 137, 372, 429–435, 445–446, 448
Block, Ned, 287–288
Boyle, Robert, 206
Bradley, Raymond, 120, 133
Brandon, Barbara, 423
Butler, (Bishop) Joseph, 212

Calculus, 10
"Can Computers Think?" (Searle). *See Minds, Brains, and Science* (Searle)
Carnap, Rudolf, 229
Cartesian circle, 259
Cartesian dualism, 256, ch. 10
Cassirer, Ernst, 229
Categorical syllogism, 25
Category mistake, 257, 274–275
Causal regress argument
  for the existence of God, 101–113
  against moral responsibility, 328–332
Causation. *See* Aristotle, four causes; Problem of induction
Cavendish, William, 412
Certainty (of belief), 169, 171, ch. 8
Chain argument, 47–49
"Challenge of Cultural Relativism" (Rachels), 393–398. *See also Elements of Moral Philosophy* (Rachels)
Charity, principle of (in interpreting arguments), 51, 53–54, 65, 68
Charles I of England, 412
Chinese Room (thought experiment), ch. 13
Chisholm, Roderick M., 349–354, 360–361
Churchland, Paul, 296–300, 301–302, 304–305
Cogency. *See* Cogent (argument)
Cogent (argument), 21, 22, 98, 107, 124
Combination indicators, 45
Commonsense morality, 423–424
Compatibilism, 321–322, chs. 15–16
Complex argument, 49–50
Concept of Mind (Ryle), 267–276
Conceptual analysis, 175
Conclusion, x, 18
Conclusion indicator, 40. *See also* Structural indicators
Conditional statement, 16–18
Confirmation (of a theory/hypothesis), 239–240, 241–247
Conjectures, 239
Conjectures and Refutations (Popper), 234–241, 249–251
Consciousness Explained (Dennett), 311–313, 315–316
"Consciousness Imagined" (Dennett). *See Consciousness Explained* (Dennett)
Consequent, 16, 17
Consequentialist ethics, 371–372, 440. *See also* Utilitarianism
Consequent skepticism, 212
Constructive dilemma, 25
Contractarianism, 371, 412–418, 425–427
Conventionalism. *See* Cultural relativism
Convergent argument, 46–47, 65, 91, 119, 120–123
Convergent argument indicator, 47
Cooper, Anthony Ashley, 206
Cosmological argument. *See also* Aquinas 90–91, 101–113
Covenant, 427–428. *See also* Hobbes, Thomas; *Leviathan*; Contractarianism
Critical thinking, x
Cultural differences argument, 393–397. *See also* Cultural relativism
Cultural relativism, 368–369, ch. 18

Darwin, Charles, 138, 144, 153–154, 303
Davis, D. Dwight, 153
Deduction. *See* Deductive (argument)

Deductive (argument), 24–28
for the existence of God, 90–91, ch. 4
against the existence of God, 91, ch. 5
Definition, 23. *See also* Necessary and sufficient conditions
Demarcation (of science from nonscience), 234–235. *See also* Popper, Karl
de Mirabaud, Jean-Baptiste. *See* d'Holbach, Baron
Dennett, Daniel, 258, 311–313, 315–316
Deontological ethics, 372, 440. *See also* Kant, Immanuel
"Descartes' Myth" (Ryle). *See Concept of Mind* (Ryle)
Descartes, René, x–xi, 165, 168–169, 187–206, 212, 221–223, 227, 256, ch. 10, 354
Descriptive (account of human behavior), 369, 429–430
Design, argument from. *See* Argument from design
Determinism, 321–322, chs. 14–16
Deterministic system, 321
d'Holbach, Baron, 323–327, 333–334, 336
Dialogues Concerning Natural Religion (Hume), 92, 137–144, 156–158
Digital computer, 308–310
Disjunction, 177–178
Disjunctive syllogism, 25
Divine command theory, 368, ch. 17
Double-life theory. *See* Cartesian dualism
Drange, Theodore, 120
Dualism, ch. 10

Easterday, Matthew, xiii
Efficient cause. *See* Aristotle, four causes
Egoism, 371, 405–412. *See also* Ethical egoism; Psychological egoism
Einstein, Albert, 101, 229
Elements of Moral Philosophy (Rachels), 379–385, 387–388, 383–397, 397–398, 405–412, 422–425
Empiricism, 206, 341, 440
English Civil War, 206, 412
Enquiry Concerning Human Understanding (Hume), 212–221, 225–227, 337–341, 346–347
Enthymeme, 55–59
Epiphenomenalism, 256, ch. 12
"Epiphenomenal Qualia" (Jackson), 289–293, 302–304
Epistemology, 4, 165–247, 440
Essay Concerning Human Understanding (Locke), 206–212, 223–225
Ethical egoism, 368–369, 372, 405–412, 412, 422–425
Ethical realism, 368–369
Ethics, 319–445
Euthyphro (Plato), 373–378, 385–387
Euthyphro's dilemma, 373–378
Evil, argument from (against God). *See* Argument from evil
Evolution, 152–155, 302, 303
Experience and Prediction: An Analysis of the Foundations and the Structure of Knowledge (Reichenbach), 229–234, 247–249

Fact, Fiction, and Forecast (Goodman), 241–247, 250–251
Fairness, principle of (in interpreting arguments), 51, 52, 53–54, 65
Feldman, Richard, 183–184
Final cause. *See* Aristotle, four causes
Fodor, Jerry, 257, 281–283, 286–287, 288
Formal cause. *See* Aristotle, four causes
Formal fallacy, 26
Forms (Platonic), 171–172
Four causes (Aristotle's), 8, 91–92, 370–371
Free will, 319–360
"Free-Will Controversy" (Wood), 347–348
Frege, Gottlob, 5, 7
Function. *See* Teleological argument; *Nichomachean Ethics*; *Groundwork for the Metaphysics of Morals*
Functionalism, 257, 281–283, 287–288, 290

Gaunilo of Marmoutiers, 99–100, 114–115, 117
General theory of relativity, 101
Gettier, Edmund, 168, 174, 175–179, 183–184
Ghiselin, Michael, 153

Golden Rule, 424
Goodman, Nelson, 170, 241–247, 250–251
Gould, Stephen Jay, 152–154
Groundwork for the Metaphysics of Morals (Kant), 440–445, 447–448
Grue, 244–247, 250–251

Happiness, 370, 372, 401–405, ch. 20
Hard determinism, 322, ch. 14
Hedonistic utilitarianism, 372, 429–439, 446
Hegel, G. F. W., 341
Heraclitus, 171
Hilbert, David, 229
Hobbes, Thomas, 412–418, 424, 425–427, 428
Homunculi, 287–288
Hooke, Robert, 206
"Human Freedom and the Self" (Chisholm), 349–354, 360–361
Hume, David. *See also* Problem of induction
 on epistemology, 165, 169, 212–221, 225–227
 on free will, 337–341, 346–347, 348
 theological arguments, 92, 6.1, 156–158, 160–161
Hypothetical syllogism, 25, 96

Identity theory, 257, 277, 281–283, 283–286, 290
"If, then" statement. *See* Conditional statement
iLogos (software), xiii
Implied statement (premise or conclusion), 55–59, 65, 68–70. *See also* Enthymeme
"The Impossibility of Moral Responsibility" (Strawson), 328–332, 334–335
Incompatibilism, 321. *See also* Hard determinism; Libertarianism (free will)
Indeterminism, 341–345, 354–360
Indicator words and phrases. *See* Conclusion indicator; Convergent argument indicator; Linked argument indicator; Premise indicator; Structural indicators
Induction. *See* Inductive (argument); *see also* Problem of induction
Induction, problem of. *See* Problem of induction
Inductive (argument), 28, 89, 212–221, 225–227, ch. 9. *See also* Problem of induction
Inductive enumeration, 119
Inferential structure, x
Innate (ideas and knowledge), xi, 169, 206–212, 223–225
Inspiration (software), xii
Instrumental value, 370, 401, 435
Intelligent design, ch. 6
Intentions (of argument's author). *See* Interpretation (of an argument)
Interactionism, 256, 264–265, 286. *See also* Property dualism
Interactionist dualism. *See* Interactionism
Interpretation (of an argument), 39, 51–55, 65, 68. *See also* Fairness, principle of (in interpreting arguments); Charity, principle of (in interpreting arguments)
Intrinsic value, 370, 373–378, 401, 435
Introduction to the Principles of Morals and Legislation (Bentham), 429–435, 445–446
Invalid (argument). *See* Valid (argument)

Jackson, Frank, 293–296, 302–304, 305
Justice, 425–427
Justification (of belief), 168–169, chs. 7–9
Justified true belief, 168–169, ch. 7. *See also* Knowledge, definitions of

Kant, Immanuel, 137, 372, 440–445, 447–448
King, Martin Luther, Jr., 398
"Knowing Qualia: A Reply to Jackson" (Churchland), 296–300, 304–305
Knowledge, 165–247. *See also* Epistemology
 classification of, 166
 definitions of, 167–168, ch. 7
 knowledge how, 166
 knowledge of, 166
 knowledge that (see Propositional knowledge)

Laws of nature, 412, 427. See also Hobbes, Thomas; Leviathan (Hobbes)

Leibniz, Gottfried Wilhelm, 10, 135, 136, 262
Leibniz's Law, 262–264, 265–266
Leviathan (Hobbes), 412–418, 425–427
Lewis, C. I., 349
Libertarianism (free will), 322, ch. 16
Linked argument, 37, 43–45, 65
Linked argument indicator, 45
Locke, John, 169, 206–212, 223–225, 227
Logic, 5–6, 7
Logical behaviorism, 257, 267–273, 281–283, 286
Logical positivism, 234
The Logic of Scientific Discovery (Popper), 234
Logik der Forschung (Popper), 234
Lottery paradox, 185
Lyceum (Aristotle's school), 8

Mackie, John (J. L.), 91, 162–132, 134–135, 136, 166
Main hypothesis, 240–241. *See also* Popper, Karl
Malebranche, Nicolas, 212
Martin, Michael, 91, 119–126, 132–134
Mary argument (against materialism), 293–296, 296–300, 304–305
Material cause. *See* Aristotle, four causes
Materialism, 255–258, ch. 11, 333–334, ch. 12
Mechanics, 101
Meditations on First Philosophy (Descartes), xi, 187–205, 221–223, 256, 259–266, 273–274
Mendel, Gregor, 148–149
Meno (Plato), x–xi
Meta-ethics, 367, 368–369, chs. 17–18
Metaphysics, 4–5, 6, 255
Metaphysics (Aristotle), 8
Metaphysics (van Inwagen), 354–360, 361–362
Mill, James, 429, 435
Mill, John Stuart (J. S.), 372, 429, 435–439, 446–447, 448
Mind-body problem, chs. 10–12. *See also* Cartesian dualism
"The Mind-Body Problem" (Fodor), 281–283, 286–287
Minds, Brains, and Science (Searle), 307–310, 314–315, 316
Modal argument (against materialism), 302
Modus ponens, 24–25, 44, 95
Modus tollens, 25, 56, 174, 176
Montanism, 89
Moore, G. E., 349
Moral argument for nonbelief (in God), 120, 133
Moral contractarianism. *See* Contractarianism
Morality. *See* Ethics; *see also* Value theory
The Moral Point of View (Baier), 424–425
Moral responsibility, 319, 328–332, 337, 347
Moral theory, 5. *See also* Ethics
Motive, 440–445, 445–446
Multiple statements within sentence, 41–43

Nagel, Thomas, 289–293, 300–301, 305
Natural selection, 152–155
Natural theology, 88–89, 102
Natural Theology (Paley), 144–145, 158–160
Necessary and sufficient conditions, 22, 167–168, 170, 230
Negative argument, 410
New riddle of induction, 242, 244–247, 250–251. *See also* Goodman, Nelson; Grue
Newton, Isaac, 10, 101, 107, 369
Nicomachean Ethics, 370–371, 401–405, 418–422, 428
Nietzsche, Friederich, 368
Nihilism. *See* Subjectivism
Noncomputational Perspective (Churchland), 296–300
Nondeductive (argument), 24, 28–29, 89, 91–92
Normative (account of human behavior), 369–370, 430
Normative ethics, 367, 369–372, chs. 19–20

Objections and replies, diagramming, 59–65, 66
Official doctrine. *See* Cartesian dualism
"On Behalf of the Fool" (Gaunilo), 99–100, 114–115
Ontological argument, 90, 93–101, 113–115. *See also* Anselm; Gaunilo of Marmoutiers
Ordinary language philosophy, 267

Paley, William, 92, 144–145, 158–160
The Panda's Thumb: More Reflections on Natural History (Gould), 152–154
Paradox, 5–6
Para-mechanical hypothesis, 267
Pascal, Blaise, 7
Passions of the Soul (Descartes), 265, 274
Phenomenology, 257–258, ch. 12
Philosophiae Naturalis Principia Mathematica (Newton), 101
Physicalism. *See* Materialism
Physics, 101, 107
Physics (Aristotle), 8, 91–92
Planck, Max, 229
Plato, x–xi, 7–8, 89, 90, 368, 401
  on the definition of knowledge, 167–168, 171–174, 175, 180–183, 184 (see also Theaetetus)
  on divine command theory, 373–378, 385–387, 388 (see also Euthyphro; Euthyphro's dilemma)
Plotinus, 89, 90
Popper, Karl, 169–170, 234–241, 249–251
Popular dualism, 256
Positive argument, 410
Premise, x, 8
Premise indicator, 39–40. *See also* Structural indicators
Principle of equal treatment, 409–412
Principle of the uniformity of nature. *See* Problem of induction; Hume, David
Principle of utility. *See* Utilitarianism; Bentham, Jeremy
Problem of evil. *See* Argument from evil
Problem of induction, 169–170, 212–221, 225–227, ch. 9
Proof, 7
Property dualism, 256
Propositional knowledge, 166, 168, 298–300
Proslogion (Anselm), 93–101, 113–115
Psychological egoism, 371. *See also* Ethical egoism
Purpose. *See* Teleological argument; Four causes (Aristotle's)
Pythagoras, 171

Qualia, 257–258, 287–288, ch. 12. See also Epiphenomenalism; Antimaterialism
Quantifier switch fallacy, 110–111
Quantum physics, 322

Rachels, James
  on cultural relativism, 405–412, 422–425, 428
  on divine command theory 368, 379–385, 387–388
  on egoism 18.2, 397–399
Rand, Ayn, 422–423
Rationale (software), xii
Rationalism, 440
Rationalism (in Popper), 237–238
Reading philosophy, ix
Red arrow (in diagramming), 60, 61
Reductio ad absurdum, 25–26, 91, 93, 97, 126, 130–131, 156, 175, 441
Reduction (of mental states to physical states), ch. 12. *See also* Mind-body problem
"Reduction, Qualia, and the Direct Introspection of Brain States" (Churchland), 301–301, 304–305
Refutation (in Popper), 239–241
Reichenbach, Hans, 169, 170, 229–234, 247–249, 251
Relativism. *See* Cultural relativism
Religion and the Modern Mind (Stace), 341–345, 347
Replies and objections, diagramming. *See* Objections and replies, diagramming
Revealed theology, 89
Rosenberg, Jay, ix
Rules for argument diagramming. *See* Argument diagramming, rules of
Russell, Bertrand, 5, 9, 349
Ryle, Gilbert, 257, 266, 267–273, 274–275

Schism, 89
Schlick, Mortiz, 234
Scholasticism, 93
Scientific laws, 28
Searle, John, 258, ch. 13

Self-interest. *See* Ethical egoism; Psychological egoism; Contractarianism
"Sensations and Brain Processes" (Smart), 277–281, 283–286
Skepticism, 212
Smart, J. J. C., 257, 277–281, 283–286, 288, 290
Social and political philosophy, 5
Social contract, 371, 412–418, 425–427. *See also* Contractarianism; Hobbes, Thomas; *Leviathan* (Hobbes)
Socrates, 7–8
Soft determinism, 321–322
Sommerfeld, Arnold, 229
Sorensen, Roy, 185
Sound (argument), 20, 98, 107, 124
Soundness. *See* Sound (argument)
Stace, W. T., 341–345, 347, 348
Statement, 16, 41
State of nature, 412–418, 426–427. *See also* *Leviathan*
State of war, 412–418, 426–427. *See also Leviathan*
Strawson, Galen, 328–332, 334–335, 336
Strawson, Peter, 328
Strength. *See* Strong (argument)
Strong (argument), 20–21, 22, 24, 89
Structural indicators, 39–40, 65
Subargument, 47, 48
Subconclusion, 48
Subjectivism, 368–369
Sufficient and necessary conditions. *See* Necessary and sufficient conditions
Summa Theologica (Aquinas), 101–113, 115–117
Sumner, William Graham, 397
Surprise Principle, 144, 147–150, 152–155. *See also* Paley, William
Surprise Test Paradox, 185–186
System of Nature (d'Holbach), 323–327, 333–334

Tabula rasa, 210
Teleological argument, 92, ch. 6
Theaetetus (Plato), 168, 171–174, 180–183
Theodicy, 91
Theodicy (Leibniz), 135
Theologia naturalis. *See* Natural theology
Thiry, Paul-Henri. *See* d'Holbach, Baron
Transitivity of justification, 179
"Troubles with Functionalism" (Block), 287–288
Truth-value, 16
Turing, Alan, 258. *See also* Turing machine; Turing test
Turing machine, 258, ch. 13
Turing test, 258, ch. 13

Unsound. See Sound (argument)
Utilitarianism, 277, 371–372, 429–439, 441, 445–447
Utilitarianism (John Stuart Mill), 435–439, 446–447

Valid (argument), 19, 20, 24, 89, 93
Validity. *See* Valid (argument)
Value, 6, 370, 401, 435. *See also* Instrumental value; Intrinsic value
Value theory, 5, 6
van Inwagen, Peter, 354–360, 361–362
Vienna Circle, 234
Virtue ethics, 370–371, 401–405, 418–422

Watchmaker. See Argument from design; Paley, William; Teleological argument
Weak (argument). *See* Strong (argument)
"What Is It Like to Be a Bat?" (Nagel), 289–293, 300–301
Wickedness, 424
Willis, Thomas, 206
Wittgenstein, Ludwig, 234, 267
Wood, Ledger, 347–348

Zeno of Elea, 5–6
Zeno's paradox, 6, 9–10, 12, 25–26